Ravenna

JUDITH HERRIN

Ravenna

Capital of Empire, Crucible of Europe

PRINCETON UNIVERSITY PRESS

PRINCETON & OXFORD

Published in the United States and Canada
in 2020 by Princeton University Press
41 William Street, Princeton, New Jersey 08540

press.princeton.edu

First published in 2020 by Allen Lane,
an imprint of Penguin Books,
Penguin Random House UK

Library of Congress Control Number 2020934134
ISBN 978-0-691-15343-8
ISBN (e-book) 978-0-691-20197-9

Jacket art: Alfredo Dagli Orti / Art Resource, NY

Set in 10.2/13.87 pt Sabon LT Std
Typeset by Jouve (UK), Milton Keynes

Printed on acid-free paper. ∞

Printed in the United States of America

1 3 5 7 9 10 8 6 4 2

To my three As: Alita, Asha and Anthony

And musing on Ravenna's ancient name,
I watched the day till, marked with wounds of flame,
The turquoise sky to burnished gold was turned.

O how my heart with boyish passion burned,
When far away across the sedge and mere
I saw that Holy City rising clear,
Crowned with her crown of towers! – On and on
I galloped, racing with the setting sun,
And ere the crimson after-glow was passed,
I stood within Ravenna's walls at last!

. . .

Adieu! Adieu! Yon silver lamp, the moon,
Which turns our midnight into perfect noon,
Doth surely light thy towers, guarding well
Where Dante sleeps, where Byron loved to dwell.

Oscar Wilde, Ravenna

Contents

PART FOUR 540–70
Justinian I and the campaigns in North Africa and Italy

PART FIVE 568–643
King Alboin and the Lombard conquest

PART SIX 610–700
The expansion of Islam

PART SEVEN 685–725
The two reigns of Justinian II

PART EIGHT 700–769
Ravenna returns to the margins

PART NINE 756–813
Charlemagne and Ravenna

List of illustrations

Note: Of the photographs taken by Kieran Dodds, nos. 7–9, 32–5 and 37–40 are reproduced with the kind permission of the Opera di Religione of the Ravenna-Cervia diocese; nos. 10–15, 50–54, 57–8 and 61 are reproduced with kind permission of the Ministry of Cultural Heritage and Tourism, Regional Direction of the Museums of Emilia-Romagna.

A note on spellings

Some readers may notice the lack of consistency in the transliteration of names. I have used proper names that are familiar in anglicized forms, for instance, for emperors Constantine, Justinian, Leo and Maurice, popes Sylvester, John and Gregory, and figures such as Arius and Boethius. Where there is no generally accepted English form of the proper name, I have distinguished rulers of Constantinople and their officials by using the Greek form, ending in -os, from those active in the West, identified by the Latin ending in -us. This means that Anastasios, the emperor, is spelled differently from Anastasius, the pope.

Similarly, for unfamiliar place names I have used the spellings employed in the sources, on both the maps and in the text, adding the modern names where necessary. Both are signalled in the Index, so you can find the contemporary name referred to in the book.

For official titles, I have cited the terms used at the time and added a definition if necessary. Again, both Greek and Latin terms have been transliterated, for example, *strategos* and *apocrisiarius*. Naturally, over a four-hundred-year period there are some anomalies.

London •

• Paderborn

Aachen •

R.Rhine

Soissons •   Trier •   • Mainz

R.Seine   • Reims   Ingelheim •   Regensburg •   *R.Danube*

Paris •   • Ponthion   Metz •   NORICUM   PANNONIA

Worms •

R.Loire   *R. Isonzo*   Singidunun •

Poitiers • ✕ Vouillé   *R.Frigidertus*
                      • Lyon   A   l   p   *s*   Trieste •   Sirmium •

Clermont- •   Geneva •   • Verona
Ferrand   *R. Rhône*   Milan •   Pola •   DALMATIA

                                      Adda ✕   *R.Po*
Bordeaux •   Bologna • Ravenna   • Split

                              Nîmes •   Pisa • Florence •   *Adriatic Sea*
Narbonne •   Arles •   Genoa •
                 Marseille •   Perugia •   *Apennines*

P y r e n e e s   CORSICA   Rome •   Dyrrachium •

Barcelona •   • Naples

B a l e a r i c   S e a   SARDINIA   *T y r r h e n i a n*   Salerno •
                                                            S e a   Taranto •

Carthagena •   SICILY
                      Hippo •   Carthage •   • Syracuse
              NUMIDIA   Kairouan •
MAURETANIA   *M e d i t e*

0   500 miles

0   500 kilometres

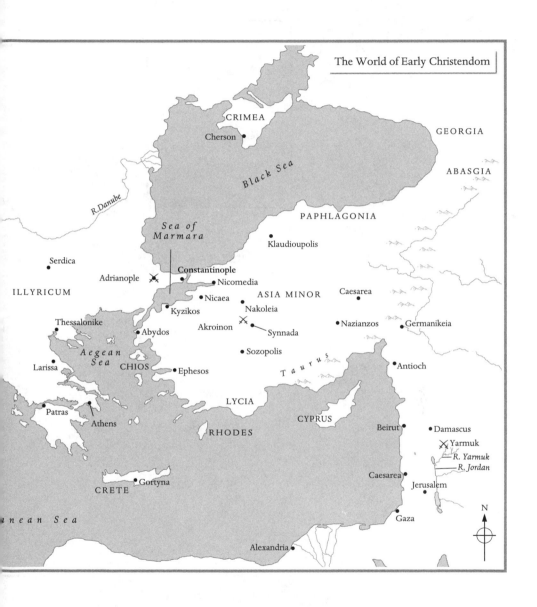

The World of Early Christendom

CRIMEA

Cherson

GEORGIA

ABASGIA

Black Sea

R. Danube

PAPHLAGONIA

Sea of
Marmara

Klaudioupolis

Serdica

Constantinople

ILLYRICUM

Adrianople

Nicomedia

ASIA MINOR

Caesarea

Nicaea

Nakoleia

Kyzikos

Akroinon

Nazianzos

Germanikeia

Thessalonike

Synnada

Abydos

Aegean
Sea

Sozopolis

Larissa

CHIOS

Ephesos

Taurus

Antioch

LYCIA

Patras

CYPRUS

Beirut

Damascus

Athens

Yarmuk

RHODES

R. Yarmuk

R. Jordan

Caesarea

CRETE

Gortyna

Jerusalem

N

anean Sea

Gaza

Alexandria

Italy, sixth to eighth centuries

N

Sabione
Zuglio
Feltria
Tridentium
Asolo
Lake Como
VENETIAE
FRIULI

Monza
Brixia
Milan
LOMBARDY
Pavia
Cremona
Mantua
Piacentia
R. Po
Bobbio †
Vulturina
Brixellum
Pollentia
VIA AEMILIA
Genoa
Bononia
Ravenna
DALMATIA
Luni
Lucca
Albenga
Florentia
Pisa
R. Arno
Salona
Split
TUSCANY

See map opposite

VIA AMERINA
VIA FLAMINIA
Tuder
Spoletium
Urbs vetus
Ameria
CORSICA
Polymartium
Narni
Chieti
Castrum Valentis
Horta
Sutrium
† Farfa
Ortona
Nepi
R. Tiber
Adriatic Sea
Rome
Monte Gargano †
Lucera
Terracina
LONGOBARDIA
Monte Cassino †
Capua
Benevento
CALABRIA
Naples
Salerno
SARDINIA
LUCANIA

Tyrrhenian
Sea

Squillace

Mediterranean Sea

Lilybaeum

SICILY

■ City
● Town
-- Road
◆ Castle
† Monastery

Syracuse

0   150 miles
0   200 kilometres

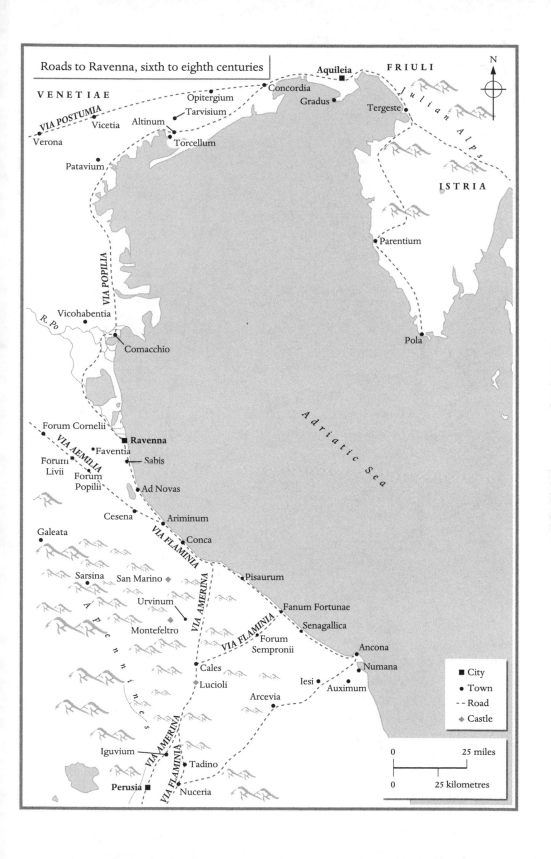

Roads to Ravenna, sixth to eighth centuries

N

VENETIAE

VIA POSTUMIA

Verona
Vicetia
Altinum
Opitergium
Tarvisium
Patavium
Torcellum

Concordia
Aquileia
Gradus
Tergeste

FRIULI

Julian Alps

ISTRIA

Parentium

VIA POPILIA

Vicohabentia
R. Po
Comacchio

Pola

Adriatic Sea

Forum Cornelii
VIA AEMILIA
Ravenna
Faventia
Sabis
Forum
Livii
Forum
Popilii
Ad Novas

Cesena
Ariminum
VIA FLAMINIA
Conca
Galeata

Sarsina
San Marino
Urvinum
VIA AMERINA
Montefeltro

Pisaurum

Fanum Fortunae
Senagallica

Apennines

VIA FLAMINIA
Forum
Sempronii
Cales
Lucioli
Arcevia

Ancona
Numana
Iesi
Auximum

VIA AMERINA
Iguvium
Tadino
VIA FLAMINIA
Perusia
Nuceria

0   25 miles

0   25 kilometres

■ City
● Town
-- Road
◆ Castle

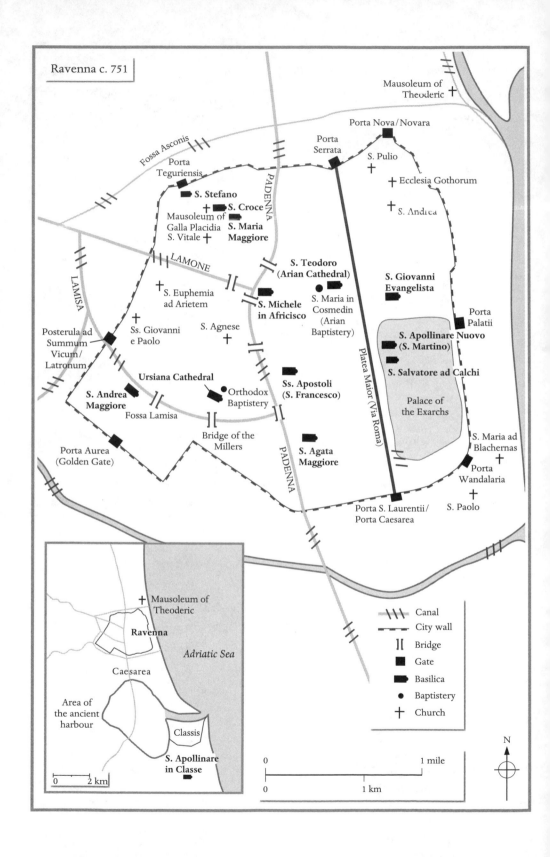

Ravenna c. 751

Mausoleum of Theoderic

Porta Nova/Novara

Fossa Asconis

Porta Serrata

S. Pulio

Porta Teguriensis

Ecclesia Gothorum

S. Stefano

S. Andrea

S. Croce

PADENNA

Mausoleum of Galla Placidia

S. Maria Maggiore

S. Vitale

S. Teodoro (Arian Cathedral)

S. Giovanni Evangelista

LAMONE

S. Euphemia ad Arietem

S. Michele in Africisco

S. Maria in Cosmedin (Arian Baptistery)

Porta Palatii

LAMISA

S. Apollinare Nuovo (S. Martino)

Posterula ad Summum Vicum/ Latronum

Ss. Giovanni e Paolo

S. Agnese

S. Salvatore ad Calchi

Ss. Apostoli (S. Francesco)

Platea Maior (Via Roma)

Palace of the Exarchs

Ursiana Cathedral

S. Andrea Maggiore

Orthodox Baptistery

Fossa Lamisa

S. Maria ad Blachernas

Bridge of the Millers

PADENNA

Porta Wandalaria

Porta Aurea (Golden Gate)

S. Agata Maggiore

S. Paolo

Porta S. Laurentii/ Porta Caesarea

Mausoleum of Theoderic

Ravenna

Adriatic Sea

Caesarea

Area of the ancient harbour

Classis

\\\ Canal

City wall

]\[Bridge

■ Gate

▶ Basilica

● Baptistery

✝ Church

S. Apollinare in Classe

0   2 km

0   1 mile

0   1 km

N

COMPETING POWERS IN RAVENNA

Political	Military	Episcopal
EMPERORS		
Honorius 395–15th Aug 423	Stilicho 394–408 *mm*	Ursus *c.* 399–13th Apr 426
John, *notarius* Sep 423–May 425	Castinus 421–424 *mm*	
Valentinian III 23rd Oct 425–455		Peter I 426–31st Jul 451
Empress Galla Placidia 425–437 d. 27 Nov 450	Boniface 432 *mm*	
	Aetius 433–454 *mm*	
	Faustus 437–438 and 442 PP	
		Neon *c.* 451–11th Feb 473
Avitus 9th Jul 455–17th Oct 457	Ricimer 457–472 *mm*	
Marjorian 28th Dec 457–2nd Aug 461		
Libius Severus 19th Nov 461–14th Nov 465		
Anthemius 12th Apr 467–11th Jul 472		
Glycerius 3rd Mar 473–24th Jun 474		Exuperantius *c.* 473–22nd May 477
Julius Nepos Jun 474–28th Aug 475		
Romulus Augustulus 31st Oct 475–23rd Aug 476		
KINGS		
Odoacer 23rd Aug 476–1st Mar 493	Basilius 483 PP	John I 477–5th May 494
Theoderic 1st Mar 493–30th Aug 526	Liberius 493–500 PP	
	Cassiodorus 503–507 PP	Peter II 494–3rd Dec 519–520
	Decius 507–511 PP	

Political	Military	Episcopal
	Faustus 509–507 PP	
	Albinus 512–513 PP	
	Opilio before 524 PP	Aurelianus d. 26th May 521
	Abundantius 526–26th May 527 PP	
Athalaric 526–2nd Oct 534		Ecclesius 522–27th Jul 532
	Iohannes before 527 PP	
	Avienus 527–528 PP	
Queen Amalasuintha 31st Aug 526–535 with Theodad Nov 534–Nov 536		Ursicinus 533–5th Sep 536
Witiges Nov 536–May 540	Fidelis 537–538 PP	Victor 537–544
	Reparatus 538–15th Feb 539 PP	
	Athanasius 539–542 PP	
Ildibad 540–41	Belisarius 540 briefly PP	
Earic 541		
Totila/Baduila 541–Jun 552	Maximinus 542 PP	Maximian 14th Oct 546–22nd Feb 557
Teias Jul 552–553		
EMPERORS Justinian May 540–565	Narses 552–568 PP	
	Antiochus 554 PP	
	Aurelianus at Ravenna 552–557	

Political	Military	Episcopal
	Pamphronius 557–557/9 PP	Agnellus 27th Jun 557–1st Aug 570
Justin II 565–572	Longinus c. 568–572 PP	
		Peter III 15th Sep 570–16th Aug 578
	Sisinnius c. 575 at Susa *mm*	
	Baduarius 575–77 *kouropalates* son-in-law of Justin II	
Tiberius 572–582		John II, the Roman 22nd Nov 578–11th Jan 595
Maurice 582–602	Decius c. 584	
	Smaragdus c. 585–589 *vir praecelsus exarchus*	
	Julianus 589?	
	Romanus exarch 589–596	
		Marinianus 595–606
	Georgius 591–25th Oct 593 PP	
	Gregorius 595 PP	
	John 598 PP	
	Callinicus 596–603 *patricius et exarchus*	
	EXARCHS John (seal)	
	Theopemptus (seal)	
	Akataphronius (seal)	

Political	Military	Episcopal
	John (seal)	
Phokas 602–610	Smaragdus 603–608 *exarchus Italiae*	John III 607–613/25?
Herakleios 610–641	Photios ?608–613	
	John I ?615–616 killed	John IV ?613/25–630
	Eleutherios, eunuch 616–619 *rebelled and killed by soldiers from Ravenna army at Lucioli*	
	Gregorios 619–625 *patricius Romanorum*	
	Isaac 625–643	Bonus 631–25th Aug 642/8
Constans II 642–668	Theodore Calliopas 643–645	Maurus 642/49–671
	Platon *c.* 645	
	Olympios 649–653	
	Theodore Calliopas 653–?666	
	Gregorios II ?–1st Mar 666	Maurus d. 671
Constantine IV 668–685	Theodore II 678–687	Reparatus 671–30th Jul 677
	Anastasios *c.* 650–700 (seal)	Theodore 677–18th Jan 691/2
	Theocharistos (seal)	
Justinian II 685–695	John Platyn II 678–?701 murdered	Damian 692–12th Mar 707/8
Leontios 695–698		
Tiberios Apsimar 698–705	Theophylaktos 701–705	
Justinian II second reign 705–711	John III *c.* 705–710?	Felix 25th Mar 708–25th Nov 723/5

Political	Military	Episcopal
	John Rizokopos 710–711	
	Eutychios 711–713	
Philippikos 711–713		
Anastasios II 713–715	Scholastikios 713–?	
	Stephanos c. 700–750 (seal)	
Theodosios III 715–717		
Leo III 715–741	Paul the patrician 723–726	John V 723/5–744
	Eutychios 727–751	
Constantine V 741–775		

LOMBARD KINGS

Political	Military	Episcopal
Liutprand 727/8–744	Pope Zacharias 3rd Dec 741–15th Mar 752	Sergius ?744/8–25th Aug 769
Aistulf 752–756	Pope Stephen II 26th Mar 752–26th Apr 757	

Pippin, King of the Franks, first campaign in Italy, 755, presents Ravenna to Pope Stephen II, Peace of Trevi. Second campaign 756, insists on donation

Political	Military	Episcopal
Desiderius 756–774	Pope Paul I 29th May 757–28th Jun 767	
	Pope Stephen III 7th Aug 768–24th Jan 772	

774 Charles incorporated the kingdom of Italy and thereafter dukes appointed by Charles probably ruled the city of Ravenna

FRANKISH RULERS

Political	Military	Episcopal
Charles 774–813	Pope Hadrian 9th Feb 772–26th Dec 795	Archbishop Leo c. 770–14th Feb 777/8
Charles/Emperor Leo IV 775–780		John VI c. 777–24th Jul 784
Charles/Constantine VI 780–797		Gratiosus c. 786–23rd Feb 788/9
Empress Irene 780–802		Valerius 789–29th Jan 801/10

Political	Military	Episcopal
Emperor Charlemagne 800–813		Martin c. 801/10–818
Bernard, son of Pippin 813–818	Pope Leo III 27th Dec 795–12th Jun 816	
Louis the Pious 28th Jun 814–20th Jun 840	Pope Paschal 817–824	
Lothar king of Italy 817–844	Pope Gregory II 828–844	Petronax c. 818–837
Lothar emperor 840–855		
Louis II 844–876	Pope Sergius II 844–847	George c. 837–846

mm *magister militum*

PP   Praetorian Prefect

Many dates are best guesses; often the death date of bishops found on their tombs is the clearest indication, though it may not coincide with the literary evidence.

Introduction

When the Allied forces prepared to invade and occupy Italy in 1943, the British Naval Intelligence Division planned four handbooks 'for the use of persons in His Majesty's service only', comprising exhaustive accounts of every aspect of the country. The first volume – of six hundred pages – was published in February 1944, five months after the first landings; packed with diagrams and pull-out maps it describes Italy's coastal and regional topography. The second and third volumes cover every element of the country's history, populations, roads, railways, agriculture and industry. The final, 750-page volume, published in December 1945, describes the country's seventy inland and forty-eight coastal towns in curt, meticulous prose. Its description of Ravenna, a small city on the Adriatic coast of northern Italy, opens with a brief, authoritative statement: 'As a centre of early Christian art Ravenna is unequalled.'

But by the time this volume was published, many parts of the city were in ruins and some of its unequalled early Christian art had been destroyed over the course of fifty-two Allied bombing raids. In August 1944 the Basilica of San Giovanni Evangelista was pulverized by bombs intended for the railway station and its sidings. This mid-fifth-century church had been decorated in mosaic. Those on the floor had already been lost when the church was modernized in the seventeenth century. In 1944 the entire building was shattered.[1]

If you have never visited the city of Ravenna, you have missed an amazing experience, an extraordinary delight, which this book aims to recreate. I open my history of its unique role and significance with a grim salute to this recent damage because it spun a thread that led me to write this study.

The Italians are among the finest art restorers in the world. Immediately after the war they set about repairing their unique heritage in Ravenna. To raise the funds for this and re-establish tourism, an exhibition was mounted that reproduced some of its most glorious mosaic images, which toured Paris, London and New York in the 1950s. As it passed through England my mother, at the time a doctor working in general practice, went to see it.

Some years later she decided to visit Italy for herself and to introduce me to it as a teenager. And so, in 1959, we approached Ravenna from the north in order to see the mosaics that had fascinated her since the exhibition. I recall vividly that we caught sight of the abbey of Pomposa, its redbrick bell tower shimmering in the setting sun. Within the city the Mausoleum of Galla Placidia made a lasting impression on me with its mosaic of the starry sky, hanging suspended above the doves and deer drinking at fountains and the fascinating geometric patterns covering every arch that supported the dome. It was a hot summer and I felt that eating figs with prosciutto in a cool restaurant was more interesting than the mosaics. But a seed of curiosity had been implanted, and a postcard with the portrait of Empress Theodora from the church of San Vitale accompanied me to university.

Also, I'm told, I often mentioned the visit. Forty years later when we were on holiday in Tuscany, as a surprise, my partner booked us onto an extended all-day trip, so that he could see what had impressed me. Refreshed and thrilled by the intense, compressed tour of Ravenna's major sites, I bought the local guidebooks and settled in for the drive back. As we sat in an endless traffic jam around Bologna I grew increasingly angry at the failure of those books to provide any adequate history as to why such an astonishing concentration of early Christian art should be there in the first place, and then how it survived.

Thus, the notion of this book flickered into life in stationary traffic in the form of a double question: how to explain why the matchless mosaics of Ravenna existed, and how they endured. The idea was sustained by my overconfidence that I could answer these problems without great difficulty. They say you only really pose a problem when you are already in a position to resolve it, and I somehow felt, perhaps immodestly, that I could do so. My first book, *The Formation of Christendom*, had surveyed the Mediterranean world and I was familiar with the critical role of the Goths who built one of the most important of Ravenna's basilicas. My second book, *Women in Purple*, showed how three empresses had reversed iconoclasm, and I was about to collect my essays on the roles of women in Byzantium into *Unrivalled Influence*. I believed I was fully able to assess the impact of Empress Galla Placidia and to appreciate the stunning presence of Theodora, wife of Emperor Justinian I. Further, at the peak of its influence, Ravenna was clearly a Byzantine city. The book I was about to publish, *Byzantium: The Surprising Life of a Medieval Empire*, crystallized my argument that, far from being devious, over-hierarchical and manipulative – as the word 'Byzantine' suggests when used as a lazy term of abuse – Byzantium lasted from 330 to 1435 because of its extraordinary resilience and self-confidence. This strength was rooted in its threefold combination of Roman law and military prowess, Greek education and culture and Christian belief and morality. Proof of this, I showed, was the vitality of its outlying cities, which, as soon as the capital was conquered in 1204, burst into a Byzantine life of their own. It was a theme I had investigated over many years in essays collected in *Margins and Metropolis*, and clearly it had a special relevance to Ravenna as an outpost of Constantinople.

The price of such overconfidence was nine years of research! I had to work on unfamiliar Latin records on papyrus and engage with scholarly and not just conversational Italian. I struggled with a history that has too many synthetic overviews of the decline of the West and fails to recognize the rise and role of Ravenna. I had to identify a completely new cast of characters, distinguishing between Agnellus the doctor, Agnellus the bishop and Agnellus the historian. I found myself in the handsome city library of Ravenna, where Dante's relics are kept, in a temperature-controlled environment, to inspire readers (he was exiled there from Florence). I travelled along the old Roman road, the Via Flaminia, to see how it crosses the Apennines, the formidable spine of Italy, that both connected and separated Ravenna and Rome, and explored the alternative military roads used by Belisarius, the sixth-century Byzantine general. I followed as best I could the route that Theoderic, the Gothic king who had such an important influence on Ravenna's history, took across the northern Balkans to the banks of the Isonzo where he overwhelmed his rival, Odoacer, and then went on to conquer Italy and much of southern Gaul. This trip also allowed me to observe the craftmanship of the Lombards preserved in Cividale: not only the Christian statues, carvings and painted decoration, but also pre-Christian grave goods in gold and garnets. Thanks to the generosity of four Ravennati yachtsmen, I sailed across the Adriatic, driven by a brisk wind, in an experiment to check how easy it would have been for mosaicists from Ravenna to work in Parenzo (Poreč, in modern-day

Croatia). There I witnessed the gleaming mosaics of the basilica of Bishop Eufrasius, which are so closely connected to the monuments of Ravenna (both were made in the sixth century).

These explorations were full of pleasures and from them three particularly challenging issues emerged, which might be labelled antiquity, perspective and location. The first is obvious enough. When we imagine going to northern Italy to admire its stunning art, we think of the Renaissance of the fourteenth and fifteenth centuries: from Siena's frescoes of good and bad government made in the 1330s to Leonardo's Last Supper of the 1490s. But the intense period of Ravenna's artistic flowering occurred nearly a thousand years earlier. The historical records that have survived are only fragmentary. It is extraordinarily hard to work out how people lived then. The secular palaces where records of government were stored have themselves been ruined, treated as quarries, dismantled for their stones. What little remains is long buried and almost all documentation has turned to dust. Sometimes, tantalizing, incomplete and very partial accounts survive, such as the unique account of the bishops of Ravenna by Agnellus, its ninth-century historian.

A simple measure of the loss of knowledge is the silence about the craftsmen and possibly women and children who created the city's mosaics. All we know is that when the Emperor Diocletian attempted to fix maximum prices across the Roman empire in 301, his edict stipulated that pay for wall mosaicists was the same as for the makers of marble paving and wall revetment – considerably below portrait painters and fresco painters, but above that of tessellated floor makers, carpenters and masons. We can imagine that there must have been families trained in the skills of making, trading and then bonding coloured tesserae, sketching the original images and portraits, calculating the repetitions of the border patterns, creating guilds in cities across the ancient world and perhaps travelling from employment in one city to the next big opportunity. What we do know is that from modern-day Seville to Beirut, from Britain to North Africa, across every island in the Mediterranean from the Balearics to Sicily and Cyprus, and in all the great cities of the Roman empire, enormous floors and endless walls were laid out with mosaic images of the gods, the myths of the ancient world, every species of beast, bird and fish, daily life and even the remains of great banquets. But we do not know the name of a single person who worked on the stupendous mosaics of Ravenna.

Although mosaic is the medium of Ravenna's unequalled early Christian art, its function and power is not merely aesthetic. It is used in a novel and distinctive fashion, which distinguishes it from its ancient predecessor. In place of the floor mosaics that had adorned every major villa of the Roman world, the apses and walls of churches become a focus. Another change lies in the replacement of a white background by a glistening gold ground, which reflects the light in a unique fashion. From the fourth century, as emperors such as Constantine I and his mother Helena patronized new ecclesiastical building in Jerusalem, Old Rome and the New Rome of Constantinople, gold was associated with Christian worship. This represented an innovative development of the inherited skill of ancient mosaic decoration, but very few skilled mosaicists of this period ever signed their work. The anonymity of the Ravenna mosaicists is itself a symptom of the enormous losses in our knowledge of this period.

The second difficulty stems from the way the time of Ravenna's flowering and influence is perceived. The period of its special history from 402 to 751, roughly 350 years, is now generally identified as 'late antiquity', which developed out of the ancient world of Greece and Rome before the identifiable medieval civilization of the Middle Ages. The book that above all others created our contemporary awareness of the period is Peter Brown's *The World of Late Antiquity*, its pages filled with the infectious vitality that characterizes his scholarship and brings the unique period to life. I am one of many historians inspired and deeply influenced by it. But in the course of writing this book I have come to doubt whether the term 'late antiquity' is appropriate, for it makes the epoch seem inextricably one of decline and antiquarianism. As I attempted to uncover Ravenna's history, the apologetic atmosphere of the term became increasingly incongruous, because it is one of the rare cities of this period in the West that did not experience the general failure clearly visible in many others.

In his great book of 1971 Brown also emphasized the innovations of the era, ranging from individual creativity, such as the first autobiography (St Augustine's *Confessions*), to the codification of Roman law, the creation of Christian canon law and the eruption of Islam, which resulted in the threefold division of the Mediterranean – which are among the tap roots of our modern world. From the process of electing the pope to the formulation of dating our calendar, it witnessed the beginnings of modernity. Nonetheless, the term 'late antiquity' assumes we should be comparing the period to the glory days of classical Rome and Greece rather than emphasizing it as a time of great change: a mid-fifth-century inscription in Ravenna proclaims: 'Yield, old name, yield age to newness!' I have therefore sought to replace the inevitably backward-looking perspective of 'late antiquity' by the term 'early Christendom', which looks forward to a newly Christianized world seeking novel forms of organization.

Crucially, antiquity was pagan, while from the foundation of Constantinople in 330, the empire was destined to become Christian. And not just the area within the frontiers of the empire. Outsiders, the so-called 'barbarians', were also attracted to Christianity's promise of eternal life in the hereafter and converted. Throughout the Mediterranean world and beyond, people were working through what it meant to be Christian. The process became even more critical after the rise of Islam and the intense divisions over the role of icons this provoked.

From an early date, and especially after the conversion of the Goths, early Christendom was characterized by disputes over the exact nature of the humanity of Christ, as recorded in the Gospel stories, the 'good news' that established the creed of power and authority. Nothing of the sort defined antiquity. Some of the fourth-century Christian emperors believed, reasonably enough, that if Christ was the son of God, he must have been born later than his Father, must be separate from him and, in this sense, secondary to him. Such views had been formulated by the deacon Arius in early fourth-century Alexandria. When the Goths adopted Christianity, it was this definition of the faith, the commanding belief of the emperors in Constantinople at the time, that they embraced. Their loyalty to Arianism was to ensure a division that extended its impact down the centuries, as we will see. Later, Islam also reflected the dispute over Christ's humanity, for it overtly worshipped the same God but identified Jesus as a major prophet, not the son of God.

Arianism was displaced by what became the generally accepted view, namely that God the Father, his Son and the Holy Spirit all shared in the same origin and substance. Nonetheless, theological arguments about the Trinity and Christ's humanity continued to frustrate Christian unity and provoked a crisis in the eighth century when some western church leaders added the phrase 'and from the son' (filioque) to the creed. Because the wording of basic belief, which had been confirmed in the mid-fifth century at the Council of Chalcedon, stated that the Holy Spirit proceeded 'from the Father', the addition of this little phrase *'filioque'* was rejected in the East, since when it has symbolized the division between Greek Orthodoxy and Roman Catholicism.

But in using the term 'early Christendom', I am not seeking to focus on such doctrinal issues. My intention is rather to characterize the period that began in the fourth century as Christianity became the dominant belief. From 380 onwards, it was a defining force in the exercise of authority as well as the organized means of transmitting community and integrating the economy. It provided many of the peoples of the Mediterranean world, often speaking different languages and battling with incomers who nonetheless thought of themselves as Christian, with a shared belief in the hereafter, and a passion to define the best means of deserving it. It was less a 'late Roman' civilization than an emerging new world, with all the confidence and confusion of great change. The exceptional achievements of Ravenna only make sense within this framework. In order to communicate the liveliness and energy of the process, I have divided each of the nine parts of this book (which broadly cover successive half-centuries) into short chapters and, wherever possible, I have identified a key figure, man or woman, in their titles. Among the Ravennate makers of early Christendom, kings and bishops, soldiers and merchants, a doctor, a cosmographer and even an historian, all take their places.

Another aspect of the period that 'early Christendom' characterizes much better than 'late antiquity' is the role of Byzantium. During the fourth and fifth centuries the new centre of imperial government at Ravenna developed in tandem with the Christian authority of its bishop, as church leaders throughout the western provinces of the Roman world took over administrative roles. They all also drew on the legacy of the emperors established in Constantinople, which became the outstanding achievement of the later Roman Empire. Constantine I's capital of New Rome continued to lead the Mediterranean world, providing guidance in legal matters, diplomatic disputes, political negotiations and theological problems. These centuries were marked by the hegemonic importance of Constantinople and it had a distinct influence in the way what we now call Italy developed.

At the same time a new force emerged in the western regions of the empire, which combined barbarian energy and prowess with Roman military, architectural and legal achievements, as well as Christian belief and organization, to create a widely diffused but unstable mixture. Gradually, it became a specifically Latin fire that spread and generated its own autonomy and influence across Italy and North Africa between 400 and 600. Ravenna was one of the cities that exemplified and sustained its growth, particularly under the long domination of Theoderic, the multilingual Gothic king trained at the Byzantine court and formed by its perspectives. His determination was crucial in the integration of the 'barbarian' and 'Roman' elements in a decisive new synthesis.

Across these in-between centuries Ravenna not only produced some of the most refined and exquisite art, it also assisted the development of what was to become 'The West'. In this process Constantinople played a key role in the emergence of institutions in Italy that is often overlooked by western medieval historians.

The third difficulty stems from the peculiar nature of Ravenna's influence. It was more shaped than shaping. When the general Stilicho and the young Emperor Honorius (395–423) decided to move his capital to Ravenna, Alaric, the feared chieftain of Gothic forces, had recently broken through the Alpine frontiers of Italy and was about to threaten the imperial government based in Milan. Milan's walls were too extensive to defend effectively, while Ravenna's position among the marshes, lakes and tributaries of the Po estuary provided a natural protection, reinforced by strong walls; it also had direct access, via its nearby port of Classis (modern Classe), to Constantinople, as well as to supplies of the trading centres of the East Mediterranean. This was an inspired strategic redeployment. Laws issued in Ravenna in December 402 record the initial stages of this relocation, which made it the new capital city.

The city was already famous for its port at Classis, a large harbour planned centuries earlier by Julius Caesar as a base for the Roman fleet in the East Mediterranean. It was from this point, in 49 BC that Caesar set out for Rome and crossed the Rubicon a few miles to the south, an act now famous as a sign of irreversible commitment. Twenty-two years later, his great nephew Augustus established the centres of Roman naval power at Ravenna on the east coast of Italy and Misenum on the west, under praetorian prefects. He also gave his name to a channel that ran through the eastern part of the city, the Fossa Augusta. The harbour was artificially created within a lagoon, its bases built on stilts, with a capacity to shelter 250 ships. Classis became a large naval centre filled with shipbuilders, sailors, oarsmen and sailmakers, whose funerary monuments record their skills. It was connected to Ravenna by a channel that permitted boats to dock close to the city, and between the harbour and the city another settlement, named Caesarea, gradually developed. In this way, the combined settlements represented a secure urban centre with access to the Adriatic and maritime communication with Constantinople.

Ravenna was built on sandbanks and wooden piles, with bridges over the many canals that flowed around and into the city, just like Venice in later centuries. It had all the components of a typical Roman city – municipal buildings, facilities for public entertainment, temples and, eventually, churches – scattered across marshy land separating the Padenna and Lamisa tributaries of the Po. Now the enormous apparatus of government, military forces, merchants and scholars all followed the emperor to their new capital. Stilicho's instinct proved correct. Ravenna became a nigh-impregnable centre, often besieged but rarely captured by force, and it developed into a capital with appropriately grandiose structures decorated in the impressive artistic styles of the day.

Nonetheless, it was a city whose importance stemmed from its location. It was, par excellence, a centre of connectivity. The tremendous forces that divided the Mediterranean and would forge a new settlement in the western half of the Roman world were enabled, focused and, in part, defined by it. Its history, therefore, is not simply the story of the city, its rulers and its inhabitants' way of life. It is also a much broader account of the far-flung powers drawn to and through it that were to make Ravenna a crucible of Europe.

I

The emergence of Ravenna as the imperial capital of the West

In the centuries before Rome adopted Christianity as its official religion, the Eternal City served as a symbol of world domination imposed by vigorous military leaders and efficient civilian administrators. Within its vast fortifications, along its famous streets, among its magnificent public buildings, emperors proclaimed their victories over distant foreign rulers in triumphal processions, statues and inscriptions. The Roman Senate commemorated those displays of power and the Roman populace joined in the celebrations, an essential element of the imperial policy of 'bread and circuses'. The imperial court, based in the great palace on the Palatine hill, processed appeals for judgment, military reports, tax returns and news from the frontiers, while priests attached to the temples ensured divine support for the empire through their sacrifices and prayers. It was to Rome that ambitious young men and women, talented poets, sculptors, merchants, mercenaries and entertainers, came to seek the patronage of Roman aristocrats and to make their fortunes. The city was the centre of the known world and all roads led to Rome.

Yet during the third century rulers no longer resided there permanently. An increasing number of emperors from military backgrounds based themselves in other, more strategically significant cities, and wherever the emperor went the court and part of the administration had to accompany him. In the ancient capital the Senate continued to appoint a prefect to govern the city and had responsibility for providing grain supplies for the urban population. On 1 January every year it bestowed the highest honour of the consulship on two individuals, nominated by the emperor, who gave their names to the year and thus established a dating system. The consuls were also expected to finance extravagant popular entertainment in the form of horse and chariot races, wild beast fights and displays of dancers, mimes and acrobats. While the Senate remained the power base of aristocratic families who had traditionally provided well-educated sons to govern the provinces, command the armies and protect the legal system, the shift away from Rome as the sole centre of empire created a novel style of imperial rule: a more direct attention to frontier security, increased military efficiency and supplies to combat hostile attacks. The reign of Diocletian (284–305) marked a distinct break, with changes that inaugurated a new era. During this period Ravenna emerged from its insignificant beginnings to become an imperial capital.

The Reforms of Diocletian

Diocletian was a military leader from Dalmatia who was acclaimed emperor by his troops in 284 and set out to reverse the economic and political decline characterized by modern historians as 'the crisis of the third century'.[1] He began by reinforcing the empire's northern borders, threatened by Sarmatian and Germanic forces, and reorganizing its administration. In a dramatic shift, in 286 he moved the imperial court from Rome to Milan, and appointed a military colleague, Maximian, as his co-emperor with authority to rule in the western half of the empire. Diocletian made his own capital in Nicomedia (modern-day İzmit in north-western Turkey), a city from which he could protect the empire from the threat of Persian invasion more effectively. This initial division of imperial authority was followed in 293 by the appointment of two junior emperors, called caesars, who would inherit full power after a fixed period. In this way, Diocletian tried to introduce a system for orderly succession that would prevent the wars frequently generated by rival claimants to the imperial title.

While the two emperors constructed palaces and administrative buildings in their new capital cities, Nicomedia and Milan, the two caesars set up their courts in bases closer to the borders: Antioch in northern Syria and Trier in the West. Other centres, such as Serdica (modern Sofia in Bulgaria) and Thessalonike (in Greece) were also used, producing new 'imperial' capitals that symbolized the extension and consolidation of Roman power far from Italy. From Milan major routes to central Europe and the East, and to transalpine Europe, the

North and West, established a more northerly communication system that partly replaced the centrality of Rome. Between 337 and 402 emperors from Constantius II to Honorius made Milan their preferred residence, and courtiers and imperial officials constructed elegant villas there for themselves.[2]

Diocletian's rule of four, the 'tetrarchy', designed to exert stronger control over frontiers very distant from Rome, was accompanied by drastic reforms to imperial government. Civilian administration was separated from military and was overhauled to increase the efficiency of tax collection. Fortifications, factories (for weapons as well as uniforms) and roads were built, while taxation in the form of food supplies for local armies was introduced, all designed to assist military success. Many provinces were divided into smaller units, which acquired a distinct hierarchy of officials under a governor and a salaried judge. As part of this process, in 297 Ravenna became the capital of the province of Flaminia, the coastal section of north-east Italy.

Today, Diocletian is generally remembered for his persecution of the Christians from 303 to 311, and his attempt to standardize prices by the Price Edict of 301. Neither policy succeeded and both were reversed by his eventual successor Constantine. His vast palace at Split marks a megalomaniac ambition that included the adoption of Persian regalia, such as wearing a crown and specifically imperial costume, and ceremonial that required visitors to bow low before his throne.[3] Although he and his co-emperor Maximian retired in 305 as planned, the peaceful transfer of power proved elusive. Military forces often refused to accept the designated caesar and instead promoted their own commanders as emperor. Constantine I was one of those, acclaimed by his troops at York in 306. He fought his way across the length and breadth of the Roman world, eliminating all rivals, to become sole emperor in 324.

The Innovations of Constantine I

In 330 Constantine inaugurated a new capital city in the eastern half of the Roman Empire, giving it his own name, Constantinople, the city of Constantine, and a Christian identity. By the late fourth century it became known as the ruling city (*basileuousa*) or queen of cities, *basilis ton poleon*, also *basilissa polis*. In recognition of the Christian faith,

Constantine also endowed large, prominently sited churches in major cities; ordered bishops to convene in councils over which he presided; and issued Christian regulations that were incorporated into imperial law. The emperor granted toleration to the Christians and stabilized prices by minting a reliable gold currency. Evidence of his building activity remains in Trier, which had developed into a magnificently fortified centre that protected the Rhine frontier of the empire for over a century, until 395. There he built the massive basilica, baths and palace decorated with frescoes, now painstakingly restored. In his new capital on the Bosporus, he established a New Rome, a name that both imitated and challenged its predecessor. Although the ancient aristocratic families who formed the Senate remained in charge of Old Rome's civic routines, republican traditions and polytheistic cults, their power was gradually weakened by Constantine's creation of an eastern senate in his new capital.

The extent of Constantine's adoption of the faith is much disputed. While Christian authors followed Eusebius in insisting on his conversion prior to the battle of the Milvian bridge outside Rome in 312, Constantine continued to promote an emperor cult in association with specific pagan gods. Nonetheless, one year later, in a decree known as the Edict of Milan, Christianity was accorded the same privileges as other cults, provided that all its followers prayed to their god for the well-being and triumph of the Roman empire, as every other group was obliged to do. Although the Christians constituted a minority and were by no means united, the emperor's patronage promoted their dominance, which was celebrated at the council that took place at Nicaea in 325. The emperor summoned all the bishops of the Roman empire and instructed them to determine a definition of Christian belief – the creed – and to resolve problems of clerical discipline. The meeting identified the doctrines elaborated by Arius, a deacon of the church of Alexandria, as unorthodox and heretical. It was later commemorated as the first Universal (Oecumenical) Council, its definition became the Nicene Creed and its supporters can be identified as Catholic Christians.

Constantine abolished the Praetorian Guard of Rome for opposing him at the Milvian bridge, and built several major churches in the city; he donated a large basilica, which became the Lateran palace, to its bishop, while his mother, Empress Helena, supervised similar building in Jerusalem, Bethlehem and Rome.[4] On his deathbed Constantine requested baptism from the bishop of Nicomedia and was the first Roman emperor to be given a fully Christian burial, in a sarcophagus in the mausoleum he had constructed for himself and his family, a rotunda attached to the church of the Holy Apostles in Constantinople.[5] After his death in 337 his sons fought each other to succeed to his position as sole emperor, but gradually a de facto division of the empire developed by which the senior emperor, who resided in Constantinople, normally appointed a junior colleague to rule in the West.[6]

In the course of the fourth century, the two halves of the Roman world gradually became less balanced. Under Constantine's dynasty the new capital of Constantinople increased in prestige as Rome waned; the transalpine western provinces remained poorer than the East, where power was more effectively exercised. On the death of Emperor Julian in 363, army officers took charge of the imperial position. One year later Valentinian, a general from Pannonia in the western Balkans, was acclaimed by the leading military and civilian officials, and he promoted his younger brother Valens as co-emperor. Both new leaders were obliged to deal with military threats, which took Valentinian to Trier and, later, Milan, while Valens settled in Antioch to deal with the Persians. Both were Christians, though Valens favoured the Arians.

The Theology of Arius

Despite the creation in 325 of the Nicene Creed to be recited at every church service, Constantine failed to settle the debate over Arianism. Some Christians thought that the insistence on one god (monotheism), which gave their faith such a different character from the cults of the ancient gods and goddesses (polytheism), was compromised by belief in the Trinity of Father, Son and Holy Spirit. Some insisted that it was improper for the Father not to take precedence over the Son, as fathers naturally created their sons. In the early fourth century, Arius had developed this objection to the equality of the three forms of God in a detailed theological argument that influenced much later thinking. His definition was countered by the Catholic assertion that all three members of the Trinity shared the same substance, essence and nature that predated the birth of Jesus, the son of God, as recounted in the Gospel stories. The Arians contended that the Son could only be of *similar* nature to the Father (in Greek *homoios*, hence the name Homoian attached to this theology). In spite of Arius' condemnation in 325, Constantine's successors observed this Homoian theology as orthodox and used missionaries to spread it among Germanic tribes. The Arians succeeded in founding a rival church that won the loyalty of fourth-century emperors and set their own 'orthodox', or 'catholic', definitions of correct belief, against those of their Catholic opponents, who claimed exactly the same terms.[7]

In Constantinople the Arian clergy drew considerable support from military commanders of Germanic and Gothic origin. The Goths had been converted to Arian Christianity as the official 'orthodox' faith, and their founding bishop, Ulfila (341–81), had devised a written alphabet for his people and then translated the Bible and liturgical texts into Gothic so that they could worship in their own language. In conjunction with the support of Constantius II (337–61) and Valens (364–78), Arianism extended to the West, notably to Milan, then capital of the western half of the Roman empire. The city's Christian population was divided into two rival factions, supporters of Arius and opponents who remained loyal to the ruling of the Council of Nicaea. In 355 a local synod held in Milan imposed the pro-Arian view and appointed Auxentius, a disciple of Ulfila from the East, as bishop.[8] Despite many attempts to unseat him, he remained in control of Milan for twenty years sustaining the doctrines of Arius, which continued to generate violent clashes as recorded by Ambrose, Catholic bishop of Milan (374–97).

In contrast, Arianism made less impact in Rome, still dominated by a largely pagan Senate. The Christian community, led by bishops who traced their line back to St Peter, had emerged very gradually from the city's profoundly embedded polytheistic cults with their impressive temples on the Capitol, where imperial sacrifices were made, and throughout the Forum where the Vestal Virgins sustained the sacred flame at the hearth of Vesta. Emperors very rarely went to Rome; the ceremonial visit of Constantius II in 357 was exceptional and was not repeated until Theodosius I made the same journey over thirty years later.[9] The fate of the empire, however, was being decided on distant borders far from the immediate concerns of the Roman Senate or the city's bishop, by Germanic military forces that had embraced Arian Christianity.

A telling weakness of the entire Roman administration can be traced to the increasing numbers of non-Roman mercenaries in the army. Often recruited in Balkan regions and commanded by their own leaders, who were paid for each campaign in which they participated, some pursued their ambition to occupy imperial territory as federate allies of the emperor, others merely threatened to invade and destroy. As the influence of these auxiliary troops grew throughout the fourth century, they began to dominate the Roman army and spread their adherence to Arian Christianity.[10] Their Germanic and Gothic generals gained senior military posts, deepened a serious division within the army, and promoted the rival form of Christian belief that was often shared by hostile groups beyond the empire's frontiers. The reduction of imperial fighting power became clear at the disastrous battle of Adrianople in 378, when Gothic forces killed Emperor Valens together with many of his generals in an unprecedented and total rout.

The Achievements of Theodosius I (379–95)

As a result of this devastating defeat, the young western emperor, Gratian, had to call on Theodosius, a disgraced Roman general who had retired to Spain after his father's execution, to save Constantinople from the Goths. Theodosius duly set out on the long journey from Spain to the East. His progress was interrupted by confrontations and then negotiations with the Goths over their determination to settle within the empire on the richer land south of the Danube. After battles with Sarmatians near Sirmium in the Balkans, Theodosius was acclaimed emperor by his victorious troops, and Gratian made his appointment official on 19 January 379 (Plate 1). Theodosius then settled a large number of Gothic families on imperial territory as federate forces, obliged to fight for the empire. His long reign constituted another major turning point in imperial history, marked by his successful campaigns against hostile forces, his promotion of Christianity as the official religion, and his decision to install his two sons as emperors, which marked the division of the East from the West.

In the history of Ravenna Theodosius is especially important as the father of Empress Galla Placidia, who ruled as regent in Ravenna from

425 for thirteen years. The emperor had married his wife Flaccilla in Spain and they had a son, Arcadius, born before 379, a daughter Pulcheria, who died young, and in 384 another son, Honorius. Theodosius also adopted his niece Serena, when her father died; he made her legally his daughter and married her to his leading general, Stilicho. After Empress Flaccilla died in 386, Theodosius negotiated a second marriage to Galla, a princess of the dynasty of Valens, which was celebrated in Thessalonike in 387. From this second marriage the only child that survived to adulthood was Galla Placidia, half-sister of the young princes Arcadius and Honorius.

Theodosius was not only a most pious Christian, strongly anti-heretic, but he also firmly opposed the polytheist cults and issued laws against their celebrations and sacrifices. Following the example of Constantine I he summoned another Universal Council of bishops to Constantinople in 381, where they repeated the condemnation of Arianism and agreed a slightly revised version of the Nicene Creed of 325. The council also issued several canons – ecclesiastical laws – including one that elevated Constantinople to a status equal to Rome.[11] Bishops of Rome considered this deeply insulting to St Peter (*Petrus*) the rock, *petra*, on which Christ had founded his church and which they claimed gave them superior authority. While the canon became a source of much rivalry between Old and New Rome, Theodosius had given legal standing to the emergent new civilization of early Christendom. Like Constantine, Theodosius campaigned throughout the entire Mediterranean world; he paid only one ceremonial visit to the ancient capital, in June 389 to celebrate a major victory. In Constantinople/New Rome he erected an Egyptian obelisk on the Hippodrome, mounted on a base that describes his achievements and portrays both the erection of the monument and the emperor receiving homage and bestowing victory wreaths to competitors in the races.

In 394 after victory over his western rival at the Frigidus, Theodosius went to Milan and summoned Serena, who was looking after his youngest children following the death of Empress Galla. Leaving Arcadius, then aged seventeen, in Constantinople, Serena duly travelled from the eastern capital with Honorius, aged ten, and Galla Placidia, about three, and all their staff, and arrived in Milan just in time to witness the emperor's death on 17 January 395. As decreed, his two sons assumed imperial power under the dominant influence of their military guardians, Rufinus in the East and Stilicho in the West. Theodosius had probably arranged for their baby half-sister to be brought up in the imperial household of Serena and Stilicho, where Galla Placidia lived for the next seven years. In planning the division of the empire, Theodosius may have hoped to prevent his sons from quarrelling over their inheritance, but rivalry between the two courts in Constantinople and Milan hampered any intended co-operation, especially when the nominal rulers were so young and inexperienced.[12]

The Child Emperor Honorius

In January 395 the ten-year-old Honorius thus became emperor of the western Roman Empire at the court based in Milan (Plate 2), where his guardian and very successful general (*magister militum*) Stilicho assumed effective control. With his wife Serena, an imperial princess in her own right, Stilicho had three children, Maria, Eucherius and Thermantia, who were all employed in advantageous marriage alliances. In 398 Maria, then about twelve years old, was married to the young Emperor Honorius, aged thirteen, and Eucherius was betrothed to Galla Placidia, integrating the orphaned imperial princess into Stilicho's family plans. It was a typical Roman betrothal of young children, though it did not lead on to marriage and the anticipated birth of a new generation. Nor did Honorius and Maria have any children before she died in about 407/8. Stilicho then persuaded the emperor to marry his second daughter, Thermantia, trying to ensure his own family's place within the ruling dynasty.

But at the turn of the fourth century Stilicho and the imperial court in Milan received news that Alaric, chieftain of the Visigoths, had ravaged Greece and was threatening to invade Italy. By 401 he had crossed the Julian Alps (at the far east of the range) and laid siege to Aquileia. He moved on to besiege Milan in the winter of 401–2 as well as capturing many cities. Stilicho defeated the Goths in the summer of 402 (although Alaric escaped with most of his cavalry), and then advised Honorius that it might be wise to move the court away from Milan to a safer centre. This was the moment when Ravenna was selected as a suitable residence for the rulers of the western half of the Roman Empire.

Ravenna, Imperial Capital

They chose the city of Ravenna partly because it was considered impregnable and partly because of its large port at Classis. The city was well served by river connections to the wide valley of the Po, rich in agricultural produce that could be stored inside the city if it was ever besieged, yet protected by treacherous marshes and lakes.[13] Built in the second century BC on sandbanks that protruded from the surrounding waters, Ravenna followed a typical square garrison pattern, the *quadrata romana*. It was considered a secure city where distinguished hostages or refugees could be accommodated. Bato of Pannonia, who had been forced to march in Emperor Tiberius' triumph, was confined in what was in effect a glorified prison; similarly, the wife of Arminius of the Cherusci brought up her son there. In AD 43 Emperor Claudius constructed a ceremonial entrance to the city, the Golden Gate, dated by his inscription.[14] The monument was demolished in the sixteenth century but drawings preserve an idea of its grandeur and a few fragments of the elegant sculptural decoration remain in the National Museum. The area around Classis also housed a school for training gladiators, who were said to benefit from the sea air. As naval challenges declined, the harbour at Classis was gradually adapted for the transport of goods across the Adriatic and throughout the Mediterranean. Shipbuilding, sailmaking and related maritime skills continued to be commemorated on funerary monuments, such as the second-century stele to Publius Longidienus, 'FABR.NAVALIS' (shipbuilder).[15]

Water-management was clearly necessary in the region where so many tributaries of the Po river descended towards the sea. Two major channels, the Padenna and the Lamisa, flowed around and into the city, creating a wide moat outside the city walls and a series of canals within them. In the sixth century Procopius described this:

> This city of Ravenna ... is so situated as not to be easily approached either by ships or by a land army ... A land army cannot approach it at all; for the river Po ... and other navigable rivers together with some marshes, encircle it on all sides and so cause the city to be surrounded by water.[16]

The Po's heavy silt also meant that the canals and river outlets were regularly blocked, and boatmen on barges stirred up the sediment with their poles as they punted around in the marshes. Visitors commented on the ubiquity of water but the lack of drinkable supplies, which was relieved by Emperor Trajan in the early second century when he ordered the construction of a major aqueduct, 35km long, to bring water from the Apennines.[17] Even so, floods and earthquakes in 393, 429, 443 and 467 caused buildings to sink with serious damage.

The three intimately linked settlements – Ravenna, Caesarea and Classis – already commanded the attention of fourth-century emperors as an important location for watching naval and commercial activity in the Adriatic. Indeed, Honorius had visited the city in 399, and in that year, he united the province of Flaminia with neighbouring Picenum, a coastal region to the south. Thus enhanced as the seat of a governor, Ravenna acquired a full array of Roman administrative and cultural buildings, as well as some impressive villas such as the *Domus dei Tappeti di Pietra* (house of stone carpets). In the circuit of its old city walls the Golden Gate made a particularly monumental, triumphal entrance that led to the heart of the city past an area associated with Hercules (perhaps a temple), the theatre and other urban facilities. The combined settlements were capable of housing and supporting a large additional force, such as the detachment of 4,000 soldiers, sent from Constantinople in the early fifth century, that remained in Ravenna. Like all Roman cities, Ravenna was governed by a local council (*curia*) of officials elected annually to collect taxation, provide basic services and maintain the city's walls and public buildings, though the council was under the ultimate authority of the commander of the fleet.

In addition to the governor and the naval commander, the city also had a bishop, whose status was rather lowly in comparison with the established sees of Milan and Aquileia. Severus is the first officially recorded bishop who attended a church council held at Serdica in 343 (Plate 52). The earliest references to a Christian presence in the area appear at Classis, which also claimed to house the relics of several early Christian martyrs, notably St Apollinaris who was later identified as the founding bishop of the city. It's quite likely that the earliest bishops resided there, but the episcopal centre was moved to Ravenna as soon as the imperial court was established, and the first cathedral building was probably begun in the early fifth century. Over the winter of 402–3, as this tripartite settlement on the Adriatic coast welcomed the emperor and his court, it took on its new role as the imperial capital of the West.

No contemporary writer provides a description of this process and how Honorius was received by the city. But we can imagine that he rode in through the Golden Gate, accompanied by his personal guards, to be acknowledged by the naval commander, the provincial governor and the bishop, cheered by the local inhabitants. The bulk of the court's equipment, furniture, records and supporting staff probably arrived by river transport along the Po from Milan. In December 402 the emperor's presence at Ravenna is confirmed by laws issued there and coins struck in his name at the new mint he established.[18] Like other capital cities created in the third and fourth centuries, Ravenna now experienced a major expansion as new and more substantial accommodation was rapidly constructed to house the court, part of the army, the imperial government's larger bureaucracy, officials and their families, Christian clergy, merchants and craftsmen, who followed the court to its new base. Transforming a fairly small Roman city with a large port into the leading centre of the western half of the empire was only achieved by substantial large-scale investment, which probably remained in the hands of the emperor and his immediate circle of officials; the city council may have found its power somewhat reduced from the full autonomous control normally exercised by such bodies. By the mid-fifth century, when fragmentary records of its activity are preserved, its role appears to be focused on the maintenance of civic archives, rather than raising taxes.

Not all the ruling elite of the western empire approved of the choice of Ravenna: some members of the Senate hoped that the emperor would return to live in Rome; other military advisers suggested that Arles should be made the new centre of government. Honorius was clearly sensitive to the disappointment of the Roman faction and made a point of visiting the ancient capital frequently, in marked contrast with his father's neglect. Late in 403 he celebrated an imperial entry (*adventus*) at Rome to mark Stilicho's military victory over Alaric at Pollentia (modern Pollenza), which had protected the city and the emperor from the Gothic leader's invasion of Italy (401–3).[19] Following the formal ceremonial of his arrival, Honorius retired to the imperial palace on the Palatine Hill, and at New Year the Senate nominated him as one of the consuls for 404. Assuming the office of consul involved more

THE EMERGENCE OF RAVENNA

choreographed processions in the palace and the Forum, culminating in the emperor presiding over military parades, games and chariot racing in the Circus Maximus, funded by him in his capacity as the new consul. These ceremonies, on which senators often spent vast sums in order to ensure the promotion of their sons, symbolized the status associated with honorific titles, as well as Roman traditions of lavish popular entertainment.[20]

While Ravenna could not compete with these ingrained traditions, Honorius returned to the task of creating facilities for the imperial court and administration in his new capital, the provision of grand churches for the Catholic population and the beautification of the city. Leaving Stilicho to manage military defence and to appoint civilian administrators, Honorius appears to have given up any ambition to rule in the manner of previous emperors. His move to Ravenna, however, ensured the survival of the Theodosian dynasty and provided his half-sister Galla Placidia with a stable court environment in which she grew up. Under his patronage, which she later continued, the city was endowed with the first of a series of extraordinary buildings that signalled its position as the new capital of the western Roman Empire.

PART ONE

390–450
Galla Placidia

2

Galla Placidia, Theodosian princess

Honorius' half-sister, Galla Placidia, plays a key role in the development of Ravenna, leaving an indelible imperial mark upon it. She was quite an unusual figure, not only in her turbulent life but also in her ancestry. Both through her parents and her experience she embodied the shifting character of the Roman empire, in which imperial rule came to be shared by different emperors in East and West who were interrelated, who governed by agreement and constantly competed for seniority and greater power, while non-Roman military leaders, often Christian, challenged the ruling families. Galla Placidia was born in Constantinople, where her mother died in 394, and her father Theodosius then ordered Serena to bring her to the West, as we have seen. After his death in January 395, her half-brother Honorius became nominally emperor of the West, and Galla Placidia, her nurse, Elpidia, and some personal servants settled in Milan close to Serena and Stilicho and their three older children.

At the imperial court in Milan, she would have heard stories about her grandmother, the powerful Empress Justina, who had vigorously promoted the Arian form of Christianity in the city against the catholic definition supported by Bishop Ambrose. She would have learned about her uncle Valentinian II who had been forced to flee from Milan in 387 when Maximus, a usurper, captured the city. The entire imperial family, including her mother, Galla, Valentinian's younger sister, sailed to the safety of Thessalonike. There, Empress Justina arranged her parents' marriage, and Theodosius agreed to restore Valentinian II to his throne. From her earliest years as an orphaned princess she carried a keen awareness of her imperial inheritance and of her grandmother Justina's dominant influence in political developments. In Milan young Galla Placidia also learned more about her parents than her nurses and servants might have been able to tell her in Constantinople.

During her lifetime Galla Placidia moved with ease across the Roman world, from Constantinople to Rome and further west into Gaul and Spain, although these regions were no longer under imperial control. They were, however, part of the new Christendom, a world united in Christian devotion that recognized the rule of Roman and non-Roman alike. Within this once Roman and now greatly expanded universe of faith, Galla Placidia was at home everywhere, although she was to spend the most important part of her adult life in Ravenna.

In 402, when the entire court left Milan for Ravenna, Galla Placidia's small entourage was also moved out of danger. Now aged about ten years old, she may have been accommodated in a palace in the newly designated imperial capital, close to Honorius, or with Serena and Stilicho, who also had a house in Rome. It is clear that she knew both cities and witnessed the exciting transformation of Ravenna as new buildings were constructed to house the court, the offices of government and troops, and as Bishop Ursus began work on the new cathedral. Serena probably arranged Placidia's education in the manner appropriate for a princess of the ruling dynasty, reading classical literature in Latin and Greek and studying imperial history. If Claudian's speech celebrating the marriage of Honorius to Maria, the eldest daughter of Stilicho and Serena, may be taken as an example of such an imperial upbringing, Serena read works of literature with her, taught her to sew and embroider and trained her in the appropriate behaviour for an empress.[1]

Barbarian Breakthrough

Three years after the court's move to Ravenna, on 31 December 405, Germanic forces broke through the Rhine frontier in a spectacular attack across the river. In Britain, Roman troops promoted their general Constantine to lead them in a rebellion, which spread across the Channel into northern Gaul. There he claimed imperial status as Constantine III. Despite a strong military response by the general, Sarus, sent from Ravenna to check the revolt, by late 407 Constantine had succeeded in establishing his authority at Arles, and issued coinage in his own name, while Sueves, Vandals and Alans continued their devastation of Gaul and advanced towards the Pyrenees. Stilicho took a major role in defeating these invaders, but the combination of an internal revolt with the incursion of such large numbers of barbarian forces greatly reduced imperial control of western territory. In the resulting turmoil and confusion, imperial officials failed to maintain military administration, leaving cities and rural landowners to defend themselves as best they could. In April 406 Honorius had issued a law promising freedom to all slaves who volunteered to fight alongside their owners against the invaders, itself an index of the growing desperation.[2]

In addition to the violent disturbances north of the Alps, Visigothic forces persisted in their efforts to invade Italy, as Stilicho had predicted. He then decided to use the Goths against the usurper, Constantine III, and made an alliance with their king, Alaric. As a result, Honorius was obliged to appoint Alaric as count of Illyricum, a military command under Stilicho's overall authority. But when the implementation of one specific military plan was delayed and Roman forces failed to participate as agreed, the Gothic leader demanded to be paid for his services, stating that 4,000 lbs of gold was due. Since the imperial court had insufficient funds, early in 408 Stilicho and Honorius went to Rome to try and persuade the Senate to provide the necessary money. The general's policy of conciliating Alaric was put to the test: after Stilicho's first speech the Senate decided against it and in favour of fighting the Goths; after his second, however, they reviewed that position and accepted the demand for 4,000 lbs of gold. Although the sum was large, it had the desired effect of sending Alaric off.

On 1 May 408 Emperor Arcadius died in Constantinople, leaving a seven-year-old son, Theodosius II, as his heir, and generating a major crisis. Honorius now became the senior emperor with authority over his junior colleague in the East, who would not be able to rule alone for a decade. While Honorius and Stilicho argued about how best to secure this authority, other advisers insinuated that Stilicho was trying to assume imperial power for himself or to set up his own son, Eucherius, as ruler. Taking advantage of these rumours Alaric invaded Italy again, prompting one section of the Roman army at Pavia to mutiny. Under this combination of political and military threats Stilicho found himself without sufficient troops or allies and sought asylum in a church in Ravenna. Honorius then ordered his death and Stilicho was beheaded on 22 August 408. The emperor not only had his own father-in-law killed, he also issued orders for the arrest of Eucherius and sent his wife, Empress Thermantia, back to her mother Serena in Rome. All

Stilicho's supporters were pursued; Eucherius was eventually executed and, in October 408, Serena was put to death in Rome, allegedly for sending support to the Goths (some rumoured that Galla Placidia had consented to her death). The conflict among the Romans opened the way for Alaric to advance on Rome.[3]

The Sack of Rome

In the winter of 408 Alaric began the first of three sieges of the city, which caused extreme hardship because the Goths secured control over all access and grain supplies. Despite a negotiated peace that briefly lifted the first siege, Honorius in Ravenna refused to honour the terms and, in April 409, the Goths returned. Embassies went back and forth between the Senate in Rome and the court in Ravenna, while Alaric repeated his desire for a treaty with the imperial government and his appointment as supreme military commander of Roman forces in the West, a demand regularly denied by the emperor. With the death of her guardians, Stilicho and Serena, Galla Placidia, now aged about eighteen, was in Rome and in extreme danger. She may have tried to leave the city, perhaps to flee to Ravenna, but in a moment of high drama she was taken hostage by the Goths who kept her in their camp.[4]

Late in 409 Alaric forced the Senate to elect a rival emperor within Rome, to replace Honorius, and insisted on his own appointment as supreme military commander. The chosen emperor, Priscus Attalus, immediately agreed that Alaric should lead a force to besiege Ravenna, where Honorius found himself threatened by the brilliant Visigothic commander. He prepared to flee from the city by boat, and was only dissuaded by the arrival of a military contingent of about 4,000 troops sent from the East and funds raised by the loyal administration in Africa, vindicating the choice of Ravenna as the capital.[5] Thus reinforced, Honorius ordered an attack on the Goths during a truce when negotiations were underway. This so infuriated Alaric that he immediately went back to Rome to besiege it for a third time. Had negotiations continued, Galla Placidia might perhaps have been released and a new settlement with the Goths agreed.

Instead, Rome capitulated rapidly. On 24 August 410 Alaric's Gothic followers entered the city and sacked it for three days. This was the symbol of unimaginable imperial decline that traumatized St Augustine in Hippo in North Africa, was mourned by St Jerome in Jerusalem, and was later attributed to the decline of pagan religious rituals by the historian Zosimus in Constantinople. There was no food in the city so Alaric had no choice but to leave the sacked capital.

Laden with booty, Alaric led the Gothic force south, taking with them the ex-emperor Attalus and a group of Roman aristocratic hostages including Galla Placidia.[6] The victors set off with their distinguished prisoners in search of supplies and a more permanent settlement, hoping to find both in Sicily. But the plan to cross to the island was thwarted by a storm and they had to turn back. Alaric fell ill and died before the end of the year and his brother-in-law and successor, Athaulf, realized that the Goths were trapped in the boot of Italy without naval forces or sea-faring skills. After devastating the southern provinces, he therefore marched the Goths back up the Italian peninsula, across the Alps and into southern Gaul. They had been on the move for nearly a decade, unable to convince the Roman authorities of their value as military allies who wanted to settle on land they could control, on the model of Theodosius I's grant made to previous Gothic tribes who had moved into the eastern part of the Roman empire in the 380s. And they took with them their prize hostage, the princess Galla Placidia, whose half-brother, Emperor Honorius, remained safely behind the walls of Ravenna.

Living with the Goths

Galla Placidia could hardly have expected to spend over three years in the wagons of the Goths moving from place to place. She was presumably treated well, both as an imperial princess and as a valuable bargaining chip, but however honoured the Roman hostages were, their lives must have been uncomfortable and their future uncertain as the Goths switched sides in numerous battles with Roman forces. Nor could she have imagined that she would marry the Gothic king, yet on 1 January 414 Placidia, now aged about twenty-one, was married to Athaulf. The contemporary historian Olympiodoros, writing in Greek in the East with detailed information from eye-witnesses, reports: 'Placidia, dressed in royal raiment, sat in a hall decorated in the Roman manner and by her side sat Ataulf wearing a Roman general's cloak and other Roman clothing.' Among his gifts to his wife were 'fifty handsome young men dressed in silk clothes, each bearing aloft two very large dishes, one full of gold the other full of precious – or rather priceless – stones which had been carried off by the Goths at the sack of Rome'. First, the Roman senator and ex-emperor Attalus sang the appropriate wedding song, and then the other aristocratic hostages joined in to celebrate the marriage in traditional Roman style.[7]

This most unusual wedding reveals a highly symbolic development, one that had a critical influence in Galla Placidia's life: the Goths who had captured her wished to display their commitment to Roman customs; the imperial princess who had been held prisoner recognized the strengths of the Goths and used the celebration to influence her new husband. The wedding followed entirely traditional Roman procedures, in which religion played no part though bride and groom were in fact both Christian, albeit of conflicting 'orthodoxies'. It generated a symbol of a new civilization, based on the combination of Gothic military and Roman cultural traditions. Later in 414, or early 415, the couple celebrated the birth of their first child, a son, naming him Theodosius after his maternal grandfather in traditional Roman style. In this way Galla Placidia presented him to the Goths as heralding a new union of Roman and Goth. Athaulf announced his intention to restore the Roman empire in a Gothic form, in which their son would rule over both communities. This would recognize the Goths' capacity to sustain the Roman empire, integrating them into its administration, enhancing their status and spreading the use of Latin and a broader Roman-style education among them. Athaulf incorporated several elements of Roman law into his own legal code, probably under Galla Placidia's influence.[8]

Since very few non-Roman authors left any account of their peoples' invasions of the Roman empire in the West, these have nearly always been understood as Roman and Christian writers experienced them: essentially violent, destructive and bloody. As a result, the fact that some groups of barbarians wanted above all to be accepted as federates of the Roman system of government, who would fight loyally for the emperor, has often been overlooked. Alaric's search for a territory where his people could settle, obey imperial laws and live peacefully led to Athaulf's marriage to Galla Placidia – a personal way of declaring the co-operation of different cultures.

The great ambition of the marriage was wrecked by the death of little Theodosius in 415, when the Goths had crossed the Pyrenees into Spain. He was buried in a silver coffin in a church somewhere near Barcelona. Shortly after, Athaulf was murdered by one of his grooms, presumably working for Sigeric, who succeeded to Athaulf's regal position and humiliated his widow by forcing her to walk 20km out of the city in front of his chariot and back. Although he was quickly replaced, Galla Placidia remained a hostage.[9]

Galla Placidia's early life has given historians of all times tremendous opportunity for imaginative reconstructions. Did she 'throw in her lot with the Goths' outside Rome because she believed they represented a more viable future than that offered by her half-brother Honorius? Did she imagine that she could survive as a Roman princess living among them? If so, how could the daughter of an emperor, educated to be empress, have tolerated the ignominy of marrying a Goth? Or did she fall in love with the young chieftain Athaulf during the three long years of being moved in wooden wagons over cobbled and unpaved roads?[10]

Such speculations about Placidia's agency are a modern misconception about the degree of individual choice open to imperial women. Because she had been raised by members of the ruling dynasty to fulfil the roles expected of an imperial princess, she had an innate knowledge of her status: she personified imperial traditions and duties, which would have empowered her to negotiate her position among non-Romans to a greater or lesser effect. But her personal views were shaped by a concept of the imperial feminine, which endowed women of the ruling dynasty with the potential power of leadership. Galla Placidia had been trained to perform that role to the highest standard. At the imperial court in Ravenna, and in Rome with Serena and Stilicho, her education had been a preparation for an imperial life, even if she found herself married to a Goth.

By 413 Honorius and his general Constantius were trying to negotiate her release, but Galla Placidia may not have been aware of their efforts. In 415 after the deaths of her son and her husband, however, her future as a hostage among the Goths cannot have seemed very promising.

3

Honorius (395–423) and the development of Ravenna

While Galla Placidia was living with the Goths, Roman power over the western provinces disintegrated still further. From 383 onwards the most northern province of the empire, marked by the border at Hadrian's Wall, gradually slipped beyond imperial control, and in 410, while the Goths were besieging Rome, Honorius responded to appeals for military assistance with a letter advising the cities of Britain that they must take care of their own defences. Although this may have been considered a temporary measure at the time, it proved to be permanent. Britain was abandoned to its indigenous inhabitants and the numerous hostile forces that raided and, later, settled in it. The emperor's letter was a clear sign that the old Roman world was shrinking back into its heartland of Italy even as it was expanding in a new eastern centre in Constantinople.

The Gothic attack on Rome in 410 confirmed that the city's overly long walls were impossible to defend without a much larger military garrison. It was also too dependent on its port at Ostia to survive a long siege. In contrast, Ravenna was clearly more secure and defendable, and as non-Roman militias continued to break through imperial defences, Honorius' decision to move from Milan to Ravenna seemed vindicated. The emperor therefore began to enhance his new capital and court with suitably impressive buildings. Although few literary sources mention this activity, archaeological evidence suggests that he resided in a large suburban villa dating back to the first century AD, which lay to the south-east of the present church of S. Apollinare Nuovo, beyond the original city walls. It was centred on a large peristyle courtyard with reception and living rooms on the north and south sides, enlarged in the early fifth century by an apsed dining room. The discovery of floor mosaics with circus scenes, including a victorious charioteer of the Green faction, suggests appropriate decoration.[1] The factions, Green, Blue, White and Red, organized chariot racing and other public entertainments in the circus of Ravenna modelled on Rome and other imperial capitals like Thessalonike. Although no trace of such a large structure has so far been found, a site close to the palace has been identified and mosaics of Hippodrome scenes reflect the pervasive love of such traditional sports. Later, Valentinian III celebrated New Year with games and chariot races in the circus at Ravenna, and in the middle of the seventh century the head of a rebel was displayed there. Honorius enhanced his palace with earlier Roman sculptures and statues of himself. A massive porphyry statue (now headless) might be one of these.[2]

New bridges over the many canals and tributaries of the Po that flowed around, through and under the city of Ravenna, as well as new fortifications around the harbour at Classis, are impossible to date precisely, but it seems quite reasonable to associate them with the arrival of the imperial court from Milan. An extensive new ring of stout brick fortifications, consolidated with re-used marble and other classical remains (spolia), was constructed to incorporate the new government buildings, villas for the courtiers, military garrison and public monuments within the city area. There is no consensus about their date, but if Honorius did not order their construction, the city presumably had adequate defences that were later expanded by Valentinian III. Honorius' building activity may have involved the adaptation and plundering of older buildings as much as new construction to accommodate his court and administrative offices.[3]

One of the key institutions associated with this immediate activity is the imperial mint, recorded in 402, the year of the court's move to Ravenna. Because the control of precious metals was always of major importance to rulers, mints were often situated within imperial residences. The first gold coins, solidi, issued in Honorius' name at Ravenna were probably struck in a building recently excavated, the Moneta aurea (for gold coinage), which seems to have been very close to, if not part of, Honorius' palace.[4] There was also another mint where bronze coins for everyday use were produced. A related monument was the Miliarium aureum, the golden milestone that was probably erected in the Forum of Ravenna, to mark the spot from which all distances should be measured. Rome provided the model for this central marker in the Forum at the very heart of the old capital, which was copied in Constantinople and now in Ravenna.

Agnellus, the First Historian of Ravenna

Much of the information about this most important period in Ravenna's growth was recorded four hundred years later, by a ninth-century local cleric named Agnellus. He is the first historian of Ravenna, a proud native of the city, assiduous in his efforts to recount the lives of all its bishops. His record of forty-six church leaders, from the mythical founder St Apollinaris to Archbishop George, Agnellus' own contemporary, is based on the similar one for all the bishops of Rome (the *Liber pontificalis, Book of the Pontiffs*), and is paralleled in other comparable lists.[5] It includes much curious detail derived from local witnesses, as well as inherited wisdom, often invented and entirely unreliable. Despite this, Agnellus was clearly determined to find out about the bishops of Ravenna, tracing their history from buildings, tombs, inscriptions, mosaic decoration and liturgical objects, such as altar coverings, that he had seen. His particular care in copying verses inscribed on buildings that no longer exist preserved many striking accounts of what individual bishops intended to achieve through their patronage. These antiquarian interests also led him to include many amusing anecdotes and stories that he learned from older citizens, probably enhanced by oral transmission and elaborated at every re-telling. Nonetheless, Agnellus is a consummate local historian and without his *Book of the Pontiffs of Ravenna* the history of the city would be very bald.

For the lives of the early bishops of Ravenna Agnellus found very little secure information and resorted to inventing suitably uplifting stories and short sermons attributed to these holy leaders or designed to characterize their activity. Since their dates are not documented, working out the order in which they held the see has provoked much debate. Wherever he found the tomb of a bishop, however, Agnellus recorded where it was and, in this way, associated church leaders with particular buildings, such as the church of St Probus in Classis, where many of the earliest bishops were buried.[6] He identified some in monasteries, preserving valuable information about the growth of such shrines, chapels or actual monastic communities in or near Ravenna, such as Bishop Liberius, 'the third of that name', who was buried in the chapel of St Pulio that he founded, 'not far from the Porta Novara', or Florentius, the fourteenth bishop, buried in another dedicated to St Petronilla, 'clinging to the walls of the church of the Holy Apostles'.[7] From the time of Bishop Ursus, however, Agnellus recorded much more detail, probably because Ravenna underwent such a major transformation in the early fifth century. And by the second half of the eighth century, when Agnellus was growing up in the city, he writes from first-hand experience.

Agnellus' *Liber pontificalis ecclesiae Ravennatis* draws on what must have been one of the most useful records of local events, the *Annals of Ravenna*, a year-by-year account of the most important events in the city, written in the fifth century but now lost. It followed the format shared with other city chronicles, which served as a form of calendar based on the names of the two Roman consuls appointed for each year on the first day of January. The tragedy for historians of Ravenna is that only half a page of the unique manuscript of the *Annals*, with its tiny images, survives in the archive of the cathedral of Merseburg (Plates 17 and 18).[8] What would have been a vital record of life in Ravenna and one of the rare illustrated annalistic chronicles of the late Roman empire has been consumed by time. From this fragment, however, we can extract useful entries for particular years and drawings that document events such as earthquakes. It is a reminder of the many texts, such as the *Histories* written by Archbishop Maximian, that have been lost.

The Papyrus Records

This lack of contemporary historical records is partially relieved by a series of documents written on papyrus, which formed the city's basic writing material and continued to be imported from Egypt well into the eighth century. The surviving papyri, some in the archiepiscopal palace of Ravenna, others scattered in many European museums, reflect the activities of traditional Roman municipal government through regular meetings, at which legal documents were witnessed and registered in the city's archive (*gesta municipalia*). From the earliest one preserved, dated 433, through to the late sixth century they record the participation of several local families who served on the city council, which

maintained some basic legal functions. Every year the council elected
its own officials who then presided over its meetings. The repetition of
family names among these *quinquinealis, decemviri, praesidii,* etc.
reflects the domination of a local elite, trained to manage the city's
finances, from taxation to purchase of grain and other basic foodstuffs.
We can thus glimpse the families who had probably participated in
local government for decades if not centuries. Names like Melminius
and Pompulius recur as sons and grandsons fulfilled the same inherited
roles, while fascinating information derives from the lists of less prominent members who witnessed the decisions recorded by municipal scribes.
Funerary inscriptions also provide names of individual citizens and
sometimes their professions, for instance, the tribute by Aurelia Domi-
tia to her incomparable husband, or the tiny sarcophagus prepared by
her parents for Licinia Valeria who lived only one year, six months and
six days.[9]

Similar records on papyrus were kept in all major Italian cities but
not many survive. In Rome, almost none; in Naples, a few. Those from
Ravenna preserve a wide range of local issues. Because legal formulas
had to be employed, the working methods are clear and individuals
with specific tasks can be identified. Part of the 433 record has been
reconstructed from six tiny fragments of papyrus later re-used in a book
binding. It concerns a dispute between two individuals (the younger
one named Lagalianus) and a church (not named), which is represented
by a notary (*notarius*), Contius. The two men had appealed to the
emperors, Theodosius II and Valentinian III, and received a rescript
(order) that imposed the payment of a fixed sum. Contius assisted at the
court hearing when the rescript was read aloud and Lagalianus' father-
in-law agreed to pay the fine. The rescript was entered in the official
court record (*gesta municipalia*). The older man also signed a *cautio*
(promise to pay) and swore under oath that he would do so within the
time limit, and then the *cautio* was also entered in the *gesta*.[10] Such a
procedure guaranteed the legality of decisions taken.

The City Council

For centuries, free-born men of all major cities within the Roman
empire who owned a certain amount of property had been obliged to

serve on the local council, which ran the city. Each council was expected to enrol one hundred members whose chief task was to collect taxes, and the city's autonomy was guaranteed only so long as the necessary sum was raised to finance local defence, provision of food, maintenance of facilities, security and festivities. The system had functioned effectively while prominent families competed to be on the council, but as the cost of curial duty rose, men who qualified were less prepared to serve. Ever since Constantine I declared that Christian clergy would be exempt from this service, many of curial status had been ordained in order to escape their responsibilities. Others tried to claim a similar exemption after fifteen years' service in the imperial administration, a privilege rescinded in 436 when Valentinian III set the qualifying level at an annual salary of 300 *solidi*, which was the equivalent of owning about 150 *jugera* of land. Yet repeated laws against the ordination of members of professional colleges, and skilled craftsmen who had fled to the country and married rural women, indicate that many were still trying to avoid curial responsibilities. In 458 these rural *curiales* were again ordered to return to their cities.[11]

Cities therefore often failed to maintain the normal figure of one hundred councillors. Many fourth- and fifth-century writers record the difficulty of finding enough local men with property, and of free birth, to qualify for duty. In Ravenna this may already have been the case before 402 when the arrival of the imperial court from Milan demoted the status of councillors. The *curia* was subordinated to imperial administration, although it continued to perform certain everyday tasks, registering trade agreements, transfers of property and, above all, wills by which local citizens disposed of their goods, especially gifts to the church of Ravenna.[12]

Bishop Ursus

Although Agnellus knew quite a lot about Emperor Honorius, he records nothing about the arrival of the court that might clarify the situation of the church of Ravenna in 402. It appears, however, that Ursus was bishop in 402, because when he died (on 13 April, Easter Sunday, probably in 426) he is said to have held the office for twenty-six years and some months and days (numbers not preserved). Agnellus often found the length of each bishop's episcopate inscribed on his tomb, though in the case of Ursus he had not seen it in person. 'Some assert', he says, that Ursus was buried in the major church of the city dedicated to the *Anastasis* (Resurrection), founded by him and called the Ursiana after him. He also notes that Ursus' successor, Peter, held the bishopric when 'the empress Galla Placidia offered many gifts to the church of Ravenna' (which indicates a date of *c.* 426–50).[13]

As the cathedral church of Ravenna was constantly embellished and (eventually) destroyed, Agnellus' early ninth-century description of it is the only record of its decoration at that date. From personal observation of the cathedral, he describes the rows of columns on the north and south sides of the church, indicating that the original building was a typical early Christian basilica. The walls were covered by most precious stones (probably coloured marbles), and the vault with multicoloured mosaics. He also records the names of individuals involved:

> Euserius and Paul decorated one wall surface, on the north side, next to the altar of St Anastasia, which Agatho made . . . Satius and Stephen decorated the other wall on the south side . . . and they carved (*inciserunt*) in stucco different allegorical images of men and animals and quadrupeds, and they arranged them with greatest skill.[14]

So here some of the patrons who paid for the original work are named, and possibly some of the painters, sculptors and carvers who recorded their activity in dedicatory inscriptions.

The Ursiana was built and embellished in accordance with the most fashionable style by local craftsmen, or others who accompanied the imperial court from Milan where comparable late fourth- and early fifth-century building and decoration is known (for example, S. Aquilino). They employed many different materials – marble plaques, mosaic, fresco and carved stucco – and displayed images of personifications (allegorical figures), birds (probably) and four-footed animals. To the east of the cathedral, Bishop Ursus built a baptistery decorated in similar style, which was used at the major feast of Easter when those who had been prepared for entry into the Christian community were admitted. In the middle of the fifth century this baptistery would be rebuilt with new mosaic decoration by Bishop Neon and is now known as the Baptistery of the Orthodox.

It seems likely that it was the arrival of the emperor and his entourage in 402 that promoted the construction of such a grand and lavishly decorated new basilica in the city previously dominated by mainly pagan monuments. As at Rome, many of the early Christian churches were attached to cemeteries outside the city walls, and the decision to build within the city reflected a new determination to replace the ancient gods: Agnellus notes that the Ursiana was situated in an area previously called Herculana (and therefore dedicated to Hercules) near the Vincileonian gate. He also mentions that Ursus built the bishop's residence, *episcopium*, attached to the church, close to the south-east wall where the Fossa Amnis canal left the city under the Bridge of the Millers, and a tower which may have been part of the aqueduct. Agnellus says the place was called Organaria because it was constructed entirely from a built device (*organa*, possibly connected with the work of millers or water-powered millstones).[15] This would echo the mills on the Janiculum in Rome and along the Tiber that operated on water power.

Honorius added to Ravenna's status by elevating the bishop of his new capital at the expense of Milan, using the argument formulated by his father Theodosius that the city where the emperor resided clearly had to be the ecclesiastical capital. He transferred six subordinate bishops from Milan to Ravenna, which thus gained considerably in territory as well as taxes and personal donations and legacies, but he did not grant the bishop independence from Rome.[16] Instead, he endorsed its subordination, perpetuating a rivalry between Ravenna and Rome, personified by many later bishops, which came to a head in the mid-seventh century.

Honorius' Government

In the aftermath of the disastrous sack of Rome, Honorius appointed Constantius as his leading military general, and the Roman poet Rutilius Namatianus took the chief civilian post of *magister officiorum*, master of offices. In 411 the emperor sent Constantius to defeat the upstart Constantine III, who was still holding power in Arles, and his victory the following year was marked by the public display in Ravenna of the usurper's head. The little fragment of the *Annals of Ravenna* includes a drawing of the heads of Constantine and two supporters set up on poles under the year 412.[17] Constantius also campaigned in North Africa to protect the provinces whose resources were so rich that their defence was central to all imperial strategy: they produced the wheat that had traditionally fed the city of Rome, as well as oil, wine and high-quality ceramic tableware, which was distributed throughout the Roman world. In 413, Honorius dispatched a naval force to blockade the coast of southern Gaul, which successfully forced the Goths established there to negotiate a peace treaty.

During the next decade Honorius celebrated his generals' victories and his additional consulships in Rome and in Ravenna. While his new capital provided a safe base for the court and became the hub of the traditional, imperial style of bureaucratic government, Rome remained the centre of imperial ritual and provided the more appropriate setting for the mausoleum Honorius constructed. In 407/8 he buried his first wife, Maria, there. With the murder of Stilicho, who had served as his guardian and very successful military commander, Honorius had shaken off the influence of an experienced adviser, repudiated his second wife, Thermantia, and also permitted the death of Serena. After the sack of Rome he visited the city on several occasions to reassure the survivors, to restore his authority with the aristocracy, and to distribute high-ranking titles to prominent senators. But he did not remarry and therefore had no heir to succeed to his imperial position. Fortunately for the dynasty, his half-sister Galla Placidia was able to fill this gap, as we shall see.

4

Galla Placidia at the western court

In 415, when the Goths in southern Gaul had been blockaded by Emperor Honorius' naval forces for two years and were desperate for food supplies, they sent several embassies to Ravenna, and late that year (or early in 416) they traded their honoured hostage, Galla Placidia, for 600,000 measures of grain. To arrange such a large shipment, imperial officials probably drew on supplies from North Africa and/or Sicily. The princess, now about twenty-four years old, widow of the Gothic leader Athaulf, was escorted back to Rome by Honorius' envoys, who also obtained the release of the other Roman hostages. She was accompanied and protected by a guard of Gothic soldiers, who remained with her thereafter.[1]

As the only daughter of Theodosius, and half-sister of both the emperors Arcadius and Honorius, Galla Placidia was the second highest-ranking woman of the dynasty, surpassed only by the reigning empress, Eudocia, in Constantinople. Before her arrival Honorius made arrangements for her future, and on 1 January 417 the emperor 'took her by the hand and gave her to Constantius', his favoured general, thus solemnizing their marriage. Olympiodoros records that this was done against her will, noting a rumour that Constantius had apparently wanted to marry her for a long time. Perhaps, as one of the negotiators with the Goths, he may have encountered her in Gaul. In any case she would clearly bring the most exalted rank to whoever married her, as well as the promise of children.[2]

Galla Placidia thus returned to the life of an imperial princess, now as the wife of a highly reputed military leader who divided his time between the imperial court at Ravenna, their home in Rome and his campaigns. She gave birth to a daughter, Honoria, in 417/18, followed by an all-important son, Valentinian, in July 419. Constantius' presence at the imperial court probably required the family to reside in Ravenna yet she also kept in close contact with Rome. In 419, for instance, when news of a disputed papal election arrived in Ravenna, she not only persuaded Honorius to intervene but also wrote her own letters appealing to the bishops of Africa and Paulinus of Nola to assist in resolving the matter. Sadly, the letters do not survive. The rivalry between two candidates, Boniface and Eulalius, was eventually settled and Placidia's close collaboration with Roman church leaders continued under popes Sixtus III and Leo I in the last years of her life.[3]

Four years after the marriage, on 8 February 421 Honorius elevated Constantius to the position of co-emperor of the West, and sent his imperial portrait to Constantinople to indicate his possible successor; he also crowned Galla Placidia empress, *augusta*, and named Valentinian, her young son, 'most noble boy' (*nobilissimus puer*) (Plates 3 and 4).[4] These promotions were not accepted in the East, however, which greatly angered Constantius. But in September 421, before he could react, he died, leaving Galla Placidia a widow for the second time. In these uncertain circumstances her young son Valentinian now became the most likely successor to the childless Emperor Honorius.

The position of the western ruler was most unusual. Although twice married, Honorius had produced no children. With limited interest in imperial government, he had relied on Stilicho until 408, and then turned to Constantius and promoted him to imperial status, presumably with the full support of Galla Placidia. His weakness and inability to engage with the imperial role now took an unexpected turn, as he developed an excessive affection for his half-sister. According to Olympiodoros, 'their immoderate pleasure in each other and their constant kissing on the mouth caused many people to entertain shameful suspicions about them'. The court scandal developed as rivalry between the empress's Gothic praetorian guard, 'the host of barbarians', and Honorius' imperial troops stationed in Ravenna provoked open fighting in the streets. In the same tense conditions Galla Placidia's steward Leontius, her nurse Elpidia and another servant Spadusa, were accused of plotting against the emperor. It's impossible to tell how these separate factors combined but the result was decisive: Honorius banished Galla Placidia and her family and servants from Ravenna. She fled to Constantinople and took refuge at the court of her nephew Theodosius II.[5]

Galla Placidia in Constantinople

When Galla Placidia, her children and servants arrived in the East in 423, they took up residence in a palace in Constantinople, later known by her name. She had returned to the city of her birth and for the first time met the emperor, then twenty-two years old, and his older sister, Pulcheria, who had prepared him for his imperial role. Pulcheria was also determined to prevent any challenge to Theodosius' authority by devoting herself and her sisters to a life of celibacy, which would protect them from becoming pawns in marriage alliances. At the meeting of these two princesses, eastern and western, they discovered that they shared basic traits: both had a grasp of imperial administration, understood the significance of traditional male leadership and sought to wield power within its constraints; they also shared a commitment to Christian observance and patronized the church. Although Galla Placidia was six or seven years older than Pulcheria and had lived through very different experiences, both had invested in their male relatives: Pulcheria in her younger brother, Placidia in her son's imperial inheritance.

On 15 August 423 Honorius died. News that John, the chief secretary (*notarius*) in Ravenna, sought to usurp imperial power reached Constantinople in October. Placidia realized immediately that her son Valentinian had a much better claim to rule the western half of the empire than any bureaucrat and set out to persuade the eastern court that he should be recognized and installed as ruler in Ravenna. In 424 Theodosius II agreed and confirmed Valentinian as *nobilissimus puer*; he also issued gold coins in the names of Galla Placidia, her daughter Honoria and his own sister Pulcheria. All these carried the title of *augusta* around their profile images with symbols of victory. The alliance between the two branches of the imperial dynasty was sealed by the betrothal of Valentinian (aged five) to Theodosius' daughter Licinia Eudoxia (aged two), in an attempt to unify and restore imperial order in the West, wrecked by Honorius and the Goths.[6]

In the summer of 424 Galla Placidia's family, accompanied by a large armed force led by the Germanic generals Ardabur and his son Aspar and a group of experienced civilian administrators, set off back to Italy. After surviving a terrifying storm at sea (later believed to account for Placidia's devotion to St John the Evangelist), they reached Aquileia in the spring of 425 where the usurper John was defeated and executed. They then proceeded to Ravenna, where Valentinian was acclaimed as emperor and prepared for his formal inauguration, which took place that October in Rome. Although seasoned political commentators, officials and military men were quick to warn that setting up a child as nominal ruler suggested weakness rather than strength at a time when strong government in the West was essential, the court in Constantinople had backed Galla Placidia.[7] For she ensured the continuity of dynastic succession in both halves of the one Christian Roman empire.

Galla Placidia and Valentinian III, Child Emperor

Empress Galla Placidia was now determined to exercise her authority within the West and for the following twenty-five years she proceeded to exploit it for her own ends. In Ravenna, the powerful group that arrived to establish the young prince Valentinian further reduced the status of the local city council and provincial administration to mundane daily activity. Any notables, such as general Castinus, who had supported John's promotion from chief secretary to emperor lost power as the praetorian commanders, Aetius and Boniface, took charge of western military forces, while administrators from Constantinople handled civilian matters. Yet the empress mother maintained a marked influence.

Through the second quarter of the fifth century, when Galla Placidia was empress in the West and her niece Pulcheria dominated the court in the East, non-Roman forces made a more determined effort to invade, occupy and settle on imperial territory. To resist this Constantinople relied not only on military strength: it also staved off attacks by diplomatic means, including payments of large amounts of gold and desirable goods like silk clothing and pepper. In the West, Ravenna was less well supplied with precious metal and, even before the sack of 410, Rome had been almost emptied of its surplus wealth by the huge payments made to Alaric. As we have seen, the military strength of the western provinces had been greatly reduced by fourth-century revolts and the capacity to recruit replacement forces dwindled as the empire shrank and tax revenues declined. Nonetheless, the court in Ravenna had to rely on Roman armies to deter the incoming forces, which gave military commanders enormous powers and responsibilities.

It was therefore unfortunate that the two leading generals, Aetius and Boniface, refused to co-operate. In addition to this harmful division in the military command, nearly all the units of the late fourth- and early fifth-century Roman army were staffed by non-Romans and often commanders identified by their non-Roman names as mercenaries. The troops that marched against 'barbarian' invaders of imperial territory in the Balkans and the West included 'barbarian' contingents from the same background, who spoke the same language and had the same customs and military skills. Not surprisingly, in cases of clear military incompetence or failure to pay, these units were tempted to desert or go over to the enemy. The military and civilian leaders who welcomed Galla Placidia and Valentinian to Ravenna in the spring of 425 knew full well how dangerous the 'barbarians' were. So did the senators in Rome.

The first and most symbolic task undertaken by Empress Galla Placidia was the inauguration of her son as emperor. After his acclamation at Ravenna, his presentation to the Senate in Rome was essential to both of them: it would confirm Valentinian in his imperial role and his mother as empress mother. On 23 October 425 the six-year-old was duly dressed in his imperial robes, crowned and hailed by the Roman population with long acclamations.[8] The imperial family remained in the city until the New Year when Valentinian took up his second appointment as consul in an extravagant ceremony with popular entertainment organized by the four circus factions: the Greens, Blues, Whites and Reds. In addition to chariot racing, a particular Roman passion, these performances also provided an occasion for the ruler to distribute gold coins, and extra supplies of bread, wine and clothing – all part of the much-loved tradition of 'bread and circuses'.[9] As the mother of the new, very young emperor, Galla Placidia signalled her position at the head of the government. The family then returned to Ravenna, where the empress ruled in the name of her son and built some of the most famous early Christian churches.

When Placidia set up her court in Ravenna, only the most elderly officials would have remembered previous empresses like Justina (her grandmother, who died in 388), but powerful women were not an unfamiliar feature of Roman imperial history. Flaccilla, the first wife of Theodosius I, and Serena, his niece and adopted daughter, who was also Galla Placidia's foster mother, had maintained this tradition. Emperor Arcadius' wife Eudoxia participated actively in imperial philanthropy and public service in the East before her daughter Pulcheria adopted the same role. They may well have taken further inspiration from stories about Helena, Constantine I's mother, who had been singled out as a major patron of the church by Ambrose, bishop of Milan.[10] At the imperial court of Ravenna the empress's authority appears to have been respected from the very beginning of her son's reign. The basic imperial machinery of the early fifth century was in place, sustained by imperial notaries who recorded all governmental decisions. Court officials, often eunuchs, knew how to organize the ceremonial aspects of imperial administration, and they adapted and rearranged previously male roles almost spontaneously. The essential feature was that the position of emperor was filled, and, in his name, government could continue even when directed by a woman. We can legitimately imagine the young Valentinian seated on the imperial throne, with his mother on another throne beside him, while leading officials and guards stood in their set positions around them.

Coins, both gold and copper, minted in Placidia's name after 425 display her regular profile portrait on the obverse and show her seated on a throne with her feet on a cushion and her arms crossed over her breast on the reverse. While this image is a modified version of coins commemorating male rulers, it shows the empress mother enthroned with the inscription, *Salus Reipublicae*, the safety of the Roman state. This symbolic association had been introduced to the coinage by Empress Eudoxia in the early fifth century, with the hand of God crowning her on the obverse – a major advance in the status of imperial wives.[11] Through Galla Placidia's coinage, minted in Ravenna, Rome, Constantinople and elsewhere, especially the bronze issues that were used for everyday purchases, inhabitants throughout the Roman empire learned of her authority. And they could see her as she would have presided over the imperial court at Ravenna, seated on a throne beside her son Valentinian III.

Initially Galla Placidia probably resided close to the imperial palace where Honorius had established his court. Clearly, she would have had to work with the council of regency that probably included leading military and civilian officials and formally ruled in the name of her son. In practice, between 425 when Valentinian was acclaimed as emperor and 437 when, aged sixteen, he was married to his cousin Licinia Eudoxia, he merely approved decisions taken by others, often by his mother. She would have attended meetings of the council in the imperial palace and presided at every formal announcement that her son made as emperor. Since her entire life (apart from the few years with the Goths) had been spent close to the circles of government and she had observed how emperors performed in both the western and eastern courts, she now stepped into the role that Honorius had neglected, and engaged more effectively in the business of imperial administration: issuing laws and enforcing them, maintaining peace through the law courts and internationally through diplomatic activity, raising taxation and paying the military, minting coins and sustaining markets, appointing and dismissing officials if they failed in their responsibilities or adopted corrupt practices, nominating western consuls, and all the other tasks normally undertaken by emperors.

Galla Placidia's Government

Much of this governmental business was conducted through reports received and responses given at Ravenna, demanding attention to written documentation as well as oral argumentation. Six tiny fragments of papyrus dating from 433, that had been re-used much later, reveal one aspect of this administration, as we have seen earlier. Two local men had appealed to the emperors, Theodosius II and Valentinian III; the particular nature of their quarrel with a church is not preserved, but a response was recorded. This must have been an order (rescript) signed off by Galla Placidia in her capacity as the official representative of the young western emperor (then aged fourteen). The appeal was settled by a fine, probably to compensate for some loss suffered by the church, and the complete document was then registered in the city's archive.[12] In addition to such routine administration, an earthquake shook Ravenna on a Sunday in September 429 and she had to deal with the damage caused. The *Annals of Ravenna* preserve a tiny drawing of this regular hazard, imagined as a monster emerging from the earth (Plates 25 and 26).[13]

From the very beginning of her son's nominal rule, Galla Placidia undertook to direct the government from Ravenna, while reassuring the Roman Senate of her great respect and good intentions. She issued a series of laws in the name of Valentinian III designed to protect the traditional rights of senators and to maintain the accepted divisions in civil society: a hierarchy of slaves under their masters' control, peasants (*coloni*) tied to the land, freedmen excluded from even the lower levels of imperial service, and free citizens. She also abolished part of the traditional gift of gold offered by the Senate to the emperor at New Year. For thirteen years, from 425 until 438, she managed the civilian and ecclesiastical administration and introduced important legal reforms. After 438, when Valentinian III assumed authority, she remained in Ravenna as the retired empress mother and, for a further twelve years, devoted herself to religious matters, philanthropy and building projects.

It is in the first period, when she acted as de facto ruler, that we can observe Galla Placidia's contribution to the survival of the western Roman empire. She rewarded her own supporters such as Boniface, who had sent her funds when she was banished from the court by Honorius – he was confirmed as count of Africa (*comes Africae*) – and nominated others whom she considered reliable to key positions, men such as Bassus, a member of the aristocratic Roman family of the Anicii, who was given the post of imperial treasurer (*comes rei privatae*) in August 425, when the imperial family was still in Aquileia. One year later he was Praetorian Prefect of Italy, a post he returned to again in 435, after serving as consul in 431.[14] From Honorius she inherited other reliable men, such as Anicius Acilius Glabrio Faustus, prefect of Rome, who had refused to recognize John the *notarius* and usurper of 423; he was appointed to the same post in July 425, and is named in five laws issued at Ravenna between 425 and 428. In 437 Placidia sent him to Constantinople to negotiate Valentinian's marriage to Licinia Eudoxia. The empress's reliance on the Anicii family was balanced by the appointment of others, such as Petronius Maximus, twice Praetorian Prefect, and Consentius, an official from Narbonne who held office at Ravenna between 437 and 450 and became Valentinian III's notary (*tribunus et notarius*).[15] But she seems to have had difficulty filling several of the key civilian administrative positions, which were left vacant. A similar neglect continues under Valentinian III (437–55), suggesting that imperial administration in the West could not compare with that in the East, where all these posts were regularly filled.[16]

Although the eastern court had provided a strong military and civilian contingent to establish Valentinian as titular emperor, none of the advisers from Constantinople could handle the rivalry among the military commanders that surfaced almost immediately. Galla Placidia tried to separate the two leading generals by sending Aetius to Gaul and leaving Boniface in Africa. In 425 she appointed a less celebrated general, Constantius Felix, as the military leader for Italy, but in May 430 he was killed on the steps of the cathedral at Ravenna with his wife and one of the cathedral deacons. Rumour held Aetius responsible for these murders. Two years later, Boniface died of a wound inflicted during a violent fight with his rival, though Aetius continued loyally to combat numerous challenges to imperial control in Gaul.[17] His persistent refusal to co-operate with other military leaders, however, weakened the court at Ravenna.

Within the imperial capital, Galla Placidia found a committed supporter in Bishop Peter, later called Golden-word (Chrysologus), one of the few church leaders not elected from the local clergy but brought in from nearby Imola. Because this was so unusual, his promotion is recorded as a miracle in the *Book of the Pontiffs of Ravenna* and is attributed to Pope Sixtus III's vision of Sts Peter and Apollinaris. A delegation from the priests and 'the whole assembly of the people' had gone to Rome to request the consecration of their own candidate, but the pope had insisted on Peter, the deacon from Imola.[18] The pope's (and empress's) candidate prevailed and Peter 'the golden word' became famous for his sermons, which were copied by later church leaders as models of outstanding preaching. Although he condemned Arians among many other heretics, the Gothic and Germanic Christians appear to have maintained their Arian worship in their own churches at Ravenna, protected by the empress. With the co-operation of the Catholics under Bishop Peter, the two Christian communities coexisted in the capital.

Establishing Precedents

In matters relating to the law, Galla Placidia also made a decisive contribution in an imperial speech delivered on 7 November 426 to the Senate in Rome. Although the author of the speech and the person who actually gave it are not recorded, it was probably due to the empress's intervention. It set out a series of new rules, which have been described as a mini law code: a serious reform of a wide range of problems in testamentary law, gifts and transfers of property through the emancipation of slaves, including both general principles and specific instances. This so-called *Law of Citations* also attempted to clarify which ancient legal authorities were to take precedence over others and how discrepancies between them were to be settled.[19] It states that the opinions of five classical lawyers of the first and second centuries might be cited, and others, provided that the texts were accurate, and in the case of disputes, the commentaries of Papinian were to be adopted, because he was 'superior to any other'.

This speech, of remarkable competence, was given in the name of the seven-year-old Valentinian III. The text originated in the West with no relation to other comparable efforts in the East, although it does seem to be in some way connected to the first legal commission set up by Theodosius II in Constantinople only three years later in 429. Normally such legal pronouncements were drafted by officials – expert lawyers – with the title *quaestores sacri palatii*, but none are recorded in the West after 412. So, who was the author of this wide-ranging initiative? Galla Placidia has been proposed as the initiator and Antiochus, *quaestor* of the eastern court, as the author; others see Galla Placidia as the chief author.[20] Her understanding of the importance of written law can be traced back to the time when she was a hostage of the Goths and influenced Athaulf to add some Roman legal principles to his rule.[21] She surely also discussed legal matters with experts in Constantinople during her stay there. And she must have had trained legal counsellors around her in Ravenna, even if no official was granted the title of *quaestor*, chief legal adviser to the emperor. Among her other early rulings, one suggests a personal interest: it was designed to facilitate the right of mothers to inherit their children's estates and reflects her own experience of the insecurity of widowhood.

Some hint of Galla Placidia's commitment may be seen in another important imperial oration, of 3 January 426, just after Emperor Valentinian assumed the consulship, which stated that emperors are bound by the law. A later one, of 25 February 429, declared that the law should be 'common to us and to private persons', that is, emperors are not above the law (which was the Hellenistic view) but are bound by it (the republican Roman view), an oration repeated on 11 June 429. This suggests that in the first four years of Valentinian's rule, when his mother had a determining influence, legal reform was strongly promoted by the imperial administration. It coincides with an even more vigorous reform of legal practice in the eastern Roman Empire. Galla Placidia's 426 *Law of Citations* echoes concerns that had resulted in changes to the professional teaching of law in Constantinople. In 425 two posts were established at the university of Constantinople, one for law and the other for statutes. Freelance teachers of law were barred from practising and approved professors were given much higher status, equivalent to senior governors and top civil servants. In this reorganization of higher legal education professorial salaries were fixed and specific facilities established. Four years later, in 429, Theodosius II set up the first commission to explore a complete reform of imperial law, which resulted in the Legal Code that bears his name.

Both imperial courts, therefore, had been concerned to clarify the contradictions inherent in the vast number of legal rulings issued over centuries. These included imperial decrees, called constitutions, which resulted from judicial decisions taken by the emperor or by magistrates in his name, and rescripts, which were imperial responses to petitions sent by individuals.[22] When the eastern commission requested copies of all the constitutions issued by emperors in the West since the time of Constantine I, Galla Placidia was ready to provide them and the Code contains a preponderance of western laws. Her officials also appear to have taken great care in the laws prepared in her son's name. In Constantinople the task of sifting through all the accumulated legal enactments was entrusted to a second commission of fourteen experts, who worked remarkably quickly to produce a compendium of Roman imperial law in just over two years.

Accession of Valentinian III

This was the impressive work Valentinian approved in 437 when he went to the eastern court to marry Eudoxia (Plate 5). The new Code of Roman Law, prepared in Constantinople, was named after the eastern emperor (the *Codex Theodosianus*).[23] After the very grand wedding in

Thessalonike, Faustus, the praetorian prefect, accompanied the young couple back to the West, sailing around Greece via the imperial palace at Split to Ravenna. He presented the codex to the Senate in Rome on 25 December 438.[24] For the first time the entire body of Roman law was made available in a compact and manageable form; it was to have an enormous influence in the barbarian kingdoms of the West.[25] Indeed, the first five books of the Theodosian Code, which are incompletely preserved, can be reconstructed from the *Breviarium of Alaric*, a Visigothic king who compiled his own law code in 506 for the Roman population under his control. This copy includes the *Law of Citations*. While Justinian's Codex of Civil Law may be better known to legal historians today, the Theodosian Code made a more lasting impact on the formation of European legal principles, and Galla Placidia's efforts were incorporated into it.[26]

The Theodosian Code of 437 provided clear guidance for solving myriad legal problems ranging from disputes over land ownership and trade contracts to the punishment of thieves, murderers and rebels, observance of traditional religious cults and the regulation of correct weights and measures. Family affairs and inheritance laws were fully covered, for example, the rights of children of a first marriage in relation to those of a second, and appropriate punishments laid down for disloyal servants and runaway slaves. The final book, Book 16, devoted to matters of religion, included a law issued in 386 by the fifteen-year-old Valentinian II to protect the right of Arian Christians to hold their services without disturbance. Those agitators who disturbed the peace of the church (by attacking the Arian community) were identified as 'authors of sedition . . . they shall also pay the penalty of high treason with their life and blood'.[27] The law reflects the tense situation in Milan at the time when Valentinian II's mother, Empress Justina, campaigned against the Catholic Christians. Although the situation had changed radically by the 430s, all previous laws had to be included in the Code, and the notion of free assembly for religious purposes remained relevant.

In 438 the newly married couple returned to Ravenna and moved into the imperial palace, obliging Galla Placidia to retire to her own palatial accommodation in the north-west of the city near the church of S. Croce (the Holy Cross), where she probably took a less prominent role in the administration. Yet she remained a formidable force and power within the West. Valentinian III, now aged nineteen, took over

44

the major tasks of government, aided and sometimes bullied by Aetius, the military supremo of the 430s to 450s. But neither Aetius nor any other adviser foresaw Vandal ambitions and took firm steps to prevent this 'barbarian' tribe from conquering and, eventually, occupying the western provinces of Africa, Mauretania and part of Numidia. In 439, devastatingly, they captured Carthage. The loss of the richest areas of North Africa brought with it further serious decline in imperial power in the West.

5

Galla Placidia, builder and empress mother

Galla Placidia is forever associated with the Mausoleum in Ravenna that bears her name. With its resplendent starry sky and blue and gold decoration, bordered by brilliantly coloured, geometric *trompe-l'oeil* patterns, garlands of flowers and fruit springing from baskets, it remains to this day one of the most beautiful burial places ever built (Plates 6–8).[1] Who wouldn't want to be laid to rest under such an array of stars, doves, deer and vines, with the Good Shepherd, the Gospel writers and St Lawrence for company? In the building's compact cross shape, dimly illuminated by light glinting through the alabaster windows (not original), three huge sarcophagi are clear – one in each arm of the cross. But despite its name, this chapel was not planned as the final resting place for Galla Placidia; it was part of a larger basilica dedicated to the Holy Cross, which no longer survives. When the empress died, she was buried in Rome in 450. The astounding decoration of what is now called her Mausoleum is a stellar part of her achievement. It is not simply an unequalled example of early Christian art. It is an architectural witness to her claim on imperial power, her grasp of the 'imperial feminine' and her belief in the utmost importance of the hereafter.

This Mausoleum was originally connected to the church of the Holy Cross, one of the major monuments built by the empress between 425 and 450.[2] Excavations indicate that the church was constructed in the form of a huge cross, with a corridor across the west end that linked the Mausoleum, to the south, with a chapel dedicated to St Zacharias to the north, now lost. The walls were decorated in coloured marble revetment, stucco and mosaic, with hexameter and pentameter verses carved on the arches, and an image of Christ acclaimed by angels above the four rivers of Paradise derived from the Book of Revelation. In his ninth-century description of it, Agnellus adds, 'some say that the Empress Placidia herself ordered candelabra to be placed on four round slabs of red marble ... with candles of specific measure ... and she would pass the night praying in tears for as long as those lights lasted'.[3] Since the Mausoleum includes a figure usually identified as St Lawrence, approaching the grid over a great fire on which he suffered martyrdom, the chapel may have been dedicated to him. Many theories claim to establish who was buried in the three sarcophagi, but they too remain disputed.[4] Because the floor level has risen very considerably above its original foundation, the chapel today appears rather squat. But the mosaic decoration has ensured its place among the best known and beloved monuments of early Christendom.[5]

When Ravenna became the centre of imperial court life in the early fifth century, builders and craftsmen of all architectural and artistic techniques had come to the city in hopes of employment. Across Italy, bishops were constructing churches and octagonal baptisteries that often portray white doves flying over an impressively contrasting dark blue starry sky while saints prayed. Whether teams of craftsmen moved from site to site to create these elegant dome and apse decorations or local artists were inspired by new models to emulate a particular style, Ravenna clearly had access to the best. What remains is breathtaking, yet it is also a signal of how much more we have lost.

S. Giovanni Evangelista

The second major church commissioned by Galla Placidia is a very large basilica dedicated to St John the Evangelist, which had been promised to the saint in recognition of his saving the empress and her family from shipwreck during a storm on their way back from Constantinople, probably in 425. As the daughter of one emperor and the mother of another, Galla Placidia connected three generations of the dynasty that she commemorated on the triumphal arch of this church. Since the empress mother was also depicted in the leading position within the apse, it was probably consecrated before Valentinian III gained his majority, which suggests a date some time between their safe arrival in the West in 425 and 437.[6] The inclusion in the apse of Bishop Peter Chrysologus confirms the same period. Although it was probably the first of Galla Placidia's churches, it may have taken several years in the early 430s to complete.

The original decoration of the interior was replaced in 1568. Then, in 1944, most of the church collapsed when it was hit by Allied bombing. However, the drawings made by earlier antiquarians provide us with vital evidence of its decoration. The triumphal arch that frames the east end of the church in front of the apse – and thus attracts immediate attention – carried inscriptions and portraits.[7] Here, Galla Placidia arranged for an unprecedented display of imperial propaganda: her own dedication in large capital letters ran over the semicircle of the arch, above twelve portraits of her ancestors and relatives, representing the dynasties of Valentinian and Constantine the Great and demonstrating her own claim to imperial authority. Her grandfather, Valentinian I, and uncle, Gratian, headed the left section, with Constantine, her father Theodosius I and her half-brothers Arcadius and Honorius on the right. These were all labelled divine, *divus*, a common attribute of emperors, as was her dead husband Constantius (misrepresented as Constantinus) on the opposite side. Below them, her two brothers, Gratian and John, who died as infants, and Theodosius, her own son from her marriage to Athaulf, all identified as *n(obilissimus) p(uer)*, most noble boy, were commemorated. On the wall of the apse she also depicted the figures of Theodosius and Eudocia, the ruling couple in Constantinople, and Arcadius and his wife Eudoxia, their predecessors, standing either side of Peter Chrysologus, who celebrated the eucharist directly behind the altar in the apse. Above the imperial portraits were more familiar elements of church decoration, the Evangelists and Christ enthroned, and inscriptions which detailed the particular assistance of St John during the sea storm. None of the other churches Galla Placidia constructed in Ravenna and Rimini made such an obvious claim to her imperial status.

After the Second World War, the church was painstakingly reconstructed using the original columns and capitals that survived. Some fascinating thirteenth-century mosaics depicting the conquest of Constantinople in 1204 by the forces of the Fourth Crusade were found during the restoration, but no trace of the original decoration.[8] Today the Gothic portico attached to the west entrance gives the church a very different appearance, but inside it has been rebuilt in its fifth-century form, a vivid reminder of the era when Ravenna assumed its new role as the western capital. In her patronage of such an impressive, large-scale basilica, Galla Placidia intended to demonstrate that her city was as great a capital as Milan, Trier or Arles that had all served as imperial centres. She may even have wished to rival contemporary churches in Rome and Constantinople and the architectural heritage of her half-brother Honorius.[9]

As well as the display of her imperial claims at S. Giovanni, Galla Placidia recorded her patronage in an inscription read by Agnellus in the mid-ninth century: it was on the lip of a gold chalice dedicated to St Zacharias, whose chapel lay at the north end of the western corridor of S. Croce.[10] By the mid-ninth century the inscribed chalice had been moved to the cathedral church (the Ursiana) and Agnellus knew that it was used in the processions that celebrated the Christmas liturgy in his day, along with golden crowns and other gold and silver vessels. In this way, his own experience of the Feast of the Nativity confirms a gift made by Galla Placidia to the chapel of St Zacharias over three hundred years earlier. The empress also endowed the church of Ravenna with a huge golden candelabrum that weighed 7 lbs. According to Agnellus, at the centre of this lamp there was a medallion with her portrait and around it an inscription which read: 'I will prepare a lamp for my Christ'.[11] The lamp may have been in a circular form that could support several candles around the edge, with a painted or relief medallion of the donor in gold at the centre. Such lamps, crowns and liturgical vessels of silver and gold were often inscribed with the names of the donors and were carried in procession on feast days.

The Expansion of Ravenna

As the seat of the imperial court, Ravenna attracted many to service its needs and others who hoped to make a career in the administration or army. To run the government trained scribes were essential to record decisions, using the normal writing materials of papyri, reeds woven into sheets imported from Alexandria, and quill pens to write in black ink made from carbon. Facilities for their activity and the storing of their archives had to be constructed. In addition to such secular building, the empress directed the work of many craftsmen and engineers to the beautification of Ravenna, to make it a centre of Christian artistic production to rival all other imperial capitals. She probably played a part in the ecclesiastical promotion of Ravenna to ensure that it was listed after Milan and Aquileia as a leading, metropolitan bishopric in 431.[12] During her regency the city expanded and consolidated its position as a major centre of commercial, religious, administrative and architectural activity in the Adriatic and beyond.

In these many tasks she was assisted by her new ecclesiastical leader, Bishop Peter, who mentions the presence of the pious empress, with the imperial family, at his inauguration in 431. They are described as 'an august trinity of emperors', and Valentinian is elsewhere named as 'her ever-august son'.[13] A later allusion to their attendance in the cathedral church suggests that Galla Placidia regularly took her children and members of the imperial court to listen to the bishop preach. In his inspiring Sunday sermons Peter Chrysologus used a Gospel reading to explain correct Christian interpretation and to exhort his listeners to live better lives, practising true Christian morality and charity. For instance, when condemning the performance of pagan spectacles at the Kalends of January, that some excused saying, 'it's only a desire to take part in the sport . . . joy over the new era . . . the beginning of the year', he warns that these are sacrilegious events, obscenities based on lies, that 'drag the participants toward Tartarus, hastening to Gehenna'. He urges his flock to liberate those who thus celebrated the New Year wearing animal masks, cross-dressing, putting themselves on the level of asses and masquerading as demons: 'Let us restrain those who are thus running to perdition.' On the occasion of St Cyprian's feast day, he warns: 'Brothers, do not think . . . that the birthdays of the martyrs should be celebrated only by meals and more elegant banquets.'[14]

His homilies mention groups of Jews, whom he hoped to convert; Arians, the worst of heretics; Epicureans and polytheists, whose paintings and statues of gods represent adulteries, incest and cruelty; and fortune-telling, divination and palm reading, which he condemns as 'instruments of the devil'. In each sermon he tackled a complex theological issue and kept the text admirably short, so as not to tire the audience. Chrysologus also describes the beauty of the imperial palace, with its gold, shining marbles and paintings, as well as gardens, which together represent the heavenly kingdom, and records the presence of slaves, sailors, lawyers working in the courts, farmers and the devastation caused by pestilence and famine. Through these sermons, which were collected together by local clerics in the eighth century, the flourishing Christian community in Ravenna under Placidia's rule comes to life.[15]

Valentinian III, Emperor (438–55)

While the empress performed her imperial duties most effectively, elevating Ravenna to a much higher status than it had previously enjoyed, she appears to have been a terrible mother. She neglected to prepare her children for their roles. Her daughter, Honoria, was not married at the appropriate age but remained in her own palace in Ravenna with her servants. Her son Valentinian was not allowed to take over the government fully in 438, and ten years later when an outsider visited Ravenna he found the empress mother 'ruling the city'. When Cassiodorus wrote a eulogy of Theoderic the Great's daughter, Amalasuintha, in 533, he employed a very unfavourable comparison with Galla Placidia, accusing her of overprotecting her son 'so that he endured what he could scarcely have suffered if abandoned'. This harsh judgement was connected with her inability to sustain the full extent of the empire: 'the empire she slackly ruled for him was shamefully diminished ... she weakened the soldiery by too much peace'.[16] Clearly, in marking the contrast with Amalasuintha Cassiodorus exaggerated Placidia's failure. But there may be some truth to the claim that she did not give her children adequate guidance for their imperial roles. Both made disastrous decisions as soon as they could shake off their mother's control.

Valentinian had been installed as a very young emperor and grew up in Ravenna while his mother handled imperial business. The betrothal arranged in Constantinople in 424 gave him an imperial princess, Licinia Eudoxia, as his bride in 437 at Thessalonike, and the couple returned to Ravenna to assume control (Plate 5). Although he remained the junior partner beside his cousin Theodosius II, the two emperors represented one ruling dynasty united under one Roman legal system. In 438 Valentinian took over nominal direction of the government in the West, using his own officials, drafting his own laws and maintaining communication with Constantinople. While he spent several years in Rome, he continued his mother's efforts to endow Ravenna with fine new monuments. He built another palace at the Laurel grove (perhaps a reflection of the name of the Daphne palace in Constantinople), which no longer survives but is described by Merobaudes, a contemporary poet. In a visual representation of the dynasty, Valentinian III and Eudoxia were displayed on the ceiling with scenes from the emperor's life that included his mother, sister, children and cousin. This palace may have overlooked the circus in Ravenna, where the emperor provided the four-horse chariots for races, but by the mid-ninth century it no longer existed.[17]

In the fifth century, however, Sidonius Apollinaris describes such celebratory races in a poem addressed to his friend, Consentius, who participated in person. These 'private games' to mark the start of the new year in Ravenna involved harpists, flute-players, mimes, rope-walkers and clowns, who quaked before the competing chariots of the Green, Blue, White and Red factions. Sidonius recalls: 'you chose one of the four chariots by lot and mounted it, laying tight grip on the hanging reins'; he then evokes the methods used to incite the horses while they are held behind the barrier of the starting gates, the excitement of the trumpet call that opens the race and Consentius' skill in winning in the sixth and final circuit (scenes preserved on mosaics excavated from the palace area in Ravenna). His friend was a tribune and notary to the emperor as well as 'an honest and skilled interpreter', employed by Valentinian on missions to Constantinople when he needed to transmit messages to his father-in-law, Theodosius II.[18]

'Empress' Honoria

Meanwhile his sister, Honoria, must have been educated in a suitably imperial style, but Placidia failed to arrange a marriage for her when she reached the right age (about fourteen) in 432. Given the disturbances and dangers of Galla Placidia's early life, it is strange that she didn't take more care of her daughter. She may have intended Honoria to follow a celibate Christian life like her cousins in Constantinople; Valentinian may also have wanted to prevent his sister from producing a male child to rival his own claims on imperial authority; other advisers may have thought it better to hold her 'in reserve', so that if anything happened to the young emperor, she could be used to perpetuate the dynasty.[19] Whatever the reason for her remaining unmarried, Honoria was not properly integrated into court life and a stray reference in the *Chronicle* of Count Marcellinus for the year 434–5 records an affair that resulted in a pregnancy. If this is accurate, Valentinian would certainly have insisted on his sister's seclusion and the child would have been concealed as far as possible. Since Marcellinus wrote in the East and is not terribly well informed about western developments, it may just be another rumour that circulated much later. But there is more reliable evidence that in 449, when she was thirty, Honoria broke away from her restricted life in Ravenna by having an affair with her steward, Eugenius. Valentinian reacted furiously and proposed to marry her to a Roman senator, which provoked a more firmly documented scandal.

In 449 Honoria appealed to none other than Attila the Hun to come and rescue her from Ravenna, sending Hyacinthus, one of her eunuch servants, to him with her request. Because Attila was the most aggressively determined enemy of the Roman empire at that time, her invitation constituted a stupendously treasonable act. And the seriousness of her message was marked by the gift of a ring, which Attila interpreted as a proposal of marriage. If he could marry the imperial princess, sister of the western emperor, she might bring at least half the western provinces as her dowry! The dangers were clear enough to both Theodosius II and Valentinian, who reacted quickly. The eastern emperor recommended that Honoria be dispatched to the Huns straight away, which might have reduced the threat of invasion, but Valentinian had reservations about allowing his sister to marry the 'scourge of God', who was known to be polygamous. Instead, he punished his sister by exiling her from the court and executing her eunuch servant and other accomplices. Only Galla Placidia's interventions and insistence upon the planned marriage to the senator Herculanus, secured Honoria's restoration. In 452 Herculanus was named consul in Rome, a mark of the emperor's gratitude for saving Honoria from total disgrace.

To explain her wild proposal to Attila, some modern historians have suggested that Honoria was merely following the example of her mother. But Galla Placidia had not proposed marriage to Athaulf in 414; she had been a hostage among the Goths when that union was imposed. Nonetheless, Honoria knew that her mother had once married a 'barbarian' and survived. Like all imperial princesses she was aware that she might be called upon to make a similar marriage for diplomatic reasons and decided to take her own very surprising initiative. In two respects, however, Attila was quite unlike other non-Roman tribal chiefs: he was not a Christian, and he already had several wives and many children, as Roman visitors to Attila's court had observed.[20]

Leaving Honoria in the company of servants for so long had been a serious mistake, and Galla Placidia had to make great efforts to save her daughter from being completely ostracized before Valentinian relented. But the news of Honoria's appeal to Attila must have caused immense anger among the military. For nearly a decade Aetius, the leading general, had been trying to rid the western empire of the invading Huns, only to find that the emperor's sister was now undermining his campaigns. Attila, however, did not attack Ravenna immediately so that he could claim 'his bride'; he marched his forces west to Metz and Trier, which they sacked. The Huns then went on into Gaul, where Aetius' stalwart defence finally bore fruit at the battle of the Catalaunian Fields in the summer of 451.

Although Attila was worsted, he gathered additional forces to invade Italy again in 452. At Aquileia a large population – perhaps 100,000, including Bishop Nicetas – fled before his attack, seeking a refuge on the island of Grado or in the lagoons at the head of the Adriatic. Like the Ravennati before them, they hid among the swampy marshlands and found new homes on sandbanks surrounded by water. Milan suffered a similar fate. Attila then moved on, not to Ravenna but further south to threaten Rome. Pope Leo I (440–61) accompanied the embassy that negotiated a peaceful retreat. The Huns never got to Ravenna to 'rescue' Honoria, and in the following year Attila died and thus brought a respite to the battered western provinces. While he remained a terrifying figure of legend for many centuries, Honoria disappeared from the historical record and her fate is unknown.[21]

The Visit of Bishop Germanus

To what extent Galla Placidia's influence was curtailed after her son's assumption of imperial authority remains unclear, as she continued to impress visitors not only within Italy but further afield. In 448 Bishop Germanus of Auxerre arrived at the imperial court in Ravenna from Gaul to plead the case of the Armoricans, the local inhabitants of his diocese. They had foolishly rebelled against Roman rule, had been defeated by Aetius and now wished to be reconciled with the emperor. The account of Germanus' visit, preserved in his *Life* written by Constantius of Lyon, notes that Galla Placidia was 'ruling the city' and emphasizes her considerable plans for his reception: not knowing whether he would arrive by day or night, she arranged for fires to be lit every evening and guards posted to alert her to his approach, to make sure that he would find an appropriate welcome. With Peter Chrysologus' participation, she celebrated the elderly bishop's visit with an exchange of gifts, and Germanus performed miraculous cures before falling ill. Placidia attended him and promised that if he did not survive, his body would be sent back to Auxerre. After his death and the appropriate period of mourning in Ravenna, the empress provided vestments for his corpse, which was transported back to his home town where miracles continued to be attested at his tomb. The empress, however, held on to the box of relics that Germanus had carried with him.[22]

Placidia's successes, as regent and agent of her administrative, legal and architectural legacy, nonetheless had damaging effects on her children. Despite her 'glorious descent and a famous reputation', she failed to prepare them for their dynastic roles.[23] Honoria's appeal to Attila was a stupid misjudgement, but she hoped it would get her out of Ravenna. Similarly, when Valentinian III moved the court to Rome and agreed to let his own daughter marry the son of King Geiseric, this alliance resulted in the Vandals' sack of Rome, after Valentinian's death in 455. Through their behaviour, her children draw attention to Placidia's inadequacy as a mother, though it should not detract from her intellectual capacity, which is most clearly manifested in the survival of two of her letters on theological issues.

The Nature of Christ

Unsurprisingly, Galla Placidia followed the theological disputes in the East that divided the Church with great interest. In 431 the imperial court in Ravenna learned of preparations for another Universal Council, to be held at Ephesus, and Bishop Peter Chrysologus wrote a letter that supported the condemnation of Patriarch Nestorios of Constantinople for refusing to allow Mary the epithet of *Theotokos* – God-bearer.[24] At Ephesus, Nestorios was duly branded a heretic and dismissed from the see of Constantinople, while Mary was recognized as the chosen instrument of the Incarnation, the Mother of God. Pulcheria, sister of the eastern emperor, had strongly supported the council's decision; she now introduced liturgical commemorations of the Virgin's life and dedicated churches in Constantinople to her role. The Virgin was already commemorated in the West, but not all the rituals which became associated with her cult were widely known. In Rome, popes Celestinus and Sixtus III celebrated her new status in the magnificent Roman church of S. Maria Maggiore, which influenced later building in Ravenna.[25]

The debate over Mary's role in the Incarnation and the nature or natures of Christ nevertheless persisted. In 448 Eutyches, leader of a large monastic community near Constantinople, was condemned for proposing that Christ had a single unique nature. Later, under pressure from Theodosius II, Eutyches was reinstated, but his opponents continued their denunciations and appealed to Pope Leo I to intervene. In February 450 the bishop of Rome wrote a doctrinal letter (*tomus*) to Patriarch Flavian of Constantinople, expressing his condemnation of Eutyches.[26] He also asked Valentinian III and his family to add their support to his position.

The letters written by Galla Placidia were kept, hidden among the records of Pope Leo I preserved from the Council of Chalcedon. They constitute the sole survival of her literary output.[27] While many educated Roman women wrote letters, the publication of their correspondence was usually determined by the recipient. If they wrote to important figures such as St Augustine or St Jerome, their texts might be put into the letter collections made for these famous men. Letters exchanged between women suffer from the absence of similar archives – their correspondence was not deemed worthy of collection and copying. Yet it's quite likely that Galla Placidia wrote personal letters to her relatives in the East, especially her niece Pulcheria. When Pope Leo requested Valentinian III's support, the empress mother was well qualified to assist.

The issue once again turned on the nature or natures of Christ, and how precisely the human and divine elements were combined. In pursuing a theory about their fusion in Christ's one nature (*mia physis*, which gives rise to the modern term miaphysite), Eutyches denied any role for the Virgin Mary.[28] This, of course, undid the declaration of the Council of Ephesus that had identified Mary as *Theotokos*, causing enormous controversy and debate. Pulcheria opposed Eutyches, relying instead on the definition of two natures united in one essence (*ousia*) that had been decreed at Ephesus. This was the position adopted by Pope Leo in his letter to Patriarch Flavian; it was also supported by Galla Placidia.

In the first of her letters, addressed to Theodosius II, 'conqueror and emperor, her ever august son', she regretted that the synod at Ephesus had disturbed the true faith and intimidated Bishop Flavian of Constantinople, because he had appealed to the Apostolic see (Rome). Emphasizing the authority of the bishop of Rome, heir of St Peter, who holds the keys of heaven, she urged Theodosius to preserve the faith, to protect Flavian and to allow the appeal to be resolved in Rome, in order 'to maintain the respect due to this great city which is the mistress of all the earth'. In the second, to Pulcheria, Galla Placidia wrote as one powerful ruling woman to another: 'So it is appropriate, most holy and venerable daughter Augusta, that piety should prevail. Therefore may your clemency in accordance with the catholic faith, as it always has along with us, now in the same way share our objectives.' These 'objectives' were to overturn the decisions taken at Ephesus by holding another universal council in the West, and to refer the issue of Flavian's position to the Apostolic see of St Peter: 'Yield to the primacy of that city which filled the whole world with the domination of its own *virtus*, and committed the globe to being governed and preserved by our empire.' This belief in the supremacy of 'our imperial power' was matched by the supremacy of St Peter in the church – a natural coalition.[29] Pulcheria probably wrote back to her aunt in the West but there is no trace of this letter, while the emperor replied to Galla Placidia that he had the matter in hand and was sustaining the faith of the Church Fathers.

The Council of Chalcedon

When Theodosius II died after a riding accident in July 450 at the age of forty-nine leaving no heir, the eastern imperial court faced a political crisis.[30] Pulcheria initially concealed the emperor's death while she decided on a strategy for the succession. She then negotiated with

Marcian, a military commander, whom she persuaded to join her in a marriage of convenience. Since she had taken a vow of virginity, the arrangement was designed to enhance his imperial credentials and to permit her to take a full part in the government as empress. Together they planned and then summoned the Council of Chalcedon, which met in 451, condemned Eutyches as a heretic, reaffirmed Mary's title of *Theotokos* and asserted the union of Christ's two natures, the divine and human, in one person (*hypostasis*). This became the official, ortho-dox duophysite definition, in opposition to the miaphysite. The *Tomus* of Pope Leo and two letters written by Pulcheria in preparation for the council were read out and incorporated in its acts.[31] The empress had valiantly overcome the problems created by Theodosius' lack of a son and had established an heir for her brother. This news probably reached Rome within a month. It must have brought some comfort to Pope Leo I that the 'correct' theology had prevailed in Constantinople. Valentin-ian, however, withheld his recognition of Marcian. Technically he became the senior emperor on Theodosius' death and no doubt believed that he should have been consulted about the succession.

Galla Placidia did not live to hear of the success of the Council of Chalcedon in 451, where Marcian and Pulcheria were hailed as a new Constantine and a new Helena. She died in Rome and was buried on 27 November 450, probably in the imperial mausoleum next to St Peter's constructed by her half-brother Honorius. At some time before her death Placidia had arranged to have the body of her first-born child, her Arian Gothic son Theodosius, exhumed from its original grave near Barcelona and brought to Rome in its little silver coffin, where it was reburied in the imperial mausoleum. This was a major ceremony at which Pope Leo officiated with members of the Senate, and it would have been appropriate for Valentinian III to arrange his mother's bur-ial in the same imperial tomb.[32] Shortly after, Bishop Peter Chrysologus died, closing the era that had been dominated by Placidia.

Galla Placidia was not the only woman to rule over a substantial part of the Roman empire during the fourth and fifth centuries, but she exer-cised power and displayed agency in novel ways that greatly enhanced the importance of Ravenna, not least through her pious endowment of churches. Other fourth-century empresses had influenced their hus-bands and sons but none as effectively as Placidia, who both initiated and embodied the fusion of Gothic and Roman that secured a new basis for imperial rule, while creating a strong co-operation between imperial and ecclesiastical forces in the capital of the West. Maintaining a firm awareness of her imperial birth and upbringing, her status as the widowed mother of a young prince recognized as future emperor, and thus protecting his rights, she sustained the ruling dynasty. But she may also have prevented her son from gaining a youthful apprenticeship in the habits of governing, and her daughter from making a sensible marriage.

PART TWO

450–93
The Rise of the Bishops

6

Valentinian III and Bishop Neon

In January 450 Valentinian III decided to move his family and the entire court to Rome on a more permanent basis. They arrived in time to attend a vigil at the seat of St Peter, a feast celebrated the following day, 22 February, a sign of his close relations with Pope Leo I. Since he had spent two and a half years in the ancient capital between 445 and 447, the decision to leave Ravenna reflected his clear preference for Rome. But it was also connected to a more independent style of government, enhanced by the surroundings of the ancient capital, far from the world of Ravenna – a repudiation of his mother's dedication to that city.[1] The move was to prove fatal both to his own survival and that of the western empire.

As Valentinian established his court in Rome, news of the death of Theodosius II in July 450 reinforced his position as he became the senior emperor.[2] His initial refusal to recognize Marcian as his eastern colleague failed to take account of the growth of Constantinople at the centre of the empire. Under Theodosius II its vast new city walls, three circuits deep, created impregnable defences. The area within had been profoundly enriched by the construction of numerous new churches, imperial and secular buildings and the large villas of leading senators, who left Rome to join the new Senate of Constantinople, as well as those of military leaders who settled in the capital. The imperial government could draw on extensive resources to buy off enemy attacks, as can be seen from the hundreds of pounds of gold carried from Constantinople to the court of the Huns by numerous embassies that negotiated peaceful settlements rather than risking military engagements.[3] Both within and beyond the Roman borders, Constantinople was increasingly perceived as the sole capital of empire.[4]

Valentinian nonetheless attempted to rule the West from Rome, assisted by Aetius who continued to defend the empire from the Huns. After the death of Attila in 453, Valentinian III felt he could safely remove his general. Whether the decision was born of jealous rivalry or a desire to assume unrestricted imperial control, it was a foolish one. By ordering the murder of Aetius, the emperor brought about his own death, for soldiers loyal to their former military leader assassinated Valentinian on 16 March 455.[5]

Valentinian's death left Empress Eudoxia in a very difficult position, comparable to Pulcheria in the East, for whoever married her would greatly strengthen his claim to imperial power (the women of the ruling family were crucial carriers of imperial legitimacy). Almost immediately a Roman senator, Petronius Maximus, attempted to abuse Eudoxia's authority by forcing himself upon her. Since Valentinian had proposed an alliance with the Vandals, to be sealed by the marriage of their daughter Eudocia with Prince Huneric, Eudoxia used this connection to send an appeal to King Geiseric in Carthage.[6] Geiseric was only too glad to come to her aid. In the summer of 455 the Vandals sailed to the rescue of the imperial family.

The Vandal Sack of Rome

News of the approaching Vandal fleet caused panic. After encouraging all the Romans who could do so to leave the city, Petronius Maximus was killed in the chaos of massed flight. The Vandals then ransacked the city for treasure and booty for two weeks, causing much more destruction than the Gothic attack of 410. Empress Eudoxia and her two daughters were taken to Africa for their safety and there Eudocia was married to Huneric. While the violence of their attack gave rise to the term 'vandalism', coined during the French Revolution, the Vandals did not attempt to occupy Rome.[7] But the sack of 455 put an end to the Theodosian dynasty in the West. In this way, Valentinian's decision to abandon Ravenna led to a disastrous impoverishment of Rome, which was reduced to a stage for rival ruling candidates with barely any power or authority, while Ravenna continued to grow and flourish under new leadership.

In the absence of the imperial court, a further distinct change occurred in the balance of power in Ravenna. Some of the routine imperial administration remained in the city, deepening the division between the senatorial elite of ancient Rome and those less aristocratic forces sustaining imperial government. The provincial governor and local city council resumed some of the basic responsibilities of city councils, including the arduous task of establishing and collecting local taxes. But, more tellingly, a series of energetic bishops of the church of Ravenna took advantage of the emperor's departure to extend their influence. In the period following the deaths of Galla Placidia and Peter Chrysologus, Bishop Neon (*c.* 450–73) took over the empress's style of patronage in splendid new buildings, which he funded from the resources of the church – taxes on its estates in Sicily and other properties, bequests of land, clerical endowments and grateful parishioners' gifts.

Ravenna and Sicily

Like the churches of Rome and Milan, Ravenna owned agricultural land in many different provinces of the empire and drew particularly on estates in Sicily that provided wheat, oil and wine as well as rents in cash. The papyrus records of Ravenna reveal these as an underlying aspect of the wealth of both the church and the city council, generating a small fleet of ships that transported these resources to the city. In 445/6, Pyrrus, a *tribunus* (tribune, a military officer), had failed in his duty to collect the taxes due from property in Sicily: only 4,216 *solidi* had been sent for the two preceding years, leaving 1,934 unpaid. At the beginning of the next year, which began on 1 September for tax purposes, the city council recorded the order issued by Lauricius to Sisinnius, the *conductor* of an estate named Fadiliana in Sicily, giving very precise instructions about how to proceed. Sisinnius was to collect the goods and taxes due from the past two years and to load them onto a ship sailing directly to Ravenna by a certain date. If no transport was available, he should send the consignment to Rome to be stored in the city's granary (*horreum*). There were further instructions for two tenants identified as Eleutherius and Zosimus. At the end of a third fragment of papyrus, the taxes owed by these two (and another tenant named Tranquillus) are listed: 2,174, 1,800 and 1,811 *solidi* respectively and the estates are identified. In an unusual detail, Lauricius signed his instructions and added his wishes for many years of good life (*multos annos bene valeas*).[8]

If we compare these figures with the minimum annual salary of a Ravenna council member (*curialis*), fixed at 300 *solidi* at the same time, it's clear that quite substantial revenues were being raised from farms in Sicily. The city council paid close attention to them and recorded its orders in the city archive. Later papyri document the ongoing importance of the island for both the city and the church of Ravenna, which may have benefitted from the gift of imperial estates under Honorius. In about 600, Archbishop Marinianus of Ravenna sent his deacon John to Sicily to find out why the *patrimonium* of the church had been reduced (and presumably tried to restore it).[9] The clearest indication of the significance of these estates comes from a seventh century dispute under Archbishop Maurus, when the sum of 31,000 *solidi* annually was divided between the church of Ravenna and the treasury in Constantinople.[10] In addition, the Sicilian rector of the *patrimonium* supplied 150,000 *quintali* of wheat; other grains and vegetables; fleeces dyed red which could be used for luxurious shoes or imitation purple-dyed parchment; silk robes and silver and brass vases, which was all transported on ships sent from Ravenna. The ninth-century Arab conquest of Sicily put an end to these taxes and shipments of goods.

This seventh-century reference to the church's fleet of transport ships reflects its close relations with the Adriatic, where Ravenna also had properties in Dalmatia, Istria and the Venetiae. As a native of Pola in Istria Archbishop Maximian sustained his contacts with the city, building a major basilica and a house for the rector of Pola. Maximian also went to Constantinople to defend the church of Ravenna's ownership of a forested area at Vistrum, south of Rovigno. In the mid-fifth century Ravenna drew on the produce of estates (*coloniae*) in Padovano in the Venetiae, which were probably transported by ship.[11] References to the *naves dominice* of the archbishop also indicate the activity of smaller ships that sailed up the riverways of Romagna, where Ravenna had scattered properties in the Pentapolis and Umbria and the areas around Ferrara, Bologna, Perugia and Gubbio. Although it proves extremely difficult to calculate the size of these estates and the value of the taxes or goods they produced, the church of Ravenna clearly derived its wealth from a very large number scattered across north-eastern Italy and further afield.

Bishop Neon's Patronage

After the departure of Valentinian III, Bishop Neon stepped into the role of Ravenna's chief patron, commissioning new buildings, both secular and spiritual, to enhance the city's standing. One of most impressive of these buildings erected in the second half of the fifth century is known today as the Baptistery of the Orthodox, which can still be admired, close to the cathedral church. The small octagonal structure had been built by Bishop Ursus, but Neon was responsible for decorating the rebuilt dome and walls with brightly coloured marbles, stucco and spectacular mosaics. At its centre is the baptismal font of white marble, with steps leading down into the pool of water and up the other side. As Christian initiates descended into it and then emerged, they could look up at their divine model in the centre of the dome, where in a golden roundel John the Baptist baptizes Jesus in the River Jordan while the Holy Spirit descends from above in the form of a dove (Plate 9). The Jordan is personified as an elderly half-naked river god almost submerged in the water, while around the scene the Apostles stand against a glorious golden background. Within the lower four arched bays that alternate with four flat walls of the octagon, Neon put up biblical texts and dedicatory verses that record his own patronage of the redecoration. Every architectural feature is picked out in extravagant floral or geometric decoration, a mass of contrasting colours that echoes the plants springing out of baskets in the Mausoleum of Galla Placidia.[12]

Since Pope Sixtus III (432–40) Roman bishops had set a new fashion for octagonal baptisteries, as well as longer and taller basilicas, and Neon was determined to endow Ravenna similarly. He even copied a line of the verses put up by Sixtus in the baptistery attached to the Lateran church.[13] In thus elevating the Orthodox baptistery – where those who had been prepared for baptism would enter the Christian community – Neon emphasized his own role with a pun on his name:

> Yield, old name, yield, age to newness! Behold the glory of the renewed font shines more beautifully. For generous Neon, highest priest, has adorned it, arranging all things in beautiful refinement.[14]

Similar buildings, often octagonal, were being built all over the Christian world to emphasize the significance of the act that admitted new converts to the faith. In 458 Pope Leo wrote to Neon precisely about the significance of baptism, a once-in-a-lifetime ceremony, which should not be repeated except in particular circumstances, for instance, when children who had been taken captive by barbarians didn't know if they had ever been baptized. In such conditions, which may have been common enough, Leo says they should be baptized even if it might be for the second time.

For many adults the ceremony of baptism was put off until they reached an age where they could undertake to sin no more. Preparation for baptism required the catechumens (adult candidates who had been accepted by the bishop) to attend services and religious instruction during the forty days of Lent. Then, on the Saturday before Easter, they were submerged in the sunken bath in the centre of the baptistery and emerged to be clothed in white garments as newly born Christians. They processed into the church to take their first communion and celebrated the Resurrection in their new identity, parading through the streets of the city and breaking the fast of Lent with feasting. Since they provided their own white shrouds, the baptized competed to display the finest Easter costumes.[15]

Icons of Christ

Bishop Neon also completed the Petriana basilica begun by his predecessor Peter Chrysologus, which housed an exceptional icon, later destroyed in an earthquake. Agnellus described it as 'an image of the Saviour . . . over the main door, the like of which no man could see in pictures; it was so very beautiful and lifelike'.[16] These were words about its power not 'art', and the ninth-century historian was far more interested in the story of the miraculous discovery of the Petriana icon than its actual form and origin. Old men had told him how a saintly figure, who lived in the wilderness, accompanied by two lions, went in search of the image and eventually found it in Classis, where he died. The two lions buried him with such vociferous roaring and mourning that they also died and were buried on either side of his tomb.[17] Similar tales of protective lions occur in the biographies of many of the Egyptian Desert Fathers, which circulated very widely throughout the Mediterranean world, and Agnellus regularly drew on such oral traditions.

Another equally fantastical story is attributed to an image of Christ flanked by saints Peter and Paul displayed in the basilica of the Apostles, where Agnellus saw it. He reports that it served as the guarantor of a loan made between two men who were already linked in the spiritual relationship of godparenthood. Since the choice of godparents for children might have a substantial influence in their lives, families often asked more powerful patrons to act as godparents. In this case, the poorer man, who wanted a loan of 300 gold *solidi*, was anxious to keep it secret so that none of the regular moneylenders, witnesses and guarantors would be involved. His friend therefore invoked the strong arm of Christ as shown in the image as the guarantor and the two Apostles as witnesses, and in the end the loan was repaid with interest.[18] Similar icons of Christ are recorded in a number of churches at this time.[19]

Legends of the power and capacity of images, also enhanced by dream visions of them, are part of a repertoire of such miraculous stories. Ravenna actively participated in the shared visual world of early Christendom in which images of saintly and holy figures were commanding an increasing devotion. In Egypt, where many icons survive thanks to the dry climate, Christ was shown with his arm around the shoulder of St Menas, or raising his hand in blessing.[20] In addition, the Ravenna image in the basilica of the Apostles was intimately connected to the all-important relationship between natural and spiritual parents created when children were baptized. Although these two images of Christ confirm the growth of icons in Ravenna, neither survives.

Bishop Neon also constructed a substantial dining hall (which no longer exists in its original form) inside the episcopal palace adjoining the cathedral of Ravenna. It would have been large enough to hold five couches on which guests would recline to dine in the traditional Roman fashion, several to each couch, and provided elegant facilities in which bishops, monks and important visitors to the city could be entertained (Plate 15). It was decorated with Old Testament scenes on one wall and the New Testament story of Simon Peter and the miracle of the loaves and fishes on the other – a suitable decoration for a dining hall. Neon's hexameter verses in the contemporary rhetorical style explained the paintings and were copied down by Agnellus:

> Hail, Simon Peter! apostolic light, whom Christ's golden mind
> takes pleasure in honoring through all the years:

in you God's holy church shines brightly,
in you the Son of the heavenly prince, brilliant through the ages,
has established the firm foundations of his house.[21]

As the successor of Peter Chrysologus, Bishop Neon held the see of
Ravenna for over twenty years, sustaining the faith as set out by Universal Councils in the East and celebrated in Constantinople, Antioch,
Alexandria, Jerusalem and Rome. He was buried in the church of the
Apostles (now S. Francesco's), which he probably founded. The crypt,
3.4m below the present church floor, has a fine mosaic floor with an
inscription in Greek recording Hesychios and Gemella, probably
donors who contributed to the cost, and another in Latin that alludes
to the bones of Bishop Neon. Several of the tombs have been excavated,
though none can be identified as his.[22]

The Arian Christians

Alongside this Catholic Christian community, however, there were other
followers of Christ, such as Galla Placidia's armed contingent of Goths
who accompanied her back to Rome in 416 and non-Roman military
forces stationed in Ravenna. Despite several official condemnations of
their Arian (Homoian) definition of faith from 325 onwards, they gradually formed a parallel Christian world with their own priests (or
presbyters) and churches for their services.[23] The existence of these Arian
church leaders is confirmed by their writings, though the hostility of their
Catholic opponents means that they are poorly preserved.[24] In the established Homoian church of Vandal Africa, a hierarchy of bishops, modelled
on the previous Catholic one, established a patriarch of Carthage who
summoned councils of all his Arian bishops. But a similar pattern did not
develop in northern Italy, where local communities in the Arian churches
of Milan, Rome, Aquileia and Grado appear to have been more or less
autonomous. Further afield in Burgundy, Visigothic Aquitaine or the Balkans there must have been methods of communication and sharing texts,
but overall there was no hierarchy of sees comparable to that of the catholics, still less a graded scale from the richest and most important down to
the most modest, often of recent creation (as revealed in the *Notitiae*, lists
of precedence of the Constantinopolitan church).

All the Arians, however, used the same Bible text, translated by Ulfila, their 'Moses', who had led a 'chosen people' away from traditional pagan cults (Plate 24). They often read it in a bilingual Latin/Gothic version and wrote commentaries on it in Latin. Despite the official condemnation of the Arian definition of faith and the Catholic destruction of as much Arian theology as possible, fragmentary texts survive, including a Gothic commentary on the Gospel of St John, *scholia* on the Council of Aquileia (381), and collections of sermons. The commentary records the Arian conviction that the Son was naturally subordinate to the Father and censored 'the impious contention . . . that the Father and Son are one'.[25] In Vandal Africa, Visigothic Spain and wherever Germanic/Gothic forces were in control of western regions, these texts insisted that the three figures of the Trinity could not share in the same essence or nature. As the imperial administration became more and more dependent upon these 'barbarian' military forces, their role became entrenched and demand for their own churches grew.

All over the Mediterranean world, nearly 150 years after the conversion of Constantine I, both Arian Christian leaders and Catholic bishops maintained their own definitions of the faith, considered themselves 'orthodox' and rivalled each other in the sumptuous decorations of their churches. In Ravenna, the Arian community used the same materials, some *spolia* from ancient buildings, some newly brought from Constantinople, and probably employed the same teams of craftsmen – skilled workers in marble revetment, fresco, stucco and mosaic. These craftsmen may have travelled from place to place, employed by bishops, imperial officials, Gothic and Germanic patrons and the leaders of the empire's Jewish communities, who all competed for the best to decorate their places of worship.[26] Ravenna's mixed population exploited the city's maritime contacts to bring building materials, new styles and skills to intensity both their cult buildings and the city's status as the imperial capital of the West. The strength and vitality of Ravenna even without the emperor's presence confirmed Valentinian's strategic folly in moving to Rome. While the western empire was decapitated and collapsed, Ravenna consolidated its prominence.

7

Sidonius Apollinaris in Ravenna

While a series of insignificant imperial hopefuls competed to inherit the mantle of Valentinian III, Ravenna was visited by an imperial official and son-in-law of the short-lived Emperor Avitus (455–6). Sidonius Apollinaris had been appointed prefect of the city of Rome for the year 467–8 and visited Ravenna on his way south. His journey along the Po river from Pavia by the *cursoria*, a boat service of the public transport system, reveals the roster of oarsmen who guided the boats downstream. As far as Brixellum (Brescello), men from the Venetiae were responsible, and then the boatmen of Emilia took over.[1]

In a curiously cryptic account, Sidonius complained in a letter to a friend about the heat, the mosquitoes and the frogs whose croaking disturbed his nights:

> In that marshland the laws of nature are continually turned upside down; walls fall and the waters stand, towers float and ships are grounded, the sick promenade and the physicians lie abed, the baths freeze and the houses burn, the living go thirsty and the buried swim, thieves keep vigil and authorities sleep, clerics practise usury and Syrians sing psalms, businessmen go soldiering and soldiers do business, the old go in for ball-playing and the young for dicing, the eunuchs for arms and the federates for culture.[2]

This dramatic description may reflect an earthquake that caused severe damage to Ravenna in 467, recorded by Marcellinus in his *Chronicle* and illustrated in the *Annals of Ravenna*, or just regular flooding (Plates 25 and 26).[3] The city lay right on the waterline with direct access to the sea, surrounded by tributaries of the Po, causing persistent subsidence. Even today, buildings sink every year and have to be shored up as water is pumped off. Sidonius' observations are in marked contrast to the typical compositions in praise of a city, for instance, the verses by Ausonius about Milan. Nonetheless, he tells us that in mid-fifth-century Ravenna there were doctors, eunuch servants and federate troops, merchants and soldiers, old and young with their own styles of entertainment, baths and houses, thieves and guards, clerics who charged interest and Syrian merchants who sang psalms – all the different sorts of people and activities associated with a thriving city, even if it was badly governed. The presence of traders from the eastern Mediterranean reflects the important maritime ties Ravenna sustained with the ports of Antioch, Gaza and Alexandria, and the island of Cyprus.

As an outside witness, Sidonius emphasizes the watery environment that protected Ravenna, with one branch of the River Po forming a moat encircling the walls while another brought numerous channels into the city, which was good for commerce. Noting its trading capacity – 'we saw large food supplies coming in' – he also alludes to Martial's first-century description of the city, characterizing it as 'that place of thirst, well-watered Ravenna'.[4] On one side the briny sea water laps the walls, while on the other local boatmen churn up the filthy mud from these shallow channels as they use their poles to get around, for 'when the people of Ravenna go hunting they get into their boats', flat-bottomed barges on which they punted to outcrops in the marshes to catch game. He connects the lack of drinking water with the absence of pure aqueduct water and bubbling springs, and the problem of dirty wells and reservoirs. Since the aqueduct had to be repaired later in the century, it was possibly failing at the time of Sidonius' visit.

The City Council

Whatever geophysical difficulties Ravenna faced, in numerous earthquakes and muddy water, its inhabitants appear to have coped with their marshy environs. We catch glimpses of the city's local government from documents, mainly wills written on papyrus, that survive from this period. They record the leading families of Ravenna – Aelius, Commodianus, Hernilius, Proiectus, Melminius, Pompulius, Tremodius, Firmilius, Firmilianus, Florianus and others – who served on the council and regularly appear at its meetings as the two presiding magistrates (with the rank of *inlustres*, *clarissimi* or *laudabiles*).[5] Below them the council required the assistance of two *quaestores*, two *aediles* and two *duoviri* (though they are not often identified by these titles in Ravenna) who took precedence over all the other councillors. The *principales*, leading men, in attendance often belonged to the same families and high ranks as the magistrates; in contrast, witnesses often had the lower status of *vir spectabilis*, *strenuus* or *devotus*, and include those of *honestus*, the lowest rank.

The individuals who appear before the *curia* to settle their legal matters are generally of this lower status. Some seek the protection of the *defensor civitatis*, set up to prevent the abuse of citizens. The key responsibility of this official, however, was to ensure the registration of property in the municipal archive so that land taxes could be collected. Whenever an estate changed hands, the tax assessment also moved to the new owner who had to pay it. Another official with a similar responsibility was the *duumvir quinquennalis*, appointed every fifth year to maintain the census, a method of ensuring that tax payers would be identified.[6] Evidence for the appointment of such officials comes from the letters of appointment (*formulae*) composed by Cassiodorus during the rule of Theoderic, but he drew on older traditions which had established city councils as a critical force in imperial administration. Local papyrus records illustrate their role in governing the city.

The main business of the council in Ravenna continued to be the official registration of legal decisions, sales of property, bequests and gifts often made in wills, through a process known as *insinuatio*. This followed a fixed procedure in a dialogue between the magistrate and the individual establishing his or her will, which recorded the status and names of different classes of individuals, including up to eight witnesses, their family relations and professional activity. Once approved it was then written into the city archive (*gesta municipalia*), thus guaranteeing its legal standing.[7] Some time before 474, Constantius, a local dyer, with his wife Pascasia, *honesta femina*, dictated his will to Domitius Johannes, the official scribe (*forensis*) and thus ensured that his property would be distributed as he wished.[8] On 27 December 480 a deacon, Colonicus, registered his will 'in Classe, castris praetorio Ravennae', revealing that the praetorian prefect continued to reside in the fortified settlement at Classis, near the harbour, and council business might be conducted there.[9] Women also appear in court to defend their inheritances, free their slaves and sign by making a cross when they are unlettered.[10]

In one case Maria, *femina spectabilis*, came to the council in 491 to request that she and her husband might be buried in the church of St Laurentius (S. Lorenzo) in Caesarea. They had previously made a gift to the church on this condition, but it had not been registered in the city's archive. She now presented another gift (a property identified as *Domicilium in Cornelinesi*) to Bishop John, leader of the church of Ravenna, in a petition written by her notary Jovinus with the support of Castorius, *vir clarissimus*, who was dear to her and promised to sign in her name. He witnessed the donation, together with Flavius Severus, a silver merchant/banker and *vir honestus*. In this way, Maria sought to ensure that 'our bodily remains should repose in the basilica of St Laurentius', and that her husband's wish could be fulfilled.[11] Proximity to the saints and their relics constituted a highly desirable final resting place for fifth-century Christians.

As we have seen, members of wealthier local families tried to escape from serving on the council by entering the church (a move officially prohibited by law to ensure that city councils could maintain their numbers), and some had managed to take their wealth with them. Agnellus records that in the 470s a subdeacon named Gemellus founded the church of St Agnes (where Neon's successor, Bishop Exuperantius, was later buried). Inscriptions in the church recorded Gemellus' endowments of gold and silver vessels and banners for the church, as well as a silver cross used in the processions to mark the birth of the saint, which were still observed in the ninth century. Gemellus had also been rector of Sicily and may have derived his resources from the island.[12]

Similar efforts to avoid curial service are documented in many Roman cities, such as in Toulouse, Clermont-Ferrand and Paris where senatorial families adopted leading roles in the church. But by the late fifth century, becoming a bishop might involve even heavier responsibilities, as Sidonius Apollinaris discovered when he was appointed to the see of Clermont-Ferrand in 471. Almost immediately the Visigoths attacked the city, and they returned every summer to besiege it until 474/5, when it fell and Sidonius was taken prisoner. After a period of captivity in Bordeaux, the Visigothic king Euric pardoned him and Sidonius returned to the city to serve as bishop for another decade.[13] Elsewhere the Burgundians and, later, the Huns put tremendous pressure on ex-Roman senators who sought a new life within the Christian church. Ravenna was again spared by its reputedly unassailable defences in the estuaries of the Po, though Agnellus preserves an entirely fictitious account of Attila's entry into the city.[14]

While Bishop Neon and his successors were not called on to meet the challenge of dealing with the Huns, they also took a dominant role in the city, continuing investments and donations that were recorded on their tombs. Agnellus had seen the tombstone of Bishop John (probably 477–94), originally placed behind the altar in the church of St Agatha and later moved to the Ursiana church.[15] It commemorated John's gifts of valuable gold and silver vessels, crowns and hanging cups to the church, which Agnellus personally handled. The fifth-century prosperity of the city is more directly confirmed by Sidonius' comments as he passed through the city on his way to Rome in 467. In spite of the contradictions he observed, Ravenna was clearly a flourishing centre during the chaotic final years of western imperial rule.[16]

8

Romulus Augustulus and King Odoacer

The years between 455, when Valentinian III was assassinated, and 476 when Odoacer established his rule in Ravenna, are often identified as the key period of the 'decline and fall of the Roman Empire'. From the Gothic sack of Rome in 410, followed by the more serious destruction by the Vandals in 455, through to the deposition of the 'last emperor', Romulus Augustulus, in 476, 'barbarian' tribes persisted in a more permanent occupation of the western provinces of the Roman world.[1] But the traditions of Roman rule did not simply disappear, for the success of the newcomers owed much to their grasp of some of the Roman principles of government: secure defences, efficient administration, application of a written law and reliable coinage. Italy, like Gaul, Spain and other parts of northern Europe, suffered many invasions and incorporated many non-Roman settlers. Ravenna, however, sustained the traditions of Roman urban life longer than most cities.

Barbarian Chieftains in Power

From the early fifth century onwards, as we have seen, military leaders responsible for the defence of the western empire found themselves increasingly dependent on 'barbarian' troops with their own loyalties and Arian faith. Between 455 and 476 these non-Roman soldiers gained an utterly dominant role, not as actual emperors – because the Senate and established aristocratic families would not promote them to that supreme position – but as king makers. Ricimer, an Arian Christian of possibly Hunnic and Gothic descent, played this role most skilfully between 457 and 472, when he held the supreme military command and high title of *patricius*. Four emperors – Avitus (455–6), Majorian

(457–61), Libius Severus (461–5) and Anthemius (467–72) – discovered in quick succession that if they failed to satisfy Ricimer their days were numbered. Using the Senate of Rome to sanction his campaigns, Ricimer set up and deposed candidates for the imperial office, and for nineteen months between 465 and 467, in the absence of any emperor, he became the effective ruler of the West. His nephew Gundobad, a Burgundian, and Odoacer, another Hun or Scirian, continued the same manipulative policy until September 476.

Initially, because it had to deal with its own 'barbarian' pressures, the imperial court in Constantinople did not send funds, troops or any form of serious support to the West. When the eastern court did try to intervene in the turbulent conditions of Italy, it was unable to reverse the growing authority of non-Roman figures. In 467, for example, Emperor Leo I appointed Anthemius to govern the West, but his candidate was ridiculed as 'the little Greek' (Graeculus). Ricimer insisted on marrying Alypia, Anthemius' daughter, which further subverted the new emperor's authority. The two men became rivals, and in the civil war that followed Anthemius lost.[2] Thereafter Constantinople effectively abandoned the West to Ricimer's dominance, which prepared the remaining provinces for a new phase in their history: rule by non-Roman kings, who were often more effective than their imperial predecessors.[3] And most of these men – like Ricimer – were Arian Christians.[4]

During these twenty-one years a total of seven emperors ruled, some for one year, others for four to five but never long enough to tackle the underlying weaknesses of the West, although Majorian and Libius Severus tried. Some of these nominal emperors tried to enlist senatorial support in Rome, while others went to Ravenna, the capital city where most of the imperial administration still functioned and laws issued by emperors were still registered. This competition between Rome and Ravenna for 'capital' status further reduced the formal existence of the Roman empire in the West. It was in Ravenna that both Majorian (in 457) and Libius Severus (in 461) were acclaimed, while Avitus and Anthemius went to Rome. But after the deaths of Anthemius and Ricimer in 472, Glycerius (473), Julius Nepos (474) and Romulus Augustulus (475) were unable to sustain any figment of 'imperial' government.[5] The historian Procopius describes their rapid turnover: 'There were, moreover, still other emperors in the West before this, but . . . they lived only a short time after attaining the office and . . . accomplished nothing worthy of mention.'[6] The citizens of Ravenna may have welcomed the promotion of Glycerius, previously commander of the local militia (*comes domesticorum*) with the expectation of donatives (gifts in coin) to loyal troops and general celebrations. But in Constantinople Emperor Leo decided to support his rather distant relative Julius (called the nephew, Nepos) to counter Glycerius.[7] Despite his imperial connections Julius proved no more successful and, in less than a year, he had fled from Ravenna.

Romulus, The Last Roman Emperor (475–6)

The man responsible for this startling development was Orestes, a military leader of Pannonian origin, who had made a career serving Attila as *notarius* and had participated in some of the Hun's negotiations with eastern emperors in 449–52. He had married the daughter of a seasoned Roman diplomat named Romulus and commanded a loyal following. In 475 he took an initiative to promote his own family rather than accept Julius Nepos as emperor: Orestes refused to lead his troops to campaign in Gaul, as ordered, and instead marched towards Ravenna. At this point Julius decided that flight was the better option and sailed from Classis to Dalmatia, where he continued to rule as emperor for several years. In the autumn of 475 Orestes thus gained possession of Ravenna and, on 31 October, his sixteen-year-old son Romulus was duly crowned emperor in the imperial palace (Plate 18). His father intended to direct the government in the same way as Ricimer had done, from behind the throne, and having put his brother Paulus in charge of the imperial court, set out to campaign against his rivals.

By 475 the dismemberment of the Roman West was more or less complete.[8] From the breaching of the Rhine frontier in 405, the Vandals had effectively conquered North Africa; Visigoths had occupied southern Gaul and Spain apart from the north-west of the country, where the Sueves established themselves. In northern Gaul the independent sub-kingdom of Soissons eventually succumbed to Frankish pressure. Under their king, Clovis, the Franks were to have a triumphant success in the early sixth century as the one non-Roman tribe to adopt the Catholic definition of Christian faith, rather than the Arian. In Italy,

Rome had been sacked twice and besieged many more times, most recently by Ricimer in 472. Sicily had been repeatedly raided by the Vandals, whose dominance at sea had also given them control over Sardinia and the Balearic Islands. Ravenna and the areas to the north, Istria and parts of Pannonia, remained an independent outpost of Roman imperial tradition, as all around them tribes of non-Roman Christians took control.

Odoacer's Revolt

As the young Romulus was set up as emperor, his father Orestes faced the dissatisfaction of a mixed group of mercenary soldiers, who demanded land to live on. This drew attention to a persistent problem of employing mercenaries rather than local troops whose families were already settled on their own farms. When Orestes refused, one of his subordinate officers, Odoacer, rebelled, promising to find the soldiers land. This daring offer won over the main army and generated a civil war between Odoacer and Orestes that was only settled by a battle near Placentia on 28 August 476. Odoacer was victorious, Orestes was killed, and the troops marched into Ravenna and killed Paulus, uncle of the young emperor. In September 476 Odoacer sent the 'little Augustus' into retirement, as Marcellinus reported from Constantinople in a panoramic perspective of Roman imperial history: 'and with this Augustulus perished the Western empire of the Roman people, which the first Augustus, Octavian, began to rule in the 709th year from the foundation of the city'.[9] The teenager was the last emperor of the West, and was fortunate to avoid the violent death of so many of his predecessors. A 'barbarian' general had finally displaced any semblance of Roman imperial authority in Italy and had settled in Ravenna.[10]

The man responsible for this decisive change was identified as a Hun on his father's side and a Scirian on his mother's. His father, named Edeco, had undertaken various diplomatic journeys for Attila.[11] Like many barbarian commanders of mercenaries, who sought work as hired fighters, Odoacer is recorded in Gaul in the 460s, with a band of Saxons, and later in Italy where he supported Ricimer. At one point he was in Noricum and sought out the holy man St Severinus who predicted his regal future, despite his very poor clothing and his Arian loyalty.[12] Although Odoacer led his own warriors brilliantly, he had never served as *magister militum* of Roman forces in the manner of so many non-Roman generals such as Orestes, and he was not as familiar with imperial customs. Yet he succeeded where Orestes and others had failed and ruled for fourteen years. Making Ravenna the seat of his Roman-style administration, he set out to create an autonomous power base by integrating non-Roman fighting forces into the regions under his control and initiated what was to become the most effective method of preserving Roman traditions in the West.

In 476 Odoacer's primary aim was to gain recognition from Constantinople of his position as ruler of Italy. Assuming the title of king, in a highly symbolic act he sent an embassy of Roman senators to Constantinople with the imperial insignia – the crown, purple cloak of office, orb and sceptre – instructing them to negotiate his position with Emperor Zeno. The ambassadors were to report that Odoacer had no ambition to usurp imperial rule; he claimed to represent the western Roman world and wished to be granted the honorific title of *patricius*. According to a later report, the ambassadors announced that 'one shared emperor was sufficient for both territories. They said, moreover, that they had chosen Odoacer, a man of military and political experience to safeguard their own affairs and that Emperor Zeno should confer upon him the rank of patrician and entrust him with the government of Italy.'[13] There was no longer any need for an emperor in the West. Zeno, however, was unwilling to grant serious support, beyond the title of patrician, to a 'barbarian' military leader in the West and ordered Odoacer to accept Julius Nepos as emperor. Repeated high-ranking senatorial embassies from Ravenna to Constantinople failed to improve the position.

Despite this underlying problem, Odoacer set up a government that was accepted by local inhabitants, who had watched the rapid turnover in imperial claimants since 473 and may have considered the deposition of Romulus as just another change of ruler. There certainly doesn't seem to have been any decisive shift in the functioning of the city council after 476. The leading families who had traditionally filled civilian positions on the city council continued to do so, and presumably included attendance at the king's court in Ravenna if invited. In one major change, Odoacer favoured his own Arian clergy, often called presbyters, who had accompanied his army, rather than the Catholic hierarchy of Ravenna. The new king and his wife, Sunigilda, supported the Arian Christian community and patronized new church building.[14]

Odoacer's Government

The new ruler's administration was based in the palace at the Laurel built by Valentinian III. Many government offices persisted unchanged: those of the *quaestor, magister officiorum, comes rei privatae* (imperial treasurer) and *comes sacrarum largitionum* (chief tax official), under the superior authority of the praetorian prefect of Italy as before.[15] To these established structures Odoacer added new ones, such as a count in charge of personal royal treasure (*comes patrimonii*), which corresponded to the Roman *domus divina*, as distinct from the management of old imperial lands (under the *comes rei privatae*).[16] The mint continued to issue gold *solidi* in the name of the eastern emperor, and silver coinage displaying the monogram and portrait of the king (Plate 19). Odoacer also introduced a new, more reliable copper coinage, which formed a model for the later eastern reform made by Emperor Anastasios.[17] No western consuls were appointed for the years 473 to 479, indicating quite a long hiatus as the fate of Romulus Augustulus was decided. In 480, however, Odoacer nominated Caecina Decius Maximus Basilius, of the Roman aristocratic family, and the Senate resumed its task of approving consuls until another break in 491–2.

Odoacer had to attend to immediate threats to his rule, notably from the Vandals of North Africa who had conquered parts of Sicily. By negotiating an annual payment of tribute, Odoacer regained possession of the island, which had always been a vital source of supplies for the elite of Ravenna, as well as Rome.[18] When faced with a revolt in Gaul, he proposed that both parties should send embassies to Constantinople for arbitration, a sign of the far-reaching hegemony of the eastern capital. Emperor Zeno supported Odoacer's party. In 480 Odoacer took advantage of the assassination of Julius Nepos in Dalmatia to invade the area and bring it under his control, thus reasserting the unity of the northern Adriatic coastlands. He also realized the importance of rewarding the soldiers who had supported him, for instance, his *comes domesticorum* Pierius, to whom he donated lands in Sicily and Dalmatia worth 690 *solidi*, recorded in a document drawn up in March 488.

It suggests a typically effective style of administration for a government very dependent on military expertise.[19]

During Odoacer's reign Roman senatorial families increasingly accepted the fact of barbarian government and put their talents at its disposal. The king recruited Cassiodorus Senior, father of the more famous Cassiodorus who played an important role in Ravenna later, to serve as provincial governor. Similarly, he appointed Opilio *comes sacrarum largitionum* and his sons Opilio and Cyprianus later served in the administration, while Caecina Decius Maximus Basilius (consul in 480) was promoted Praetorian Prefect in 483 and became *patricius*. Odoacer clearly drew on skilled Roman administrators such as Rufius Achilius Sividus, his *quaestor palatii* before 483, later prefect of the city, *patricius* and consul after 488. Other members of the Roman aristocracy in Odoacer's chancery included Flavius Rufius Postumius Festus, the head of the Senate (*caput senatu*) in 490, and Anicius Probus Faustus Niger, nominated consul in the same year, both experienced diplomats.[20]

The *Life* of Epiphanius, Catholic bishop of Pavia in north-west Italy, records visits he made to Ravenna to obtain tax remissions and other material assistance from Odoacer. The author, Ennodius, who was a deacon of the church in Pavia, claimed that the sack of that city during the battles of 476 had caused severe damage, and that punishingly harsh tax demands would have wrecked its revival. Epiphanius went on several embassies to Odoacer, making him aware of the distress in the region of Liguria, and won relief from the *coemptio* tax (a compulsory levy of supplies for the army).[21] This hagiographical account of the bishop's deeds, one of the rare contemporary sources for the reign of Odoacer, reveals the king in a favourable light. 'The time of King Odoacer' is also used as a dating mechanism in the Roman *Book of the Pontiffs* at the election of Pope Felix III in 483. It marks the resumption of the traditional method of dating papal events missing from many of the pontifical biographies between 384 and 483 and preserves a memory of Odoacer as the legitimate ruler of Italy.[22]

The king, his court and the army represented a considerable body of Arian believers, whose basic needs – performing baptisms, blessing marriages and burying the dead, probably in separate cemeteries, distinct from Catholic space – were performed by the Arian clergy of Ravenna. The most exhaustive study of these Arian officials has identified twenty-seven named clerics including three bishops (*episco-pus*), five presbyters and four individuals whose names are not recorded. While none of these leaders of the *ecclesia Gothica* or *ecclesia legis Gothorum* can be dated to the reign of Odoacer, it's clear that a strong Arian presence continued without a break into the sixth century.[23] Two papyri from Ravenna document the use of Gothic as a written language.

Odoacer and the Catholic Church

Being an Arian Christian, Odoacer may not have concerned himself with theological disagreements among the Catholics, yet his dominance did not prevent their bishops from caring for their own Christians; there is no hint of repression. Exuperantius (473–7) and John I (477–94) who governed the Catholic church in Ravenna during Odoacer's reign, patronized some new building, though Agnellus confessed that he had no information about the former; he 'constructed' a very short and uninformative biography, describing this bishop as 'humble and gentle, wise in good works ... What his predecessors built he kept safe.' In an entirely invented description of Attila the Hun's visit to Ravenna, Agnellus praises Bishop John's extraordinary courage in negotiating with the enemy, possibly evoking Odoacer's Hunnic ancestry.[24] These Ravenna churchmen were, however, drawn into the long dispute over the nature and essence of Christ generated by the Council of Chalcedon of 451, and were regularly summoned to Rome for meetings with its bishop. In 482 Emperor Zeno had issued the *Henotikon*, an attempt to reconcile the definitions of the council with its miaphysite opponents who stressed the single nature of Christ. The document, written by Patriarch Akakios (Acacius) of Constantinople and Peter Mongos, the miaphysite patriarch of Alexandria, proved unacceptable to both sides and was condemned by Pope Felix III in councils held in Rome in 484 and 485. This opened a breach between Rome and Constantinople, known as the Acacian schism (see Chapter 12).[25]

In contrast to the prevailing Roman hostility to heretics, Ravenna generated a more tolerant attitude. While the leading Arian clergy of the capital gained prestige from ministering to the regal court in Ravenna, benefitting from their proximity to the ruler and his patronage, the Arian and Catholic communities appear to have co-existed without the violent quarrels and fights that had dominated the city of Milan in the late fourth century. Ravenna was enhanced by a greater acceptance of Christian difference, in contrast to Roman practice, where several bishops ceremoniously burned the books of heretics on the steps of S. Maria Maggiore.[26] During the fifth century the persecution of Manichaeans (dualists, quite distinct from Christians) and heretics such as Donatists (in North Africa) and Priscillianists (active mainly in Spain) culminated under Pope Gelasius (492–6), who wrote five books against Nestorios and Eutyches and two against the Arians.[27] There is no evidence that Odoacer ever visited Rome, though he permitted repairs to the seats in the Colisseum.

It seems likely that the king would have celebrated his military victories in Ravenna and erected statues of himself with inscriptions that praised his achievements, but these were not recorded at the time or remembered in oral traditions. Nor did the king attract talented rhetoricians to his court who could compose panegyrics of his reign. Yet he must have been a judicious ruler and a competent administrator, as well as a successful general, to have survived for so long. As king from 476–93 he recognized the superior authority of the emperor in Constantinople but was determined to govern independently within the imperial system. He persuaded Roman senatorial administrators to work for him, tolerated their Catholic belief and the pope's leadership of their churches, yet he remained an Arian Christian. Above all, he integrated his own mixed bag of military supporters into a Germanicized imperial system run with the help of Roman office holders. This emphasis on co-operation and co-existence secured his rule and established a template for his successor.

PART THREE

493–540
Theoderic the Goth, Arian King
of Ravenna

9

Theoderic the Ostrogoth

In 489 Ravenna was under King Odoacer's control when a large Gothic force (plus dependants) approached Italy from Pannonia through the Julian Alps, led by their chieftain, Theoderic. Like Moses, he had grown up in the palace of his enemies and had led his followers on a long march to a promised land. Now in his mid-thirties, he was a seasoned military leader with exceptional talents.

Theoderic was born in about 453, probably in the region of today's Hungary, at a time when several Gothic tribes were, alternately, attacking the Roman empire and co-operating with it by trying to convince emperors that they would fight as loyal allies. All these Germanic peoples, both eastern Ostrogoths and western Visigoths, based in the Balkans, had been converted to Arian Christianity in the fourth century, but they were not united and fought constantly among themselves. In 461 Theoderic's uncle, Valamir, who commanded one particular tribe, arranged a truce with imperial forces, which was sealed by the customary exchange of hostages. In this case his nephew Theoderic, then about eight years old, was sent off to the court of Emperor Leo I in Constantinople.[1]

The boy was known as Theuderic, a common name among the Goths, which was Hellenized to Theuderichos by the historians Malchus and Procopius but has become Theodoric in most modern histories. (It does not derive from the Greek Theodore, meaning 'gift of God'.) The name and long and spectacular life of this son of a rather obscure Gothic chieftain gave rise to a myth, preserved in a medieval German epic, which identifies him as Dietrich of Bern; it is also recorded in verses carved on the Rök stone, made in ninth-century Sweden. His fame generated many stories that convey the extraordinary historical transformation of a young boy who arrived at the imperial court of

Constantinople in the mid-fifth century, accompanied by Roman troops that had until recently been his father's enemy.

As we have already seen with Galla Placidia, hostages were regularly exchanged at the conclusion of alliances and were held in the opponents' camps as a guarantee of the terms agreed.[2] Any serious failure to observe the conditions set by the older generation might endanger the life of the young hostage. Earlier in the fifth century the twelve-year-old Georgian prince Murvan was sent to Constantinople as a hostage from Iberia in the Caucasus and spent several years there. According to a much later record, 'He received a royal education and held military rank', but became obsessed with Christian relics and ascetic devotions.[3] The adventurous story of his escape conveys the privileged and religious atmosphere of the Palace but indicates that the hostages who sustained important political alliances were well cared for in the imperial court and were induced to internalize the Roman traditions that surrounded them. This established practice was based on a belief that educating young enemies would transform them into adult allies. The investment in their formation according to imperial norms, and exposure to the passions, skills and power of the court, would ensure co-operative relations when they returned to their own countries.[4]

Theoderic in Constantinople

During his crucial formative decade in the 460s Theoderic grew up in Constantinople, probably in part of the Palace with other foreign hostages, obliged to attend official events as a demonstration of the emperor's power.[5] Despite the somewhat humiliating conditions, Theoderic was educated in Greek and Latin and participated in courtly activities such as hunting and military training.[6] Only hints of his experience are preserved in later records, which emphasize the learning he acquired in the imperial capital and his appreciation of Roman technology, law and warfare.[7] Theoderic also watched how the imperial administration functioned, how the Romans prepared for war, conducted diplomatic relations with foreign powers and organized court ceremonial. He participated in the great celebrations and feasts, when the emperor and empress appeared in public or invited foreign visitors into the court for banquets and entertainments. By witnessing these

ceremonies, Theoderic observed how to perform the rites symboliz-
ing the superiority of the ruler, how to demonstrate a truly imperial
authority.

The court was by no means a homogenous entity. During Theoderic's first years in Constantinople, two Germanic military leaders
occupied the highest civilian positions (consul, *magister officiorum*) as
well as controlling the armies. Aspar and his son Ardabur (named after
his grandfather) were also Arian Christians, and so were obliged to
celebrate their faith beyond the city walls. Theoderic joined these
Alans, Goths and other Germanic soldiers in special churches for their
services. Although the Ostrogothic prince was identified by the imperial court as an outsider, in more ways than one, he cannot have failed
to notice how military and political skills had brought non-Roman
leaders and Arian Christians like himself to such exceptionally powerful positions. After the death of Emperor Marcian in 457, Aspar
maintained his influence by promoting Leo, one of his subordinate officers, as emperor, intending to keep him in an entirely dependent
position. While Aspar thus appeared to be the undisputed authority in
the eastern empire, Theoderic would also witness the political upheaval
when Leo later asserted his independence.

The great city of Constantinople was unlike any other and would
have enormously impressed the young Goth, who had never lived in an
urban environment. From its massive triple walls to the broad avenues
leading to great palaces and churches, decorated with ancient and
imperial statues, it must have induced a sense of wonder.[8] In addition
to his first impressions of Constantinople, many events of the decade
when he lived there influenced Theoderic's later life: the grand celebrations for the weddings of Leo I's two daughters, the baptism of Leo's
grandson in 467, and the return of the western empress Eudoxia and
her younger daughter Placidia from Vandal Africa in 462. Theoderic
would have seen the emperors participate in processions to mark the
most important Christian festivals and enjoyed the regular displays of
chariot and horse racing, theatrical displays, dances and gymnastics
held in the Hippodrome. He lived through a great fire that broke out in
464 – a terrifying event that burned so much of the central city that the
emperor was forced to move the court to the suburban palace of St
Mamas for six months.[9] Theoderic may have seen a famous icon of the
Mother of God (*Theotokos*), that showed Leo I and his wife Verina

kneeling before her in veneration. It was painted to commemorate the acquisition of a relic, Mary's veil or mantle, for which the emperor built a special chapel at the Blachernai church dedicated to the Mother of God.[10] In placing this icon above the reliquary that held the veil, Leo brought a portrait of a reigning emperor into a sacred space – the first time a depiction of secular rulers had been allowed inside a Christian building in the eastern capital. The young hostage may have remembered this event later when he set up his own portraits in the church he constructed as his palace chapel.

Theoderic also watched the decline of Aspar's influence as Leo sought alternative military support from an Isaurian chieftain, Tarasicodisa, who was recruited into the emperor's new elite bodyguard, the *exkoubitores*, created to counter the powerful Germanic leaders. In 466–7 the Isaurian leader adopted the Greek name Zeno and was married to Leo's daughter Ariadne. A year later Ariadne gave birth to a son, named Leo after his grandfather, and the baby was recognized as the heir to the imperial title. Much later, when Theoderic negotiated with Zeno, now emperor, he could recall participating at these momentous occasions. By 471 the influence of Aspar and Ardabur was so greatly reduced that Leo could have them murdered without risk. Theoderic witnessed the ruthlessness. He also noticed the preparation of a huge fleet for the 468 campaign against the Arian Vandals settled in North Africa. This very costly effort to regain the most prosperous western provinces ended disastrously and was held responsible for emptying the imperial treasury.

The failure was partially compensated by a victory in 469 when imperial forces in the West defeated Attila the Hun's son, variously called Denzic, Dinzerich or Dengizich, and his head was sent to Constantinople. 'It was paraded along the Mese and carried away to the Xylocircus and fixed on a pole. And the whole city went out to view it for number of days.'[11] The ceremonial procession of this trophy along the main road that led from the city walls to the palace and its public display dramatically reinforced the imperial propaganda of victory. While the inhabitants of the capital saluted this visual performance of their ruler's authority, Theoderic was reminded of the fate of non-Romans who unsuccessfully challenged the empire.[12]

As a highly intelligent young man, one of the key lessons that Theoderic would have drawn from his experience in the imperial capital was the relative weakness of emperors when contrasted with military leaders. First Aspar and Ardabur, Alans and Arian Christians, were unusually successful; then the Isaurians and Zeno demonstrated how outsiders could secure the title of *patricius* and honours – even the consulship – as well as the highest military posts and incomes. These non-Roman military commanders could protect and promote their own families, followers and allies, even Goths far off in the Balkans. But emperors still had power to deny them the right to settle within the empire, and to exclude them as Arian Christians, as well as humiliating them as enemies, whose heads were put on display. Theoderic could hardly have avoided learning that non-Romans needed Roman technology: education, mastery of the law, money and minting, military strategy.

When Theoderic was about eighteen years old, Leo I sent him back to Pannonia where his father associated him in his rule and designated him as his successor. This journey of over 1,000km today (and considerably less direct on fifth-century roads) took him through the Balkan provinces of the Roman empire and along the Danube frontier towards Lake Balaton (today in Hungary). It must have taken several weeks. Soon after his return, the young chief marked the abrupt shift from hostage at the imperial capital to future king of the Ostrogoths by launching a surprise and unplanned attack on the Sarmatians. During this campaign he captured the fortress of Singidunum (modern Belgrade), a key site on the Danube that had served as a centre of imperial defence for centuries, and to the irritation of the authorities in Constantinople he refused to relinquish it. Despite his long training at the imperial court, he was already determined to display his independence.

Theoderic the Chieftain

By the time he was twenty, Theoderic had shown his people he could conquer and hold an imperial outpost, negotiate its surrender and defy Constantinople while maintaining relations with the capital. He had made his mark and established himself among the Goths. He never looked back. During the 470s and 480s he developed a double ambition: to unite more of the Gothic tribes under his command, and to negotiate a permanent settlement for his people within the empire where he could rule under the overall authority of the emperor.[13] In contrast to other non-Roman tribes who settled within the imperial frontiers illegally, Theoderic aimed to win recognition as a reliable ally who should be rewarded by official permission to occupy territory permanently. This plan was regularly blocked by Emperor Zeno and led to intermittent conflict, as the Gothic leader marched his supporters from the Balkans to the Peloponnese and back to Thrace again, seeking to secure a base for his soldiers and their families.

In 483, when Theoderic was threatening Larissa in central Greece and Zeno faced a civil war in the East, the emperor was forced to make peace with the Goths; Theoderic gained permission to settle on lands in the Danubian provinces of Dacia and Moesia with the position of *magister militum*. He also won the even greater honour of being named consul for the year 484, which meant that he was welcomed back into Constantinople with great festivity, awarded patrician status and commemorated in an equestrian statue erected in the capital.[14] But the improvement in relations did not last, and a year later Theoderic's forces were plundering Thrace again.

After nearly twenty years of constant movement and insecurity, Theoderic determined to find a lasting solution and advanced to the walls of Constantinople. In 487 the Goths encamped around the city and cut off the water supply. They could not capture it but neither could the emperor destroy the entire Gothic army. Zeno was forced to negotiate with a leader who was familiar with the ways of the imperial court, had served in the imperial army, and held the title of *patricius*. Whether the resulting treaty was proposed by Theoderic or Zeno's court, it appears to have been agreed that the Gothic leader could march to Italy, seek to remove Odoacer from Ravenna and then rule the West in the emperor's name. The precise terms are unknown but Theoderic interpreted them to suit his ambition.[15] He retired to his base at Novae in Moesia (Romania today) and in the autumn of 488, with his entire Gothic following, set off on the long journey through the challenging terrain of the Balkans to cross the Alps and descend into north-east Italy.[16] On the way they were joined by a band of Rugians and probably other adventurers, too, who hoped for a better future under Theoderic's leadership.

The Gothic Migration to the West

About 20,000 warriors and perhaps 80,000 dependants may have been involved, but these numbers are only estimates.[17] Certainly it was a vast group that must have moved slowly across the Balkans, following the course of the Danube. They travelled with the emperor's permission, using local guides to advise them on the best routes, and had agreed to respect the provincial inhabitants. Just north of Singidunum, however, a large force of Gepids opposed the Goths and Theoderic had to capture the city of Sirmium before he could pitch his tents beyond the imperial border, where his forces wintered. The following year they continued north along the River Sava and west over the Julian Alps to enter Italy from the north in the summer of 489. Odoacer immediately fought to defend his kingdom on the frontier at Pons Sontii (today where the River Isonzo forms the border between Slovenia and Italy). In two vital battles he was defeated and retreated back into his capital, while Theoderic occupied Milan and made his base at Pavia. When the Gothic forces experienced difficulties there in 490, Theoderic was able to recruit his Visigothic cousin, Alaric, from Toulouse, to come to his assistance and together they defeated Odoacer on the River Adda in August.[18] By 491 this great Gothic movement had breached the defences of Italy and occupied large parts of the north of the peninsula.

Even before he had overcome some strenuous resistance to his initial conquest, Theoderic sent Festus, the head of the Roman Senate, to inform Constantinople of his campaign. This embassy was unsuccessful because of the death of Zeno and the elevation of Anastasios as eastern emperor in 491, but Theoderic was determined to adhere to the terms of the agreement – that his Gothic followers should legitimately occupy the fertile regions of Italy. When Odoacer retired behind the walls of Ravenna the Goths settled down to starve him into surrender. After a three-year siege, which imposed great hardship on the defenders, terms were agreed and hostages exchanged. The two men agreed to share the kingdom, but Theoderic allegedly discovered a plot against him and ordered men to assassinate Odoacer. When they were too scared to act, Theoderic personally killed Odoacer, claiming 'there certainly wasn't a bone in this wretched fellow'.[19] Through this combination of murderous ambition and military skills, in 493 he became the ruler of Italy, with nominal authority over Rome, the south and Sicily, as well as parts of Istria, Dalmatia and southern Gaul. He was nearly forty years old, a highly effective military commander with clearly superior political skills and a rare understanding of Roman ideals.

Theoderic in Ravenna

According to a contemporary record known as the Anonymous Valesianus, written in about 550, Theoderic 'was a man of great distinction and of good-will towards all men . . . although he himself was of the Arian sect, he nevertheless made no assault on the catholic religion'.[20] The same source alleges that Theoderic's mother Erelieva had converted to the Catholic faith, adopting the name Eusebia. While there is no indication of when this happened, Theoderic had offered his mother and sister as hostages to Constantinople, confirming his understanding of the Roman tradition. Indeed, Empress Ariadne had entertained the Gothic hostages in her private quarters within the Great Palace. Possibly Erelieva converted to the Catholic definition of the faith with Theoderic's approval, in order to facilitate better relations with the imperial court. Pope Gelasius (492–6) addressed a letter to her, believing that she had influence with her son.[21]

Three centuries later the historian Agnellus claimed that in 493 Theoderic promised to bring peace to the citizens of Ravenna and to all the Romans. He records that between 27 February and 5 March, Bishop John went out to Classis to welcome 'the new king from the east', the clergy chanting psalms and carrying the Gospels, crucifixes and incense burners.[22] Although bishops often played a major role in such negotiations, always moments of high tension, this account may be imaginary.[23] The Arian presbyters who had ministered to Odoacer and the city's Germanic and Gothic garrison troops are not mentioned, although they must have welcomed the new ruler. Theoderic immediately occupied the imperial palace and ordered the minting of bronze coins in his own name, reserving gold coinage for the eastern emperor. Nothing is known of Theoderic's previous relationships in Moesia, but when he arrived in Ravenna he didn't have a wife who could assume the role of queen. His mother, Erelieva, sister Amalafrida and daughters Ostrogotho Areagni and Thiudigotho, however, all required appropriate accommodation, as well as his other relatives, such as Theodagunda, *illustris femina*. His military followers also expected to be given suitable palaces or villas in the capital, as well as landed estates. While they followed instructions to hunt down and kill any of Odoacer's supporters who would not come over to the new ruler, there must have been a period of considerable upheaval until Theoderic's people had replaced the previous regime.

After the long siege it was essential to repair the city walls and restore confidence among the inhabitants. Theoderic persisted in his efforts to win recognition of his success from Constantinople, to reassure the Roman senatorial elite of his intention to govern equably and to reward his Gothic and Germanic followers. He dispatched a second embassy to the East led by Faustus Niger, a Roman senator, to announce his victory over Odoacer and his intention to rule as king over both Goths and Romans.[24] Before that embassy returned the Goths had elected Theoderic as their king and he had begun to address two of the most pressing consequences of his invasion: the distribution of land to his supporters, and the construction of more impressive Arian churches. First, where were the Goths who had been on the march from Thrace into Italy going to live? Since the promise of land had been a fundamental motive of their migration, Theoderic had to satisfy the demand of several tens of thousands of Goths for a permanent place to settle. Continuing the process of integration initiated by his predecessor, he promoted an experienced Roman administrator, Liberius, to the position of Praetorian Prefect and put him in charge. In the redistribution of properties, Liberius managed to dispossess Odoacer's supporters in north Italy, who were replaced by Goths, while leaving the landed estates of local Romans largely intact, which pleased both parties. Even if the methods used to establish control of land and the taxes to be paid on it remain obscure, the Goths clearly now became landowners.[25] They always remained a small minority within the local population, however, perhaps 14 per cent under Theoderic, a figure that was probably halved later in the sixth century.[26]

A second requirement was for suitably imposing churches for the Goths' Arian worship. One of the first structures commissioned by Theoderic in 493 became the cathedral of the Arian clergy of Ravenna. It was a basilica church that survives today in a renovated form dedicated to S. Spirito, with an octagonal baptistery close by. This Arian baptistery is clearly modelled on the one built by Bishop Neon, with almost the same proportions and a very similar internal decoration in mosaic (Plate 10). In the dome, the scene of the baptism presents Christ as a distinctly younger, unbearded and very human figure. John the Baptist stands on his left and an elderly figure representing the River Jordan sits on the opposite bank. In contrast, the earlier baptistery rebuilt by Bishop Neon depicts a bearded Christ, appropriately aged about thirty, with John the Baptist on his right, and the Jordan personified in a figure half submerged in the water. In both structures the font is placed in the centre of the building below the dome, so that all Christians would experience the same sense of rebirth as they emerged from the water. The Arians, however, would look up at a young Christ, who confirmed their belief that the Son did not share the same essence as God the Father, he was merely 'like' the Father. But Theoderic clearly intended that his followers should be inducted into the Arian Christian community in an equally dazzling golden building.

Near the cathedral and baptistery, the leading Arian minister was provided with a residence (*episcopium*), complete with a bath and other annexes for the clergy, including a villa known as the *domus Drogdonis* (house of Drogdo). In 512 or 517/18 Bishop Unimundus added another church, dedicated to St Eusebius, outside the city walls.[27] The use of impost blocks and polygonal apse exteriors suggests Constantinopolitan practices, in contrast to local construction methods, and may imply that the masons came from the East, possibly with Theoderic.[28]

Symbols of Empire: Imperial Regalia

When Emperor Anastasios (491–518) received Theoderic's requests for the imperial regalia, which the victorious general felt was due after the Gothic triumph in the West, he refused. While Theoderic understood his subordination to Constantinople, he persisted in his demand for the symbols of power. Finally, after four years of diplomatic negotiations Anastasios conceded that 'all the ornaments of the Palace' and the 'ruling robe' that Theoderic desired (clothing and objects that symbolized imperial power), should be transported back to Ravenna.[29] Since Theoderic never wore a crown, according to the Anonymous Valesianus, it seems unlikely that the crown and sceptre of Romulus Augustulus, which had been sent to Constantinople by Odoacer in 476, were returned. But the Gothic king took the arrival of the other elements of imperial regalia as a recognition of his title and, from 498, began to wear the purple cloak of imperial office. While he never assumed the full powers of a Roman emperor, Theoderic is described by contemporaries as a ruler endowed with an imperial authority; he was sometimes addressed as *semper augustus* ('forever august', a term usually reserved to emperors).

Theoderic maintained the basic administration that had functioned in Ravenna under Odoacer while he dealt with immediate challenges. He therefore did little to change the imperial system he inherited, though he sought to introduce key roles for his Gothic supporters within it. As *comites* (counts) and *saiones* (regal agents, retainers of the king), individual Goths were endowed with plenipotentiary powers, for instance, *saio* Grenoda, who investigated charges brought against an ex-praetorian prefect.[30] In addition to this major shift, Theoderic devised a rough division of labour to meet the task of integrating the new arrivals into Italian society: local inhabitants (*Romani*, now somewhat clumsily identified as 'Italo-Romans') were expected to pay taxes, as before, while the Goths provided military service in the traditional style. The regime and court would be sustained through regular taxation and the kingdom defended by reliable fighting forces. The Italo-Romans were not allowed to carry arms, which became the prerogative of the highly militarized Gothic minority (with a few notable exceptions). Theoderic thus created a clear separation between local inhabitants and the incoming Goths, even though some of these newcomers had already adopted Roman names in addition to those given at birth. Intermarriage was not prohibited but appears to have been rare. While some Goths converted from Arian to Catholic beliefs, three of the Arian clergy of the church of St Anastasia have Roman names and six sign in Latin.[31] But in general Gothic identity and naming patterns were passed on through the generations into the late sixth century.[32] While references to 'our law' indicate the survival of traditional Gothic legal practice, Theoderic stressed that there should be an innovative combination of complementary Gothic and Roman customs that he identified as the *res publica Romana*.[33]

In couching this negotiation in traditional Roman rhetoric designed to assimilate his Gothic forces into the ancient civilization of Rome,

Theoderic delineated the area now governed by a specifically Gothic and imperial system of administration from the regions ruled by other non-Roman forces beyond its border. Although he maintained close contacts with his distant Gothic relatives and with the Vandals in North Africa, he did not respect their right to rule, and was quick to take advantage of any disputed successions. While the Visigoths in Toulouse and Spain and the Burgundians and Franks in Gaul had also adapted Roman-style administration for their kingdoms, Theoderic considered his own understanding of imperial institutions to be superior, for example, his laws, his use of the court and propaganda. It was an understanding grounded in the time he spent in Constantinople in the 460s, as well as the knowledge he had gained of imperial mechanisms of control as he negotiated with Zeno. Once established in Ravenna, he set about rebuilding the Roman empire in the West, under the suzerainty of Constantinople. In this he consolidated his predecessor's pioneering integration of senatorial officials into the regal government, creating an ideological framework in which Gothic and Roman elements coalesced in a powerful new political system.[34]

10

Theoderic's kingdom

Regardless of whether Theoderic presented himself to the inhabitants of Italy as the chosen representative of Emperor Zeno in Constantinople, he certainly derived much prestige from his familiarity with the eastern court. He held the highest honorific title of *patricius*, had served as consul in the East and had been appointed *magister militum*, commander of imperial forces; he had observed at first hand how the empire was ruled. He was thus a completely new type of non-Roman military leader, different from all those who had marched into Italy since the early fifth century. He knew enough Latin and Greek to follow what the most educated Roman senators said and wrote, yet he remained a Gothic leader who addressed his own people in their language and promoted their version of the Christian faith. This trilingual ability that enhanced both his military and governing credentials also set him apart as a Goth of particular distinction, who impressed all who came into contact with him.

From his capital in Ravenna he created a kingdom which extended far beyond the boundaries of modern Italy. It encompassed the territory of Istria, at the head of the Adriatic, some regions further north and west (the provinces of Rhaetia I, Noricum Mediterraneum, Pannonia II and Dalmatia, which included the eastern Adriatic coast). Beyond the Alps it included large parts of southern Gaul (the provinces of Narbonnensis I and II and Viennensis to the north), though his authority was disputed with the Burgundians, based at Lyon, and the Visigoths, whose capital was at Toulouse in Aquitaine. Outlying regions of this large area were often under less permanent or effective control, though garrisons were set up on many borders that were critical to the security of the kingdom. The settlement of the Ostrogoths who had accompanied Theoderic from the East was concentrated around Ravenna, Pavia and in Picenum, the coastal region south of Ravenna. From this central hub Gothic forces campaigned regularly to enforce Theoderic's authority over distant regions. And through Gothic counts his administration was extended over the entire island of Sicily, and into the northern province of Pannonia II based on Sirmium on the Danube in 508.[1]

Theoderic's Court in Ravenna

Once established in his capital, Theoderic deployed all the trappings of authority, referring to himself as prince (*princeps*) and king (*rex*), and using these titles on his coins.[2] Although gold coinage was issued only in the name of the eastern emperor, one commemorative triple *solidus* minted in Rome displayed Theoderic in imperial stance and wearing imperial robes (Plate 16). This single surviving portrait – with its Gothic hairstyle – records his titles: King Theoderic, the pious and always most invincible *princeps*, and Theoderic, king, conqueror of the barbarians (*victor gentium*). The silver and bronze coins repeat his regal title, which encircles his monogram or a laurel wreath, as well as the traditional theme of unconquered Rome (*Invicta Roma*) and fortunate Ravenna (*Felix Ravenna*).[3] In addition, bronze coins used as small change were minted with images of the city of Ravenna as a turreted woman and the words *Felix Ravenna* on the reverse (Plate 28). Theoderic appointed a hierarchy of trusted Gothic allies to supervise the daily routine of the palace and employed eunuchs to guard his *cubiculum*, private quarters, in the imperial style. His doctor, a deacon named Helpidius who was approached by those who wanted favours or a decision from Theoderic, appears to have been a local inhabitant.[4]

Because the Goths did not keep written records comparable to those of the traditional imperial administration, it is not easy to document the activity of the inner circle of the king's Gothic advisers and servants. The military leaders who had accompanied Theoderic on the migration from East to West made up his *comitatus*, the permanent entourage of the king, together with advisers who gained the king's confidence. They represented the king's ability to impose his decisions by force and moved with him wherever he went (though the court was not peripatetic).[5] When he sent Roman senators on diplomatic missions, the Goths provided a military escort, for example the *spatarius* (sword bearer) Inigis or the *scutarius* (shield bearer) Witterit.

From the ranks of this court entourage Theoderic chose the counts (*comites*), who supervised the bureaucracy, and agents (*saiones*), who had authority over Roman officials. The counts had the status of *illustri* (highest-ranking senators) and exercised judicial powers in conjunction with Roman legal experts.[6] The Gothic *saiones*, who were given estates around Ravenna and in northern Italy, were endowed with wide powers and formed a quite distinct cohort of the king's officials. They were drawn from military personnel and could control all other officials, even the praetorian prefect. Their terms of appointment were defined by the king and varied depending on their responsibilities: some were appointed to protect individual Romans, others supervised transport and the food supply. To judge by complaints made against them, they regularly used their weapons to enforce decisions and acted as a rough police force. As they had to mediate between Goths and local inhabitants, they were probably bilingual.[7]

Although Theoderic intended that Gothic warriors should defend his kingdom, the Goths were not numerous enough to defend all Theoderic's territories and, in exceptional circumstances, he also called on experienced Roman military commanders. Liberius is one of the most remarkable, notable for managing the establishment of the Goths on their estates in Italy as well as leading several successful military campaigns, for instance in Gaul. During his very long life – he died aged eighty-nine some time after 554 – he also held challenging positions under Emperor Justinian in Egypt and in Spain.[8] When he finally retired, he returned to his ancestral lands in Italy and was buried in Rimini. All military leaders could draw on local resources for the army but some military campaigns against distant rival powers in southern France (Provence) and Burgundy were led by Roman officers, with their own personal armed forces as reinforcements.

Theoderic's Administration

Gothic warriors formed the inner core of Theoderic's administration, but he also took over several skilled chancery officials and diplomats from Odoacer's government: Flavius Rufius Postumius Festus, consul in 472 and leader of the Senate in 490, and Anicius Probus Faustus Niger, nominated consul in 490 by Odoacer. Both served as ambassadors to Constantinople: Festus in 490 and 498; Faustus in 492–4.[9] Theoderic retained other senatorial figures recruited by Odoacer in Ravenna: Opilio and his sons; Albinus, the son of Caecina Decius Maximus Basilius, chosen by Theoderic as consul in 493; and Liberius, all members of the Roman elite.[10] While the king was careful to respect the power of the Roman senatorial aristocracy, endowed with inherited wealth and bearers of long inherited names, the adherence of these old Roman families, such as the Decii, to the new regime helped Theoderic to maintain an essentially traditional style of government.

The Cassiodori were one of the most important families to assist in establishing Gothic rule. Cassiodorus the Elder was a Roman senator with estates in southern Italy that provided a supply of horses for the army. In 490, when he went over to Theoderic, he was governor (*consularis*) of the province of Sicily and ensured its loyalty to the incoming Gothic leader. His seniority and experience of Roman administration made him a very important ally. His son, Cassiodorus the Younger, known by the epithet Senator, would become the leading spokesman for Theoderic, starting his career at the court as *quaestor* in 507 and then moving on to higher positions, including Praetorian Prefect (533–7). For over twenty years Theoderic and his successors addressed instructions, made appointments and issued advice through letters composed by Cassiodorus. His edited record of these documents, the *Variae*, provides detailed information about Theoderic's rule as well as revealing the writer's literary skills and personal interests. In a highly elaborate classical style, very different from normal speech, Cassiodorus no doubt exaggerated Theoderic's achievements, but without the *Variae* the record of his reign would be very colourless.[11]

In addition to the participation and incorporation of these representatives of the highest levels of Roman society, the civilian administration at Ravenna employed established provincial governors, such as Gaudentius of Flaminia, and experienced civil servants, including three who held the post of *magister officiorum* (master of the offices, the leading imperial bureaucrat), and another three praetorian prefects of Italy.[12] While many of the senatorial class preferred to live in Rome, members of less aristocratic families often moved to Ravenna. Mastery of the legal system provided many young and ambitious men from such backgrounds with an entrée to the court: as a youth Florus was educated in the law at Ravenna and became *advocatus*.[13] Eugenes (or Eugenetes), a brilliant orator and lawyer, served as *quaestor sacri palatii* in 506–7, and then as *magister officiorum* (507).[14] Other lawyers of similar status included Decoratus and Honoratus, brothers from Spoleto, who both rose to the post of *quaestor sacri palatii* in the 520s.[15] It's possible that the appointment of less socially eminent Romans into Theoderic's civilian administration deliberately brought about a downgrading of senatorial positions, which became merely honorary. In this way the Gothic court restricted most of the senatorial aristocrats to titular positions and concentrated much power in Ravenna in a different group of elite individuals.[16]

Theoderic's Buildings

To house his court Theoderic expanded the palace with new buildings and complemented them by improvements to the city's facilities: attention to the water and grain supply is clear from new sewers, repairs to the aqueduct, baths, granaries and bakeries (Plate 29).[17] Almost none of these survive, secular buildings being less well cared for than ecclesiastical. The most important additions to Ravenna, however, remain his palace church and his own mausoleum, testimony to his determination to glorify the city.

When he arrived in Ravenna, Theoderic must have been struck by the grandeur and richness of the major churches and the display of imperial portraits at the east end of the basilica of St John the Evangelist. Here were the dynastic claims of the ruling family put up by Galla Placidia – with the significant exception of those who embraced the Arian heresy. Her novel idea almost certainly provoked Theoderic's plan for an even larger basilica to be attached to his palace that would commemorate his own family and their Arian belief. It was originally dedicated to Christ the Saviour and is now known as S. Apollinare Nuovo. Since it originally had a gilded roof and three tiers of mosaics set against a gold background running the entire length of the church, it was called 'the Golden Heaven'. On a sunny day the whole building makes an extraordinary impression, glistening with spectacular bursts of colour between the large windows (Plate 11).

For the decoration of his church, Theoderic ordered a series of scenes from the life of Christ to adorn the highest level, the miracle stories to be illustrated on the north side and the Passion on the south (Plates 14 and 15). Between each square panel, exquisite arrangements of peacock feathers and flowers evoke a heavenly glory. In the second tier he commissioned a series of male figures, apostles and saints, each characterized by specific features such as hairstyles elegantly executed. In the lowest tier of mosaic decoration, two processions of saints and martyrs (male on the north side, female on the south) advance from the west end to large images of Christ and the Virgin at the east end. Since these mosaics of the third tier have been heavily restored, their original form is not clear – possibly Theoderic had himself portrayed leading the male procession while his wife or daughter led the women. In the apse an inscription recorded the king as the founder, and he may have been displayed in person. After the collapse of this part of the church during an earthquake in the eighth century, the inscription was no longer in situ, but it was still visible where it had fallen when Agnellus recorded it in the ninth.

Perhaps the most unusual element of the decoration is the depiction of the twin cities, Ravenna and Classis, on either side of the nave at the west end, the former dominated by a colonnaded structure labelled PALATIUM (Plate 12). This is one of the rare images of an imperial palace, including an open portico with the throne room at the centre where Theoderic was depicted. According to one contemporary text, Theoderic built a portico around the entire palace, and this mosaic may display part of that structure, an external feature where he could appear to receive his subjects' applause. On either side of the throne, courtiers raised their arms in acclamation. In this magnificent scene of the king enthroned in his palace Theoderic appeared as the new ruler of a walled city enclosing a variety of buildings, shown in the background. On the opposite wall is Classis, with its port and ships riding at anchor, and officials (possibly including the king) standing in front of a long fortification wall. Since Classis had always been so closely connected with Ravenna, it formed an obvious counterpart to the palace and reflects the importance of communication and trading networks throughout the Mediterranean and up and down the Adriatic. Although the Goths had little experience of naval warfare, towards the end of his reign Theoderic decided to strengthen sea defences by building a fleet.

In displaying his cities so elegantly Theoderic claimed responsibility for them in the palace church in which he worshipped according to his Arian belief, close to the *Palatium* depicted in mosaic.

Originally, Theoderic occupied the central panel of the Palace mosaic, but today we only see a golden space with curtains at either side. The ruler's image, and those of his courtiers who stood between the columns of the portico, were all removed in the 560s when the Catholic bishop took over the church. The surviving hands of some of the courtiers embedded in the mosaic columns are all that remain on the south side, and on the north the feet of four figures standing in front of the wall of Classis, which were finally removed in the early twentieth century (Plate 13). This transformation has been interpreted as a *damnatio memoriae*.[18] But within the church, one can still experience the glowing aura of the original decoration in the basilica erected by the Gothic king for Arian veneration in Ravenna. The novelty of the mosaics – especially the miracle scenes from the life of Christ (which include the Samaritan woman, the poor widow who gave what she could to the collecting box, the woman with an issue of blood, and the serving girl who accused Peter) – and the long processions of holy martyrs that draw the eye towards the east end, though not specifically Arian, are a very striking testimony to the king's Christian faith. And even with considerable rebuilding (such as the seventeenth-century apse, reconstructed in the 1950s), we can appreciate Theoderic's representation of Gothic rule and Christian belief as his response to Galla Placidia's imperial claims laid out at S. Giovanni Evangelista.

There is much debate about the identity of the craftsmen responsible for these monuments; were the builders and mosaicists also from the eastern capital? Or from Rome? Or were they recruited locally among the descendants of those responsible for the churches of Galla Placidia and Bishop Neon? The fact that Theoderic requested skilled marble workers, craftsmen and building materials from Rome, and imported Proconnesian marble capitals and columns from Constantinople (with the Greek masons' marks), implies a desire to have the very best. From his visit to Rome in 500, when he saw the great Roman churches, he may have considered their builders superior to the local workers in Ravenna.[19] For decades, the bishops of Rome had been nurturing these craftsmen and Pope Symmachus (498–514) constructed many churches, chapels and the fountain at St Peter's, which was decorated in mosaic with lambs, crosses and palm fronds, all traditional Christian symbols.[20] An obvious model for the form of S. Apollinare Nuovo was the immense Roman basilica of S. Maria Maggiore dating from the mid-fifth century, which also portrays scenes from the Old Testament and the life of Christ at its highest level, while Theoderic's decade in Constantinople provided at least eastern inspiration, if not craftsmen.

Although there are hints of external responsibility for the Arian churches in Ravenna, we know that the city sustained teams of skilled workers who had built and decorated secular as well as ecclesiastical buildings for generations. Quite possibly, local guilds of artists who were active in Ravenna assembled the imported materials and decorated Theoderic's palace chapel in its unusual and independent style, as well as other Arian churches. One of these, later demolished and now known only as the church of the Goths, had elaborate capitals decorated with Theoderic's monogram. (These can now be admired supporting the Venetian portico on the Piazza del Popolo, Plate 27.) In addition, a small church near the mausoleum of Theoderic was dedicated to St George, and a chapel to St Peter. During Gothic rule the Arian bishops of Ravenna built two more residences or palaces known to Agnellus, who also records another palace constructed by Theoderic on an island just off the Lion Port. Many of these Gothic buildings fell into ruins or were later demolished to provide building material for Catholic re-use – Agnellus himself used *spolia* from Theoderic's island palace in the construction of his own house.

The choice of a palace to represent the city of Ravenna in the mosaic in S. Apollinare Nuovo reflects Theoderic's pride in extending and enriching the building initiated by Honorius nearly a century earlier. Archaeological signs of his additions made between the late fifth and early sixth centuries include another, larger, dining room, the *triclinium ad mare*, overlooking the sea; many structures with fine mosaic floors; walls relating to additional buildings; and lead pipes stamped with the king's name and recording his restoration of the city (Plate 29).[21] In expanding the palace Theoderic was obviously inspired by memories of the Great Palace in Constantinople, for instance in the area called *scubitum* (from the Greek *exkoubiton*, a garrison building for the elite imperial guard created by Emperor Leo I). This imitation is most obvious in the palace gate named *Calchi*, after the imposing ceremonial entrance to the Palace in Constantinople, the *Chalke*. Like the imperial model, Theoderic probably decorated this entrance with statuary, images of himself and his family, and classical *spolia*. Harking back to even older Roman traditions, an equestrian statue of Theoderic was installed in front of the palace. (Nearly three hundred years later, this was the monument that Charlemagne removed from Ravenna to help instil a sense of imperial power in his new capital city of Aachen.)

The Power of Images: Regal Statuary

Theoderic clearly understood regal statuary, decorating the palaces in Ravenna and Pavia with statues and portraits of himself to promote his rule. Agnellus had seen the immense image of Theoderic on horseback in the king's palace at Pavia, which was taken over by later Lombard rulers for their own use.[22] By insisting that Gothic military units should come to the capital to collect their pay, he showed an understanding of the impact such regal images, set in a quasi-imperial setting, could have. He also marked his building projects with his name in the way that Roman rulers had claimed credit for constructing aqueducts, bridges, roads and inns. He restored the imperial transport system in the areas of the West under his control, and constantly encouraged the local populations to improve and beautify their cities and estates by draining and reclaiming marshy land, repairing fortifications, building new ones or participating in their maintenance. In all this, he benefitted from the appreciation of those who erected inscriptions to his honour: the most sycophantic occasionally praise the king as *semper augustus* (although he himself never used the imperial title, *augustus*), *gloriosissimus, victor ac triumfator, clementissimi principis* (most glorious, triumphant victor, most merciful prince). This may reflect appreciation for the king's repairs to monuments in Rome, where he restored the city walls and part of the palace.[23]

Similar images of the king and references to his patronage are found in palaces in Verona, Pavia, Galeata and Monza, near Lake Como where he spent time in the summer. (Like other rulers of Ravenna, he appreciated the cooler climate there.) Procopius knew of a mosaic portrait of him in the market place at Naples.[24] While his decrees indicate that he visited these cities, especially Pavia, on numerous occasions, the concentration of regal attention on his capital reflects Theoderic's determination to create a little Constantinople in the West, where he could rule as an emperor, patronizing the best artists, craftsmen and scholars. The portraits and statues erected in other cities may have been put up at his command, but they represented local appreciation of his rule, special provisions made in time of need (as in Liguria) or simple admiration recorded in inscriptions.

Gothic Court Culture

Under Theoderic the court at Ravenna became a centre of patronage that attracted not only skilled Goths and Arians, but also the best scholars, builders and artists, most of whom appear to have been Roman. The most notable intellectual figure at Theoderic's court was Boethius, famous for his translations from Greek of Aristotle, Plato, Pythagoras, Ptolemy, Nicomachus, Euclid and Archimedes, his knowledge of water clocks, sundials (displayed in a letter to Gundobad, king of the Burgundians), scientific and musical instruments.[25] From 507 onwards, Theoderic consulted Boethius and expressed his enormous pride in the high culture of his court: 'May the foreign tribes realize, thanks to you, that my noblemen are famous authorities.' Boethius was already established as an outstanding scholar of Greek texts – scientific, mathematical and philosophical – and held the title of *patricius* before he moved to Ravenna. In 522 when his two young sons were made consuls (a notable joint honour), Boethius agreed to take the position of *magister officiorum* at Theoderic's court. Although some Gothic military leaders remained hostile to Roman culture, Boethius brought immense lustre to the ruling family.

His presence, together with other Roman scholars, certainly distinguished the court in Ravenna from other Germanic centres that looked to King Theoderic for advice. One measure of their brilliance was their mastery of Greek, rare in the West in the sixth century. As well as Boethius, there was for example a man from Ravenna named Marius Novatus Renatus, whom Severus of Antioch met in Constantinople in around 510. They conversed in Greek. Renatus owned a manuscript of Boethius' work on logic, which had been copied in the eastern capital by a certain *antiquarius* named Theodorus, and he may have acquired it there.[26] Lesser figures also provided specialist knowledge, like Helpidius,

Theoderic's doctor (*medicus*), who was also a deacon, and the *comes archiatrorum* (chief doctor) mentioned by Cassiodorus, who dealt with the medical profession in the city. Since advanced medical knowledge, based on Greek texts, was unfamiliar in the West and translations of such texts were made in Ravenna, Theoderic's court became an important centre attracting Jewish and western doctors. Greek traders in Classis included *argentarii* (bankers or money changers), such as Julianus, and several Syrian merchants, who signed documents using Greek letters.

Gothic Bibles

A specifically Gothic contribution to this intermingled culture may be illustrated by one magnificent manuscript with letters written in gold and silver ink on purple-dyed parchment. This extremely high-quality, de luxe exemplar is a text of the Gospels in Gothic with lavish decoration and wide margins, preserved in the University Library at Uppsala (Plate 24).[27] Through it, we can see the rivalry between two different interpretations of Christian faith that both produced sumptuous biblical texts, in a very expensive object probably intended for display rather than regular use. A Gothic scribe (*bokareis*) named Wiljarith is associated with the Uppsala manuscript.[28] The enormous investment in fine parchment, purple dye and gold and silver lettering suggests royal patronage and an origin in Ravenna. Similar workshops existed to provide religious texts for Arian Christians in less expensive formats, but since most of them were later condemned to the flames as heretical, the Uppsala Gospel book is a rare survival.

In addition to the production of Arian religious texts, fragmentary bilingual texts in Gothic and Latin, as well as Greek and Latin, imply a team of translators who were active in making theological, historical, philosophical and medical documents available in the three languages used in Ravenna. Theoderic supported a very broad education in Gothic, Latin and Greek for his daughters and the children of his courtiers. Writing to the Senate in 533, Cassiodorus praises the education of Theoderic's daughter Amalasuintha:

> She is fluent in the splendour of Greek oratory; she shines in the glory of Roman eloquence; the flow of her ancestral speech brings her glory;

she surpasses all in their own languages, and is equally wonderful in each . . . no one needs an interpreter when addressing the ear of our wise mistress . . . to this is added, as it were a glorious diadem, the priceless knowledge of literature, through which she learns the wisdom of the ancients.[29]

He goes on to commend her capacity to 'untie the knots of litigation . . . quietly calm heated conflicts' and insists that her firmness of mind 'surpasses even the most famous philosophers'. He lavishes similar appreciation on the skills of Amalaberga, Theoderic's niece, who was sent to marry the king of Thuringia with valuable gifts befitting a royal marriage: a herd of silver-coloured horses, 'very well-fed, and thus gentle, swift from their great size, good to look at and pleasant to ride . . . they are trained to a steady and enduring speed', but 'she who adorns the glory of royal power rightly outdoes them all'.[30] As usual, Cassiodorus exaggerates but there was surely some truth to his claims. Ennodius' record of a woman named Bona who was summoned to Theoderic's court in 509/10 has been connected to the education of Amalasuintha and her cousin. Whoever was responsible, the aim of preparing these royal women to hold their own in this early sixth-century Romano-Gothic world clearly reflected standards of education and knowledge at the court of Ravenna.

Another Gothic element of court culture in Ravenna derives from the work of three geographers, Athanarid, Heldebald and Marcomir (although their names are not recorded in sixth-century sources). They used Roman itineraries such as the Peutingeriana map, as well as their own sources of information, and listed towns according to their position on rivers, indicating the routes taken by those travelling by boat. In addition to useful information about northern peoples identified as 'the Finns', they provided the names of towns that had been changed under Roman rule. Despite their shadowy existence, these geographers seem to have plotted the long tortuous movement of Gothic tribes from the Far East to the West and to have identified names of places and rivers that had been previously unmapped.[31] Their evidence was put to very good use by a later geographer known only as the Anonymous Cosmographer of Ravenna at the turn of the seventh century.

Bread and Circuses

While Theoderic took pleasure in surrounding himself with Roman as well as Gothic intellectuals, he did not ignore the imperial policy of 'bread and circuses' and took care to provide large cities with sufficient grain as well as popular entertainment. Cassiodorus presents him as hostile to gladiatorial combat and fighting with wild beasts, but his support for circus games – charioteers in Rome and Milan, the amphitheatre in Pavia – indicates a firm grasp of their importance in Roman culture. In a letter to King Herminafrid of Thuringia, he acknowledges gifts of trained wild animals, possibly dancing bears, while to celebrate the consulship of Eutharic in 518–19 unfamiliar wild beasts, possibly lions or giraffes, were brought from Africa, and their display in Rome was repeated in Ravenna.[32] Particularly skilful charioteers were rewarded, such as one called Thomas who had come from the East to compete in western circuses, and pantomime artists, dancers – male and female – as well as athletes, gymnasts and musicians were highly appreciated. Theoderic was allegedly unenthusiastic about chariot races but considered it necessary to finance what the people most desired: a huge spectacle of the Green, Blue, White and Red teams of horses and men challenging each other to race six times around the hippodrome. In Cassiodorus' long description of how this came to dominate Roman popular entertainment, the king criticizes the frenzy generated by chariot racing while conceding that 'sometimes it is useful to play the fool, and so control the joys people long for'.[33] In contrast, Pope Felix IV (526–30) condemned the clergy of Ravenna for showing too much interest in circus entertainments, which, he said, damaged their souls.

Living in Ravenna in the Early Sixth Century

While Theoderic laid on popular entertainment for the city's inhabitants, he left the traditional system of city government in Ravenna unchanged, viewing some city autonomy as a valuable source of local pride and social distinction. He insisted on the principle of collective responsibility for taxation, especially when the richer council members tried to avoid paying their share. An edict issued between 507 and 512 stipulates that the greatest landowners are to pay their full proportion of taxes, either in three instalments or in one payment, so that their debts or arrears of tax shouldn't fall on poorer town councillors (*curiales*).[34] After 493 the local council, dominated by a few aristocratic families, continued to administer the city, appointing the nightwatchmen and other municipal officials.[35] Among the *principales* who presided at its meetings we find representatives of families well established in the city, such as Johannis Aelius and Tranquillus Melminius, who oversaw the registration of land sales. This was vitally important because whenever property changed hands the tax responsibility was transferred to the new owner.[36] In 504, for instance, Flavius Basilius, described as a *vir honestus* and *argentarius* (money changer), sold land in a place called Vetereca to the church of Ravenna, represented by Rusticus, an assistant (acolyte, *acolythus*).[37] The presiding magistrate Firmilianus Ursus orders the document, drawn up by the official clerk (*forensis*) Flavius Vitalis, to be read out, the sale price of 18 *solidi* is agreed and the document is signed and sent to be registered in the city archive. The *defensor civitatis* was responsible for ensuring that the church of Ravenna assumed responsibility for the tax due.[38]

Another papyrus preserved in the city's archive is the will of Bishop Aurelianus. Dated the Ides of January in the year of the western consul Valerius (521), this record stipulates that the bishop wishes to leave all his property to the church and that all his slaves, male and female, are to be freed. In the 550s it was copied and read aloud in front of the councillors, and witnessed by a large group of city residents, identified by name, who signed it.[39] The reason for repeating this performance may lie with the former slaves, who might have needed to reassert their free condition and therefore demanded the registration of a new copy. Their insistence has preserved evidence of wealth accumulated by one of the city's bishops, which he left to the church and which could be used by later Christian leaders in their ambitious architectural projects.

Theoderic's Gothic court attracted skilled craftsmen such as Daniel, a marble worker to whom the king bestowed a monopoly on carving sarcophagi, with the instruction not to exploit those grieving a death by charging too much for his work, and ambitious young men like

Senarius, as well as supporters of a more traditional Roman background such as Liberius.[40] Senarius was a young man who sought employment in the new ruler's court and rose from the position of page to be an honoured adviser and *patricius*, while Liberius had devoted himself to Theoderic's service in a long and varied career since 493. Both acted as the king's envoys and composed elegant verse epitaphs to be engraved on their tombs in Ravenna and Rimini respectively, which describe their careers under the Gothic king and his rewards.[41]

With his grasp of the centripetal forces provoking the disintegration of the Roman world in the West, Theoderic remade an imperial style of government, becoming emperor in all but name. Like no other non-Roman chieftain Theoderic created a hub around which later forces circled, eager to brush against his aura and carry it away to enrich their own centres of power. Theoderic's rule in Ravenna thus transformed the fifth-century period of Roman collapse into a new period of early Christendom, under the aegis of Constantinople. It opened a future in which the integration of Gothic and Germanic strength with Roman skills and essential features of imperial administration made Ravenna a crucible in which the alloy of Europe was formed.

I I

Theoderic's diplomacy

Theoderic elevated his court at Ravenna into the centre of a network of diplomatic connections that stretched around the entire western half of the Roman world and reinforced the city's imperial credentials. Even before his first victory over Odoacer he was sending out embassies to other rulers, and when he needed military assistance in 490, he persuaded Alaric II, the Visigothic ruler of Toulouse, to come to his aid. Like kings and emperors throughout history, he used marriages very effectively as a method of reinforcing political links and avoiding warfare. In 493 he negotiated an alliance with the Frankish king Clovis that was sealed by his own marriage to Audefleda, Clovis's sister; his daughter Thiudigotho, was given as a reward to Alaric of Toulouse in 494. His other daughter, Ostrogotho Areagni, was later married to Sigismund, son of King Gundobad of Burgundy. In 500, Theoderic betrothed his recently widowed sister, Amalafrida, to Thrasamund, king of the Vandals of North Africa, which helped to reduce Vandal attacks on Sicily and southern Italy.[1]

Sometime between 507 and 511 Theoderic sent his niece Amalaberga to marry Herminafrid of Thuringia, a northern kingdom to the east of the Rhine. In the panegyric that described her accomplishments, Cassiodorus reported: 'Fortunate Thuringia will possess what Italy has reared, a woman learned in letters, schooled in moral character, glorious not only for her lineage but equally for her feminine dignity.' He also insisted that her contribution would improve the kingdom: 'With you she will lawfully play a ruler's part, and she will discipline your nation with a better way of life.'[2] In another major initiative Theoderic selected a Visigothic noble, Eutharic, as the husband for his sole surviving child, his daughter Amalasuintha. This promoted Eutharic to the position of potential heir, though his untimely death in 522 caused the project to fail, to the king's great regret.

Theoderic's carefully constructed family network enhanced his status and authority and helped to avoid warfare, but it could not maintain co-operative alliances for ever. He was unable to check his brother-in-law Clovis, whose ambitions threatened both the Alemanni and the Visigoths. Early in 507, when the Frankish king was trying to gain military support from the Burgundians, Thuringi, Heruli and Warni (the last two settled in the northern reaches of the Rhine and Elbe), Theoderic wrote to all the parties to counsel peace. Since he was related by marriage to both Clovis and Alaric, the principal opponents, he stressed restraint and negotiation rather than war. He sent envoys to King Gundobad in Burgundy, who were instructed to persuade the king to join in an effort to settle the dispute by arbitration.[3] But Clovis refused these attempts and in 507 his forces defeated and killed Alaric at the battle of Vouillé. This obliged the remaining Visigoths to retreat south into Septimania and Spain, leaving the Franks in control of most of Gaul.[4] The following year Theoderic prevented the Burgundians from capturing Arles in a military campaign that allowed him to incorporate Provence into his own kingdom.

In a period dominated by volatility, insecurity and violent struggles for power, diplomacy was still not as effective as military intervention. The king's alliances, consolidated by his female relations, could never guarantee loyalty to the Ostrogothic court at Ravenna. In Visigothic Spain, for example, Thiudigotho's son eventually inherited power, but was murdered in 531. Theudis, who had been Theoderic's shield bearer, then inherited the kingdom. In North Africa, in spite of her five-hundred-strong Gothic guard, Amalafrida was unable to survive her husband's death. She died in prison while the new Vandal king Hilderic made sure all her Gothic protectors were killed.[5] And as we shall see, after the death of her husband in 534, Amalaberga had to flee from Thuringia.

Yet Theoderic's network of connections to many parts of the transalpine West provided useful information about distant regions. Through diplomatic and trading contacts, often assisted by spying, he gained news of other rulers and their ambitions. The practice was modelled on his knowledge of the eastern empire, where he had witnessed the value of such measures and the importance of appropriate gifts. When Clovis requested a cithara or lyre player, Theoderic consulted with Boethius about the best man to send to entertain the Frankish king at his banquets.[6] Boethius also provided a water clock and a sundial for Gundobad in Burgundy.[7] After the death of Eutharic in 522, Theoderic received complaints about the Visigothic administration in Spain and instructed his officials there to protect the poor from exploitation by the Gothic garrisons.[8] Through his officials in Pannonia, Istria and Dalmatia he learned of developments in the form of petitions, like one from a merchant in Salona who complained to Theoderic about the bishop's refusal to pay for oil he had provided for the church lamps. The bishop was promptly instructed to pay. Another embassy from Dalmatia brought the young barrister Arator to the court to plead the suffering of local inhabitants in rhetoric that left a lasting impression in Ravenna and resulted in Arator's later employment in the Gothic administration.[9]

Another measure of the importance of Theoderic's court is the number of foreign embassies and bishops who made their way to Ravenna. Epiphanius of Pavia was among the first, coming to plead for Liguria, the north-western region of Italy devastated by Burgundian attacks, and in 493 the king responded by employing him, accompanied by another Catholic bishop, Victor of Turin, on an embassy to the Burgundians charged with the ransom of Ligurian prisoners of war. Another early visitor to Theoderic's court was Laurentius, bishop of Milan, who also sent his deacon, Ennodius, to Ravenna on several occasions to promote the interests of the northern church. In 513 Ennodius was promoted to become bishop of Pavia and, in that capacity, Theoderic appointed him to serve on two important embassies to Constantinople in an effort to resolve the Acacian schism. His career illustrates Theoderic's insistence on using Catholic bishops for certain diplomatic missions, which continued throughout the most serious diplomatic row over Arian churches in the eastern capital.

The Gothic king also understood the importance of the bishops who ministered to the dominant, Catholic population in the area of Provence, after he had taken over that part of the Visigothic kingdom of Toulouse. When major ecclesiastical centres such as Arles and Carcassonne were besieged, he came to their relief, and appointed the elderly general Liberius as Praetorian Prefect of Gaul to re-establish 'Roman' (that is, Gothic) rule. But in 513 Theoderic caught wind of rumours that Bishop Caesarius of Arles was in contact with the king's Burgundian enemies; he immediately summoned the bishop to Ravenna. At their meeting, however, the king's determination to co-operate with the Catholic clergy led to respectful discussions and, while in Ravenna, Caesarius performed two miraculous cures. Theoderic presented many gifts to the bishop, who proceeded to Rome where Pope Symmachus settled a dispute between the sees of Arles and Vienne and appointed Caesarius as papal vicar for the region of southern Gaul. This satisfied both the bishop and Theoderic.[10]

Cassiodorus documents a wide range of decisions taken by Theoderic in response to appeals from many different regions: from the Green faction in Rome over the death of one of their members; from traders in Sipontum (Siponto), who were granted two years' relief from compulsory purchase while they restored their businesses; from the city of Arles, for food supplies and funds to restore the walls and towers; from some inhabitants of Campania and Samnium who complained that they were being forced to take over the debts of others; from the Jews of Genoa about rebuilding their synagogue; and from the blind Anduit, who had been reduced to the status of a slave despite a previous legal ruling that he and his family were free. Between 507 and 511, the king asked the Senate to delineate the area of Decemnovium, a 30km stretch of the Via Appia north of Terracina, which the patrician Decius had promised to drain. As Cassiodorus puts it:

> It is a notorious desolation of the age, which through long neglect has formed a kind of marshy sea ... and has destroyed the kindly arable equally with shaggy woodland ... All the space that the mud of the marshes occupied through stagnation of the incoming water shall be marked by fixed boundary stones ... When the promised work reaches completion, the ground restored will profit its deliverer.

A long inscription erected at Terracina records the success of the operation, with excessive praise for Theoderic (*semper augustus*) and a less fulsome tribute to Decius, ex-prefect of the city, ex-praetorian prefect, consul and patrician, whose right to own the land drained was thus guaranteed.[11]

Theoderic also received numerous requests for help after disasters and often allowed relief from taxes to stricken areas. In the early sixth century, when famine was reported in Liguria, he ordered supplies of corn to be shipped from Ravenna to the region.[12] And when this was shipwrecked, he instructed private merchants from central and southern Italy to go and sell their products in Gaul. He renewed the privileges of Marseille, a major port of entry to the region, and granted the city a temporary remission of taxes in order to boost its mercantile activity.[13] When informed about a Gothic army's looting of the area, he sent funds to a Bishop Severus, to be distributed to those people who had suffered losses. In addition to financing constructions designed to improve fortifications, land use and transportation, Theoderic insisted on the participation of local people in draining marshes and regaining cultivatable land. Through his correspondence, which is frequently enlivened by Cassiodorus' personal comments, Theoderic's efforts to impose justice and prevent undue poverty come into sharp relief.

In the letter to Boethius about the best lyre-player, Cassiodorus enthuses on the joys of music and the skill of the player.

> Harmful melancholy he turns to pleasure, he arouses sleepy sloth from its torpor, restores to the sleepless their wholesome rest, recalls lust-corrupted chastity to its moral resolve, and heals boredom of spirit which is always the enemy of good thoughts . . . Among all men this is achieved by means of five *toni* [scales or modes] each of which is called by the name of the region where it was discovered.

He then proceeds to give Boethius, the great expert in musical theory, a lecture on the Dorian, Phrygian, Aeolian, Iastian [Ionian] and Lydian modes. 'By this means, Orpheus held effective sway over the dumb beasts . . . the mermen fell in love with dry land, Galatea the sea-nymph played on firm ground . . . the bears left their beloved woods; lions abandoned their reed beds.' Continuing through other classical allusions to the power of music, he gives a digression on metre, the power of hymns and the technique of plucking the strings of the hollow cithara that resonate sweetly and vibrate harmoniously in a diversity of sound. Finally, he concludes, always speaking for Theoderic:

> Now that I have had the pleasure of this digression – for I am always glad of learned discussion with experts – let your wisdom select the superior cithara player who will perform a feat like that of Orpheus, when his sweet sound tames the savage hearts of the barbarians . . .[14]

Theoderic and Constantinople

In a much-quoted letter to Emperor Anastasios written in about 507/8, Theoderic described his kingdom, using the traditional Roman term of republic.

> Our royalty is an imitation of yours, modelled on your good purpose, a copy of the only empire, and in so far as we follow you do we excel all other nations ... We think that you will not suffer that any discord should remain between two republics, which are declared ever to have formed one body under their ancient princes.[15]

This undivided Roman kingdom, *Romanum regnum*, is later contrasted with the two constituent kingdoms, *regna*, which were united not merely by love, but also by the active support they gave to each other. 'Let there be always one will, one purpose in the Roman Kingdom.' Through Cassiodorus' carefully crafted formulations, Anastasios is praised as the emperor and Theoderic is granted an almost-equal status, as *princeps* of the west. A similar emphasis is evident in an inscription in Rome that refers to both Anastasios and Theoderic as lords, *domini*, though it reserves more honorific adjectives for the former. Theoderic recognized Constantinople as the acme of power in the Roman world, the supreme source of authority, and tried to maintain a policy of co-operation with Anastasios, who had inherited a complete repository of imperial epithets (and rituals to match), and was quite unbothered by any pretensions assumed by the Gothic ruler in the West.

Within this single empire, however, Theoderic insisted on the acceptance of a variety of religious views. As he stated in a letter of 502 to the Catholic bishops, his policy of dealing justly with all was based on his understanding of the Gospel. He considered it quite wrong that bishops both 'catholic' and 'of our religion' had been thrown out of their churches and deprived of their lands on account of doctrinal differences.[16] His emphasis on permitting all Christians – and also Jews – to express their own beliefs in their own ways may resonate particularly with us today. At the time this was not a principled theory of toleration, but a recognition of the Goths' minority presence in the territory they had conquered. Even so, it distinguished Theoderic's rule from that of other Arian kings. Between 457 and 487 the Vandal King Huneric had intensified the official opposition to Catholics in Africa, forcing 302 bishops into exile, including 46 sent to Corsica to cut wood for the royal navy. Eighty-eight of the exiled bishops died and two were martyred. Similarly, Visigothic rulers persecuted non-Arian Christians as well as Jewish communities in Spain.

In contrast to this active persecution, Theoderic allowed Catholic bishops of Ravenna to continue to build their churches alongside Arian ones and to sustain their definition of the faith.[17] During his reign Bishop Peter II (494–520) patronized a baptistery attached to the Petriana basilica in Classis; a small chapel of S. Andreas decorated with Proconnesian marbles that 'shined with bright light'.[18] He also began the construction of a chapel called Tricollis, 'constructed with great ingenuity' inside the episcopal palace, which was continued by his successors Aurelianus (521) and Ecclesius (522–32). With the help of Julianus, a banker, Ecclesius also dedicated a church to the Virgin Mary on his own property, and in the vault of the apse put up a huge golden mosaic image of the Mother of God and Child with the Angel Gabriel, as recorded in the metrical verse below the image.[19] Theoderic also employed the Catholic bishops of his kingdom in diplomatic missions, where he thought their allegiance might assist in a positive outcome. As we have seen, Epiphanius of Pavia was sent to Burgundy to obtain the release of prisoners, and his successor Ennodius served on several embassies for the king. In 525 Ecclesius of Ravenna accompanied Pope John on an embassy to Constantinople to prevent the closure of Arian churches there, and on his return planned the even more ambitious structure of San Vitale, which would eventually compete with Theoderic's mighty Golden Basilica.

Theoderic and the Jews

Because Theoderic appreciated the need to accept theological disagreements while trying to promote a social unity that could overcome them, he extended a surprising degree of toleration to Jewish communities. In contrast to the frequently punitive measures taken against them both in eastern and western parts of the empire, he allowed them to follow their religious practices. Between 507 and 511 when Cassiodorus, in the king's name, wrote to the Jews of Genoa, 'We cannot command

1 and 2. (*Left*) Gold *solidus* of Theodosius I (379–95), *Dominus Noster, Pius Felix Augustus* (Our lord, dutiful, fortunate emperor), minted in Constantinople between 379 and 383. (*Right*) Gold *solidus* of Honorius (395–423), with the same inscription as 1, *DN PF AVG*, minted in Constantinople, 408–20.

3 and 4. (*Left*) Gold *solidus* of Galla Placidia (424–37), also identified as *Domina Nostra, Pia Felix Augusta*, minted at Ravenna, 426–30. (*Right*) Gold *solidus* of Constantius III, *DN PF AVG*, briefly emperor (421), minted at Ravenna.

5. Gold *solidus* of Theodosius II struck in Constantinople in 437 to mark the marriage of his daughter Licinia Eudoxia to Valentinian III, shown on the reverse, with the emperor joining their hands and the words *Feliciter Nubtiis* (To the happily married).

6, 7 and 8. The 'Mausoleum' of Galla Placidia, Ravenna (425–50), the chapel attached to the church of S. Croce (Holy Cross) she founded. (*Below*) An interior mosaic of St Lawrence (or possibly Christ), carrying a long cross and an open book, with the burning grid and cupboard of Gospel books. (*Right*) The dome of the 'Mausoleum'. The starry sky and supporting structures are completely covered with symbolic and colourful bands of mosaic, including doves drinking at a water basin.

9 and 10. The central domes of the two baptisteries at Ravenna: (*above*) the Orthodox, commissioned by Bishop Neon (*c.* 450–73), with a mature, bearded Christ; (*opposite*) The Arian baptistery, built by Theoderic (493–526), with a distinctly younger, more human Christ.

11. Theoderic's towering palace church of S. Apollinare Nuovo. An interior view of the south wall, with scenes from the Passion, male figures and the procession of male saints in three tiers of mosaic (493–526).

12. The Palace mosaic (PALATIUM) with the walled city of Ravenna behind it, at the west end of S. Apollinare Nuovo. Originally, Theoderic was shown enthroned under the central arch. This image of the heretical Arian king with his courtiers on either side was removed by Archbishop Agnellus in the 560s, leaving only some hands still visible, and replaced by curtains.

13. The walled city of Classis, CIVITAS CLASSIS (opposite the Palace mosaic), where Theoderic and his officials were portrayed standing in front of the fortifications. When Archbishop Agnellus converted the church to Catholic use, they were also excised and replaced by golden bricks.

14. A mosaic of Christ healing the paralytic, whose bed was let down through the roof on the north wall of S. Apollinare Nuovo, as recounted in Mark 2.4 and Luke 5.19.

15. On the south wall, a mosaic of the Last Supper, with Christ (now bearded) and the twelve disciples reclining on dining couches, around a semi-circular table with loaves and fishes, as described in Matthew 26, Mark 14, Luke 22 and John 13.

your faith, for no one can be forced to believe against his will', he was laying down a very significant principle.[20] By permitting such behaviour, which distinguished his rule from many fifth- and sixth-century examples of intolerance, Theoderic established a precedent that was to be much cited by later reformers. He would not permit the Jews to add a larger extension to their synagogue, but he allowed them to rebuild the roof.[21]

Their presence in Ravenna is confirmed by the find of part of an amphora, now in the Archaeological Museum, with a Hebrew inscription on the neck, which reads *Shalom* (peace), and by the later conversion of at least one synagogue.[22] Despite Theoderic's ruling, there were regular attacks on Jewish communities in Ravenna and in Rome. In 519–20 when Theoderic was visiting Verona and Eutharic had been left in charge in the Gothic capital, the synagogues were burned by local people. Eutharic supported the Jews' appeal to the king, who ordered Bishop Peter and the leader of the Ravenna city council to arrange their rebuilding, using local labour.[23] The contrast with similar attacks on Jewish property in the eastern empire is striking. When monks in Kallinikos, an important commercial centre in the East, destroyed the local synagogue, the emperor in Constantinople took the side of the local bishop, who refused any assistance in financing its rebuilding.[24] And the Jews of Genoa acknowledged Theoderic's rule as binding different communities together in one society, while in Naples the Jewish community remained loyal to the Gothic cause when faced by imperial troops in the 530s.

Although 'crowds' of refugees from Theoderic's kingdom arrived in Constantinople, according to Priscian, and an eye-witness, Dominic or Domnicus, fled to the eastern capital from the 'tyrant', the king appears to have been generally appreciated by the local Italo-Romans.[25] Part of this approval must be due to his insistence on justice, and efficient government, but diplomacy also played a part. Using trusted ambassadors such as Senarius, who undertook twenty-five embassies for Theoderic to Constantinople, Spain, Gaul and Africa, Theoderic kept in touch with the entire Mediterranean world. Following imperial traditions developed in Constantinople the king absorbed the benefits of negotiating peace rather than risking war; he organized his international relations with care and reinforced them with suitably impressive gifts. Deploying Cassiodorus' mastery of different genres of letter writing, he flattered his correspondents and praised their co-operation, as in a letter thanking the king of the Warni for his swords, so sharp they could be 'the work of Vulcan . . . May Providence grant concord, that, as we carry on this pleasant intercourse, we may unite the hearts of our peoples, and, as we show concern for one another, we may be linked by mutual obligations.'[26] This high-flown style of diplomacy reflected his youthful training in the eastern capital, where the reception and treatment of foreign envoys had been one of the most impressive ceremonies of the court, and diplomatic skills were transmitted across the generations by a professional body of ambassadors.

12

Theoderic the lawgiver

Seventy years after Galla Placidia's assumption of the regency, and over forty years after Valentinian III's disastrous decision to leave Ravenna, Theoderic took control of the city that continued to embody its imperial inheritance. To consolidate the process of fusing the Roman and non-Roman populations begun by Odoacer, the Ostrogothic king drew up a new law code. This is the Edict, a short legal text probably issued in Rome in 500.

After the two sacks of Rome by Goths and Vandals (in 410 and 455), ravages caused by Ricimer's troops in 472, and the loss of the African wheat supply after 439, the ancient city's population and extent had been considerably reduced. By the end of the fifth century it was down to about 500,000, which was still larger than the populations of other Italian cities, but constantly declining.[1] When Theoderic and the Goths arrived Ravenna possibly had 10,000 inhabitants and this number expanded rapidly as the king set up his new government. The city attracted local 'Italo-Romans' as well as non-Roman peoples, who sought work in the centre dominated by this figure with the elevated title of *patricius*, who brought personal knowledge of the eastern court to Ravenna. In contrast, the underlying population trend in Rome was downwards, out of the city, as some of the oldest aristocratic families left to join the new Senate in Constantinople and ascetic, celibate patterns of life disrupted the ancient emphasis on family continuity. Despite the loss of their estates in provinces of the western Roman empire, especially North Africa, senators were still the wealthiest individuals, but Christian dominance contributed to a reduction in their resources as Roman bishops, who were regularly drawn from aristocratic circles, donated much of their wealth to the church.

'Rome' still implied much more than just the city, despite the fact that for over two centuries the working capital had been moved first to Milan and then Ravenna. It was a term as well as a place. Rome remained the site of a great imperial legacy, especially from the pre-Christian era, and emperors continued to celebrate triumphs in their ceremonial visits to Rome. What remained of the Senate of Rome continued to meet in its Curia in the Forum and maintained the calendar of associated festivities, such as the anniversary of the city's foundation. Apart from the appointment of an urban prefect to run the city, the senators' formal role was to propose the names of the consuls nominated by the king and confirmed in Constantinople, which were still used as a system of dating. At the same time, bishops of the city began to elaborate a novel ecclesiastical attribute to the term 'Roman'. As the heirs of St Peter, these leaders of the church of Rome claimed a superior status and authority over all western bishops, which they exercised by settling appeals, resolving quarrels and holding councils that issued legally binding resolutions in the form of decretals or ecclesiastical canons. Their definitions of theological doctrine were applied with the force of law against opponents, who were branded as schismatics and heretics. In this way, 'correct' Catholic belief became identified as Roman.[2]

Theoderic and Rome

In his relations with the ancient capital Theoderic had to attend to these two different constituencies: Senate and church. He was aware of the power of the leading families and set out to win their support, urging senators to continue their traditional funding of popular entertainment (chariot races, theatrical performances and wild beast displays, if not actual fights), which bankrupted at least one of them – Asterius in 494:

> I provided banners in the circus and erected a temporary stage on the spina [the middle of the hippodrome] so that Rome might rejoice and hold games, races and different sorts of wild beast shows . . . Thus do the games preserve the expenditure of my riches and the single day that saw three spectacles will last, and hand on Asterius to a lively future, Asterius who spent the wealth he had won on his consulship.[3]

In connection with the traditional chariot races, however, church leaders like St John Chrysostomos and St Augustine had expressed their strong disapproval, linking circus entertainments with the frenzied enthusiasm and immoral behaviour generated by such crowds of men and women.[4] Theoderic was perfectly aware of this attitude and was careful in his correspondence with Roman church leaders. He also recognized the high educational standards maintained in Rome and encouraged senators to support this tradition too. For their part, the senators of Rome needed Theoderic's protection as he re-established control over the disintegrating imperial structure in the West. Without him they could not defend or maintain the extended circuit of the city's walls, aqueducts and mills.

Although the early-sixth-century sections of the Roman *Book of the Pontiffs* were written in about 535, after Theoderic's death, they make no reference to his Arian beliefs until the last year of his reign (525–6).[5] In the *Lives* of the seven bishops of Rome between 492 and 530 events are dated in a neutral fashion: 'in the time of King Theoderic and the Emperor Zeno [or Anastasios]'. Theoderic does not appear to have been seen primarily as a heretic and was not denounced by these bishops. Yet the identification of the Goths as a separate people, with a version of Christian scripture written in their own language, meant that Theoderic was an Arian leader. He did not wish to abandon such a fundamental identification of his people, but his ambition to create a Gothic kingdom within the empire involved a subordination of religious differences to the larger sphere of Roman civilization. While remaining loyal to Arian definitions of the faith, Theoderic was able to use his position outside the Catholic community to exercise an unexpected authority in theological issues, and as the supreme secular power in the region he was invited to act as arbiter in disputed ecclesiastical elections.

Theoderic's reputation for fairness was confirmed in 498 when he received an appeal to arbitrate in a papal quarrel. It arose when two candidates were elected to the bishopric of Rome on the same day, causing a deep division among both the clergy and the Senate. The rival parties sought to resolve the dispute by going to Ravenna for the king's judgment. The decision to appeal to a ruler known to be an Arian Christian must reflect confidence in his capacity to adjudicate equitably in what was a purely Catholic matter. And Theoderic seems to have provided a solution: 'he made the fair decision', according to the papal record, namely that the first candidate elected and by the largest party should become bishop.[6] This was Symmachus, a deacon of the Roman church, whose opponent, Laurentius, was persuaded to accept the see of Nuceria (Nocera).[7] Symmachus then called a synod to draw up rules for papal elections – an instance of the inventiveness of this period of early Christendom.

Theoderic's Visit to Rome

As a result of this successful intervention, Theoderic made an official visit to Rome in 500, his only lengthy stay in the ancient capital. The Anonymous Valesianus identifies this as a celebration of his *tricennalia*, the thirtieth anniversary of his assumption of regal power (and possibly an imitation of Constantine the Great's *tricennalia* of 335). It could also have been taken as marking the tenth anniversary of his rule in Italy, *decennalia*, a suitable moment to make an extravagant display of imperial-style largesse – chariot races and games in the Circus Maximus, and distributions of food and wine. Before his official entry to the city, Theoderic went to venerate St Peter 'as if he were a Catholic', probably at the basilica which lay outside the north-western walls of the city.[8] Then there was an official ceremony of welcome involving Symmachus, so recently confirmed as bishop, the entire Senate and the populus, who escorted him into Rome. There he visited the Senate and addressed the people at the Palm, a point in the Forum between the Senate house and the arch of Septimius Severus. 'He entered the Palace in a triumphal procession for the entertainment of the people and exhibited games in the Circus for the Romans.'[9] All this was typical of an *adventus*, an imperial visit to the ancient heart of empire, such as Constantius II made in 357. Very few emperors had been seen in Rome since that year.

Theoderic's familiarity with imperial tradition was immediately displayed in his actions. From the emperors' former residence on the Palatine Theoderic announced that he would make an annual distribution of grain for the people (a function normally performed by the Senate) and committed tax funds for a much-needed restoration of the city walls and for the repair of public buildings, including some parts of the vast palace.[10] Like all emperors, he distributed honours to the senators and promoted officials to new posts. He also concluded an important alliance with the Vandal kingdom of North Africa by betrothing his sister Amalafrida to King Thrasamund. Amalafrida's departure for Carthage must have occasioned another grandiose celebration; she was escorted by a ceremonial guard of a thousand noble Goths and a troop of five hundred warriors. In addition, Theoderic gave her the north-west promontory of Sicily, Lilybaeum, as her dowry, so she became a queen in her own right, with her own financial resources.

Theoderic's Law Code

Theoderic never presumed to issue laws, as only an emperor could do that, but he wrote many edicts and regulations which drew heavily on Roman precedent and, from the very first years of his rule, he adopted a Roman style of legal administration that took account of Gothic traditions. When he received appeals, such as one from a Roman widow dispossessed by a high official, his harsh punishment of the man responsible and his insistence that the law be observed set the tenor of his administration: corruption of any kind would not be tolerated; and the purchase of office, abuse of privilege or misuse of public funds were all outlawed. This attitude is clear in a letter Cassiodorus wrote in the king's name in about 510 to two officials (one Roman, one Gothic) who had been appointed to resolve disputes about the barbarian occupation of Roman estates by force: 'You who have taken up the work of proclaiming law to the people should observe and cultivate justice. For a man who is supposed to restrain others under the rule of law must do no wrong . . .'[11] The ideals later recorded by Cassiodorus were clearly deeply held, whether his administration always lived up to them or not. As we will see from his law code, the king demonstrated a strenuous effort to make the administration of justice available and effective.

Theoderic also knew that it was traditional for emperors to pronounce their legal regulations at Rome and to inscribe them on stone. So, during the six months that Theoderic spent there in 500, celebrating his role as *princeps*, ruler over the Goths and Romans, he promulgated a short legal code, the *Edictum Theoderici*. This very important text unites the two traditions – Gothic and Roman – in a joint legal administration that had been prepared in Ravenna, was taken to Rome for its formal promulgation, and then inscribed on stone to be displayed in public places.[12] It was designed to ensure peace and order within the new state that Theoderic ruled by establishing one law for all – a *ius commune* for both Goths and Romans.

> We, taking into consideration the [desired] peace of the state and having before Our eyes the irregularities that can often occur . . . command that the present edicts be posted for ending matters of this sort, so that both barbarians and Romans (*barbari et romani*), while maintaining the respect due to the public laws and dutifully preserving in their entirety the rights of everyone, may clearly know what they are obligated to follow concerning the items specified in the present edicts.[13]

If judges were unable to enforce the regulations that followed, drawn from recent laws and previous Roman codes, they were to report immediately to the king. In this way Theoderic aimed to prevent the influence over, and corruption of, judges by powerful landowners (both Roman and Gothic) and perhaps military leaders.

The first ten regulations are devoted to the activity of judges, who at that time were drawn from all those in authority and often had no legal expertise. They were not a professional class.[14] To improve this situation Theoderic appointed Gothic counts to preside in courts when Goths brought legal disputes, and Roman judges to oversee cases brought by the local Italo-Romans, and ordered the correct implementation of the law according to Roman precedent. In problematic circumstances that brought representatives of the two communities into conflict across ethnic boundaries, the two authorities were to work together to resolve them. He insisted that circuit judges were to be a benefit not a burden to provincials, and they were not to claim more than three days' maintenance when they visited.[15] In his own resolution of disputes, Theoderic emphasized the ideals of common justice and appropriate treatment that the Edict intended to inculcate. Concerning a man who had struck and hurt his brother very badly, Theoderic recommended that for such fratricidal hatred the perpetrator should be exiled from the province, as one undeserving of the company of fellow citizens.[16]

Like all the 'barbarian' law codes, the *Edictum* draws particularly on the *Codex Theodosianus*, a key source, and addresses a wide range of conflicts that often arose over the treatment of slaves, the arrangement and dissolution of marriages, the enforcement of wills, the punishment of cattle rustlers, thieves, illegal occupation of property and the use of torture and oaths. In 154 short regulations it underlines the importance of officials behaving appropriately, whether they are in charge of public weights and measures or tax receipts. The text of Theoderic's *Edictum* employs a clear, unembroidered language normally used by jurists, lawyers and legal experts such as the *quaestores*, who must have been responsible for the selection and adaptation of Roman precedent to suit the new code.[17] The Edict preserved the privileges of Jews, whose disputes should be resolved by 'teachers of their own observance' (title 143), and set out penalties for those who buried corpses within the city of Rome (title 111) – both of these titles repetitions of Roman law – or those who committed fraud through forgery, including clipping gold coins (title 90). 'If a condemned curial should leave behind children, they shall take possession of everything which he forfeits; if he has no children, his assets shall be conferred on the municipal council', with the exception of cases of high treason when the children get nothing (title 113). Regarding the protection of women from rape, titles 17–22 repeat the *Codex Theodosianus*, including the provision that if a slave discovers that a complaint of abduction (*raptus*) has been concealed through the connivance of his owners and he reports this to the court, he shall be freed. Title 23 is an innovation concerning those who die intestate: the closest in degree and title among the agnates and cognates of the deceased inherit, though the rights of the children and grandchildren must be preserved. Such concerns are paralleled in other legal collections, even the short *Ecloga* (Selections) issued by Leo III and his son Constantine V in 741 in the eastern half of the empire.[18]

In assuming this imperial role, Theoderic used the historic standing and religious authority of Rome to augment the impact and legitimacy of his legal code. He then left the city for Ravenna, never to return, imposing its regulations from his own capital for another quarter of a century. His solution to the disputed papal election of 498 did not last long. In 502 two senators, Festus and Probinus, accused Pope Symmachus of numerous crimes, recalled his rival Laurentius and asked Theoderic to appoint a neutral figure with authority, a visitor, to the church of Rome to investigate. There were clear precedents for this procedure; Emperor Honorius had used the same method to resolve a quarrel in 419.[19] But Pope Symmachus refused to recognize the visitor (Bishop Peter of Altinum) and the dispute provoked so much violence on the streets of Rome that Theoderic had to send three Gothic *saiones*, Gudila, Bedeulphus and Arigern, to impose order. The king insisted that the bishops should themselves decide who should be their leader, and Symmachus was finally confirmed in his position by a synod held in 502 (with the help of the two consuls). It was signed by 103 bishops, led by Laurentius of Milan and Peter of Ravenna.[20]

The Acacian Schism

Long before Theoderic arrived in Italy a breach had developed between the sees of Constantinople and Rome, which complicated his relations with them both. It was related to the persistent problem of Christ's human and divine qualities, debated at the Council of Chalcedon in 451, which Emperor Zeno had attempted to resolve in a compromise drawn up by Patriarch Akakios in the *Henotikon* (Edict of Union) in 482. But this edict was condemned as too close to the miaphysite belief in the union of the human and divine in one nature, and two years later Pope Felix III, with the support of a synod at Rome, condemned it as a betrayal of the Chalcedonian duophysite definition of two distinct natures that shared the same essence. As a result, Roman popes refused to name the Constantinopolitan patriarchs in their daily prayers or to take communion together, and the easterners responded in kind. Peter, Catholic bishop of Ravenna, was one of the most prominent church leaders who supported Pope Felix and maintained the schism with the East, which continued long after the death of Akakios in 489.[21]

When Hormisdas was elected to the see of Rome in 514, he renewed efforts to end the schism with Constantinople, and took Theoderic's advice on three separate occasions. The first time, the king recommended Bishop Ennodius of Pavia as a negotiator, and Ennodius then led two missions to Constantinople. Both were rebuffed. It was only after the death of Emperor Anastasios and the accession of Justin I in 518 that the new emperor could revoke the *Henotikon* (on 28 March 519). The Roman *Book of the Pontiffs* records that Pope Hormisdas again took King Theoderic's advice about the delegation that would travel to Constantinople to celebrate this event. Later, he went to Ravenna to consult the king about reinstating those bishops who had resisted the schism, realizing that restoring them would mean removing others who had approved of it. With Theoderic's agreement Hormisdas then drew up a document ordering the withdrawal of the *Henotikon* and the pardon and reinstatement of all its opponents, which he sent with his warrant, seal and signature to Emperor Justin.[22] This re-established the unity of the Catholic church and endorsed the authority of the Council of Chalcedon. While the Arian Gothic ruler had not been a party to the dispute, his stature as a political leader again allowed him to rise above doctrinal divisions: his Catholic Christian subjects consulted him and followed his advice.

Theoderic's visit to Rome in 500 had confirmed his respectful appreciation of the Catholic Church and Senate, to which many responded by supporting the Gothic government in its diplomatic initiatives. But it seems that officials attached to the court in Ravenna, such as Cassiodorus, developed a distinct attitude at variance with some of the older senatorial aristocracies based in Rome. Theoderic's tendency to turn away from those families with the closest connections to Rome became apparent in the 510s, as he began to appoint new men (*novi homines*) to his court, often senators from Liguria and northern Italy.[23] This split between the older and less prominent Roman aristocrats may have contributed to the accusations that led to the arrest and death of Boethius and his father-in-law, Symmachus, a very distinguished Roman senator, although the real and immediate provocation was the threat to Arian worship in Constantinople.

Arian worship in Constantinople

In 522–3 the eastern Emperor Justin began to curtail the celebrations of Arian Christians in Constantinople, a symptom of the much greater intolerance that would later result in outright persecution of minorities. The closure or takeover of Arian churches in the East obviously attacked Theoderic's Arian co-religionists and damaged his generally cordial political relations with the imperial court. The Roman *Book of the Pontiffs* gives a clear account of this development:

> the orthodox emperor Justin . . . wanted to drive heretics out: in the deep
> fervour of his Christianity he adopted a plan to consecrate the churches

of the Arians as catholic ones. That was why when the heretic king
Theoderic heard of it, he was incensed and wanted to put the whole of
Italy to the sword.[24]

From Theoderic's point of view, Justin and his young nephew, Justinian, who was already preparing to assume greater imperial control,
were breaking the arrangement with emperors Zeno and Anastasios by
which the king had assumed Gothic leadership of the Roman empire in
the West and which involved a respect for the differences between
Catholic and Arian Christians. The king's sharp reaction was therefore
immediate and was doubtless exacerbated by rumours that certain
Roman senators were plotting with forces in Constantinople to replace
his government by direct rule from the eastern capital. Rome's support
for measures against heretical Arian practice was being exploited by
opponents of Gothic rule for political reasons. Theoderic therefore sent
an embassy to investigate, forcing Pope John, Bishop Ecclesius of
Ravenna and several senators to participate.

At the king's court Cyprian, a *referendarius* (judicial official), publicly
accused Albinus, the senator and Theoderic's consul and ambassador, of
communicating with allies in the eastern capital in a treacherous plot to
impose a ruler in the West nominated in Constantinople. When Boethius
heard this, he immediately protested. 'Cyprian's charge is false, but if
Albinus did it, both I and the entire senate have done it acting together.
The business is false, lord king.'[25] This declaration that Boethius and all
the Roman Senate would stand by Albinus did not reassure Theoderic,
who pressed Cyprian to provide proof of his claim. Forged letters were
then concocted that implied Albinus and his allies were intending to
restore Roman freedom (*libertas Romana*), that is, to overthrow the
Gothic kingdom. Any suggestion that Constantinople might re-impose
direct rule in Ravenna was, naturally, anathema to Theoderic, who
arrested Albinus and Boethius. The tensions were heightened by the failure of the embassy he had sent to the East, which did not secure freedom
of worship for the Arian Christians in Constantinople. On its return
Theoderic imprisoned the Roman participants and Pope John died in
prison in Ravenna.[26] Since Boethius had dedicated some parts of his
Opuscula Sacra to John, a Roman deacon before his election as pope,
this may have added to Theoderic's hostility to the scholar whom he had
so warmly patronized.[27]

The Consolation of Philosophy

While Boethius was awaiting trial, he composed his famous text, *The Consolation of Philosophy*, which was to have an extraordinary influence in later centuries. He describes the inspiration of philosophy, personified as a lady who encouraged his analysis of what makes a good life. Plato had advised that good men should rule in order to prevent the wicked from having authority, and Boethius cites this as his reason for accepting a governmental position at Theoderic's court. He stresses his love of justice, which prompted him to defend those who were already suffering hardship from higher taxation, and justifies his own role in the defence of Albinus. He details the love of philosophy already expressed in his intention to translate all the works of Plato and Aristotle into Latin. Although Theoderic seems to have appreciated the amazing range of Boethius' scholarship, which made available in Latin so many critical texts of Greek science, mathematics, philosophy and music, he considered treasonable activity (even if unproven) too dangerous not to be punished. The king ordered that the philosopher should be tried in absentia and summoned the urban prefect of Rome to Pavia to adjudicate. Boethius was condemned to death without any appeal, even though all senators, if accused of serious crimes, had the right to be tried by their peers. In addition, the witnesses brought to support Cyprian's charge were not investigated and may well have been bribed.

Shortly after Boethius' arrest, his father-in-law Symmachus, a distinguished elderly senator who had spoken out in his defence, was also charged with treason and later killed. This additional insult to the Symmachii suggests that Theoderic was convinced by Cyprian of a plot launched by high-ranking Romans to undermine his own authority. Knowing that Emperor Justin was ready to close Arian churches in Constantinople, or to re-dedicate them to Catholic use, Theoderic reacted in such a way as to impose comparable punishment on adherents of 'the other religion' under his control. It was a Gothic interpretation of a Roman and Catholic threat, carried out with a ruthlessness typical of imperial rule that Theoderic had observed as a teenager.

In a forceful reaction to the murder, Boethius' widow, Rusticiana, ordered the destruction of statues of Theoderic in Rome, which nearly provoked her own death later.[28] Among courtiers in Ravenna there was little if any critical response. Since Cassiodorus apparently did nothing to defend Boethius and Symmachus and fails to report the arbitrary nature of the murders, he has been associated with Theoderic in the same guilt. Loyalty to the king overrode any qualms Cassiodorus may have felt as he succeeded to Boethius' job as *magister officiorum* and maintained it beyond Theoderic's death for a further fourteen years. Whether his attitude was shared by all Theoderic's officials or not, it seems that no one defended Boethius and Symmachus when they were threatened with death. Later, many commentators insisted on the unjust and unjustified deaths, emphasizing the trope of the 'barbarian' ruler, uncivilized and violent.[29]

Theoderic's responsibility for the death of Boethius has preoccupied many modern historians seeking to elucidate the balance between 'barbarian' (Gothic) and 'civilized' (Roman) features of Theoderic's rule, and of the whole history of the western half of the Roman empire as it was occupied by non-Roman forces. One recent interpretation presents the scenario as an unusual type of rebellion: Boethius wished to replace Theoderic as ruler, to reassert the Platonic ideal of a philosopher-king. Another, more convincingly, argues that the death of the king's son-in-law Eutharic had created a succession crisis that Theoderic was unable to resolve.[30] Above all, as we have seen, the persecution of Arian Christians in Constantinople threatened Theoderic and provoked the process that led to Boethius' death. Nonetheless, the arrest and murder of Boethius and Symmachus makes an unavoidable contrast with Theoderic's emphasis on law. Had the king's treatment of the two senators conformed to Roman precedent, his reputation as a lawgiver might have been salvaged. Instead, it coloured his entire reign and continues to obscure appreciation of his *Edictum*, which set up a legal framework for the peaceful cohabitation of Italo-Roman and Gothic populations in sixth-century Italy.

13

Amalasuintha and the legacy
of Theoderic

In 526 when Theoderic died, at the great age of about seventy, he had
ruled in Ravenna for thirty-three years. Such longevity was unusual, as
was the very particular tomb he had prepared before his death. While
Ravenna, like most Roman cities, is built of local brick (even today it
remains the normal building material), the king ordered a special shipment of white Istrian marble for his mausoleum. Theoderic's spectacular
two-storey resting place is the only major monument in Ravenna constructed entirely of marble, visible on both the exterior and the interior,
with a dome formed of an enormous monolith. Under this incredibly
heavy roof, which rested on vast substructures and required considerable skill to erect, the king was laid to rest, probably in the large
porphyry bath now on the upper level of the mausoleum.[1] Although no
text recounts the funeral rite, it must have included a very solemn procession from the palace to the mausoleum, led by his young grandson
Athalaric, his daughter Amalasuintha accompanied by the priests of
the Arian cathedral and Gothic military leaders, followed by the entire
court and city.

In commissioning this particular style of tomb, Theoderic followed
the fourth-century Roman precedent of imperial tombs, which were
circular domed buildings. He had seen the examples of Constantia's
tomb in Rome, Diocletian's in the imperial palace at Split, as well as
those of the eastern emperors in the church of the Holy Apostles in
Constantinople. Theoderic magnified this entirely Roman model with
a second storey and added a specifically Christian element – the names
of the Apostles were carved on spurs of the exterior blocks – and a
Gothic feature in the sculpted external decoration that runs around the
base of the dome with an echo of Germanic metal- or woodwork.[2] In
arranging this striking combination in the construction of his tomb just

beyond the city walls in the Gothic cemetery area, Theoderic made sure that it would remain a perpetual memory for later generations. Although it was adapted for different use, over the centuries the marble structure has resisted decay and still impresses the visitor today.

Theoderic's standing had been commemorated in a speech written by Ennodius, the deacon from Pavia, who had accompanied his bishop Epiphanius on a diplomatic mission to the Burgundians in 494. Ennodius knew that Theoderic had been educated in Constantinople and would have witnessed the rhetorical tradition of panegyrics (speeches of praise) given at the imperial court. He therefore had to produce his very best prose and characterized Theoderic as a most just ruler, whose outstanding *civilitas* preserved the peace and co-operation between Goths and Romans. He described Theoderic as the *princeps* 'who rules Italy, cherishes Rome and honours the western senate', and thus governed (*imperare*) in the manner of a Roman emperor.[3] Similarly, the Anonymous Valesianus would later hail Theoderic as *optimus princeps*, the best prince, 'a new Trajan'.[4] Praising him as a Christian from birth and an ideal Christian ruler, Ennodius avoided any mention of his loyalty to Arian definitions, and compared him favourably with Alexander the Great, who is dismissed as not even a virtuous pagan. On another occasion Ennodius reported that Theoderic kept the Christian faith safe, even though he followed another.[5] After comparing him to the Old Testament King David as an ideal Christian ruler, Ennodius asked: 'Is it in your justice, or your skill in battle, or what is more excellent than both of these, your piety that I should mention that have surpassed all prior emperors?'[6] With such superlatives Ennodius characterized the ruler whose presence in Ravenna remains, even when churches that he founded are redecorated, converted to Catholic use or demolished.

After the burial of Theoderic in his mausoleum, his daughter Amalasuintha took charge of the Gothic state in the name of her young son Athalaric, then aged ten (Plate 20).[7] She faced a problem because Theoderic's agreement with Emperor Zeno had not envisaged its continuity into the next generation and both the principals were now dead. In spite of the underlying tensions between Ravenna and Constantinople, the queen mother tried immediately to renew warm relations with Emperor Justin. In the name of the young king, Cassiodorus wrote, 'Let hatreds be shut up with men entombed', and recalled the alliances that dated back generations:

You exalted my grandfather in your city to the Consul's ivory chair; in Italy you distinguished my father Eutharic with the Consul's robe of office . . . he was adopted as your son by arms, although he was almost your equal in age . . . The name of son which you bestowed on my elders, you will grant more fittingly to a lad. Your love should now take up a father's role . . . I have assumed a royal inheritance: let me find a place in your thoughts also.[8]

He thus presented Athalaric to the imperial court in the East as the legitimate heir to the Gothic kingdom of Italy, over which he would rule with his mother's guidance. Cassiodorus noted that the ambassadors who carried this official letter to Constantinople would also transmit oral messages, a clear indication of the traditional way of conducting diplomacy and a sign that additional arguments would be made to secure the Gothic inheritance.

In another letter composed for Athalaric, Cassiodorus wrote to the Senate at Rome praising their acceptance of Pope Felix IV (526–30), who had been elevated to the bishopric as a result of Theoderic's intervention in a dispute. In making this claim that a king 'of alien faith' had resolved the rivalry between two candidates, Cassiodorus draws attention to the 'judgement of a good prince' and reminds the Senate of Theoderic's desire 'that religion in all churches should flourish with good priests'. He thus linked the new Gothic king's personal dedication to the Arian Christian faith with his authority over Rome, a combination that the young prince intended to continue, since Athalaric assured the Senate of his pleasure in 'conversing with the chief men of my realm'.[9]

One year later Cassiodorus was writing to the governor of Lucania, Severus, about the city councillors (*curiales*) of southern Italy who had abandoned their cities in order to live in the countryside of Bruttium. This instance of neglect had to be corrected immediately. Here Cassiodorus extrapolates on the delights of urban living: 'visiting the forum, looking on at honest crafts, legislation, entertainments such as playing at draughts, going to the baths or exchanging splendid dinner parties.' In particular, he stresses the importance of the city for the education of children, who are otherwise condemned to an ignorant life in the wilderness surrounded by slaves. Behind this instruction we can sense the same pressures of heavy curial responsibilities addressed by earlier emperors and the importance of local elites in sustaining city life. Severus was also ordered to ensure that the annual fair of St Cyprian was safely celebrated at Marcellianum in Lucania, because it provided a market for sea-borne trade, foreign goods and regional exports and an outlet for products from Campania, Bruttium, Calabria and Apulia.[10]

The History of the Goths

Before his death Theoderic had given Cassiodorus a most important task: to write the official history of the Goths, recording for posterity the origin of his people and their history prior to their arrival in the Roman world. His most experienced and skilled speech writer was therefore obliged to research how the tribal group had developed its own self-awareness, its historic activities and its migration into Italy – a long saga from mythic origins, through many battles, up to their domination of the Roman West. In composing this history Cassiodorus found valuable evidence in the works of the Gothic geographers, who had noted many place names and routes followed by the tribes. He appears to have written it between 526 and 530, under the patronage of Theoderic's daughter Amalasuintha, and naturally highlighted the importance of the Ostrogoths among all the other Germanic and Gothic tribes. The *Origo Gothica* provided a genealogy, which extended from Theoderic's father Valamir down to his grandson Athalaric, in twelve books that preserved much unusual, first-hand evidence about the Gothic migrations. The text does not survive, but it served as the basis for Jordanes, when he wrote his *Getica* (*De origine actibusque Getarum*, The Origin and Deeds of the Getae/Goths) in Constantinople in about 551.[11] At the time Cassiodorus was in the eastern capital, having accompanied King Witigis and his family into exile in 540, taking the text with him.

His *Origo Gothica* is typical of the process of ethnogenesis, an account of how tribal peoples construct their identity and history, which is often provoked by their coming into contact with others who already have a sense of their own history. Among the Franks, for instance, the story of origins is traced back to Troy and Aeneas is claimed as their father-founder. Isidore of Seville, a Visigoth in Spain, similarly compiled biographies of famous men that included his own

Gothic heroes. The Visigoths in Toulouse and the Burgundians in Savoy also aspired to synthesize their Germanic traditions with Roman customs to gain a quasi-imperial status.[12] But they did not have the lasting impact created by Cassiodorus' work, which presented Theoderic's collaboration, co-operation and relative tolerance as exceptional achievements, informed by his youthful exposure to the eastern court in Constantinople. In Jordanes' *Getica* these features were naturally employed to accord a superior status to the Ostrogothic court at Ravenna.

The Regency of Amalasuintha

Cassiodorus frequently alludes to his own role in sustaining the Gothic kingdom in the first years of Athalaric's reign, claiming to have been a great support to the queen mother as she formed a link between her father's rule and the uncertain succession of her son. In 533, when Athalaric, now aged seventeen, was old enough to take over the government, Cassiodorus composed a eulogy to Amalasuintha, who had 'achieved the glory of either sex', as 'one who surpasses all the praise given to men'. In the queen, he continues, 'her ancestors' – he proceeds to list them – 'would see their glory reflected as in a clear mirror' and would recognize the superiority of her throng of virtues. He praises her government, identifying Theoderic and his daughter as famous leaders of the Gothic kingdom at its zenith, and makes a long, disparaging comparison with Galla Placidia.[13] Procopius also noted that Amalasuintha directed the government wisely, 'displaying to a great extent the masculine temper', keeping the peace between Goths and Romans.[14] Although royal women, widows and daughters of kings, often had the best claim to rule, contemporaries perceived their gender as a weakness that nearly always affected their innate capacity. And Amalasuintha's position was subtly different from her fifth-century imperial counterpart, Empress Galla Placidia, in that she ruled over a kingdom under the authority of the eastern emperor, who remained the supreme overlord.

When Amalasuintha prepared her son for his task as ruler of the Ostrogoths using the same classical upbringing that had given her such authority, some sections of the Gothic nobility objected. In particular they criticized the Roman style of education, and made military training their priority, insisting that Athalaric master more warlike skills appropriate for a Gothic king who would lead them in battle. Amalas-uintha had to dismiss the tutors she'd put in charge of her son's education and permit others to instruct him in a military, Gothic style. Yet she persisted in stressing the importance of education in the classical style to the Senate in Rome, insisting that the professors of grammar, rhetoric and law had to be paid their full salaries. Grammar, in particular, is singled out as 'the mistress of words, the embellisher of the human race ... barbarian kings do not use her ... she remains unique to lawful rulers.'[15]

The Goths' hostility to her training in classical literature may also have extended to the queen's relationship with the imperial court, where Justinian ruled from 527. In the last years of Theoderic, Constantinople's moves to curb Arian worship had provoked the murder of Boethius and polarized the difference between Goth and Roman. Amalasuintha's warmer contacts with the emperor were interpreted as dangerous to the Gothic state, and she found it much harder than her father to unite the two factions within her kingdom. In addition, she could not emulate her father's commanding presence, due to his military skill, and the absence of a male leader became more pronounced as Athalaric displayed little interest in this role.

The eight years of her regency, 526–34, are characterized by a clear emphasis on justice, which can be traced in letters and decrees written by Cassiodorus in the name of young Athalaric. One of the first was the decision to restore the properties of Boethius and Symmachus to their children. An edict issued in the young man's name included many provisions, such as those against bribery and against adulterous men, who are to be denounced and punished.[16] Other decrees stress the need for improvements in court procedure, against the purchase of ecclesiastical office and for the rule of law and the promotion of good order (*civilitas*) throughout society. Similarly, the appointment of a man highly skilled in letters, possibly the well-known Arator, as count of the bodyguards, or adviser, *conciliarius*, to the military official Tuluin, reflects Amalasuintha's concern for good administration at the highest level, since the 'magnificent patrician Tuluin' was entrusted with 'handling the secrets of my empire'.[17] When the court learned of the death of the queen's aunt, Amalafrida, in Africa, Amalasuintha ordered a severe condemnation of the Vandal king. The rebuke, however, remained entirely rhetorical because the Goths in Ravenna had no way to avenge her murder.[18]

The queen maintained the court at Ravenna as the centre of both Gothic and Roman culture, keeping in contact with the Senate and bishop of Rome as well as the imperial court in Constantinople through special envoys and diplomatic missions. She also held the keys to the Gothic treasury, accumulated by Theoderic, kept in the palace, which continued to be a focus and sanctuary for all Goths.[19] When the queen's cousin Amalaberga was forced to flee from Thuringia, she took refuge in Ravenna with her children (Belisarius, Justinian's general, later took the children back to Constantinople).[20] Ravenna was constantly enriched by the port activities at Classis that linked it with so many parts of the Mediterranean. Commercial and political opportunities attracted investment in the city, for instance, in opulent houses such as the *Domus dei Tappeti di Pietra* that was independent of the court, though the occupant of this particularly fine building may have been employed there.

Divisions among the Catholics

It was during Amalasuintha's regency that a serious quarrel broke out among the Catholic clergy of Ravenna who objected to the way Bishop Ecclesius set their salaries. They split into two factions, divided rather evenly between those who supported the bishop and the rest led by the archdeacon Mastulus. An appeal to Pope Felix IV resulted in a document that the historian Agnellus found in the archives and copied into his *Book of the Pontiffs of Ravenna*. The Catholic cathedral church had built up a very large annual income of 160 lbs of gold (12,000 *solidi*), of which one quarter, 40 lbs or 3,000 *solidi*, was set aside for the sixty clergy enrolled in the church.[21] Of this total eleven were priests, ten deacons, five subdeacons, twelve acolytes, twelve readers, four cantors, three defensors, two deans and one was the superintendent of stores.[22] Income on this level put Ravenna into the first rank of all ecclesiastical sees, directly below those of the patriarchs, and well ahead of the 30 lbs of gold considered appropriate to the top bishoprics in 546 when Justinian issued an edict on ecclesiastical matters. Of the 3,000 *solidi* divided between the staff of sixty at Ravenna, the eleven priests and ten deacons probably got a larger portion, to which they added their share of offerings from the laity.[23]

This income had accumulated during the fifth century to make Ravenna one of the richest churches in the empire. In 482 it was already substantial, as we learn from a priest named Gregory, who complained that on his election to the provincial bishopric of Mutina he would earn less than as a priest in Ravenna. He angrily demanded an estate with an annual salary of 30 *solidi* to maintain his income.[24] Under Bishop Aurelianus (in 521) church revenues were increased by additional donations: farms that provided taxes in kind (oil, wine, corn), forests, villages and subordinate country churches, such as the territory of Comaclio, where the church (or chapel, *monasterium*) of St Mary *in Pado uetere* was built. Some of the property donated to the church was leased to secular figures: Pope Felix alludes to such leases when he recommends that the archdeacon Mastulus should reclaim all those properties, both rural and urban, that had been given 'through no necessity of friendship' to secular men. His stress on keeping up-to-date written records of leases and having tighter control over secular landlords must reflect a common problem of sixth-century church leaders. The bishop of Ravenna had seven notaries to copy and file all documents relating to the patrimony of the Catholic church.[25]

Pope Felix also instructed the clergy who held urban or rural estates belonging to the church to withhold only what was due to them from the revenues so generated. All the rest of the money should be brought into the church 'for the benefit of ecclesiastical profit'. The bishop was responsible for all the churches of his diocese as well as monasteries for men and women, and Felix gave advice about maintaining 'reason, justice, peace and discipline' in all of them. His letter appears to have put an end to the quarrel with Mastulus, and Ecclesius thereafter 'was with his sheep like a father with his sons . . . he ruled his church in peace'.[26]

With this considerable income and the help of the banker Julianus, who donated an additional sum of 26,000 *solidi*, Bishop Ecclesius commissioned the building of the most striking church in Ravenna, the one dedicated to San Vitale, discussed in Chapter 15. The bishop ensured that his portrait appeared in the apse, while Julianus was thanked in inscriptions and through his monograms in both Greek and Latin. In addition to their joint patronage, Ecclesius also commissioned a manuscript of the Bible, which was emended by Patricius, as recorded in an inscription in a ninth-century copy.[27] The Gothic queen mother did nothing to obstruct the ambitious building plans of the Catholic community and tolerated their architectural competitiveness. No specific foundations are attributed to Amalasuintha, but it seems likely that she extended her father's patronage of the Arian churches. The historian Agnellus associates her with the building of a house on her property, where a chapel of St Peter, called *Orfanotrophium*, still existed in his time.[28] The use of a Greek term suggests that it may have been connected to an orphanage comparable to those in Constantinople.[29] Within Ravenna the two Christian groups co-existed in pronounced contrast to the contemporaneous Arian persecution of Catholic Christians in North Africa and Spain and the condemnation and exclusion of Arian Christians in Rome.

In her relations with the Catholic church, Amalasuintha intervened in papal elections, as her father had, in her case to ensure that candidates did not distribute huge sums to buy the votes of the poor. A letter of 533 instructed Pope John II to inform all the bishops under his control that they would be punished by canon law if they were found guilty. A similar letter to the prefect of Rome ordered him to have the measure inscribed on marble tablets and placed in the atrium of the church of St Peter. And an official was sent with the letter to see that the engraving was made and duly erected, so that there could be no room for doubt.[30] As with other legal measures, this practice of engraving the law and setting it up where everyone could see it continued the traditional Roman method of law enforcement. It also commemorated Gothic control over Rome as part of the kingdom ruled by Theoderic's daughter and grandson, even though Cassiodorus expressed this most politely.

Ravenna's Control over Istria

From 480 until 539, when it was conquered by imperial forces from Constantinople, Istria, at the head of the Adriatic, formed 'the storeroom of the royal city'. Wine, oil, corn and dried fish paste (*garum*) were produced in abundance, as well as fish, oysters and other seafoods; the church of Ravenna owned forests there that provided wood for building. The Ravennati also had villas there and relaxed in the cooler climate, creating summer resorts only a day's sailing across the

Adriatic, equivalent to those of Campania cultivated by the Romans. The queen may have moved to the delightful settlements of Pola (Pula), Ruginium (Rovinj) and Parentium (Poreč) to avoid the summer heat. Close contact by sea is documented in several of Cassiodorus' letters to officials based in Istria in 537: hearing from travellers that there was an exceptionally rich harvest, the praetorian prefect sent an official to assess the crops and then establish a fair price for them. He also informed local shipowners that they should transport the crops without delay. And when he received a petition from a bishop in Venetia where the harvest had failed, he cancelled the normal army requirements in kind (wine and corn) and arranged for wine to be supplied from Istria at market rates.[31]

In the early 530s, when it was evident that the young king Athalaric was often too inebriated to fulfil his regal duties, hostility towards Amalasuintha increased, perhaps driven by her pro-Constantinopolitan policy maintained through regular diplomatic contacts with Justinian. Fearing an insurrection against her rule, Amalasuintha wrote to the emperor asking for his protection, and he ordered the preparation of a refuge for her in Dyrrachium (ancient Epidamnus, modern Durrës), a port on the eastern coast of the Adriatic within the East Roman empire. In 534, she loaded all her possessions and a large part of Theoderic's treasure onto a ship and sent it off to Dyrrachium ahead of her own possible flight. But then she successfully arranged the deaths of her chief opponents and felt confident enough to recall the ship.[32] Both of these moves must have scandalized the Goths at court.

Athalaric's death in October 534 deprived Amalasuintha of the role of regent and seriously weakened her position within the court. She then felt an overwhelming need for a male figure to act as her consort and invited her cousin Theodahad, the son of Theoderic's sister Amalafrida, to become king (Plate 21). Announcing her choice to the Senate in Rome, she declared that she had preserved the palace in Ravenna for a noble Amal (the family name). She described Theodahad as a man of royal stature, a scholar known for his enviable literary learning, including ecclesiastical letters, his charity and hospitality, and one who had been admonished by the virtues of his ancestors and effectively guided by his uncle Theoderic.[33] Against this, his unlawful accumulation of estates in Tuscany had already provoked serious criticism among the Goths, and Amalasuintha had instructed him to desist. Their co-operation as a ruling pair did not start out well. In addition to the queen's established contact with Justinian, Theodahad also sustained close contact with both emperor and empress through an imperial envoy, Peter the patrician.[34] Before 535 he appears to have suggested that he would hand over control of the Gothic kingdom if the emperor would allow him to retire to Constantinople and pursue his interests in Neoplatonic texts, a proposal that may reflect the reality of eastern ambitions over Italy.

While he cheerfully accepted Amalasuintha's offer to become king, Theodahad exploited his new position by plotting against her. Amid a flurry of diplomatic embassies between the court and Constantinople, sent by both Amalasuintha and Theodahad, the queen was taken from Ravenna to an island probably in Lake Bolsena in central Italy. When Justinian sent Peter the patrician to Theodahad to threaten war if any harm came to her, the Gothic king tried to reassure him that all was well and forced Amalasuintha to write a similar letter in her own name. Shortly after this, however, late in 535 or early 536, Theodahad ordered her death and imprisoned the eastern envoy, and as soon as this news reached Constantinople, Justinian made it the pretext for a determined attack on Italy.[35]

PART FOUR

540–70

Justinian I and the Campaigns in North Africa and Italy

14

Belisarius captures Ravenna

Thanks to Procopius, who wrote a *History of the Wars*, we have a lengthy description of the campaigns fought on Emperor Justinian's orders in North Africa and Italy. This records the close relationship between Procopius and Belisarius, a leading military commander, that dated back to 527 when Procopius was sent to the Persian frontier as the general's legal adviser. There he observed Belisarius' heroic character, his magnanimity and restraint in dealing with enemy prisoners and conquered populations during a campaign that culminated in a peace treaty with the Persians in 532. In Justinian's determination to end what had been a prolonged conflict, stretching from Lazica (in modern Georgia) and Armenia south to Syria and Palestine, his ambassadors negotiated an 'Eternal Peace' for the vast sum of 11,000 lbs of gold.

Even before this was achieved, an internal revolt of the Greens and Blues, the two dominant circus factions that organized Hippodrome entertainments in Constantinople, caused a more dramatic threat to the emperor in person, right under the imperial palace. Chanting 'Nika!' (conquer), the two groups, normally rivals, united to demand the dismissal of some high officials and then set fire to the centre of Constantinople. When Justinian's attempts to satisfy their demands failed to end the rioting, the crowds elevated an alternative ruler. Procopius reports that Theodora, the emperor's wife, refused to flee from the city, with the famous statement that it is better to die in the imperial purple than to lose your status as empress: 'royalty is a good burial shroud'.[1] Other accounts emphasize the skill with which the emperor disposed his military contingents who attacked the populace in the Hippodrome. On Sunday, 18 January 532, Belisarius was one of the leaders of the massacre in which up to 35,000 people were killed. For several days afterwards 'Constantinople was quiet, and no one dared to go out, but only the shops which provided food and drink for needy people were open.'[2]

The Wars in the West

Belisarius had won the emperor's gratitude and was chosen to lead a most ambitious campaign against the threats to the empire in the West in 533. For several years refugees from Vandal persecution had urged Justinian to overthrow the Arian kingdom in North Africa and restore the Catholic bishops to their sees. Even more pressing appeals for military assistance came from the governor of Sardinia and the leader of a revolt in Libya, both intent on removing the Vandal King Gelimer. With this encouragement, Justinian sent Belisarius with an expeditionary force of 10,000 infantry and 5,000 cavalry, plus his own militia (*bucellarii*). Compared to the 52,000 troops sent against Persia in 503, or the 6,000 to reinstall the Monophysite patriarch of Alexandria in 535, 16,000 overall was not a large force – certainly small in relation to the massive armada constructed by Leo I for the attempted conquest of 468 that had failed so miserably.[3] The 533 expedition nonetheless reflected Constantinople's capacity to transport probably more than 5,000 horses with sufficient water and fodder, as well as 10,000 infantry, who dreaded the possibility of having to fight at sea, in 500 ships protected by 92 warships that set sail from Constantinople around the spring equinox.

The armada sailed slowly from Abydos on the Dardanelles across the Aegean to Greece and on to Sicily, where Belisarius learned that the Vandal fleet had gone to Sardinia, so he decided to land his troops in Libya immediately. With surprising speed his troops advanced to capture Carthage and King Gelimer himself.[4] His brilliant success was celebrated by a triumph in his honour in Constantinople, the procession of prisoners led by the Vandal king and his foremost warriors. The immense booty displayed included golden treasures from the Jerusalem Temple captured by Emperor Titus in AD 70. After the Vandal sack of Rome in 455 these had been carried off to Carthage, and they were now added to the imperial treasury in Constantinople. In 534 Justinian issued a law designed to restore imperial government in the North African provinces, under the supreme military commander, a praetorian prefect based at Carthage, with a staff of nearly four hundred civil servants, plus governors appointed to the seven provinces, each with fifty administrative staff, and five dukes to maintain order and defend the region.[5] If the loss of the North African provinces in 439 had marked a turning point in the decline of the Roman empire in the West, Belisarius had now reversed it, bringing these rich areas back under direct rule from Constantinople. This also symbolized the replacement of Old Rome by New Rome: the Queen City was clearly now the sole source of imperial power. The African provinces reinvigorated Roman rule from Constantinople over the West for another century. North African exports of grain, wine and oil to Italy increased, and the famous burnished red slip ware pottery from the region turns up on sites throughout the Mediterranean world and further afield.[6]

After this victory over the Arian Vandal kingdom, Justinian was deeply angered by the news of Theodahad's treatment of Amalasuintha. Her detention – and rumours of her murder – gave him an opportunity to extend the western military campaign against the Gothic government both in Italy and Dalmatia. In 535 Justinian planned a two-pronged campaign led by Mundus, who was to march overland to Dalmatia to consolidate control on the eastern coast of the Adriatic, while Belisarius would sail to occupy Sicily, the crucial link to Italy.[7] The two forces were then to combine in an assault on Ravenna to defeat the Ostrogoths and capture Theoderic's treasure – booty was always an essential element of military campaigning.

The emperor may have been misled by the quick victory in Africa into thinking that a similar campaign would succeed in Italy, and indeed Belisarius captured Sicily without difficulty and advanced up the west coast of Italy. But in November 536 at Naples his forces encountered stiff resistance, in which the Jewish community sided with the Gothic commander in charge of the city's defence. After a twenty-day siege the city capitulated and was sacked. The imperial troops moved north towards Rome and in December the pope and notables petitioned Belisarius to enter the city peacefully, while the Gothic garrison, greatly outnumbered, decided to leave.[8]

Ancient Rome was once again under direct imperial rule from Constantinople, a major triumph for Justinian. Belisarius appointed a duke to rule the city in conjunction with the remaining senatorial families and consolidated his control over central Italy. After their defeat at

Naples, the Goths deposed King Theodahad, suspecting his military weakness, and selected an experienced soldier, Witigis, as king. He immediately marched to Ravenna where he married Matasuntha, the daughter of Amalasuintha, against her will.[9] By allying himself with the ruling dynasty in this way, he counted on imperial forces being reluctant to attack the Gothic capital while a descendant of Theoderic was queen.

In the court at Ravenna Cassiodorus celebrated the union in his own typical style, thus continuing his long service to the Gothic kingdom. He had begun this career under Theoderic, had been trained and generously rewarded by three generations of Gothic rulers and remained loyal to the family that held power in Ravenna.[10] Late in 536 (or early in the new year) he composed an epithalamium or marriage poem for the wedding, which has only survived in parts. After praising her genealogy at length, he addresses the queen, *domina*:

> You have also built, O Lady, a palace which would make you famous clearly also to those who do not know you, because from such a huge dwelling can be deduced the magnitude of the resident. The coating of the marbles shines with the same color as the gems, the gold scattered about shines on the columns ... mosaic works decorate with stone the rounded vaults; and all is adorned with metallic colors wherever waxen paintings are discerned. One remembers that the Queen Semiramis had the circular walls of Babylon built with bitumen mixed with sulphur ... It is said that the house of Cyrus was built with stones bound together with gold, in Susa ...[11]

This reference to lost mosaic and marble decoration confirms its ubiquitous use not only in the imperial palace, probably where the epithalamium was delivered, but also in other palaces, such as the one where Matasuntha had previously lived, enjoying radiant mosaic, gold and bejewelled wall coverings.

Perhaps Witigis believed that he could avoid a war with Constantinople by negotiating a return to Theoderic's arrangements, 'so that either commonwealth may endure in harmony restored', as Cassiodorus puts it – with Ravenna representing the western and Constantinople the eastern government. But this is in stark contrast with the king's militant declaration to the Goths that he had been raised on a shield 'among the swords of battle in the ancestral way ... as the trumpets blared so that the Gothic race of Mars roused by the din and longing for their native courage might find themselves a martial king.'[12] Invoking the Roman god of war, Witigis claimed:

> All that I do will look to the benefit of our race . . . I promise to pursue what will honour the royal name . . . I promise that my rule will be such as the Goths should possess following the glorious Theoderic. He was a man peculiarly and nobly formed for the cares of kingship . . . hence he who can imitate his deeds should be thought of as his kinsman.[13]

The Gothic population of Ravenna may have cheered, but the Catholics must have found the situation dangerous.

Living in Ravenna in the 530s

Even under these unsettled circumstances, some aspects of regular life continued in Ravenna and those areas of eastern Italy that remained under Gothic control. Two papyrus records from nearby Faventia (Faenza) tell us something of what it was like to live in the Gothic kingdom nearly fifty years after its foundation. In these sales, dated 539 and 540, poorer landowners negotiate with wealthier buyers. The first by Thugilo, *honesta femina*, the widow of Parianis, her daughter Domnica and son Deutherius, is of 20 *jugera* of land in the territory of Faventino to Pelegrinus, *vir strenuus*, for 110 *solidi*.[14] The land seems to have been near the coast close to property owned by two *dromonarii* (who owned or managed swift ships) and Witterit, a Gothic *scutarius* (shield bearer). One of the witnesses was Julianus, the money-changer (*argentarius*), who is also identified as the son-in-law, *gener*, of Johannis *pimentarius*, who supplies herbal pigments for painters as well as herbs used in medicinal remedies.[15] Other witnesses included officials from the office of the postal service, *de scrinio cursorum*, the tax office, the guild of landowners and a caterer – provisioner – of the lord (*obsonator domini nostri*, that is, King Witigis).[16]

In the second sale (the size of the estate is lost but the price was 40 *solidi*) a clause stipulates that Dominicus, the seller, had inherited the two estates from his mother, free from all possible taxes, debts and other obligations (a long list is given) or legal controversy (*a sorte barbari et aratione tutelaria*).[17] The seller is of modest rank (*vir honestus*), and the buyer, Montanus, and all his witnesses, colleagues or friends, are *clarissimi*. Montanus is a notary of the king's wardrobe (*notarius vestearium*) and two of his witnesses are also involved in the civil administration: Reparatus, *praepositus cursorum dominicorum* (head of the couriers who handled the regal postal system and its network of roads and staging posts), and Romanus, *silentiarius* (a palace official, *apud Ravennati Urbe*), while Paulus is a banker or money-changer, and Vitalis works in the mint (*monitarius*).[18] The presiding magistrate at the court is Plautus Pompulius and the high-ranking *principes* in attendance come from some familiar families: Flavius Florianus, Firmianus Ursus, Fl. Severus Junior, and Fl. Quiriacus Junior.

In these records both the women, Thugilo and Domnica, make the sign of the cross because they cannot write their names, and Deutherius signs; they are among the *honesti*. The money-changer Julianus uses Greek letters, quite a common phenomenon (though whether it implies high status or is just a snobbish affectation is unclear) and gives his father-in-law's name and occupation. The property near Faenza is identified by boundaries with three landowners who have some fighting capacity. In contrast, the group of officials who worked at the Gothic court of Ravenna all sign their own names. Like Cassiodorus, they are Catholics who serve the Gothic king, in the palace administration established by Theoderic.[19]

The Brief Reign of King Witigis

Late in 536 the new Gothic leader, King Witigis, hoped to avert an outright war by proposing peace terms to Justinian. When these efforts failed, he turned the tables on Belisarius by leading his Gothic troops to besiege Rome. For over a year the Goths attempted to reduce the city to such great hunger that Belisarius would be obliged to surrender, staging sixty-seven attacks, some of which Procopius witnessed at first hand. In detailed descriptions of the medical extraction of arrows and javelins and the story of two soldiers (one of each side) who both fell into a deep hole and pledged to support each other to get out, which they did and then went back to fighting, he documents the violent, hand-to-hand conflict. At one dangerous moment Belisarius had to smuggle his wife, Antonina, out of the city; at Naples she experienced the rumbles of Vesuvius that threatened a volcanic eruption.[20] But the Goths were unable to gain entry to Rome and, in 537 during a truce in the fighting, they sent another embassy to Constantinople in an effort to secure peace, while the besieged Romans brought in supplies and reinforcements. Belisarius now sent one of his commanders to threaten other Gothic cities further north. With the assistance of the fleet based in Dalmatia, these imperial troops captured Rimini, very close to Ravenna, and Witigis was obliged to abandon the siege of Rome in March 538 in order to defend his capital.[21]

Although Belisarius had conquered Sicily with only 7,500 men, to which he added reinforcements during the siege of Rome, he remained greatly outnumbered by Gothic forces and had to divide his troops among the captured cities in order to maintain control in southern Italy. In response to his request for further military assistance, in 538 Justinian sent Narses, an elderly eunuch, courtier and keeper of the royal treasuries, with additional forces. After some disagreements, the two imperial commanders focused on securing the surrender of key garrisons in order to capture Ravenna, the allegedly impregnable Gothic capital city. When Belisarius finally arrived at the walls late in 539 or early 540, he aimed to force the city to surrender by cutting off all supplies. Under this pressure, Witigis renewed his appeals to Justinian and obtained a peace offer that would have allowed the Goths to remain in control of the area north of the Po. According to Procopius, Belisarius opposed this because he was confident of winning a decisive victory and taking the Gothic king to Constantinople in chains. Many embassies were exchanged, not only between Belisarius and Justinian, but also between Belisarius and some of the Goths in Ravenna, who had decided that he would make a better overlord than Justinian. They offered him the title 'emperor of the west', *basilea tes hesperias*, and Belisarius initially considered this proposal favourably – or gave the appearance of doing so to win over Gothic support. Later he refused it, but not in a sufficiently clear fashion to prevent rumours of his ambition from circulating among his own soldiers and, of course, the rumours reached the East.[22]

After several months and lengthy negotiations, Belisarius entered Ravenna in May 540. Procopius commented:

> Although the Goths were greatly superior to their opponents in number and in power, and had neither fought a decisive battle since they had

entered Ravenna nor been humbled in spirit by any other disaster, still they were being made captives by the weaker army and were regarding the name of slavery as no insult. But when the women, as they sat at the gate, had seen the whole army ... they all spat upon the faces of their husbands, and pointing with their hands to the victors, reviled them for their cowardice.[23]

This description seems to reflect the view of some Goths that Witigis had been tricked into surrendering Ravenna without even fighting a major battle for control of the city. While several Gothic garrison commanders joined in the plan to make Belisarius their ruler, Justinian got wind of it and summoned his general back to Constantinople. Belisarius therefore prepared to take the Witigis, his wife and supporters, together with the treasure of Theoderic seized from the palace, to the East, abandoning those Goths who had been deceived by him to regroup. They elected Ildebadus, commander of the Gothic garrison at Verona, as their king and fought on for twelve years, though they never regained their capital, Ravenna.[24]

Despite his success in bringing another 'barbarian' king to Constantinople, the emperor refused to grant Belisarius another triumph and did not even display the booty from Ravenna in public. Procopius contrasts this coolness towards the general with the enthusiasm of local people, who welcomed the hero home and brought gifts and tributes to his house. Later he was represented in a mosaic put up on the Chalke Gate of the Palace commemorating his two major conquests:

the general Belisarius [who] returns to the Emperor, his whole army intact, and offers him booty, namely kings and kingdoms and all other things that are prized by men. In the center stand the Emperor and the Empress Theodora both seeming to rejoice as they celebrate their victory over the kings of the Vandals and the Goths, who approach them as captives of war being led into bondage.[25]

Although it does not survive, this mosaic was a public acknowledgment of Belisarius' military victories, erected in a most prominent place. And many years later, in 559, when Justinian was worried by a Slavic attack near the Long Walls of the Queen City, he called on Belisarius, who successfully drove them off, despite having a much smaller force.[26] So although fortune may not have favoured him throughout his long career, the aged general finally retired after a long life full of victories. The myths of his poverty-stricken old age recounted in Robert Graves's compelling novel *Count Belisarius* are quite untrue.[27]

The most important result of Belisarius' Italian campaign was therefore the capture of Ravenna, and the removal of the Gothic king, queen and courtiers to Constantinople. For the Goths to relinquish their capital city without a fight implies serious divisions among them: the surrender of Witigis was followed immediately by the election of Ildebadus as the remaining Goths set out to reverse Belisarius' conquest. Although they captured Rome and many other cities, they failed to win back control of Ravenna, further proof of its very well-protected position. The city thus passed under the direct rule of Constantinople and became the centre of imperial administration in Italy for the next two hundred years.

15

San Vitale, epitome of Early Christendom

In May 540, when Ravenna was restored to Constantinopolitan control, the Catholic bishop, Victor (537–44), gave the imperial troops a particularly warm welcome. The departure of the Gothic king and his courtiers meant that the Arian clergy had lost their patron and were reduced to the church of the conquered minority. No immediate steps were taken against them, but the pressure of the restored Catholic community may perhaps be perceived in a fragmentary record dated after 16 July 541, in which Minnulus, a cleric of the Gothic church of Ravenna, son of Cristodorus, the presbyter, sold land to Isacius, a soap maker/merchant (*saponarius*) of Classis.[1] It is one of the rare occasions when a leader, presbyter, of the Gothic clergy is mentioned, together with his son Minnulus, who is also *clericus legis Gothorum*. The pattern of son following father into the same priestly profession is one common to early medieval Europe; popes Boniface, Felix III and Agapitus were all sons of priests, and Silverius (the short-lived pope of 536–7) was the son of Pope Hormisdas. It took many centuries before clerical celibacy was successfully imposed.

Reinvigorated contact with Constantinople as a result of the imperial conquest encouraged Bishop Victor's investment in the Catholic church's furniture and fittings. From four inscriptions that survived into the ninth century, we know that he replaced an old wooden canopy over the altar of the Ursiana church (the cathedral founded by Bishop Ursus) with a silver one made of 120 lbs of silver.[2] Agnellus thought that such a luxurious object could only have been constructed with imperial assistance and claims that the taxes from the whole of Italy were allotted to Victor for this purpose. Some of the funding was used for new liturgical vessels that Agnellus could identify three centuries later because they continued in use. Bishop Victor was responsible for a beautiful altar cloth for the same church, which was made of very heavy silk threads, golden and scarlet, with five images that included Christ and Victor. An inscription woven into the cloth in purple stated that it was to be used at Easter services and dated its production to the fifth year of Victor's episcopate (542–3). The bishop also restored the bathhouse attached to his episcopal palace and recorded its re-dedication in hexameter verses set in gold mosaic; Agnellus quotes the regulation that on two days (Tuesdays and Fridays) the clergy of the city should be allowed to wash without paying.[3]

A very impressive marble calendar, which inscribes the date on which Easter should be celebrated according to the nineteen-year cycle computation established by St Cyril of Alexandria in the mid-fifth century, may also date from the period of Bishop Victor. These complex calculations, based on solar and lunar phases, were translated into Latin by Dionysius the Lesser (*exiguus*) in 525 in Rome, and covered the years from 532 to 626. Although they resolved a major problem of when to celebrate the most important festival of the Christian calendar, they were only slowly adopted. In Ravenna a fraction of these calculations is recorded on marble in a circular form divided into nineteen sectors with the appropriate computation. Similarly neat lettering is also found on the funerary epitaphs of Gerontius, dated December 523, and of Bishop Ecclesius on his sarcophagus of 532, indicating a skilled mastery of late-imperial styles of marble carving that continued into the second half of the sixth century.[4]

The Beginnings of San Vitale

After 540 the now dominant Catholic population of Ravenna had access not only to talent in the form of builders and craftsmen, but also to financial support provided by an exceptionally wealthy citizen, the *argentarius* Julianus, who invested much of his fortune in Bishop Victor's building projects. Chief among these was the completion of the octagonal church of San Vitale, the most surprising of Ravenna's monuments. This had been begun at the very end of Theoderic's reign by Bishop Ecclesius, who was responsible for its unusual, octagonal plan and insisted on depicting himself in the apse above the altar. Since he died probably in July 532, the design of the apse mosaic was agreed and may have been completed by that time. But San Vitale continued to be a building site under bishops Ursicinus, Victor and Maximian, who completed and dedicated the church in 547. In Constantinople it took five years to erect the almost contemporaneous church dedicated to Holy Wisdom (Hagia Sophia), the largest ever constructed, which contemporaries acknowledged was an amazing achievement. Only imperial funding on the most extravagant scale and the forced corvées by huge numbers of workers made it possible.

In contrast, the construction of San Vitale had continued through all the vicissitudes of Amalasuintha's regency and the Gothic wars, the different parts reflecting a history of overlapping ambitions and authorities. The original design is captured in the apse, where Ecclesius presents a model of the domed church on an octagonal base to Christ (Plate 31). Where did Ecclesius find the inspiration for such novel features, not familiar in the West at this date? Domes were normally associated with imperial tombs, such as the impressive rotunda built by Emperor Hadrian in Rome, now known as the Castel Sant'Angelo, the tomb of Diocletian at Split, or the Pantheon, originally a temple. The mausoleum of Constantia, also in Rome, emphasized the central tomb, surrounded by an ambulatory, a plan that was copied at several martyr shrines to enable pilgrims to walk around the relics. Although, as we have seen, the so-called mausoleum of Galla Placidia in Ravenna and the larger one built for Theoderic are domed, both are shallow, quite unlike the lofty dome of San Vitale. Similarly, the two baptisteries in Ravenna, both constructed on an octagonal base, have shallow domes made of ceramic cylinders and blocks of pumice, designed to lighten the load on their narrow walls.

The chapel of Sant'Aquilino attached to the church of San Lorenzo in Milan, probably constructed in the late fourth century, has an octagonal plan supporting a tall dome, which might have provided a model for San Vitale. It is often suggested, however, that Ecclesius may have been inspired by his visit to Constantinople in 525, when Theoderic sent him with the delegation to protest against the restriction of Arian worship in the eastern capital. The members of the western embassy would certainly have been taken to admire the major churches of the city: the church of the Holy Apostles with the imperial mausoleum attached, and the cathedral church of Hagia Sophia, an impressive basilica, though not the building we are familiar with today. They might have seen the large fifth-century Rotunda with its heavy masonry dome, and would have heard about the basilica of St Polyeuktos, recently constructed by the wealthy aristocrat Juliana Anicia, possibly domed and decorated with the most extravagant carved marble cornice and elegant furnishings. Its immense grandeur had irritated Emperor Justinian.[5]

None of these buildings in the eastern capital had an octagonal base covered by a dome. Yet precisely that structural plan is found in several early Christian buildings in and near Jerusalem, such as the churches of the Anastasis and the Ascension, with domes whose measurements were replicated in nearly all other early Christian domed structures, including San Vitale. Architects and builders could calculate the base of a building capable of supporting a dome with a diameter of fifty or even seventy feet (15m and 21m respectively). A fairly simple geometric formula was employed to plan concentric buildings and could be applied on the ground using tools such as rods and ropes to fix the proportions of base to dome. In this way, the churches commissioned by Constantine I and dedicated to Christ, and the first churches dedicated to Mary, the Mother of God, in the fifth century, may derive from 'an eastern earlier prototype that does not survive'. At Kidron, where Mary's tomb was identified, and at the Kathisma (seat) where she was supposed to have rested on the flight into Egypt, concentric church structures were covered by domes. The Kathisma also had an octagonal plan and a dome 15m in diameter, modelled on that of the church of the Ascension.[6]

Emperors and bishops, who were usually the patrons of these new buildings, provided the finance, while architects, normally called engineers or technicians (*mechanikai, technitai*), drew on shared plans and ideas that circulated among builders. Thus, the very innovative plan of both San Vitale and its contemporary, the church of Sts Sergius and Bacchus in Constantinople, probably derive from eastern building practice that circulated in the sixth-century Mediterranean world. At his accession in 527 Justinian began an ambitious building programme with the church of Sts Sergius and Bacchus, which was the first in the capital to use the complex plan of an octagonal base that supported a domed roof. The effect of this design is to create a very high, well-lit interior that draws the eye up from the ground, past the gallery at the first-floor level to the brilliantly designed, segmented dome. From the long inscription running around the cornice at the base of the first-floor gallery, it is clear that Empress Theodora took a major part in the patronage of the church.

Sts Sergius and Bacchus may have been under construction at the same time as the even more astonishing structure of Hagia Sophia, conceived on a vaster scale and completed in 537. The church of Holy Wisdom is roofed by the largest dome ever built, 32m in diameter, which floats 55m above ground level, supported on four massive piers with two large semi-domes to the east and west. In 558 part of the eastern semi-dome and the dome above collapsed, but Justinian summoned the son of the original architect to restore it. This was achieved by raising the height of the dome, which was not surpassed until Michelangelo put up the dome of St Peter's in Rome.[7] In 525 Justinian's plans may have been discussed by the western visitors, who were also interested in building churches.

Whatever the source of his inspiration, it was Bishop Ecclesius who commissioned the church that continues to command most attention in Ravenna today (Plate 30). The workmen he employed to construct San Vitale could have used an established architectural model that had been tested and shown to work. From the beginning of the work Ecclesius was assisted by Julianus the *argentarius*, who is recorded in several inscriptions and his monograms in Greek and Latin as a major donor to the church. Julianus provided 26,000 *solidi* for the construction of San Vitale and supported the building of S. Apollinare in Classe and S. Michele *in Africisco*. The term *argentarius* was used of dealers in coin, who provided small change for those who wished to break gold *solidi* into the bronze coins normally used for purchases, and for bankers.[8] *Argentarii* were also involved in maritime trade, specifically the insurance of the goods carried and the ships themselves. Given the frequency of storms and shipwrecks, increasingly revealed by underwater archaeology, it was an occupation that demanded very considerable resources and tight control. Such insurance activity is best documented in Alexandria, an important port of entry to the Mediterranean trade routes, and Julianus may have been of eastern origin and used a Greek monogram; since Classis was also a trading station on the Adriatic, he may have been involved in underwriting shipments of goods in and out of that port. However he had accumulated his fortune, he invested it in the church of Ravenna and assisted bishops Ecclesius and Victor in their grandiose building plans, as well as commissioning an extravagent silver reliquary. From the endowments recorded in inscriptions copied by Agnellus, we can see that Julianus was well established by 520 and he may have lived until 550.[9]

With the help of this generous local patron, Bishop Ecclesius set out to construct a most striking and original monument to the local saint, Vitalis, who is recorded with his sons Sts Gervasius and Protasius in an inscription. These two saints, however, were from Milan, where Bishop Ambrose miraculously discovered their relics in June 386, and ingeniously contrived to spread news of the discovery by distributing phials of their blood to places in Italy (Bologna) and further afield (Rouen). It is not clear how their relics came to Ravenna; possibly Emperor Honorius had brought some when he transferred the imperial court from Milan to Ravenna in 402.[10]

The new building was probably planned on Ecclesius' own land in the north-west corner of the city and may have been intended as a private foundation. A very substantial base must have been dug to create a platform strong enough to support the structure that sustains the dome at a considerable height of 30m. Its diameter of 17m is slightly larger than earlier churches but follows the established ratio of the size of the dome to the outer width of the octagon. Unlike other buildings that re-used *spolia*, the bricks for San Vitale were all new and slightly larger than the normal size.[11] Before he died, Ecclesius he had ensured that he would be commemorated in the apse mosaic as the donor of the church, identified by his name and in a style that appears to reflect his physical appearance, opposite St Vitalis who receives his martyr's crown (Plate 31).[12]

Once the dome was constructed, the mosaicists began their work at the highest point and worked down. They had to work quickly while the plaster was still the right consistency for the scene to be sketched and the important figures picked out in tesserae inserted at specific angles so as to be viewed from the ground. Master craftsmen completed the features of each individual in smaller stones, while the background might have been filled in by less skilled workers.[13] How much of the mosaic decoration was installed before the death of Ecclesius is unclear. Below his portrait, there is a large area of mosaic that covers the entire sanctuary, an extended chapel forming the east end of the church. The ceiling above, the walls on either side of the altar and the triumphal arch leading into this area are all decorated in mosaic scenes, separated by bands of brilliant animal, floral and vegetal patterns in a glorious range of blues, greens and reds. Eventually this entire area became a glowing ensemble, which commands the attention of every visitor to the church: the Lamb of God at the centre of the apse roof supported by four angelic figures (Plate 32); the Old Testament scenes that recall visions of God – Moses at Mount Sinai, Abraham preparing to sacrifice his son, and Melchizedek the high priest officiating at the altar – and the twelve Apostles that adorn the triumphal arch flanking the Lamb, with portraits of male saints enclosed in frames of dolphins and peacocks.

After the death of Ecclesius, his successor, Ursicinus (533–6), is cele-brated as the founder of the basilica of S. Apollinare in Classe, although how much of this vast church was built in his reign is unclear (Plate 53). Victor (537/8–44) took over the completion of San Vitale, probably after the imperial capture of Ravenna in 540. He claimed responsibility for the ambulatory supported on columns and capitals, which are iden-tical to ones used in Constantinopolitan churches of the same date. They were certainly carved in the East before being shipped to Ravenna and are incised with his monogram (Plate 33). Since many churches of Ravenna had already been decorated with similarly imported marble furnishings, Victor was following not only a local tradition but also a fashionable Mediterranean-wide practice: the brilliant white marble quarried on the island of Proconnesus in the Sea of Marmara provided much sought-after furnishings for patrons throughout the Roman world.[14] Bishop Victor probably ordered the stucco decoration and marble covering of the outer walls of the ambulatory, which echo the mirror-image revetment of the church's main pillars. A similar extrava-gance and splendour mark the decoration of the apse where the bishop would sit enthroned with the clergy beside him. Since marble was the most expensive element in interior wall covering, the astonishing variety of colours and shapes, inlay and contrasting patterns, reflects a deter-mination to enhance San Vitale with the most prestigious materials.[15]

The Imperial Panels

The most striking images in the church are the two large panels that flank the altar. They display Emperor Justinian in full imperial regalia with his guards and clergy, opposite Empress Theodora, also crowned and swathed in a deep purple cloak, accompanied by her ladies-in-waiting

and priests (Plates 37 and 38). Both the central figures are shown participating in a liturgical procession, bringing their gifts to the altar.
Not only are such secular figures extremely unusual, but they are also
within the area of the altar, a space forbidden to women. The emperor
is flanked by Archbishop Maximian, priests and soldiers, and the empress by two unbearded officials (possibly eunuchs), the further one
holding back a curtain to reveal a fountain. Some of the court ladies
and soldiers are so crowded that their feet have been omitted altogether.
In contrast, Theodora stands alone in a shell-like alcove frequently
used to frame important figures.

In order to create such portraits, mosaicists could have used representations of the rulers in their official court costumes, such as the
icons sent out from Constantinople to announce the accession of a new
ruler. Theodora's companions wear their courtly garments of highly
coloured and patterned silks with red shoes and elegant jewellery. Fragments of silk with identical patterns of small ducks and birds survive in
museum collections and similar representations are found in the chapel
of S. Andreas in the episcopal palace. The clerics and officials in white
garments create a marked contrast with the imperial costumes and the
magnificent dresses of the court ladies, who are clearly intended to
compete with Theoderic's Golden Church of Christ the Saviour, with
its impressive processions of martyrs and saints advancing from the
cities of Ravenna and Classis towards Christ and the Mother of God.[16]

The extraordinary detail, setting and authority of these two full-
length portraits of the emperor and empress with their entourages in
San Vitale have, if only through their survival in such a defining place,
played a shaping role in the imagination of power ever since. Here we
can see the full display of official imperial dress and jewellery that goes
back to Diocletian's adoption of Persian royal insignia and purple
robes. Crowns, orbs and sceptres associated with this style of ceremonial dress come down to us today in court rituals around the world and
in the official attire of high priests, popes and bishops.

Yet Justinian and Theodora never went to Ravenna. Their presence
in the church of San Vitale has therefore provoked an enormous amount
of research devoted to the significance of the panels, their date and
sponsorship. Since Ecclesius is rightly understood as the patron of the
original church, he could also have designed the rest of the mosaic decoration, including the imperial panels. This would provide a date of

about 532, though the work might not have been completed until several years after the bishop's death. But it seems very unlikely that the Gothic rulers of Ravenna would have permitted such a prominent display of the eastern emperor and his wife. Even Amalasuintha, who relied on Justinian for protection, would not have accepted his powerful presence in a Catholic church under her Arian rule. And by the time of Theodahad, relations with Constantinople had deteriorated to the point when to put up an imperial portrait would have amounted to treachery. So, a date after the recapture of the city by Belisarius in May 540 appears most likely, bringing us back to the time when Victor was bishop.

This, in turn, raises the question why the bishop portrayed standing next to Justinian is clearly labelled 'Maximianus', not Victor. It has recently been suggested that the imperial portraits could have been planned by Bishop Victor and Belisarius in 540, as a thank-offering to the emperor for funding the successful military campaign; that is, between the recapture of Ravenna in May 540, and Belisarius' departure from the city in July, when he took King Witigis and the Gothic nobility to Constantinople.[17] According to this theory, the design of the portraits of the emperor and empress and the figures accompanying them, identified as Belisarius and his wife Antonina, was planned and approved in a very short time.[18] Bishop Victor was shown next to Justinian until Maximian became archbishop, when he replaced the image with his own.

The mosaics of the imperial panels were therefore set during the episcopate of Bishop Victor, between 540 and 544, to celebrate the liberation of Ravenna from the Goths with a portrait of Justinian, and in this way to rival other mosaic depictions of rulers in Ravenna. After the bishop's death a delegation of the clergy and people of Ravenna went to Constantinople to inform Justinian and to request the pallium of office for a new bishop. When they arrived in the capital, Maximian a native of Pola on the eastern coast of the Adriatic, was there – he travelled widely in the East Mediterranean and presumably had connections to the imperial court.[19] Justinian seized the opportunity to appoint a reliable supporter of his theological views to the crucial western see of Ravenna, so recently won back to imperial control. He promoted Ravenna to the status of an archbishopric, gave Maximian his pallium of office and instructed Pope Vigilius to consecrate him. As he had already summoned the pope to come to Constantinople, the emperor arranged for the two men to meet at Patras on the western coast of

Greece: Maximian on his way back to the West, while the pope was en route to the emperor. The new archbishop of Ravenna was thus consecrated in Patras on 14 October 546, and effectively became the senior ecclesiastical leader in the West, temporarily replacing the bishop of Rome who had left the see of St Peter in the hands of subordinate clergy. Maximian presented himself at the gates of Ravenna as the newly consecrated archbishop late in 546.

Archbishop Maximian

When the Ravennati travelled to Constantinople, they had intended to propose a member of their own clergy as bishop, according to the regular pattern of the recruitment. Instead, the emperor had insisted on a 'foreigner' and the community of Ravenna objected to the fact that Maximian was born, educated and ordained a deacon in Pola (today Pula in Croatia). Crossing the Adriatic only takes a day's sailing in summer with a fair wind, and contacts in the sixth century were frequent, but Maximian was not a local cleric and he had been chosen by the emperor in Constantinople. So the city did not welcome him. Instead, he was forced to wait outside the walls, where he stayed with his entourage in what had been the Arian episcopal palaces of Unimundus and of St George. He then invited prelates and city leaders to visit him one by one, hosting banquets and providing gifts of gold that gradually won them all over.

In an interesting observation about the city's inhabitants in 546, Agnellus describes differences among the citizens, who ranged from the leading people, the big figures, down to the little people, with the middling sort in between. These were all civilians rather than clerics or imperial employees.[20] Even if his definitions conform more to his own time rather than the mid-sixth century, they help to illustrate the mixed community that went out to welcome Archbishop Maximian in 546, with crosses, banners and flags, when the entire city finally decided to accept him as their religious leader. In this collective action we can see Ravenna's symbolic acceptance of its new status, subordinated to the authorities in Constantinople.

Once Maximian had persuaded the Ravennati to accept him, he then altered the imperial panel in San Vitale, replacing the image of Victor with his own. He labelled this new portrait so that no one would ever mistake the new rulers of the city: Archbishop Maximian, the outsider, intimately linked with Emperor Justinian, the distant but all-powerful political master. The archbishop thus took over most of Victor's body and feet, which demonstrated his power by putting his foot on top of his subordinate's, in the same fashion as the emperor who treads on his neighbour's feet. As a result, Bishop Victor's role in the construction was reduced to the monograms on capitals that support the ambulatory around the octagon. The mosaic panel with Maximian's image was in place when the new archbishop dedicated the church on 19 April 547.[21] It is a statement of imperial ideology that marks the transition from Ravenna's relative autonomy to a new position dominated both politically and ecclesiastically by Constantinople.

This revision of the mosaic decoration and re-dedication of the church in 547 fits with a policy enunciated in Constantinople to mark the recovery of Italy, Dalmatia, North Africa and the southern tip of Spain. Having sponsored the building of churches dedicated to the Mother of God in every major city in the east of the empire, Justinian now instructed his bishops to do the same in the West. Maximian not only completed the mosaics of San Vitale and at S. Apollinare in Classe but also built a large basilica dedicated to Mary in his home city of Pola, as well as several churches in Ravenna (Plate 45). This extensive programme of building was sponsored and partly funded by the imperial treasury on Justinian's orders. It drew on teams of technicians who had mastered the art of church building (often military architects and engineers attached to the army, which also provided the manpower), such as the *archiergatus* (master worker), whom Maximian chastised for not finishing a building. When the man complained of lack of materials, the archbishop immediately arranged supplies of 'plaster and tiles, rocks and bricks, stones and wood, columns and stone slabs, gravel and sand' – everything that was needed.[22]

The Basilica Eufrasiana at Parentium

The emperor's ambitious schemes to commemorate Mary are illustrated by another major basilica at Parentium (Poreč on the Adriatic coast of

Croatia), which was reincorporated into the empire by the imperial campaign of 536. Here Bishop Eufrasius constructed a new basilica church and episcopal complex in his see just north of Pola (Plate 43). While the date of his construction is not recorded, Eufrasius ordered a substantial part of the materials for his church directly from Constantinople – capitals, columns and stucco. Even the hooks to hold curtains over the main entrances, which are identical to those installed at Hagia Sophia, were made in the eastern capital. In Parentium a very particular episode in Mary's life is emphasized in two large mosaic panels that recount the Annunciation and the Visitation, where Elizabeth and Mary are shown as quite clearly pregnant (Plate 44). This highly unusual stress is also echoed in the choice of saints to adorn the triumphal arch – all of them female. Bishop Eufrasius clearly wished to distinguish his church from any others dedicated to the Mother of God.[23]

As at San Vitale, the founder commissioned the apse mosaic to reflect his association with the local martyr, St Maurus, as well as his patronage. Bishop Eufrasius is shown holding a model of the church, which he presents to the Virgin, flanked by angels, beside Maurus who holds his crown of martyrdom. The figures are presented in exactly the same fashion as in the apse at Ravenna. In addition, the remarkable similarity of marble, stucco and mosaic decoration at the Eufrasiana at Parentium and at San Vitale, particularly noticeable in the borders, frames and linking bands between the figural scenes, strongly suggests that both monuments were decorated by the same craftsmen.[24] Clearly, pattern books existed for many common features: the semi-circle of rays descending from a dove at the centre of the side chapels is found at the mausoleum of Galla Placidia as well as the Eufrasiana (and doubtless in numerous other churches). Similarly, the wavy bands in red and blue that form such striking divisions between scenes are copied all over Ravenna and at Parentium. The care given to the bishops' faces may also reflect the skills of expert mosaic setters who had worked for Maximian and Eufrasius.

While the mobility of such skilled mosaicists, masons and workers in marble revetment, inlay and stucco seems very likely, local teams in Parentium had been designing mosaic floors for the city's churches for centuries. The extensive use of mother-of-pearl in the exquisite inlaid panels that surround the bench (*synthronos*) on which the clergy sat in the apse indicate a local material not so widely used in Ravenna. And although invisible to the visitor, because they are behind the altar, tiny slivers of ivory embedded in some of these panels suggest access to the highly prized, rare material generally controlled by the emperor. Eufrasius thus exploited a wide range of sources in the creation of his basilica.[25]

The Template for Majesty

The imperial panels in San Vitale obviously constitute an exceptional and startling choice of subject, with the secular rulers accompanied by court ladies and soldiers within the most holy part of the church, flanking the altar table and close to the marble *synthronos*. In Constantinople Justinian and Theodora were celebrated in numerous mosaics and statues erected in public spaces as part of a developed scheme of imperial propaganda – for example, with Belisarius on the Chalke Gate of the palace, as we have seen – but never in churches there. Even in their foundations of Sts Sergius and Bacchus, St Eirene or Hagia Sophia, there were no portraits of them on the walls, and at St Catherine's monastery on Mt Sinai their names are preserved only on roof beams invisible from the ground. They barely travelled outside Constantinople and never went to Ravenna, so why were they commemorated in San Vitale?

Let us return to the building activity of Galla Placidia and Theoderic. The most unusual feature of Placidia's decoration of the church of S. Giovanni Evangelista was the portrayal of her ancestors and family members on the triumphal arch of the east end and in the apse. As I've already suggested, this insistent dynastic claim provoked Theoderic to celebrate his own family in the church of S. Apollinare Nuovo, where he was probably depicted in the apse wearing the imperial purple and shown seated in his palace under the inscription PALATIUM. Such depictions of rulers in churches were altogether a novelty in the fifth and sixth centuries. The first record of portraits of an imperial couple set up in a church in Constantinople were those of Leo I (457–74) and his wife, Verina, on an icon. They were depicted venerating an image of the Mother of God, together with the officials who had presented the relic of her garment to the Byzantine court in the 460s.[26] A century later, when Paul the *silentiarios* commemorated the repair of the dome of Hagia Sophia, he recorded images of Justinian and Theodora with Christ and the Virgin woven into an altar cloth.[27] But never full-length portraits of living rulers, with their entourages of soldiers, clerics and ladies-in-waiting, set in mosaic on the walls of a church.

The panels in San Vitale are an innovation, provoked by images of earlier rulers of the city to emphasize the new phase of direct imperial rule from Constantinople, which would last for two centuries. The church symbolizes the replacement of the Arian Gothic kingdom, incorporating both a Catholic and an imperial victory. Just as the Gothic king Theoderic outdid Galla Placidia and her basilica of S. Giovanni Evangelista, so now Justinian and Theodora outdid Theoderic. The eastern rulers' joint patronage of many other churches and philanthropic institutions was known in the West, and Belisarius would have confirmed the empress's tremendous power and influence in affairs of state.[28] Theodora's portrait within the holiest space flanking the altar nonetheless remained a unique example, unparalleled in Constantinople or any other church.

Today, although heavily restored, the depictions of Justinian and Theodora constitute the template of how to be truly imperial. They encapsulate a majestic power, marked by the regalia and clothing of the eastern emperors, which are so different from the togas or military uniforms worn by ancient Roman emperors. Throughout the medieval period the San Vitale mosaics were a reminder of the ruling couple who dominated the Mediterranean world in the sixth century, eliciting reactions that changed as political power assumed different forms. Charlemagne, who visited Ravenna three times, and his German successors in the second half of the tenth century, Otto I, Otto II and especially Otto III, contemplated their meaning in novel circumstances. Nearly 1,500 years later they continue to attract and amaze crowds and have made the names of Theodora and Justinian more familiar than any other Byzantines.

16

Narses and the Pragmatic Sanction

While bishops Victor and Maximian were completing the church of San Vitale in the 540s, the war between Gothic and imperial forces continued. Despite the loss of their capital in 540, the new Gothic leader Ildebadus defeated a major military contingent near Treviso later that year. When he was murdered in 541, his nephew Totila (also called Toutilas, Badua and Baudilas) took his place. Under this young energetic general, the Goths began to reverse all Belisarius' victories (Plate 22).[1] Their tenacity extended the war from 540 to 552, contributing to terrible destruction of agriculture (and the ruin of the farmers who grew crops, harvested olives and grapes and maintained food supplies), of fortifications, bridges, aqueducts and roads, and of many lives.

Constantinople had clearly not anticipated such a vigorous revival of Gothic power and Justinian had not arranged an adequate restoration of imperial administration in the reconquered regions of Italy. One reason for this failure was a catastrophic development in the East, where Chosroes, the Shah of Persia, broke the 'Perpetual Peace' and invaded the empire in the spring of 540. He marched across the eastern provinces, capturing major cities including the great centre of Antioch, and bathed in the Mediterranean.[2] This symbol of his extension of Persian control to the coast of the Roman sea had to be countered. But in the summer of 542 the first outbreak of a devastating plague took its toll on conqueror and conquered alike. The movement of this sixth-century 'Black Death', from the south-east corner of the Mediterranean right across the Roman world, can be traced in records of many thousands dead and entire villages abandoned. It was carried by fleas clinging to rats that had travelled on ships from the Far East, bringing a deadly poison to all human life. Once established in Egypt the pestilence spread rapidly throughout the Roman world.[3] In Constantinople, the living were too few to bury the dead, and the emperor himself suffered the swellings that usually predicted death. Unlike many, he survived. But Justinian was hardly in a position to reinforce the recent imperial conquest of Italy while Chosroes remained in control of large regions of the empire in the East and the army was devastated by the plague. He concentrated what forces he had on preserving power in Egypt, the most fertile and prosperous province that provided the grain for Constantinople's bread supply, and left Italy to fend for itself.[4] The Persian campaign was a harbinger of the even more successful challenge of Islam.

After the reconquest of North Africa, Belisarius had appointed men on whom he could rely, often his own commanding officers, to leading positions within the newly imposed administration, and it seems reasonable to assume that he did the same in Italy before he left Ravenna in June 540. Among the junior military leaders who had served under him, several remained in charge of Italian garrisons in key areas: Conon in Naples, Cyprian (Perugia), Bessas (possibly Spoleto), Justin (Florence), Vitalian (Venetia) and Constantianus (Ravenna).[5] But their presence was not enough to secure all the territory that had been reoccupied. In 542, Constantinople appointed Maximinus Praetorian Prefect for Italy with overall military responsibility, but he never ventured further than Syracuse in Sicily. When he eventually sent the fleet to Naples to confront Totila, it was destroyed in a storm. This remarkable failure was not corrected by immediate reinforcements, partly because the eastern capital was in the grip of the pestilence that killed so many, but partly because the Gothic king had his own fleet, which consolidated his control over southern Italy.[6]

Within Ravenna, now the provincial capital of Italy, officials appointed from Constantinople jostled for the best facilities and most prestigious accommodation. Among civilian officials sent to Italy, Procopius only mentions Alexander, the *logothetes* (controller) of state finances (known as 'Snips' from his skill in clipping gold coins), who was condemned for his meanness in settling military claims for compensation, and making unreasonable tax demands. The introduction of imperial taxation was one of the consequences of Belisarius' campaign and widely resented. A disastrous shift from the victorious entry into Ravenna in 540 to military defeats two years later may be attributed both to inadequate armed support and to Snips's niggardly attitude to pay, which reduced the willingness of the garrisons of Ravenna and other cities to fight. His reputation was well known, as Totila reminded the Senate when he compared the good deeds of Theoderic and Amalasuintha to the new governors from the East: 'You know full well what guests and friends you have found them, if you have any recollection of the public accounts of Alexander.'[7] Procopius also records Snips's failure to co-operate with Constantianus, when the two shared the leadership of a large force sent to capture Verona from the Goths. They failed to agree a strategy, which led to a major defeat for the imperial forces. From Ravenna Constantianus wrote to Justinian complaining about the lack of reinforcements. While the ineffectual praetorian prefect Maximinus refused to leave Sicily and 'Snips' imposed his rule in Ravenna, the new Gothic leader rallied his forces to regain many of the key fortresses of southern Italy.[8]

In this indeterminate situation, the deadly pestilence spread throughout the Mediterranean world, although Italy does not appear to have suffered such dramatic losses as the East. Agnellus alludes to its effects in Ravenna under Bishop Victor who lived through these years, mentioning pestilence, hunger and strife and great dissention between Christians, as if the world was about to end. Quoting the Book of Revelation, he describes the signs and wonders and unnatural phenomena that heralded the Apocalypse, claiming that evil men had destroyed what Victor had achieved.[9]

The Final Defeat of the Goths

In 544 Justinian had to send Belisarius back to counter the Gothic threat. When he arrived in Ravenna, via Salona and Pola, Totila was besieging Rome. Since the imperial general's own forces were quite inadequate to the task of relieving the city, he attempted to win over any Goths who would change sides. But, in the protracted war from 544–9, Totila captured Rome and reoccupied most of Italy and Sicily, thus reversing the balance of power. Belisarius' campaign was ineffective and he was recalled to Constantinople. In 552 Justinian provided more substantial funding for Narses, an Armenian general, to resume the anti-Gothic campaign. Narses was a eunuch who had held the court position of *praepositus* (treasurer) and had served briefly under Belisarius before 540. He was a remarkably skilful military leader who would have a major influence in shaping imperial administration in the West for the next twenty years.[10] With the help of John, another commander familiar with the region, he initially outwitted the Gothic forces sent to oppose his entry to Italy at the Julian Alps by taking the coastal route around the head of the Adriatic, using the small boats of local inhabitants of the Venetia to construct pontoon bridges across the many river outlets that normally made the route impossible. In May/June 552 these troops appeared unexpectedly at Ravenna, having avoided the established road through Verona.[11]

Late in June 552, before what was to be the decisive battle of the campaign, Totila gave a prolonged bravura display of horsemanship in front of the imperial troops, making his horse prance and dance while he threw his javelin up and caught it in a demonstration of military skills.[12] At this clash at Busta Gallorum in the Apennines, the Gothic forces were routed and their leader was fatally wounded; in August Justinian received Totila's jewelled cap and cloak as proof of his death. Although the Goths elected another king, Narses defeated them again the following year and marched in victory to Ravenna, to be welcomed by Archbishop Maximian. He then proceeded to Rome, which he made his base of operations. After eighteen years of highly destructive warfare the provinces of Italy had been won back into imperial control. But Justinian had little to celebrate. The war had totally disrupted the civilian population, administration and, most critically, agricultural production, which made it very difficult to collect the regular taxation destined for Constantinople.

The Pragmatic Sanction

Nothing daunted, in August 554 the emperor issued an edict in Latin now known as the Pragmatic Sanction, to rebuild a working government in Italy based in the imperial capital, Ravenna.[13] Although it was directed to Antiochus, the newly appointed praetorian prefect, as well as Narses, the victorious commander took precedence, following the model of imperial administration recently restored in North Africa. This arrangement, with priority given to military needs and considerable overlap between the military and civilian spheres, broke the strict separation traditional in Roman administration and took a clear step towards their fusion that would characterize all governments of the early medieval West. The Pragmatic Sanction was primarily designed to restore land ownership, which had been disrupted by the long war. It insisted on the validity of laws issued and grants made by Athalaric, Amalasuintha and Theodahad, but not those of the usurper Totila – 'utterly abominable', 'of criminal memory' – as well as concessions and grants made by Theodora 'of pious memory' (she had died in 548). This effort to maintain legal ownership of property and livestock encouraged landowners who had fled, like Cassiodorus, to return to Italy. Those who had bought or sold property under the Goths would not be threatened by restitution, and all property owners would continue to pay the basic land tax. The effort to reaffirm conditions that existed before the time of Totila was attributed to a petition of Pope Vigilius, who was still in Constantinople in 554.

In addition, Justinian ordered the circulation of his Codex, originally in Latin, and subsequent new laws (*Novellae*), written in Greek and translated into Latin, to regulate the judiciary; the maintenance of courts of justice; the payment of teachers, rhetoricians, doctors and lawyers (according to the practice of Theoderic); the use of correct weights and measures, as issued 'to the most blessed pope or the most eminent Senate', for payments in cash or in kind; avoidance of double taxation; the return of slaves to their owners, and of virgins dedicated to God to their monasteries or churches. Senators were guaranteed the right to travel to the emperor's court and to go to their estates in Italy for as long as they needed. A specific set of regulations covered the maintenance of public works in Rome, relating to the channel of the Tiber, the Forum, the port and sewers, which were to be financed from taxes assigned. The city was to be governed by a military duke (*dux*), a subordinate of the praetorian prefect based in Ravenna. Since Justinian had abolished the consulate in 541, and the Senate had been greatly reduced by the flight of so many distinguished members to Constantinople during the war, the bishop of Rome was obliged to assume greater responsibility for the city's well-being.[14]

This was part of a system of much closer governmental co-operation with the Church, drawing particularly on the assistance of bishops. Justinian ruled that bishops and local notables, landowners and inhabitants were to select governors of the reconquered provinces to apply the law justly and legally, and if these men were ever found to have exacted excess taxes, or to have used inaccurate weights or light-weight *solidi* to cause losses, they were to provide compensation out of their own resources.[15] This was another major innovation. Previously provincial governors had been nominated by the highest authority (emperor or praetorian prefect) and had been moved from one region to another, rarely serving in their own provinces; government had been highly centralized. Now much power was devolved to local elites who could select governors from among their number. These men were to be appointed without paying anything for the office and were charged with the collection and transfer of public taxes to the imperial administration without extorting any additional payments.

While Rome remained the home of the Senate and probably the chief centre of legal instruction, Ravenna was confirmed as the capital of the reconquered Italian provinces and the base for restored civilian administration. Around six hundred officials would be required to run such a centralized government, and each senior figure would have his own *officium*, a team of subordinates, secretaries and scribes.[16] The influx of trained officials and their entourages, which probably brought additional influence from Constantinople, together with an increase in the military establishment, must have led to a considerable expansion in the size of the city. In addition, regulations that promoted bishops to replace city defenders, *defensores civitatis*, and other laws addressed specifically to church leaders rather than military officials, increased ecclesiastical authority.[17]

In spite of Justinian's insistence that the selection of good governors could reinstate imperial administration in its best possible form, the Pragmatic Sanction of 554, and subsequent rulings, failed to address the underlying problem caused by so many years of warfare. The plague of 542–3 had also taken a toll on the survivors. How were landowners and tenants to pay their taxes when agricultural production had been so severely disturbed that they had no basic resources, crops, oil or wine, to sell, when urban life had been disrupted by sieges, many inhabitants displaced, and castles, bridges and roads destroyed to limit enemy movement? During the war soldiers had regularly complained about the lack of pay and were still roaming the countryside looking for sustenance. Even those who had returned to their homes and could begin to cultivate their land often had no money. Many aristocratic families had spent much of their fortunes during the military upheavals, supporting the population during city sieges, such as the long siege of Rome in 545–6, and would have exhausted their reserves.

The same problem may be observed in many urban centres, where the mechanisms of taxation levied by local councils to support local defences, military needs and court expenditure were reinstated by the Pragmatic Sanction. Whether Justinian intended it or not, a conservative tradition maintained by local scribes prolonged methods of resolving property quarrels and recording sales and gifts with only slight changes to the formulae employed. There was an underlying shift to a more local authority, in the person of the provincial governor elected by bishops and notables, and military men who acquired land assumed greater prominence in almost all parts of the post-Roman world. Ravenna was an exception in that it became the seat of the imperially appointed ruler with overall authority throughout Italy.

But the city had experienced some of the upheavals and disorders of the war period, which surface in muddled form in Agnellus. He appears to have copied material from a chronicle such as the poorly preserved *Annals of Ravenna* (where information was recorded and dated by year) that involved the vigorous punishment of a group of Manichaeans, heretics according to the established Church, who were discovered in the city. They were thrown out and died in the *Fossa Sconii* next to the river. Further omens, visions and terrifying events, such as a red sign in the sky on 11 November, may be related to the year 560, as the entry immediately precedes Agnellus' note about the death of Pope Pelagius on 3 March 561. This red sign (a star or comet?) persuaded the citizens to put marks on their homes so that they would be recognized at the end of times. It was associated with a series of visions, followed by the claim that the people of Ravenna made war on those of Verona and conquered them on 20 July, possibly an allusion to Narses's siege of that city and its eventual capture in 561. Another comet that appeared between August and October, together with red signs in the sky and the burning of the town of Fano and the camp of Cesena, is associated with the death of Justinian in 565.[18]

Living in Ravenna in the Mid-Sixth Century

Thanks to the survival of papyri records from the mid-sixth century onwards, the *curia* of Ravenna can be observed perpetuating city administration, which seems to have survived longer in Italy than elsewhere. In 552 the will of George, a silk merchant, son of a silk merchant from Antioch, was re-entered in the municipal archive, George signing in Greek letters. On this occasion the council met in Classis in the presence of the praetorian prefect, Flavius Aurelianus, with Bonifatius Pompulius serving as magistrate, Andreas Melminius, defender of the city, and Johannes the *proemptor* (agent) as witness. Like many local inhabitants, George donates all his property to the church of Ravenna. In 564 Germana, *clarissima femina* and widow of Collictus, drew up a charter appointing Gratianus, subdeacon of the church of Ravenna, as tutor of her young son Stefanus.[19] A fascinating inventory of his inheritance, written by Johannes, one of the city's scribes (*tabellio civitatis Ravennae*), was appended to the charter with a detailed description of all the gold and silver (in coin and objects such as silver spoons), household furnishings (carpets, cushions, bed coverings, kitchen ware), tools, clothes and jewellery, plus portions of three houses, in Ravenna and outside the city in Bologna and Cornelia, which had been sold on Collictus' death. The slaves Guderit and Ranihilda had been freed (the latter now deceased), and Guderit had received an impressive list of clothing: a silk tunic, a decorated shirt, an old wool coat, a cloak and a cloth (*mappa*) worth one silver *siliqua*, all stored in a locked chest. The inventory of the clothing provides a startling example of the sumptuous dress of high-ranking inhabitants of Ravenna: a silk shirt in red and green (worth three and a half gold *solidi*), a green silk tunic with decoration (one and half *solidi*), a silk tunic with short sleeves, and linen trousers.[20] Their brightly coloured garments echo those worn by the three kings depicted in S. Apollinare Nuovo as Persian or the ladies-in-waiting in San Vitale, and the survival of silks in contrasting colours confirms the same appreciation.

Germana's petition was accepted and entered in the council's records to ensure that Stefanus would in due course receive his inheritance. His male guardian, the subdeacon Gratianus, signed with a cross, indicating that he was illiterate. Other witnesses included Stefanus, *vir devotus*, and the secretary of the prefect (*scriniarius gloriosae sedis*), probably Pamphronius named in several documents. The civilian administration of the city and the council's regular activity clearly continued despite the devastation of warfare.

Narses and the Military Administration of Italy

While bishops and local elites were charged with the selection and installation of provincial governors, Narses tried to impose an effective military occupation, sending dukes to the remaining cities and stationing troops in the fortress garrisons that defended the borders of Italy.[21] In 553–4 the imperial administration was challenged by the Franks, who with their allies the Alemanni and Heruli, attacked unwalled cities in northern Italy and ravaged the countryside. This brought Narses to Ravenna, where he presumably occupied the palace that had been expanded and redecorated by Theoderic and his successors. While he was there the Gothic defender of Totila's treasure came to Classis to hand over the keys to Cumae (south of Naples), where the accumulated booty had been secured. Narses then returned to Rome to organize a final campaign against the invaders. In 555 Narses attended the inauguration of Pelagius as pope, who repeatedly asked him for military assistance. He restored at least one bridge destroyed by Totila, the *Pons Salarius*, commemorated in two inscriptions and a parapet with pilasters decorated with Greek crosses. In gratitude for the assistance of the Veneti, who facilitated his unusual route into Italy, he dedicated churches at the head of the Adriatic (on what became the Rivus Altus, much later the centre of Venice), and in Vicenza, but there is no evidence of his patronage in the imperial capital. In 561 Verona's was the last Gothic garrison to capitulate.

Despite Narses's efforts, the disruption caused by prolonged military activity made it very difficult for imperial officials to reimpose order. Newcomers vied with the settled populations in all the western regions previously part of the Roman empire. Africa too was threatened by many revolts. As late as 565 Narses had to put down a rebellion in northern Italy led by Sindual, a *magister militum* previously associated with an invasion of the Heruli. Was this a band of wandering mercenaries or another group of discharged soldiers without land, homes and families? Narses defeated the revolt and 'hung Sindual from a lofty beam', according to Paul the deacon.[22]

In his efforts to establish firm administration, Narses appears to have generated opposition among some members of Roman society. In

568 Emperor Justin II received letters that denounced the general, accusing him of 'subjecting the Romans to slavery', and recalled him to Constantinople.[23] The general went off to Naples as if to sail back to the East, but when Pope John III learned of this, he insisted on Narses returning to Rome. When he finally died at the great age of ninety-five, perhaps in 574, his body was shipped back to Constantinople in a lead coffin to be buried in the monastery he had founded in Bithynia.[24] Justin II and Empress Sophia took part in this grand funeral. In his burial, as in his life, Narses embodies the unity of the Roman world, in which the Armenian eunuch had served with such distinction in the western provinces while preparing his own tomb in an eastern setting, where he would be commemorated in perpetuity by monastic services on behalf of his soul. But he left Italy in a very unstable condition.

17

Archbishop Maximian, bulwark of the West

At the end of the war, Italy was economically exhausted. But it was also caught up in a different struggle that weakened the entire Christian world – a long theological controversy that came to a head in 553 when Justinian summoned the Fifth Universal Council of the Church to Constantinople. His aim was to gain ecclesiastical confirmation of the heretical nature of three particular texts by Theodore of Mopsuestia, Theodoret of Cyrrhus and Ibas of Edessa (which came to be known as the Three Chapters).[1] Justinian hoped that by identifying them as dangerously close to the writings of Nestorios, condemned at the Council of Ephesus in 431, he could clarify the precise form of the union of the human and divine natures of Christ, and thus bring those Christians who maintained the theological doctrine of Christ's one nature (*mia physis*) back into communion. And he wished to impose this interpretation throughout the Roman world, despite its doctrinal and regional tensions, emphasizing how his sole authority mirrored the Christian belief in one God – one faith, one empire.[2]

Western opposition to this development was based on the firm belief that Pope Leo I had contributed the defining statement on the natures of Christ in his letter (*Tomus*) read at the Council of Chalcedon in 451. Ibas and Theodoret had also participated in that meeting without provoking any hostile comment. Bishops of Rome, including Pope Vigilius (537–55), therefore considered anything that modified the decisions taken at Chalcedon as threatening to the true faith, and against papal authority. This opposition prompted Justinian to arrange for Vigilius to be escorted from Rome to Constantinople, via Patras where he consecrated Maximian as archbishop of Ravenna. While the pope spent the next eight years in the eastern capital, the newly appointed archbishop brought the conflict over the Three Chapters to Ravenna.

After much negotiation, increasingly harsh treatment and even imprisonment in his own Constantinopolitan palace, Pope Vigilius eventually agreed to endorse the condemnation of Theodore of Mopsuestia, while preserving the integrity of the Council of Chalcedon. But he refused to participate in the Fifth Oecumenical Council, which met in May 553 under the leadership of Patriarch Eutychios (552–65), with representatives of the patriarchs of Alexandria, Antioch and Jerusalem. Officially, Rome was the most honoured among these five patriarchates whose agreement was essential for council decisions to be binding throughout the *oikoumene*, the whole Christian world.[3] Although the Fifth Council met without Pope Vigilius, it duly condemned the three texts selected by the emperor. However, seven bishops from Africa and many of the nine bishops from Illyricum refused to accept its decrees. After months of violent treatment, Vigilius finally accepted the council, condemned the Three Chapters on his own terms, and was allowed to return to Rome. But he only got as far as Syracuse, where he died on 7 June 555.[4]

The coincidence of a deteriorating military situation in the West, as Narses struggled to curtail Gothic and Herulian forces, and what proved to be an unpopular and ultimately divisive theological decision greatly reduced effective imperial control. Bishops in Aquileia and several African cities immediately repudiated the council of 553, opening a schism with both Constantinople and Rome. In contrast, Archbishop Maximian of Ravenna, chosen and promoted by Justinian, upheld the council in co-operation with military officials and, later, with the new pope, Pelagius (556–61).[5] His role may be illustrated by the consecration of Vitalis as the new bishop of Milan to replace Datius, who had accompanied Vigilius to Constantinople and died there in 552. Because Milan was still controlled by the Goths, the man Justinian had selected could not be installed in his see. Instead, an imperial military official escorted Vitalis to Ravenna where the ceremony took place, and he probably died soon after for he was buried in the church of San Vitale.[6]

Archbishop Maximian

According to Agnellus, Maximian was a scholar and writer who had travelled in the East, visited Alexandria when Patriarch Timothy IV

(517–35) was ruling the church there, and Constantinople, where he made himself known to Justinian. He wrote the *Histories*, twelve books in one volume, warmly recommended by Agnellus who quotes a passage describing the rioting that accompanied rival patriarchs in the Egyptian capital and an earthquake that caused the city of Anazarbas in Cilicia to collapse, reportedly with the loss of 30,000 lives. Maximian had new copies made of the two Bibles that were still in use, as well as missals 'for the whole cycle of the year and for all the saints'. He studied the biblical text and amended it where he found improvements in St Augustine's comments or Jerome's text of the Gospels. Agnellus quotes the colophon of the Bible that records the archbishop's cautious emendations to the text, so that the text 'should not be corrupted by illiterate or evil scribes'.[7]

In addition, Maximian may well have written the *Life* of Apollinaris, supposedly a contemporary of St Peter and the founder and first bishop of the Christian community of Ravenna. The 'invention' of the saint, who is portrayed as a soldier martyred in the reign of Vespasian, could have been promoted by Maximian. In this way the archbishop enhanced the city's standing, just as Ambrose had raised the status of Milan. When he dedicated the huge new basilica at Classis to St Apollinaris, Maximian could cite this *Life* as proof that Ravenna had also nurtured a great hero of earliest Christian times.[8] In the apse of the basilica, moreover, the local saint is clearly depicted as a bishop wearing his episcopal pallium, participating in the liturgy (Plate 51). Agnellus noted that Maximian's writings had been taken to Rome, but none now survives.[9]

Maximian visited the eastern capital in 547 to make sure that the forests of Vistrum in Istria should belong to the church of Ravenna in perpetuity; this was confirmed by Justinian. On another occasion he obtained building material in Constantinople, and also tried to remove the body of the Apostle Andrew. In this he was foiled by the emperor who insisted that the relic remain in the Queen City, pointing out that as St Peter and St Andrew were brothers, so Rome and Constantinople were sister cities, and it was appropriate for each of them to have one of the apostolic brothers. Maximian nevertheless managed to remove the saint's beard, which he took back to Ravenna together with other relics obtained with the emperor's permission.[10] In the ninth century, when Ravenna was firmly under Roman control, Agnellus wrote that if

Maximian had obtained the body of St Andrew and buried it in the city, 'the Roman popes would not thus have subjugated us' – implying that with an apostolic relic to rival St Peter, Ravenna would have been able to resist Rome more effectively.[11]

The apparently close relations between the two men and their meetings 'when he and the emperor both had grey hairs',[12] have led some scholars to suggest that the emperor may have rewarded Maximian with the ivory throne – probably for display rather than use – that survives today in the Archiepiscopal Museum of Ravenna (Plate 36). On the front, Maximian's monogram is centred above a row of five large rectangular plaques that depict St John the Baptist flanked by the four Evangelists holding their Gospels. Within the decorative scrolls above and below these figures, animals and birds accompany two peacocks, and two lions and other wild beasts prance among the flowers and leaves. Although twelve of the original plaques are lost, thirty-two, of different sizes but all of elephant tusk, are used to form the sides and back of the throne, carved with scenes from the Old and New Testaments (many from the life of Joseph, which prefigured that of Christ).

Alexandria was known as the centre where such work was produced, and similar thrones are recorded as gifts. Cyril of Alexandria is reported to have given several as bribes to win favour after the Council of Ephesus.[13] If Justinian had this exceptionally expensive, high-status throne made for Maximian, perhaps he also financed some of the building that the archbishop organized both within Ravenna and in Pola. Procopius' account of the emperor's vast programme of construction (the *Buildings*) records numerous churches dedicated to the Virgin Mother of God and other saints in very distant parts of the empire, from Sinai in Egypt to Jerusalem and Justiniana Prima in the northern Balkans. Huge sums were also expended on secular buildings: fortresses, bridges, charitable institutions for the sick, elderly, and widows and orphans, and inns along the major highways where the imperial post carriers, merchants and other travellers could stay overnight.[14] But Procopius' description does not cover the western regions. The throne could have been an acknowledgment of Maximian's support for imperial theology.

Surviving inscriptions, however, make it clear that Maximian cooperated with Julianus the banker and Julianus' relative Bacauda. The two men helped to finance the most famous churches of the city, San

Vitale and S. Apollinare in Classe, and another dedicated to the Arch-angel Michael *ad Frigiselo* (now S. Michele *in Africisco*, which survives only in part). Thanks to Agnellus, we know the text in the narthex of San Vitale that records Julianus as the builder, the date of Maximian's consecration of the church (19 April 547), and the attribution of the original initiative to Bishop Ecclesius. On the imperial panels, Agnellus merely notes 'the image of this same Maximian and of the emperor and empress are beautifully created in mosaic'.[15] He also quotes other inscriptions from S. Apollinare, consecrated by Maximian on 9 May 549, and from S. Michele.[16] In none of the three churches connected with Julianus is there any mention of an imperial contribution, such as that recorded in inscriptions from Sinai or Jerusalem, for instance.

In addition to the completion of churches already partly con-structed, Maximian built a new church dedicated to St Stephen, the first Christian martyr and deacon, not far from the Ovilian Gate. Here the archbishop installed relics of many saints and set up his own image in the vaults of the apse 'in multicoloured mosaic surrounded by wonderful glasswork', with a dedicatory inscription that recorded its consecration on 11 December 550. He added side chapels, *monas-teria*, with 'new gold mosaics and various other stones fixed in plaster', and his own name carved above the capitals of the columns.[17] Other construction work attributed to Maximian includes the church of S. Maria *in Formosa* in Pola (Plate 45) and a house for the rector of that church; the completion of the Tricollis chapel, where he was depicted with his predecessors, and the church of S. Probus, where Max-imian preserved the body of the saint with aromatics and decorated the façade with mosaic images of Sts Probus, Eleuchadius and Calocerus.[18] He also replaced the old wooden columns in the church of S. Andrea, not far from the Ursiana, by new ones of Proconnesian marble.

In keeping with episcopal traditions Maximian put his own image on many of the liturgical objects he commissioned, such as two special vessels to hold chrism (holy oil), one identified by an inscription with his name, which survived to Agnellus' time. He provided four altar cloths, one of fine linen with the whole story of the Saviour embroi-dered on it, which was used in the Ursiana cathedral on the day of Epiphany. Agnellus says it had unrivalled, life-like images of Maxim-ian and his predecessors, as well as of beasts and birds.[19] Another altar cloth displayed all his predecessors woven in gold, and at least one of the last two cloths was decorated with pearls and had biblical inscriptions woven into it. The archbishop had also ordered a very heavy gold cross decorated with gems to hold a fragment of the True Cross, one of the many relics he had collected.[20]

Maximian was also associated with a secular building, the barracks for a regiment called the *bandus primus* (First Flag or Banner), built with tiles stamped with an inscription, 'Maximian, bishop of Ravenna'. It was not far from the Golden Milestone and must have been erected at the time, if not actually at the instigation, of the archbishop.[21] It serves as a reminder of the pride rulers and patrons took in the production of building material in Ravenna. This regiment, *numerus*, was one of several military bodies attached to the city that served as guards and were identified by their distinctive banners and flags. At the beginning of the eighth century there were twelve cohorts known by similar names: First Banner, Second Banner, New Banner and so on.[22]

Agnellus concludes his account of Maximian's life with a fascinating description of the transfer of the bones from his grave next to the altar of the church of S. Andreas to a more elevated central position in that church. This reburial took place under Archbishop Petronax in about 833. Agnellus supervised the opening of the sarcophagus, which was full of water, and the removal of the bones which were placed on the altar in a shroud and sealed by Petronax with his ring. The bones, which were all complete 'except one tooth on the right side', were then washed in choice wine, embalmed in spices and replaced in the sarcophagus with due ceremony. Agnellus also measured all the water that was removed from the tomb in little bronze vessels: it filled 115 of these *siculi*, as they were known in common parlance, full of the water made holy by contact with the bones. He says that the incident provoked much fear and trembling 'as if blessed Maximian himself stood in our sight', perhaps because of the disturbance of his tomb.[23] The first archbishop of the city clearly remained a significant presence in ninth-century Ravenna; a prolific builder, a scholar and writer, who dominated his community for eleven years until his death in 557, had visited Constantinople several times and spoken to Justinian himself.

Maximian had also upheld the decisions of the Fifth Oecumenical Council, against persistent opposition from the bishops of Illyricum and Africa who had attended and denounced it. They in turn inspired church leaders in northern Italy, particularly those of Milan and

Aquileia, to omit any mention of the emperor or patriarch of Constantinople in their daily prayers. Pope Pelagius was horrified by their refusal, which put them out of communion with the entire Church, and considered them 'schismatics, making sedition in the church'.[24] He particularly criticized Paulinus (or Paulus), patriarch of Aquileia, who set about the creation of an independent church in the northern Adriatic. By 559 the quarrel over theological texts had become a more political one as the pope demanded that Valerius, *patricius*, arrest Paulinus and send him to Constantinople to be judged. He also asked Archbishop Agnellus of Ravenna (557–65) to select and consecrate a reliable replacement to head the dissident Aquileians.[25] Although the pope had accused some of his opponents of very serious crimes (murder in the case of Eufrasius, who may have been bishop of Parentium), no secular officials took action against them until 566, when Narses arrested the bishop of Altinum. Opposition to the Council strengthened into a distinct local loyalty that fractured ecclesiastical unity without clarifying any theological division.

At the head of the Adriatic in Venetia and Istria, this sustained resistance extended the schism for many years, weakening the Christian presence in regions that had already been disrupted by many years of military violence. Despite efforts to find a solution that would reunite all Christian bishops in a shared definition of belief, several regions of northern Italy and Africa remained in outright opposition. While the western imperial capital benefitted from the presence of military leaders, in Rome the pope complained repeatedly of the lack of support in imposing the correct theology. Observing the turbulence in Italy, a hostile Lombard force based in Pannonia (beyond the north-east frontier of the Danube) decided in 568 to launch an invasion, a military development that was to have momentous consequences for Ravenna.

18

Archbishop Agnellus and the seizure of the Arian churches

After the death of Maximian in 557, the Ravenna clergy elected a local priest, Agnellus, as their archbishop. Unlike most church leaders, this Agnellus, who came from a wealthy noble landowning family, had pursued a military career, married and had a daughter. After the death of his wife, he decided to devote himself to God, was ordained deacon by Bishop Ecclesius in the 520s and served as priest of the church of the martyr Agatha. He occupied a house attached to the building, which survived into the ninth century.[1] Agnellus had therefore lived through the reign of Theoderic, the long period of the Gothic wars and the arrival of imperial troops under Belisarius in 540. When Justinian ordered the transfer of all Arian properties to the control of the Catholic community, he was governing the church of Ravenna.

The precedent for this elimination of Arian observance lay in the edict of 535 directed to the churches in North Africa, which insisted that all property there, taken over by the Arians during the period of Vandal rule, should be returned to the orthodox, that is, the Catholic church. And any remaining Arians, Donatists, Jews and pagans, now branded as heretics, were not permitted to hold public office, or to celebrate their own religious ceremonies.[2] Despite lingering loyalty to Arian beliefs, the Vandal ecclesiastical hierarchy in North Africa appears to have disintegrated with Gelimer's kingdom and the Catholic clergy resumed control. When Justinian considered how to restore his imperial theology to the conquered areas of Italy, he had a model that had recently worked. But the Arian churches in Italy had been independently endowed by the Goths, who had not taken over Catholic churches in the same way as the Vandals. Between 557 and 565, however, the emperor sent a new instruction to transfer all Arian ecclesiastical properties to the Catholic churches of Italy.

As a good antiquarian, Agnellus the historian quotes from this imperial letter preserved in the city's archive, which praised 'the holy mother church of Ravenna . . . the true mother, truly orthodox'.[3] Archbishop Agnellus duly supervised the process in which nine churches of the Arians, four outside the city (St Eusebius, St George, St Sergius in Classis and St Zeno in Caesarea), and five within, including the cathedral and baptistery, were all re-dedicated to the Catholic rite.[4] Although the process was called 'reconciliation', probably in hopes of reconciling the Gothic Arian Christians to the Catholic definitions of the majority, it effectively integrated them by non-violent means: the confiscation of their churches and property, and laws which denied them the right to make wills and thus pass their inheritance to their children.

S. Apollinare Nuovo

In Theoderic's Golden Church of Christ the Saviour the forced conversion can be traced in the major changes to the Palace mosaic that removed images of the king.[5] All the courtiers were replaced by curtains inserted between the columns, though some outstretched hands remained (Plate 12). On the opposite side of the nave, at the harbour of Classis, the feet of four figures standing in front of the port were left behind, and even these have now been removed (Plate 13).[6] The most serious alteration concerned the replacement of Theoderic and his wife Audefleda from their leading positions each at the head of a procession of saints. St Martin of Tours, to whom the church was re-dedicated, became leader of the male procession, while St Euphemia was set at the head of the women.

The choice of St Martin, a Christian hero of opposition to Arianism, was another symbol of the domination of the majority faith.[7] St Euphemia's prominence derives from her association with the Council of Chalcedon that met in her church in 451. Among the twenty-one female martyrs that follow her, Agatha, Agnese, Cecilia, Valeria, Vincenza, Perpetua and Felicity, Lucia, Daria and Eugenia had cults at Ravenna; the others, Pelagia, Crispina, Eulalia, Giustina, Anastasia, Emerenziana, Paolina, Vittoria, Anatolia, Cristina and Sabina, have no specifically local connections. A similar emphasis on female saints and martyrs is clear from sixth-century monuments at Rome and at Parentium on the eastern coast of the Adriatic, close to Pola, where Euphemia again leads a group of six.[8] While the presence of so many female saints at S. Apollinare is not exceptional, the equality of the two processions, male and female, that advance towards the East, is most unusual.

In addition, much of the northern wall of the church suffered damage, which meant that some mosaic figures had to be restored in the nineteenth century. In recreating the three kings, restorers were aided by Agnellus the historian, who provides a fascinating analysis of their costumes. The colour of their clothing is related to their gifts, each highly symbolic. Thus, Caspar offers gold and wears a reddish garment that signifies marriage; Balthasar carries frankincense and is dressed in yellow, which signifies virginity, while Melchior, who brings myrrh, has a multicoloured garment that signifies penitence. The gifts also have important associations, of course: gold represents regal wealth, frankincense the priesthood (or God), and myrrh death, all symbols of Christ. And for Agnellus the number three is critical, since it stands for the Trinity of God the Father, the Son and the Holy Spirit.[9] Today, visitors to the church may be more surprised by the unusual decoration of the trousers worn by the Magi. These very fancy striped and spotted garments are, in fact, the only original bits of the mosaic, and they are very similar to the trousers of the three kings in the mid-fifth-century church of S. Maria Maggiore in Rome. The Magi from the East were portrayed in startlingly coloured 'oriental' attire, complete with Phrygian caps, that became a tradition reproduced in Ravenna.

Archbishop Agnellus also put up a mosaic of himself with Emperor Justinian, possibly in imitation of the imperial panel in San Vitale, or by transforming an earlier image of Theoderic with his Arian bishop. He thus commemorated his role in the conversion of Arian churches and baptisteries for Catholic use, and a part of this mosaic may survive in the portrait of the emperor currently mounted on the west wall of the church of S. Apollinare Nuovo, labelled IUSTINIAN. It was restored in the nineteenth century, when the inscription was added. But the imperial portrait in S. Apollinare is much fatter than the one in San Vitale, with a heavy jaw and a large and awkward upper arm and is altogether less imposing. Some historians have suggested it may be of Theoderic, who founded the church, rather than Justinian, but it is very unlikely that a portrait of the Arian king would have survived the 'reconciliation'. Neither does the image resemble the portrait of Theo-deric preserved on the Senigallia medallion where the king wears his long hair and clipped moustache in typically Gothic fashion (Plate 16).[10]

The local Gothic communities that used to worship in these churches are very visible in the papyrus records, for example a document of 553 that records the donation of silver, land, jewels and clothes by Ranilo and her husband Felithanc (not obviously Roman names) to the church of Ravenna. She had inherited this from her father Aderit and wished to share her fortune with her half-brother, Ademunt also called Andreas, an illegitimate son of her father. Her gifts comprised 50 lbs of silver and an income of 100 *solidi*, plus properties in Formidiana, Urbino and Lucca and elsewhere (some places quite distant from Ravenna). In an echo of the war-time disruption, Ranilo insisted that the city's procura-tors should find and bring back all the slaves who had run away 'in this barbaric time'. It implies, nonetheless, that in this case a Gothic family had also weathered the period of war despite the flight of slaves and agricultural workers.[11]

It is also evidence of the devotion of this family to the Catholic church rather than the Gothic community of the city. Ranilo had already given up her Arian belief and no longer supported the Gothic clergy, who had been so disadvantaged by the imperial reconquest; her half-brother Ademunt had adopted a more Roman name in the form Andreas. This is a common naming pattern among Goths who con-verted to the dominant Christian faith.[12] Earlier, the Gothic nobleman Gudila had abandoned his Arian beliefs and donated property to a Catholic church. His legal battle to guarantee the bequest involved Belisarius and Pope Vigilius as well as a Gothic bishop, *episcopus Gothorum*, in Rome.[13] Slaves are also mentioned in another papyrus, probably of the mid-sixth century, in the more common context of their liberation by Laurentia, the mother of Adauctus, who stipulate in their joint will that Bilesarius and his wife Sifilo are to be freed.[14]

S. Anastasia

Even before the official decision to eliminate Arian observance, some of the Goths had been under pressure, as is clear from a record of 551 that concerns the clergy of the church of S. Anastasia, one of their major churches. The sale of its marshy land to a Catholic, Petrus, *defensor ecclesiae*, for 180 *solidi* suggests that they may have been in financial difficulties. It is witnessed by nineteen Gothic clergy, of whom the four highest-ranked signed in Gothic, another six use Latin, and the rest make their crosses. The Gothic subscriptions, by a *papa* (priest), two *daikon* (deacons) and a *bokareis* (*spodeus*, scribe), appear to follow a formulaic declaration with the phrase 'with the deacon who stands for all of us' (using the words *diakuna alamoda*). In contrast, the Latin witnesses formulate their own distinct declarations, though they identify themselves as clerics of the church of the law of the Goths and the entire text is in Latin.[15] Two priests (presbyters), one deacon and one subdeacon, three *clerici*, six *spodei*, five *ostiarii* (door keepers) and one *defensor* are listed. The use of Gothic is also recorded in a sale of 538, involving two different Gothic deacons: Gudilibus identifies the purchaser, Alamud, in Gothic (*dkn Alamoda*) and translates the name of the farm he sold as *Hugsis Kaballarja*.[16] These were the Arian clergy who were dispossessed by Archbishop Agnellus when all their property was transferred to the Catholic church.

In 527 Justinian had forbidden Manichaeans and all heretics 'who do not follow our universal and orthodox church and our holy faith' to make wills. This was extended in Novel 37 of 535 – addressed to the government of North Africa – to encompass the ungodly: Arians, Donatists, Jews and pagans. Goths who clung to their traditional Arian beliefs were thus not permitted to pass on their property to their heirs.[17] Five years later, the 540 reconquest of Ravenna brought much greater imperial support for the Catholic population there, and in the 560s the city's Arian churches were finally transferred to Catholic control. It was remarkably difficult for the Goths to sustain their Arian faith once Justinian's laws deprived them of their places of worship and all the land and dependants attached to those churches. Some Goths may have found refuge in other cities that remained under Gothic control, where the Arian definition of Christian faith was sustained – such as Milan – or among other groups, like some of the Lombards, who adhered to Arianism. But, increasingly, the Goths in mid-sixth-century Italy were obliged to abandon their traditional adherence, a process quickened by Justinian's *reconciliatio*. Like Henri IV of France ten centuries later, they may have felt that Paris was worth a mass.

Even before the fundamental change of conversion, many Goths seem to have adopted Latin names, sometimes used together with their original Gothic ones, as we have seen. Double names continued to be recorded, for instance by two of the Gothic clergy attached to S. Anastasia: Igila who signed the 551 document as Danihel, and Willienant, also known as Minnulus; or Gundegerga, *spectabilis*, who was also called Nonnica (in Modena in 570). And Gothic naming patterns persisted. In the early seventh century Wililiwa may have identified herself as a Goth, *gutae*, and Pope Pelagius II (579–90) was the son of Unigildus. As late as 754 Uviliaris, archdeacon among the Catholic clergy of Ravenna, continued to use his Gothic name.[18]

In these records, preserved on papyrus, the mixed population of the city is brought to life as colleagues and friends act together to safeguard their wealth beyond their deaths. Whether they were of Gothic, East Mediterranean or Syrian origin, or local Italo-Romans, they all made use of the legal procedures overseen by the city council, which appears to have continued in active existence into the seventh century. In 572, Bonus the trouser maker, *bracarius*, and his wife Martyria, gave half of their properties (both urban and rural) to the church of Ravenna, and the text was drawn up by Gunderit, an official of the city council with a clearly Germanic name. In 600 the Goth Sisivera, *honesta femina*, freed by her mistress, Theudifara, donated land from Rimini to the church of Ravenna, an act witnessed by a wide range of men including Adquisitus, *vir clarissimus, optio* of the *numerus Mediolenenses*; Jannes, a Syrian *negotiator* (merchant), who signs in Greek letters, *souros nagouzatro*; Juvinus, *vir honestus* and *horrearius*, in charge of the granaries, and Julinus, who had assisted Theudifara's husband Marcator. In *c.* 625 a subdeacon, Deusdedit, and his wife Melissa donated properties but not their slaves. Some of the land was named: an estate (*fundum*) called Carpinianum, a mill, two hostels (*hospitia*) and a little garden.[19]

Another example of the wealth of the church of Ravenna occurs in a fragmentary papyrus from about the same time, listing some of the church properties (*coloniae*) and the taxes due in gold *tremisses* and *siliquas*. It mentions Victor, a priest (*presbyterus*), who held two ponds (*palude*) named Micawi and Pampiliana, presumably recorded because they provided a supply of fish. Contributions in kind (*voluntarius munus*) were also to be made: hens, eggs, geese, 1 pound of honey and 100 pounds of milk (cheese?).[20] It is impossible to calculate the overall sums involved, but clearly the Ravenna notaries kept precise records and officials expected these payments to be made.

The lands donated and thus registered in the city council archive came from a wide area, ranging from Salona, on the other side of the Adriatic, to Lucca on the west coast of Italy. Most of the documents concern properties of the church of Ravenna and how they were acquired, suggesting a devotion to the church that was shared by all the different groups living in the area. The church also appointed officers to inspect its properties and ensure that the correct taxation could be paid and contributions in kind were collected. As the full force of the imperial administration became clearer, many Gothic families found it necessary to adopt the majority definition of Christian faith, abandoning their ancestral inheritance and linguistic formation. Yet Gothic influenced the early medieval Latin that was slowly evolving in Italy. It left traces of the enforced integration that Constantinople demanded and Archbishop Agnellus executed.

Agnellus as Patron

Following the example of his predecessor Maximian, Archbishop Agnellus put his name and portrait on monuments, such as a large silver cross and a fine linen altar cloth which Maximian had commissioned but not completed. He also marked his patronage of a chapel of St George built on an estate named Argentea that he acquired for the church of Ravenna (possibly it had belonged to a Goth).[21] According to Agnellus two centuries later, this was a wonderful image of the archbishop, whose work was recorded in metrical verses over the entrance to the chapel, although he does not reproduce them. However, he read and copied another dedication, from the chapels of Sts Matthew and James attached to the sides of the baptistery of the Petriana church in Classis, which may allude to Archbishop Agnellus' role in the decoration:

> This apse has been decorated in mosaic from the gifts of God and of his servants, who have given them for the honor and adornment of the holy apostles, and the remaining part was decorated from the sum of the servants who had been lost and were found with the aid of God.[22]

This sounds very much as if it refers to Arian priests or presbyters of the Goths who had converted to the majority faith.

When Archbishop Agnellus died at the great age of eighty-three, as recorded on his marble tomb in the church of St Agatha, he left all his property to his granddaughter, his daughter's daughter, 'five silver ornamental vessels for the table and many other things'.[23] Rather than elaborate on this inheritance Agnellus the historian then reminds his audience that married men may become bishops under certain conditions, and avoids any further discussion of women, though he promises to return to the subject. Perhaps he objected to the accumulated family wealth being passed down to a female relative, rather than coming into the treasury of the archbishopric. For whatever reason, Agnellus felt it necessary to explain how the twenty-seventh leader of the Ravenna church did not conform to a typical clerical career, although he presided over one of the most important changes to that church, which brought it great benefits. Even after his death Agnellus' work continued as property and taxes were transferred to the Catholic church, as is clear from the protocol relating to the transfer of property and taxes to the church made by Adon, Eventius and Honorius. *In scrinio suburbicario et canonum*, they declare what they've done according to the orders of the late archbishop.[24]

Ravenna as a Centre of Learning

While Agnellus was archbishop of Ravenna, a young man from the Venetia, Venantius Fortunatus, came to the city, probably between 557 and 565, where he received his training in classical Latin literature, studying Virgil, Ovid, Horace, Statius and Martial. He also mastered Christian authors (such as Arator, Claudian and Sedulius) and may have had contact with Archbishop Maximian, an intellectual scholar, and his successor Agnellus. By 566 Venantius had moved to the court of the local Merovingian dynasty based at Metz in time to compose a fitting wedding speech for King Sigibert.[25] He 'acquired a poetic fluency in the schools of Ravenna', manifested in his hymns, epitaphs, royal panegyrics, hagiographical verses and poems for every sort of commemoration. At a banquet, his declamation would add 'a conspicuous display of literary consumption that complemented the message . . .

and impressions made by the dinnerware, servants and architectural setting'.[26] As he also displays some knowledge of Greek language, and legal and philosophical texts, Ravenna seems to have given him a much wider secular education than was generally available in the West in the middle of the sixth century. Venantius and his friend Felix, later bishop of Treviso, also visited the church of Sts John and Paul in the city, where the poet was cured of blindness by an image of St Martin, which resulted in his dedication to the saint.

Although Venantius says nothing about his teachers, there were many educated people in Ravenna, including Theodosius, *magister litterarum*, who witnessed a will in 575 and might well have trained him.[27] Among the civilian officials attached to the praetorian prefect's office, Stephanus acted as *scriniarius* (secretary); Eugenius, *palatinus*, was the son of a Greek doctor, Leontios, and Apolenaris, son of Florentinus, *pater pistorum*, head of the guild of bakers, became *cancellarius*, chancellor, of the prefect Longinus.[28] A considerable number of secretaries, *tabellioni*, and scribes such as Gunderit, *exceptor* of the Ravenna *curia*, kept track of all legal documents and recorded the numerous gifts to the city's church.[29] Even a relatively lowly administrator required some training and knowledge of accounting, so there must have been teachers and schools to educate these bureaucrats. From what he described as a northern exile in a cold climate, Venantius recalled 'sipping a few tiny drops from the water of grammar, taking a small draught from the stream of rhetoric, I have barely had my rusty edge sharpened by the whetstone of law'. He missed 'his dear (*cara*) Ravenna', where his teachers had the skills to train a young man like Venantius not only in the basic *trivium* of grammar, rhetoric and logic, but also to give him a serious grasp of different poetic metres and styles.

Through the career of Venantius we can begin to see the critical role that Ravenna would play in the development of the West during the seventh and eighth centuries. As the Italian arm of the imperial government of Constantinople, the city was positioned at the hinge of East and West where it could transmit influence both ways. It was the port through which many ambassadors, military commanders and merchants passed, the link between northern Italy, transalpine Europe and the Byzantine capital in the East Mediterranean. As a result, the Adriatic became a busier waterway, and the ports on its eastern shore in Istria, Croatia and Dalmatia developed in relation to the western route, from Ravenna south to Sicily and beyond. Although Sicily retained its own independent administration, and other ports grew to rival Ravenna, from 554 the city gained a new infusion of international contacts, which were consolidated by the creation of the exarchate.

The final stage in the conquest of Ravenna by Constantinople had been marked by the imposition of imperially defined Christian belief, which brought the Gothic domination of the city to an end. Ravenna had been gloriously decorated, endowed with high status and invigorated by Byzantine influence. This moment, between 557 and 565 when Emperor Justinian died, marks the beginning of nearly two hundred years of rule from the East, a new phase in the life of the city and northeast Italy that deeply influenced Venantius. From the schools of Ravenna, Venantius took skills fast becoming unfamiliar north of the Alps that enhanced the power of a succession of Frankish kings in Metz and the famous Queen Radegund, founder of the Holy Cross monastery near Poitiers. Remembering his exposure to the monuments of the imperial capital of Italy, Venantius drew on the Mediterranean culture of early Christendom to praise new patrons:

> The beautiful church is aglow, raised to a venerable height,
>> and dedicated to God in the name of St Martin.
> So brilliant gleams their faith in the virtue of his life
>> that he bestows on the people all their holy prayers seek.
> Faustus, a bishop of devout heart, constructed this church
>> and brought happy gifts to his own Lord.[30]

PART FIVE

568–643

King Alboin and the Lombard conquest

19

Alboin invades

In the spring of 568 a band of warriors, identified by their long beards (*longobardi*), crossed the Julian Alps and captured Forum Iulii (Friuli) in north-east Italy. King Alboin and some of his warriors knew the territory because they had fought as auxiliaries under Narses in the final campaign of the Gothic war of 552. The general had paid them well and then escorted them back to their base in Pannonia along the northern border. A group of these Longbeards, or Lombards, signed up for further imperial service and fought on the Persian front, where they witnessed imperial rule in the East. In 568 their immediate success in Italy initiated yet another phase in the settlement of the peninsula, as another group of outsiders determined to become masters of her territory.[1] But the Longbeards left a permanent presence in the regions of Italy still known as Lombardy and Longobardia.

At this time Lombard settlements in Pannonia were under pressure from the Avars, a hostile force settled in what is today central Hungary, which gave them a good reason to move south to the rich, fertile lands in Italy.[2] After the final defeat of the Goths in 552, imperial forces had taken inadequate measures to ensure the safety of the remaining inhabitants, despite Narses's extended military activity against enemies such as the Alemanni and the Franks. By 568, when the elderly general was probably in his eighties, the new emperor, Justin II, decided to replace him by a younger man, Longinus. The coincidence of the first references to the Lombards' invasion of Italy in precisely this year gave rise to a scandalous suggestion that Narses had 'invited' them in – a claim found in the life of Pope John III (561–74) in the Roman *Book of the Pontiffs*.[3] The passage that preserves the legend of Narses's 'betrayal of the empire' may be a later insertion and thus a forgery, which probably reflects local prejudice against the Armenian eunuch who played such a major role in the restoration of imperial control in Italy.[4] The accusation was without foundation and Narses remained in Rome until his death in about 574.

Constantinople's plan for a direct imperial administration of Italy had been barely conceived and was still unrealized when the appearance of a powerful new group of outsiders proved almost fatal to it. The Lombards had to be either excluded or accommodated. But Justin II may not have been aware of the danger, for it did not cause as much anxiety as hostilities on other borders. In the second half of the sixth century when the empire was poorly defended across so many regions – Spain, Africa, Italy and Dalmatia in the West, the Balkans in the North, and the long eastern frontier with Persia – many of its neighbours, such as Slavonic tribes, sensed its weakness and attacked. The Lombard challenge was mirrored along several frontiers separated by huge distances, in combinations that greatly reduced the empire's capacity to respond effectively.

Like Theoderic before him, King Alboin led his people across the Alps, bringing women and children as well as livestock with him. They wintered in Friuli, creating a great burial mound near Cividale, where rich grave goods reflect their love of gold, garnets and other gems (now beautifully displayed in the National Archaeological Museum). In 569, the Lombard warriors attacked a small imperial garrison in Milan, which was unable to resist; the bishop fled to Genoa with some local aristocratic families and the city was sacked. The patriarch of Aquileia also fled to the nearby island stronghold of Grado, taking the whole church treasure with him. Right across northern Italy, from the eastern frontier to Como in the north-west, the Lombards defeated imperial forces and Alboin established his own garrisons. Pavia held out for three years, defended by local forces (largely Gothic, as the city had been one of the few centres of resistance to Belisarius) augmented by people seeking the protection of strong walls. When it succumbed in 572, King Alboin took over Theoderic's palace there and appointed military dukes to subdue the other major cities.[5]

Longinus, Praetorian Prefect of Italy

While the Lombards extended their control over the inland regions of northern Italy, Ravenna remained secure behind its fortifications in the marshy delta of the Po, with its direct access to the Adriatic and the East Mediterranean. After the long period of Narses's rule, Longinus assumed control of everything south of Pavia with the title of Praetorian Prefect of Italy. When his ship docked at Classis, probably in the summer of 568, we can imagine his ceremonial entry into the city through the historic Golden Gate in the southern fortification wall, where he was greeted by the local elite: Archbishop Agnellus, local councillors (members of the city *curia*), landed aristocrats from the region, and leading citizens from Ravenna, Caesarea and Classis. The wealthiest inhabitants would have been wearing their colourful clothing, the guilds carrying their banners, the garrison soldiers their flags. This was a thriving centre, which made quite a contrast with Rome, impoverished by repeated sieges.[6]

The new prefect took up residence in the palace of Theoderic and established his staff and troops in their quarters. Longinus served as governor of the area that later became known as the Exarchate of Ravenna and the Pentapolis, five cities along the eastern coast of Italy: Rimini, Pesaro, Fano, Senigallia and Ancona. If Longinus had been instructed to stop and reverse the Lombard occupation, he appears to have been singularly inactive. Apart from his construction of a fortification wall (though its location is not specified), he undertook little military action. He appointed subordinate commanders who defended key castles and major bridges, particularly on the frontiers of the area that remained under imperial control; one, named Sisinnius, is recorded as *magister militum* in *c.* 575 at Susa near the Alpine border in Piedmont. Yet as early as 571 some Lombards were established at Nocera Umbra, very close to the Via Flaminia in the central Apennines.[7]

Several years of procrastination, therefore, elapsed before the eastern court was able to give a considered response to the Lombards' military challenge. Another reason for the delay may have been Justin II's lapses into insanity, which were hidden from the court by his wife Sophia. And, in 572, imperial policy against Persia led to outright warfare and a devastating defeat for Constantinople, so even less attention could be paid to the situation in Italy. The imperial authorities in the East may not have realized the severity of Lombard military activity, which was concentrated on the west of the peninsula.

In his *History of the Lombards*, Paul the deacon, who wrote towards the end of the eighth century, two hundred years after the events, describes how King Alboin died – one of the stories of female revenge that Paul particularly enjoyed.[8] In Pannonia the Lombards had jostled for dominance with the Avars and the Gepids, another hostile tribe, for some time. After killing the Gepid king and capturing his daughter, Rosamund, Alboin had transformed the Gepid leader's skull into a golden drinking cup, decorated with pearls and precious gems, which he loved to use. Alboin ordered his captive to drink wine from the same cup, that is, from her own father's skull. Rosamund did so, while secretly vowing to have him killed. After arranging for one of her retainers to murder Alboin in 572, she fled to Verona and from there contacted Longinus, requesting transport to Ravenna. He duly sent a boat through tributaries of the Po to collect her and she came accompanied by her daughter Albsuintha, the retainer and many Gepids and Lombards. She also brought the entire royal Lombard treasury. Rosamund then quarrelled with the retainer and both died, supposedly from drinking poisoned wine. Longinus appropriated the treasury and sent it, together with the Lombard princess Albsuintha, to Constantinople, for which he was duly rewarded.[9] Despite much embellishment, the story captures the rivalry and intense volatility among different Lombard leaders who freely switched allegiance, the confusion this caused, and the financial and military subordination of Ravenna to the eastern empire.

The Lombards Threaten Rome

From their main centres of Milan and Pavia in northern Italy, the Lombards sent ambassadors to the emperor seeking recognition as allies, with the right to settle in the cities and regions they had already conquered.[10] This was never granted. In a repetition of imperial dealings with the Goths, such requests and rejections provoked a constant tension in Lombard relations with the empire. Some Lombard forces pressed on down the west coast towards Rome, and others advanced into the central Apennines and occupied territory around Spoleto and Benevento, further south. Under Pope Benedict I (575–9), these hostile forces are mentioned for the first time in the Roman *Book of the Pontiffs*; they are associated with a terrible famine that forced even well-defended cities to surrender to the Lombards.[11] When Justin II learned that Rome was under siege by the Lombards in about 575, he sent his son-in-law Baduarius to Italy and organized the transport of grain from Alexandria to relieve the hunger. But the Lombards defeated Baduarius, who died in Italy probably in 576. According to Agnellus, however, he was responsible for a church in Ravenna dedicated to Sts John and Barbatianus, suggesting that Baduarius spent enough time in the city to devote resources to a new ecclesiastical building.[12]

The Lombard invasions of northern Italy posed an insuperable challenge for the empire – how to campaign on two very distant frontiers at the same time. In the 530s Justinian had tried to avoid this by signing a thirty-year truce with Persia before sending Belisarius to recover North Africa from the Vandals. One reason for the length of Belisarius' later campaign against the Goths in Italy was imperial anxiety about eastern frontier defences. Since it took a long time to transfer military units from Persia to the West or vice versa, it was always difficult to provide adequate numbers in both regions simultaneously. This critical issue would determine the later history of the western provinces of the empire, which were often starved of effective military forces when they were needed more urgently in the East. The dilemma became even more pronounced in the late sixth century as Persia launched another major invasion and Arab tribes moved beyond their desert base in Arabia and into the fertile Roman provinces of the Near East.

The imperial policy of paying one 'barbarian' group to fight another was more successful when an experienced mercenary commander of Alemannic origin, named Droctulft, was persuaded to abandon the Lombards and join the imperial forces. Such a clear betrayal provoked the Lombard King Authari (584–90) to attack Droctulft, who was forced to retreat from Brescia to Ravenna, where the imperial commander, Smaragdus, welcomed him.[13] Droctulft then aided the Ravennati to regain Classis (temporarily occupied by a Lombard force), by helping them to build a fleet so that they could attack the city by sea. With the harbour back under imperial control, the city could reassert communication with the wider world, as well as reinforcing the linked urban sites of Ravenna–Caesarea–Classis. Several years later, in gratitude for this valuable assistance, Archbishop John II authorized Droctulft's burial in the church of San Vitale. This signal honour is commemorated in a long verse inscription that preserves his life's story, recording his successful campaigns against the Avars and suggesting that he may have travelled to Africa to serve in the forces of the exarch Gennadios of Carthage.[14] In addition to celebrating the great general, the archbishop took advantage of the recapture of Classis to complete the construction of a church begun by his predecessor.

King Authari's success in reviving the military capacity of the Lombards demanded a concerted strategy to defend Italy, which began in about 584 with the appointment of more experienced military leaders. Emperor Maurice sent Decius, followed by Smaragdus in 585 with enhanced authority that prefigured a novel administration built up over the course of the next twenty years, making Ravenna the seat of a commander of patrician status with the title of Exarch. No sixth-century emperors ever visited the western regions to observe local problems at first hand; they relied, as usual, on reports from their officers, fiscal as well as military. Men like Belisarius and Narses, who had served for long periods in Africa and Italy, must have emphasized the challenge of reasserting imperial control to the non-combatant administrators and emperors in the eastern capital. In both regions, and in southern Spain, which was conquered by the aged patrician Liberius in about 552, the growth of a new system of administration was slow. The Lombard occupation of much of the inland and mountainous terrain of Italy forced imperial officials to concentrate on securing the major ports and coastal cities, but they were unable to dislodge the newcomers. Similar problems beset the government in North Africa, where Moorish tribes controlled the interior regions and pressed on the southern borders of all the provinces, while in Spain the Visigothic kings whittled away imperial control.[15] All the western outposts of Constantinopolitan power were regularly attacked by local forces and the eastern capital was too far away to support them.

The Three Chapters

To these military deficiencies, opponents of the Fifth Oecumenical Council of 553 added a religious schism. Under the patriarch of Aquileia, who had taken refuge in Grado, they formed an independent church and resisted all efforts to convince them of their errors, from the time of Pope Pelagius I (556–61) right through the sixth and seventh centuries. To modern sensibilities there is something incomprehensible in the way the Three Chapters continued to envenom ecclesiastical relations.

Emperor Justinian had ensured that Ravenna remained a bastion of imperial authority and from the time of Maximian all its church leaders supported the Fifth Council, not least because the decision to transfer all the property of the Arian church to the Catholics enormously benefitted Archbishop Agnellus and his successors. Their loyalty to the emperor extended to local inhabitants through the church. When Archbishop Peter III returned from his consecration in Rome in 570,

> with great joy the citizens of Ravenna received him; the [populace of] Classe hastened to meet him . . . at the ninth mile. Then everyone rejoicing sang the acclamation: 'God has given you to us, may his Divinity preserve you.' Then the boys went before him with prayers.[16]

In this welcoming procession that illustrates local pride in the city's new ecclesiastical leader, we catch a glimpse of the very strong links between the church and the community of Ravenna–Caesarea–Classis, where Peter III later laid the foundations of the church of St Severus in an area called 'the district of safety'.[17] Political leaders didn't inspire the same enthusiasm.

After Peter's death, however, at about the same time as the establishment of the exarchate, a major shift occurred in the position of the city's bishops. In 578, for the first time, pressure from Pope Benedict ensured the selection of a Roman cleric, born and trained in that city, to lead the church of Ravenna. Normally the Ravenna clergy elected their bishop from their own ranks and, unsurprisingly, they resented this papal intervention. In a short notice, the historian Agnellus twice condemned Archbishop John II (578–95) for his foreign origin – 'not of this flock . . . born in Rome, sent here from that see'.[18] The pope's intervention was related to the issue of the Three Chapters, which continued to divide the churches of the West. Although the see of Milan had been won round to the imperial position by 572, Aquileia stubbornly refused, and many bishops, like Frontius of Dalmatia and several African leaders, were exiled to Egypt.[19]

John the Roman

Archbishop John 'the Roman' proved a loyal ally to Pope Pelagius II in the campaign to convince the schismatic community of its errors. Pelagius' letters to Elias, patriarch of Aquileia, document his intense efforts to justify condemnation of the Three Chapters.[20] But they were unsuccessful. On the death of Elias in 588/9, John the Roman called on the power of the Ravenna exarch, Smaragdus, to prevent the election of a schismatic successor. The exarch went to Grado to oppose one candidate, named Severus, and

> dragged him out of the church and brought him with insults to Ravenna together with three other bishops from Istria, that is John of Parentium, another Severus from Trieste, Vendemius of Cissa and also Antony, now an old man and *defensor* of the church [of Grado].[21]

Smaragdus forced these five opponents of the imperial policy to hold communion with John the Roman (that is, to accept the bread and wine dedicated in the communion liturgy performed by Archbishop John) and detained them in Ravenna for a year before allowing them to return to their sees.

When they got back to Aquileia, however, the five bishops were rejected by their own communities and other bishops. The schismatic group then held a council on Marano in 589/90, where Severus confessed his error in taking communion at Ravenna with those who had condemned the Three Chapters. He was readmitted, as patriarch of Aquileia, to the group of ten bishops who controlled large areas of northern Italy and Istria, mainly under Lombard administration: Altino, Concordia, Sabione, Trento, Verona, Vicenza, Feltre, Asolo, Zuglio and Pola in Istria.[22] The other four bishops stuck by their 'conversion' in Ravenna, but overall the intervention by Smaragdus had failed to increase obedience to the imperial and papal position.

John the Roman also took personal action against the schismatics, as is clear from an extraordinary, anonymous document that is preserved among material relating to the Three Chapters' controversy. The text, written by a cleric or monk who felt that the archbishop had punished him unreasonably by refusing to readmit him to communion, takes the form of a plea for mercy and forgiveness. The unknown author relates that he has been absolved by the pope's legates, but the political authorities have imprisoned him. He complains that he has already written several times to Archbishop John, who refuses even to open his letters. Since he appears to have been reconciled with the imperial view (hence the reference to papal legates accepting him), it may have been the Lombard authorities who considered him a traitor to the 'schismatic' church and had detained him. His text must have been written between 593 and 595, and was probably copied because it was associated with a collection of arguments in favour of the 553 Council, several drawn from works by Gregory the Great.[23] While nothing is known of the author's fate, his record displays some rougher aspects of the Three Chapters' controversy.

Living in Ravenna in the 570s

Ravenna remained the lynchpin between Constantinople, Italy and northern Europe, with control of the Adriatic that ensured contact with Sicily. It was the conduit for many ideas about imperial government, artistic influences and forms of religious devotion, and the point of entry for many ambassadors sent to negotiate with western rulers, merchants and military commanders, also marked by their Greek influence. Despite the failure of the imperial administration to prevent the Lombards' steady expansion in western and central Italy, Ravenna continued to enjoy a fairly peaceful civic life, which is illuminated by local records such as the will of the Goth Mannas, son of Nanderit. This was drawn up in March 575 to ensure that Albanionus and his wife and daughter were to become free Roman citizens. This act, in which a Goth grants freedom to a local family, is witnessed by a long list of interesting figures: Johannis, son of Januarius, an assistant to the praetorian prefect; Emilianus, one of the prefect's *scriniarii* (secretaries); Riccitanc, son of Montanus; Theodosius, a master of letters (*magister litterarum*); Andreas, a scribe; Quiriacus, *horrearius* (in charge of the granary); and Petros, *kolektarius* (*collectarius*, tax collector, who signs in Greek), son of Thomas *defensor*. The document was drawn up by Julianus and his assistant, Johannis, the *forensis* (clerk). The presiding magistrate was Cassianus Junior, one of the Melminius clan.[24] Another papyrus records the gift made by Bonus the trouser maker and his wife

Martyria, of half of all their possessions to the church of Ravenna, written by Gunderit, *exceptor curiae civitates Ravennatis*, with two Melminii as witnesses.[25]

These records document the integrated, mixed, local society that used the municipal archive to register their legal decisions: Goths, local Italo-Roman craftsmen and officials with some knowledge of Greek – telling evidence of the continuity from the time of Theoderic. A number of scribes appear to have been based in specific spots in the city, such as the house of Otratarit, below that of Zenobius (*cata ipso Zenobio*), or at St John the Baptist (either a church or statue), places where officials could be found to draw up legal documents. Another *forensis* worked close to the Mint for gold coins in the portico of the palace.[26] Several witnesses worked in the prefect's tax office (*sacrarum largitionum*), including a Mint official, Paschalis, whose father had also been employed in the Mint for gold, and Eugenius, who was the son of Leontios, a doctor from the Greek school (*medicus ab schola greca*). The pride of these educated, middle-ranking officials in the city of Ravenna, which they identified as most splendid (*splendidissima*), is matched by the persistence of higher-ranking families among the magistrates presiding at meetings of the city council in the 560s and 70s. The Melminius family is particularly well represented by Laurentius, magistrate for the second time, Bonifacius and Johannis Junior as *principales* and *defensores* of the church of Ravenna in 572, and Cassianus Junior, magistrate in 575.

From such records we can see how city administration survived in Ravenna, and its very diverse groups were spared much of the disruption that accompanied the Lombard invasion of this decade. Scribes worked in clearly appointed places in the city where people could go to dictate their wills or to discuss gifting their properties to the church. Among the witnesses several individuals identify themselves by professional qualifications (doctors, minters, trouser makers and those in charge of grain supplies). Under Constantinopolitan influence, the city sustained imperial standards of administration and legal skills, encouraging a high standard of education and engagement in civic responsibility.

The Catholic church also flourished, extending its control over properties both near and far away from the city. Archbishops Peter III and his successor, John the Roman, constructed a church dedicated to St Severus, the bishop of Ravenna who had attended the Council of Serdica in 343 and was much commemorated in the area of the port of Classis.

In the late ninth century this basilica, which is currently being excavated, was re-used to form part of a Benedictine monastery.[27] Since the same area outside the old harbour also contained the major church of St Apollinaris consecrated by Archbishop Maximian, Classis was clearly an important centre of Christian cults. There was another church dedicated to St Probus in Classis, next to the church of St Euphemia 'by the sea'. According to Agnellus, this had been wonderfully decorated by Maximian with mosaics, but the church 'is now demolished'.[28] Another tantalizing mid-sixth-century record mentions the place of the deaconesses (*in sanctas diaconissas*), as a familiar landmark and perhaps also a community of nuns. If so, this is the only evidence for nunneries in Ravenna at this time. In all parts of the Christian world women founded nunneries and often became abbesses, so it is very likely that the church of Ravenna also supported such institutions.

In the 570s the Lombards occupied the Veneto, captured Pavia and established individual dukedoms in Spoleto and Benevento, in defiance of imperial troops and military forces from the East. Ravenna, however, remained unassailable among the marshy tributaries of the Po, a thriving stronghold that Constantinople now chose to become the centre of a new form of government – the exarchate of Ravenna.

20

The exarchate of Ravenna

The origins of the exarchate, as imperial territory in north and central Italy became known, have been much disputed ever since the great Byzantinist George Ostrogorsky suggested that the exarch combined military and civil powers in a new fashion later adopted in Asia Minor. He saw the regions of Ravenna and Carthage as experiments in a more overtly military administration geared for regular warfare that developed into the eastern *themata* (large provincial units). Although the creation of these *themata* took place much later than he believed, the principle of putting an army officer in supreme control of all elements of government does go back to the sixth century. In North Africa, Belisarius' quick victory permitted Solomon, his *domesticus*, another eunuch commander, to take full control of the administration in 534.[1] After a much longer Italian campaign, the Pragmatic Sanction subordinated judicial and fiscal elements to the needs of the army, a process of militarization that followed the same tendency.[2] Although civilian titles persisted, praetorian prefects took second place to military commanders. The conquests set in train the shift that eventually led to a different system of government – the establishment of two exarchates in the provinces of North Africa and Italy.

The combination of all power in the hands of one military commander had occurred earlier, usually as a temporary measure required by adverse circumstances. What is distinctive about the sixth-century change in Africa and Italy is that it becomes the norm, and previously high-ranking civilian officials are subordinated to a military hierarchy. Yet no laws were issued in Constantinople to establish the new system in its far-flung western provinces. Instead, it evolved through the appointment of a series of military figures endowed with great powers and high court titles, such as 'most eminent' or 'most distinguished' (*eminentissimus*, *excellentissimus*). Most of these commanding officers held the title of *patricius*, which carried membership of the Senate (in most cases of Constantinople), and were described by observers beyond the imperial court as 'outstanding' (*praecelsus*), or 'glorious' (*gloriosus*). They were the new governors of extremely large regions ruled from Constantinople via the two centres of Ravenna and Carthage.

Before 584 the title *exarchus* had also been held by several different ranks of military men, not exclusively those in charge of the areas that became exarchates. Nevertheless, when Decius, followed by Smaragdus (585–9) and Romanus (589–96) held the title, it's clear that they were specifically empowered in a new fashion. The official title, exarch of Italy (*exarchus Italiae*), occurs for the first time in an inscription dated 1 August 608, erected in the Forum in Rome, which honours Emperor Phokas (Plate 48).[3] The exarch Smaragdus, on his second tour of duty between 603 and 608, was responsible for the monument thanking the emperor for ensuring the peace of Italy and for preserving liberty (a rather hollow flattery). The title would remain in use for nearly 150 years to designate the governor appointed by Constantinople, with authority to negotiate alliances and treaties with foreign forces (subject to later confirmation by the emperor) and responsibility for the overall administration of imperial territory in Italy and its military defence, including Rome, Naples, Genoa and all the cities and territory in between not occupied by the Lombards. His control over Sardinia is also marked by inscriptions and construction work.[4]

The Italian exarchate consisted of two major regions, centred on Ravenna in the north-east and Rome in the west, linked by ancient roads over the Apennines that divided the areas of Lombard rule. The Roman roads Flaminia and Amerina, which followed the river valleys up to the mountainous spine of Italy and down the other side, had been constructed with tunnels, bridges and dramatic Z-bends. They were tortuous and difficult to defend, though guarded by numerous castles such as Perugia on the Via Amerina, which became critical to communication between Ravenna and Rome.[5] Despite its narrowness, this corridor remained the vital connection between eastern and western Italy throughout the existence of the exarchate.[6] South of Rome the city and region of Naples formed an extension of the duchy of Rome, also under the exarch's control, although the Lombard principalities of Spoleto and Benevento regularly threatened it.[7]

While north-western Italy, especially the area around Milan and the Lombard capital at Pavia, had been lost to imperial control during the first phase of Lombard invasions, the exarch still had access to some cities of the Po valley, linked by the river to Ravenna. He commanded a substantial region in the north-east, including the Pentapolis, as well as territory around the head of the Adriatic (Istria), south to Pola (Pula, in Croatia) and down the eastern shore (Dalmatia). He was assisted by subordinate army officers, normally identified as *magistri militum*, tribunes or dukes, who maintained garrisons in frontier towns and for tified castles, by praetorian prefects of Italy with responsibility for civilian matters, and officials who collected the taxes, a part of which was now sent back to Constantinople.[8]

The *Numeri* and Other Military Forces

Although exarchs often complained of inadequate military strength to check further Lombard expansion, they had regular forces that could be supplemented by the army of the Pentapolis and other regions. By the late sixth century most soldiers stationed in Italy derived either from the army of Narses, who continued on active duty into the 560s, or from eastern units drafted in later (for example with Baduarius). It seems that the exarch normally had a group of soldiers, his *obsequium*, who accompanied him on all military campaigns and acted as a guard of honour when required; they may have been personal retainers, *bucellarii*, who came from the East with the exarch.[9] The praetorian prefect was accompanied by a military guard whenever he travelled, which also fought under the command of the exarch in campaigns against the Lombards. In Ravenna there was a regular garrison, probably recruited locally to defend the city, known as the *exercitus Ravennatis*. Additional troops could be raised from other cities and regions where soldiers had been settled as garrison troops, or in winter quarters, or on land for which they were required to serve in the army. These armed groups, whose high status went back to the Gothic settlement under Theoderic, became the dominant feature of the exarchate. In an increasingly militarized situation, many may have volunteered hoping to receive an endowment of land, which would ensure their future prosperity.[10]

The survival of several Roman military groups, *numeri*, is recorded in Ravenna well into the seventh century. The name indicates a military unit of three to four hundred men established in imperial times. Several *numeri* of Theodosius are mentioned in the *Notitia dignitatum* (list of offices, updated in 425) and recorded in Ravenna in 491. Other *numeri* may have been formed after the defeat of the Goths (in Milan, the *Mediolanensium*, or in Verona, the *Veronensium*), or were named for the regions in which their members were recruited: Sirmium, Dacia or Armenia.[11] Gradually sections of the army were settled in cities and castles as garrison troops and became more of a local force.[12]

In Ravenna military officers attached to such units are frequently named in the papyri. A donation of *c.* 600, records that Johannes, *vir clarissimus*, first officer (*primicerius*) of the Theodosian *numerus*, gave half of all his property to the church of Ravenna.[13] He had previously been the bodyguard of George, a *magister militum*, and was now his assistant. The gift was witnessed by the same George and Marinos, a banker, who both signed in neat cursive Greek, two counts, and John, judicial clerk of the praetorian prefect. The donor, however, declared: 'I made the sign of the holy cross with my own hand because I do not know letters.' He dictated his wishes to the clerk of the city of Ravenna, Vitalis, who acted as his *rogatarius* (proposer) and drew up the document.[14]

The relationship between the army of Ravenna (*exercitus Ravennatis*), and the army of Italy, *exercitus Italiae*, is not clear. In 668 the *exercitus Italiae* is recorded as having units from Istria in the north and Campania in the west, so it drew on very distant resources. Representatives of this army attended a ceremony in Constantinople with the exarch in 687, and some detachments later served in the imperial Palace there. In contrast, the *exercitus Ravennatis* appears to have functioned in and around the city, as did other local forces that might be called on to defend their own centres. Some of these troops had barracks in the city and were named after specific urban quarters, which they were expected to defend from attack. The *banda* (flags) of each unit, carried by special bearers, and the *vexillum*, military standard, often housed in a special church when not in use, were important features of loyalty.[15] A unit specifically named *bandus Ravenna* appears in the early eighth century.

Under Narses the mixed troops that defeated the Goths were well trained and probably retained their traditional military skills into the exarchate. Certainly, the assumption in Constantinople was that imperial forces had to remain ready for battle. The late sixth-century military manual known as the *Strategikon*, which is attributed to Emperor Maurice (582–602), assumes a well-trained, equipped and disciplined army that still practised manoeuvres and tactics.[16] Although these forces were paid, booty always remained an additional and expected resource, and comments on successful campaigns often cite the quantity and type of booty and loot. In Italy, the exarch Romanus appears to have planned his campaigns of reconquest in the 590s with a grasp of the tactics and leadership demanded by the *Strategikon*.

Greek and Latin

From his court in the palace of Theoderic in Ravenna the exarch executed orders from Constantinople and transmitted information back in Greek. His court was also the place where delegations from western rulers came to negotiate political and military arrangements, where regional officials came to plead for tax reductions when their crops failed, and where disgruntled bishops from other cities came to complain. All this was done in Latin and, in a world where bilingualism was no longer common, the linguistic divide between official business conducted in Greek and more local affairs in Latin was an undoubted weakness. Very few people in the West read, spoke or understood Greek. In late sixth-century Rome Pope Gregory I complains of the difficulty of finding translators. Ravenna and Naples were two of the rare places outside Sicily and southern Italy where witnesses sometimes preferred to write their names in Greek letters. Although some exarchs had a command of Latin, their regular use of Greek put them at a disadvantage.[17] This bilingual environment might have encouraged the use of *glossae*, lists of useful words with Greek and Latin equivalents. Only a few early examples are known, and Ravenna could well have been the centre where such simple aids to mutual understanding were developed.

In contrast to the governor who used Greek, Ravenna's ancient municipal administration vested in the city council continued to function in Latin. The enhanced ecclesiastical presence of the Catholic archbishop is very obvious in the papyrus records – an invaluable source of information about the exarchate in its early years. Between

16. The gold triple *solidus* of Theoderic (493–526). It identifies him as REX, King, 'PIUS PRINC(EPS) I(NVICTUS) S(EMPER)' (pious ruler, forever invincible). In his left hand he holds the orb topped with a symbol of winged victory that presents a victory wreath to him. His hairstyle and moustache are Gothic; his costume, and jewelled fibula and symbols are entirely imperial.

17. Theoderic's Mausoleum, just beyond the walls of Ravenna, constructed before his death in 526.

18 and 19. (*Left*) Gold *tremissis* (one third *solidus*) of *DN Romulus Augustus PF AVG*, minted at Ravenna in 476. (*Right*) Gold *tremissis* minted by Odoacer at Ravenna in the name of the Emperor Zeno between 476 and 491 (*DN ZENO PERPI(tuus) AVG(ustus)*).

20 and 21. (*Left*) Silver quarter *siliqua* of the young King Athalaric (526–34), minted in Ravenna in the name of Emperor Justinian. (*Right*) Bronze coin of King Theodahad (535–6), (*DN THEODAHATUS REX*), also minted in Ravenna.

22 and 23. (*Left*) Silver half *siliqua* of King Baduila/Totila (549–552), minted in Pavia. (*Right*) Silver half *siliqua* of King Witigis (536–40), minted in Ravenna.

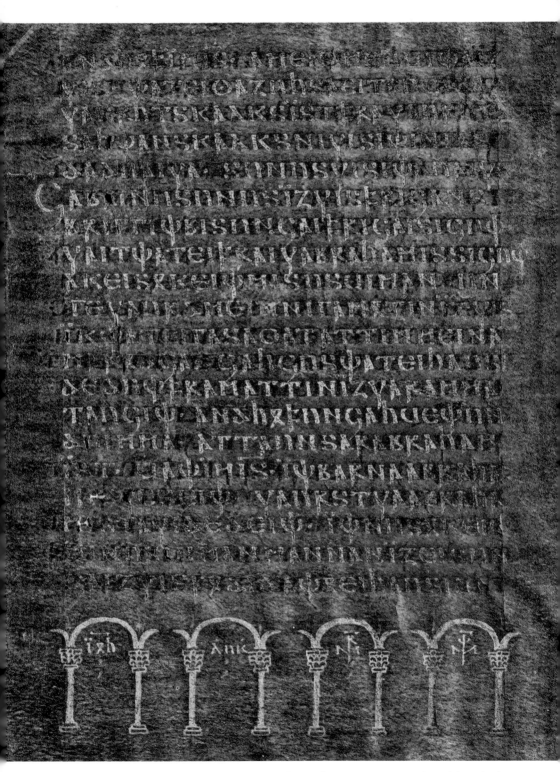

24. Folio 99r of the sixth-century Gothic Bible made in Ravenna, with gold and silver lettering on purple dyed parchment, showing the text of part of Christ's debate with the Pharisees (John 8, 34–40). The arcades below the text provide corresponding passages from the Gospels of Luke, Mark and Matthew in the form of canon tables.

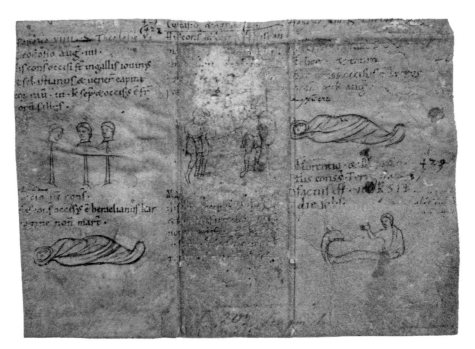

25. The Annals of Ravenna. One half page of a manuscript, with entries for the years from 412, including the display of the head of the usurper Constantine III on a pole (*top left*) and a monster emerging from the earth representing an earthquake (*bottom right*). Deaths are indicated by shrouded corpses.

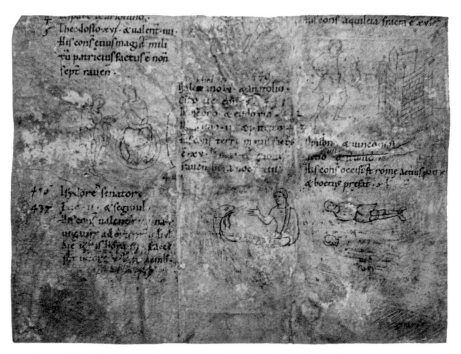

26. The other side of the same fragment, with Theodosius II (the emperor seated on a globe) promoting Aetius to the dignity of patricius in 435 (*top left*) and entries for 436 and 437; another earthquake (*centre*); a siege of Aquileia (*top right*) and the deaths of two individuals (*bottom right*).

27. Capital from a dismantled Gothic church, with the monogram of Theoderic at the centre, re-used at the Venetian loggia on the Piazza del Popolo, Ravenna.

28. A Ravenna penny, a sixth-century bronze coin of 10 nummi, minted in Ravenna, with (*left*) a turreted woman representing the city, identified as FELIX RAVENNA, and (*right*) a monogram R(avenna) F(elix) surrounded by a wreath.

29. Lead pipe stamped with the inscription, 'Our Lord King Theodericus restored [it] to the city'; part of Theoderic's repair to the aqueduct and water channels (493–526).

30 and 31. San Vitale, Ravenna (526–40). (*Above*) The exterior from the west, showing its octagonal form, and (*below*) the apse mosaic, a detail of Bishop Ecclesius presenting the domed church of San Vitale to Christ.

32. (*Opposite*) The apse of San Vitale, with Christ seated on a globe flanked by angels. The two famous imperial panels (37 and 38) are immediately below to either side. The central medallion in the dome displays the lamb of God, supported by four angels, and floral garlands with animals and birds.

33. Impost block with the monogram of Bishop Victor (537–44) above a capital imported from Constantinople, on the ground floor of San Vitale.

34. A sarcophagus lid inscribed with Exarch Isaac's Greek epitaph, commissioned by his widow Susanna in 643.

35. Early Christian sarcophagus with the Three Kings presenting their gifts to the Virgin and Child, re-used for the burial of Exarch Isaac in San Vitale.

613 and 641 the Goth Wililiwa, *clarissima femina*, dictated her will to Deusdedit, the secretary (*tabellio*) of the city of Ravenna. The now fragmentary document notes that this high-ranking lady signed by making her cross and preserves the name of one witness Dulcitius. Another, later document (of June 625) also records a magistrate still presiding over the local court, when a subdeacon, another Deusdedit, and his wife Melissa listed the property they intended to donate to the church: one estate was called Carpinianum; another, close to the gate of St Apollinaris, before the arches of St George, included a mill (*pistrino*), two lodging houses (*hospitia*) and a small garden (*horticello*). They insist on the freeing of all their slaves wherever they are housed. This papyrus is the last in the series that preserves the official traditional dialogue between an unnamed magistrate and the court notary, Donatus.[18]

By the seventh century none of the older family names occur in these papyri – a big change in the way people are identified. Many witnesses and officials are now clerics and lower administrators, though the office of prefect maintains some continuity with the sixth century. In 639 Paulacis made a gift of thirty-six gold coins of good weight to the church of Ravenna. He was a soldier in the Armenian *numerus* and the son of Stefanus, first officer of the Verona one. The act was witnessed by Germanus, *exceptor* of the most eminent prefect, and Johannis, *scolaris* of the sacred palace (i.e. the exarch), as well as Theodoracis, *exscriba* of the Armenian *numerus*.[19] In this typical example the preponderance of military titles is hardly surprising, given the newly militarized form of government, but it seems clear that the previously dominant families have either moved into military occupations or adopted a simpler style of identification. Use of a Christian baptismal name and an occupation has replaced the traditional Roman naming pattern.

Within the city distinct levels of government became clearer as the exarchate took shape. At the top, the exarch and his close assistants, who were appointed from Constantinople and reported back to the emperor in Greek, dealt with major concerns of war and peace; below them a subordinate level of civilian government, headed by the praetorian prefect (sometimes just called prefect), managed local issues. These two sectors of government covered all the remaining imperial territory in Italy. Much ecclesiastical and urban civil administration was dominated by local bishops, who appointed priests to the city churches and held their own courts to settle disputes. The old pattern of Roman provincial government had been swept away, together with the provision of the Pragmatic Sanction of August 554 that notable landowners and bishops could elect governors of particular regions.[20] Beyond the city how did exarchs manage to control the increasingly military landowners? Were they really such exceptional governors? While some historians view the office of exarch as one endowed with extraordinary power, subordinating all previous systems to policies decided in Constantinople, others have minimized its novelty.[21] Since a similar structure was applied in North Africa, some comparisons may help to show how the new system operated.

A story recorded by Gregory of Tours in the later part of the sixth century reflects how the system of exarchal, prefectorial and city administration worked in Carthage. At some point before 590 Childebert, king of the Franks, sent a friendly embassy of three men to Constantinople, which travelled via Carthage (presumably from the south of Gaul across the Mediterranean and then on to the eastern capital). There a servant of one of the ambassadors stole an object in the marketplace, refused to return it and then killed the merchant involved. 'The Prefect of Carthage summoned a squad of soldiers, enlisted the help of such passers-by as were bearing arms and dispatched this force to their lodgings.' In the fighting that followed, two of the ambassadors were killed and Grippo, the third, went on to Constantinople to demand that the emperor punish those responsible for insulting him at Carthage. Here the prefect, or city magistrate (elected once a year to preside over the city council), sought to impose order using local forces. Such quarrels may have been common enough and, in Carthage as well as Ravenna, there was a hierarchy of authority, with lower levels to deal with these matters while the exarchs dealt with more serious issues.[22]

The Failed Frankish Alliance

In the early years of the exarchate Constantinople's main ambition was to persuade the Franks to campaign against the Lombards by offering substantial bribes in gold. When Faroald, the Lombard duke of Spoleto, whose territory lay to the south of Ravenna, captured and plundered Classis and held it for some time in 580, Emperor Tiberios II tried to negotiate such an alliance with the Frankish king Childebert II (575–95).[23] The emperor's successor, Maurice, also pursued this policy, sending Decius and Smaragdus, high-ranking patrician officials, to Ravenna in 584 and 585 with instructions to buy Frankish military support. The enormous sum of 50,000 *solidi* was transferred to King Childebert but the proposed joint military action did not take place. Smaragdus initially continued this strategy and, when it failed, he organized a three-year truce with the Lombards.[24]

Many diplomatic envoys passed through Ravenna to try to negotiate terms with Childebert in Gaul. In 590 the Frankish envoy Grippo, whose retinue had been attacked in Carthage, returned from Constantinople with a treaty promising co-operation between Franks and imperial forces in Italy against the Lombards. This was the moment for an all-out battle to drive the Lombards out of Italy. The Franks duly invaded but failed to make contact with the new exarch, Romanus, who described his anger in two letters sent to Childebert. His imperial forces had attacked and captured Modena, Altino and Mantua, and were about to reach Verona, by river and land, to join the Franks in a combined attack on the Lombard capital Pavia, when they learned that Cedinus, one of the Frankish leaders, had signed a ten-month truce with King Authari and marched back to Gaul.[25] This misunderstanding was typical of the protracted negotiations. Large amounts of gold changed hands and Frankish armies did cross the Alps to attack the Lombards, but never achieved the much desired, crushing victory. On several occasions, Frankish dukes, or their mercenary forces, quarrelled among themselves; imperial forces failed to meet them at the arranged rendezvous, and they suffered from dysentery brought on by the summer heat. As a result, both Constantinople and Ravenna had to come to terms with the permanent presence in Italy of the Lombards.

The invaders persistently sought to reduce the exarchate by further conquest, and the precise extent of the territory under imperial control remained disputed. In the 580s, on an island in Lake Como in the far north of Italy, the *magister militum*, Francio, loyal to Constantinople, was guarding a great treasure, valuables that had been deposited on the island for safe keeping. He was besieged by the Lombards and after six months surrendered, having negotiated his own safe passage to Ravenna with his wife and household goods, and the treasure fell into Lombard hands. Clearly, Ravenna was the place where one could find passage to

Constantinople and protection from the Lombards. But Francio's surrender also meant that Lake Como and the area around it passed out of imperial control and ceased to form part of the exarchate. In 602 Padua, which had resisted Lombard control for a long time, finally fell to King Agilulf when his forces projected fire barrels into the city. He then ordered the burned city to be demolished, although some of the defenders were allowed to return to Ravenna.[26]

Despite the more permanent Lombard settlements in north-west Italy, Ravenna remained the centre of imperial government under the eighteen officials who held the title of exarch until 751 (see Chart). The territory of the exarchate was placed onto a more regular administrative base, while a comparable but less well-documented process took place in North Africa until 698, and in southern Spain until about 629. Many exarchs are known only from their seals of office and are difficult to date, but the large number indicates regular turnover: they served for a limited number of years and then returned to the East (apart from Isaac). Such brief tenures of office were intended to ensure closer supervision from Constantinople as well as preventing the growth of strong local loyalties. Given the exarchs' enormous powers, emperors must have been aware of the danger of them developing too much independence, which might lead to rebellion. In this respect the system failed, for there were several revolts. Yet this inventive new form of administration succeeded in keeping considerable areas of north and central Italy within the imperial sphere of government, sustained effective monetary control and represented Constantinople's global influence, with all the concomitant political and cultural ties, for about 150 years.

21

Gregory the Great and the control of Ravenna

Although the exarchs maintained imperial control over the corridor between Ravenna and Rome, the inherent weakness of this narrow link between the two parts of the exarchate left it vulnerable and reflected the precarious nature of imperial power in Italy. Opponents of the Fifth Oecumenical Council of 553 further challenged its effectiveness.

In these disturbed conditions Pope Gregory I, later universally acknowledged as Gregory the Great, was elected bishop of Rome on 3 September 590, when he was about fifty years old. His life spans a decisive period in the Christianization of Roman senatorial families, symbolized by the transformation of his family palace into a monastery in about 573. He retired from secular life into this monastery and, in 579, Pope Pelagius II ordained him a deacon and included him in the papal team sent on a major diplomatic mission to Constantinople. There he remained as papal ambassador until 586. During these crucial seven to eight years in the eastern capital Gregory witnessed the power of the city of Constantine and the imperial court at the centre of the Roman world. Through his friendship with emperors Tiberios and Maurice, he gained an experience of imperial administration and was integrated into the ruling family, acting as godfather to Maurice's son Theodosios. However, he preferred to maintain a monastic routine in the Palace of Placidia, which served as the papal residence in the eastern capital, where he prepared some of his most important commentaries on the Old Testament Book of Job, as well as other spiritual writings. He was also drawn into theological debates with Patriarch Eutychios (restored to his office between 577 and 582) and became very familiar with the problems raised by the Fifth Universal Council that had condemned the Three Chapters.

Leaving Constantinople in 586, Gregory returned to his monastery in Rome, extended his skill as an exegete, manifested in many later commentaries on the Gospels and the Book of Ezekiel, and wrote sermons and studies of local saints including St Benedict, which became the famous book of *Dialogues*. After his election as bishop of Rome in October 590, a promotion confirmed by imperial support, he held the see for nearly fourteen years. His pontificate is particularly well documented by over 850 letters on all manner of topics, his *Book of Pastoral Care* (*Regula pastoralis*) – a guide for bishops – and many other writings connected with his administration. While he regularly complained of the weight of secular duties attached to the position and longed for the peaceful monastic environment, his skills as a leader of western Christianity and the initiatives he took to expand and deepen the spiritual traditions of the western Church make his pontificate especially significant in the development of the medieval papacy. It is also the period when a more distinct separation between the churches of the East and West begins to emerge.[1]

One of Gregory's first tasks was to deal with the schism over the Three Chapters within the western Church. With vigorous determination Gregory set out to convince the Aquileians of their errors, writing letters, arranging meetings, focusing all his persuasive powers on the issue. In 590–91, when Gregory summoned a council to judge the schismatics, the north Italian bishops who had remained under Lombard control formed one group, while the coastal cities (that is, Ravenna, Rome and Naples, which were under imperial control) formed another. Both wrote letters to the emperor, as did Severus, patriarch of Aquileia. The north Italian bishops' letter includes a complaint against the exarch's efforts to convert them. They argue that they will not appear at Pope Gregory's council because they have renounced his communion, and if they are forced back into it their churches will be less loyal to the emperor. While Gregory went on to condemn the north Italians *in absentia*, he was ordered by Emperor Maurice to stop putting such pressure on them. In subsequent letters to the exarch and archbishop in Ravenna, Gregory had to tell them not to use force in their efforts to persuade the schismatics.[2] He appointed a papal official to reside in Ravenna and continued to send the north Italians theological arguments to induce them to condemn the Three Chapters.[3] He also criticized Archbishop John the Roman for sending help to Severus of Aquileia after a fire destroyed the city. Gregory argued that Severus was in Constantinople, where he would misuse the funds in his efforts to win imperial support.[4]

After the death of John the Roman in 595, Pope Gregory sent firm instructions to Castorius, his official notary residing in Ravenna, about the correct procedure to be adopted in electing a successor. Acknowledging the tradition of Ravennate autonomy, he suggested that five senior presbyters and five leading citizens should bring their choice to Rome. But when the Ravenna clergy sent their nomination to the pope for his approval, Gregory rejected both their first candidate and their second. Instead, he insisted on another cleric from Rome, Marinianus, who was a nephew of John the Roman. When Marinianus expressed no enthusiasm to take up a position where he would clearly be unwelcome, he had to be persuaded by Gregory, who dedicated his *Book of Pastoral Care* to him.[5] The pope then wrote to the clergy and people of Ravenna on their duty to honour their new archbishop, who correctly venerated the four universal councils of the church.[6] Here he makes a clear reference to the Council of Chalcedon and pointedly ignores the Fifth Council of 553. In this way, he tried to ensure a strictly pro-Roman position in Ravenna.

Agnellus the historian knew that Marinianus had held the see of Ravenna during the pontificate of Gregory, and reports 'He humbly held the metropolitan see, taught by apostolic dogma', possibly a reference to Gregory's *Regula pastoralis* dedicated to the archbishop.[7] To fill out the *Life*, Agnellus includes bits of sermons and tirades against bishops of his own time, clerics who buy and sell offices, run up debts, bribe officials, corrupt others and generally behave like avaricious civilians.[8] Marinianus, he says, was not like these ninth-century bishops. Agnellus did not mention the beautiful ambo that Marinianus commissioned from Constantinople for the church of Sts John and Paul in 596/7, which can now be admired in the Archiepiscopal Museum, but he copied the long epitaph on Marinianus' tomb at S. Apollinare in Classe, which now became the designated resting place of Ravenna's archbishops. All subsequent leaders of the church were buried there, some in sarcophagi that survive and many with inscriptions that describe their achievements.

Even after Pope Gregory had imposed his own choice for the archbishopric of Ravenna, and instructed Castorius to keep him informed about ecclesiastical life in the city, relations between Rome and the imperial capital were not always peaceful. The pope received reports from junior clergy, such as Adeodatus, a deacon of the church of

Ravenna, who told him that bishops in the Ravenna archdiocese wore the pallium on many more occasions than the four or five ceremonies when it was permitted. In a letter to Castorius, Gregory complains that the exarch, prefect and other noble men of Ravenna have requested this enhanced use of the pallium, and insists that the regulations must be observed.[9] Local abbots, such as Claudius, of the monastery of Sts John and Stephen at Classis, also appealed to Gregory against Marinianus' abusive behaviour: the archbishop had usurped the monastery's properties, tried to impose his own candidate for abbot, and removed monks to serve in other churches. When he came to visit the monastery he insisted on lengthy and lavish entertainment, which reduced it to poverty. In response, the pope ordered Archbishop Marinianus to perform his visitation of the monastery in one day. (Claudius had also attended Gregory's oral exposition of several books of the Old Testament, and later the pope wrote to John, subdeacon of the church of Ravenna, asking him to check if Claudius had left any written records.)[10]

Through his own network of administrative officials, Gregory learned that even the saddle bags used when the archbishop rode out to visit his suffragans were a subject of serious dispute. Horse trappings and harness decoration was one of many issues regulated according to the ecclesiastical hierarchy, and this use of special saddle bags probably overstepped the permitted status. The underlying cause, however, was a distinct rivalry between Ravenna, the imperial capital of Italy, and the older capital of Rome, now transforming itself into the centre of leadership over the Christian West. The political superiority of the new centre of secular power had to confront a greater ecclesiastical authority held by the representatives of St Peter, who sought to exercise a titular primacy of control over all churches. Tensions were therefore inevitable. In the long construction of Roman claims, Gregory the Great played a vital role, drawing on his experience in Constantinople to insist on the subordination of Ravenna.

Under the leadership of Exarch Romanus, imperial troops had regained considerable territory from the Lombards, including key cities and castles in the Apennines that controlled one of the main routes from Ravenna to Rome. According to the Roman *Book of the Pontiffs*, Romanus came to Rome when Gregory was pope, and went from there to Ravenna, retaking the cities of 'Sutrium, Polymartium, Horta, Tuder, Ameria, Perusia, Lucioli and many others'. These were on the

Via Amerina, the trans-Apennine route via Perugia, which had to be secure for effective communication between the exarch and his subordinate, the duke of Rome.[11] In this all-important city Romanus left the Lombard Duke Maurisius in charge, who had come over to the imperial side.

In retaliation, the Lombard king Agilulf marched from Pavia to Perugia and besieged the city. He killed Maurisius and then moved south to threaten Rome, where Pope Gregory was so terrified that he negotiated a truce with the king, and for this he was roundly criticized by Romanus. Through the intervention of Queen Theudelinda, the Catholic wife of the Arian king, a peace was agreed in 598/9; Paul the deacon quotes Gregory's letter to her, thanking her for her help, and to Agilulf. In this example of papal diplomacy, the authority of Constantinople, represented by the exarch, was outflanked by the bishop of Rome.

After the death of Romanus, his successor Callinicus (596–602) sent an army to attack Parma, where it captured the (unnamed) daughter of King Agilulf and her husband Gudescalc, and brought these valuable hostages to Ravenna.[12] They remained there after the death of Callinicus, who was replaced as exarch by Smaragdus, returning on his second tour of duty in 603. But Agilulf was furious at the capture of his daughter and, in July 603, he left Milan to attack Cremona with the assistance of Slavs sent by the king of the Avars. By 21 August, he had razed Cremona to the ground and went on to Mantua, where he broke through the walls on 13 September, and advanced to Vulturina (Valdoria), which surrendered to the Lombards rather than suffer the same treatment. The troops that had defended Mantua were permitted to return to Ravenna, where presumably they told Exarch Smaragdus what was happening further north. Smaragdus then agreed to release King Agilulf's daughter and she returned to Parma with her husband, children and all her property. A truce was agreed on 1 April 605 and Pope Sabinian (604–6), Gregory's successor, continued to respect the terms of the peace treaty with the Lombards.[13]

Exarchs were regularly instructed to contain Lombard power without being given sufficient troops or funds to do so effectively. This remained the crux of Ravenna's problems throughout the seventh century and into the eighth. Smaragdus preferred to make a truce with the Lombards rather than fight, and in November 605 when Constantinople sent 12,000 *solidi* as tribute to Agilulf, the exarch negotiated for him to keep cities in Tuscany that he had seized: Balneus Regis (the King's bath, Bagnarea) and Urbs vetus (Orvieto). But the peace lasted for only three years, until 610, and the Lombards continued their attacks.[14]

In these, sometimes fraught, circumstances, the exarchs tried to resolve ecclesiastical disagreements and to maintain cordial relations with the pope. Callinicus intervened in a dispute between Gregory and the bishops of Salona, on the eastern shore of the Adriatic. Gregory had been angered by reports that Bishop Natalis had been selling off the liturgical vessels of his church and thoroughly neglecting his ecclesiastical duties. When Natalis held a synod at which he deprived Honoratus of his position as archdeacon of the see, Gregory objected forcefully. Although Honoratus was eventually reinstated, and then elected to succeed Natalis as bishop, other factions schemed against him and his rival, Maximus, gained control of the church of Salona. The pope identified him as someone who had obtained the see by simony and supported heretical views.

At this point Callinicus tried to persuade the pope to recognize Maximus. While Gregory insisted that Maximus should come to Rome so that these issues could be resolved, at one point demanding his presence within thirty days, Callinicus found a way to end their quarrel. In July 599 he arranged a ceremony of submission at Ravenna, where Maximus was formally readmitted to communion with the pope in the presence of Archbishop Marinianus.[15] As well as resolving the dispute in a symbolic act, the exarch's ceremony confirmed Ravenna's centrality in the political and military affairs on both shores of the Adriatic.

Despite Pope Gregory's efforts, the ecclesiastical division in Italy continued with coastal cities under imperial influence and mainland bishops living in Lombard territory, and often influenced by Lombard kings, remaining fiercely independent, although not always united. When Severus of Aquileia died in 606/7, two patriarchs were elected, one in favour of the 553 Council and one against. This reflects the high state of tension and mistrust over Lombard support for the schismatic bishops. The theological dispute over the Three Chapters could not be resolved while the north Italian bishops maintained their separate ecclesiastical community under Lombard suzerainty. And, as none of the exarchs proved capable of destroying the Lombards' military hold on the area, theology and politics combined to frustrate both Constantinople and Rome.

The schism over the Three Chapters persisted until 698, when the Lombard king Cunincpert abandoned opposition to Constantinople's policy in a council that celebrated reunion with the other churches of the West, with no reference to the writings of Theodore of Mopsuestia, Theodoret and Ibas. Instead, Paul the deacon's account stresses the title Mother of God, given to the Virgin Mary by the Council of Ephesus in 431, as if this was the decisive novelty.[16] By the end of the seventh century the Marian feasts were celebrated throughout western Christendom and Ravenna had five churches dedicated to her cult, including S. Maria *in Cosmedin*, previously the Arian baptistery, and S. Maria *ad Blachernas*. Agnellus proudly explains the name Cosmedin, saying that this is not from the Greek for world, *kosmos*, but from the Latin *cosmi* meaning ornate. Since he was also the abbot of S. Maria *ad Blachernas*, he knew it was modelled on the Blachernai church in Constantinople, another reminder of the city where the Three Chapters dispute had originated.[17]

22

Isaac, the Armenian exarch

During the early seventh century a series of capable exarchs in Ravenna consolidated control over the Italian provinces, ensured the payment of local taxes to Constantinople and attempted to enforce the official theology adopted in the eastern capital. Ravenna's maritime connections with the East facilitated the movement of envoys, pilgrims, merchants and soldiers, who all continued to travel throughout the Mediterranean world, often using the port of Classis.

In November 602 a military revolt in the East threatened this relatively settled arrangement, when a junior officer, Phokas, was acclaimed emperor by his fellow soldiers in the Balkans. After their immediate refusal to campaign north of the Danube in winter, the rebels marched to Constantinople and, in a surprisingly rapid coup, murdered Emperor Maurice and his sons and established Phokas on the throne. While this caused great anxiety in Constantinople and provoked the Persians to invade the empire in the East, in Italy Exarch Smaragdus accepted the new regime.[1] Even though Pope Gregory had known Maurice and Empress Constantina in Constantinople during his time as papal representative, he too urged support for Phokas, going out to greet the portraits of the new imperial ruler and his wife on 25 April 603. After this ceremonial reception, Gregory displayed the images in the chapel of St Caesarius within the ancient palace on the Palatine to mark the change of regime in the East. He wrote to Phokas and his wife, Leontia, recommending that they follow the model of Constantine the Great and his mother Helena, always considered the archetype of Christian rulers.[2] Had he learned of the murder of the widowed Empress Constantina in 605, he might have been less supportive, but on 12 March 604 Gregory died after a momentous papal reign of fourteen years. While his mission to Canterbury to convert the Angles is often considered his supreme achievement, his organization of the papal office, with efficient record keeping, administration of estates and care for the poor (probably including many refugees from Lombard attacks) was certainly more important for Italy.

His successors, Sabinian and Boniface III, continued to co-operate with the new emperor, and in 608 Boniface IV (608–15) negotiated permission from Phokas to adapt the Pantheon for Christian use. This was the first conversion of a pagan monument in the centre of Rome, and the emperor sent many gifts to mark its transformation into a church dedicated to St Mary and all the martyrs.[3] Smaragdus the exarch was also involved in the process and commemorated it in a very striking new monument put up on the Roman Forum on 1 August 608: an honorary column. Not since the fifth century had an emperor been honoured in Rome in this way. The exarch and the pope thus collaborated in renewing control over Rome, imperial and papal respectively, under the aegis of Constantinople's authority.

Smaragdus' Inscription

The long inscription carved on the base of the column records Smaragdus the exarch who took responsibility for erecting it in honour of Emperor Phokas (Plate 48). Both column and base were re-used; the original inscription to Diocletian was scraped off, and the gilded statue that was erected on top may also have been recycled. Nonetheless, the dedication to 'our most clement and pious ruler, lord Phokas, perpetual emperor crowned by God, the forever august triumphant [prince]', in gratitude for his innumerable benefactions, and the peace and freedom of Italy, reflects an appropriate devotion to the emperor in Constantinople, the supreme ruler of Italy. Acknowledging Smaragdus, currently exarch of Italy and *patricius*, as previously holding the position of *praepositus sacri palatii*, it also notes the height of the column (at 13.6m, the tallest on the Forum), all part of the effort to commemorate the emperor's glory.[4] The ceremonial dedication was obviously a most unusual event at the time and drew attention to the real master of Old Rome, who now resided in New Rome. And although no one at the time knew it, this was also to be the last in the tradition of raising columns on the Forum.

To judge by the numerous revolts that took place during his short eight-year reign, Phokas was a cruel and incompetent ruler, a soldier who had been promoted by his troops but had very little imperial skill. He might well have suggested the erection of the statue in Rome, but in the very same year of its dedication, disaffected senators in Constantinople appealed to Herakleios, the exarch of Carthage, to oust the emperor. In response, he sent his son (also named Herakleios) by sea, and his nephew Niketas by land, to assist their plans. The following year (609) Herakleios the Younger sailed into Constantinople and removed Phokas. The role of the North African exarchate in providing military muscle to this senatorial revolt drew attention to the power of the western provinces within the empire. Once installed as emperor, Herakleios (610–41) appointed competent men to govern the exarchates, though local leaders – and indeed some exarchs – tried to take advantage of these resources to create their own independent states.[5]

Exarchs of the Early Seventh Century

In 615–16 a revolt broke out in Naples led by John of Compsa, and the exarch, also called John, and other imperial officials identified as *iudices rei publicae* (notables, often military) were killed.[6] The unrest was probably provoked by cuts or delays in paying the army. Herakleios dealt with this effort to shake off Constantinopolitan control by sending Eleutherios, a eunuch, to punish the assassins. He arrived in Ravenna in 616, went to Rome where he was welcomed by Pope Deusdedit with all solemnity, and proceeded to Naples to put down the revolt of John of Compsa. The Roman *Book of the Pontiffs* records that he returned to Ravenna, paid the soldiers and 'a great peace was achieved throughout Italy', that is, in both parts of the exarchate, Ravenna in the north-east, and Rome and Naples on the west coast. But three years later, in 619, Eleutherios in turn decided to set himself up as ruler and demanded that Archbishop John IV of Ravenna should crown him. Instead, John suggested that he should go to Rome to establish his authority, and at the castrum called Lucioli on the Via Amerina between Ravenna and Rome, he was killed by 'soldiers from the army of Ravenna'. They put his head in a bag and sent it to Constantinople to prove that he was dead.[7]

This episode exemplifies the dangers inherent in governing an area so far from the centre of the empire. Constantinople had to invest the position of the exarch with sufficient authority to ensure the collection of taxes and obedience to rule from the eastern capital. In this, the exarch also relied on support from the archbishop of Ravenna, who represented another powerful but independent institution, and the city council and other local bodies not controlled from Constantinople. With this remarkably powerful capacity, several governors were tempted to try and establish their own little kingdoms in the West. In 619 Archbishop John and a section of the local militia found an effective way to get rid of Eleutherios, one of these over-ambitious officials. Their combined action makes plain the inevitable tensions within Ravenna, which were common to many regions of the empire.

Following the death of Eleutherios, Herakleios appointed as exarch Gregory the patrician (619–25), followed by Isaac, who, like the emperor, also claimed Armenian descent. The first must have rewarded the troops from the army of Ravenna who had obstructed the attempted coup of his predecessor. He also dealt with the Lombard dukes of Friuli and Slavs settled in Carinthia (southern Austria).[8] This was an area whose bishops persisted in their opposition to the Council of 553; they had elected a rival patriarch of Aquileia to represent them and resisted all Exarch Gregory's attempts to win them over to the imperial view. His successor Isaac, who held the position of exarch longer than any other, from 625 until 643 (perhaps a sign that he was a most trusted and reliable supporter of the emperor), had to continue the campaign. In 625 Pope Honorius wrote to Isaac to request his help in curbing the activity of these persistent supporters of the Three Chapters, but the exarch was preoccupied by a revival of Lombard military action.

The Energy and Will of Christ

When he first arrived in Constantinople in 610 Herakleios 'found the affairs of the Roman state undone, for the Avars had devastated Europe, while the Persians had destroyed all of Asia and had captured many cities and annihilated in battle the Roman army'.[9] For two decades the new emperor had to confront a determined Persian invasion, followed by the occupation of Syria, Palestine and Egypt, which greatly reduced his resources, while Slavs and Avars threatened the Balkan frontier. In his efforts to rebuild military resources he was strongly supported by Patriarch Sergios, who permitted the melting down of liturgical silver to increase the supply of coin for military pay. Herakleios then transferred military units from Europe to Asia Minor and in 622 set out on a long campaign against Persia.[10] Following a complex and brilliant strategy, in 628 he destroyed the Persian capital, Ctesiphon, and celebrated his decisive victory in appropriate triumphs and a new Greek title, *basileus pistos en Christo*, king faithful in Christ. This reflected Herakleios' determination to unite all the Christians of his empire, by regaining the support of the Monophysite communities of the Near East, who had never accepted the decrees of the Council of Chalcedon.[11] In this effort to find a theological compromise that would command their agreement, the emperor became mired in debates over the single energy and single will of Christ (Monotheletism), which only deepened divisions.

The argument that Christ had only one energy, not two corresponding to his divine and human natures, was initially accepted by Pope Honorius.[12] But the more developed Monothelete doctrine of Christ's single will, pronounced in 638, immediately provoked a strong reaction among a group of eastern monks whose sophisticated grasp of theology made them serious opponents. The death of the pope in October the same year not only opened the western reaction to Monotheletism but was also accompanied by rumours in Rome that Honorius had retained funds sent to pay the army in the papal residence, the Lateran palace. Taking advantage of these ideas and the power vacuum that existed before the consecration of the new pope, the *cartularius* Mauricius, one of Isaac's subordinates, broke into the Lateran and wrote to inform the exarch of the great wealth accumulated by many earlier bishops. Isaac went to Rome and decided to remove the treasure, partly to provide pay for the army and partly to support the emperor by sending a portion of the wealth to Herakleios. In order to do so, he had to exile the Roman clergy to other cities temporarily.[13] They later complained that in plundering the palace Isaac had exhausted funds bequeathed to the Church for distribution as alms to the poor, for the redemption of captives and of the souls of many Christian donors. But Isaac had to pay his military forces, as well as imposing the imperial theology, and used the funds to ensure the policy of Herakleios. After a long gap of nineteen months Severinus was ordained pope on 28 May 640, but he died only two months later.

This plunder of the Lateran palace coincided with increasing opposition to the Monothelete doctrine of Christ's will, led by Patriarch Sophronios of Jerusalem and Maximos, a monk later known as the Confessor, who went to Rome to warn the pope of the danger of a new heresy. Pope John IV (640–42) and his successor Theodore (642–9) both condemned Monotheletism as contrary to the traditions of the ancient church, thus opening a schism not only between the sees of Rome and Constantinople, but also between Rome and Ravenna where Isaac the exarch supported the imperial position. When Herakleios died in 641 his religious policy had failed in both the East and West. In some regions, the persistent upholders of the Three Chapters suspected that Constantinople was now the source of unreliable, if not heretical, beliefs.

The Resurgence of Lombard Power

All this theological turmoil developed while Exarch Isaac faced military threats from the Lombards under kings Ariold (626–36) and Rothari (636–52), invigorated by a revival of their traditional Arian beliefs. While this recreated the earlier rivalry between religious leaders – 'there were two bishops throughout almost all the cities of the kingdom, one a Catholic and the other an Arian' – the resurgence of Arian communities among the Lombards strengthened their military ambitions to conquer all imperial territory. In addition to the usual diplomatic efforts to play off one hostile force against another, Isaac sent imperial forces to confront a Lombard invasion of the duchies of the Venetiae, north of Ravenna, and campaigned in north-west Italy, where Rothari consolidated his rule over Liguria when he captured Genoa and Albenga and Luni in Tuscany. Paul the deacon claims that the Lombards defeated Isaac near the River Scultenna (Panaro) where eight thousand troops fell – a terrible loss for the exarch, if true.[14]

In the Venetiae the Lombards occupied much of the mainland,

forcing the inhabitants of Oderzo and Altino to flee to islands in the lagoons at the head of the Adriatic, where they formed the settlements of Cittanova, which later became the core of Venice, and Torcello, respectively. The local bishop, Maurus, recorded the patronage of Isaac in the foundation of a church dedicated to Holy Mary, Mother of God, on Torcello, reflected in the inscription of 639:

> On the order of the pious and devout Lord Isaac, most excellent exarch and patrician, for his benefit and that of his army this was built from its foundations by Mauricius, the glorious master of the soldiers of the province of the Venetiae . . .[15]

Isaac may also have intervened when an invasion of northern people, often identified as Bulgars, fled the domination of the Avars in Pannonia and advanced into Gaul and Italy. Some were settled in central Italy by the Lombard duke of Benevento, others reached the Pentapolis, under Isaac's control, and in both regions their presence is reflected in the names of places and people.[16]

The Revolt of 642

When Pope John IV died in October 642 Mauricius, the devious *cartularius*, launched an even more brazen rebellion with the help of those local troops who had plundered the Lateran. Claiming that Exarch Isaac intended to set himself up as emperor, Mauricius tried to persuade all the people from Rome and the neighbouring cities to swear loyalty to himself alone. Isaac reacted by sending Donus, *magister militum*, and a *sacellarius* (treasurer), to put down this revolt, and they captured Mauricius and killed him. His head was carried into Ravenna and displayed on a pole in the middle of the circus there, a typical punishment for a rebel. Before he had decided how to punish the others who had taken part in the revolt, Isaac died in 643.[17]

The Roman *Book of the Pontiffs* records his death as an act of God, a divine punishment for his loyalty to the Monothelete doctrine opposed by Rome. His grieving widow, Susanna, acquired a late antique sarcophagus for his tomb and a lid on which she had his life and achievements recorded in Greek iambic trimeters. These claim that 'he kept Rome and the West safe for the serene sovereigns', and praise his Armenian origin and his unusually long tenure of office (Plates 34 and 35).[18] This magnificent sarcophagus, which can still be admired inside the church of San Vitale, dates from the fifth century and displays the three kings presenting their gifts to the Virgin and Child, an elaborate cross flanked by peacocks on the two long sides, with Daniel in the lions' den and the raising of Lazarus on the short ends. Bishops of Ravenna were all buried in these impressively carved sarcophagi.[19]

Isaac's epitaph was probably chosen by Susanna who paid the author of the verses and the carver, who very skilfully created their record on either side of the cross that was already on the lid. The Greek letters were very accurately and precisely carved and are quite different from contemporary Greek inscriptions in Rome or Vicenza, displaying no influence from Latin inscriptions. Accents and breathings must have been added much later, probably in the Renaissance when a Latin translation of the verses was added on the other side of the lid.[20] The entire Greek inscription is presented in such a fashion that the verses can be read from left to right across the central divide formed by the cross, or in two sections separated by it. In the use of Greek, Susanna displayed her appreciation of the language employed at the highest levels of government and identified the governor as one who belonged to the cultural milieu of imperial Constantinople. While his Greek epitaph would not have been understood by most local inhabitants, on his seal Isaac was also identified in Latin (as *patricius et hexarchus*).[21] Like his predecessors he must have used Latin for writing letters to local officials, Lombard kings and popes, while employing Greek for communication with Constantinople.[22]

Isaac is also known from another inscription in Greek, at Comaclum (Comacchio) near Ravenna devoted to his nephew Gregory, who died at the age of eleven, which is equally carefully executed.[23] The Armenian exarch's trilingual identity reflects the very mixed population both of the eastern empire and of the western exarchates, where skilful military commanders and experienced administrators could make their careers. One of them may be Paulacis, a soldier of the Armenian *numerus*, who sold a property named Terriatico to the church of Ravenna for 36 *solidi* in 639. A *schole gentilium* (cohort of guards) is recorded at Classis and another *schola forensium* existed for secretaries, who represented the literate lower-level administrators. As we've seen, there were several Greeks in Ravenna who signed acts using Greek letters, while other merchants, moneychangers and officials witness legal documents writing their names in Greek characters.[24] Educated people still wished to understand and extend their knowledge of Greek. Ravenna was just the sort of place where such bilingual knowledge was preserved, reinforced by the regular arrival of officials appointed by Constantinople and by the study of medical, liturgical and geographical texts.

23

Agnellus the doctor

In the rich and varied cultural environment of Ravenna at the turn of the seventh century, the city was also a centre of medical learning. There was a Greek school of medicine represented by Leontios, *medicus ab schola greca*, and probably another *schola*, a guild or professional group, of Latin experts.[1] Since Cassiodorus mentions a city official who had responsibility for settling any disputes between doctors, different medical traditions were practised in the city.[2]

The most famous local doctor was Agnellus, who gave lectures in Latin on the most important elementary texts of Galen, which were written down by a student or younger scholar, perhaps his amanuensis, named Simplicius.[3] This scribe signed his manuscript three times with the declaration: 'from the voice of Agnellus, *yatrosophista*, I, Simplicius, with God's help, read and wrote in Ravenna successfully' (Plate 46). He gave Agnellus the titles of *archiatros* (chief doctor) and *yatrosophista* (someone who teaches medicine) and identified himself as *medicus*. From Dr Agnellus' oral presentations, Simplicius made notes – probably using the well-known short-hand system for taking dictation – and created the most complete surviving account of Galen's *Ars medica* in Latin. The second-century Greek original is today reconstructed from this source.[4] Since Agnellus followed the commentaries of Olympiodoros, an Alexandrian expert, whose work reached Ravenna around 550, his activity may be dated in the second half of the sixth century or later, perhaps a generation after Leontios, and he belonged to the same medical school in Ravenna where ancient Greek techniques were taught and practised.[5]

Dr Agnellus' lectures consisted of a series of commentaries in Latin on the most important works of Hippocrates and Galen, whose writings had been copied and commented on by generations of teachers in the East but were little known in the West. These founders of ancient Greek medicine had investigated both theoretical and practical aspects, which were taught in schools, particularly in Alexandria, into the seventh and eighth centuries. Agnellus introduced students to Galen's writings beginning with the most elementary, *De sectis* (On different schools and approaches to medical problems), and moving on to the *Ars medica* (The art of medicine, later known by the name *Techni*), *De pulsibus ad tirones* (On the pulse for beginners) and finally an anonymous Latin commentary on Galen's *Therapeutica ad Glauconem*: 'because we can't cure fevers unless we know from the pulse the changes in nature'.[6] He also taught some more advanced courses on aetiology. In Alexandria, the students began with Hippocrates' *Aphorisms* and then went on to sixteen books of Galen in seven consecutive grades, in the same way that they had to master Aristotle's *Organon* before they could tackle Plato. The medical education established in Alexandria inspired the school at Ravenna, which has been described as 'clearly the epicenter of the most advanced medical learning in late antiquity . . . [it] was the Latin West's answer to the Greek East's Alexandria, which was the primary center of medical instruction and practice in the Byzantine world through the seventh century'.[7]

In his lectures Agnellus added to the commentaries on Galen's medical texts with an explicit condemnation of the 'methodist' school of medicine that ignored internal and external factors in sustaining health (*De sectis*); he supported the 'empiricist' school committed to observation of all possible influences. He also gave greater emphasis to the four causes that may modify the pulse (*De pulsibus*).[8] But the major innovation occurred in his comments on Galen's *Ars medica*, where Agnellus appears to have incorporated ideas of the fourth-century Greek authors Nemesios, a Syrian bishop, and Posidonios of Byzantium, a doctor, who linked the function of three human qualities – imagination, intelligence and memory – to specific ventricles of the brain: the anterior, central and posterior.[9] Developing the Greek texts, he emphasized the softness and humidity of the front of the brain, likened to wax in which an image can be stamped, which becomes harder towards the back. The capacity to learn is facilitated by a substance that can take an impression, or be imprinted; this *logismos*, reason, is an abundant and subtle spirit that penetrates the nerves. In contrast, memory springs from a more stable substance associated with the posterior ventricle.[10]

These divisions are also related to the Hippocratic concept of the four humours of the body – blood, yellow bile, black bile and phlegm – which with the equivalent temperaments determine the character of the soul. Agnellus, following this tradition, attributed the bad judgement and excessive anger of a tyrant to a choleric, hot dryness, in contrast with the royal *imperator* who is just, wise and tries to restrain anger with a cool temperament. He suggested that bad habits, which may be inherited, can be corrected by philosophical training and obedience to the laws, an idea that Galen derived from Plato.[11]

Simplicius' written account of these presentations preserves all that is known about Dr Agnellus. His text survives in a ninth-century copy made in Milan, now in the Ambrosiana library there. Oral delivery, integral to the ancient method of teaching, was the normal pedagogic method of communication in all fields. And from the records of what a teacher said the development of different subjects can be traced. This was the procedure that transmitted most of Galen's teaching; the original Greek text of his *De sectis* may have been compiled from the notes dictated to students or taken down in lectures.[12] Similarly, when Julius Honorius made oral presentations on the geography of the world, probably in late fourth- or early fifth-century North Africa, a student was instructed to write down his explanation of the *sphaera*, a round map of the world.[13] Later, the anonymous Cosmographer of Ravenna would expound his knowledge of geography verbally and, much later still, Agnellus, the historian, read his *Book of the Pontiffs of Ravenna* to an audience.[14]

Agnellus and Leontios were undoubtedly products of the medical schools of Ravenna, patronized by Theoderic and his successors, where the translation of Greek texts, including commentaries on Galen's four fundamental texts and Oribasios' huge compendium of medical knowledge – the *Aphorisms* of Hippocrates – were made.[15] The translator of Oribasios had recorded that he worked in Ravenna with the Gothic court's encouragement, using similar Latin terms to those found in the Latin versions of the Hippocratic corpus.[16] Boethius was actively translating Aristotle and other major Greek authors at the time. In the new Latin medical texts the preponderance of Greek terms is pronounced; literal translations of technical terms are followed by a Latin equivalent, or the contrast between 'what the Greeks say and what we say [in Latin]'.[17] This fits with the established practice of commentaries written in the East Mediterranean, for example by John of Alexandria, Palladius, Gessius and Stephanos of Athens, who often take a point from the translated text to initiate a discussion, and go back to the Greek originals, implying the circulation of both versions.[18] Although there is no evidence that Dr Agnellus studied in Alexandria, it is likely that he did and another local doctor, named Martyrius, is cited as one who had studied with experts from the East.[19]

In the Latin versions of Galen's preparatory courses there are also two references to the study of urine – a fundamental diagnostic instrument in ancient medical practice. Both are concerned with obstructions to the bladder caused by fat and glutinous humour or stones. Treatments to remove both fat and stones are then described, and if these are unsuccessful, 'we must then use those instruments that are able to move the stone from its position, for example a catheter. If the catheter is also unsuccessful we must then proceed with a surgical procedure that we call lithotomy.'[20] So Agnellus knew the practical way to remove painful gall stones, and a modern doctor who has studied him believes that he probably practised these methods; his expertise may have extended to surgery based on ancient principles.

The manuscript that preserves the text of Simplicius also contains three texts of Hippocrates translated in Ravenna, as well as chants to celebrate the feasts of S. Severo and S. Andrea, emphasizing the local origin of Dr Agnellus and his followers.[21] Further evidence of Ravenna's medical traditions is found in the existence of several palimpsest manuscripts, literally 'twice scraped', that have traces of an earlier text erased to create a fresh parchment. Several eighth-century copies of the *Etymologies* of Isidore of Seville were written on such re-used parchment that preserves an undertext of fragments of Galen in Greek, of the Gothic Bible, of another Latin Bible and a Greek mathematical text of Anthemius of Tralles. Although these were traditionally associated with the monastery of Bobbio, they are more likely to have come from Ravenna, which provided some Greek and Gothic manuscripts to be washed and then re-used by the scribes of the *Etymologies*. Other Arian texts from Ravenna remain barely legible under a text of the Council of Chalcedon, probably commissioned by King Cunincpert when he decided to abandon the Three Chapters, a symbolic end for heretical documents.[22]

As a result of these discoveries, other Latin texts that can now be attributed to Ravenna include the *Aphorisms* of Hippocrates, and pseudo-Hippocrates' *De observantia ciborum* (two medical texts now in the Vatican and Naples), and the second Latin version of Oribasios' *Euporista*.[23] This mentions Johannis, *pimentarius* at Ravenna, who supplies herbs for medical purposes and can provides good *tymia*, thyme. Could he be the same Johannis *pimentarius* recorded in a papyrus of 539 (Chapter 14)?[24] The most important compendium of herbal properties and pharmacological treatments, *De materia medica* compiled by Dioscorides in the first century AD, was certainly known in the city. While responsibility for making its first Latin versions is claimed by many centres, one translation, now preserved in Munich, was definitely made from a Greek model that came from Ravenna.[25] Another short text, *De herbis feminis*, also attributed to Dioscorides, similarly betrays a connection with the city.[26] Ravenna probably provided an early seventh-century collection of medical recipes in Cassiodorus' library at Vivarium, which is now in Lucca.[27] The earliest Latin manuscript of the anthology of treatments known as the *Alphabet of Galen*, Hippocrates' gynaecological treatises and the Latin version of Rufus of Ephesus' *On Gout* confirm that Ravenna was a major centre of medical manuscript production, with scribes competent in Greek, Latin and Gothic.[28]

This unusual concentration of medical expertise is paralleled only in the exarchate of North Africa, the other imperial western enclave, where Greek texts were also translated into Latin before the Arab conquest of 698. Both Ravenna and Carthage thus demonstrate cultural connections with the East Mediterranean, but Ravenna is the centre in which a serious practice of medicine can be documented. In his commentaries on the chief works of Hippocrates and Galen, Dr Agnellus represents a development of Alexandrian teaching and a curiosity about difficult Greek texts that was already rare by the end of the sixth century.[29] His work influenced the much later Beneventan manuscripts of the Latin translation and commentary of Hippocrates' *Aphorisms*, the commentaries of Barthelemy of Salerno in the eleventh century, and many later medieval writers on medicine.[30] His unusual style of teaching must be related to the city's direct links to Constantinople and Alexandria, although it's impossible to recreate the precise syllabus of lectures or to date his activity more closely. Agnellus' interests probably encouraged the knowledge of Greek later manifested by a local bilingual translator who displayed such skills that the emperor summoned him to the Queen City (see Chapter 25). And, clearly, he inspired Simplicius to write down several complex treatises on medical treatments with a clear summation of ancient Greek medical knowledge that became a key source in its transmission to the Latin West.

PART SIX

610–700

The expansion of Islam

24

The Arab conquests

For centuries the Roman empire had confronted the other great power of the Middle East, Persia. The ancient Persian empire had always challenged the Mediterranean world and its threats had forced all sixth-century rulers, like Justinian, to campaign on Rome's eastern frontiers. Between 622 and 628 Emperor Herakleios battled to crush Persia's power and eventually succeeded. The official dispatch of victory was sent to the patriarch, who read it to the people of Constantinople in the church of Holy Wisdom, capturing the triumphant moment:

> Let all the earth raise a cry to God; and serve the Lord in gladness, enter into his presence in exultation, and recognize that God is Lord indeed. It is he who has made us and not we ourselves. We are his people and sheep of his pasture . . . For fallen is the arrogant Chosroes, opponent of God . . . his memory is utterly exterminated from the earth . . . he who was exalted and spoke injustice in arrogance and contempt against our Lord Jesus . . . and his undefiled Mother, our blessed lady, Mother of God and ever-Virgin Mary, perished is the profaner with a resounding noise.[1]

This was a Christian victory over a Zoroastrian leader who had forced the patriarch of Jerusalem, with his Christian flock and the relic of the True Cross, into a Babylonian captivity in Ctesiphon. With great solemnity, on 21 March 630 Herakleios restored the True Cross to its rightful place in Jerusalem.

The emperor now reimposed Roman administration in the eastern provinces of Palestine and Syria and installed a pliant, pro-Roman ruler in Persia, but both empires had been drained by the long war that exhausted their military forces. Although he knew the importance of intelligence provided by 'the Saracens who are subject to our

Christ-loving state' – Ghassanid and Lakhmid tribesmen who lived in the desert that bordered eastern Syria and Palestine – imperial officials, insensitive to disturbances in the region of Arabia, refused to pay them the customary regular tribute. Whether this was an ill-considered change of policy or an initiative of local commanders, it led some tribesmen to give up their traditional role, leaving parts of the south-east frontier unobserved and unguarded. Raiders from Arab tribes soon found it much easier to ride north on their camels and attack the flourishing regions of Palestine.

The combination of a change in frontier policy and the introduction of Monotheletism proved fatal to imperial control in these regions: doctrinal disagreement increased divisions among the Christian population, while a traditional way of gathering intelligence was abandoned. From the early seventh century a contrary development towards greater political unity and a new religious purpose among the desert tribes of Arabia transformed their raiding into occupation of provinces of both the Roman and Persian empires. Inspired by the Prophet Muhammad, who dictated his vision of Islam (submission to Allah, God) as the final divine revelation to humanity, his family, his tribe and, gradually, many other Arab tribes adopted the new Arabic monotheism. In 622 Muhammad moved his community from Mecca to Medina and marked the event as the start of a new Muslim lunar calendar: year 1 of the Hegira (AH). He united many of the warring factions under his leadership so that they could regain Mecca in 629, where he destroyed the 360 pagan idols at the pilgrimage site of the Kaaba. Emphasizing the spiritual nature of Islam, he gave his followers a mission to spread their new faith beyond the deserts of Arabia. After his death in 632, they rapidly occupied the prosperous provinces of Palestine, capturing Jerusalem between 635 and 638, occupying Syria after 636, and Alexandria and most of Egypt by 642.[2] The speed of their conquests must be related to the new monotheistic doctrine pronounced in their own language (classical Arabic), which was transmitted orally until written down in the Koran, a holy book intended to replace both the Old and the New Testaments.[3]

After witnessing a most serious defeat at the battle of the River Yarmuk, a natural barrier in Palestina 11 (636), Herakleios withdrew imperial forces behind the Taurus mountains of eastern Asia Minor and the Arabs established their capital at Damascus. From this base they overran the entire area of the Persian empire and raided Asia Minor almost every year, determined to capture Constantinople. This threat was real and continuous: the once-nomadic people integrated the cities and lands they conquered into the sphere of Islam, creating a new self-contained power. Their ambition was frustrated initially at the Taurus frontier and later by the will and the walls of Constantinople, but emperors were never able to reverse the original Arab conquests of the 630s.

An immediate effect of the Arab campaigns was the catastrophic loss of tax revenue together with manpower for the army and mercantile activity.[4] In addition to regular raids by land, the Arabs pressed the maritime skills of the Christian populations of Alexandria, Syria and Lebanon into service, to build ships and begin naval warfare against the islands of Cyprus, Rhodes and even settlements in the Aegean. When Herakleios died in 641, the disputed succession of his son caused a major crisis for about ten months, until his twelve-year-old grandson, Constans II, was acclaimed as sole ruler under the guidance of a council of regency. The new emperor's age, repeated defeats suffered by imperial military units and the emergence of Islam with its claim to supersede both Judaism and Christianity, did not augur well for the survival of the empire. If the followers of Muhammad had indeed taken over the resources of the eastern capital, the history of the world would have been very different, but thanks to the regency council that sustained young Constans II, his own reign (c. 650–68) and those of his son and grandson (Constantine IV, 668–85, and Justinian II, 685–95 and 705–11), the city resisted. In the process of adapting to a greatly diminished territory, the East Roman empire was transformed.

The Arabs' rapid conquests resulted in a tripartite division of the Mediterranean world into an eastern and southern littoral, dominated by Islam, a greatly reduced Christian empire based on Constantinople, and isolated and fragmented regions in the Christian West, still under Germanic pressures. In Carthage, Exarch Gregory saw the Arab advance as a chance to assert his independence, but his rebellion failed, and he was killed in 649. At the time witnesses underestimated the permanent nature of the Arab advance into the Mediterranean, though the continuators of Fredegar's *Chronicle* recorded the defeat of Arabs near Poitiers in 732 (also noted by Bede in northern England). Anonymous Spanish chronicles of 741 and 754 both cite Emperor Herakleios's nightmares about rats from the desert, who would ravage him (without specific references to Islam).[5] Refugees arrived in Italy with stories of their flight from the Arabs, and the Roman *Book of the Pontiffs* reports that the Saracens were living in Sicily in the 650s, with no reference to the scale of the Islamic conquests. By the end of the eighth century, however, Paul the deacon mentions the Saracens, 'unbelieving and hateful to God', who had advanced from Egypt into Africa and captured Carthage.[6]

For Constantinople the emergence of Islam clearly marked a turning point, but the overall impact of the Arab conquests is highly disputed. The hundred-year-old thesis of Henri Pirenne – 'Without Muhammad Charlemagne would be inconceivable' – continues to provoke debate over the decline in Mediterranean-wide trade. But growing evidence for small-scale coastal transport, from shipwrecks and reports of piracy, and the co-operation of Muslim and Christian merchants (and rulers on Cyprus), suggest that the demand for papyrus, spices and eastern luxury goods in the West was met by continuing trade.[7] New finds of imported ceramics at Classis add to the evidence of continuing contacts between Ravenna and the East Mediterranean, though less than in earlier centuries.[8] In Constantinople the western regions of the empire took on much greater importance, both as a resource to assist the beleaguered East and as a refuge from continual pressure on the frontier now developing along the line of the Taurus mountains. The extent of imperial losses, particularly control of Egypt and its supply of grain on which Constantinople had depended for centuries, resulted in a search for alternate supplies nearer the capital and, probably, a change of diet.

The Reign of Constans II

The council of regency established in Constantinople from 641–50 had to concentrate all imperial military capacity to defend what remained of the empire against regular Arab attacks. And when Constans II turned twenty-one and insisted on ruling without its advice, his youthful bravado and inexperience almost led to his death four years later in 654. At a naval battle fought off Phoinike on the south coast of Lycia (in Asia Minor, today's Finike in Turkey) he escaped from near disaster by disguising himself in the clothes of a loyal guard who perished, while the Arabs sailed into the Aegean capturing Rhodes and Kos and raiding Crete. The Arab armada intended to link up with land armies sent from Damascus in an attempt to besiege the capital, where only an act of God saved it. According to the Armenian historian Sebeos, 'a great tempest stirred the sea . . . the waves piled up high like the summits of very high mountains and the wind whirled around over them, it crashed and roared like the clouds and there were gurglings from the depths'. For six days this violent turbulence broke up the Arab fleet, throwing its crews overboard, where a few survived by holding onto planks until 'the sea opened its mouth and swallowed them'.[9] The Arab military commanders waiting at Chalcedon to be transported across the Bosporus to besiege Constantinople were obliged to retreat. The capital had survived a serious military threat, but the Arabs had not given up their aim of capturing it and would try again in 667–9 and 717–18.

Challenged by the new Islamic monotheism, the government of Constantinople renewed its efforts to unite the Christians within the empire. Constans II was committed to the theology developed by his grandfather Herakleios – the doctrine of the single energy and will of Christ, rather than both the human and divine energies and wills – which had been promoted in the *Ekthesis* (statement of faith) of 638.[10] The Monothelete doctrine had been debated in churches in Cyprus, North Africa and Italy, and its arguments over Christ's single will must have been rehearsed in Ravenna, where Exarch Isaac upheld the imperial position. In Rome, however, Pope John IV had condemned the *Ekthesis* and opposition to Monotheletism was stiffened by the election of Theodore, son of a bishop from Jerusalem, as his successor.[11] He was the first in a series of eleven Greek-speaking popes, elected between 642 and 715 and identified by their births in Syria, Greece (which designates the eastern empire), Sicily and southern Italy; their knowledge of Greek proved very important during the theological disputes of the period. Because this group marks such a clear break from the normal recruitment of bishops from among the Roman clergy, there must have been a distinct preference for such candidates and an organized pressure from Palestinian refugee communities in Rome to secure their promotion.[12] Pope Theodore had been warned by Archbishop Sergios of Cyprus about the disagreements over Monotheletism and it was during his reign that the theological problem of Christ's will or wills became entwined in political loyalty to Constantinople.

Rome, Champion of Orthodoxy

As we have seen, initial opposition to Monotheletism was led by eastern theologians, particularly Maximos the Confessor and his teacher and friend Sophronios, patriarch of Jerusalem, who had established the significance of the two wills operating in Christ. They were able to demonstrate that the divine will corresponded to the will of the Father, and the human will to the incarnate Christ, completely undermining the imperial position. In addition, they also championed the role of Rome as an apostolic foundation that sustained Christian orthodoxy against such heretical developments in Constantinople.[13] In a public debate held in Carthage in 645, their arguments persuaded Pyrrhos, the Monothelete ex-patriarch of Constantinople, to recant, and Maximos accompanied him to Rome to be welcomed by Pope Theodore. In combination with Palestinian and Syrian monks, refugees from the Muslim invasions, Rome now became the centre of opposition to Monotheletism and championed the doctrine of two wills (Duotheletism). There Pyrrhos changed his mind again, and as the *Book of the Pontiffs* puts it, 'went back again like a dog to the vomit of his own impiety'. Pope Theodore organized a gathering of local priests and clergy to condemn Pyrrhos, who fled to Ravenna, and from there returned to the East. The pope sent his own legates to Constantinople to convince the new patriarch, Paul, of the error of Monotheletism and their failure opened a schism between Rome and Constantinople.[14]

The schism put the authorities in Ravenna in a difficult position. Through the seventh century a series of experienced military officials, Isaac's successors, continued to govern the exarchate, defending the territory and collecting taxes destined to support the East: Theodore Kalliopas (643–5), Platon (*c.* 645), Olympios (649–53), Theodore Kalliopas (for the second time, 653–66), Gregorios II (recorded in 666), Theodore II (678–87) and possibly two more known only from their seals (Anastasios and Theocharistos).[15] In contrast to Arab threats to the Aegean, the Adriatic remained a relatively safe naval link between Ravenna and the eastern capital, while the Lombards constituted the primary land enemy that demanded the attention of successive exarchs during the crucial period from 641 to 685 when Ravenna was a vital outpost of empire.[16] But the tension between the exarch, who represented the city's political authority derived from the eastern capital, and the archbishop, its ecclesiastical authority, subordinated to Rome, came to personify the growing differences between East and West.

Monotheletism developed in response to the triumphs of Islam and generated little support in the West, where Maximos the Confessor's sermons, writings and public debates promoted opposition. Under papal leadership this new theological split was added to the schism over the Three Chapters that dated back to the Fifth Oecumenical Council of 553. Although emperors intended their definitions of faith to unite Christian believers, their initiatives only deepened divisions. Worse, some western churchmen began to identify Constantinople as a source of unorthodox argumentation that generated heresy.

Pope Martin

In 647/8 the regency council that ruled in the name of Constans II had issued an imperial edict known as the *Typos tes Pisteos* (Outline of the Faith), which forbade any further discussion of the Monothelete doctrine. To Pope Martin (649–55) this ruling countered 'the statements of the holy Fathers with the utterances of the wickedest heretics to give no definition or acknowledgement of either one or two wills or operations in Christ our Lord'. He condemned both the *Typos* and Patriarch Paul (641–53), who had authorized an attack on the papal legates in Constantinople: 'lawlessly and presumptuously he went so far as to have the altar of our holy See . . . consecrated . . . in the house of Placidia overthrown and destroyed, thus stopping our *apocrisiarii* from . . . receiving the sacraments of communion'.[17] As part of his response, Pope Martin summoned a synod of 105 bishops to the Lateran palace in Rome to condemn those who had introduced such novelties to the faith. This put Archbishop Maurus of Ravenna in a very awkward position: he refused to attend and thus avoided declaring his support for either the eastern or western position on Monotheletism.

Once the synod had issued its anathema, Martin sent copies of it to 'all the districts of East and West'.[18] For Constantinople such flagrant opposition to imperial policy could not go unpunished, and Constans instructed the new exarch, Olympios, to have the *Typos* read in all the churches of Italy in order to get the clergy to agree with it. If the pope remained obdurate, he was to be removed. Olympios duly set out, leading the army of Ravenna, with plans to link up with the army of Rome and thus impose the imperial policy. But his plans to arrest the pope or to assassinate him as he officiated in the church of S. Maria Maggiore were frustrated, and by another miracle: the soldier designated to do the deed was blinded at the crucial moment![19] The exarch then abandoned his 'wicked' mission and was reconciled with Pope Martin. Instead of carrying out imperial instructions, he decided to attack the Arabs in Sicily, and the *Book of the Pontiffs* notes that the Roman forces suffered defeats and the exarch himself died of disease.[20]

As soon as Constans II learned of this disastrous failure, he sent another exarch, Theodore Kalliopas, and an imperial chamberlain Theodore Pellourios to arrest the pope. When Martin realized that he might not be able to escape a second time, he selected a group of his clergy to travel with him to the East and justify his own criticism of the Monothelete theology. But the imperial officials arrested him in the Constantinian basilica, a famous Roman church founded by Constantine I, and secretly put him on a ship that sailed before dawn so that his companions would not be able to accompany him. This opened a new phase in the campaign to enforce Monotheletism. Pope Martin was put on trial by the Senate in Constantinople; he was not allowed to discuss any aspect of the Monothelete theology and was condemned to death for assisting the revolt of Olympios, clearly a political charge. In June 655 the sentence was commuted to exile and Martin was sent to the Crimea, where he died a year later.[21] Eugenius (654–7) was elected to replace him, and Rome rejected Patriarch Peter's customary encyclical letter as 'unintelligible ... failing to be explicit about the operations and wills in our Lord Jesus Christ'.[22]

The Divisions Harden

The emperor then summoned a council of all the bishops under his control to establish Monotheletism as the official doctrine of the church; it met in late May–early June 662.[23] With the patriarchs of

Constantinople, Antioch and Alexandria, together with the Senate of Constantinople, they condemned the Duothelete doctrine and put its defenders on trial: Maximos the Confessor, the monk Anastasios and Anastasius the papal legate were beaten, mutilated and ordered into perpetual exile.[24] Constans believed that by uniting his Christian subjects the empire would secure a more effective defence, but his aim of winning over the many Monophysite communities living in the Near Eastern regions was not very successful. Their failure to resist the Arabs was probably related to the fact that the Muslim conquerors were willing to let Christians and Jews pay an extra tax rather than converting to Islam. Both groups may have been tempted to adopt this new status of *dhimmi* (non-Muslim subjects) under Arab rule. Such concerns did not apply to bishops of Rome who could insist that the dangerously incorrect theology of Monotheletism had to be opposed. Although Constans II made an example of Pope Martin and Maximos the Confessor, he was still unable to convert the Christians of the West to his theological beliefs.

Part of Constantinople's failure to reverse the Arab conquests and regain the provinces of the Near East was due to this obsessive concern with theology and the divisions unleashed by Monotheletism. While doctrinal differences remained a continuing preoccupation, the Arabs consolidated their control over Jerusalem and Damascus, making it much harder for the empire to contemplate a successful reconquest. In this upheaval Ravenna was the centre from which exarchs appointed dukes to rule over Rome and attempted to force the popes to accept the eastern theological definitions. The city remained pivotal to the Adriatic connection with Constantinople but lacked the resources to recreate its role as an alternative western capital – as it had been under Theoderic the Gothic king. Through Ravenna we can thus witness the waning of Constantinople's influence and the rising defiance of Rome, in a process that divided the Mediterranean world into three separate sectors under the impact of Islam, leaving the eastern empire to adapt to its medieval form, which we know as Byzantium.[25]

25

Constans II in Sicily

Emperor Constans' relations with the West had been laid down by his treatment of Pope Martin, which remained a constant reminder and symbol of imperial authority over Rome. Constantinople now used the exarchs of Ravenna to control the city: with their military and civilian powers fused, they also ensured that diplomatic links were maintained despite theological differences. Some improvement in relations is reflected in the *Life* of Pope Vitalian (657–72), who sent his *apocrisiarii* with his synodical letter to the 'pious emperors' in Constantinople, and they received a splendid Gospel book 'decorated with pearls of wondrous size' to take back to Rome.[1]

By this date two distinguished Ravenna church leaders, archbishops Maurus (649–71) and Reparatus (671–7), were preoccupied by the desire to free their church from its subordination to Rome.[2] This gained strength under the leadership of Archbishop Maurus, previously abbot of the monastery of St Bartholomew, who may have calculated that Ravenna's loyal support for the imperial theology deserved a reward. When Pope Martin summoned all his bishops to the synod held in Rome to denounce Monotheletism, Maurus had prevaricated, writing to the pope that he couldn't leave Ravenna because of the Lombard threat.[3] Perhaps he was already preparing an appeal to the emperor for Ravenna's autonomy. In the 650s Maurus went to Constantinople on several occasions to negotiate his church's freedom from papal control, and Constans II seems to have taken a positive view of Ravenna's claims. The emperor granted Maurus his pallium of office, a clear indication of the see's independence.[4] After this initial victory in Ravenna's struggle to avoid Roman control, the central issue became how its archbishops should be consecrated: were they obliged to go to Rome to be installed by the pope, or could this ceremonial dedication be made in

Ravenna by three of their subordinate bishops as happened in other western sees?

The Emperor Leaves
Constantinople

Once the leading opponents of Monotheletism had been sent into exile on 8 June 662, Constans exploited the Arab civil war that followed the assassination of Caliph Uthman to secure a peace treaty, which required the Muslims to pay a substantial amount in tribute.[5] In an unprecedented move, the emperor decided to go to Sicily where he could draw on the resources of the western provinces to reconstruct his naval and military forces, and in the summer of 662 he set out with a considerable army that marched via Thessalonike to Athens and Corinth (where a statue base and numerous bronze coins record his visit), the more direct route on the Via Egnatia across the Balkans to Dyrrachium being blocked by Slavic tribes. From Corinth they crossed the northern Peloponnese to Patras, where ships from Sicily transported the troops by the shortest crossing of the Adriatic to Taranto in the instep of Italy.[6] The arrival of the ruler of Constantinople in the West marked an extraordinary transition as the emperor devised a strategy to enable him to defeat the Muslims. Sicily was a Greek-speaking island naval base that formed a key link between the eastern and western basins of the Mediterranean. After his disastrous defeat at Phoinike in 654, Constans had realized that effective naval power was essential to counter the maritime triumphs of the Muslims. His move to the West was therefore closely connected to the construction of new warships to be manned by local men.[7]

In 663 the newly disembarked imperial troops engaged the Lombards in Benevento and marched to Naples, where the local duke must have arranged a suitable celebratory arrival ceremony (*adventus*) for the emperor. From there Constans went on to Rome and, on 5 July of that year, he was welcomed by Pope Vitalian and the clergy 'at the sixth mile from Rome' and escorted into the city of which he was the undisputed overlord and master. Even though this was the emperor who had caused the death of Pope Martin and had issued doctrinal statements condemned by many previous Roman bishops as heresy, the ceremonial honours had to be performed. Vitalian accompanied the emperor to St Peter's where they prayed and then Constans retired to the ancient palace on the Palatine hill. The *Book of the Pontiffs* describes his twelve-day visit in detail, recording the Sunday liturgy at St Peter's, attended by the whole army, all carrying candles, where the emperor laid a pallium woven with gold thread on the altar. He presented other gifts to all the Roman churches he visited. He also bathed and dined at the basilica of Vigilius in the Lateran palace. And throughout his stay, as if to remind the Romans of his sovereignty over them, he ordered his soldiers to pillage the city. He 'dismantled all the city's bronze decorations, he removed the bronze tiles from the roof of the church of St Mary *ad martyres*, and sent them to the imperial city'. Then, like a conqueror laden with booty, Constans returned to Naples, went on to Rhegium and sailed across to Sicily, choosing Syracuse as the base for his court.[8] The governor of the island put his palace at the emperor's disposal, from which Constans could enjoy watching chariot and horse races that still took place in the local hippodrome.

Once established in Sicily the emperor ordered an accurate census of properties so that he could raise funds for military needs, which was greatly resented, as the *Book of the Pontiffs* records:

> He imposed such afflictions on the people, occupiers, and proprietors of the provinces of Calabria, Sicily, Africa, and Sardinia for years on end by the registrations of land and persons and by imposts on shipping as had never before been seen, and such as to separate wives from their husbands and sons from their parents.[9]

After the construction of new naval forces, rowers, sailors and captains would be required to man the new style of lighter fighting ships – this explains the references above to taxes on shipping and the enforced separation of men from their families. They were sent to run the navy that fought to check Arab naval successes. Initially, Constans exploited the resources of Calabria and Sicily, Africa and Sardinia (all within fairly close maritime contact) and ordered the exarch and archbishop of Ravenna to add financial assistance. Maurus drew on the resources of the church of Ravenna to provide funds for these military campaigns and received privileges from the emperor, while Sicily's relative security created a safe haven for the imperial court and the troops that accompanied the emperor to Syracuse.[10] Despite efforts to bring his family to

Sicily, the senators of Constantinople (who had been left in control of the capital), refused to allow the emperor's wife, Fausta, and their three children, Constantine, Herakleios and Tiberios, to leave the city (Plate 47). Syracuse did not become an alternative capital; Constantinople remained the centre of empire defended by young prince Constantine from Arab attacks.

The Celebration of Autocephaly

It was, therefore, to Sicily that Archbishop Maurus sent Reparatus, abbot of the monastery of St Apollinaris in Ravenna, to negotiate a stronger statement of his church's independence from Roman control, carrying a copy of the *Life* of St Apollinaris, and a forged edict of Valentinian III that promoted the see to an archbishopric with authority over all the local bishoprics and provided the pallium of office.[11] On the basis of these somewhat unreliable claims, Constans II issued an imperial diploma, dated 1 March 666, that guaranteed Ravenna its autonomy. Agnellus the historian saw a document that was kept in the church archive and summarized the critical part:

> [that] no future pastor of the Ravennate church need ever afterward go to Rome to the bishop of the Roman see for consecration, nor that he should have the pope's rule over him, nor that he should at any time be under the dominion of the Roman bishop, but might consecrate his choice [for episcopal office] with three of his own bishops . . .[12]

Archbishop Maurus thus gained Ravenna's independence from Rome, and the church's contribution to the emperor's campaigns in Sicily finally brought about the much-desired result.

So, on three separate occasions when Archbishop Maurus subsequently received letters from Pope Vitalian demanding his presence in Rome to submit to papal approval, he always refused and sent the legates back empty-handed. On the third occasion, in 671–2, both sides formally excommunicated each other, opening a schism between Ravenna and Rome. As a result, neither side commemorated the other in the liturgy. Agnellus reports that as Maurus was dying, he summoned his clergy and warned them: 'Do not place yourselves under the Roman yoke. Choose a pastor from yourselves and let him be consecrated by his bishops. Seek the pallium from the emperor. For on whatever day you are subjugated to Rome, you will not be whole.'[13] And subsequently, every Thursday, all the clergy gathered together after Vespers and privately shared a loaf of bread and fish with some wine (a funerary feast?), and the most senior priest said a prayer for the soul of their independent archbishop.

The achievement of Archbishop Maurus was later commemorated in a mosaic panel (heavily restored in modern times) that was inserted into the decoration of the church of S. Apollinare in Classe. It depicts Maurus at the centre, flanked by Archbishop Reparatus and Emperor Constantine IV, who hands a scroll marked PRIVILEGIA to Reparatus (Plate 54). The saintly Maurus, depicted with a halo, puts his hand on his successor's shoulder. To the left of the archbishop are three clerics, and to the right of the emperor three secular figures, two with haloes, who are Constantine's brothers, Herakleios and Tiberios, recorded in the inscription above. Another inscription below praises Archbishop Reparatus, who made a new decoration for the hall 'that shines for eternity'.[14] The identity of the third secular figure, wearing a short purple tunic and holding a model of a ciborium or altar canopy, is much disputed. Often named as Justinian, the young son of Constantine IV, Salvatore Cosentino has recently suggested that this is the exarch Theodore, who held office from 678–87 (Plate 55), and who may have donated a ciborium to the church.[15] He associates this with Maurus' decision to move the relics of St Apollinaris from the narthex to the centre of the church, where they were probably deposited under the altar (frequently covered by a ciborium). In commemorating this important *translatio* in the mosaic, the two priests holding an incense burner and a chalice participate in the ceremony, while Theodore the exarch is the donor of the ciborium.[16] In 673 Reparatus went to Constantinople and obtained very specific privileges from the emperor, which indicate that Ravenna had contributed to Constans II's tax demands (particularly for taxes on mooring boats, a shore tax, gate, sales and customs taxes). These were lifted after the archbishop's visit.

The panel is a narrative in tesserae marking a very significant moment in the history of the church of Ravenna. It clearly imitates the imperial panel in San Vitale that displays Emperor Justinian with Archbishop Maximian.[17] The same multicoloured border, the same curtains and geometric patterns above, even the priests' feet overlapping each other, all reflect a determination to re-make the sixth-century image in a new form. Reparatus also added another panel opposite, which reproduces the depiction of Melchizedek and Abel standing either side of an altar from San Vitale. The altar table is almost identical but here Melchizedek is placed directly behind it, with Abel bringing his lamb from the left, and Abraham presenting his son Isaac from the right, while from above the hand of God blesses the scene. These commemorations of the Old Testament sacrifices and the imperial grant to the church of Ravenna are powerful statements about the figures represented.[18] Emperor Constantine IV and his brothers are brought into immediate contact with Archbishop Reparatus, with the saintly Maurus between them.

The privileges bestowed by Constans II represented a moment of great prestige for Archbishop Maurus and a key moment in the city's history, celebrated with tremendous festivities. The archbishop's successor Reparatus strengthened this independence by securing additional tax privileges from Constantinople, as the people of Ravenna were reminded every time they worshipped in S. Apollinare in Classe. The inscriptions emphasize Ravenna's intimate contact with the most powerful ruler of the time, projecting a message about the church's universal claims.[19] On Maurus' tomb in the same church, they could also read: 'Here rests in peace Archbishop Maurus, who lived for very many years, sixty-seven, who in the time of the lord Emperor Constantine liberated his church from the yoke of servitude to Rome.'[20]

Most exarchs of this period were recruited in Constantinople and sent to Ravenna to serve a limited term of office. Platon, who held office in about 645, is recorded as one of Constans II's advisers in Constantinople in 649 and 654; his son-in-law Theodore Chilas may have accompanied him to Italy, where he is found having a conversation with Maximos the Confessor in Rome in c. 650.[21] Olympios, previously *koubikoularios* (imperial chamberlain), and Gregorios, mentioned only in a document of 666, and two other governors known from their seals were all easterners. 'The men of the exarch' also appear to have accompanied Pope Martin to Constantinople when he was arrested, as they attended some parts of the trials of both Martin and Maximos. Soldiers from Italy, some of Lombard origin, are known to have participated in action in the East and were serving in the palace of Constantinople in 687.[22]

Among the exarchs, Theodore Kalliopas is unusual in that he had local roots; his father, Apollenarius, held a position of some importance and owned property (6 *oncia/uncia*) in Uttianus near Rimini, 8okm south of Ravenna; in addition, he had an estate of San Giovano in Computo that was bordered by the public road, another called Organiano and a two-storeyed house in Rimini, which is described in detail.[23] Before 665/6 Theodore Kalliopas and his wife, Anna, and their sons secured a lease from the bishop of Ravenna of a house in Rimini on two floors with 6 *oncia* of land attached; another 6 *oncia* of *familiarice* (a courtyard and garden); and 4 *oncia* with a bath with basin and drains (*bagno cum baso, fistulas et omne ordinatione sua*). An additional plot of 6 *oncia* suggests a farm with equipment on the river next to the *bagno* and at the garden with *puto et puteales* (a well), *lavello* (washing place), *arca saxe* (stone reservoir?) *in curte, pistrino cum furno* (a mill and oven), *macinas* (*machinas*? possibly any sort of machine) and *rota* (wheel). Despite his local origins, Theodore used Greek seals.[24] Whether he was already in Italy in 643 when Constans II appointed him exarch with instructions to arrest Pope Martin, his success in that task appears to have resulted in a second term of office between 653 and 666, which coincided with the episcopate of Maurus.

During his stay in the West Constans II did not visit Ravenna (perhaps happily for the condition of its monuments), leaving Exarch Gregory and his successors in control. Gregory was preoccupied by Lombard attacks on the imperial territory and further incursions of Avars and Slavs, some of whom penetrated into Italy and were settled by the Lombards further south. In 668 the emperor must have sent troops to campaign against the Slavs in an area north of Istria, or substantial payments designed to stop their attacks, since hoards of his coins are found on sites even further north.[25] In addition to rebuilding his naval forces, the emperor also supported military activity in North Africa, which can be traced through the seals of officials (*kommerkiarioi*) responsible for army supplies, and in the Balearics and Sardinia, where churches were dedicated in traditional fashion.[26]

The First Arab Siege of Constantinople

By 663, the general Muawiyah had emerged as the new leader of the Arabs and renewed efforts to capture Constantinople. He found allies both in the Caucasus, where the prince of Albania went over to the Arabs, and within the empire where Saborios, governor of the Armenian region, led a revolt in 667. Muawiyah sent his son Yazid to support the rebels with a massive land army while naval forces sailed to blockade the imperial capital. Although Saborios was killed in a riding accident, the Arabs persisted in their blockade and siege of Constantinople, which began late in 667 and lasted two years.[27] When news of this major assault reached Sicily, court officials in Syracuse took measures to ensure their control of the western provinces under a leader of their own. Fearing that Constantinople might fall to the Arabs, the emperor's eunuch servants executed a clearly planned operation: Constans II was bludgeoned to death in his bath by an attendant, Andreas Troilos, and local officials immediately proclaimed a young Armenian named Mizizios as emperor. Although Mizizios struck coins to proclaim his authority, imperial forces in the West refused to accept him and combined to protect the dynasty of Herakleios. From Ravenna, Istria and Campania, with additional support from North Africa and Sardinia, troops identified as the army of Italy under the command of Exarch Gregory converged on Syracuse and killed Mizizios.[28]

As soon as the news of Constans' murder in Sicily became known, his son Constantine was acclaimed emperor in Constantinople, with new coins minted in his name while the capital was under siege. The Arab forces were seriously reduced by hunger and pestilence. In the winter of 668/9 Constantine IV and his advisers prepared 'Greek fire' – small boats with siphons to project burning oil – which destroyed much of the Arab fleet.[29] He then negotiated a peace treaty with Yazid, and the Arabs withdrew, allowing the inhabitants of Constantinople to celebrate a victory that was to be annually commemorated on 25 June. Later in 669 Constantine IV probably sailed to Sicily to assert his authority over the judges who had supported the revolt of Mizizios and then moved the imperial court back to the capital.[30] While Syracuse resumed its role as the provincial capital of Sicily, Constantinople reasserted its imperial position for the next five hundred years.

Throughout the seventh century regular contact between Constantinople and Ravenna continued, with military governors and bishops travelling to and fro, negotiating with imperial figures in the East with adequate knowledge of Greek and Latin. At the time of Archbishop Theodore (677–91), however, the exarch's notary died, leaving a serious gap in the administration's ability to compose the reports and letters sent to Constantinople. The ninth-century historian Agnellus reports the solution with obvious pride, since it honoured one of his own relations: a young man called Johannicis, 'instructed in Greek and Latin letters' and very well educated in other fields too, was summoned to take the job. At first sight the exarch was not impressed as the youth was short and ugly, but when tested he proved very capable – he translated at sight a charter written in Latin into Greek – so the exarch employed him as his notary and ordered him to be present in the palace every day.[31] For three years he carried out the tasks of chief secretary to the governor, writing official letters to the emperor, possibly translating instructions written in Greek into Latin, and running the palace administration. He also composed poems, which came to the attention of the emperor, who ordered that the author should be sent to Constantinople. Johannicis was therefore dispatched to the eastern capital where his expertise in both Latin and Greek was exploited for several years. Around the beginning of Archbishop Damianus' episcopate in 692 he was allowed to return to Ravenna, where 'his wisdom was famed in all of Italy'.[32] Clearly, Agnellus may have praised his relative excessively, but there can be no doubt about the very particular skills that Johannicis was able to acquire in his native city.

Archbishop Theodore

The archbishop who was obliged to send Johannicis off to Constantinople was Theodore, a figure who profoundly antagonized his clergy. Within a year or two of his consecration the elders of the church forcefully protested against Theodore's refusal to pay the clergy their rightful salaries. Furthermore, he had collected and burned all the records of the church's traditions that had been settled in the time of Bishop Ecclesius, had hoarded grain at a time of famine and had set the junior clergy against each other by favouring first one group and then another. Eventually all the clergy rebelled against his authority and, on Christmas Eve (of 678 or 679), after celebrating the vigils at St Mary the ever Virgin, they consulted Theodore the archpriest and Theodore the archdeacon, his maternal cousin, who agreed to lead the clergy to S. Apollinare in Classe. They completed the night liturgy in the church of the Apostles and then, as dawn was breaking, they walked out to Classis and celebrated the Christmas service there together. No clergy remained in the city and Archbishop Theodore was totally perplexed. He sent his notary twice to find the priests and then withdrew. The people were amazed and could not understand why their archbishop didn't come to preside at the festival of Christmas with them.[33]

Instead, Theodore sent noblemen with swift horses to Classis to make peace, only for them to be silenced by the crowd of clergy, who said, 'Turn back, since we do not have a shepherd but a killer!' And then they addressed the saint: 'Rise, St Apollinaris, celebrate with us the mass of the day of the nativity. Holy Peter [the Apostle] gave you to us as a shepherd. Therefore we are your sheep. We gather round you, save us.' They threatened to go to Rome to blessed St Peter to beg him to 'give us a new shepherd, who will defend us from the mouth of the serpent who lives within our walls'. And they continued, 'If he will not hear us, we will travel to Constantinople to the emperor and seek from him a father and shepherd.'[34] When Theodore heard what his clergy had said, he went to the palace and begged the exarch (also called Theodore) to mediate. Civilian officials were sent to Classis but met another refusal when the people there said if they went to Constantinople they would also complain about the exarch, since he was not prepared to correct the archbishop. Eventually the exarch ordered his horse to be saddled – with appropriately decorated harness – and rode out to Classis, where he promised the people that Theodore would agree to their complaints and persuaded them to come back and celebrate Vespers with the archbishop.[35]

From Agnellus' account of this telling incident, we can see that the Ravennati understood the difficulty of getting rid of a bad leader and took exceptional measures to force Theodore to reform his practices. In Classis they created an alternative cathedral where their patron saint Apollinaris was buried, and threatened to appeal to the emperor in Constantinople to settle their dispute.[36] This persuaded the exarch that he had to come and witness their refusal to co-operate with the bishop and thus they gained his support to hold a trial. On the next day the exarch went to the episcopal palace and sat with the archbishop and all the priests, with the deacons standing behind them as in a court. And after much conversation, the archbishop restored all the honours and dignities that he had removed, and agreed to share all the revenues correctly – even the bailiffs and suburban estates got a part.[37] So with the exarch's assistance the disagreements among the clergy of Ravenna were settled.

Despite this resolution Archbishop Theodore continued with his plans, intending to grant the property of the church to his relatives. Agnellus can't explain how the Ravenna church lost its autonomy but associates it with Theodore's visit to Rome in 680. Pope Agatho had sent out a general order for all western bishops to come and discuss the orthodox faith. Theodore read this letter to the clergy and asked their advice, saying he would only go if they agreed, and because they thought they should all 'undergo the danger of death for the orthodox faith and the holy church of God', they allowed Theodore to leave Ravenna and go to Rome. When he was there, he treacherously gave up his church's claim to independence.[38]

A more likely scenario is that Constantine IV yielded to papal objections to the independence of the church of Ravenna. At the time of Pope Donus (676–8) the emperor also abandoned the eastern determination to impose Monotheletism, as we shall see, and set about restoring good relations with Rome. Donus might well have demanded control over the church of Ravenna as part of the preparation for a universal council to reverse the one-will theology. After the death of Pope Agatho in 681, the subordination of the church of Ravenna to Rome was reaffirmed by Pope Leo II, with many additional stipulations in the relations between the two churches: that the priests of Ravenna would be permitted to choose their bishop, who would go to Rome to be consecrated by the pope; he would not stay for more than eight days; and that the pope would not come to Ravenna on the day of the birth of the Apostles (an annual visitation?) although he might send a legate.[39] In the ninth century Agnellus deeply regrets these developments and records that clerics curse and insult the memory of Archbishop Theodore every time they pass his tomb in the narthex of S. Apollinare in Classe (Plate 57). The epitaph had been damaged and Agnellus was unable to read it, surely a symbol of extreme local hostility.[40]

Theodore the Exarch

In contrast with the despised archbishop, Agnellus praised the exarch and *patricius* Theodore (Plate 55), a devoted Christian who gave three gold chalices to churches in Ravenna and built the *monasterium* (a chapel) of St Theodore the Deacon not far from the Chalchi gate, next to the church of St Martin the Confessor (that is, the church of Golden Heaven – S. Apollinare Nuovo – built by Theoderic). He also worked with the archbishop to transform what had been a synagogue of the Jews into the church of the blessed Apostle Paul near the Wandalaria gate in the south-east of the city. He commissioned a most precious purple altar cloth for the monastery of S. Maria *ad Blachernas* (where Agnellus was later abbot), and he and his wife, Agatha, were both buried there.[41] And the exarch may have donated a ciborium to the church of S. Apollinare in Classe, if he is the person depicted on the mosaic there. The exarch's benefactions, which compared so favourably with the actions of Archbishop Theodore, confirmed his serious responsibility for the city.

Although the seventh-century exarchs had sustained Ravenna and protected all the western provinces during the rebellion of Mizizios, the Ravennati reserved their greatest honour for Archbishop Maurus and his successor Reparatus, who had won independence, however temporary, from Roman control. And in the mosaic panel in S. Apollinare in Classe that commemorates the city's privileges, they created a permanent record of this historic achievement. When admiring it today, one can sense the city's determination that this particular moment would never be forgotten.

26

The Sixth Oecumenical Council

Although Constantinople had withstood the Muslim siege of 667–9, Constantine IV was unable to consolidate his authority until he defeated the Arab naval forces off the coast of Asia Minor, near Syllaeum in 672 and again in Lebanese waters in 677/8. These two victories demonstrated the vital importance of maritime supremacy and Constans II's success in rebuilding the Byzantine navy. They permitted the emperor to negotiate a very favourable peace treaty, which obliged the Arabs to make annual payments of 3,000 gold coins, 50 captives and 50 horses.[1] This was partly necessary in order to confront a new enemy in the Balkans, where the Bulgars crossed the Danube frontier. Constantine IV's appreciation of the wealth of the western provinces and Pope Vitalian's support for his imperial inheritance against the claims of Mizizios in Sicily in 668 probably influenced the emperor's decision to reverse Monotheletism and end the schism with Rome.[2]

In 678, the emperor initiated the repudiation of Monothelete belief by announcing that he would summon an oecumenical council to Constantinople to reunite all Christians in belief in the two wills of Christ. This fundamental change involved removing the Constantinopolitan Patriarch Theodore in 679 and replacing him with a new leader, George (679–86), chosen to preside at the council.[3] Pope Agatho welcomed the proposal as a return to the doctrine approved in Rome and throughout the West. As we have seen, he summoned the western bishops to respond and Archbishop Theodore of Ravenna went to Rome in 680 to participate in this Roman synod. The pope's long response to Constantine IV was read out and signed by all the 125 bishops present.[4] Agatho then appointed a team of educated men with some knowledge of Greek – bishops John of Portus, Abundantius of Tempsa and John of Rhegium, two priests and a deacon from the Roman see, and his vicars in the East: the bishops of Thessalonike, Corinth and Gortyna (in Crete), plus Theodore, a priest from Ravenna – to represent him at the council. In contrast to this enthusiastic western approval, many bishops in the East who had embraced the definition of Monotheletism in 662 remained loyal to it and refused to attend the opening of the council.

In the history of such universal gatherings the definition of correct belief was always the most important aspect. The first council, held in Nicaea in 325, and all subsequent meetings had devoted much attention to this. At Nicaea, however, regulations had been agreed (for example, the age at which priests could be ordained) and these became known as canons. They were incorporated into civil law and canon law thus developed in parallel with imperial law. Additional canons had been issued by the Council of Chalcedon in 451 but none since. The Sixth Council of 680 was dominated by the restoration of orthodox doctrine (Duotheletism) and then, twelve years later, the Council *in Trullo* promulgated 102 canons to provide rulings on clerical behaviour, discipline and religious art – issues that had evolved since 451. Both these seventh-century meetings were held in the Great Palace of Constantinople in a hall with a dome (*troullos*), but the first was known by its place in the series of universal councils, while the second of 692 is usually identified by the place where it was held – *in Trullo*.

Ravenna at the Sixth Council

Theodore, the Ravenna priest, travelled to Constantinople with the papal delegation to the Sixth Oecumenical Council and is listed among the bishops who participated. He was probably chosen because he was already familiar with Constantinople or knew Greek. His presence is recorded from the first session, held in November 680, through to the final decrees of the eighteenth session on 16 September 681, which he signed as Theodore, presbyter of the church of Ravenna, representing Archbishop Theodore. As the only individual from the capital of the exarchate, he was appointed to an elevated position (eighth) in the order of signatories, immediately after the three papal representatives (who occupy the first place), four other patriarchs and two senior metropolitan bishops of Thessalonike and Cyprus. He thus signed the acts ahead of the bishops who acted as legates of the Roman see (John of Portus, Stephanos of Corinth and Basil of Gortyna) and the two papal *apocrisiarii*.[5] It was the first time a priest from the church of Ravenna had attended such a gathering and his place in the order of precedence was a sign of the importance of the city in the eyes of Constantinople.[6] At most previous oecumenical councils the pope or his representatives had spoken for the entire West, and very few, if any, bishops from other parts of Italy took part. On this occasion, the presbyter Theodore participated in the council as part of the papal team and returned to Ravenna with personal information about its conclusions.[7] Neither the archbishop nor the general populace of Ravenna could have remained ignorant of the major doctrinal change that had taken place in order to reunite the Christians of East and West.

Theodore's position in the ecclesiastical hierarchy highlights one big difference between the eastern church and its western counterpart: the patriarch of Constantinople ordered the sees under his control according to a fixed ranking, which also determined their salaries. To be appointed to the see of Caesarea in Cappadocia, the first in rank (*protothronos*), was not only the highest honour but also carried a more substantial income than any other bishopric.[8] By the same token, the newly created bishoprics that appear in the lists of signatories of 680–81 and 692, such as Aurillioupolis (number 165), some of the islands of the Aegean and inland sees recently reconquered from the Slavs, had much smaller incomes.[9] Candidates for some of these poorer sees might refuse the appointment on the grounds that they wanted to wait until a richer one became vacant. For one deacon in the wealthy church of Ravenna such a 'promotion' would have meant a reduction in his income and he demanded compensation. Among the well-established churches, such as Thessalonike and Corinth, there was always an element of competition for greater honour, as clerics hoped to attain a higher rank.

Nothing comparable existed in the West where the bishop of Rome consecrated all the metropolitan bishops and their age determined the hierarchy – the oldest-living metropolitan held the highest rank and authority after the pope. Suffragan bishops under their metropolitan shepherds may have competed for priority and greater honour and they all derived their incomes from local properties and gifts. But the western sees were not ranked in a particular, unchanging, order, which would have been very difficult to establish in the seventh century. At individual councils and synods, the order in which representatives of individual churches signed their agreement was based on the seniority of those attending, and just for that event.

While there is no evidence that young Johannicis, the poet and scribe from Ravenna, was in Constantinople at the time of the Sixth Council, he may have been involved in the dissemination of the council acts. A fragmentary papyrus discovered in Ravenna preserves a unique list of thirty-six episcopal signatures in Greek, made at the council or copied shortly after, which displays the very different ways in which these individuals wrote their names. Some used majuscule letters (*grammata ekklesiastika*), others minuscule in a form called half-cursive, which is only documented from the ninth century.[10] This partial list is therefore the earliest record of such a Greek script used in the context of the penultimate session of the council, dated September 681, which was attended by those who signed in their own personal styles. The only complete record of this session is preserved in the Latin acts.

How did the fragment get to Ravenna? It seems unlikely that Theodore the presbyter would have brought it with him, since the city's archive contains no other papyrus records of the Sixth Council. But Johannicis, a skilled translator and scribe, might well have been interested in the different scripts employed and could have carried it from Constantinople to Ravenna when he returned before the end of the seventh century. However it travelled from the imperial capital to the Italian city, the fragment is the sole witness to original Greek signatures of thirty-six bishops at the council, and another mark of the close relations between Ravenna and Constantinople.

Eastern attachment to the single-will doctrine, which had been observed throughout the empire since the early seventh century and enshrined as correct belief by Constans II in 662, appears to have been widespread. Many bishops refused to attend the first sessions of the Sixth Council; only after the condemnation of the Monothelete leader Makarios of Antioch on 7 March 681 did larger numbers participate, and the final declaration of the council in September, signed by 165 bishops, substantiated the claim that this was a universal gathering.[11] Monothelete loyalty also persisted among the military and, in the summer of 681, soldiers of the Anatolikon army marched to Chrysopolis demanding that Constantine IV rule with his brothers Herakleios and

Tiberios, as a symbolic holy trinity. The emperor had the leaders of the revolt impaled at Sycae and mutilated his brothers by cutting their noses, exiling them so that they could never rule.[12] After the condemnation of Monotheletism, Makarios of Antioch and several other supporters were exiled to Rome, where Pope Leo II tried to convince them of their heretical views.[13] The council of 680–81 had achieved Constantine IV's major aim of recreating unity with Rome, which he hoped would strengthen the Christians in their battles with Islam and other 'barbarians'.

Justinian II

In July 685, four years after presiding over the Sixth Oecumenical Council, Constantine IV died and his eldest son Justinian, named after his famous predecessor who was commemorated on the sanctuary walls of San Vitale, acceded to the throne. Continuing opposition to the council's condemnation of Monotheletism forced him to reaffirm its decisions. Fearing that the text of the Sixth Council might be corrupted and altered by falsifications and intrusions, he sent an order dated 17 February 687 to the pope, instructing him to keep it unchanged. In this letter he recorded how he was doing the same in Constantinople, having the acts read to a gathering of all church leaders including the pope's *apocrisiarius*, the Senate, palace workers, members of craft guilds and representatives of the people (probably drawn from the Blues and the Greens), and all his military leaders, so that they would know the correct definition. When they had all listened diligently, he made them signal their agreement.[14] In this way, without circulating copies of the proceedings, which might become corrupted through faulty copying or deliberate alteration, he assured the pope that everyone in his empire understood the importance of the decision to approve the two wills of Christ. The letter was addressed to Pope John V, who had died in August 686, so it was delivered to Pope Conon, bishop of Rome from October 686 to September 687.

In the list of military units that were summoned to this gathering, Justinian names those from the East – the Exkoubitores, and the armies of the imperial Opsikion, the Anatolian, Thracesian and Armeniakon provinces – followed by those from the West led by the army of Italy, the Cabarisian, Septensian and Sardinian forces, and finally the army of Africa. The precise significance of the names of the eastern forces is disputed, but the roles of the exarchs of Ravenna and Carthage, who commanded the armies of Italy and Africa, and the governor of the island of Sardinia are perfectly clear. Theodore II, who was so devoted to the ecclesiastical life of Ravenna, was exarch in 686.[15] The names Cabarisian and Septensian refer to the Caravisiani, a unit equipped to transport troops by sea, and other naval units based in the Balearics and the tip of North Africa (Septem/Ceuta). It seems very plausible that Justinian had commanded the leaders of these military and naval units to come to Constantinople for the proclamation of the true Christian faith, if they were not already in the capital. Organizing their presence required time, at least several weeks in good sailing weather for the westerners. So, although the letter reporting this meeting was sent in February 687, the orders to attend probably dated back to the previous year, before the seas became too dangerous for regular sailing, and the gathering may have taken place towards the end of 686. It must have been one of the first important tasks the young emperor set himself.

As the leader of the army of Italy, Theodore the exarch received the summons to Constantinople and left Ravenna in the autumn. His successor, John Platyn, was nominated to replace him and set out from Constantinople in the spring of 687. It is probable that both of them would have participated in the meeting in 686 when the decrees of the Sixth Oecumenical Council were read out to re-confirm the doctrine of two-wills in Christ. The theological agreement meant that exarchs, who had responsibility for the confirmation of every new pope as the emperor's representative, could leave the administration of the duchy of Rome to their officials and did not intervene in local matters unless quarrels over papal elections demanded their presence.

Disputed Papal Elections

This was precisely what happened in August 686 when the army of Rome under its duke (*dux*, appointed by the exarch) supported one candidate, while the clergy favoured another. In this case the quarrel was resolved by the election of an alternative, Conon. But in September 687, when Pope Conon died, his archdeacon Paschal tried to gain the papal throne by bribing the new exarch John Platyn. The Roman *Book of the Pontiffs* is quite clear that John Platyn went along with this by ordering the judges (whom he appointed) to make sure Paschal was elected. Again, the two rival parties eventually agreed on a third candidate, Sergius, but Paschal secretly appealed to the exarch and his judges to come to Rome, promising a bribe of 100 lbs of gold to secure his own election. When John Platyn arrived completely unannounced (the Roman army didn't even go out to meet him at the customary place with flags and standards), he realized that everyone except Paschal had accepted the nomination of Sergius. He abandoned the cause of the archdeacon but then demanded that the bribe he was expecting should be paid by the church of Rome. Pope Sergius, understandably, protested that he had played no part in the scandal and could not pay. He even handed over the chandeliers and crowns that hung in front of the altar of St Peter's as a pledge, but John demanded the full amount, which had to be raised. Paschal was later stripped of the rank of archdeacon and imprisoned in a monastery.[16]

John Platyn's discreditable intervention in the election of Pope Sergius emphasizes the power of the exarch. But in the case of Theophylaktos, who was promoted from the post of *strategos*, commander in Sicily, to exarch, Pope John VI (701–5) had to protect him from local opposition to his appointment. News of his imminent arrival in Rome caused at least sections of the army of Italy (*militia totius Italiae*) and certain 'lower elements of the Roman population' to riot.[17] It seems that these poorer people were accusing certain individuals of acquiring wealth illegally and wanted the exarch 'to strip them of what they owned'. The presence of the army became so threatening that the pope closed the city gates and sent priests out to pacify the crowds. In this case, the pope protected the newly appointed governor, who would otherwise have faced considerable danger before he even reached Ravenna.

Living In Ravenna in the Late Seventh Century

Papyri of this period confirm the importance of protecting legitimate claims to property, such as the gifts made to the church. In one such gift, made around 700, Johannis and his wife, Stefania, present a small plot of land to Johannia, the abbess of the monastery of St John the Baptist, which is called *ad Navicula*, suggesting that the nunnery was situated near the sea or port.[18] The donor, Johannis, is described as *vir clarissimus* and *primicerius* of the *numerus Ravennatensium*, revealing his membership of the local military unit, and Sergius, one of his witnesses, was *domesticus numeri Armeniorum*, an official of the Armenian detachment. The foundation of nunneries to house dedicated Christian women was a feature of early Christian devotion, well documented at Rome, Constantinople and in Lombard cities where rulers adopted the same practice (often, it seems, to dispose of their female relatives). As Ravenna was ruled by an imperial official rather than a monarch, the same need didn't arise, but there must have been many quite wealthy women who preferred to live in religious communities and therefore needed nunneries.[19] In another fragmentary papyrus of *c.* 650, a similar mixture of military and ecclesiastical officials come together to witness the gift of a city garden made by Gaudiosus, *defensor* of the Ravenna church, to his church. The three witnesses, whose names are lost, were all military men: two were *domestici* of the detachment of Leti, and a *vir honestus* was a guardsman, *scol[aris??]*, in Classis. They testify to Gaudiosus' gift in Latin and he signs his name using Greek letters for his Latin titles.[20]

Such documents to guarantee the legality of gifts are common to all parts of the West in this period of early Christendom. But by the last decade of the seventh century, Ravenna had risen in stature – both in ecclesiastical terms, as seen by its eighth position in the rankings of the patriarchate of Constantinople, and in terms of its military strength, when the exarch commanded the army of Italy in putting down the revolt of Mizizios. Its inhabitants identified themselves as loyal subjects of the emperor in Constantinople, to whom they would turn if their secular or religious leaders failed them. The city housed facilities that encouraged teachers, poets like Johannicis, scribes like the unnamed copyist of theological texts, and scholars curious about the world, like Odo and his brother who could use local resources to compile a fascinating seventh-century cosmography, as we shall see.

27

The Anonymous Cosmographer of Ravenna

While Constantine IV and Justinian II were ensuring the orthodox faith of the empire's inhabitants, Ravenna was nurturing an unknown author who wrote a *Cosmographia*, a geographical description of the universe in five books. This anonymous scholar introduces himself in this way:

> Although I was not born in India, nor travelled in Scotia or Mauritania or Scithia, or through the four quarters of the world, yet by theoretical learning I have understood the whole world and the various peoples who live in it, just as the world is recorded in the books [of those philosophers] in the times of many emperors.[1]

He was therefore not an explorer, or even a traveller, but a reader of books by philosophers (which is the name he gives to geographers) to which he had access in Ravenna.

The motive for his effort to explain and document the known world came from the author's 'most dear brother Odo', who had asked him how to interpret what Scripture records of the creation of the world (Bk I, 1). He therefore began his study with the Book of Genesis and tried to incorporate all the information he could glean from ancient Greek, Roman and more recent writing about the universe. He found these resources in 'the most noble' city of Ravenna, which he placed at the very centre of this world, in the middle of the Mediterranean. While he reserves the epithet *nobelissima* for Ravenna and Constantinople, he accepts that Rome is even more noble, *insignis nobelissima*. Alexandria is most famous, *famosissima*; Petavia, very old, *vetustissima*.[2] His work appears to have been prepared to be read aloud, as auditors as well as readers are mentioned, perhaps in a school organized by the archbishop or the abbot of a monastery.

While the author was clearly based in Ravenna, he provides no evidence about the date of his composition and does not mention any events that would help to establish when he lived.[3] But he cites seventh-century authorities like Isidore of Seville, whose writings would have become known in Ravenna by about 650, so he must have been active between that time and the Lombard capture of the city in 751. His *Cosmographia* is not concerned with the political authorities of his time: it does not record any eastern emperor or imperial official by name; there is no mention of the Lombards or Arabs.[4] It draws heavily on late Roman administrative records of provinces and cities, rivers and mountains, as well as myths about foreign peoples. Only three copies survive, made in the thirteenth and fourteenth centuries, and the very lengthy period of transmission may account for some of the duplications, errors of spelling and garbled Latin. But in the early twelfth century the *Cosmographia* was available in Pisa, where a cleric named Guido incorporated the whole text into his *Geographica*, a geographical encyclopaedia. Guido's copy was more accurate than the later ones; he identified place names better and tried to improve the original Latin.[5] With his help we can study the Anonymous Cosmographer of Ravenna's extraordinary synthesis of world geography, written around the year 700.

The first of his five books is a literary *mappa mundi*, an account of the entire universe from its creation by God across the four corners of the world; the second, third and fourth books detail over five thousand cities in the three regions – Asia, Africa and Europe – that Noah allotted to his sons, and the fifth includes a circumnavigation (*periplous*) of the Mediterranean, listing all the ports around the Magna Mare and the islands within it.[6] Although the *Cosmographia* is based on lists of cities within the provinces of the Roman empire with their rivers and mountains, it stretches outside the imperial frontiers to the Baltic islands, the Orkneys and *ultima Thule*. 'Britannia', he declares, 'is said to form part of Europe', although it had not been Roman since the early fifth century. In the south, he identifies the two provinces of Arabia by their traditional names: *Omeritia* (land of the Homeritai), which is *eudaemon* (Greek for *felix*, prosperous) and full of cities, though neither Mecca nor Medina (previously Yathrib) are mentioned, and *Arabia maior* (Bk II, 6–7).

Biblical inspiration is fundamental to his work. He opens Book I with the divine order of the world created by God as recorded in Scripture, and links this to 'the edict that went out from Caesar Augustus that all the world should be taxed' (Luke 2.1: *'exiit edictum ex Augusto Caesare ut describeretur universus orbis'*). He understands this more as a measurement of the world rather than a census. In order to describe the universe, he uses previous records of peoples, tribes, cities and rivers, recording the conflicts that made some *gentes* oppress others, *ut barbarus mos est*, 'according to barbarous custom', a much-used phrase. Repeatedly stressing that he can do nothing without Christ's help, he insists that Christ made everything from nothing and put the great lights in the heavens, by which the most skilful men are able to compute movements and times according to the order of the creator.[7]

His description of the known world proceeds from East to West, from the Indian subcontinent to islands off the coast of Britannia, listing the places and peoples who inhabit those regions. He explains that the sun's movements through the whole day along the line of the meridian enable us to fix both the hours of the day and the passage of time through the year, and to designate the countries of all the peoples placed within the great circuit of the unnavigable Ocean's shore. In this way he introduces a concept of the world depicted within a circle – a plan familiar from late antique T-O (Isidoran) maps – ringed by the great ocean that surrounds the inhabited landmass. He measures the hours of the sun's progress at the vernal equinox (21 March), adds the six winds that blow, followed by a long digression on where the sun goes at night.

At this point he cites Rigilinus, a *philosophus*, whose twenty-four lines of verse on the daily journey of the sun confirm that by night it moves through the *partem arctoam* (arctic region).[8] Thanks to this otherwise unknown geographer/poet, the Anonymous Cosmographer can follow another tradition: that of prefacing serious intellectual endeavour by verses that enhance its authority and power.[9] In the fifth century two craftsmen who created a map for Theodosius II also wrote a poem of dedication to the emperor.[10] The verses by Rigilinus here support the Ravenna cosmographer's argument that the sun does not hide behind huge mountains during the night, or sink below the waters of the Ocean, but returns to its seat in the East, whence it rises again in the morning. That the nightly movement of the sun continued to perplex early medieval philosophers is demonstrated by his conclusion that the means by which this happens 'is known only to our God'.[11] Then he records the hours of darkness going back from West to East, listing the regions of the north, from Germania and Britannia, via the Baltic islands of the Fini, to the Caucasus, Scythia, Sarmatia and the Caspian Gates to Bactrian India. He tries to fit all the peoples of the north into these twelve hours and draws attention to the importance of midnight with several scriptural references, such as the moment when Judith struck off the head of Holofernes.[12]

Although many of the ancient sources appear to be cited from later compendia and florilegia, there's no doubt about the range of books available to the author in seventh-century Ravenna or his ambition. The Cosmographer begins by acknowledging his predecessors, 'philosophers' such as Ptolemy, Herodotus and Strabo, and Orosius, Solinus and a certain Castorius, among the Latin authors. He knows of Persian philosophers who wrote in Greek, uses Josephus for the regions of Palestine where the Hebrews live, and quotes several Greek Church Fathers: Basil of Caesarea, Epiphanios of Cyprus, Athanasios of Alexandria, and Gregory the Great, the most famous of the Latin Fathers known to him. In addition to sixth- and early seventh-century authorities such as Procopius, Cassiodorus and Stephanos of Byzantium, he also mentions Pentesileus as a reliable source for the Amazons and their region of Cholchia in a mixture of the fantastical and serious. He follows the typical early medieval habit of providing an extravagant etymological explanation of strange names, for example, 'Altinum was once called Altilia because it was captured by Attila the Hun'.[13]

One of the chief sources he uses is attributed to Castorius, an otherwise unknown author, whom the Anonymous Cosmographer associated with a list of itineraries that linked cities across the Roman world, similar to the celebrated *Tabula Peutingeriana*.[14] Whenever he cites Castorius as his source for specific city names, they can be traced to this document, which only survives in a twelfth-century medieval copy over seven metres long.[15] Since the original Peutinger map was probably made in the Tetrarchic period, about AD 300, it's likely that a copy was kept in Ravenna, where the Cosmographer thought it had been made by Castorius.[16] And because he describes this philosopher/geographer as 'learned in both languages', there were probably both Greek and Latin references in this source, in contrast to the firmly Latin base of the surviving Peutinger map.[17] It's likely that he also had a circular map that showed the division of the universe into the portions distributed to Noah's sons: Asia to Shem, Africa to Ham, Europe to Japheth.[18]

Gothic Geographers

In frequent references to three – probably Gothic – experts, the Anonymous Cosmographer provides information about the extreme north and the outlying frontiers of Christendom. While 'Athanarich', 'Ildebaldus' and 'Marcomirus' could certainly be Gothic names – Athanarid, Heldebald and Marcomir – no individuals with these names are recorded elsewhere.[19] The destruction of Gothic documents (especially those containing texts of Arian doctrine, which were all condemned to the flames) ensured their work did not survive. This probability is supported by the growing number of Gothic palimpsests identified, mainly Arian Christian texts, which originated in Ravenna and were re-used in Verona for the production of new records.[20] It's difficult to judge what the alleged Gothic geographers added to the Ravenna Cosmographer's knowledge of the Goths, which is largely derived from Jordanes' *Getica* and Isidore of Seville, whose works would certainly have found a place in a library in Ravenna.[21] The archbishop, exarch and the abbots of the numerous monasteries in the city maintained their own libraries and would have regarded these Gothic geographers as a further source of esteem – experts who provide specifically Gothic names of settlements mostly unfamiliar to the Mediterranean world.

In addition to such Gothic texts, the Anonymous Cosmographer was clearly aware of the history of Ravenna, and that it had been ruled by the famous King Theoderic, whose palace, churches and mausoleum remained a constant feature of the cityscape. In particular, the equestrian statue that stood in front of his palace with its impressive basilica, rededicated to St Martin in the 560s, demonstrated his power and patronage. Even if the Gothic language had not survived the extinction of Arian theology, it left an influence in the spoken language and certain technical terms. The Cosmographer was heir to this integration of Germanic and Roman cultures, which is so evidently reflected in his text, and he therefore cited his Gothic informants, whether they were very useful or not.[22] The Gothic names gave later readers problems as they were not familiar with the alphabet.

In Book V, a *periplous* of the Mediterranean, the Cosmographer makes Ravenna the starting and end point of his coastal journey and travels anticlockwise. In contrast, earlier descriptions of sailing around the Mediterranean began at the Pillars of Hercules in the extreme West and moved clockwise around the littoral. The text takes his audience south down the Adriatic coast of Italy and then up the western coast to Salerno, Rome and Genoa to Ventimiglia – and on via Nice, Marseille, Nîmes and Narbonne to the Pyrenees and Spain. Crossing over into North Africa and on to Alexandria, he travels north to Palestine, Syria, round Asia Minor into the Sea of Marmara past Chalcedon, up the Bosporus into the Black Sea, anticlockwise round the sea, and back to Constantinople. Then on to Thessalonike, south down the coast of Greece and up the Eastern Adriatic past Salona, Pola, Parentium, Tergeste, Aquileia and back to Ravenna. Pride in the most noble city of his birth, and an individual approach to maritime routes, which note some little-known harbours, confirm the author's focus on his own locality.

In a note attached to the list of coastal cities south of Ravenna, the author advises his reader that there may be a discrepancy between the names of cities already given and those which follow.

> They are the same but men use different letters (*diversis vocabulis*) according to their custom and the diversity of their languages (*linguarum diversitas*). Just as men vary in their appearance (*facie*) so speech (*loquela*) divides men and cities. Don't worry if despite a similar appearance you find the word (*loquelam*) used by men for cities varies. (Bk V, 1)

And indeed, when comparing the lists of cities in earlier books with those in the *periplous* there are some slight and other more notable differences, such as Pensarum/Pensaurum; Floxo/Flosor; Pinna/Tinna; Pausas/Pausulas. In contrast to other geographical lists of cities, the spelling of names is quite idiosyncratic, and there are duplications and undocumented sites. The Cosmographer's attention to the spoken Latin of the time and the different spellings of city names reveals the difficulty of finding an established form.

The original text of the *Cosmographia* may well have been illustrated with a map of the world (*mappa mundi*), but no images accompany the surviving manuscripts, and the map created by Guido of Pisa in 1119 does not record any debt to the Anonymous Cosmographer. Such maps were highly appreciated, as we know from Pope Zacharias (741–52), a Greek, probably from southern Italy, who had one in Rome, and another noted in the 822/3 library catalogue of the monastery of Reichenau on Lake Constance. At Aachen, the great Frankish king Charles had a very heavy silver table 'which shows the entire universe in three concentric circles', as well as a copy of the *Tabula Peutingeriana*.[23] When he was planning his military campaigns in Italy in 773 and 776, Charles acquired important topographical information from Martin, the envoy and deacon of Archbishop Leo of Ravenna (770–77), who 'showed to the Franks the route into Italy'.[24] The lists of cities in the *Cosmographia*, probably based on itineraries, may have generated practical value as well as an intellectual interest.[25]

Quite apart from any military usefulness, the *Cosmographia* of the anonymous scholar of Ravenna excels in its range of evidence and combination of geographical sources. This wealth of information played a critical part in the transmission of geography and cartography from Roman times via Guido of Pisa in the early twelfth century and on to a more sophisticated art of mapping, which encouraged new systems of recording sea voyages in the earliest portolan maps.[26] An even more intriguing influence of the Anonymous Cosmographer is found in a copy of the *Tabula Peutingeriana*, discovered in the fifteenth century.[27] The Renaissance scholar Pellegrino Prisciani, librarian of the d'Este collection, saw this manuscript on display in the bishop's palace in Padua and copied a section of it, noting the Greek glosses for certain names, which he had difficulty reading. These Greek additions appear to have been made in Ravenna and may well have derived from the Anonymous Cosmographer.[28] Since the copy of the *Peutingeriana* attested at Charles's court appears to have had only Latin names, the removal of any Greek names that may have gone back to the anonymous Ravenna scholar could be the result of Carolingian scholars' demand for 'exclusive Latinity'.[29]

Despite the paucity of evidence for schools and teachers of Greek and secular learning in Ravenna, the presence of Johannicis, Rigilinus and the Anonymous Cosmographer implies a high standard of education and an interest in Greek and verse as well as maps and computation, which is not at all common in the early Middle Ages. And although some later emperors were not interested in supporting this bilingual

36. Ivory throne of Archbishop Maximian in Ravenna, sixth century, made entirely of elephant tusk, with his monogram at the centre, flanked by peacocks. Below are John the Baptist and the four Evangelists holding their books, while the sides are decorated with scenes from the Old and New Testaments.

MAXIMIANVS·

37. The imperial mosaic panel on the north wall of the presbytery of San Vitale, showing Emperor Justinian with Archbishop Maximian (labelled) with priests and soldiers. The emperor in full imperial regalia presents his gifts to the church.

38. The panel on the south wall opposite Justinian showing Empress Theodora presenting her gift of a chalice, flanked by her ladies in waiting and eunuch officials. On the hem of her purple cloak the Three Kings are bringing their gifts to the Virgin and Child.

39 and 40. How was Christ to be portrayed? (*Above*) Detail of the young unbearded Christ enthroned on the globe in the apse of San Vitale contrasted with (*below*) the mature bearded Christ holding the Gospel at the head of the arch in front of the apse.

41. (*Left*) Gold *solidus* of Justinian II (second reign 705–11), displays the young curly-haired Christ, IhS CRISTOS REX REGNANTIUM (King of Kings), blessing and holding the Gospel. (*Right*) On the reverse, a bust portrait of the emperor (identified as the servant of Christ, Servus Christi), holding the cross on steps and an orb marked PAX (peace) surmounted by a cross.

42. (*Left*) Gold *solidus* from the same period, showing the mature bearded Christ blessing. (*Right*) On the reverse, Justinian II standing holding a tall cross on steps.

43 and 44. (*Opposite*) The church of Bishop Eufrasius of Parentium, Parenzo (Poreč), across the Adriatic from Ravenna, decorated with comparable mosaics of the mid-sixth century. (*Right*) A mosaic panel of the Visitation, when the Virgin Mary greets Elizabeth, mother of St John the Baptist. Both are clearly pregnant, a most unusual feature.

45. The small chapel of S. Maria *in Formosa*, Pola (Pula), as seen from what would have been the western entrance to a large basilica church commissioned by Archbishop Maximian in his home town. Now isolated like the 'Mausoleum' of Galla Placidia, this chapel attached to the apse, is all that remains of a substantial mid-sixth-century monument.

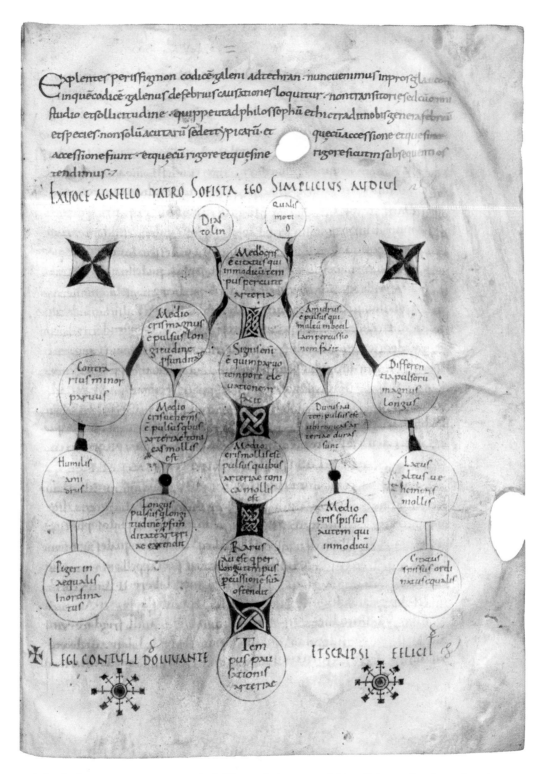

46. A ninth-century copy, now in Milan, of the text of Simplicius, who 'heard and wrote down' the lectures of Doctor Agnellus, 'YATRO SOFISTA', in Ravenna in the seventh century, illustrated in a genealogical table. This commentary on the texts of Galen became a core feature of the teaching of medicine in the medieval West.

atmosphere, Ravenna's close ties to Constantinople constantly invigorated and refreshed it. Translation skills were at a premium and texts originally in Greek were made available in Latin as and when required. The same skills were evident in Rome at this time but were directed specifically to the translation of religious documents. While some influence from the East may have encouraged the Anonymous Cosmographer, much of the information required for his research into ancient geography appears to have been local. And since it had practical application, as King Charles later found, it was probably patronized by the exarchs, in whose palace Johannicis found employment.

As the head of imperial administration in the West, the exarch obviously had responsibility for maintaining written records of all that happened, based on a bureaucratic tradition developed in Constantinople – where records were kept in triplicate. The exarch's palace must have had secure places for storing such papyrus documents, as well as a library for texts that might be useful.[30] Similarly, within the city the archbishops were responsible for keeping all the documentation of land ownership, the church's contracts, leases, rents and taxes paid in kind, safely stored in locked chests. And at precisely this date, around 700, a scribe in Ravenna copied a collection of sermons in Latin and stories of the Desert Fathers that had been translated from Greek into Latin by Pelagius, later pope (556–61). The manuscript is now sadly fragmented, but it reflects the widespread interest in such tales 'good for the soul', known in Greek as *Apophthegmata Patrum* (Plate 56). The unknown scribe may have been attached to a monastery where records were also carefully kept.[31] The city had more than one library where records and important documents could be consulted and cited.

Was the Anonymous Cosmographer one of the officials appointed to look after such collections? He was almost certainly a cleric, like his 'brother Odo', given the restriction of more advanced learning to those dedicated to ecclesiastical careers by the mid-seventh century. But the verses composed by Rigilinus serve as a reminder that early medieval clerics often sustained a serious interest in pre-Christian culture. They studied and copied texts and emulated earlier styles in their own writing. They may have cited ancient authors such as Ptolemy and Strabo without actually reading the originals, but from one perspective this was another reflection of the high esteem in which classical learning was held. The Ravenna cosmographer displays an exaggerated dedication to the transmission and elaboration of Greek and Latin culture. In his work we can see the germs of an early medieval culture that emerges in western Europe personified by Charlemagne, with its combined Latin, Christian and Germanic tributaries, transalpine energies welded to those of Rome. For the Anonymous Cosmographer, however, 'Rome' still designated a single world empire, now centred on Constantinople, drawing on translations of Greek works. In this text we can see how these different forces influenced his world. Ravenna not only nurtured expertise in Greek, but also preserved a curiosity about the physical world, mountains and rivers, as well as imperial geography. It was a fulcrum for the combination of Gothic, Latin, Greek and Christian elements, made possible only by the wealth, culture and direct role of Constantinople itself, presented in the surprising range and confidence of a scholar who 'explored the whole world' from his vantage point in *nobilissima* Ravenna.

PART SEVEN

685–725
The two reigns of Justinian II

28

The Council *in Trullo*

While the Anonymous Cosmographer of Ravenna was listing all the coastal cities of the Mediterranean, the inland sea that he regarded as the centre of the world, its perpetual division between Christianity and Islam was underway. The losses suffered by the empire can be measured by the magnitude of the Christian population that passed under Muslim control. In 646 the North African ecclesiastical dioceses of Proconsularis and Byzacena recorded 109 bishops in their local synods. By the eighth century they were gradually dwindling, and the Arabs had advanced into Spain.

Another stage in this process of division occurred in 692, when Emperor Justinian II ordered the Sixth Oecumenical Council that had begun in 680 to reconvene in Constantinople in order to complete its work by revising the canons – ecclesiastical laws – of the church. This meeting is variously known as the *Quini-Sext* (Fifth-Sixth), meaning that its task was to complete the work of the Fifth and Sixth Councils, or as the Council *in Trullo*, because it met under the dome of the same hall in the Great Palace as it had in 680. It issued 102 disciplinary canons, which reviewed church rules, for example, on the authority of bishops over their diocesan monasteries. Once again, the position reserved for the church of Ravenna was very high, eleventh in the list, although no representative actually attended.[1] And it is clear that other western bishops who had not been present were expected to add their assent to the final document agreed in 692. Thus, immediately after the signature of the emperor (in red) on the acts a space is left for the signature of 'the most holy pope of Rome'; at seventh place, the archbishop of Thessalonike is indicated; at ninth, Sardinia; and at eleventh, Ravenna. Bishops of Herakleia in Thrace and Corinth would have added their signatures at positions twelve and thirteen.[2]

No canons for the whole Christian world had been issued since 451 and that world had changed irrevocably with the spread of Islam. Muslim rule over the huge provinces of Palestine, Syria, Egypt and North Africa prevented any bishops from these areas attending the council in either of its meetings, although the patriarchs of Alexandria, Antioch and Jerusalem were represented. The first stage of the council a decade earlier had dedicated itself to theological issues of doctrine, and Ravenna had been recognized as one of the leading churches. The second stage, which Justinian II presided over, intended to provide legal regulations governing a wide range of religious behaviour and practice, from issues of celibacy and church discipline to the condition of Christians living 'in barbarian lands'.

Although the council sought to add a unified set of canons that would apply to bishops and believers throughout the Oecumene, it failed to secure Rome's support and thus lost considerable authority in the West, particularly in Ravenna. Instead of sending a special team to the meeting in which Ravenna might have participated, Pope Sergius (687–701) was represented by the papal legate resident in the capital and Bishop Basil of Gortyna (on Crete).[3] Other bishops who had attended in 680–81 now returned to Constantinople, together with a number of more recently appointed clerics, many bringing specific legal problems to the meeting so that new canons could be formulated – for example, for Christian bishops fleeing from Muslim rule. For several months they discussed a wide range of issues, including measures to curb superstitions and irreverent practices, such as interpreting clouds as divine messages, that might deceive uneducated Christians (the simple-minded). Two canons were devoted to appropriate Christian art, the first stipulating the human depiction of Christ rather than his symbolic representation as the Lamb of God, and the second forbidding any artistic representation that might generate improper feelings.[4] This emphasis on the incarnation, through Christ's earthly life, both drew on and also encouraged the cult of icons. Justinian sent the final list of 102 regulations to all the leaders of the pentarchy, so that Christians everywhere would be aware of them.

Among these regulations canon 3 established that the see of Constantinople should be given the same honour as the see of Rome, while conceding the overall primacy of St Peter. This followed the imperial tradition that the city where the emperor resided should also have the highest ecclesiastical status. Pope Sergius, however, took exception to Constantinople's claim to equal honour, as well as other rulings that he considered 'outside the usages of the church', offensive to the heirs of St Peter and even contrary to Roman practice, such as traditions of clerical celibacy, fasting and genuflecting.[5] The Roman *Book of the Pontiffs* describes how 'six copies of the acts had been written out, signed by the three patriarchs of Constantinople, Alexandria and Antioch, and by the other prelates . . . confirmed by the hand of the emperor and placed in the despatch-box called *scevrocarnalis* and sent to Rome.' The pope was to sign them at the top 'as head of all the priests (*sacerdotes*)', and he refused.[6]

Reaction to the Council *in Trullo* in Italy

In Ravenna Archbishop Damianus, who was elected after the death of Theodore in January 692, had been consecrated by Pope Sergius and shared his opposition to the council. There is no evidence that he was asked to sign the copies of the acts that had been sent to Rome; no western church leaders did so.[7] The emperor therefore took urgent measures to acquire their agreement. First, Justinian sent Sergios, a *magistrianus*, to persuade the pope to sign, and when he failed in that task, the emperor retaliated by ordering the arrest of John, bishop of Portus, who had participated in the council of 680–81, and Boniface, counsellor of the papal see. The two were taken off to Constantinople and nothing more was heard of them.[8] Justinian then sent a military officer, Zacharias the *protospatharios*, to arrest and remove the pope himself. In response to this drastic threat, local soldiers, specifically those of Ravenna, the Pentapolis and neighbouring regions, set off for Rome, determined to protect Pope Sergius and to prevent him being taken to the East. They arrived after Zacharias and found the city gates closed against them, because the *protospatharios* feared for his life and had begged the pope to protect him. According to the *Book of the Pontiffs*, he was so frightened that he took refuge inside the Lateran palace, even hiding under the pope's bed.[9]

When the army of Ravenna learned that Zacharias was in the city, they forced their way through the gate of St Peter and marched to the palace to expel him. They also demanded to see the pope, fearing that he had already been smuggled out and put on board ship, a reaction that was obviously related to the treatment accorded to Pope Martin and to the other papal officials, who had not returned from Constantinople. When they arrived at the Lateran palace, Pope Sergius went out to reassure 'the common soldiers and the people' that he was alive and well. Only once the army of Ravenna had ensured that Zacharias had left the city, expelled 'with injuries and insults', did the troops abandon their defence of Rome and return home.[10] Though the presence of the exarch is not noted, this military intervention by local forces from Ravenna and the Pentapolis was the first explicit defiance of Constantinopolitan authority; it implies that their loyalty to the imperial administration had been replaced by a determination to protect the bishop of Rome from arbitrary arrest.

The canons of 692, therefore, were not recognized in the West. In his anger at this refusal, Justinian may have transferred the ecclesiastical diocese of East Illyricum from Rome's authority to that of Constantinople.[11] This substantial area of the Balkans, Greece and the Aegean islands had been under the control of the bishop of Rome for centuries. Its transfer to Constantinople created another major disagreement between West and East, and popes would continue to demand the return of the diocese for centuries, to no avail. For his part, Justinian never forgot the antagonism of the army of Ravenna, which had humiliated his official Zacharias between 693 and 695.

The Mutilation and Exile of
Justinian II

The overthrow of Justinian II in 695 is a critical event in the history of Ravenna. The emperor believed that some of its citizens played a major role in this coup d'état, though the activity of his unscrupulous financial officials and their violent methods of extortion were more likely responsible for his downfall. The emperor's increasing unpopularity in Constantinople came to a head when rumours began to circulate that he had ordered the murder of the city's patriarch and all members of the Blue circus faction. In response, a rival military officer, Leontios, was persuaded by a prediction that he would become emperor to lead a military coup. He broke into the central prison, armed the inmates and ordered them to go through the city, shouting 'All Christians to St Sophia!' The population and the patriarch joined in the revolt, arrested and killed the hated financial advisers, and mutilated Justinian in a public ceremony in the Hippodrome.[12] While the new emperor spared Justinian's life, the symbolic act of cutting his nose and ears was designed to disqualify him from ruling, and Leontios (always identified as Leo on his coinage) exiled him to the Crimea.[13]

Paul the deacon correctly describes this extremely unpleasant operation: 'Leo in banishing him cut off his nostrils.'[14] This quite common procedure of nose-cutting, *rhinotomia*, gave Justinian the nickname *rhinotmetos*, the emperor whose nose was cut. It was intended both to disfigure him and to prevent him from ever resuming his imperial dignity. To hold the office of emperor required a whole person, which is why eunuchs were never permitted to aspire to rule. It was in this extremely unattractive condition that Justinian was sent into exile in Cherson, a major port on the north coast of the Black Sea. His departure from Constantinople inaugurated a period of instability, in which other military officers decided to take their chances in capturing the post of emperor.

The Fate of Carthage

Meanwhile, in 697, the Arabs finally captured Carthage, the capital of the North African exarchate, and Leontios demonstrated a clear grasp of its strategic importance by sending a major sea-borne expedition under John the patrician to recapture the city. These forces successfully occupied the capital and surrounding territory but were unable to resist the Arabs' counterattack, which defeated them in 698.[15] The imperial forces withdrew to Crete where a subordinate officer, Apsimar, rebelled and sailed on to Constantinople. He overthrew Leontios and ruled as Tiberios III (698–705). Caliph Abd al-Malik ordered the defences of Carthage to be razed and the harbours destroyed; then his forces pressed on with the conquest of western North Africa, which was completed by their crossing into Spain at the Pillars of Hercules in 711.

The loss of Africa marked a massive reduction in the empire's tax base and the removal of a wheat supply that had sustained the inhabitants of Rome for centuries. Fortunately, with a greatly reduced population and alternate sources in Sicily and southern Italy, Rome could survive, even with an increase in Christian refugees from Africa.[16] But the destruction of Carthage was a symbol of imperial failure that made the remaining western provinces all the more important: Ravenna, still the centre of an exarchate, the island of Sicily, promoted to an independent *thema*, and Sardinia and the Balearics. Particular significance was attached to the Sicilian mint of Catania, which gained a superior position to that of Ravenna because the greater agricultural production of the region could furnish higher taxation to Constantinople. This shift heralded the key role that Sicily would play in eighth-century imperial politics.[17]

Against this background of Arab triumph in Africa and continuing campaigns against major cities in Asia Minor launched from Damascus, Justinian plotted to regain his throne. Despite the mutilation designed to prevent him from ever exercising imperial power again, he negotiated an alliance with the Khazar ruler of territory north of the Black Sea, who gave him his daughter (or possibly sister) in marriage, and won Bulgarian support for his return to Constantinople. In the summer of 705 he sailed back to the capital, assisted on land by a Bulgarian army. When the gates of the city remained closed to him, he was able to find a way into it through the aqueduct. Both Leontios and Tiberios were paraded in the Hippodrome and beheaded; military leaders were impaled on the walls of the city; and the patriarch himself was blinded and exiled to Rome.[18]

The Second Reign of Justinian II

Once the mutilated Emperor Justinian II had resumed the throne in Constantinople, he summoned his wife, whom he had renamed Theodora, and their son, Tiberios, from Crimea and 'they reigned jointly with him'.[19] The emperor clearly aspired to recreate the glory of his sixth-century predecessors, Justinian I and Empress Theodora.

The emperor immediately attempted to have the canons of the Council *in Trullo* recognized throughout Christendom, sending an embassy to Rome led by two metropolitan bishops to demand the pope's agreement. But John VII (705–7), like his predecessor Sergius, refused to sign and sent the acts back unchanged.[20] Justinian then devised a different way to coerce the church of Rome and commanded the pope to travel to Constantinople. Since the instruction arrived after the death of Pope John, it was delivered to Pope Constantine (708–15), who accepted the emperor's order.[21]

News of Justinian II's imperial reinstatement was not greeted with any enthusiasm in Ravenna, where local soldiers had rallied to the defence of Pope Sergius. The city realized that if any Ravennati had also participated in the emperor's mutilation in 695, he might institute reprisals. In this respect they were correct, as Justinian II displayed a level of revenge against both Cherson and Ravenna that led to an unprecedented disaster. The restored emperor was initially preoccupied with defeating the Bulgars (who were no longer allies) and regular Arab raids, but Agnellus the historian, writing with hindsight, believed that Ravenna was also on his mind. 'What shall I initiate against Ravenna?', he reports the emperor as saying. 'These people inimical to me, through fraudulent counsel, have cut off my nose and ears.'[22] Justinian knew that the army of Ravenna had prevented his envoy Zacharias from obtaining Pope Sergius' signature to the canons of 692. In revenge for the disfigurement, which he may have associated with the Ravennati, as well as their clear opposition to imperial orders, Justinian instructed a reliable military commander (the *strategos* of Sicily) to sail up the Adriatic, capture the rebellious city and transport its archbishop and leading citizens to Constantinople to be put on trial.[23]

Agnellus relates the skilful deception by which the commander of the fleet ensnared and kidnapped Archbishop Felix, Johannicis, the leading citizens as well as the less exalted and sailed away. 'The soldiers who were left behind went inside the city walls and used fire against the remaining citizens', causing a terrible commotion and the people 'groaned and wept'. The attack did not destroy Ravenna and Classis but was intended to remind the inhabitants of their necessary loyalty to Constantinople. It was a devastating example of the long arm of the emperor, who could draw on loyal resources in Sicily to punish the inhabitants of his capital city in the West.[24]

Ravenna's New Defences

In the absence of their archbishop and leading citizens, the remaining Ravennati decided to take action to defend themselves. They chose a new leader, George, who was the son of Johannicis, and all agreed to follow his orders.[25] George then rode around the exarchate and planned its defence. He divided the entire shoreline of the Adriatic coast so that close watch could be kept for any fleet, allotting duties to the cities of Sarsina, Cervia (at Nova on the sea), Papia (at Cesena), Forlimpopoli (at the port of Sava), Forlì, Faenza (at Lacherno), Imola (at the Coriandrum field) and Bologna at the Lion Port, and to farmers (at Candiano). Within Ravenna itself he created twelve military units in specific quarters, to which the local population were attached. These may have been based on already existing quarters, some of which were related to particular gates into the city such as the Porta Teguriensis or Posterula Latronum. And he identified eleven of the new units by a banner, named First, Second, Unconquered, Constantinopolitan, etc., and a twelfth was entrusted to the clergy and those not worthy in honour or family.[26] In this way the people were all associated with a particular banner, which represented their area within the city.

This was clearly a rebellion designed to reassert the city's independence and to repel any further naval force sent from Constantinople as well as Lombard attacks. George is reported as saying that they had all 'drunk of the foul poison from the mouth of the serpent, which was brought from the Byzantine sea'. He continues, 'Let us not flee from the Greeks (*Danais*) who are swollen in heart.'[27] George had inspired the populace and the factions of Ravenna to put aside their old quarrels; he set them all to work at the tasks they could do best, young men to cut down poplar trees and virburnum bushes to mix with oak (presumably for ships) and tent-makers to make sails, instructing them to protect their heads from the heat.[28]

George had effected an entirely new defence system for Ravenna and its neighbouring regions by creating a citizen force based on city quarters. It probably replaced or incorporated the limited military capacity that had remained under the command of the imperial governor. No exarch is associated with the development, even though it must have drawn on inherited traditions of civic pride and responsibility.[29] Such an independent civilian organization, created without any deference to Constantinople, makes Ravenna the prototype of an Italian city-state, a model for the later development of Venice and other north Italian republics. Since Agnellus said that the arrangement survived to his day, it was probably incorporated under the exarch's control and persisted even after 751, when the Lombards took control. Its development reflects Ravenna's notion of its own importance and confidence, as well as the capacity to respond with determination to the terrible news that Archbishop Felix had been blinded and banished to the Black Sea, just like Pope Martin.[30]

Justinian was, nonetheless, aware of the dangers to the exarchate and, in 710, the emperor sent another exarch, identified by the Roman *Book of the Pontiffs* as John Rizokopos (possibly serving a second term of office). Rather than sailing directly to Ravenna, the new exarch disembarked at Naples, presumably because Ravenna was already considered to be in a state of rebellious opposition to Constantinople. There he met Pope Constantine and a large clerical team that had set off from Rome on 5 October 710 on their way to the East. While the papal party left for Sicily, John proceeded to Rome where he murdered the four senior clerics who had been left in charge.[31] He then crossed the Apennines to assert imperial order in Ravenna. Instead, he met with a hostile reception and 'by God's judgement on his atrocious deeds he died an ignominious death'.[32] As soon as the death of the exarch was known in Constantinople, the emperor appointed another to take his place: Ravenna had to be brought to heel under the empire's control, so that it could repel Lombard attacks.

The Canons of the Council
in Trullo

Meanwhile, on his journey to the East Pope Constantine was received with great honour by the patrician and *strategos* Theodore in Sicily and passed the winter in Otranto. In the spring of 711 the papal party proceeded via Greece and the Aegean islands and was welcomed into Constantinople by the entire Senate and the patriarch, led by the very young prince Tiberios. As Justinian was in Nicaea in Asia Minor, he asked the pope to meet him in Nicomedia, where they resolved all the disagreements over the canons of the Council *in Trullo*. The emperor renewed all the Roman church's privileges and allowed the pope to return home. The Roman *Book of the Pontiffs* naturally records this visit in glowing terms, dwelling on the highly respectful ceremonies put on by commanders at every stage of the journey, the pope's affectionate reception by the emperor and his safe return to Rome in October 711. The canons agreed in the East, however, were never assimilated into western canon law. The claim made in canon 3 that Constantinople should have the same high status as Rome, though retaining primacy of honour for St Peter's successors, continued to rankle. Indeed, many of the issues covered by the canons concerned communities in the East – such as law students who celebrated their final qualifications in pagan fashion, Armenian priests who added hot water to the communion wine, or those who did not use the correct liturgical form of the *Trisagion* ('Holy, Holy, Holy') prayer – that were irrelevant to western Christians. In the gradual separation of the two halves of Christendom, imperial decisions such as the transfer of the diocese of East Illyricum and the papal patrimonies of southern Italy to Constantinople probably took on much greater significance.

In November 711 Justinian II was overthrown in a military coup. When the news arrived in Ravenna, the city celebrated his death. The new ruler of Constantinople, Philippikos, ordered the disfigured head of his predecessor to be carried on a lance and displayed through all the cities of the West.[33] This might have been appreciated as a token of apology for Justinian's vicious actions and of reconciliation with the western provinces of Italy, whose wealth was so necessary to the East in the battle against the Arabs. It also legitimated the earlier rebellion of the Ravennati against the emperor. When the relic arrived in Ravenna, Johannicis' sister was anxious to witness the proof that the ruler who had ordered her brother's death in such a monstrous manner was really dead, predicting that once she was convinced of it, she would die. The decomposing remains of Justinian II were carried to her house, where she asked the bearer to stand still so that she could contemplate them from an upper window. After giving thanks for this sight she fell dead.[34]

29

The heroic Archbishop Damianus

During the confused period of Justinian II's overthrow and subsequent imperial upheavals, Archbishop Damianus emerges as both the spiritual and secular leader of the city, working to maintain order and reinforce local unity and identity. His family was from Dalmatia, where his parents dedicated him to the church and sent him across the Adriatic to be educated in Ravenna. He rose within the clergy to be elected archbishop in 692 and then went to Rome to be ordained by Pope Sergius, a confirmation now incumbent on the leaders of the church of Ravenna.[1] Throughout his rule, from 692 until 705/8 (thirteen or sixteen years, the dates are disputed), there is one mention of an unnamed exarch, before the arrival of Theophylaktos, exarch under Pope John VI (701–5). John Platyn and another John, Rizokopos, are known to have held the post in the early eighth century, with Eutychios and Scholastikos at imprecise dates. But none of these military officials made any impact in comparison with Archbishop Damianus. For Agnellus, the ninth-century historian, he was a local hero, with miraculous powers, passed down the generations by oral histories.

Here is one of the stories Agnellus tells. A woman came to the archbishop's residence carrying her very young son who was desperately ill; she feared he would die before being baptized and was very anxious for Damianus to anoint him immediately. But as the archbishop was being shaved, his staff told her to wait, to her great distress since she knew that babies who died unbaptized would go straight to Limbo, or even to Hell. The issue was very urgent. While she waited, however, the baby died in her arms. She became distraught and attracted Damianus' attention with her wailing. When he learned how his attendants had delayed telling him the news and then tried to cover up their mistake, he wept and groaned and, taking the baby in his arms, he went into the church and prostrated himself 'behind the apse'.[2] His prayers were so effective that the child revived long enough for the archbishop to baptize him before he died again.

Another exceptionally dramatic story documents the regular fighting that took place every Sunday between different groups of citizens. It concerned the inhabitants of the city quarter next to the Teguriensan Gate and those of the Posterulan, which was also called *Summus Vicus*, and was next to a canal called the *Fossa Lamisem*. These local residents went out of the city on Sundays to fight each other in an area where boys used to play with hoops. Not only young men were involved; interestingly, Agnellus records that the middle-aged, elderly and children of both sexes took part, using slingshots, throwing stones, beating each other with sticks. One week the Teguriensans broke the bolts and bars on the gate of the Posterulans, and the next they killed many on the Posterula side with their swords. Even the elders of the city couldn't remember such a blow, 'the first disaster, grief and woe in the region'. Worse still, it provoked the Posterulans to plan a revenge that took an even more deadly form. Every member of the Posterula faction separately invited a Teguriensan opponent to a reconciliatory lunch after Mass at the Ursiana cathedral and swore him to secrecy. Each Posterulan then killed his Teguriensan guest and enemy in a co-ordinated massacre, and all the deaths were hidden from everyone else.

After the fighting and these unexplained disappearances, Damianus ordered a fast for three days. Then he arranged a penitential procession through the city in which the population was divided into clerical and lay; the laity into male and female; and a crowd of the poor made up the final section. Priests walked barefoot, wearing sackcloth with ash on their heads; nobles and commoners wore hairshirts and did not wash or comb their hair, while women took off all their jewellery and dressed in mourning clothes. In this manner each group walked in a separate chorus, a stone's throw apart, lamenting and weeping. And as a result, there was some sort of eruption in the area of the amphitheatre, near the Golden Gate, that made a huge sound and gave off a great cloud of smoke, and in the hole that emerged the dead were found and could be identified. The murderers were then arrested, their wives and children punished, their homes razed to the ground and their property burned at the Milvian bridge outside the city. Through this ritual expression of guilt and grief, peace returned to Ravenna, thanks to

Archbishop Damianus' wise formula of the penitential procession that revealed the bodies of the Teguriensans and resolved their unexplained deaths.[3] The violence was brought to an end temporarily.

Yet the Sunday fighting continued into the ninth century, indicating that local factions persisted with their rivalries. Even within a relatively small community such as Ravenna, particular districts developed a distinct character that may have been based on different trades, family connections or origins. An area that Agnellus incorrectly identifies as 'the Criminals' took its name from a guard house (*latronum*); similarly, a leper house near Classis gave its name to the area called the Lepers. These districts became more prominent in the early eighth century when the city had to devise a more serious civil defence system that contributed to the growth of local militias with specific denominations. Ravenna's pattern of Sunday violence also seems to have influenced the nascent community of Venice, where both military training with weapons and fist fighting without sticks or stones led to boxing competitions, which were later held on bridges over canals, giving the victor the pleasure of tipping his opponent into the water below, to the delight of the spectators.[4]

Such competitive sporting activity had dominated Roman cities, with their teams of chariot drivers, horses and circus entertainers. In Constantinople and a few other cities, two major groups, the Blues and the Greens, dominated entire neighbourhoods and maintained these traditions. In addition to their roles in the hippodrome, when the city was under threat, emperors issued weapons to their members to assist in the defence. While Ravenna may not have preserved circus factions, it's clear that different districts within the city cherished a fighting rivalry. The great annual horse race of Siena, the *pallio*, had comparable roots in inner-city factions, later supported by guilds of craftsmen. Horse races, cock fights, displays of unfamiliar animals, dancing bears, dogs or monkeys, and disfigured individuals were all part of lively civic entertainment in medieval times.

Damianus also had to deal with more serious threats to his church. At some point a fire in the city had destroyed part of the *archivus ecclesiae*, the church's collection of important documents, such as gifts of land and records of rents due on its property. Damianus suspected that many had not been burned but had been stolen and 'hidden by wicked men', presumably to revoke the legal agreements.[5] Rather than preaching a sermon on the issue, he summoned all his priests to a city tavern where he issued anathemas against anyone who was in possession of these documents. He also declared that if they brought such records back, they would be absolved of all blame.[6] In this secular manner the Ravenna church may perhaps have regained some of its archive.

The Resurgence of Lombard Hostilities

Both bishops and exarchs of this period were challenged by the Lombards, still battling among themselves for leadership of the 'longbeards' over a century after their settlement in Italy north of the Po. In the 680s Duke Ansfrit usurped power in Friuli, tried to attack King Cunincpert and was punished by blinding and exile.[7] At the same time a terrible pestilence swept through the cities, causing many deaths in Rome and a total devastation of the Lombard capital, Pavia, which was abandoned as survivors fled to the country. Against this background of constant rivalry and insecurity, Cunincpert decided to reverse traditional Lombard hostility to the Fifth Oecumenical Council and to accept its rulings over the Three Chapters as a true definition of the faith. In 698 he summoned all the bishops in Lombard territories to a council in Aquileia (also known as the Synod of Pavia), at which those who had supported the schism agreed to end it and to accept the leadership of the bishop of Rome. The Roman *Book of the Pontiffs* attributes this conversion to the power of Pope Sergius, but the king and the patriarch of Aquileia undoubtedly played a part.[8]

Despite this solution to a very old dispute, Cunincpert was unable to control the fractious southern dukes, Faroald of Spoleto and his son, Transamund, nor could he ensure the inheritance of his own son Liutpert. After Cunincpert's death in 700, a decade of in-fighting followed, only finally resolved in 712 when the Lombards accepted Liutprand, the son of a duke of Asti, as their king. Liutprand had passed his youth in exile in Bavaria, and now returned to Pavia with his bride, the daughter of the duke of Bavaria, consolidating the transalpine alliance that strengthened both the Lombard kingdom in Italy and its Catholic faith. Liutprand also displayed great respect for the bishop of Rome and the Latin Church Fathers. According to Paul the deacon, after

Lombard forces overran the patrimony of the Cottian Alps, Liutprand decided to give it back to the pope. He also donated Sutri and other cities of Latium to 'the blessed apostles Peter and Paul' in 728.[9] When he learned that Sardinia had been subjected to Arab attacks that threatened the tomb of St Augustine, the king arranged to retrieve the bones and bring them with due reverence to Pavia, where he constructed a special chapel to house them.[10]

Although the Lombards' novel religious orientation altered the balance of forces in Italy, it did not unite the rival Lombard dukes, nor did it stop their attacks on Ravenna and particularly Classis. After Faroald of Spoleto attacked the port city of Ravenna, Liutprand insisted that it be respected as part of Roman (that is, imperial) territory.[11] Yet, later, the king also laid siege to Ravenna and may have captured Classis, from which he 'took many captives and removed untold wealth'.[12] In the course of his long reign (from 712 to 744) Liutprand frequently threatened the imperial enclaves in Italy, and besieged Rome despite his respect for St Peter. Only by appointing his nephews, Agiprand and Gisulf to rule in the dukedoms of Spoleto and Benevento was there any peace in Italy.

The Lamb of God

When Johannicis returned from Constantinople to Ravenna in the time of Archbishop Damianus, he brought news of the canons issued by the Council *in Trullo* held in 692, which decreed that Christ should be shown in his human form rather than as the Lamb of God (number 82).[13] Such symbolic depiction was very common in Ravenna, for example in the apse of S. Apollinare in Classe, where the eponymous saint stands among twelve lambs (representing the apostles), and in many other churches (Plate 51). In Rome too the symbol was very widely used and beloved. Pope Sergius displayed his appreciation of it when he added a new section to the Mass entitled *Agnus Dei* – 'the Lamb of God who taketh away the sins of the world'.[14] So the instruction to replace images of the Lamb with those of the human Christ was not well received.

Part of the opposition may have arisen from the difficulty of defining the correct representation of Christ that churches should use. In the apse of San Vitale, decorated in the time of Bishop Ecclesius early in the sixth century, Christ was shown as a young man with short curly hair seated on the globe. Yet at the apex of the apse the older, bearded Christ is depicted with long hair (Plates 39 and 40). Similarly at the church of Sts Cosmas and Damianus in Rome, a contemporary sixth-century mosaic shows him as a fully adult man with a long beard.[15] In the church of S. Apollinare in Classe the bust of Christ at the centre of the jewelled cross is of the older type, with long hair and a beard. Both styles were employed by Emperor Justinian II when he introduced the image of Christ on his gold coinage – an extraordinary move but one made in line with the same canon (Plates 41 and 42). Adding a Christian image to the imperial coinage was also closely related to Caliph Abd al-Malik's minting of new coin types at precisely this time, inscribed with Koranic texts in Arabic.[16]

In Damascus and Jerusalem, Christians and Muslims initially shared their places of worship, and a specifically Islamic architecture for mosques only developed slowly. The construction of the Dome of the Rock in 691–2, an octagonal building on Jerusalem's Temple Mount, marked a key moment. Its radiant mosaic decoration was entirely aniconic (that is, with no figures), and the craftsmen responsible, together with the supply of tesserae to make the mosaics, came from Constantinople. Muslim–Christian rivalry and the superiority of Islam was made very evident in a long inscription.[17] The entire interior was decorated with exquisite images of nature: trees, flowers and baskets of fruit. Similarly at the Great Mosque of Damascus, the mosaics evoked gardens of paradise filled with palaces, streams, trees and flowers, but not a single person. Non-figural decoration in mosques, on liturgical objects and manuscripts of the Koran contrasted with portraits of the human Christ, which stressed the significance of the incarnation, as ordered by canon 82. Although many of the craftsmen and techniques were shared, and motifs from a wide range of monuments including Persian were incorporated, these fundamentally contrasting approaches to symbolism and decoration separated newly constructed Muslim places of worship from Christian churches.

The impact of the Trullan canon 82 is echoed in a strange conversion story from Ravenna. Without citing the background that provoked this new regulation, Agnellus the historian describes how a Jew rushed to the altar one Sunday after Archbishop Damianus had consecrated the host and demanded to be given a piece of the lamb that was being pulled apart. When the archbishop replied that he was holding bread that represented the body of Christ, the Jew insisted that he saw lamb, not bread. Since the man was a Jew and considered unclean, Damianus insisted that he should be converted and baptized a Christian before he could partake of the Mass, saying, 'Receive the sign of the Lamb and eat of the Lamb with us.'[18] The Jew immediately gave up his ancestral faith and received his new identity as a Christian.

It is unlikely that the Lamb was regularly invoked in this particular way. Rather, Agnellus has caught an element of the opposition to canon 82, which continued through the episcopate of Damianus and was not resolved until 710. Lambs continued to feature in Christian art as symbols, while artists developed different ways of representing the human Christ. For Muslims, the Old Testament commandment against the making and worshipping of graven images meant that no human images were permitted in mosques. The debate among Christians about how to represent Christ was partly a reflection of this more insistent Islamic avoidance of human figures that might be construed as idols.[19]

Abbot John Journeys to Constantinople

While Damianus was archbishop, the monastery of St John *ad Titum* in Classis was attacked by men who tried repeatedly to gain control of its farms and property, to the distress of its abbot, a priest also named John. Normally these quarrels should have been resolved through the law courts, or by an appeal to the exarch, but Abbot John decided to go to Constantinople in person, in order to win imperial confirmation for the monastic properties.[20] Agnellus relates his extraordinary journey with great delight, elaborating the account with mythical inventions. Believing that an official letter from the emperor would curb any further efforts to expropriate his monastery, the abbot waited in the eastern capital for an audience. When it was time for the Invitatory to be performed, he duly recited the entire liturgy, unaware that the emperor was listening in a room above. A doorkeeper wanted to remove the stranger who was chanting, but the emperor enjoyed listening and insisted on hearing it to the end. He then summoned the abbot and demanded to know his business in Constantinople. Once this was clarified he issued an edict for the monastery and a letter to the exarch to insist on its implementation. After this astonishing success, the abbot looked for a ship to take him back to Sicily or Ravenna but could not find one in the harbours of the capital. Eventually, through miraculous means of flight, he was transported back to the roof of his monastery. When his monks recognized him and helped him down, he went to the palace of Theoderic to display his imperial documents to the exarch. This unnamed governor refused to accept their authenticity, 'because there is no one who can go to Constantinople and return within three months'. But Abbot John insisted and invited the exarch's officers to come with him to Archbishop Damianus, where he explained his night flight back from the eastern capital. Damianus encouraged him to 'make true repentance', and 'he finished his days in peace'.[21] Presumably the exarch was forced to accept the emperor's edict and letter.

Such inexplicable divine intervention in the human world is an integral element in the repertoire of popular accounts of people assisted by miracles. Like stories told of saintly monks and ascetic Desert Fathers, they circulated widely as oral traditions before they were written down in many versions and different languages. What excited Agnellus and his audience in ninth-century Ravenna was the idea that a local abbot could appeal to the emperor in Constantinople, gain an audience and obtain an imperial guarantee of his monastery's sole ownership of its estates. They knew that archbishops like Maximian, Maurus and Reparatus had often travelled to the eastern capital for the same purpose. But this story reflects an ingrained perception of the immensely far-reaching power of the emperor in Constantinople, which could still override the governor of the Italian provinces, the ruling power in Ravenna. It also shows that the city's inhabitants acknowledged the supreme authority of an edict, confirmed by an official letter (presumably written on papyrus), which the abbot brought back to the West. Roman law, as dispensed in Constantinople, was still perceived as superior. The links between the city and the eastern capital (even the non-supernatural ones) gave Ravenna access to this, the highest source of justice, which probably continued to protect the monastery of St John *ad Titum* into the ninth century and beyond.

In the neighbouring church of St Apollinaris, Archbishop Damianus commissioned a marble archiepiscopal throne with his name inscribed on it. Admiration for him is conveyed by the inscription over his tomb:

Blessed bishop coming from the lands of Dalmatia, you preserved holy Ravenna by your prayers ... Such a tomb proves that you merited a grave in these temples, that you pleased God. And since as a priest you carried out his duties correctly, may you have holy rest in his grounds.[22]

Damianus thus joined other leaders of the Ravenna church in a large, late antique sarcophagus in the church of S. Apollinare in Classe. He may have been buried in a shroud of purple silk, such as the one retrieved when these tombs were opened in 1949.[23] He was neither a man of the East, formed by Constantinopolitan traditions, nor a man of the West schooled in the ecclesiastical replacement of civic authority, but a striking product of the church of Ravenna, a city that straddled the Mediterranean world and linked its shores.

30

The tempestuous life of Archbishop Felix

After the death of Damianus, in March 708 the clergy elected Felix, abbot of the monastery of St Bartholomew, as their thirty-eighth bishop and he went to Rome to be ordained by Pope Constantine. According to the regulations laid down in the *Liber diurnus* (the papal journal containing ecclesiastical formularies), three oaths were required of bishops: to observe the oecumenical councils (the *promissio fidei*); to promise never to pay for ordination or to accept money for baptism and other church rituals (the *cautio*); and to swear loyalty to St Peter and his heirs (the *indiculum*).[1] The Roman *Book of the Pontiffs* claims that Felix refused to provide 'the normal tokens and expressions of his faith' in the customary form (probably a reference to the third oath) and instead expressed his own declaration of obedience.[2] The local judges appointed by the exarch in Ravenna apparently supported his unorthodox behaviour.[3] When Felix's written declaration (called his bond) was placed in the tomb of St Peter and later retrieved, it was found to be grimy as if burned, a very bad omen that may have been reported to the emperor. It added another element to the rivalry between Rome and Ravenna and increased Justinian II's determination to punish the city.[4]

In the middle of the ninth century, the historian Agnellus succeeded to Felix's position as abbot of St Bartholomew's. Through this connection, he had access to records preserved in the monastery that may have informed his *Life* of Felix, which is one of the longest and fullest in his book. He describes Felix's notable efforts to enrich the local liturgy, with the help of Johannicis, the bilingual scribe and poet who had returned to Ravenna from Constantinople while Damianus was archbishop. First, Felix instructed Johannicis to revise the antiphons (short chants set to the text of the psalms) in both their Latin and Greek versions. These were chanted by alternating choirs at several points in the liturgy and must have kept knowledge of some Greek alive among the Ravennati. Here the historian can't resist praising his ancestor Johannicis, recording his gifts to the monastery of St Andrew the Apostle, which was called *Jericomium*: bronze vessels of enormous weight, and cords of gold such as 'the most noble virgins of Ravenna use' as belts, which he hung from the front of the altar, where the crown (or crowns) hung from bronze chains.[5] Secondly, Felix himself edited a collection of the sermons of Bishop Peter Chrysologus, who had presided over the city during the regency of Galla Placidia.[6] He also wrote his own sermons and many other books, including an exposition on the Day of Judgment, which clearly continued to impress the local populace nearly a century and a half later.

In the process of preserving sermons by Ravenna's most famous bishop and revising the antiphons sung on various Sundays in its churches, Felix and Johannicis performed a task regularly undertaken in leading bishoprics. The provision of liturgical books was an essential feature of every church, and when one copy became too worn to use, it was copied. This work was performed in *scriptoria* in Ravenna that dated back to the earliest period of the city's growth. Since the arrival of the imperial court in 402, Ravenna had provided numerous educated scribes as well as secretaries, who kept records in triplicate in the traditional Roman style. No government could survive without competent writers to document all its business: laws, legal decisions, military orders, financial matters, communications with foreign powers, and so on. From the papyri that record the city council's normal activity it's clear that such men were vital to the efficient running of the municipal archive.[7] By the early sixth century, as we've seen, King Theoderic patronized the production of de-luxe copies of the New Testament for use in Arian churches. Similar workshops later produced the medical and geographical texts associated with Agnellus the *yatrosophist*, recorded by the scribe Simplicius, and the Anonymous Cosmographer. Taken together they confirm a rich history of writing and copying in the city, although very little of what must have been a mountain of records actually survives.

During Justinian II's first reign (685–95), two exarchs called John, the first given the nickname Platyn (*platys*, the blade or oar), and his successor John Rizokopos (root cutter), represent an influx of officials from less elite backgrounds into the administration of the empire.[8] Even if they implemented imperial orders, both were remembered for particularly corrupt or violent acts – Platyn's scandalous intervention in the papal election of 687; Rizokopos' murder of four Roman clerics. The status of exarch may also have been reduced by their relatively rapid turnover: between 678 and 713, six named governors held office for an average of seven years (and three more, known only from their seals, may also belong in this period). In contrast, only three archbishops were in power in the same period, each in office for nearly fifteen years.

The constant presence of a respected bishop who served for well over a decade, in comparison with some of the exarchs' short appointments, is one reason for the gradual assumption of more civilian responsibilities by the church. If we exclude Isaac and Eutychios, who served for unusually long periods, the average term of office for an exarch in the seventh century is five years, whereas that for bishops is nearer sixteen. Such continuity in ecclesiastical leadership meant that the church inevitably became a more permanent and dependable resource for the population, and the standing of an indigenous religious figurehead, chosen by the local clergy, such as Damianus or Felix, became higher than a governor appointed from Constantinople. While this is particularly obvious in Ravenna, a similar development was already common in most parts of the West and in many eastern cities. It foreshadows the ecclesiastical influence that would become paramount after the fall of the exarchate in 751.

Archbishop Felix in Constantinople

As we have seen, after the naval raid on Ravenna, Archbishop Felix, Johannicis and other citizens were taken to Constantinople. For his account of their treatment in the capital Agnellus must have drawn on oral sources, doubtless elaborated in the re-telling. One particularly arresting image is of the imperial reception of the captives in the Great Palace. 'They found the emperor Justinian sitting in a gold and emerald seat and wearing on his head a crown, which his royal wife had decorated for him with gold and pearls.'[9] The Ravennati had been brought into the throne room, a regular way of impressing visitors to the Queen

City, whether captive or free, with the magnificence and the ceremonial of the court. Empresses were known to commission new crowns or to decorate old ones for their husbands, so the idea that Theodora had personally added gold and pearls to the imperial crown is quite possible.

At this reception the emperor ordered all the Ravennati to be imprisoned, then had the citizens of senatorial rank killed, and devised a hideous torture to blind the archbishop: he was forced to stare at a very hot silver tray on which bitter vinegar was poured and thus he lost his sight. He was then exiled to Cherson in the Crimea. Johannicis was killed in an equally vile manner, being crushed between huge boulders.[10] When this news was brought back to Ravenna by a survivor, there was great weeping.[11] In the mid-ninth century when Agnellus was reading his history aloud to his audience, he reported that 'almost thirty days ago' he had finally learned where Johannicis had been buried. Maurus, a deacon, had found his tomb in a small chapel in the city walls of Constantinople near the Golden Gate.[12] Agnellus' announcement of this discovery is one of the personal details that makes his book so compelling.

When Justinian II ordered that the blinded Archbishop Felix should be exiled to Cherson, his fate must have appeared as grim as Pope Martin's. But he was saved by a rebellion within the city. A naval force sent to suppress this rebellion instead proclaimed its leader emperor; an Armenian general Bardanes thus became emperor with the name Philippikos. In November 711, Philippikos and his Crimean supporters set sail for Constantinople and overthrew Justinian.[13] Whether Archbishop Felix left Cherson at this moment or later, his eventual return to Ravenna was the result of a coup d'état in the East.

Turbulent Events in Constantinople

Philippikos found support for his usurpation among many military and civilian officers, but his brief reign extended the instability of Justinian's second reign. According to eastern sources, he believed that his rise to power was dependent upon a renewal of the Monothelete doctrine. As soon as he was successfully enthroned, Philippikos therefore removed the official image of the Sixth Oecumenical Council of

680–81 and replaced it with portraits of the Monothelete leaders, patriarchs Sergios and Pyrros. When this news reached Rome, the new emperor was repudiated as a heretic. The Romans refused to commemorate him in the liturgy, to accept his official image or even his coinage. Instead, they set up an image of all the six Oecumenical Councils, called the Botarea, in St Peter's, to demonstrate their condemnation of Monotheletism.[14]

In contrast to Rome, Ravenna benefitted from the new emperor in one very important way: the blinded Archbishop Felix had accompanied, or followed, Philippikos from the Crimea to Constantinople and was later allowed to return to his city. When Felix explained to the new emperor that all the church treasures of Ravenna had been stolen when he was taken captive, Philippikos ordered heralds to go through the city of Constantinople and announce that these liturgical vessels and other treasures from Ravenna had to be returned. All but one were then, indeed, brought to the palace. This most unlikely story is capped by the list of additional gifts of precious objects and jewels that were supplied from the imperial treasury: bowls of crystal and onyx decorated with gold and gems; containers of glass, wine ewers, pitchers, basins, ladles and a crown of ordinary gold decorated with immensely valuable gems. Agnellus had clearly seen a written inventory of these objects that was preserved in Ravenna. Much later, when the Frankish king Charles saw this very crown during one of his visits to Ravenna, he asked a Jewish merchant how much he could sell it for. The merchant replied, 'If all the wealth of this church and all the ornaments and houses were sold, it would not make up the price.' It disappeared, says Agnellus, in the time of Archbishop George (837–46).[15]

The blinded Felix was thus reinstated in control of the Ravenna church and reconciled with the pope. 'He provided the normal tokens and expressions of his faith which all bishops put in the church office', as the Roman *Book of the Pontiffs* puts it.[16] While the Ravennati celebrated Philippikos for permitting their religious leader to return from exile endowed with great treasure, in Rome the emperor was condemned as a heretic. The presence of several stubborn Monothelete priests who had refused to recant in 681 at the conclusion of the Sixth Oecumenical Council, remained a constant reminder of the eastern movement to install the doctrine of one will.

When Philippikos proved incapable of checking the annual Arab raiding of Asia Minor and Muslim forces closed in on Constantinople again, the army deposed him and acclaimed Artemios, renamed Anastasios as emperor (713–15). He prepared the city for siege by repairing the walls and stockpiling food. He also condemned Monotheletism, restored the doctrine of the two wills and energies of Christ and sent a new exarch, Scholastikios, to Italy carrying an official letter with his declaration of the Duophysite faith addressed to the pope.[17] From Rome Scholastikios went on to Ravenna where he found Archbishop Felix governing the church, and George in charge of the city's military organization. There is no suggestion that the exarch disagreed with either of them over theology. Felix had not been involved in the Monothelete revival.

The archbishop's dominance in the city was striking. He had a house built within the episcopal palace and continued to command the respect of his parishioners, remaining their ecclesiastical leader for twelve years after his return from Constantinople.[18] A bronze cross erected on the Orthodox baptistery, inscribed with the names of Felix and another patron called Stephen, indicates their joint responsibility. The archbishop may also have built a two-storey set of arches and arcades attached to the tower outside the Cappella Arcivescovile – the Archbishop's Chapel – which had a *vivarium* (pen for small animals or fish pond) mentioned by Agnellus.[19] Improving the dilapidated western entrance of the cathedral church, Felix constructed a special chamber where his clergy could gather before the service. As the *Introit* (Entrance) was sung, the group would pass between the people gathered in the nave of the church, who could thus see their archbishop walking to the altar at the east end, reciting the words of God and blessing them. The building of this chamber (*salutatorium*) was commemorated in an inscription over the doors. Felix also placed many relics of saints, cased in silver, behind the shrine of the church and described them in verses set in the curve of the arch.[20]

Living in Ravenna in the Early Eighth Century

Surviving papyri from the archive maintained by the church of Ravenna to authenticate its legal possession of lands provide interesting evidence of local activity at the time of Archbishop Felix. As well as older armed units, the city's division into twelve *numeri* set up by George are frequently mentioned; for instance, the Ravenna troop (*numerus Ravennatis*), represented by John, its leader, *primicerius* (the man whose name came first).[21] A later document records Apolenaris, *domesticus numeri invicti*, a subordinate official attached to the Unconquered.[22] And the continuing existence of these groups in Ravenna is illustrated by two *domestici* of the first *bandus* (*bandi primi*) who signed a document of 767,[23] a *scholarius* (guardsman) of the Classensian *numerus* and many military personnel. Gifts to the church are made by simple individuals, such as Leontius, *clericus et cartularius* of the holy church of Ravenna and husband of Barbara, between 689 and 705.[24] A reference to Johannia, an abbess in charge of a nunnery, is one of the rare records of a group of dedicated Christian women.

By the seventh century traditional family names such as Melminius and Pompulius that dominated the earlier series of papyri have disappeared, together with the last traces of an independent city council and the method of recording documents in the public archive. The established families were being replaced by a new military aristocracy, in which family was not as important as an official post within the *numeri*. This classification of citizens by their occupations or official positions appears to be a general phenomenon observed elsewhere in the Romanized West, where military figures asserted greater control over civilians. In an episode describing a naval battle, however, Agnellus identifies the citizens of Ravenna using a classical term, Melisenses – an ancient name to match that of Pelasgians for Greeks.[25]

Among these new local residents, the Jewish community must have continued to exist, since there was a Jewish merchant who was consulted about the value of the crown in the church's treasury. But the Jew who begged Archbishop Damianus to give him a bit of the lamb doesn't appear to have had any traditional association with financial matters. Possibly some synagogues in Ravenna were transformed into churches, as elsewhere, but the Jewish community survived.[26] The existence of monasteries, some with Greek monks, others Latin-speaking, and the nunnery at Navicula, suggest a thriving population of dedicated religious, alongside the bishopric run by the blind Felix.

The Death of Felix

In 723, when he felt he was dying, Felix commanded the clergy to collect his writings and to burn them all. He explained that being blind he was not able to review what he had written, and didn't want any errors, or mistakes made by scribes who copied his writings, to survive. Only the text on the Day of Judgment was saved by some disobedient cleric (but this has not survived to be read today). Instead, the archbishop recommended the sermons of Peter Chrysologus, 'who wrote ingeniously and most brilliantly', and which Felix himself had edited before losing his sight.[27] His determination to prevent errors in the copying of texts was exactly the same as Justinian II's restriction of the number of authorized copies of the acts of the Sixth Council. By having the acts read aloud to his leading ecclesiastical, civilian and military officers, the emperor sought to preserve an accurate record of the official condemnation of Monotheletism agreed in 681.

Agnellus found Archbishop Felix's tomb without difficulty since he was buried in S. Apollinare in Classe with most of his colleagues (Plate 58), and gives the text of the long epitaph, which dwells on the hardships Felix endured:

> Exile, injuries, hunger, nudity, violence, dangers, contempt, banishment, terrors, chains, cudgels . . . Snatched from his borders, he was deprived of his see. Lacking sight in his body, divine light arose there. He was taken to a narrow cliff in the land of Pontus, where he was lacking the necessities of life, but Christ was there as bread; buried with his whole body and virtue, the bishop was consoled by the highest grace of God, and was raised from the heavy prison on the island of Pontus . . .[28]

After this most dramatic episode of his life, Felix had returned to his church in Ravenna, sustained by the devotion of his parishioners, while emperors in Constantinople came and went in rapid succession. Despite the violent retribution Justinian expended on Ravenna, he failed to crush the city, which preserved its independent character for nearly thirty years after Felix's death.

PART EIGHT

700–769
Ravenna returns to the margins

31

Leo III and the defeat of the Arabs

In the 630s Arab tribesmen had won their first major battles against the East Roman empire, when they defeated the emperor Herakleios. They quickly occupied Palestine and Syria and extended their control over Egypt, then Persia and places even further East.[1] By the early eighth century they presented a novel threat to Constantinople. They did not act like the Huns, who destroyed and moved on; for example, in the way Attila devastated Aquileia in 452. Nor did they, like the Goths or Lombards, adopt Christianity, for the Arabs already had their own form of Mosaic monotheism, recorded in their own language and script. They did not aspire to be a recognized and legitimate part of the polity they had invaded. Instead, the fighters of the desert incorporated the resources of the cities and settlements they conquered into a new Muslim civilization, the Caliphate.

Their aim was to make the huge, strategically placed, imperial capital of Byzantium their own. Constantinople, with its impressive defences, excellent harbours, wealth of artefacts and many craftsmen, would not only give them control of the eastern Mediterranean; it would also be the gateway to the Balkans and expansion into central and northern Europe, as well as the Black Sea and access to the riches of central Asia. Just as the capture of Carthage in 698 had opened the way to Spain, Constantinople's fall would have allowed the forces of the Prophet a similar entry to the West, and Rome, surrounded and defenceless, would have been theirs too.[2]

During the early eighth century, the unstable, transitory rule of emperors such as Philippikos offered Muslim rulers renewed hope for the realization of their ambition. Their previous attempt to take the imperial capital in the years 667–9 had been rebuffed, despite great effort. Now, the entire resources of the Caliphate based in Damascus were bent to achieve the supreme conquest. In 716 Caliph Suleiman began a well-planned, massive encirclement of the Queen City by land and sea, to starve it into surrender or force an entry and capture it. The threat was terrifying enough for leading military commanders, the Senate of Constantinople and Patriarch Germanos to persuade Emperor Theodosios III to abdicate, and they then selected an experienced and competent general named Leo to direct the defence. The process highlights the inner strength of the Roman imperial system. Its institutions of the Senate – a forum for the ruling elite – alongside a trained bureaucracy and a centralized court hierarchy gave it the capacity to respond. In this way, on 25 March 717 a soldier from Isauria, who had made a career in the army and risen to become commander of the Anatolikon province (*thema*), was elevated to the imperial throne as Leo III.[3]

The Siege of Constantinople

Five months later, Arab land forces closed in to begin the siege, followed a month later by their naval forces, 1,800 ships in all. Since many of the bigger ships were heavily laden they couldn't move quickly, and even the lighter transports guarding them couldn't manoeuvre when the wind dropped. When part of the fleet was becalmed close to the sea walls of the city, Leo sent out fire-bearing boats from the harbour on the Golden Horn, which spread flames among the enemy ships and sank many. This use of 'Greek fire', flammable oil that could be projected towards the enemy and burned on contact with water, terrified the Arabs. Crucially, it prevented the Arabs from completing the blockade of the capital as they were unable to close off its access to the sea.

The Muslims were, however, prepared for a long siege of the vast land walls that were impenetrable if well defended. Nature then aided the Christians with extreme, drawn-out winter weather. The besiegers were covered in snow and ice that killed many of their camels and horses. Even the arrival of a second fleet from Africa in the spring of 718 with fresh supplies failed to advance the attack, while imperial forces in Bithynia (Asia Minor) and Bulgarian allies on the European side harassed the Arabs. After exactly a year, the Arab forces withdrew on 15 August, the feast of the Dormition of the Virgin, and the inhabitants of Constantinople celebrated a great victory.[4]

Four main elements secured this triumph. First, the imposing defences of the city and its position on a steep-sided promontory into deep water enabled it to escape complete encirclement. Secondly, the long duration meant that the besiegers had to endure a severe Anatolian winter, so inhospitable to desert cavalry. Thirdly, the deployment of Greek fire, which demanded skilled craftsmen and seafarers, routed the naval blockade. Finally, and most importantly, the inner 'Greek fire' of the empire itself, which had flourished for over four hundred years in its magnificent capital of Constantinople. Its government and people, who prided themselves in being Roman, had fused ancient Greek education and Christian faith with Roman law and military prowess into an imperial system of exceptional self-belief, determination and inventiveness. They had particular faith in the divine protection of the Mother of God, who had defended the city in 626.

The Sicilian Revolt

In Sicily news of the enormous forces gathered to besiege Constantinople in 717 enticed the local general Sergios to take advantage of what he assumed would be the imperial capital's inevitable defeat. He set up one of his officers as emperor, choosing a man who came from the Constantinopolitan family of Onomagoulos and acclaimed him as Tiberios. Clearly, the aim was to replace Leo III by a ruler based in the more secure western part of the empire – perhaps in imitation of Constans II. The news was transmitted to the capital by fast ships within weeks, rather than the three months it took for regular naval transport. As soon as Emperor Leo learned what had happened he sent a reliable official, Paul the *chartoularios*, to suppress the challenge.

Together with a few men and two high-ranking guardsmen (*spatharii*), and armed with an official letter (*sacra*) signed by Leo himself, Paul slipped past the Arab blockade and sailed for Sicily. He managed to restore order by reading the *sacra* to the people of Syracuse, who realized that Leo III was in control and Constantinople was well defended. Sergios fled to the Lombards in Calabria. Tiberios and his officials were handed over to Paul who punished them all; the heads of the leaders were pickled in vinegar and taken back to Constantinople by the *spatharii*, and 'all the western parts were pacified'.[5] Even when besieged by land and sea, New Rome manifested its long reach and confidence, which was reciprocated by an underlying loyalty to its legitimate authority in what was still experienced as a single empire. Sicily would remain within the orbit of the eastern capital for another century. And news of Leo's triumphant victory over the year-long Arab siege in August 718 would inaugurate a period of self-confident rule in Constantinople, which had considerable influence in Ravenna.[6]

Although Constantinople was able to defend its own internal legitimacy in this way, it was unable to curb the Arab threat. After their defeat in 718, Muslim forces did not abandon their campaign to capture the Queen City, and mounted regular raids against Asia Minor, taking prisoners, crops and livestock. While Leo III was preoccupied by this challenge, he was unable to provide forces to secure the western provinces.[7] In 718 Ravenna was not involved in the Sicilian revolt, but it faced increasingly severe pressure from the Lombards, no longer divided by the Three Chapters controversy and thoroughly Christianized. Both Lombard centres of power – Pavia (the northern kingdom) and Spoleto and Benevento (the southern dukedoms) – attacked Ravenna and its harbour at Classis, as we have seen. The emperor responded by appointing competent officials – Paul, who had restored order in Sicily, as exarch in Ravenna and Marinus, imperial *spatharios*, as duke of Rome – but did not send them any serious military assistance.[8]

Because of the parlous condition in which he found the empire, Leo III was determined to secure his own authority, to put an end to the rapid turnover of rulers since 695 and to establish his family as a ruling dynasty. After his wife, Maria, gave birth to a son, he crowned her empress on Christmas day 718, and had their son baptized with the appropriately imperial name of Constantine, making the leading military commanders and members of the Senate pledge to honour him as if they were his godparents. At the celebration of Easter in 720 the two-year-old Constantine was crowned as co-emperor in a forthright declaration of his designation as the next ruler.[9] Leo also announced his heir on coins struck in the names of both father and son, and minted a new silver coin, the *miliaresion*, for public distribution, which identified the rulers by name only – without imperial portraits – and displayed a cross on steps on the reverse surrounded by the words 'Jesus Christ is victorious'. The change in design signalled an innovation comparable to Justinian II's introduction of the image of Christ on his coinage.[10] The emperor consolidated his control over the imperial armies, marrying his daughter to his ally Artabasdos, who headed the Armeniakon *thema*. His subordination of all aspects of government to the overriding needs of military defence led to higher taxation, and this is what western sources identified as the particular scourge of his rule.[11]

From these accounts, in the year 722–3 the demand for higher taxation was enforced in the West, linked to a new census of the population, the registration of all male children on a special list, and the transfer to the public treasury of taxes previously paid to the church.[12] Since these new measures to secure higher financial levies fell more heavily on the richer provinces of Sicily and Calabria, from which the church of Rome drew grain, oil and other resources to feed the city, Pope Gregory II (715–31) led the opposition to imperial policy. When he 'was preventing the imposition of tax in the province', Leo III sent orders to Paul the exarch to remove the pope, elect someone else in his place and collect the money, that is, to 'strip the churches of their wealth'.[13] Despite the efforts of local officials and Duke Marinus, Paul had no success in replacing the pope with a more pliable cleric, and another imperial *spatharios* was sent from Constantinople with orders to force Pope Gregory from his see. When the exarch sent 'some men he was able to pervert, along with his count and some other men from the *castra*', to enforce the imperial order, they were defeated by Lombards from the duchy of Spoleto and others from Tuscany (Benevento and probably Pavia).[14] In a display of loyalty to Pope Gregory II that Paul had not anticipated, these Lombards defended the Milvian bridge on the approach to Rome and forced the exarch's small force to retire.[15]

The Murder of Paul the Exarch

Reaction to the demand for increased taxation took a different form in Ravenna, where the citizens were divided between those who remained loyal to the emperor, led by the exarch, and those who supported the pope's opposition. In November 723 Archbishop Felix died and the Ravennati elected a local cleric, John, as his successor, but he was unable to prevent fighting between the two factions, in the course of which the exarch was killed.[16] Given that George, the son of Johannicis, had only recently organized the local troops into their city units, it seems very likely that he directed these new forces in attacking Paul. Perhaps they nominated George or another leader as duke, as the city displayed a determination to assert its autonomy from Constantinople.

The murder of the exarch marked a decisive moment for Ravenna. The city was no longer the trusted bulwark of imperial power in Italy and elements within it felt a stronger allegiance to the pope in Rome. It was uncertain as to its own resources: a faltering independent city-state, a rebellious outpost of the Greek-speaking empire of Constantinople, an untrustworthy ally of the Latin-speaking papacy – the stresses within Ravenna encapsulated the divisions of the Mediterranean world in a local, symbolic form.

The likeliest date for Paul's murder is the summer of 726, though news might have taken six or eight weeks to get to Constantinople. Leo III obviously had to avenge the murder of his official and restore control in Ravenna. The emperor therefore appointed a new exarch, Eutychios, but he does not appear to have set out immediately. He may have waited until the dangerous winter sailing season was over, i.e. until March 727, and then he sailed to Naples, which remained under more effective imperial control, rather than to Ravenna. From Naples Eutychios sent officials to Rome with orders to get rid of the pope, as this remained his major responsibility. With this in mind, he also made contact with the Lombard dukes in central Italy.

Further north, the Lombard king Liutprand, based in Pavia, took advantage of Paul's death to press on in his conquest of Emilia. Six named castles or towns fell to his troops and Ravenna may have been temporarily occupied in about 728.[17] In the summer of that year the southern Lombards captured Sutri, on the border of the duchy of Rome, and held it for forty days. Then Pope Gregory managed to persuade Liutprand to return it, not to the duchy of Rome but to the blessed apostles Peter and Paul.[18] To mark this highly symbolic donation, the king brought his army to the Campus Neronis and agreed a peace treaty with Pope Gregory. In a dramatic act, Liutprand laid down his royal insignia, 'cloak, corslet, sword belt, broad sword and pointed sword, all gilded, and a gold crown and silver cross', and received them back from the pope.[19] His power as the legitimate military ruler in northern Italy was thus confirmed. Liutprand also made a pilgrimage to the Greek monastery of St Anastasios *ad aquas Salvias* in Rome, which contained the relic of the martyr's head. The visit is described in a Latin inscription recorded at the king's foundation at Corteolona near Pavia, which draws attention to his devotion to icons. The episode emphasizes the vital importance of conversion in promoting a fusion of 'barbarian' and 'Roman' forces among the Lombards, now bypassing Ravenna, which had once been the fulcrum of this development.

Inside Ravenna itself an earthquake struck the city during the rule of Archbishop John V (723/5–44) and completely destroyed the Petriana church, as well as the apse of the church of St Martin (S. Apollinare Nuovo, founded by Theoderic) and doubtless many other buildings.[20] Although the earthquake occurred on a Sunday, the service had already ended but the apse decoration was shattered and the mosaics of the nave may also have been damaged.[21] Local workmen rebuilt the apse and probably collected the mosaic tesserae, which were often recycled. The inhabitants of Ravenna had long experience of earthquakes and must have developed ways of coping, like those who lived high in the Apennines and had to rebuild their settlements repeatedly.

Archbishop John V

The murder of Paul the exarch left Archbishop John with greater authority within the city, but he failed to bring the two factions together. He appears to have been criticized by both sides – the party that remained loyal to the imperial government and the other, pro-papal party. At some point, unspecified, John was forced to flee into exile in the territory of the Venetiae, to the north, where he remained 'in untimely discomfort and affliction' for a year.[22] The reasons for this unprecedented banishment of the archbishop are not known, nor are the identities of those responsible. The city's determination to assert its autonomy and to escape from imperial rule, especially if led by George the son of Johannicis, as well as a temporary Lombard occupation of the city, must have been factors. During the period of John's absence while the new exarch Eutychios remained in central Italy, Ravenna for a moment had neither ecclesiastical nor civilian government.

According to Agnellus, the archbishop's return was achieved through the intervention of the *scriniarius* (keeper of records), Epiphanius, who reconciled him with the men who had forced him into exile.[23] Epiphanius suggested that John should give the exarch, who must be Eutychios, a great *palarea* of silver (a bribe) in order to bring his enemies to justice, promising to recoup all the money tenfold from the guilty men. As a result, these individuals, still unnamed, were summoned to court, where Epiphanius read out an indictment against each one for attacking their archbishop, and the judge fined them. From this fine, a twentieth part was given to the exarch, and the rest (presumably ten times the amount of the original bribe) to John. Edicts were drawn up listing the properties of the men found guilty, as a guarantee that they would never write anything against their ecclesiastical leader.[24]

In an elegant inscription erected at S. Apollinare in Classe in 731, Archbishop John recorded his donations of property to the church of Ravenna, noting that Exarch Eutychios was then in post (Plate 61). This suggests that Eutychios had reasserted Constantinopolitan control in the city in 729–30, imposing fines on the men responsible for the archbishop's flight and thus facilitating John's return.[25] The long inscription lists a number of estates, *fundi*: Gammillaria, with its cottages and fertile lands, acorn and fruit trees (*silvarum glandifera poma*), and supplies of fire wood; Tregintula in the Faventino, and Pitulis in the region of Corneliese, all of which John had inherited from his parents, together with a legacy of silver to maintain the *collegio monachorum*. None of these estates is ever to be alienated or changed or leased out by contracts of emphyteusis on pain of eternal condemnation like the traitor Judas and anathema by the 318 Fathers (of the Council of Nicaea).[26] The record is dated by the reign of the most pious emperors Leo and Constantine, in sharp contrast to the Roman *Book of the Pontiffs* that stresses Emperor Leo's heresy, impiety and wickedness at precisely this date (731).[27]

Ravenna thus returned to the dual leadership of its official governor working in a close alliance with its archbishop. Yet an underlying process of separation from imperial control was deepened by an alleged victory of the Ravennati over a 'Greek' naval force, an event commemorated in an annual celebration right into the ninth century. Agnellus gives a lively, detailed (and perhaps imaginary) description of the clash between the Melisensians ('that is, the citizens of Ravenna') and 'Pelasgians', the epic name for Greeks – literary terms, which may be another clue to the somewhat mythical nature of the event that was passed down orally from the participants over a hundred years before the local historian wrote his account.[28] While the young men went out to fight, John V and all the priests and elders lay prostrate with ash on their heads praying for victory. And the victorious Ravennati prevented the Greeks from fleeing in their ships and threw their dead bodies into the River Po. As a result, it was said, no one ate fish from that part of the river for six years. The victory occurred on the feast of Sts John and Paul, which was subsequently celebrated in the city with processions to church, decorations and banners as if for the Easter festival, as a regular reminder of a local victory over distant 'Greek' enemies.[29]

Since the event took place during Archbishop John V's reign and he organized the prayers that assisted Ravenna's victory, it may represent the city's first successful defeat of Byzantine forces between 726 and 744. John's care for the city is made clear; the archbishop contributed to a successful military outcome. In contrast to the earlier naval attack that had sacked the city and taken Archbishop Felix and Johannicis off to the eastern capital, this time the Ravennati defeated the 'Greeks'.[30] This marks an important stage in the process of gaining independence from Constantinople, as well as the eastern capital's now chronic inability to maintain control over its historic western provinces.

As both the imperial enclaves of Ravenna and Old Rome were increasingly left to their own resources when threatened by the Lombards, they distanced themselves from the empire. In the first half of the eighth century, the western, Latin-speaking Christian world under Rome grew further apart from the eastern, Greek-speaking Christian empire, while both had to confront the new Arabic-speaking world of Islam in control of the entire southern shore of the Mediterranean. As Islam embedded itself, Christendom divided. While Emperor Leo III was frustrating the Arabs' determination to conquer the imperial capital, he was irrevocably losing what was now becoming 'the' West. Ravenna, which had gained so much of its significance from its position straddling the overlapping regions of Greek and Latin influence, was marginalized.

32

The beginnings of Iconoclasm

It is an injustice of historical memory that Emperor Leo III is not celebrated for his defence of Byzantium from the Arab military challenge that threatened to destroy the empire for ever. Instead, he is renowned as the infamous instigator of iconoclasm, the destruction of icons. During the first phase of this battle over icons (*iconomachia*), which was to last on and off for over a century, Ravenna freed itself from Constantinople and became an integral part of the West in closer association with the bishop of Rome. The issue of iconoclasm shaped developments far from its eastern origins.

Leo came from a family that had lived under Arab rule in northern Syria until they moved to Isauria in central Asia Minor. Then in the 690s they had been transplanted to Mesembria in Thrace, in a typical forced movement of population, when Justinian II needed to build up defences against the Bulgars. Leo had witnessed at first hand the emperor's transfer of people to protect outlying regions as part of an overall military strategy. Perhaps this meant that he saw military service as the best route for his ambitions. In 705, aged about twenty, Justinian appointed him *spatharios* (sword bearer, an honorary court title) and sent him to campaign against the Arabs in the eastern provinces, negotiating with their military leaders and rival Armenian, Alan, Abasgian, Apsilion and Laz forces.[1] A decade of observing Arab methods of warfare, diplomacy and propaganda allowed him to gain a good measure of Muslim military leaders, the coherence of their beliefs and their ambition to capture Constantinople.

Once established as emperor in March 717 Leo was determined to protect the capital, which he did with great success. Yet even after his brilliant defence, which forced the Arab armies and fleets to retire, rival generals challenged his role, the Sicilians rebelled and the deposed

Emperor Anastasios plotted against him. Leo dealt harshly with these revolts. Then, in the summer of 726, a terrifying subaquatic volcanic eruption in the Aegean threw up a new island between Thera and Therasia. From the boiling hot sea a great plume of fire and molten lava, vast clouds of ash, and pumice stones 'as big as hills' were projected when the tectonic plates deep below the sea bed collided (as had happened when the volcanic rim of the island of Santorini was created in c. 1400 BC).[2] As the monstrous deposits of ash and solid lava were borne to the shores of the Aegean in a tsunami, Leo III sought an explanation of what everyone perceived as a manifestation of divine wrath. Some of his advisers replied that it was due to the excessive veneration of religious images, which led to idolatry – a grave sin prohibited by the Second Commandment issued by God to Moses.

In addition to this cataclysmic event in the Aegean Sea, the Arabs resumed their annual attacks on the heartland of the empire in Asia Minor, terrifying the local population, capturing prisoners and livestock, and destroying communities. In 727, within a year of the tsunami, they began a siege of the major city of Nicaea, 185km from Constantinople, where the first Oecumenical Council had defined the Christian creed in 325. Despite some destruction of its walls the city survived, but when the Arabs withdrew they took with them large numbers of captives from the surrounding area. At about the same time, troops from the region of Hellas in central Greece and the Aegean islands launched a naval attack on Constantinople. It was easily repelled but Leo realized that he needed to reinforce his military strength against external and internal enemies.[3]

He identified Christian idolatry as the cause of divine anger and exploited the anxieties generated by the Aegean explosion by proposing an effective application of the Old Testament prohibition of graven images: 'Thou shalt not make unto thee any graven image, or any likeness of any thing that is in heaven above, or that is in the earth beneath, or that is in the water under the earth. Thou shalt not bow down thyself to them, nor serve them.'[4] In expressing in religious form his determination to stiffen Byzantine morale and military opposition to Islam, he also drew on the nascent iconoclasm practised by three bishops of Asia Minor, Constantine of Nakoleia, John of Synnada and Thomas of Klaudioupolis, who had already removed icons from their churches. In January 730 Leo summoned the patriarch and demanded that he support the policy of taking down icons and whitewashing painted images in order to avoid idolatry. Germanos refused and handed back his pallium of office to the emperor, who bestowed it on a more willing cleric, Anastasios. The emperor then ordered the five senior leaders of the Christian world (the pentarchy of bishops of Rome, Constantinople, Alexandria, Antioch and Jerusalem) to adopt this condemnation and get rid of all the icons in their churches.[5]

The Role of Images

Ever since early Christian times, images large and small of Christ, the Ever-Virgin Mother of God, *Theotokos* (as Mary was entitled in Greek), saints, martyrs, bishops and holy men and women had become an essential part of ecclesiastical life in the East Mediterranean. Christians honoured them with profound veneration: they kissed the icons, lit candles in front of them, bowed before them and directed their prayers to them. Numerous stories of requests being answered by the figure represented on an icon generated an expectation of an improvement in health or wealth, the birth of children, or simply relief from sickness, sin and guilt.[6] Icons were carried in liturgical processions and displayed for particular attention on feast days, such as the Nativity. Although relics of the saints were also extremely important objects of veneration, icons were ubiquitous and memorable. Small, often primitive icons in metal, ceramic and paint also decorated homes and this domestic use probably preceded their appearance in churches, while giving icons a greater prominence in the lives of Christians, especially women and children.[7]

The veneration of icons was justified by a theological argument that the respect and honour paid to the image was transmitted through it to the figure represented, a belief that went back to the fourth century when St Basil of Cappadocia noted that the honour paid the emperor's image passed on to the ruler himself. Such a demonstration of respect had been demanded of Christians during the great persecutions launched by Diocletian in the late third and early fourth centuries, and their refusal to acknowledge imperial images often resulted in death, making them martyrs. Portraits of the saints inspired Christians to lead a holy way of life; similarly, pictures of the great councils of the church reminded them of the correct belief decreed at such meetings.[8]

The practice of icon veneration reproduced an ancient appreciation of statues and images of pagan gods and goddesses that were washed, dressed, decorated with flower garlands and honoured with lights and other signs of respect and affection. In addition to large-scale statuary, such as the massive representations of Athena set up in the Parthenon on the Acropolis of Athens, smaller terracotta statues of household gods (*lares*) were displayed in kitchens. Imperial portraits painted on wooden panels were sent around the empire to announce the inaugura-tion of a new ruler.[9] The first Christian icons adopted the same format of small wood panels, similar to the portraits of ancient gods that have survived in the dry conditions of Egypt and which would have been in use all over the Roman world. Such painted panels were sometimes laid over the faces of deceased Christians in a comparable fashion to funer-ary portraits painted to cover Egyptian mummies.[10] The gestures associated with the veneration of images of Christian holy figures were taken over from the ancient world: bowing and putting lights before the icon, kissing and addressing prayers to it. Icons were considered doorways to the spiritual world in which the holy figures had unimagin-able power.

Such veneration had always been distinguished from idolatry, as defined by the Second Commandment that forbade the worship and making of images. The invisible God could never be represented and was always to be worshipped spiritually.[11] So Christian leaders stressed that icons were merely a visual reminder, never objects of adoration. Occasional outbursts of iconoclasm occurred, when holy images were removed as dangerous, or even attacked and rendered impotent by gouging out the eyes, for example. In the late sixth century when Bishop Serenus of Marseilles decided to take down the icons in his church, Pope Gregory the Great protested, formulating the classic defence of the role of images in Christianity: 'Pictures are the Bibles of the illiterate. What they cannot read they understand through images.'[12] There was another brief attempt to purge religious images in Armenia during the seventh century. But Christian icons were deeply ingrained in religious practice in a way that was far more than just instrumental, even if pictures designed to instruct the laity dominated the decoration of churches – for example the images of Christ's mir-acles and the narrative of his death and resurrection in Theoderic's palace church in Ravenna. Icons, in the sense of painted wooden panels, were more widespread in the East than the West, but symbolic as well as figural images of the holy were employed throughout the Christian world.

Today we tend to look at icons as 'works of art' that demand an aesthetic response. But in early Christendom they were endowed with power and integrated into Christian lives, familiar as a way of communicating with the past and the uncertain future, bound up with Christian authority. The lines between devout Christian veneration and an improper pagan style of worship were inevitably blurred and a constant danger lurked even in the production of icons. Craftsmen were commissioned by covert traditional pagans to paint an icon of Christ that resembled Zeus, and painters who did so were miraculously punished by losing the use of their painting hand.[13] Another danger arose when Christian icons were worshipped as if they were themselves holy objects. This was the issue that bishops Constantine of Nakoleia and John of Synnada had brought to Patriarch Germanos' attention in the early eighth century. In some parts of their dioceses, they reported, Christians were devoting all their love and veneration on icons as if they were holy.[14] This type of total veneration (*latreia*) had to be reserved to the invisible God. The icons were merely a medium through which relative veneration (*proskynesis*) could pass to the holy figure depicted. They must never be allowed to usurp the place of the Almighty who had created Heaven and Earth. Patriarch Germanos had explained this to Bishop Constantine, who visited Constantinople between 720 and 730, and had communicated the correct theology by letter to Constantine's superior, John of Synnada. But the bishop had returned to his province and removed the icons from his churches, so that no one would be tempted to commit idolatry. Given their faith, it wasn't irrational for the bishops to fear this plausibility. Yet Germanos protested that the proper veneration of icons was an ancient tradition of the church; it was helpful to ordinary people who relied on their local saints and benefitted from their cults.[15]

The Roman Reaction

In Rome the events of January 730 are reported by the *Book of the Pontiffs* as Leo's decree 'that no image of any saint, martyr or angel should be kept, as he declared them all accursed'.[16] The emperor was determined, it maintained,

> to force his way on everyone living in Constantinople by both compulsion and persuasion to take down the images, wherever they were, of the Saviour, his holy mother and all the saints, and, what is painful to mention, to burn them in the middle of the city.[17]

Painted churches were to be whitewashed and the people who opposed such activity were beheaded or mutilated. What Leo actually stated is not known, as later iconophiles destroyed the records, but there is no trace of the alleged burning of icons. On every occasion Pope Gregory II refused to comply with the imperial order and sent the emperor firm denunciations of his iconoclast policy.[18]

The pope encouraged a more general opposition to Constantinople, writing to Christians everywhere to warn them 'against the impiety that had arisen', and associating Leo's extra taxation with the prohibition of icons. Initially, the inhabitants of the Pentapolis and the armies of the Venetiae defended the pope while resisting tax demands, with no reference to holy images. They elected their own dukes to take over from those loyal to the exarch, and then planned (with 'the whole of Italy') to choose a new emperor whom they would take to Constantinople to replace Leo III. The pope restrained the leaders of this revolt, hoping that the emperor would change his mind.[19] But Leo, long familiar with the effectiveness of Muslim iconoclasm and seeking to legitimate his own distinct rule, insisted on visual purification.

Although the account in the Roman *Book of the Pontiffs* is doubtless exaggerated, and there is no other evidence for the wholesale burning of icons in Constantinople, it is an undeniably contemporary witness to the imperial order of 730 as it was experienced in Rome. It doesn't mention the participation of Ravenna, where no attempt to destroy its icons or glorious mosaics, filled with human representation, is recorded. Unlike some churches in the East, Ravenna's were never whitewashed or plastered over. But Exarch Eutychios was unable to stop neighbouring regions from joining in the general opposition and Archbishop John V did nothing to implement the imperial order. There is no record of any desecration of the many images that adorned the walls and ceilings of its buildings. Ravenna resisted iconoclasm: its icons and representations of holy people went untouched.[20] In this way, the city adopted an independent attitude, defining its own character as part of Latin Christendom. Loosening its ties with the empire involved opposition to the exarch and to any hostile force from Constantinople, as in the naval victory later commemorated every year. The process also implied greater co-operation with the other major authority in the West, the bishop of Rome, who was taking the lead in the defence of images and making a claim to the overall direction of the entire world of western Christianity.

Learning from the Enemy

The destruction of Carthage in 698 facilitated the expansion of Islam across western North Africa and into Spain, creating more Christian refugees and depriving Constantinople of tax revenue, which had to be made up by higher taxes on the remaining areas of the West. As imperial demands for taxation increased, Ravenna's political loyalty declined in conjunction with a cultural and ecclesiastical break. Papal opposition to the proposed destruction of icons became a rallying call the Ravennati could follow.

These indirect consequences of the Arab conquest of North Africa were matched by more direct influences: Caliph Umar II (717–20) initiated the forced conversion of Christians and wrote to Leo III, urging him to abandon his Christian beliefs and recognize the final divine revelation made to the Prophet Muhammad. His successor, Caliph Yazid II, attempted to correct the iconophile practice of his own Christian subjects through an edict in 723 that commanded them to get rid of all representations of persons from their churches and homes.[21] Leo III's response was to emphasize the cross, the supreme symbol of Christian faith, which was made a dominant feature of church decoration to replace images of holy people. One of the first of these substitutions is found in the apse mosaic of the church of Hagia Eirene, Holy Peace, in the capital, which was rebuilt after an earthquake in 740 and survives. Later, images of the Mother of God in the apse of churches at Nicaea and Thessalonike were replaced by similar monumental crosses.

The inhabitants of Synnada, Nakoleia and Klaudioupolis, cities that lay directly on the routes of Arab armies invading Asia Minor, reacted in similar fashion to Islamic military victories. In the 730s, when

Bishop Thomas of Klaudioupolis removed icons from his churches, whole regions threatened by the Arabs followed his example. His decision to destroy the miracle-working icon of the Mother of God at Sozopolis because it no longer manifested its healing power prompted Patriarch Germanos to insist on avoiding any suggestion that the icon had failed. Germanos warned Thomas not to allow the 'enemies of the cross' to draw any comforting conclusions from the break in miraculous cures. Elsewhere he stressed the danger of giving unbelievers, that is Jews and Muslims, any grounds for claiming that Christianity was in error, and insisted that traditional icon veneration should be maintained.[22] Here we can see how the argument over the best way to mobilize against the Arabs was articulated in religious terms.

Islamic visual culture, so clearly expressed in the Dome of the Rock in Jerusalem and the mosques built in Damascus and Kairouan (in Tunisia), also spread awareness of Islam's strict avoidance of idols, which threatened the Christian use of icons in a more focused way than before.[23] In obeying the Second Commandment and promoting the Christian cult of the Cross, Emperor Leo gave visual force to his reaction to the Islamic prohibition of idolatry.[24] He thus found a way to purify Christian worship and strengthen imperial opposition to further Arab military victories. And, indeed, iconoclasm fortified the armies in their constant operations against the Caliphate and built up a great store of loyalty to the emperor and his son, Constantine V. This does not mean that the idea of iconoclasm was an invention of Leo III alone, since bishops in Asia Minor had already embraced iconoclast practice. But it does suggest that when the empire was under the greatest threat of extinction, one specific aspect of Christian belief – worship in spirit and in truth – was used most effectively to secure its survival by an iconoclast emperor.

By the early eighth century the combination of Islamic expansion and Byzantine resistance divided the Mediterranean world, while Christendom fragmented, leaving Italy and the transalpine regions to set out on their own course. Over the next hundred years this western sphere would take on its European character under the leadership of Frankish kings allied with bishops of Rome. Although this new form of 'the West' had a much less elaborate tradition of iconic art than the East, it adopted the defence of images as part of its internal development, in opposition to eastern influence and the political dominance of Constantinople that had been exercised through Ravenna and Sicily.

The mosaic, fresco and sculpted decoration of churches throughout Italy thus remained intact, while comparable images and figural sculptures in Byzantine churches were whitewashed, replaced or destroyed. Iconoclasm would eventually generate a completely novel formulation of symbolic decoration achieved by Charlemagne's advisers, Theodulf of Orleans and Alcuin. In a curious twist, this Frankish position was never accepted in Rome, whose bishops emphasized their dedication to iconic art and commissioned their own portraits, which were frequently incorporated into figural church decoration. The rejection of eastern iconoclasm was therefore by no means uniform. But by raising questions about the legitimacy of figural representation and the potential of idolatry and future punishment, iconoclasm hastened the division of the ancient Mediterranean world, setting Muslim areas in visual rivalry with both Byzantine and western regions, and preserving the rich narrative and figurative mosaics in Ravenna as nowhere else.

33

Pope Zacharias and the Lombard conquest of Ravenna

Since their arrival in the late sixth century the Lombards had settled on the land they conquered, adopting Latin as their language and establishing their own forms of government, including a legal code. In 698 they abandoned support for the Three Chapters and accepted the pope as their Christian leader. Yet the dukes of Spoleto and Benevento refused to recognize the Lombard king in Pavia as their superior, and failed to co-operate in a united campaign to bring the entire peninsula under their joint control. Even though they attacked both areas of the exarchate, Ravenna and Rome, they did so in separate campaigns that allowed imperial officials, such as Stephen, duke of Rome, to exploit their divisions in the 730s and 740s.[1]

These rivalries complicate the already confused chronology of King Liutprand's Italian campaigns that are variously recorded in the Roman *Book of the Pontiffs* and in the later *History of the Lombards* by Paul the deacon. The latter presents King Liutprand as regally settling differences between dukes and bishops in Forum Iulii and Carniola, while also fighting victoriously against the troops of the exarchate in the Pentapolis. He shows the king distracted by conflicts with the Slavs in northern Istria and by requests from the Frankish ruler Charles Martel (the Hammer), for military assistance against Arab pirates in southern Gaul. In his relations with Rome, however, Liutprand was often torn between hostility to the military government of the imperial duke, and Christian devotion to the pope, as heir of St Peter.

In 729 when King Liutprand visited Rome he made a pilgrimage to the monastery of St Anastasios the Persian *ad aquas Salvias* in Rome, where he venerated the martyr's head, a relic brought to the West by Greek monks.[2] He later constructed a church at Corteolona dedicated to the saint, which was celebrated in a Latin inscription contrasting the schismatic Emperor Leo III and the pious Lombard King Liutprand.[3] In addition to this condemnation of the iconoclast emperor, Liutprand also expanded and redecorated the church and monastery of St Peter *in caelo aureo* in Pavia where a Greek inscription commemorated an 'igona' of St Peter in gold.[4] This golden icon was commissioned from a Byzantine artist in Rome, possibly a craftsman attached to the monastery of St Anastasios, together with dodecasyllable Greek verses. In the non-Greek environment of Pavia, the inscription might not be understood but it was a status symbol, a claim to superior culture.

The Flight and Exile of Eutychios

During the mid-730s King Liutprand may have succeeded in occupying Ravenna briefly, but not for long. In about 739, however, Liutprand's nephew, Hildebrand, joined forces with Peredeo, duke of Vicenza, to make an unexpectedly serious attack on Ravenna, which may not have been sanctioned by the king. The two Lombard leaders captured the city, forced Eutychios, the exarch, to seek refuge in the area of the Venetiae and took prisoners: the consuls Leo, Sergius, Victor and Agnellus are named as hostages.[5] When Pope Gregory III (731–41) became aware of the exarch's plight he wrote to the patriarch of Grado in Istria requesting military help to restore control in Ravenna.[6] His tone is virulently anti-Lombard and rather pro-Byzantine, suggesting that the pope, like his predecessor, continued to believe that imperial forces would protect Rome, despite the estrangement provoked by the order to remove icons. The appeal was entirely successful, in that troops based in Istria loyal to the empire marched south to restore Ravenna to imperial control and the exarch to his palace.[7] In an effective military campaign they killed Peredeo, captured Hildebrand and reinstated Eutychios.[8]

At the same time as the pope learned about Hildebrand and Peredeo's temporary capture of Ravenna, he was also threatened by Lombard activity nearer to Rome. In 739 Duke Transamund of Spoleto had rebelled against King Liutprand, who marched on Spoleto, installed his own candidate as duke and forced Transamund into exile in Rome. Liutprand's aim, however, was to capture Rome and he tried to exploit Transamund's presence there to achieve it. Within the city Duke

Stephen, the imperial commander, in conjunction with Pope Gregory, refused to hand Transamund over, and Liutprand began to blockade Rome by capturing four key cities within the Roman duchy. The pope resolved this threat by skilful negotiation, and the Lombard king retired back to his capital at Pavia.[9] Gregory knew, however, that this was only a temporary retreat and that Liutprand's determination to capture Rome would result in further attacks. At Gregory III's death in November 741, his successor Zacharias inherited a critical situation.

Zacharias, Pope and Diplomat

Zacharias was another learned pope of Greek origin, trained in Rome, who exemplified the tradition of electing spiritual leaders who knew Greek, could provide expert criticism of Monothelete theology and championed the primacy of St Peter.[10] He was a particularly gifted Hellenist who translated the *Dialogues* of Gregory the Great into Greek, which proved remarkably popular among eastern Christian readers. He also commissioned the painting of a map of the world in the Lateran palace. During his reign, Pope Zacharias assumed a key position in Italian politics and his personal assistance was sought to resolve all subsequent problems between the exarchate and the Lombards. His immediate challenge was to regain possession of the four fortified sites recently captured by King Liutprand: Amelia, Orte, Bomarzo and Blera, and to assert papal control over the surrounding area.[11]

In a series of diplomatic initiatives and journeys, Zacharias secured not only the return of these four sites, but also 'the patrimony of Sabina, which had been stolen early thirty years ago, those of Narni too and Osimo and Ancona, along with Numana and the valley called Magna in the territory of Sutri'. These properties became the tentative beginnings of territory later known as the Papal States. They were called *domuscultae*, estates to be held in perpetuity by the church of Rome, with the aim of generating supplies to be distributed to the poor, as well as additional resources for the maintenance of the papal court.[12]

As a result of the Lombard–papal alliance, prisoners were freed including the four consuls captured by Hildebrand in his earlier attack on Ravenna.[13] But in 742–3 Liutprand focused more serious attacks on Ravenna, which provoked Exarch Eutychios and Archbishop John V to

unite with all the people of the Pentapolis and Emilia in begging Pope
Zacharias to intercede with the king.[14] The pattern of papal diplomacy
was now repeated in an effort to curb further Lombard aggression
against Ravenna.

First, Pope Zacharias sent an embassy to Liutprand to try and restore
Cesena, a castle on the frontier between Lombard and imperial territory, to the exarchate. The king had already announced his capture of
the site to Constantinople and sent the papal party back unsuccessful.
Zacharias then set out to meet the Lombard leader in person, leaving
Duke Stephen in charge of Rome. The papal party crossed the Apennines via the ancient Via Flaminia (or perhaps by the military road via
Todi and Perugia[15]) and Eutychios came to meet the pope at a church
in Aquila, 80km from Ravenna. Together they proceeded to the city
and all the people, 'men and women of Ravenna, both sexes and every
age' came out to greet him as their shepherd.[16] It was on this very
important visit that Zacharias dedicated an altar cloth to the church of
S Apollinare in Classe; Agnellus describes it as 'of alithine [pure] purple
wonderfully decorated with pearls and his name is written there'.[17]

From Ravenna, Zacharias sent another embassy to Liutprand to
inform him that he intended to visit him. Although the envoys were told
at Imola that the papal party would be prevented from entering Lombard territory and warned the pope of this danger, Zacharias insisted in
making his way to Pavia, where another round of ceremonial meetings,
Masses and negotiations took place. As a result, Liutprand agreed to
give up some land around Ravenna and two-thirds of the territory of
Cesena, reserving one-third for himself until his ambassadors returned
from Constantinople. The peoples of Ravenna and the Pentapolis thus
'were filled with grain and wine', which suggests that Liutprand restored
land that had previously formed part of the exarchate to the exarch's
control.[18]

Pope Zacharias also wrote a synodical letter to the church of Constantinople and another for Constantine V, who had inherited imperial
power on the death of his father Leo III in June 741.[19] These letters have
not survived but they probably urged the new emperor to give up the
policy of iconoclasm. When the papal envoys arrived in the capital,
probably in 742, they found that Constantine's brother-in-law, Artabasdos, had proclaimed himself emperor in the city. The envoys duly
presented their letter to him and reported the situation to Rome. But

young Constantine mustered troops in Asia Minor and fought his way back into Constantinople in November 743. He then pardoned the papal *apocrisiarii* for having presented their letters to the usurper and made a donation of two estates at Ninfa and Norma to the church of Rome. These were added to the papal *domuscultae*.[20]

In his diplomatic contacts with the eastern capital Pope Zacharias acted entirely independently of the exarch, effectively taking over leadership in Italy from the figure of purely nominal authority appointed by the emperor in Constantinople. The exarchate in northern Italy was reduced to one city, Ravenna, while the duchy of Rome was expanded and developed under the pope's guidance. While the Lombards remained a constant source of anxiety to both, there was no doubt about which had the better capacity to resist hostile ambitions.

The Capture of Ravenna

King Liutprand's death in 744 inaugurated a brief respite in Lombard attacks on Ravenna. But the hostile net was closing around the city and, in 749, his successor Ratchis advanced against Perugia, threatening to blockade this critically important castle on the military road linking Ravenna with Rome. Again Pope Zacharias set out to restrain him and 'at the cost of very many gifts to the king ... and with the Lord's assistance' Ratchis withdrew from the blockade.[21] Indeed, he also decided to withdraw from public life; some days later he went to Rome where he abdicated his regal authority and embraced the monastic life.[22] This rapid transformation from hostile military ruler to submissive monk occurred under additional pressures from his half-brother, Aistulf, who had inherited his position as duke of Friuli and advocated a more aggressive Lombard policy against Ravenna and Rome.[23] Early in July 749 Aistulf was acclaimed king.

In the East, once Constantine V had put down the rebellion of Artabasdos, he remained preoccupied by Arab campaigns against Constantinople, which continued even after a major Byzantine victory at Akroinon in Anatolia in 740. He also faced Bulgarian threats to the empire's western border, which prevented him from sending any military support to the exarch in Ravenna.[24] Instead the emperor cultivated better relations with Pippin, king of the Franks, trying to build an alliance against the Lombards.[25] This was at least a coherent diplomatic policy, but in the short term it left Ravenna and Exarch Eutychios isolated. Although troops loyal to Constantinople remained in Istria and the Pentapolis, the exarch failed to employ them to resist the Lombards. Without any record of a battle, Aistulf entered the city and issued his first decree *in palatio* (from the palace) in July 751.[26] Eutychios escaped to Naples, leaving the archbishop to negotiate the terms of the Lombard occupation. This put an end to Ravenna's long role as the imperial capital in Italy.[27]

When Emperor Constantine learned that his western capital had fallen to the Lombards, he realized that they would not only control the exarchate of Ravenna but would also threaten the remaining imperial territory in southern Italy. He therefore acted to consolidate Byzantine control over Sicily and Calabria, instructing officials to occupy rich local estates there known as the papal patrimonies – lands that had been attached to the church of Rome for centuries and supplied it with food stuffs, building materials and rents. All the revenues and resources of these estates were to be transferred to the public treasury and were to be collected by imperial officials.[28] While the precise date for the confiscation is not recorded, the neat way in which the loss of the exarchate of Ravenna in the north of Italy was compensated by the acquisition of papal patrimonies in the south suggests the period immediately after 751.[29] As a result, Greek-speaking communities and orthodox monasteries remained predominant in southern Italy for centuries.

34
Archbishop Sergius takes control

After Archbishop John died in 744 and was buried at St Apollinare in Classe with his predecessors (Plate 61), the Lombard threat to Ravenna may have played a part in the choice of his successor. Most unusually, the clergy accepted a married layman, not an ordained priest, as their next leader. This man, Sergius, may have been one of the consuls taken hostage by Hildebrand in 739 and released as a result of Pope Zacharias's diplomacy. Since nearly all the seventh- and eighth-century archbishops of Ravenna had risen to that position through the ranks of the local clergy, most frequently from that of archdeacon, the promotion of Sergius was a major change, probably imposed by the city's secular elite. He was 'young in age, short of body, smiling of face, pleasing of form, with grey eyes, sprung from most noble family'.[1] Following canon law, he had to divorce his wife, Euphemia, who became a deaconess and was probably sent to a nunnery. Sergius then went to Rome to be consecrated by Pope Zacharias, who made no objection to his election.

The church of Ravenna thus acquired a new leader drawn from the local aristocracy and this immediately generated hostility among the clergy. When Sergius returned from his consecration in Rome, none of the priests or deacons would accompany him to the altar; they refused to serve with him. He therefore ordained new deacons to replace them, and these younger clergy too were spurned by the older ones. In recounting the rivalry between the old, established group of priests and deacons, who insisted on standing closer to the altar than those newly ordained by Archbishop Sergius, Agnellus reports that a compromise solution involved liturgical costume. The younger deacons would not wear the dalmatic, a tunic with sleeves traditionally reserved to deacons, but would use the *superhumeralis* 'after the Greek custom'.[2] The *superhumeralis* or *orarion* (*epitrachelion* in Greek) was a long narrow stole made of silk (originally linen) which symbolized the humility of Christ who washed his disciples' feet and dried them with a towel (Latin *orarium*).[3] Greek deacons wore the *orarion* over the left shoulder with the two ends hanging down back and front; the ends were sometimes decorated with the words 'holy, holy, holy', chanted by deacons as part of the *Trisagion* hymn.[4] If the deacons of Ravenna took off the dalmatic and wore their basic *indumentum* (undergarment) with the *superhumeralis* on top, they would have looked distinctively different.[5]

Agnellus continues, 'from that time on the number of deacons increased, although the canons forbid it', but Sergius managed to impose a 'truce of peace' between the newly ordained (Greek) and the older (Latin) clergy.[6] His election, backed by an elite faction within the city, may reflect the weakness of Exarch Eutychios, who was failing to defend Ravenna. As a powerful layman, the new archbishop represented the local aristocracy who were fully aware of the danger of Lombard hostility close at hand, in contrast with the very distant and ineffective power of Constantinople. This was the man who had to deal with King Aistulf after the Lombard capture of the city in the summer of 751.

However violent and effective in their military activity, the Lombards were also observant Christians, devout patrons of churches and monasteries. King Liutprand in particular had established or enhanced Christian institutions with extravagant decoration. The new rulers of Ravenna respected Sergius' authority as the leader of one of the largest and richest episcopal sees in Italy. Although Aistulf had 'a most ferocious' reputation, during the five years of his rule he began to rebuild the Petriana church that had been destroyed in an earthquake, setting up the bases and columns that were still visible in Agnellus' time. He also laid a golden *chlamys* (cloak) on the altar of the Ursiana church (the cathedral of Ravenna) with due reverence.[7] Sergius worked with the new ruler of Ravenna, seeking to ensure a measure of independence for his church under Lombard occupation by taking over the leading position of the exarch.

Here we can observe the consolidation of a new form of medieval power held by ecclesiastical leaders, distinct from the political rule of military men. Archbishop Sergius negotiated a balance between his own authority and that of the Lombard king. Whatever the precise arrangements made in 751, archbishops of Ravenna were determined to dominate the city through their spiritual role and physical presence, regardless of the nominal source of political power. A similar style of ecclesiastical leadership had accompanied the transition from late Roman rule to early Christendom in many western cities. Now Ravenna's archbishops embodied a comparable pattern.

Pope Stephen II's Appeal to the Franks

For King Aistulf, however, the conquest of Ravenna was a step in his wider ambition of uniting his northern kingdom with the central Lombard duchies of Italy to form a consolidated state. Leaving a duke in charge of the city in 751, he marched south. Inside Rome, Stephen II was consecrated as Zacharias' successor as pope on 26 March 752 and was immediately faced by Aistulf's threatened siege.[8] The pope initially sent letters to the Lombard king, demanding that he return the city of Ravenna and all the other places he had conquered to 'God's holy church of the state of the Romans'.[9] The king ignored them. Stephen then gathered 'the whole Roman assembly' to participate in a barefoot procession and carried on his own shoulders the *acheiropoieta* image of Christ (i.e. one not made by human hands) and other *sacra mysteria* to the church of S. Maria Maggiore in a litany of intercession.[10] When this failed, he secretly sent a message to the Frankish leader, Pippin, with an urgent request for military assistance. In response, he received an invitation to visit Pippin. As a result, in October 753 Frankish courtiers accompanied Stephen II and a large clerical group from Rome in an unprecedented journey across the Alps, leaving the pope's brother Paul in charge of Rome.[11] When they entered Lombard territory, King Aistulf attempted to dissuade them from making the journey, but Pope Stephen insisted and they continued. In this striking example of the Lombards' respect for papal authority, we can see an early example of the separation of ecclesiastical from military power.[12] It opened the way to the historic growth of papal authority that gradually asserted a novel form of government within Christendom.

Previous popes had corresponded with the transalpine rulers of Gaul and knew of Charles Martel's triumph over the Arabs at the battle of Poitiers in 732. The Franks were not only successful warriors, but they had also adopted the Catholic version of Christian faith when their king, Clovis, was baptized in about 500, and they had given up their unwritten Frankish language for Latin. Their settlements in northern Gaul, around Paris, and further east in today's Belgium and the Netherlands, created kingdoms in fertile river valleys, where they enjoyed the Moselle wines and showed no interest in moving south into Italy.

Pippin was not a direct descendant of Clovis, however. Like his father Charles Martel, he controlled the Merovingian state as mayor of the palace. In 751, after consulting Pope Zacharias, he had assumed regal power by cutting off King Childeric III's long hair and sending him into a monastic exile. By inviting Pope Stephen to visit, Pippin hoped to gain the highest spiritual approval of his right to rule, while Stephen intended to secure Frankish military help against the Lombards. After a difficult crossing of the Alps in the winter of 753, Pippin sent his eldest son Carl, or Charles, later known as Charles the Great, Carolus *magnus* or Charlemagne, to greet the pontiff in an important ceremonial ritual. The young prince, probably five years old, then led him on the final stage of his long journey.[13]

The momentous meeting of pope and king at Ponthion on the Feast of Epiphany, 6 January 754, resulted in Pope Stephen's recognition of Pippin and his family as rulers of the Frankish kingdom (Francia), and Pippin's commitment to the defence of Rome. At the monastery of St Denis in July the pope performed a sacral anointing, which established Pippin's regal status. He also anointed Pippin's wife, Queen Bertrada, and their sons Charles and his younger brother Carloman, who were named kings. In this way the pope became *compater*, spiritual father, to the young men, linking the head of the western church with the ruling dynasty of Francia in a religious bond.[14] In meetings over the next few months, Pippin agreed to tackle the Lombard danger to Rome, and invited Pope Stephen to stay and celebrate the feast of Christmas in 754 at the Frankish court.

While this new alliance was being sealed, Constantine V summoned a church council to meet and institute an official theory of iconoclasm. After preparing a clear, sophisticated justification for the removal of idolatrous icons, the emperor presided at the meeting of 338 eastern bishops that took place in the imperial palace at Hieria on the Asian coast of the Bosporus.[15] Although all the records of this council, apart from its Definition of Faith (*Horos*) were later destroyed, the invigorated policy was distributed throughout the empire. However, since no western bishops attended, these decisions did not become known in the West until their refutation at the Second Council of Nicaea in 787.[16]

Pippin's Italian Campaigns

After the failure of further diplomatic exchanges with Aistulf, in the spring of 755 the Frankish army marched into Italy.[17] As they besieged the Lombard capital of Pavia, Pope Stephen begged Pippin to negotiate a peaceful surrender. Aistulf agreed to the terms: namely, that he should give up all his conquests including Ravenna. But, despite swearing the most solemn oaths, he did nothing of the sort. Although Pope Stephen was re-established in Rome in 755, before the year was out he was writing to Pippin again to beg for further military assistance. In January 756 the Lombards besieged the city again and Pippin received a letter written in the name of St Peter, commanding the king to fulfil his promise to defend Rome. At the same time imperial envoys from Constantinople arrived in Rome, charged with negotiating the return of Ravenna and the exarchate to the emperor.[18]

Control over Ravenna therefore became the object of several alliances, as Constantine V accused Aistulf of illegally occupying imperial territory, while Pippin set out on his second invasion of Italy in 756 to replace Lombard rule by papal administration. The Byzantine envoys went to meet Pippin near Pavia, and while Frankish forces began another siege of the Lombard capital, imperial and papal diplomats debated the key question: to whom should the lands of the exarchate belong? The Roman *Book of the Pontiffs* records that George, an imperial ambassador, promised the 'western' king many stupendous gifts if he would return Ravenna, and other walled cities of the exarchate, to imperial control, rather than to the pope. Although Constantine could not send a military force to dislodge the Lombards from Ravenna, he had instructed his ambassadors to use every possible means to buy the exarchate back. But they could not sway King Pippin, who had sworn to return territory he conquered to St Peter.[19] At the same time, the Lombards had no intention of giving up their prize possession. Three forces, therefore, competed for control of Ravenna.

From the moment Pope Stephen realized he could not defend his church and the city of Rome against the Lombards, he took great risks to achieve an alliance with the Franks. And through the ritual elevation of King Pippin's family, and then the Franks' successful military campaigns of 755 and 756, this novel Frankish-Roman alliance completely overturned the traditional West–East axis of the Mediterranean. In place of the historic, culturally powerful and symbolic connection between Old and New Rome, a North–South axis was established to link Rome with transalpine Europe where the Franks were consolidating their power. This introduced an entirely new configuration of power in Italy, based on the pope's dependence on northern military forces and sealed by Frankish loyalty to the church of Rome. The religious bond that made Stephen II godfather to Pippin's sons expressed this political and military alliance in sacred terms.[20]

After his second campaign of 756, Pippin made sure that the exarchate would indeed become a papal domain, with its cities recorded in a document now known as the Donation of Pippin.[21] Ravenna heads the list, followed by Rimini, Pesaro, Conca, Fano, Cesena, Senigallia, Iesi, Forlimpopoli, Forlì with the castle of Sussubium, Montefeltro, Arcevia, Mons Lucati, Serra, the castle of San Marino, Vobio, Urbino, Cagli, Lucioli, Gubbio and Comacchio, together with the city of Narni which had been taken by the duchy of Spoleto in 717–18. Pippin also instructed his official, Abbot Fulrad, to go around the territory of the exarchate, receiving the submission of all these cities, collecting their keys and taking hostages to confirm the peace. Fulrad then took the Donation and the keys of all the cities and laid them symbolically in the *confessio* of St Peter (the area in front of the main altar and directly above the saint's tomb) in Rome.[22] In this way Ravenna passed at least officially under papal control.

The Trial of Archbishop Sergius

The fate of Ravenna was now disputed by three powers: the pope, to whom the lands of the exarchate had been given by Pippin I; the emperor in Constantinople, who maintained his historic claim to the same territory; and the Lombard King Desiderius, who succeeded Aistulf in 756 and declined to give up effective control. Before the end of 756, the pope appointed a duke, Eustachius, with military forces to govern the city of Ravenna and a presbyter, Philip, to guide the church.

This papal administration of the city was deeply resented by Archbishop Sergius, who called on the Lombards for help in removing the
Roman army (*exercitus Romanus*). Faced with such overt rebellion,
Pope Stephen ordered Sergius to come to Rome, using his allegedly
illegal promotion from lay status as a pretext – even though Sergius had
been governing the see of Ravenna for twelve years. The archbishop
was taken to Rome claiming that he had been betrayed by King Aistulf
to the papal authorities – 'deceived by trickery'.[23] There he was tried by
a synod of bishops, who accused him of 'invading the throne of Ravenna
like a thief and obtaining the see through secular favour'. Sergius
defended himself by pointing out that he had told Pope Zacharias all
about his previous married life and had been consecrated by the same
pope without any difficulty. This put the other bishops in a quandary;
they did not want to impugn the memory of Pope Zacharias.[24]

Sergius was detained in Rome for three years (roughly 755–8), and
during that time Pope Stephen's officials ran both the urban and ecclesiastical government of Ravenna. The pope also insisted that all local
officials should go to Rome to receive their orders and swear oaths of
loyalty, like those taken by rectors of the papal patrimony; he was trying
to reduce Ravenna to the same status as one of the papal *domuscultae*.[25]
The archbishop's imprisonment in Rome was dramatically resolved by
Pope Stephen's death in April 757, when Stephen's brother Paul, who
later became pope, 'released all captives and conceded indulgence to all
offences'.[26] A month later Sergius was allowed to return home. Pope Paul
I also gave back to the church of Ravenna the monastery of St Hilarion
at Galeata, which Stephen II had removed.[27] Indeed, the new pope
decided to reinstate Sergius as archbishop, with the powers previously
held by the exarch. This meant that his reception in Ravenna was not
enthusiastic: 'there was a little congratulation and a little peace'.[28] The
local population got rid of the papal administrators only to find that
their own church leader was acting as a proxy for Roman control.[29]

Living in Ravenna in the
Mid-Eighth Century

That Ravenna retained its mixed population and resources is illustrated
by a legacy made to the Greek monastery of S. Maria *in Cosmedin* in

the city, a telling example of these overlapping histories at a time of great change. In 767 the nun Eudokia, widow of a certain Basilios, made a substantial donation to Anastasios, presbyter, monk and abbot of the monastery. The date was established by reference to the ruling emperors, Constantine V and his son Leo IV, and indiction 5 (a system of dating events based on fiscal periods of fifteen years in use in the East), as well as the fifth year of Pope John (although these do not coincide).[30] The monastic community was governed by Anastasios, identified as the *hegoumenos* – the Greek term for abbot, which also occurs in Naples. The names of the donor and the abbot suggest possible Greek influence, as do references to the chanting of hymns in both Latin and Greek (recorded under Archbishop Felix) and deacons wearing the *superhumeralis* 'in the Greek style'. There is a strong impression of the presence of Greek-speaking monks in Ravenna and presumably their icons too. Archbishop Sergius was sympathetic to these Greek communities: he went first to that of S. Maria *in Cosmedin* after his return from Rome.

Eudokia's donation consisted of two groups of properties in the areas of the Faventa and Cornelisia, which had come into her possession through family inheritance, and included arable land, vineyards, fields, pastures, woods and fruit trees. She guaranteed that the gift was irrevocable, but in return the abbot and the monastic community had to agree never to alienate any part of the gift. The original document was drawn up by the scribe of the city, Vitalianus, and witnessed by Constantinus, tribune of the detachment of Leni (*numerum Lenonum*), Marinus, *domesticus bandi primi* and Tophanus, *bandi primi domesticus*, indicating the survival of the military divisions established by George at the turn of the eighth century. The three military officials who witnessed the document reflect the participation of the population in typical economic transactions of everyday life that continued under Lombard rule. Ravenna's bilingual capacity and already established orthodox groups would have made it a welcoming environment for eastern monks.

The Legacy of Ravenna

Despite the Donation of Pippin, the Lombards continued to dominate Ravenna, for twenty-three years until 774, but they never sought to displace Archbishop Sergius and his successors. The moment of Lombard conquest in 751 was, nevertheless, a crucial stage in the city's turn away from Constantinople. Ravenna passed first under Lombard and then papal control and, from 757 until his death in 769, Sergius performed his role with Roman support. Of course, he also found ways to assert his independent authority, not only over the church and its many estates but also over the exarchate. Agnellus reports that Sergius 'had jurisdiction over the whole Pentapolis . . . he ruled everything like the exarch'.[31] Although this clear substitution of exarch by archbishop marks the end of Ravenna's imperial status, the enduring loyalty of Istria and other parts of the Adriatic coastline to Constantinople ensured that imperial officials, sailors, merchants and spies were a constant presence in the region. The mosaicked churches of Ravenna also continued to inspire transalpine visitors as they became monastic centres, ensuring their preservation while all around the palaces of secular power crumbled.

PART NINE

756–813

Charlemagne and Ravenna

35

The long rule of King Desiderius

While Archbishop Sergius sought to extend ecclesiastical control over the area that had been the exarchate of Ravenna, to the irritation of both Lombard and papal officials, he soon had to confront a more vigorous Lombard leader, Desiderius. The new king established himself in Pavia and ruled for nearly twenty years, from 756 to 774. To secure his hold on the Lombard kingship, Desiderius had sworn to uphold the arrangements made between Aistulf and the papacy, namely, to return the territory of the exarchate to the pope, not to the emperor in Constantinople. But the new Lombard ruler also had his own plans, which brought him into prolonged conflict with the papacy. Under three popes – Paul I (757–67), Stephen III (768–772) and Hadrian (772–95) – Lombard forces repeatedly threatened Rome, and in 767–8 they actively supported an 'intruder', Pope Constantine II.

The fate of Rome would now decide the future of Ravenna. Had King Desiderius succeeded in his determination to capture the see of St Peter, he would have secured complete control over Ravenna and its territory in northern Italy. In 757 he met with George, an imperial ambassador, to discuss an alliance with Constantinople, and one year later he embarked on an expansion of his kingdom, first taking over the duchies of Spoleto and Benevento, and then advancing to Naples.[1] For nine years he persistently refused to return territory to St Peter, provoking great anxiety both in Rome and in Francia. He captured Senigallia (south of Ravenna on the eastern coast) and Castrum Valentis in Campania, and then brought his army to the gates of Rome, only to discover that Pope Paul was dying.[2]

At this moment of increased danger the city was divided by rival factions – elite military officials based in the surrounding country and clerical bureaucrats of the Lateran palace in the city.[3] The news of

Paul's death on 28 June 767 unleashed these rivalries, as Toto, the self-styled duke of Nepi, gathered an army of supporters in Tuscia and, on 5 July, imposed his brother Constantine, a layman, as pope. Under the threat of military violence, this highly irregular election was then confirmed by bishops George of Palestrina, Eustratius of Albano and Citonatus of Porto, who were forced to consecrate Constantine II. The new pope had to be protected by armed men when he went to St Peter's to celebrate Mass. Although many in the papal chancellery disputed his elevation to the papacy, it was recognized by King Pippin in Francia. After months of factional rivalry, the Romans who opposed Constantine turned to the Lombards and approached King Desiderius as a figure with sufficient force to remove the 'intruder'. This resulted in outbreaks of violent disorder and the mutilation of enemies by both sides, until a Roman priest, loyal to the memory of Paul I, was ordained as Pope Stephen III on 7 August 768, partly thanks to Desiderius.[4] The Lombards then withdrew from the city and the new pope immediately sent an envoy to the Franks, requesting theological, rather than military assistance. Since King Pippin had died leaving his two sons, Charles and Carloman, to share his inheritance, they agreed to send a party of Frankish bishops to Rome to assist Stephen III in establishing his authority.

The Roman Council of 769

Against this very contested local background, Pope Stephen III summoned a council that was attended by the twelve episcopal delegates from north of the Alps, in addition to a large number of Italian bishops. It marked a decisive stage in the process of defining a formal western iconophile response to iconoclasm with the involvement of Frankish bishops, who participated both in the trial of the 'intruder', Pope Constantine, and in the justification for religious icons. Their presence in Rome symbolized the rising power of the two young Frankish kings, and demonstrated the Frankish bishops' mastery of theological texts, as a question of religious practice was used to distinguish Latin from Greek Christendom.

The first and most pressing issue was what to do about the clerics ordained by the illegally installed Pope Constantine, who had held office for just over a year. Many papal officials and priests, including Stephen, had recognized the 'intruder', so their error also had to be corrected.[5] Further, the council had to decide how to prevent any future repetition of secular interventions in papal elections. When the ex-pope Constantine was examined by the council, he cited the example of Sergius, who had been made archbishop of Ravenna from similarly lay status. This would have embarrassed Archbishop Sergius had he participated; instead, he sent a deacon, John, and a priest, Valentine, to represent him at the council.[6] The assembled bishops refused to accept Constantine's argument, however; they ejected him from the church and decided to burn all the records of his acts as pope. They agreed a series of canons designed to limit the eligibility of papal candidates to clerics trained within the Lateran palace, 'who had risen through the separate grades and had been made cardinal deacon or priest'.[7] This established the committee that would eventually evolve into the conclave of cardinals to elect popes.

The other matter to be addressed was the Roman response to the Byzantine Council of Hieria, which was not discussed until the very last session.[8] In 767 King Pippin had hosted a debate about icon veneration at Gentilly in Francia with Byzantine and papal envoys. For the first time Christians from different backgrounds met at a theological discussion of eastern iconoclasm, and the Definition of Hieria was rejected.[9] Similarly, the Roman council was bound to condemn eastern iconoclasm and Pope Stephen had instructed participants to bring theological writings that justified iconophile opposition to it. At this session, Archbishop Sergius' deacon presented a text attributed to St Ambrose on the Acts of Sylvester, among other sources concerning the importance of icons.[10] Not surprisingly, the council condemned the iconoclasts and confirmed the iconophile arguments made at the Roman synod held in 731.

The council's hostility toward Constantinople is demonstrated in one very specific detail: the synod is dated *regnante Domino nostro Jesu Cristo*, 'under the rule of our Lord Jesus Christ', rather than using the regnal years of the eastern emperors, as was usual. This was no small difference. It was a bellwether reflection of Roman loyalty: in times of increased hostility, dating from the Incarnation occurs; when relations are easier, the year is calculated from the accession of the eastern rulers. The new system of identifying the years would also mark a revolution in authority.

In April 769 John and Valentine returned to Archbishop Sergius in Ravenna with the new canons that aimed to prevent the election of any but the most qualified Roman clergy to the papacy. Four months later, Sergius' death provoked a major crisis in Ravenna. While some of the clergy duly elected Leo the archdeacon as their new archbishop, Michael, the record keeper, *scriniarius*, appealed to Maurice, duke of Rimini, to assist in his own bid for the position. In an almost identical imitation of the disputed papal election of 767, external military support proved decisive. With the approval of King Desiderius and some leading citizens (*iudices Ravennati*), the layman Michael was installed by Duke Maurice's militia while Leo was imprisoned in Rimini. The firm Roman declaration against lay candidates and secular pressures in the election of bishops was totally ignored in Ravenna.

Although Michael sent many bribes and gifts to Pope Stephen and King Desiderius in an effort to gain broader support, the pontiff refused to consecrate him as archbishop. Meanwhile Leo the archdeacon remained under Duke Maurice's guard in Rimini. This grave division was only resolved by another external intervention, this time by the Franks. In a rather surprising development, the widowed Queen Bertrada had arranged for her eldest son Charles to marry the daughter of King Desiderius.[11] The prospect of a Frankish-Lombard alliance caused the pope great fury and the queen travelled to Rome in 770 to explain her intentions to him. In discussions with Stephen III, she suggested that after marrying the Lombard princess Charles would be able to influence Desiderius to return key cities to the see of St Peter and to settle the dispute in Ravenna.[12] A Frankish envoy named Itherius was deputed to negotiate with the Lombard king, and another, Count Hucbald, was sent with papal envoys to deal with Michael. According to the Roman *Book of the Pontiffs*, when the Ravennati learned of this plan, 'they all immediately rose up against Michael and threw him out of the *episcopium* in disgrace'.[13] Hucbald took the 'usurper', backed by the Lombards, to Rome in chains, and freed Leo from prison so that he could be consecrated as archbishop.[14] This Frankish initiative consolidated the importance of transalpine forces in the internal problems of the papacy and the city of Ravenna.

In the early 770s, King Desiderius returned to his campaign to win control of Rome and Pope Stephen III intensified his appeals to the Franks for protection. The Lombards used an agent, Paul Afiarta, who held a secular position as chief military officer (*superista*) of the Roman church, to intercept papal communications with the Franks and to arrange the murder of two notaries. In 772 the short *Life* of Stephen III concludes with the extreme disorder this provoked in Rome and the prompt election of Hadrian – a typically Roman candidate of noble birth. The new pope considered Afiarta a traitor and asked Archbishop Leo of Ravenna to arrest him. Leo, however, went further and arranged for Afiarta to be put to death in Ravenna, to Hadrian's intense displeasure.[15]

Charles's First Campaign in Italy

Pope Hadrian's anger was also related to Desiderius' military threats, which had heightened the desperate tone of Stephen III's letters to Charles. These letters, preserved in the *Codex Carolinus*, a collection put together on the king's orders in 791, document the significance of the novel relationship between the Frankish kings and the bishops of Rome.[16] When Pope Hadrian put the request for Frankish military intervention into the mouth of St Peter himself, the urgency of his position became clearer and harder to ignore. In Ravenna, where the possibility of repeated campaigns by transalpine rulers was surely understood, it set up a triangular framework of relations between the Franks and the two cities.[17]

Eventually, in 773, Charles somewhat unwillingly ordered the Franks to march to the relief of the see of St Peter. In the spring of the next year, using two ancient Roman routes across the Alps, the king set out from Geneva taking the Mont Cenis pass, while his uncle Bernard went over the Great St Bernard. These western passes, used by Pope Stephen II in his adventurous journey to the Franks in 753 and by Pippin when he first entered Italy, gave access to Rome over the Ligurian Apennines and down the western coast of the peninsula.[18] In 774 when Archbishop Leo of Ravenna heard that Charles had come down from the Mount Cenis pass and was marching through the valley of Susa, he sent his deacon Martin to assist the Frankish army. Thanks to Martin's detailed knowledge of the area, the king was able to surprise the Lombards by attacking unexpectedly from the rear, in a battle which proved decisive.[19] Desiderius' Lombard militia were unable to confront the battle-hardened

Frankish warriors, and Charles established a siege of Pavia that led ultimately to the collapse of the Lombard kingdom.[20] He also decided to celebrate the most important Christian feast of Easter in Rome, to Pope Hadrian's surprise. Charles's visit offered an opportunity to discuss what was to happen in the Lombard territories to be ceded to papal control, which included 'the whole exarchate of Ravenna as it once existed, the provinces of the Venetiae and Istria, and the whole duchy of Spoleto and Benevento'.[21] The Roman *Book of the Pontiffs* records that a document of donation was drawn up and placed in the tomb of St Peter, and the king took a copy of the same agreement away with him.[22]

After the fall of Pavia in June 774, the thirty-year-old Charles put on the iron crown of the Lombards, adding the title king of the Lombards to his already prestigious regal name (king of the Franks and *patricius Romanorum*). He installed a provisional government in Pavia and sent counts to demand the submission of the most important cities. To ensure that Desiderius had no further opportunity to renege on his promises, Charles took the Lombard king off to Francia in chains, where he died in a monastery.[23] His son Adelchis fled from Verona to Constantinople, where he nurtured hopes of returning to reclaim his inheritance. But Charles countered this possibility by maintaining the Lombard kingdom of Italy as a separate political unit. In 781 he appointed his four-year-old son Carloman, renamed Pippin, as sub-king; made Pope Hadrian anoint him as king of Italy, and, after Pippin's death, promoted his son Bernard as king. They both ruled under Charles's orders for nearly forty years, and then Charles's successor, Louis the Pious, gave Bernard permission to remain king of Italy.[24]

The Independence of Archbishop Leo

Once the kingdom of the Lombards had been subsumed into the Frankish sphere, Archbishop Leo of Ravenna cultivated his own relations with the Frankish monarch. He even made a personal visit to Charles, crossing the Alps at some point before 778.[25] Just as previous archbishops had often travelled to the imperial court at Constantinople to obtain privileges, so now Leo could see that the Frankish court would better serve his interests. When Pope Hadrian learned of this visit he was understandably outraged.

Leo allowed Ravenna to be used as a prison for enemies of Rome but refused to execute papal orders. He imprisoned one of Hadrian's counts; denied the papal *saccellarius*, Gregory, access to Imola and Bologna; replaced papal officers appointed to various cities by his own nominees and, in October 775, broke the seals on a letter that Patriarch John of Grado had written to Hadrian, to learn what plans were being made for action against the Lombards. The pope considered this treasonous because Leo would have revealed the contents of the letter to the Lombard duke of Benevento.

A measure of Pope Hadrian's anger at Leo's independence can be found in two letters written to Charles in October and November 775, which denounce the archbishop of Ravenna in very strong language: 'how false is the faith of Archbishop Leo of Ravenna [who] holds this apostolic loyalty in such contempt . . . and refuses to obey our commands . . . Only that archbishop stands alone in the pride of his savagery.'[26] They also indirectly criticize Charles, who had allowed Leo to attend his court when the archbishop tried to further his own ambitions. For the Frankish king, therefore, Ravenna and its ecclesiastical ruler represented a significant force that he could set against the pope; Charles was playing one bishop off against another to enhance his own authority.

The relationship that Archbishop Leo had built up with Charles persisted even after Leo's death, to Hadrian's continuing distress. Despite the pope's wild condemnations, city officials in Ravenna went on regarding the Frankish king as their overlord.[27] Hadrian accused two *iudices*, who had gone directly to Charles, of terrible crimes including the sale of individuals to pagan peoples, and demanded that they should be brought to trial in Rome.[28] In 790–91 he was still complaining that the Ravennati and Pentapolenses were seeking justice from Charles rather than coming to Rome as he had ordered. They were denying the pope's legal authority (*dicio*).[29] So, in spite of agreements dating back to the time of Pippin, Charles's father, that gave the territory of the exarchate to the heirs of St Peter, Ravenna refused to admit papal control and its government remained disputed – encouraged partly by Charles's keen interest in it.

The *Donation of Constantine*

Faced with the continuing dispute over who should rule over what had once been the Byzantine exarchate and its capital city, Ravenna, some clerical officials inside the Lateran palace ingeniously devised a document that would demonstrate the pope's rights to the territory and redefine relations between the church of Rome and the most powerful ruler in the West.[30] In their skilful forgery, probably made in 776, they invoked the first Christian emperor, Constantine I, and attributed to him an imperial decree that endowed Pope Sylvester (314–35) with control over the western regions of the Roman world.[31] This was intimately linked with the myth that Sylvester had miraculously cured the then-pagan emperor of leprosy, which persuaded Constantine to accept Christian baptism and to entrust 'the city of Rome, and all the provinces, places and cities of Italy or the western region' to the pope. The decree continues: 'we have provided for our empire to be transferred to the eastern regions ... and for a city to be built in the province of Byzantia', a reference to Constantine's new capital. Constructing the *Donation* to fit fourth-century circumstances, papal officials carefully used genuine imperial laws, Pope Sylvester's known decrees and particularly his *Life* as recorded in the Roman *Book of the Pontiffs* to justify papal rule over the western part of the empire. They also codified the superior authority of the church over lay rulers.

The *Donation* is more than simply an attempt to legitimate papal sovereignty over Ravenna. It should be seen as part of the underlying change of authority that involved an enormous psychological shift. From the perspective of the Mediterranean as a whole, the most important disruption of established patterns of authority was the permanence of the Islamic conquests. The Arabs' assault on the Queen City in the early 700s had been rebuffed, but the consequence was not the re-establishment of Roman imperial rule from Constantinople throughout the Near East. On the contrary, the empire was permanently diminished by the Arab occupation of that region, and was forced into its new form as Byzantium, implacably determined to survive – as it did until the Ottoman Turks overran it in 1453. In the mid-eighth century, however, it was unable to defend Italy from the Lombards. But, unlike the Muslim enemy, the Lombards were Christian, as were the Franks.

Both respected the authority of the heirs of St Peter and looked to them for guidance. The extraordinary achievement of the early medieval papacy was to inspire and organize an extensive and lasting Christianization of zones and people beyond Byzantium's reach and under Rome's spiritual leadership. This process drew distant territories into allegiance to the world of Christendom.

Of all the apostolic churches, Rome was now the only one outside the much-reduced Byzantine empire that had not fallen to the Arabs, as Alexandria, Antioch and Jerusalem had. In addition, it had two unique and influential legacies: the biblical primacy of St Peter was the first and most vital, recognized everywhere in Christendom, if reluctantly in Constantinople; and the second drew on the senatorial experience, wealth and authority of Old Rome, which fed into the church's administration and power structures. As a result, it had the will and capacity to exercise its authority over ever more extensive papal territories, although it continued to need a much greater secular power to protect it – hence the approach to an historic new ally north of the Alps. The *Donation* sprang from a deep sense that legitimacy stemmed from Constantinople. Only now, its imperial authority was used by western representatives to transform their own claims and to strike out in a quite different direction.[32]

The forgery was not produced in triumph as a discovery, but Pope Hadrian alluded to it in a letter to Charles of May 778, when he anxiously attempted to enforce the monarch's military duty to return the territory of the exarchate to Rome.[33] He noted the fact that Emperor Constantine had granted Pope Sylvester authority '*in his Hesperiae partibus*' – that is, the West – and added: 'we have many donations hidden in our sacred archive of the Lateran, and for the guarantee of your most Christian rule we advise you to demonstrate your words by deeds'. While the letter falls into the pattern of earlier appeals, this direct citation of the *Donation* reflects a claim now supported by a forged document supposedly written in the fourth century at the time of the founding of Constantinople. Through this passing reference and the *Donation*'s later incorporation into collections of ecclesiastical decrees, it gradually established a legitimacy its drafters were aware it never had. Their inventive care managed to convince nearly all readers for about seven hundred years, although a few challenges to its authenticity were raised (notably by opponents of papal authority such as

Hincmar of Reims and Emperor Otto III). Only in the mid-fifteenth century were the inconsistencies of vocabulary and context unpicked by Lorenzo Valla.

In 778 Charles had not reacted with enthusiasm to his role as a 'New Constantine', but three years later when he visited Rome with his wife Hildegard to have their two youngest sons anointed and crowned as kings of Italy and Aquitaine respectively, he agreed that the territories of the Ravenna exarchate should be returned to the apostles Peter and Paul.[34] In practice the transfer took much longer, partly because archbishops of Ravenna refused to support it. But the fiction behind the *Donation of Constantine* bore fruit in the permanent presence of Frankish rule in northern and central Italy in alliance with the overall spiritual authority of the bishop of Rome. This marked the fundamental shift of religious and political identity in early medieval Italy, from association with the eastern half of Christendom led by Constantinople to a western assertion of separate and superior power in what was to become known as 'Europe'.[35] In this way the dispute over Ravenna helped to forge western Christendom, in spite of the city's increasingly marginal position.

36

Charles in Italy, 774–87

The collapse of Byzantine authority in Ravenna in the 750s opened a period of instability. Despite the rivalry of papal and Frankish claims, the city's wealthy archbishops, installed in their imposing palace attached to the cathedral, manifested an undeniable physical and symbolic authority. There are almost no references to a civilian figure of comparable power in the city.[1] The archbishops drew on revenues from many estates, which financed a militia with sufficient power to arrest, imprison and kill opponents. They also commanded the loyalty of a large section of elite landowners imbued with an East Roman model of social hierarchy, who continued to use their Byzantine titles and sustained traditions inculcated over centuries of influence from Constantinople.[2] Not until the late ninth century did these local inhabitants begin to intermarry with the families installed in Italy as a result of the Frankish conquest.[3] How did the city and surrounding territory of the Pentapolis, capable of governing itself and incapable of threatening others, appear to the king of the Franks and the Lombards after his capture of Pavia?

Charles did not visit Ravenna until 787. His Italian campaigns would have made clear to him its strategic significance as an important staging post on the route which led from the easternmost part of his kingdom (in modern Austria), through the passes south of Chur into Friuli, and then south to Treviso and Ravenna.[4] This was the route used in 776 when Charles made a quick campaign south of the Alps to put down the Lombard rebellion of Count Hrodgaud, when Pope Hadrian hoped that the king would curb Archbishop Leo's powers. But Charles did not go to the city; instead he returned home, sending envoys to Spoleto to secure the loyalty of Duke Hildebrand.[5] In addition to Leo's opposition to Roman officials, the pope feared that Charles would set up his own administration in Lombard areas that had been promised to the papacy. Two years later, Pope Hadrian reminded the king of his obligation to St Peter, citing the forged *Donation of Constantine* to justify papal claims to the West.[6]

Charles's Second Visit to Rome

In 780 Charles, his wife Hildegard and their two youngest sons, Carloman and Louis, and two daughters set out from Worms for Rome 'for the purpose of prayer'. On this second visit to Rome at Easter, 781, Pope Hadrian baptized the king's four-year-old son Carloman, giving him the new name of Pippin and acting as his godfather. He also anointed Pippin and his younger brother Louis as kings of Italy and Aquitaine respectively. This spiritual relationship of *compaternitas*, modelled on Pope Stephen II's anointing of Charles in 754, bound the king and pope more tightly together.[7] Pippin and Louis were immediately set up as kings, with their own courts and appropriate guidance, and the kingdom of Italy remained under Charles's control until his death nearly forty years later, in January 814.[8] In 781 Charles also ceded to Hadrian the previously Lombard duchies of Spoleto, Tuscia, Campania and part of Benevento, though the pope must have known that it would be very difficult to pursue his claim on lands to the east of the Apennines.[9] There, the archbishops of Ravenna continued to exercise considerable authority and Leo's successor, John, had no intention of giving up his effective rule.

While in Rome, Charles received an embassy from Constantinople with a proposal of marriage between his daughter Rotrud (aged six) and the young Byzantine prince Constantine (who was probably eleven years old).[10] Charles's father Pippin had maintained diplomatic and often cordial relations with Byzantium, despite the adoption of iconoclasm, and had discussed a similar marriage proposal in 766. After the death of her husband, Emperor Leo IV (775–80), Empress Irene assumed the power of regent, ruling for her young son with a council of ministers and the patriarch of Constantinople, and decided to renew the idea of a marriage alliance. The coincidence of these two events – settling relations with Pope Hadrian over the exarchate in Italy and opening new relations with the eastern empire – reminded Charles that he could now take a role in the wider Mediterranean world.

Constantinople retained a great significance for the Franks as the unconquered capital of an empire, a court dominated by glamorous rituals in colourful processions, ceremonies and banquets, that had been attended by Frankish ambassadors. In the Queen City itself Constantine V, his son Leo IV and daughter-in-law, Empress Irene, demonstrated their political authority through embassies led by skilled diplomats laden with gifts of silk, spices and jewels. Since silkworms remained unknown in the West, bolts of glistening silk, often decorated with jewels and gold thread, or woven with circles enclosing animal images in contrasting colours, were very highly prized. Constantine V also sent a water-powered organ to King Pippin that deeply impressed western rulers.[11] While the Franks had problems getting the organ to work, later references to Charles's son Louis the Pious enjoying the sound of organ music indicate that it survived and remained in use.

The Marriage Alliance with Byzantium

In 781 these earlier diplomatic contacts were renewed and Empress Irene's son was betrothed to Rotrud; oaths were sworn and a Byzantine eunuch, Elissaios, remained in the West to teach Rotrud 'Greek letters and language and educate her in the customs of the Roman Empire'.[12] Six years later Irene decided that it was time for Constantine VI to be married and sent an embassy to the West to collect his bride. The Byzantine diplomats caught up with Charles at Capua just before Easter 787, when he was campaigning against the Lombards in southern Italy. Despite the importance that he seemed to have attached to the proposed marriage, Charles declined to allow Rotrud to go off to distant Constantinople, thus breaking off the engagement.[13]

Among the many theories for the failure of this union, the most persuasive is that Charles did not want his daughters to give birth to sons who might threaten his dynastic line.[14] Since he already had three legitimate sons in 786 (Charles, Pippin and Louis), as well as several illegitimate, he had more than enough heirs to deal with. They each had to be given authority – but not too much – and the three designated to inherit his kingdom would have to share it, in the same way as

Charles and his brother Carloman had done. In 806 the *Divisio regnorum* arranged this most precisely. But if Charles allowed Rotrud to marry Constantine VI and they then produced a son, would that child have rights to his grandfather's lands in the West, perhaps making a particular claim on Ravenna? And if the same child also inherited the entire eastern empire, would that not threaten the independence of the Frankish one in the West? Charles could have foreseen the rivalry that might result, the possible military challenges and dangers to his kingdom, and thus decided to keep Rotrud (and most of his other daughters) with him. He preferred them to enjoy unofficial love affairs within his court than to venture into foreign marriages that could bring troubling claims back to threaten him.

The Ending of Official Iconoclasm

Prior to this rebuff, in 784 Empress Irene had reported a momentous change of policy to Pope Hadrian: that the eastern church was ready to abandon iconoclasm and wished to resume close relations with the church of Rome. Although Constantine V's military victories against the Arabs had been attributed to iconoclast avoidance of idolatry, Irene decided that restoring good relations with icon-venerating Christians in both East and West was more important.[15] Irene was acting with the support of the newly appointed iconophile patriarch, Tarasios, previously her lay chancellor, and a large body of monks. For thirty years, however, iconoclasm had been the official doctrine of the eastern church and many bishops were convinced that it was correct. Against their inevitable antagonism, Irene and her supporters exploited the approval of iconophile writers such as John of Damascus, a Palestinian monk living under Muslim rule, who had developed a sophisticated justification of icon veneration and its importance in Christian worship. When Pope Hadrian learned of the proposal to reverse iconoclasm, he approved of the eastern church's return to the Roman position and, in 785, nominated his delegates to represent the see of St Peter at the council to be held in Constantinople one year later.[16] However, this meeting in 786 was inadequately prepared and broke up in disorder when military troops loyal to iconoclast principles threatened to kill the patriarch, and a few iconoclast bishops chanted their definition of the true faith over efforts to change it. The participants dispersed without reaching any decision.

Despite this set back, the empress persevered in her determination to put an end to iconoclasm. She dismissed the army units that had opposed it and settled upon Nicaea as the city that could host a successful council. Famous as the site of the first Universal Council of the 388 Church Fathers, held in 325 under the auspices of Constantine I, Nicaea was also firmly under imperial control. She recalled the papal delegates, who had reached Sicily on their journey back to Rome, and re-summoned all the bishops. In October 787, 365 participants gathered at Nicaea and identified their meeting as the Seventh Oecumenical Council. Under precise imperial direction, the doctrine of iconoclasm was condemned, some iconoclast bishops who abjured their heresy were then readmitted to the church and the veneration of icons was reinstated. When his legates reported this, Pope Hadrian expressed his pleasure and had the Greek record of the acts translated into Latin and deposited in the papal library.[17]

The restoration of icons, as recorded in a Latin version of the acts of 787, was not well received at Charles's court, where his theological advisers, Alcuin and Theodulf of Orleans, were deeply shocked by the arguments employed. They were not iconoclasts, but they could hardly believe that icons were used as guarantors of the faith, as godfathers to infants at baptism, as cures for all sorts of illnesses and other flagrantly superstitious associations. Unlike Pope Hadrian, they refused to accept these eastern traditions of icon veneration. At Charles's insistence, the liturgy used in Frankish churches had been reformed, with a much deeper understanding of its theological and symbolic foundations. The king's religious experts had also investigated the eastern opposition to idolatry which lay behind iconoclasm, as well as Trinitarian issues such as the theory of Adoptionism (that Jesus was only the adopted son of God), which had developed in Spain. Instead of welcoming the decisions taken at the Council of Nicaea in 787, therefore, Charles set up a commission to examine them in detail. The *Libri Carolini* (Books of Charles), which resulted from this investigation, criticized the eastern church and condemned outright some of its theological justifications for the use of icons. At the Synod of Frankfurt in 794 bishops from all parts of Charles's territories and papal representatives from Rome discussed these issues and condemned what they called 'the pseudo Council' of 787, opening a much more serious conflict between the Frankish church and the Constantinopolitan. This left Pope Hadrian in the impossible position of having agreed with both.[18]

Medieval historians often surmise that Charles had been vexed at not being invited to attend the council, although as the leading member of the pentarchy of major Christian sees, Pope Hadrian was authorized to speak for the entire western Christendom.[19] There was no precedent for additional 'territorial' churches to be invited to send representatives to such meetings. According to a mid-ninth-century source, however, Charles did send his palace chaplain Witbold to Constantinople in 787.[20] Witbold spent eighteen months in the imperial capital and must have witnessed the arrival of the papal legates who attended the council; at the very least he would have heard what was planned. After the council's conclusion, he would have seen the participants returning to Constantinople, where Constantine VI and Irene were acclaimed as a new Constantine and a new Helena.[21]

Charles's refusal to allow Rotrud to marry Constantine VI thus occurred in the context of a serious theological difference that defined the remarkable maturity of Carolingian rule. When Irene received the news of the rebuff, she took two steps: first, she decided to marry her son to a Byzantine bride; secondly, she embarked on an aggressive anti-Frankish policy in southern Italy. The first decision involved a particular Byzantine institution, a bride-show, set up so that Constantine could chose his princess. Officials were duly sent around the empire to find only the most beautiful girls, who had to conform to particular measurements – the Cinderella story of the shoe that fits makes its appearance here. And in 788 Constantine was married to the successful contestant, Maria of Amnia, from Paphlagonia. The procedure encouraged all the wealthier families throughout the empire to imagine the imperial status, patronage and wealth that would accompany the marriage of their daughter to the crown prince. It allowed Irene to send trusted officials to remote parts of the empire to investigate attitudes to her government. Under cover of bride selection, they talked with leading provincial families, examined local conditions and collected information in conversations designed to generate loyalty to Constantinople. The contest brought several hopeful families to the imperial capital with their most beautiful daughters, and once Maria had won all her relatives were provided with suitable rewards; two of her sisters were married to court officials and her parents were established in a fine palace in the capital. In this way, not only were closer ties established with the province of Armeniakon (in the east), but Irene also benefitted from more detailed news from other regions. All the families visited the famed Queen City, experienced the imperial court and returned home with rewards and stories to entertain their neighbours.[22]

Battles over Southern Italy

The second consequence of the failure of the marriage alliance was Irene's decision to attack Charles's authority in southern Italy, where he had been assisting Pope Hadrian in controlling rebellious Lombard groups. After the loss of Ravenna, the island of Sicily and Calabria (nearer to Constantinople although requiring a sea crossing), as well as the coastal area further north surrounding the independent duchy of Naples became the focus of imperial concern. According to Pope Hadrian, the local dukes were always plotting against papal authority. Irene now decided to exploit her western military forces in conjunction with Prince Adelchis, son of the Lombard King Desiderius, who had fled to the eastern capital in 774, to reduce Charles's influence. After fourteen years as an honoured guest at the imperial court, Irene sent Adelchis back to Italy to build an alliance with his brother-in-law, Duke Arichis of Benevento.[23] There was no question of Adelchis returning to what had been the Lombard capital of Pavia, now firmly under Charles's control, but it was hoped that he could strengthen opposition to Charles among the Lombards in the south. The empress offered Duke Arichis the elevated title of *patricius* and instructed the governor of Sicily to make military preparations for a campaign against the Franks.

Although Arichis died before his new patrician insignia arrived, the plan to attack Charles went ahead and this dramatic change in Byzantine foreign policy naturally enflamed Frankish hostility to Constantinople while generating tension in Rome. To counter Irene's military threats, Charles allowed the younger son of Duke Arichis, Grimoald, to claim his inheritance. Charles had been holding Grimoald hostage in the Frankish court, and, as a condition of his freedom, he had to agree that the Lombards would cut off their beards and place Charles's name on their charters and coins.[24] Despite Pope Hadrian's doubts about the young prince's loyalty, he returned to Salerno in 788 with military forces to oppose the Byzantines. In the ensuing clash between Lombard rivals, Grimoald, backed by the Franks, confronted his uncle Adelchis, supported by military and naval units under the command of the Byzantine *sakellarios* (treasury official) John. Grimoald triumphed, defeating the Byzantine expedition. Subsequently, the Lombard victor reneged on his oaths of loyalty to Charles and set himself up as an independent duke. Irene then rewarded him with an imperial bride; at some point between 789 and 791 Grimoald married Euanthia, Maria of Amnia's youngest sister and sister-in-law of Constantine VI.[25] Lombard rulers of Benevento in central Italy developed a vibrant blend of Lombard and Byzantine culture, drawing on the neighbouring southern regions that remained under imperial control for centuries. Like the maritime centres of Gaeta, Naples and Amalfi, these areas nurtured a rich Byzantine inheritance that cherished ancient Greek learning as well as eastern monasticism.

Charles in Ravenna, 787

After campaigning in southern Italy, Charles stopped in Ravenna on his way back to Francia in 787. Gratiosus was then archbishop, having previously been abbot of the monastery of St Apollinaris not far from the church of S. Croce, and archdeacon of the see.[26] When they learned that the king of the Franks intended to visit the city, the clergy were concerned that Gratiosus, who was 'filled with the grace of God' but also a very simple man, according to Agnellus, might say something inappropriate.[27] The king was doubtless received in the episcopal palace, constructed by Bishop Ursus and embellished by all later church leaders. During the feast when Gratiosus said things that the king couldn't understand, the clergy interpreted them as the sort of soothing noises a mother makes when she wants her child to eat. And Charles is reported to have acknowledged this as a sign of true piety: ' "Behold an Israelite in whom there is no guile". And after these things, whatever the bishop requested from him, he obtained.'[28]

Charles was prepared to honour the archbishop because he came to

Ravenna with a specific purpose. He wanted to remove columns, capitals and marbles from the city to decorate the new palace and church he planned at Aachen. Pope Hadrian had already given his permission for the king to take similar monumental building materials from Rome, and now Charles came to see what Ravenna had to offer. Such recycling of building blocks of good solid marble or stone was very common and was often the only way to acquire the large columns, capitals or revetment panels needed for new church building. Parts of the exarch's palace may have already been in ruins and other palaces, villas and abandoned Arian churches could provide suitable material, such as the four porphyry columns from the palace that had been re-used in the rebuilding of the apse of the church of S. Apollinare Nuovo. Charles was searching for elegant coloured marble columns, capitals and revetments to adorn his palaces north of the Alps.[29]

San Vitale and Aachen

During his 787 stay in Ravenna, the king visited the city's magnificent churches, and in San Vitale he saw the imperial panels – the mosaic images of Justinian and Theodora, accompanied by their courtiers, clergy, soldiers and Archbishop Maximian. Here, for the first time, Charles gazed upon the defining images of imperial glory: the great sixth-century emperor, wearing the imperial regalia, the crown set with precious stones and pearl pendants, the purple cloak fastened with an enormous jewelled clasp at the shoulder, a glistening tablion of golden silk decorated with birds in green encircled in red, and brilliantly decorated shoes, an unforgettable image of how to display oneself as an emperor. And this emperor had also given his name to a famous legal code that was still recognized as the basis for many eighth-century civil regulations. Opposite him stood his wife Theodora, the empress whose costume is even more extravagant than the emperor's, with her ladies-in-waiting all dressed in luxurious multicoloured silks. The joint portraits also present the imperial rulers participating in the liturgy and bringing their offerings to the altar. In the pose of Justinian, Charles saw a role, a title and an imperial model for the creation of his palace at Aachen.

The church of San Vitale also made a deep impression on him and inspired his own place of worship at Aachen. An octagonal structure roofed with a dome had not been constructed in northern Europe before and must have demanded all the skills at the king's disposal, perhaps including the assistance of experienced craftsmen from Ravenna. It would not have been extraordinary for him to insist on taking back to Francia workmen who knew how to construct such a building, to assemble the marble revetment and put up the mosaic decoration that made the new palace chapel such a striking monument. Charles collected experts in many fields (Alcuin from York, Theodulf from the Pyrenean border with Spain, Paul the deacon from Italy) to enhance the standing of his court, and skilled craftsmen from Ravenna to decorate its setting would have been perfectly in order.

In this way, the central building of what had once been the imperial capital in the West, containing glamorous images of the authority of Constantinople, was reworked for Charles's new palace chapel at Aachen. Nor were the imperial panels illustrating the authority of Justinian over the city's history the only source of inspiration: Theoderic constituted another, perhaps even more telling model for Charles as a fellow 'barbarian'. In particular, the Gothic king's mausoleum of white Istrian marble standing outside the city walls, and the mosaic images of his palace and the port of Classis in the church of S. Apollinare Nuovo displayed a Gothic and Germanic regal authority with which the Frankish king could identify: Theoderic represented a non-Roman king who had left an indelible imprint on the city. Although Charles did not commemorate Justinian or Theoderic among the older Roman emperors whose portraits decorated his palace at Ingelheim, he sought to equal both.

In the late eighth and early ninth centuries Ravenna preserved ideas of imperial domination that had been almost completely lost in Rome, now increasingly smothered by papal pretensions. Rome could also provide good building material, but its churches were full of papal portraits beside images of Christian saints, for instance at Sts Cosmas and Damian, rather than late Roman Christian emperors. Only Ravenna combined the figures of Theoderic and Justinian that were particularly appealing to Charles. Archbishops from Gratiosus (786–9) through to Martin (810–18) invited Charles to dine in the episcopal palace and impressed him with their collections of late antique silver, ivory and silks. Perhaps they persuaded themselves to acquiesce in the Frankish monarch's determination to remove late antique building material from Ravenna because it would spread the fame of their city north of the Alps. Whether it was later called *Roma Ventura* (the future Rome) or the Second Athens, Charles's ambitions for Aachen reflected his exposure to the concentration of buildings and culture he found in Ravenna. The city's archbishops certainly cultivated close relations with Charles and his family in order to secure the importance of Ravenna in Frankish eyes.

Archbishop Valerius (789–810) demonstrated this awareness in 792–3 when Ravenna hosted Charles's son, King Louis of Aquitaine, who spent that winter in the city in preparation for a joint expedition against Benevento with his brother King Pippin. Both young men were teenagers (fourteen and fifteen years old respectively) practising the art of warfare against Duke Grimoald and his Byzantine wife. Valerius welcomed his royal guest and put the dining hall of his episcopal palace to good use. Such high-ranking visitors were always entertained at banquets, which performed a major function both in conviviality and in the negotiations that accompanied such meetings. And banquets were always preceded by hunting, a regal sport that constituted the chief source of deer, wild boar, smaller animals and birds to be consumed. In Ravenna, given the copious supply of fish, there may not have been so much hunting on horseback, but game was somehow acquired. Possibly some parts of the ancient imperial palace provided accommodation for the young king and his entourage during their long stay.

The Death of Pope Hadrian

The last years of Hadrian's pontificate were full of anxiety expressed in his growing condemnation of the rulers of Constantinople – identified in a derogatory fashion as 'Greeks' – who were threatening Rome through their most wicked (*nefandissimi*) allies in Naples.[30] In 793 the pope sent envoys with many gifts to Charles, though relations between the king's court and Rome were strained.[31] But two years later, when he learned of the pope's death, Charles commissioned a profuse and affectionate funerary tribute, probably composed by Alcuin, which was engraved on black marble. It can still be admired in St Peter's where

Hadrian was buried on 26 December 795.[32] One of Hadrian's junior clerics, Leo, a subdeacon, was named pontiff the very next day, indicating a united decision among the electoral committee. Pope Leo III immediately sent envoys to Charles with the customary gifts, adding the keys to the tomb of St Peter as well as the banners of the city, objects redolent of Rome's loyalty.[33] Leo thus demonstrated his determination to continue the Frankish alliance. And for Ravenna this implied an extension of the subordination it had suffered since 751, despite its archbishops' cultivation of close relations with Charles. The city had become a source of imperial symbolism rather than a site of strategic power.

37

Charles claims the stones
of Ravenna

The *Royal Frankish Annals* that recount Charles's activities year by year are dominated by unrelenting campaigns against his eastern enemies – Saxons, Slavs, Huns and Avars. In 774, while the king celebrated his conquest of the Lombard kingdom, the Saxons had murdered his ecclesiastical envoy, Boniface, who had been sent to convert them. Almost every year thereafter the king crossed the Rhine and the Elbe and fought to subdue these heathen peoples, who regularly accepted baptism, swore to become Christian, and then reneged on their oaths. After his visit to Rome and Ravenna in 787, Charles was preoccupied by these campaigns and did not return to Italy for thirteen years. From 788, he regularly stayed at his new palace in Aachen, now embellished by the ancient building materials brought from Italy, as well as the older palace at Regensburg, where he received envoys from the Muslim ruler of southern Spain, King Alfonso of Galicia, the emperors of Byzantium, the Avars and the Persian king (the caliph). Representatives of the Bretons, Saxons, the Balearic Islands and a monk from Jerusalem made their way to Aachen to acknowledge his authority. As he turned forty, in 788, he was hailed as the supreme overlord of the West, who had united a large kingdom of diverse regions and imposed both an improved legal administration and effective Christian rule over it.[1]

In 793/4 his status was marked by the issue of a new coin type, an addition to the regular issues of silver pennies produced in numerous mints that constituted the bulk of Frankish currency. It took the form of his signature, the Latin monogram made up of the letters from his name, Karolus (and, in a few instances, in Greek letters – ΚΑΡΩΛΟΣ), surrounded by his titles.[2] Charles was clearly aware of the immense value of coins as propaganda, and intended the use of Greek to impress his subjects in Ravenna and other parts of Italy where Greek was

understood. Later, when he was concerned at the growing power of the
Arab Caliph, Harun al-Rashid, in the Holy Land and decided to send
funds to support the Christians, he minted special 'portrait' pennies
with an image of the Jerusalem temple on the reverse and the legend
Religio Xristiana.[3]

The King and the Empress

In Constantinople, Constantine VI and his mother, Empress Irene, were
also aware of Charles's recent military successes and enhanced status.
In 797 the emperor, now aged twenty-six, sent an embassy to Aachen to
make peace, probably in order to recover prisoners taken captive in the
south Italian clash a decade earlier. The following year, however,
Charles received another embassy, this time from Irene in her own right.
She had removed her son from power by having him blinded and now
ruled alone, the first occasion on which a woman was officially acclaimed
as emperor in Byzantium.[4] Irene needed peace in Italy in order to focus
resources against Harun al-Rashid, who had defeated her generals. Her
envoys negotiated a treaty with Charles and secured the return of Sisin-
nios, brother of Patriarch Tarasios, held prisoner since 788.[5]

Charles was, in fact, in diplomatic contact with Harun over the
Christian holy places in Jerusalem, as Irene was well aware. These
exchanges between Aachen and Baghdad would eventually result in the
arrival of an elephant at the Carolingian court.[6] In 797 Charles may
have asked the caliph for such an exotic animal because he was familiar
with the story of Hannibal's great military campaign with elephants
that crossed the Alps. While Roman statues and ivories of elephants,
and Byzantine silks produced in the imperial workshops, made them
familiar, no one living in northern Europe in the late eighth century
had ever seen one. Frankish ambassadors to Constantinople might have
heard stories of the elephant that had been kept in the city and was
commemorated in life-size statues.[7] We can imagine the excitement at
the Frankish court when Muslim envoys informed Charles that the one
surviving member of his embassy, Isaac the Jew, was on his way back
from Harun with the much-desired elephant. Plans were made to transport it from North Africa to Italy, where it arrived in October 801 and
remained to avoid crossing the Alps in the winter. In July 802 Isaac

duly presented all the caliph's gifts to the emperor – 'the name of the elephant was Abul Abaz' – and Charles took great pleasure in displaying his elephant, and took it on campaigns until its death in 810.[8]

While Charles was waiting for the return of his embassy to Harun, he received another highly unusual message from Irene acting as emperor. In 799 this was secretly brought to the king in Aachen by an envoy of the governor of Sicily.[9] It suggested that she and Charles should unite the eastern and western parts of the ancient Roman empire in a marriage of convenience. The proposal is reported by both Byzantine and Frankish sources, each claiming the initiative. According to western records, Irene's embassy 'offered to hand over the empire to Charles' – that is, it was interpreted as a measure of her weakness as a female ruler.[10] Eastern sources suggest that Irene proposed a political union that would have permitted her to rule over the East in Constantinople while Charles controlled the West from Aachen. Whether he seriously contemplated such a diplomatic union with Irene or not, he sent envoys back to Constantinople. They arrived in 802 to witness Emperor Irene's overthrow by her finance minister Nikephoros, and any hope of what would have been the marriage of the millennium evaporated.

The Attack on Pope Leo III

In the summer of 799, Charles had also received information about an even more important visitor: Pope Leo in person. Leo had been attacked by Roman opponents during the major liturgical Easter procession in the city and had escaped via Spoleto. He was escorted over the Alps to Charles, who was at his new palace at Paderborn in Saxony, now pacified. The king welcomed him and promised to sort out the rivalry that had led to the attack. After spending the winter with Charles, the pope was accompanied back to Rome with Frankish bodyguards. In August 800 Charles set off with an army from Mainz and went to Ravenna for the second time, where he met his son, Pippin, king of Italy. After a week there, they proceeded together to Ancona, where Charles instructed Pippin to go and plunder the territory of the rebellious Lombards in Benevento, while he crossed the Apennines to Rome.[11] In a carefully prepared, lavish ceremony of welcome, the pope came out to meet him 20km from the city and then escorted him into the ancient capital. From 24 November 800 until the following spring Charles remained there, re-establishing Leo's position. It was during this long visit that the pope arranged to crown him with the title of emperor at the Christmas liturgy in St Peter's and the choir duly acclaimed Charles as *serenissimus augustus a deo coronatus magnus pacificus imperator Romanum gubernans imperium* (most serene augustus crowned by God, the great and peaceful emperor, ruling over the Roman empire).[12]

After his coronation, Charles presented numerous gifts to St Peter's, including 'a silver table with its legs', a gold crown weighing 55 lbs and a large bejewelled gold paten inscribed with his name in capital letters. He and his sons and daughters visited other churches to donate gold and silver liturgical vessels, and a Gospel book with a gold cover.[13] The emperor remained in Rome until Easter, sent Pippin on another campaign against the Beneventans, and then went to Spoleto and on to Ravenna, where he spent a few days in May 801.[14] Later in 801 and 802 the Lombard cities of Chieti, Ortona and Lucera in Benevento were finally subdued, and Carolingian garrisons were established.[15]

The Statue of Theoderic

On this, his third visit to Ravenna, Charles may have found the phrase 'ruling over the Roman empire' (*Romanum gubernans imperium*) in documents preserved in the imperial archives.[16] It was a formula that probably dated back to the time of Galla Placidia and her son Valentinian III and Charles used it, almost always avoiding the title *imperator Romanorum*.[17] This fits the report by Einhard that the king would never have agreed to attend the liturgy on 25 December 800 at St Peter's had he known that Pope Leo intended to crown him as emperor.[18] If this form of the imperial title was brought to his attention in Ravenna, he was reminded of the city's historic role as the capital of the Roman West.[19]

In addition to the formula probably adopted from imperial records in the city's archive, and the building materials he had already removed, Charles clearly intended to absorb the fame of Theoderic, the Gothic king who had created his capital in Ravenna. He admired the mosaic representation of the palace in the church dedicated to St Martin

47. (*Left*) Gold *solidus* of Emperor Constans II (641–68) and his eldest son Constantine, minted in Constantinple between 659 and 661. (*Right*) On the reverse, his younger sons Herakleios and Tiberios, either side of a tall cross on three steps, with the inscription VICTORIA AUGV (*Victoria augustorum*, victory of the emperors). When Constantine IV became emperor (668–85), he mutilated both his brothers and exiled them.

48. Remains of the honorary column of Phokas, erected on the Forum at Rome in 608 by the Exarch Smaragdus to emphasize the authority of the emperor in Constantinople. After the death of Phokas in 610 his name was chiselled off – it would have filled the diamond shaped hole in the inscription after the word Domino (*detail, right*).

49. S. Apollinare in Classe, the basilica consecrated by Archbishop Maximianus in 549.

50. The interior of S. Apollinare in Classe, with the set of matching Proconnesian marble columns and capitals ordered from Constantinople. The original mosaic and marble decoration of the walls was lost and partly replaced by fresco roundel portraits of the bishops of Ravenna.

51. The apse mosaic of S. Apollinare in Classe, with the patron saint wearing episcopal robes and twelve lambs representing the Apostles, under a golden jewelled cross.

52 and 53. Two mosaic panels between the apse windows. (*Left*) S. Severus, the fourth-century bishop of Ravenna, holding a Gospel book. (*Right*) A portrait of Bishop Ursicinus (533-36), who began the building of the church with the help of Julianus the *argentarius*, during the reign of Queen Amalasuintha (526–35).

54. The mosaic panel in S. Apollinare in Classe commissioned by Archbishop Reparatus (671–7) to celebrate the autonomy of the church of Ravenna, granted by Constans II in 666. Although the mosaic has been heavily restored, it is clearly based on the earlier imperial panel of Justinian I and Maximian in San Vitale (see 37).

55. Lead seal of Exarch Theodore (678–87) from the seventh century, used to prove the authenticity of his orders: (*left*) on the front, 'Mother of God, help your servant' and (*right*) on the reverse 'Theodoros, patrikios and exarchos'. Attached by a string to the document, these lead seals are now the only witness to such record-keeping.

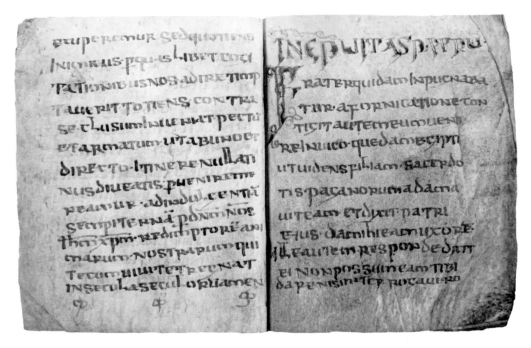

56. Manuscript of the *Vitas Patrum*, Lives of the Fathers, copied in Ravenna on parchment by an unknown scribe in *c.* 700. Attached to a collection of sermons, it demonstrates the activity of clerics probably attached to the episcopal scriptorium.

57 and 58. (*Left*) The Hand of God in the centre of the apse mosaic in S. Apollinare in Classe, directly above the golden cross with a bust portrait of Christ at the centre, and below it S. Apollinaris officiating at the altar. (*Right*) The Garden of Paradise behind the saint in the apse. In all the buildings of Ravenna such flora and fauna create an idyllic scene of birds, animals and plants.

59 and 60. (*Above*) An early Christian sarcophagus re-used by Archbishop Theodore (677–691/2), for his burial in S. Apollinare in Classe. His funerary inscription is engraved across the lid below the three wreaths. (*Below*) An early eighth-century sarcophagus of Archbishop Felix (708–25), reflecting the much lower quality of carving on newly made tombs, also in S. Apollinare in Classe.

61. (*Opposite*) Sarcophagus of Archbishop John (725–44) in S. Apollinare in Classe, another very simple tomb with poorly carved inscription, placed below a much longer and elegantly executed inscription recording his gifts to the church of Ravenna.

INN PATRIS ET FILII ET SP SCI IMP B PIISSIMIS D D N N LEONE ET CONSTANTINO A DO CORONAT PACIFIC MAGNIS IMP B LEONE
QVIDEM CLEMENTISS IMP ANNO X V CONSTANTINO VERO A DO CORON IMP ANNO X I C GVERNANTEM ITALIA DN EVTVCHIO EXCEll PATRICIO
ET EXARG IIII KAL FEBRVARIA SIND X IIII HIC TITVLVS MONSTRAT OP VS LAVDAVILI FACTV M Q VOD PIO CNSILIO CNCEPIT MENE PRAESVl
IOHANNES ALMVS PONTIFEX IVNIOR IN NOMINE QVINTVS Q VI CVRA PERVIGILI AETERNI PREMIAR EGNI FIDA SVT POSSIDATA CNORVM MACHINA
PRAE CANTV MINIBVS SACRIS HOC SIBI MONVMENTVM LOCAVIT APOLLENARIS C COMMENDANS PVLVERE A MEMBRA CVAES VR RECIVR A C REDIT
CARNIS RESVRMTO VIGORE CNVLIT ET DONVM Q VOD SERVIS DNI PROST QVI LAVDES ADSIDVAS MARTVRIS CLIB A FVNDVM CAMMILLARIA CA SALIBVS
VNDIQVE VALLATVM CVMS VISTERMINIBVS SICVT TEXTVS DONATIONIS DESIGNATAPTVM SERVIS DNI RAVENNATI ER R STVM FERTILE M FECVND VM ICNI S
AD VSVM LIC VAMEN ET SVESTO Q VOD PABVLENS I LVARVM CLANDIFERA POMA DANS SCAE CCL COMMVTATA AD VICEM LO CA FVND VM TRE CINT VLA
FAVEN IN TERR CNSTITVT ATQ FVND VMPIT VLS CRNII ERR REA CENEM SIM V LO VE ARGENTO VATER DENA P VND ERAM VDVM Q VOD SIBI LECTIME
CENTORVM MCNTV LIT IV RA VT SITINI IVATV M NEC REVOCETVRVM QVIAM Q VOD VTI CCLEGIO MONACHORVM STIPENDIIS AD VICEM CESS IT EXCVIVS
REDITIBVS PRAEPARENTVR AFFAVILES DAPES HIS QVI EIVS NOMINI ANNVAE COLVER INT DIEM QVO IVSS O DOMINANTIS MICRAVERIT
AD CAELESTIA REGNA HOC QVORAM CONCILIO STAT VIT ATQVE FIRMAVIT VT SI QVIS VCCESSOR SED IS ECCLESIO Q ACTOR VEL ABBA
PREPOSITVS HVIVS VENERAVILIS TEMPLI PRAE NOMINATI FVNDVM CAMMILLARIA EX PARTEM VEL TOTVM PER QVO VIS INCENIO ABVSVM SERVOR DI
HIC DESERVIENTIVM MALIENARE PRAESVMSERIT VEL COMMVTARE AVT PERENFVTES VEL EOS CHARTVLA LARGIRE AETERNAM CNDEMNATIONE
SVSTINE AT CVM TRADITORE IVDAE T HIS QVI PETIERIT ET QVILARGIRE TEMTAVERIT CNSTRICTV ANATEMATIS VINCLIS CR TRECENTOR DECE ET OCTO PATRVM I

† HIC TVMV LVS CLNSVM SERVAT COR PVS DN

IOHANNIS SCISSIMI AC TER BE ATISS ARCHIEP

62. Charlemagne's palace chapel in Aachen (794–813), showing how he adopted an octagonal plan with a dome modelled on San Vitale. Some of the columns and marble revetment were almost certainly taken from Ravenna.

(S. Apollinare Nuovo) even if the king's image had been removed from the throne, as well as the Christian panels of the miracles and earthly life of Christ. He sensed and appreciated the pride Theoderic had taken in depicting his walled city and its fortified port at Classis, with ships riding at anchor (Plates 12–15). Visiting the king's mausoleum that stood just outside the city walls, with its awesome dome – the largest single stone roof anywhere – and enormous purple sarcophagus, Charles perhaps considered how to be buried in a comparably impressive fashion (Plate 17). Theoderic's combination of Germanic aggression and Byzantine statecraft created a startlingly relevant model for the Frankish king so recently raised to imperial status. The Gothic ruler embodied an adaptation of the most important elements of Roman imperial culture that Charles wished to impose in his *renovatio imperii*: a commanding Christianity, Roman law, efficient administration, and high standards of education. The integration of ancient Mediterranean traditions with now more vigorous, northern customs, personified by the new emperor, was symbolized by the equestrian statue of Theoderic.[20]

This famous statue no longer exists, but Agnellus describes it as 'a horse of bronze covered with gleaming gold, and its rider King Theoderic bore a shield on his left arm, holding a lance in his raised right arm'. Since he was born in the late eighth century, Agnellus could very well have seen the statue before it was moved some time after 801. It was set on a tall plinth, 6 cubits high; birds nested in its belly and flew in and out of its mouth and nostrils. It is said that it had been made for Emperor Zeno in the fifth century and Theoderic had embellished it with his own name. The antiquarian adds: 'whoever does not believe, let him make a journey to the land of the Franks, there he will see it.' On his third visit to Ravenna Charles declared he had never seen its equal and arranged its removal to Aachen, where he erected it directly in front of his palace – an exact imitation of its position in Ravenna, which was in turn modelled on Justinian's equestrian statue in Constantinople. It dominated the area between the palace and Charles's new chapel, inspired by the octagonal plan of Ravenna's San Vitale.[21] In 829 Walafrid Strabo wrote a poem about it, though he suggests that it engendered an evil presence, so we can be confident that it made the journey.

On both occasions when Charles was in Ravenna, Archbishop Valerius took great trouble to entertain him as he had done for King Louis in 792–3. He may have helped Charles to examine documents in the city archive that preserved the formula 'governing the Roman empire'. Valerius also knew that the most powerful ruler in the West, nearly sixty years old in 801, had assisted his predecessor Archbishop Leo in regaining the see of Ravenna from the intruder, Michael, and Leo in turn had cultivated very friendly relations with the Franks. Indeed, the archbishop continued this policy of close Carolingian contact as a way of countering papal claims to govern the now defunct exarchate. Charles reciprocated by not installing a civilian official in the city, thereby leaving Valerius in charge.

After the coronation of December 800, Pope Leo III also determined to consolidate stronger relations with Charles. He commemorated the ceremony by commissioning a magnificent gold mosaic to decorate the apse of a very large dining room (*triclinium*) he constructed in the Lateran palace, modelled on those in the Great Palace in Constantinople where visiting popes had been entertained. The main scene was of Christ and the Apostles, with two smaller images either side: on the left Christ handing the keys to Pope Sylvester and a banner to Emperor Constantine I, and on the right St Peter handing the papal *stola* (the equivalent of the pallium) to Leo III while he presented Charles with a standard.[22] Clearly, the pope was likening Charles to Emperor Constantine, while putting himself in a position equivalent to Pope Sylvester, drawing on the ideology of the *Donation of Constantine*. In this way, he intended to emphasize the authority of the bishop of Rome, who had endowed Charles with an imperial title that could be traced back to the first Christian Roman emperor. But Charles never saw it.

Charles returned to Francia in the summer of 801, sending envoys (*missi*) to Italy who exacerbated the rivalry between Rome and Ravenna over the territory and resources of the one-time exarchate. On Palm Sunday of 804, Archbishop Valerius of Ravenna invited these envoys to dine with him, leading Pope Leo to suspect that they were plotting against him 'in a disgraceful manner' (*turpitudo*).[23] He was convinced that the archbishop was not supporting the claims of St Peter to the exarchate, and feared that the emperor was also more interested in advancing his own authority in north-east Italy.[24] These anxieties provoked the pope's hasty visit to Francia, where he celebrated Christmas 804 with Charles at Quierzy.[25] After a very short stay, only eight days, Charles arranged for Leo to be escorted back to Ravenna, where he may have presented gifts from St Peter to the church of S. Apollinare in Classe : 'a white silk cloth with roses, with a gold-studded cross in the centre' and scenes from the life of the Lord 'and a fine silver canister with its chains weighing 15 lb'.[26] On this occasion he was informed of the decay of the basilica's roof beams and arranged for their replacement. But in letters to Charles, Leo continues to complain about Helmengaudus and Hunfridus, '*fideles vestros*', who had despoiled the resources of the *palatium*.[27]

While Archbishop Valerius could do nothing to prevent Charles from removing building material and even a large statue from Ravenna, he had himself been engaged in demolishing buildings no longer in use so as to construct new ones. Two old Arian *episcopia* sited outside the city walls provided materials for the building of his own *Domus Valeriana*.[28] A member of his clergy, a priest named Peter, used four elegant twisting columns in the construction of the magnificent ciborium of St Eleuchadius that may have come from an earlier monument and can now be admired at S. Apollinare in Classe.[29] Valerius also accumulated many valuable objects that he bequeathed to the church of Ravenna, including one described as 'a table in the form of a plane tree, entirely filled with silver vessels'.[30] His successor, Archbishop Martin, later presented it to John of Arles. A table in the form of a plane tree is rather difficult to imagine. If a central support represented the trunk, the table part could perhaps have been the leafy canopy of a plane tree, which in turn could have been filled with objects made of silver and gold.[31]

Archbishop Martin

In about 810 Valerius died and Martin, archdeacon of the church of Ravenna and abbot of the monastery of St Andrew, was elected archbishop. It was Martin who had been sent by Archbishop Leo to show Charles the little-known routes into the valleys of northern Italy, which allowed the king to surprise the Lombards in 774. He would therefore have met Charles over thirty years before. Now, immediately after his consecration as archbishop of Ravenna by Pope Leo, Martin 'sent his messengers to Francia, to the Emperor Charles, and the emperor was pleased'.[32] In the early ninth century when Agnellus was a young boy he was endowed with the monastery of S. Maria *ad Blachernas* by Martin. For this privilege, he handed over 200 gold *solidi* and the archbishop was so fat and strong that he could hold this weight in his left hand alone. From these coins, Martin made a gold liturgical vase in the shape of a seashell, which was still used for the chrism when Agnellus was writing.[33]

While Archbishop Martin cultivated good relations with Charles, he also tried to keep on good terms with Rome. He knew of the pope's extensive construction projects in the city and persuaded Leo III to lend him experienced workers to help restore the roof of S. Apollinare in Classe, which had collapsed in an earthquake.[34] As a result, Crisafus, the pope's *cubicularius* (a most trusted assistant) and other *caementa rii* (experts in building in brick), came from Rome and set up the new roof beams. To assist in this major restoration, Martin had ordered the suburban cities to bring materials and the citizens of Ravenna to work in a corvée of teams 'with ropes and other devices'. And once the church's roofing with its 'square colonnades' was repaired, Martin 'ordered the floors to be laid with *hypocartosis*' (marble opus sectile).[35] The archbishop also undertook the restoration of the church of St Euphemia called *ad Arietem*, which had been flooded.[36] In the marshy environs of Ravenna such incidents must have been frequent and techniques to control the water level were necessary.

The rivalry between Ravenna and Rome persisted beyond Charles's death in 814. After Pope Leo III's protests about 'irregularities' in the diocese of Ravenna, he appealed to Louis the Pious, Charles's successor, to intervene.[37] As a result, Louis instructed John, archbishop of Arles, to go to Ravenna and accompany Archbishop Martin to Rome. Agnellus, now a young man, might have witnessed his arrival and the enforced departure of Martin for Rome. But when the archbishop got to Nova, Agnellus tells us, he delayed 'pretending infirmity'. He sent word to the pope that he was so ill he couldn't ride his horse and was too weak to come. Leo III then gave up and Martin returned to Ravenna, where he entertained Archbishop John with much feasting.[38] Martin marked his success in thwarting the pope with a particularly lavish gift for John, the 'table in the form of a plane tree' selected from the treasury of Archbishop Valerius.

After the death of Leo III, Stephen, a deacon who had made a typical ecclesiastical career in the Lateran palace, was elected as Pope Stephen IV and immediately planned a visit to Emperor Louis. In October 816 the two met at Reims where they exchanged many gifts, attended many banquets and reinforced a papal–imperial alliance. The new pope also negotiated the successful return of Roman exiles who had been banished to Francia after the attack on Pope Leo III in 799. On the way back to Rome Stephen stopped in Ravenna, where he was welcomed by Archbishop Martin with full honours. The two prelates kissed and the pope 'celebrated mass in the Ursiana church, and displayed the sandals of the Saviour, which all the people saw'.[39] In this very public way, the church of Ravenna projected its profound devotion to the apostolic see, and resolved the problems that had disrupted their relationship. The presentation of Ravenna's most famous relics to the people of the city, probably a rare event, made an impact that Agnellus remembered. Pope Stephen's visit was clearly one of the high points of Archbishop Martin's episcopate.

Charles's Gifts to Ravenna

The friendly relations that Martin had cultivated with Charles produced a quite unusual result when the emperor's will was made public. He had laid out in careful detail how his accumulated wealth was to be used, and the church of Ravenna was to be a major beneficiary. It was to receive a silver table with an image of Rome, as well as various silver vessels and a cup of gold, which continued to be used in Agnellus' day. The historian emphasizes that the circular table was of solid silver without wood, with square silver feet, and had 'the image of all of Rome engraved' on it.[40] From Einhard's account of Charles's other benefactions, we know that a square table with an image of Constantinople engraved on it was sent to Rome.[41] These exceptionally valuable silver tables clearly represented Old and New Rome, the two leading patriarchal sees of the Christian world in the early ninth century.[42] Thus Charles sent an image of Rome to Ravenna, an evident reminder of the city's subordinate status; similarly, by sending an image of Constantinople to Rome he indicated that another capital city was superior to the pope's, a role that Aachen had now taken. Einhard adds that the emperor retained for his successors a third golden table, 'which is far superior to the others . . . which shows the entire universe in three concentric circles'.[43] It was to be added to the third part of Charles's inheritance reserved for his heirs, and distributions to the poor.

This was part of the considered, judicious and exact division of his glittering treasury that Charles had instigated before his death. Two-thirds of the valuable and precious objects collected in his treasury had been set aside for distribution to the twenty-one metropolitan sees under his rule. Ravenna features as the second on this list, immediately after Rome and followed by Milan, Cividale and Grado. The Italian bishoprics therefore dominated the highest ecclesiastical positions in his empire. The emperor had arranged for all this treasure to be divided into twenty-one coffers, each with the name of the city to which it was to be sent, so that the archbishops could distribute it. Similarly, they were instructed to send out two-thirds of this treasure to their suffragan bishops, keeping only one third for the metropolitan church. In this way the emperor's alms (*eleemosyna*) were to reach the largest number of people living in his empire.[44]

The recognition by Charles of Ravenna's particular eminence and the reconciliation between Archbishop Martin and Pope Stephen IV form a high point in the city's relations with the Carolingians. After the great king's death in 814, his heir, Louis the Pious, and his successors had serious problems on the Spanish, Saxon and Dalmatian frontiers of the empire and spent less time in Italy. In the ninth century Rome continued to criticize Ravenna, giving rise to several conflicts involving the imperial court in Constantinople and patriarchs Ignatios and Photios.[45] Archbishops gradually ceded control of outlying estates to the kings of Italy based in Pavia, and of maritime trade and communication to Comacchio and the rising centre of Venice to the north. Ravenna continued to be a source of plunder for forceful individuals such as Emperor Lothar, who ordered a fine piece of porphyry to be taken from San Severo and reinstalled as an altar table in a church of St Sebastian in Francia. Agnellus was ordered to make sure the workmen didn't break it as they raised it and its departure made him weep.[46] And not only the Carolingians but also other Italian rulers continued to regard Ravenna as a source of valuable building material. In about 831 Theodore, bishop of Bologna, stole an early Christian sarcophagus for his own burial.[47] Powerful visitors arrived, inspected the monuments and selected the elements they would take away.

In spite of these continued removals, archbishops of Ravenna sustained and increased their local resources in a way that seems typical for wealthier cities in the ninth century. They benefitted from 'a convergence of interest between the economic expansion of the cities and the ambition of the bishops to play an ever more important political role.[48] Numerous donations to the church reflected local loyalty and civic support for Ravenna's most powerful leader. From the moment when Exarch Eutychios failed to defend the city against Lombard attack, the citizens had selected prominent men to take over the task. In Archbishop Sergius they called on a layman, whose success in winning some degree of independence from the Lombard conquerors had been extended by his successors. This was how the city tried to deal with all overlords, even the most prominent rulers of the West such as Charles. Its archbishops were able to consolidate their hold on territory, arrange favourable leaseholds to lay owners, and collect more donations and bequests from local Christians in a web of patronage and agricultural exploitation that lasted for centuries.

The churches of Ravenna, staffed and maintained by clergy who received higher salaries than many provincial bishops, were also supported by monastic communities, whereas secular buildings were not so well protected. Similarly, when they decayed the naval facilities that had made Classis a great port were not renewed. Decades of silt from the estuaries of the Po clogged up the channels that linked Ravenna to the sea, and deterred sailors from using them. In the ninth century the city was unable to participate in the development of the Adriatic as one of the most important seaways of the Mediterranean, where the adventurous merchants of Comacchio and, above all, Venice, forged new links with all the ports of the eastern coast, from Istria to Dalmatia. They continued south around southern Greece and on to Constantinople, the Levant and, especially, Alexandria, creating a permanent presence.[49] Imported pottery, coins and artefacts now being excavated at San Severo in Classe indicate that Ravenna kept in touch with Adriatic trade, but its part in this expanding commercial world was reduced.

Instead, Venice took over its role as the pivot of relations between East and West. From the ninth century onwards, the Venetian republic developed its unique archipelago of trading warehouses that were both secure from land attack and had direct access to the sea. Ravenna's exclusion from the new networks of trade and communication meant that its small, compact centre survived and its churches, with their unique mosaic records, remained under the guardianship of clerics who had the means and the determination to preserve them without the need to modernize. While Venice became the chief point of entry into western Europe for Byzantine artefacts, political ideas and culture after 800, the formative role of early Christian artistic achievements remained enshrined in Ravenna. There the confidence and promise commemorated in the mosaics that adorned its churches, the inscriptions and monuments that recorded its prominence under Roman emperors, Gothic kings and Byzantine exarchs, continued to inspire generations of visitors even as they puzzled over its gradually forgotten role in European history.

Conclusion
The glittering legacy of Ravenna

In 751 the Lombards captured Ravenna and thus strengthened their capacity to threaten Rome; the Frankish leader Pippin assumed the kingship with papal approval; the Abbasids established a new regime at Baghdad; and the eastward expansion of Islam clashed with imperial China near the Talas river.[1] Whether these coincidences form a critical turning point in global history or not, there was a fundamental shift in Europe that forced Pope Stephen II to seek a military alliance with the Franks. This freed Rome from its traditional relationship with Constantinople and set the papacy on a new trajectory, immediately reinforced by the forged *Donation of Constantine*. If the role of Ravenna was crucial to this history, why did it not produce its own historians to celebrate its importance?

It probably did, but the zenith of the city's influence occurred too early and most records from that time have not survived. Before he died in 526 Theoderic commissioned Cassiodorus to write a *History of the Goths* but it only survives in Jordanes' version. Archbishop Maximian, who inserted his image and name next to Justinian's in the famous San Vitale mosaic, wrote a history. In the ninth century Agnellus told his listeners, 'read the chronicle of Archbishop Maximian: there you will find many things about her [the Empress Galla Placidia] and about many Emperors and Kings.'[2] We cannot do so for the chronicle is lost to us. Nor do we have a copy of the illustrated *Annals of Ravenna*, the calendar that recorded the city's life and times. Such losses that we know about are matched by others of which even the memory has been vaporized. There is a great deal of losing and forgetting about Ravenna as well as physical dismantling, which is also a form of forgetting.

The fate of Cassiodorus' writing and his library is a striking example of the centrality and dissipation of Ravenna's influence. His father served as provincial governor and, from his estates in Scyllacium (Squillace) in southern Italy, supplied horses for the army. He supported the Goths against the enfeebled late fifth-century Roman administration and sent his bookish son to the court of the new Gothic king, who had spent his formative years in Constantinople. Cassiodorus became a leading mandarin – the man who wrote official letters for the Gothic rulers and sprinkled them with his own rhetorical expertise on a wide variety of topics, designed to show off his skills. After the capture of Ravenna in 540, Belisarius took King Witigis and many Goths and members of the administration back to Constantinople, including, it seems, Cassiodorus. He stayed in the Queen City for about fifteen years, editing his own correspondence, known as the *Variae*, while finding, copying and having unfamiliar texts translated.[3] In 554, when Justinian's Pragmatic Sanction guaranteed their estates to exiles or émigrés who had fled to the East, he returned to Scyllacium and founded a monastery called Vivarium after its fishponds. His collected manuscripts formed the base of the library, where he drew up clear instructions, the *Institutions of Divine and Secular Learning*, that taught monks to cherish secular as well as spiritual works.[4] When he died at a great old age, well over ninety, his collection was dispersed or lost. Some scattered volumes were later found at the Benedictine monastery of Monte Cassino, others disappeared. But his great work of instruction, *De orthographia*, on how to make and copy manuscripts, remained a guide for later monks in Italy and beyond.

Without Ravenna and its multilingual traditions Cassiodorus might have been no more than a studious Roman monk. But identifying the city's role in the formation of western Christendom is as challenging as filling the many gaps in the history of Cassiodorus' scriptorium. We do, however, have one historian, Agnellus, writing in the mid-ninth century three hundred years after Cassiodorus. His *Book of the Pontiffs* is an absolutely crucial testimony to the history of Ravenna, listing the lives and times of all the bishops of the city from its conversion to Christianity.

Its effect is to set out how the bishops of Ravenna played a vital role in the continuity of its administration. Through his determination to glorify these ecclesiastical rulers, Agnellus captured the rise of a civic, city-anchored identity in Ravenna, with both religious and secular components. Constricted by its structure as a list of the holy fathers, it is leavened by its discursive storytelling and asides, such as the one just quoted about Maximian's *Chronicle*. Agnellus' *Book of the Pontiffs* often embellishes half-remembered, sometimes mythic accounts that imagine triumphs and conveniently invented episodes. For all his unreliable details, he demonstrates how the church of Ravenna was a major force in Italy. He shows how its leaders built up resources, keeping close control over its landed estates in remote areas (Sicily, Istria, Dalmatia), and attracted additional gifts of land and produce from local inhabitants. It then used its accumulated wealth to beautify the city with monuments decorated in the most extravagant, fashionable styles, using the most sought-after, imported materials.

In other cities throughout the West, bishops assumed leadership roles that gave them authority in the political sphere and confirmed their importance to the well-being of their sees (for instance, in Clermont-Ferrand, Arles, Seville or Trier). But more than any of these, in Ravenna bishops such as Maximian, Damianus, Felix and Sergius, whom I have tried to bring to life, focused the loyalty of local inhabitants into a self-confidence that ensured the city's self-preservation and also projected its power across north-east Italy and even further afield. We sense the force of this civic religion in the welcome given to Archbishop Peter in the 570s when he returned from his consecration in Rome and the Ravennati went out to greet him with celebratory songs. Such formal ceremonies for the arrival of a newly appointed archbishop, accompanied by chants in Greek and Latin, were later reworked for Charlemagne and other western emperors. A similar collective spirit endorsed the reconciliation organized by Exarch Callinicus and Archbishop Marinianus in 599 when Maximus of Salona came to Ravenna to be readmitted to communion with Pope Gregory I, and when Archbishop Damianus successfully resolved the bloody intercommunal battles of the late seventh century with a penitential procession involving the entire population. Another key moment occurred when Exarch Theodore persuaded the clergy at S. Apollinare in Classe to return to the city and resolve their dispute with Archbishop Theodore. At these solemn and carefully arranged ceremonies the authority of the church of Ravenna, represented by its leader, often with the collaboration of the exarch, concentrated the inhabitants' attention on their city. With immense pride they exalted their leaders and celebrated their own participation in symbolic instances of the 'most noble' Ravenna, as its mosaics glittered from the walls.

Whether or not Agnellus exaggerated these moments, as he read his book out loud to his audience, he also reminded them of the existing inscriptions that recorded the activity of these bishops, their contribution to the city's appearance and the elegant sarcophagi that marked their final resting places. As S. Apollinare in Classe gradually became the church in which most archbishops elected to be buried, close to the early Christian patron of the city, their tombs were designated as places for ritual veneration, where annual commemorations of past leaders could be performed. In these ways, the civic role of church leaders became deeply implanted in the collective memory and could be reasserted when the city needed confirmation of its achievements.

Today the historian of Ravenna has to work with surviving evidence that is only a very partial trace of what was once recorded and even less of a record of what happened. Indeed, already in the ninth century Agnellus often referred to buildings and monuments that had been dismantled or decayed. Hence the need to treat the sources that do survive forensically, to work out what they can tell us about both the major events and how life was lived in Ravenna. It is a process that demands imagination and rethinking the role of Ravenna. For while the historian must be tethered to the tangible evidence of primary accounts, she can't limit herself to their remains. So, I've joined a close investigation of life in Ravenna, including legal and medical as well as religious and cosmographical ideas, with the larger panorama of shaping influences to try and overcome some of the gaps caused by such losses.

An instance of the physical loss is visible in the impressive basilica dedicated to Christ that Theoderic built as his palace church, now S. Apollinare Nuovo. The mosaic image of the Great Palace of the king dominates the southern wall at the western end, opposite another of the harbour at Classis. From these secular representations of the twin cities, two immense processions of saints, male and female, advance towards the Virgin and Christ. Within the image of the PALATIUM a colonnade of eight chambers flanks a larger central space in which Theoderic was enthroned. Here, acclaimed on either side by courtiers, the great king was pictured in his glory.

But we do not see him.

Let's pause on the extraordinary example of an image of a secular ruler and his court so prominently put up in a church. In palaces and city squares equivalent images would be normal. There is a long tradition of such displays of power, for instance in Constantinople, where Theoderic would have seen them as a young man. Emperors, their wives and victorious generals like Belisarius were portrayed in mosaic in public spaces, even though none have survived. Indeed, Agnellus refers to the existence of mosaics of Theoderic in his palaces at Pavia and elsewhere. But in Ravenna Theoderic followed the example set by Galla Placidia, who had erected portraits of herself, her children and her ancestors in the church of S. Giovanni Evangelista, which she had commissioned about seventy years earlier. Placidia was probably the first Christian from a ruling imperial family to place an image of herself within the sanctuary of a church – a boldness that appears to have been limited to Ravenna for many decades. When Theoderic did the same on a spectacular scale, it was to counter the example of an empress who had once been married to a Goth.

At the same time, through his wise management of the separation of Gothic Arians from local Catholic Christians, Theoderic insisted on a degree of toleration and permitted Bishop Ecclesius to plan the construction of San Vitale. After the king's death and the successful reconquest of Gothic Italy by imperial troops under Belisarius, Bishop Victor and Ravenna's new rulers made their counterclaim to imperial authority. The unique representation of Justinian and Theodora right in the sanctuary of a very unusual octagonal church was their response to Theoderic's blazing presence in his golden palace church. And it is because they are in churches that have been in continuous use that they have survived.

Or at least partially, for within about fifteen years of the dedication of San Vitale's imperial panels in 547, Arianism was prosecuted. Theoderic's basilica was converted to the Catholic faith. The mosaic images of the two cities were left intact. But within the palace and in front of the harbour wall, the images of the heretic Arian king and his courtiers were cut away. The central space that had been Theoderic's was filled with gold tesserae as if in his honour, while curtains replaced the figures within the colonnade. Only the hands of courtiers that overlapped with pillars and the feet of those who stood in front of the harbour wall were left behind, while the bodies were obliterated. Of Theoderic's portrait not even a fingernail survives.

It is easy to imagine how Theoderic might have appeared enthroned. Agnellus relates that in the palace there was a mosaic of him on horseback holding lance and shield, flanked by personifications of the cities of Rome and Ravenna. Ravenna was said to have one foot in the sea and another on land, a symbolic vision of the watery environment.[5] In its prime his palace would have been covered with such mosaic images of Theoderic and his victories, now reduced to dust. Indeed, the best construction elements of the palace were later recycled so thoroughly for new uses that excavation has revealed only traces of their foundations. Possibly when Charlemagne visited the city, he could have seen some of them.

What is certain is that in 787, 800 and finally, as the newly crowned emperor in 801, Charlemagne looked upon the panel of Justinian, whose faith he shared, whose laws he respected, in the apse of San Vitale. His gaze, however, was not that of a tourist, primed to experience the unparalleled achievements of 'early Christian art'. For him, the representations of Christ, of scenes from the Old Testament and of the emperor and empress bearing their gifts to the altar, were expressions of the power of God, with Justinian as his true representative on earth. The images proclaimed a social order and its purpose, setting an example for Charlemagne to follow.

This he did by ordering the construction of his palace chapel at Aachen to adopt the unfamiliar octagonal form of San Vitale with building materials taken from Ravenna. In Rome, where he was crowned, Charlemagne doubtless admired the Christian churches and mosaics put up by bishops in the vast ancient capital, now depopulated and still filled with collapsing monuments to a failed pagan empire. But it was Ravenna, built for purpose as a Christian capital, that the Frankish ruler determined to emulate. And he also took with him the great statue of a mounted emperor that Theoderic had made to represent himself. The Gothic king may have been an Arian, but he was also an invader reshaping the legacy of Rome, with whom Charlemagne could identify. In addition, the most powerful western ruler of the late eighth century saw himself as the successor to the Emperor Justinian as portrayed in the mosaic panel, opposite his wife Empress Theodora, both of them participating in a liturgical procession. In this integration of Christian philanthropy, imperial distinction and exceptionally rich symbolic costume, Byzantium set the standard: this is what it means to be an emperor.

If Ravenna was so central to the process of fusion that Constantin-ople initially oversaw and Charlemagne eventually personified, why has this not been recognized? The city's monuments have attracted many academic studies; its mosaics continue to inspire with continuing vital-ity across one and a half millennia. Yet Ravenna itself seems voiceless. This creates a second level of loss due to the fact that its leading role was thrust upon it by outsiders, first by Honorius, the emperor who abandoned Roman Britain to invading forces, then found himself faced with similar problems in Milan and moved his capital to Ravenna. Almost certainly it was Stilicho who calculated that this small centre had advantages that would protect the court from attack: a well-constructed harbour at Classis that ensured immediate access to the sea route to Constantinople, as well as to imperial territories in Istria and Dalmatia across the Adriatic; a setting dominated by water and marshes that made it very hard to besiege, with a relatively undevel-oped urban plan that allowed the imperial court to impose its presence, while – in strategic terms – its conquest was uninviting for an army determined to control the Italian peninsula.

Ravenna was in effect chosen again by Theoderic as the capital for his kingdom, as this reinforced his claim to be the legitimate repre-sentative of the East Roman empire. His realm would extend over the whole of Dalmatia as well as today's southern France and Catalonia – territories at least as great in extent as modern Italy, which he also ruled. Under his regal authority and informed by his experience of the imperial court, Ravenna became the fulcrum of energies that engendered early Christendom. Perhaps if Theoderic had been able to pass on this achievement to a capable son, born and trained in Ravenna, the kingdom would have become an independent state. But he produced only a daughter, though she made a remarkable effort to continue his rule. The problem of the succession was also related to the particular form of Theoderic's authority. As a Gothic king ruling in official association with the emperor in Constantinople, he was unable to create the equivalent of a senate, such as existed (however feebly) in Rome, in the eastern capital and, later, in Venice. His Gothic *comitatus* of noble counsellors and largely Roman-style administra-tion represented distinct interests that could not unite to secure the power and interests of the city when the succession crisis became real.

Instead, Theoderic's achievements were claimed directly by Constantinople. After Belisarius' successful reconquest of Carthage in North Africa, his eastern forces arrived in Ravenna in 540 to impose a government appointed by Emperor Justinian. The two exarchates of North Africa and Italy received imperial investment and kept the ideal of city life alive in what remained of the western empire. By 540 Ravenna was a perfect centre for the exercise of imperial influence, whose power originated elsewhere. The city became Constantinople's entry point into western Europe for government personnel, imported goods such as papyrus from Egypt, silks, spices and ivory, legal, liturgical and theological texts and changing ideas about imperial rule that circulated in the Mediterranean world. It was a hub for the dissemination of Justinian's new laws (*Novellae*) as well as fashions in architecture, court etiquette, saints' *Lives*, Neoplatonic philosophy and even dress. Through Constantinople's insistence on the closer integration of Germanic, Gothic and Arian loyalties, Christian laws promulgated in the East also protected women, children and slaves in a firm legal framework that endured and influenced other legal codes. While Carthage, Syracuse and Naples also provided entry points, ease of access to transalpine regions via the Po valley gave Ravenna primacy in this role of disseminating imperial decrees and benefits.

The administrative pattern of the exarchate meant that Ravenna was dependent on Constantinople. It did not lack a culture of self-belief, as is clear both from its pioneering, belligerent contests that became a mark of city life in northern Italy, and its Cosmographer who placed the 'most noble Ravenna' at the centre of the known world. But it could not generate and direct its own future. And the external forces that dominated the city were themselves constrained and redirected by much larger developments across the four hundred years of Ravenna's prominence, from the arrival of Honorius in 402 to the third and last visit of a very different emperor in 801.

The city rarely 'made history' in an obvious, shaping fashion. Despite its intellectual, artistic, legal and medical contributions, in the fraught centuries that generated early Christendom, Ravenna was never fully its own agent, as classical Rome had been, as Byzantium became and as Venice would become. Local writers surely attempted to record the city's history and achievements, but more powerful centres did not feel the need to acknowledge its influence.

In two phases the Roman empire gave way, first in the West and later in the South-East, bringing a shared emphasis on belief and religious observance, which lay at the heart of the world of Islam as well as early Christendom in both its eastern and western forms.[6] Although Islam made little immediate impact in the city of Ravenna, the wider consequences of its rapid spread resulted in a basic transition, 'from bread and circuses to soup and salvation'.[7] For the Roman world had been built on control of the Mediterranean coastline and the granaries of Egypt and North Africa had fed Rome and Constantinople.

Recent studies of 'the decline and fall of the Roman empire' in the West have taken quite opposite positions. Some insist on the highly destructive nature of barbarian incursions that led to a catastrophic and total collapse, followed by impoverishment and division after Charlemagne. They brand Byzantium's effort to sustain its authority as one of these hostile external forces, a perspective that updates but narrows the 'decline and fall' of Rome so brilliantly documented and mourned by Gibbon. Others find more evidence of piecemeal assimilation and gradual integration.[8] Against both views, I have attempted to show that creation and innovation accompanied the conflicts and immiseration; that what had been the western Roman empire experienced the birth pangs of a new social order as much as the death throes of the old one. A long process engendered the new social, military and legal order we can call early Christendom.

As we have seen, many distinct forces destabilized the influence of classical Roman authority once based on the Tiber, both internal – the overextension that expanded the empire beyond its own capacities – and external – the pressure of many 'barbarian' forces along the frontiers that were now too long to defend. And all these coincided with the threat of alternative centralized powers – Persia and, later, Arabia – to replace the entire Roman order with their own language, religion and legal structure. Constantine I's creation of a new eastern capital was partly motivated by the need to mobilize against such serious threats, as well as the greater wealth of the eastern provinces. It transferred and thus sustained the Roman empire in an overtly Christian setting, combining ancient administrative, technical and legal capacities with the popular energies and theological claims of Christian faith, and the learning and culture of Greece. Through this transformed legacy of antiquity Constantinople eventually achieved the ambition that had eluded classical Rome: it inspired its armies under the banner of Christ, the symbol of the cross and the icon of Mary and crushed Persia.

But this eastern shift weakened the western half of empire and the poorly defended ancient capital, where a very different transformation took place. The western challenge of the Goths, Burgundians, Franks and Lombards was quite different to that of the great Persian empire at Ctesiphon or of the Arab centre at Mecca. Although the Huns were primarily destructive, most of the newcomers, having lived for several generations in close contact with the empire, sought to make the Roman way of life their own on imperial territory. They deprived it of essential tax revenue and supplies, while adopting many of its features. Crucially, they all embraced Christianity as their faith and most used Latin for their written texts, though the Goths maintained their own Arian Christian definitions celebrated in Gothic. They brought undeniably novel ideas and practices into the world that had been dominated by polytheistic Roman political rule for centuries, and assailed classical attitudes towards city life and the countryside, commerce and overseas trade, diet, dress, education, the family and religious belief. But they did so while claiming to reproduce the new Roman faith of Christianity and absorbing the Roman legal system codified by Theodosius II and Justinian. Many had been recruited into the Roman armies or held at arms-length by alliances and treaties that also began to integrate them into the Roman world, which was itself changed in the process and then overrun. In the north-western region of the Roman world this process led to what we know as the medieval civilization of the West, with its ferocious, restless dynamics.

During the turbulent fifth century, across the West, the result was an overall urban decline accompanied by ruralization.[9] It is particularly marked at Rome, where the vast population that had been accommodated within very extensive city walls dropped from perhaps 600,000 before the sack of 410 to only tens of thousands by the sixth century.[10] This meant that there were never enough men to defend the city, although when the city gates were firmly closed it was still difficult to capture by assault. As the enormous palaces, baths, temples, theatres, villas and *insulae* (large blocks of apartments) were no longer regularly used, they inevitably fell into disrepair. Christian monuments slowly took their place, adapting some old buildings to new uses or re-employing their solid building material for new constructions.[11] Similar stories fill the pages of contemporary chronicles, describing how, throughout the West, cities shrank.

The exception was Ravenna. The source of its flourishing was the eastern Roman empire, which renewed and consolidated its authority not only in the capital but also across its provinces, where new palaces, churches, aqueducts, baths and charitable institutions surpassed the monuments of ancient Rome. As Rome became depopulated, Constantinople expanded, adding a third to its size in 413 by the construction of the huge ring of walls with towers, later supplemented by an outer wall and a walled moat that stand to this day. Ravenna shared in this imperial expansion, as Honorius, Galla Placidia and local bishops patronized new buildings, making it an outstanding exception to the degeneration of most classical cities and settlements. With Constantinople's approval, Theoderic integrated eastern influence into Ravenna's Christian Gothic administration that made the king more Roman than most Romans. While he appeared to conform to Gothic ideas of kingship, he brought to the West a grasp of imperial traditions that consolidated a very particular combination of elements: an understanding of the importance of law and the administration of justice; an acknowledgement of the differences in Christian belief that made a degree of toleration essential; a respect for superior Greek education; and a capacity to collaborate with the best-qualified and most-skilled individuals who could assist his ambitions. Through these features, observed and adopted in the East, Theoderic oversaw the symbiosis of Germanic and Roman elements into a meaningful unity, which would be continued under the exarchs thereafter.

As well as his great church of S. Apollinare Nuovo, Theodoric's mausoleum is a telling witness to this integration of 'barbarian' and imperial Roman qualities. Here the king who had dominated the West, governing in the name of the eastern rulers of Constantinople, had constructed a domed tomb fit for an emperor. Visitors even today can marvel at the single slab of Istrian marble that forms the roof – how on earth did they raise it in the early sixth century? And once installed, why did it survive? Most early Christian buildings that remain standing today do so because they have been continuously occupied, renovated and kept in use as sacred buildings, often by monastic communities in Ravenna. The more secular palaces, residences, assembly halls, houses and trading places that make up medieval settlements rarely retain such attention, were often pillaged for building material and then replaced by grander, better constructed, more fashionable or serviceable edifices. At some date Theoderic's tomb was transformed from its funereal function into a nunnery, and this kept it in use. But its original purpose was not forgotten, and the king's fame was preserved in the huge purple sarcophagus still visible.

In other western regions a similar symbiosis occurred, from Visigothic Spain to the Anglo-Saxon, Frankish and Burgundian kingdoms, where court rituals, coinage, imperial costume and patterns of patronage were imitated. But in north-east Italy the imperial framework provided by the eastern capital in Constantinople requires particular emphasis. For without Byzantium, there would have been no 'western Europe'. After the Arab conquests of the eastern and southern coasts of the Mediterranean, Constantinople barred their expansion into the European continent through the seventh and eighth centuries. In defending the Queen City in 667–9 and 717–18, the eastern emperors provided the shield that excluded Islam from further advances into the West; they scattered a massive Arab mobilization, which would otherwise have unified the entire Mediterranean under its sway. In 732 Charles Martel's victory at Poitiers also frustrated Umayyad expansion north of the Pyrenees, but this was an opportunist raid seeking treasure and weakness, not the full-scale mobilization by land and sea that fell upon – but failed to take – the Queen City.

The significance of Constantinople in the transformation of western Europe was not merely that of an outward shield, however. The imperial framework exercised a cultural hegemony that facilitated a fusion of non-imperial forces and transmitted a variation of its own policy of acculturation to the West via the Gothic king Theoderic and the exarchs. Through its capital in Ravenna the empire sustained the ideal of efficient government sanctioned by law within the West itself. In multiple ways its benefits commanded respect and a tinge of admiration for the eastern emperors among even the most hostile enemies, and in Italy an underlying loyalty to Constantinople persisted through the sixth century and beyond. The influence of Byzantium was diffused especially through Ravenna. The city acted as an essential catalyst to the development of a society that would eventually outstrip it. In this way the Christianized New Rome was a constant, built-in inspiration for the powers that took over the West. Charlemagne has traditionally been hailed, in Alcuin's phrase, as the 'father of Europe', as if he acted alone.[12] But the foundations of western Christendom that he exemplified were laid in Ravenna, whose rulers, exarchs and bishops, scholars, doctors, lawyers, mosaicists and traders, Roman and Goth, later Greek and Lombard, forged the first European city.

Notes

Primary texts

AASS	*Acta Sanctorum*, 71 vols. (Paris 1863–1940).
ACO	*Acta Conciliorum Oecumenicorum* (Berlin and Leipzig 1922–74); new series II (Berlin 1984–92), III (Berlin 2008).
Annales of Ravenna	B. Bischoff and W. Koehler, 'Eine illustrierte Ausgabe der spätantiken Ravennater Annalen', in *Medieval Studies in Memory of A. Kinsley Porter* (Cambridge MA 1939) vol. I, pp. 125–37.
Anon. Vales	*Anonymous Valesianus,* ed. T. Mommsen, in MGH *AA* IX; ed. and tr. J. C. Rolphe (London 1952) in vol. 3 of *Ammianus Marcellinus.*
CC	Codex Carolinus, ed. W. Gundlach in *MGH Epp* III (Berlin 1957).
CCL	Corpus Christianorum Latinorum. Series Latina (Turnhout 2003–)
CIG	*Corpus Inscriptionum Graecarum*, ed. A. Boeckh, 4 vols. (Berlin 1828–77).
CIL	*Corpus Inscriptionum Latinarum*, 16 vols. (Berlin 1862–1989).
CJC	Corpus Juris Civilis, ed. T. Mommsen, P. Krueger et al., 3 vols. (Berlin 1928–9).
CLA	*Chartae Latinae antiquiores. Facsimile Edition of the Latin Charters Prior to the Ninth Century*, eds. A. Bruckner and R. Marichal (Olten 1954–).
CSEL	*Corpus Scriptorum Ecclesiasticorum Latinorum* (Vienna 1866–)
CTh	*Codex Theodosianus*, ed. T. Mommsen, 2 vols., tr. C. Pharr, *The Theodosian Code and Novels* (New York 1952, repr. 2001).

Eunapius	in *Fragmentary historians*
Fragmentary historians	*The Fragmentary Classicising Historians of the Late Roman Empire*, ed. and tr. R. C. Blockley, with Historiographical Notes (Liverpool 1953), ARCA Classical and Medieval Texts, Papers and Monographs, 10.
Gregory the Great, *Regesten*	MGH *Epp. I and II, Registrum epistolarum*, eds. P. Ewald and L. M. Hartmann (Berlin 1887–99).
ILS	*Inscriptiones Latinae selectae*, ed. H. Dessau (Berlin 1856–1931, repr. 1951–5 and Dublin 1974).
John of Antioch	*Ioannis Antiocheni fragmenta quae supersunt omnia*, ed. and tr. S. Mariev (Berlin 2008). Selections in *Fragmentary historians* and in C. D. Gordon, *The Age of Attila. Fifth-century Byzantium and the Barbarians* (Ann Arbor 1972).
Laurent, *Médaillier*	V. Laurent, *Les sceaux byzantins du Médaillier vatican* (Vatican City, Rome 1962).
LP	*Liber pontificalis. Texte, introduction et commentaire*, ed. L. Duchesne, 2 vols. (Rome 1886–92); tr. R. Davis, vol. 1 *The Book of the Pontiffs (Liber pontificalis). The Ancient Biographies of the First Ninety Roman Bishops to AD 715* (Liverpool 1989); vol. 2 *The Lives of the Eighth-Century Popes* (Liverpool 1992); vol. 3 *The Lives of the Ninth-Century Popes* (Liverpool 1995).
LPR	*Agnellus of Ravenna. The Book of the Pontiffs of the Church of Ravenna*, tr. with an introduction and notes D. M. Deliyannis (Washington DC 2004).
	Latin text with German trans. C. Nauerth, Agnellus von Ravenna, *Bishofsbuch*, 2 vols. (Freiburg im Breisgau 1996)
Malalas, *Chronicle*	*The Chronicle of John Malalas*, tr. E. Jeffreys, M. Jeffreys and R. Scott, Byzantina Australiensia 4 (Melbourne 1986).
Malchus	in *Fragmentary historians*.
Mansi	J. D. Mansi, *Sanctorum Conciliorum nova et amplissima Collectio*, 53 vols. (Paris and Leipzig 1901–27).
Marcellinus	*The Chronicle of Marcellinus*, tr. B. Croke, Byzantina Australiensia 7 (Sydney 1995).
Marini	G. Marini, *I Papiri diplomatici, raccolti ed illustr.* (Rome 1805).
MGH	Monumenta Germaniae Historica
AA	*Auctores Antiquissimi*, 15 vols. (Berlin 1877–1919), including vol. XI *Chronica Minora*.

Epp	*Epistolarum*, 8 vols. (Berlin 1887–1939).
SRG	*Scriptores rerum Germanicarum in usum scholarum*, n.s., 13 vols. (Berlin and Weimar 1920–67).
SRL	*Scriptores rerum Langobardicarum et italicarum saec. VI–IX* (Hannover 1878).
SRM	*Scriptores rerum Merovingicarum*, 7 vols. (Hannover 1885–1920).
SS	*Scriptorum*, 32 vols. (Hannover 1826–1934).
Nikephoros, *Short Chronicle*	Nikephoros Patriarch of Constantinople, *Short History*, ed. and tr. C. Mango (Washington DC 1990).
Olympiodoros	in *Fragmentary historians*.
Orosius	Orosius, *Historia adversos paganos*, tr. R. J. Deferrari, *Seven Books of History Against the Pagans* (Washington DC 1965, repr. 2001).
Paul the deacon, *HL*	*Historia Langobardorum,* ed. G. Waitz, MGH *SRL*; tr. W. D. Foulke (Philadelphia 1907), repr. with an introduction by E. Peters (Philadelphia 1974).
PG	*Patrologia Graeca*, ed. J. P. Migne, *Patrologia cursus completus, series Graeco-Latina* (Paris 1857–1903).
PL	*Patrologia Latina*, ed. J. P. Migne, *Patrologia cursus completus, series Latina* (Paris 1844–1974).
PLRE	*Prosopography of the Later Roman Empire*, ed. J. Martindale, vol. IIA and B (395–527), (Cambridge 1980); IIIA and B (Cambridge 1992).
PmbZ	*Prosopographie der mittel-byzantinischen Zeit (641–867),* ed. R.-J. Lilie et al., 6 vols. (Berlin and New York 1999–2002).
Priscus	Priscus in *Fragmentary historians*.
Procopius	Procopius, *Wars*, ed. and tr. H. B. Dewing, 6 vols. (New York 1914–40).
Pros. Chrét. Italie	*Prosopographie de l'Italie chrétienne (313–604)*, ed. c. Pietri, 2 vols. (Rome 1999).
Prosper Cont.	Prosper of Aquitaine MGH *AA XI Chronica Minora* I, Continuation of Prosper, tr. A. C. Murray, *From Roman to Merovingian Gaul* (2003).
Regesta	Regesto in *Storia di Ravenna* vol. II/1, with additions in II/2.

RFA	Royal Frankish Annals, ed. F. Kurze, MGH *SRG* (Hannover 1895), tr. B. W. Scholz in *Carolingian Chronicles* (Ann Arbor 1972).
Schlumberger, Seals	G. L. Schlumberger et al., *Sigillographie de l'empire byzantin* (Paris 1884).
Socrates	Socrates, *Church History*, in *A Select Library of Nicene and Post-Nicene Fathers of the Christian Church*, ed. and tr. P. Schaff, second series, (Edinburgh 1989).
Sozomen	Sozomen, *Historia ecclesiastica*, ed. and tr. P. Schaff as above.
Theophanes, *Chron-ographia*	*Theophanis Chronographia*, ed. C. de Boor, 2 vols. (Leipzig, 1883, 1885); tr. C. Mango and R. Scott, *The Chronicle of Theophanes Confessor*, (Oxford 1997).
Tjäder, *Papyri*	J.-O. Tjäder, ed., *Die nichtliterarischen lateinischen papyri Italiens aus der zeit 445–700*, 3 vols. (Lund 1954–82).
Var	Cassiodorus, *Variae*, MGH *AA* XII; tr. S. Barnish *Cassiodorus:* Variae (Liverpool 1992).
Zacos, Seals	G. Zacos and A. Veglery, *Byzantine Lead Seals*, vol. I in 3 parts (Basel 1972).
Zosimos	Zosimos, *New History*, tr. R. T. Ridley, Byzantina Australiensia 2 (Canberra 1982).

Secondary works

Brown, *Gentlemen and Officers*	T. S. Brown, *Gentlemen and Officers. Imperial Administration and Aristocratic Power in Byzantine Italy, A. D. 554–800* (Rome 1984).
Bury, *LRE*	J. B. Bury, *History of the Later Roman Empire from the Death of Theodosius to the Death of Justinian*, 2 vols. (New York 1958).
Cirelli, *Archeologia*	E. Cirelli, *Ravenna Archeologia di una città* (Ravenna 2008).
Cosentino, *PiB*	S. Cosentino, *Prosopografia dell'Italia bizantina (493–804)*, 2 vols. (Bologna 1996–2000).
Deichmann, *Ravenna*	F. W. Deichmann, *Ravenna. Hauptstadt des spätantiken Abendlandes*, 4 vols. (Stuttgart 1958–89), I (1958), II/1 (1974), II/2 (1976), II/3 (1989).
Deliyannis, *Ravenna*	D. M. Deliyannis, *Ravenna in Late Antiquity* (Cambridge 2010).

Guillou, *Régionalisme*	A. Guillou, *Régionalisme et indépendance dans l'empire byzantin au VIIe siècle; l'exemple de l'Exarchat et de la Pentapole d'Italie* (Rome 1969).
Jäggi, *Ravenna*	C. Jäggi, *Ravenna: Kunst und Kultur einer spätantiken Residenzstadt: die Bauten und Mosaiken des 5. und 6. Jahrhunderts* (Regensburg 2013).
Jones, *LRE*	A. H. M. Jones, *The Later Roman Empire, 284–602*, 3 vols. (Oxford 1964).
Mango, *Art*	C. Mango, *The Art of the Byzantine Empire 312–1453* (Englewood Cliffs, NJ 1980, repr. Toronto 1986).
NCMH	*New Cambridge Medieval History*, vol. I, *c.500–c.700*, ed. P. Fouracre (Cambridge 2005); vol. II, *c.700–c.900*, ed. R. McKitterick (Cambridge 1995).
ODB	*Oxford Dictionary of Byzantium*, ed. A. P. Kazhdan et al., 3 vols. (Oxford and New York 1991).
Storia di Ravenna	*Storia di Ravenna*, 5 vols. (Ravenna 1990–1996); vol. I, *L'evo antico*, ed. G. Susini (1990); vols. II/1 and II/2 ed. A. Carile (1992).
Wolfram, *Goths*	H. Wolfram, *History of the Goths*, tr. T. J. Dunlap (Berkeley/Los Angeles/London 1990).

Journals

BMGS	*Byzantine and Modern Greek Studies.*
CARB	*Corsi di Studi sull'Arte Ravennate e Bizantina.*
DOP	*Dumbarton Oaks Papers.*
EME	*Early Medieval Europe.*
GRBS	*Greek Roman and Byzantine Studies.*
JÖB	*Jahrbuch der Österreichischen Byzantinistik*
PBSR	*Papers of the British School at Rome.*
REB	*Revue des études byzantines.*

INTRODUCTION

1. http://www.resistenzamappe.it/ravenna/ra_liberazione/bombardamento_chiesa_di_s_giovanni_evangelista.

CHAPTER I

1. A. R. Birley, 'The third century crisis in the Roman Empire', *Bulletin of the John Rylands Library* 58.2 (1976), pp. 253–81.

2. M. P. Lavizzari Pedrazzini, ed., *Milano, capitale dell'impero romano 286–402 d C.* (Milan 1990); R. Balzaretti, *The Lands of St Ambrose: Monks and Society in Early Medieval Milan* (Turnhout 2019), pp. 116–19, 137–53.

3. S. Williams, *Diocletian and the Roman Recovery* (London 1985), pp. 111–14.

4. R. Krautheimer, *Three Christian Capitals. Topography and Politics* (Berkeley/Los Angeles/London 1983).

5. The practice of burial had gradually replaced the ancient tradition of cremation on a funeral pyre.

6. W. V. Harris, *Roman Power: A Thousand Years of Empire* (Cambridge 2016) and de facto division of empire with senior and junior emperors, pp. 170–85, 188–91, 219–40.

7. E. Prinzivalli, 'L'Arianesimo: La prima divisione fra i Romani e la prima assimilazione dei popoli migranti', in *Cristianità d'Occidente e Cristianità d'Oriente (secoli VI–XI)*, Settimana 51 (Spoleto 2004) I, pp. 31–60; origins of the Arian hierarchy, F. R. Whelan, *Being Christian in Vandal Africa: The Politics of Orthodoxy in the Post-Imperial West* (Oakland, California 2018).

8. On the acts of the Council of Aquileia, *Religions of Late Antiquity in Practice,* ed. R. Valantasis (Princeton 2000), pp. 275–88; on Arianism in Milan, N. B. McLynn, *Ambrose of Milan. Church and Court in a Christian Capital* (Berkeley/Los Angeles/London 1994), pp. 102–5, 124–37.

9. See the famous description in Ammianus Marcellinus, bk 16, 10, 1–16, cf. J. Matthews, *The Rome Empire of Ammianus* (London 1989), pp. 10–12.

10. P. Heather and J. Matthews, *The Goths in the Fourth Century* (Liverpool 1991).

11. S. Williams and G. Friell, *Theodosius. The Empire at Bay* (London 1994), pp. 52–5; J. H. W. G. Liebeschuetz, *Barbarians and Bishops* (Oxford 1991).

12. E. Demourgeot, *De l'unité à la division de l'empire romain 395–410* (Paris 1951); S. Mazzarino, *Stilichone: la crisi imperiale dopo Teodosio* (Rome 1942), pp. 317–24, 334; Harris, *Roman Power*, pp. 228, 237–40, 279–89.

13. P. Squatriti, 'Marshes and mentalities in early medieval Ravenna', *Viator* 23 (1992), pp. 1–16; *idem, Water and Society in Early Medieval Italy, AD 400–100* (Cambridge 1998); P. Fabbri, 'Il controllo delle acque tra technica ed economia', in *Storia di Ravenna* II.1, pp. 9–25.

14. G. B. Montanari, 'L'impianto urbano e i monumenti', in *Storia di Ravenna* I, pp. 229–32; Cirelli, *Archeologia*, pp. 33–5.

15. G. Maioli, 'Classe', in *Storia di Ravenna* I, pp. 375–414 and App. 1, pp. 415–55; V. Manzelli, *Ravenna* (Ravenna 2000).

16. Procopius *Wars*, V. i. 16 (he had visited the city); Squatriti, 'Marshes and mentalities'.

17. *Flumen aquaeductus*, ed. L. Prati (Bologna 1988), pp. 13–56, 95–123; Y. A. Marano, '"Watered . . . with the Life-giving Wave". Aqueducts and water management in Ostrogothic Italy', in *Ownership of Land and Natural Resources in the Roman World*, eds. P. Erdkamp, K. Verhhoeven and A. Zuiderhoek (Oxford 2015), pp. 150–69, esp. 154–7, 164–9; *Acqua*, Settimana 55 (Spoleto 2008); *Cura Aquarum*, ed. G. Cuscito, *Antichità Altoatriatiche A* 87 (2018).

18. S. Corcoran, 'Roman law in Ravenna', in *Ravenna, Its Role in Earlier Medieval Change and Exchange*, eds. J. Herrin and J. Nelson (London 2016), pp. 163–97, at 163–4.

19. Claudian, Panegyric (404), tr. M. Platnauer (Loeb, vol. II), pp. 74–123; S. Mazzarino, *Stilichone: la crisi imperiale dopo Teodosio* (Rome 1942), pp. 99–103; Alan Cameron, *Claudian: Poetry and Propaganda at the Court of Honorius* (Oxford 1970), pp. 37–45.

20. P. Veyne, *Bread and Circuses: Historical Sociology and Political Pluralism* (London 1990); H. Lejdegård, *Honorius and the City of Rome. Authority and Legitimacy in Late Antiquity* (Uppsala 2002).

CHAPTER 2

1. Claudian's *Epithalamion*, speech for the wedding of Honorius and Maria, tr. Platnauer (Loeb, vol. I), pp. 240–67; Alan Cameron, *Claudian: Poetry and Propaganda at the Court of Honorius* (Oxford 1970), pp. 98–101; J. Herrin, 'Mothers and daughters', in *Unrivalled Influence: Women and Empire in Byzantium* (Princeton 2013), pp. 80–114.

2. Olympiodoros, fg. 13; CTh VII 13.16 and 17, dated April 17 and 19, 406, in Ravenna.

3. Sozomen, 9. 4. 4–8; Olympiodoros, fg. 5, tr. p. 157. Serena was then put to death in Rome by order of the Senate, Zosimus, 5.34, 35, 38, 38. Whether Placidia had any part in this decision is unclear; V. A. Sirago, *Galla Placidia e la trasformazione politica dell'Occidente* (Louvain 1961), pp. 84–9 claims that she approved.

4. Marcellinus, anno 410, pp. 9–10; Olympiodoros, fg. 6, tr. p. 159. On Olympiodoros, an easterner writing in Greek, see P. van Nuffelen, 'Olympiodorus of Thebes and eastern triumphalism', in *Theodosius II: Rethinking the Roman Empire in Late Antiquity*, ed. C. Kelly (Cambridge 2013), pp. 130–52.

5. Olympiodoros, fg. 14.

6. Olympiodoros, fg. 6; two other senatorial figures, Rusticius and Phoeba-
   dius, were among the hostages. They and the ex-emperor Attalus later
   assisted at her wedding.
7. Olympiodoros, fgs. 22, 24. Pointing to the proximity to Narbonne of a villa
   recently excavated to reveal its late antique decoration, H. Sivan, *Galla Placidia: The Last Roman Empress* (Oxford 2011), pp. 9–36 suggests that it
   might provide a setting for such a sumptuous event. Olympiodoros, fg. 26,
   records that Athaulf had been married before and had children from his first
   marriage whom a Bishop Sigesarus tried to protect.
8. Orosius, *Historia adversus paganos*, 7.43, stresses her influence on Athaulf,
   see J. F. Matthews, *Western Aristocracies and Imperial Court AD 364–425*
   (Ann Arbor 1995), pp. 316–18 on Athaulf praising 'her political wisdom';
   M. Harlow, 'Galla Placidia: conduit of culture?' in *Women's Influence on
   Classical Civilisation*, ed. F. McHardy (London 2004), pp. 138–50.
9. Olympiodoros, fg. 26; Wolfram, *Goths*, pp. 164–6.
10. J. Salisbury, *Rome's Christian Empress: Galla Placidia Rules at the Twi-
    light of the Empire* (Baltimore 2015), pp. 92–4.

CHAPTER 3

1. A. Augenti, 'Archeologia e topografia a Ravenna: il Palazzo di Teoderico
   e la "Moneta Aurea" ', *Archeologia medievale* 32 (2005), pp. 7–33; *idem*, ed.,
   Palatia. Palazzi imperial tra Ravenna e Bisanzio (Ravenna 2003); Jäggi,
   Ravenna, pp. 78–9, and ill. 49, p. 80; Cirelli, *Archeologia*, pp. 90–91.
2. *Anon. Vales* 80, tr. p. 559, mentions the circus on the occasion of Euthar-
   ius' consulship. Circus mosaics, Jäggi, *Ravenna*, pp. 80–81; Sidonius
   Apollinaris, *Poems,* tr. W.B. Anderson (Loeb 1936), XXXIII to Cosen-
   tius, ll. 307–427, with a long description of the private games given at
   Ravenna by Valentinian III, in which Consentius participated with success, see also Ch. 5; Alan Cameron, *Circus Factions* (Oxford 1976), p. 67;
   LP 75.2 tr. p. 69, the head displayed on a pole. For the porphyry statue
   currently in the Archiepiscopal Museum, Jäggi, *Ravenna*, ill. 34, p 72.
3. Cirelli stresses the destruction of older buildings to provide material for
   new ones, 'Spolia e riuso di materiali tra l'Antiquità e l'alto Medioevo a
   Ravenna', *Hortus Artium Medioevum* 17 (2011), pp. 39–48; Cirelli,
   Archeologia, pp. 54–69; N. Christie, 'The city walls of Ravenna: the
   defence of a capital AD 402–750', *CARB* 36 (1989), pp. 1–38; N. Christie
   and S. Gibson, 'The city walls of Ravenna', *PBSR* 66 (1988), pp. 156–97.
4. Augenti, 'Archeologia e topografia a Ravenna'.
5. *Agnellus of Ravenna. The Book of the Pontiffs of the Church of Ravenna*,
   tr. with an intro. and notes D. M. Deliyannis (Washington DC 2004);
   A. Carile, 'Agnello storico', in *Storia di Ravenna* II.2, pp. 373–8; T. S.

NOTES TO PP. 26-30

Brown, 'Romanitas and Campanilismo: Agnellus of Ravenna's view of the past', in *The Inheritance of Historiography 350–900*, eds. C. Holdsworth and T. P. Wiseman (Exeter 1986), pp. 107–14 (fairly negative about Agnellus as historian); M. Pierpaoli, *Il libro di Agnello istorico. Le ricerche di Ravenna antica fra storia e realtà* (Ravenna 1988); M. Sot, 'Local and institutional history (300–1000)', in *Historiography in the Middle Ages*, ed. D. Deliyannis (Leiden 2003), esp. pp. 100–104.

6. *LPR* cc. 3, 6, 7, 9, 12 (burials at St Probus), tr. pp. 105, 106, 107, 108, 109; J.-C. Picard, *Le souvenir des évêques. Sépulture, listes épiscopales et culte des évêques en Italie du Nord des origines au Xe siècle* (Rome 1988), pp. 123–30.

7. Liberius, *LPR* c. 22, tr. p. 118; Florentius, *LPR* c. 21, tr. p. 117.

8. K. Weitzmann, 'The selection of texts for cyclic illustration in Byzantine manuscripts', in *Byzantine Books and Bookmen*, eds. I. Ševčenko and C. Mango (Washington DC 1975), pp. 69–109 and pl. 15; B. Bischoff and W. Koehler, 'Eine illustrierte Ausgabe der spätantiken Ravennater Annalen', in *Medieval Studies in Memory of A. Kinsley Porter* (Cambridge Mass. 1939), recorded in the year 412, vol. I, pp. 125–37.

9. Plaque in the Archiepiscopal Museum and sarcophagus at S. Apollinare in Classe.

10. Tjäder, *Papyri* I, no. 59, pp. 252–3, and commentary p. 309. Although this record consists of three tiny fragments of papyrus later re-used, the dialogue between Contius and the other men can be partly reconstructed, because the court proceedings follow a formulaic routine. A similar protocol recorded in 504 follows the same pattern. Contius, the church notary, is also called *prodecurius*, i.e. he takes the place of one of the three *decuriones sacri consistorii* attached to the court. F. Santoni, 'I Papiri di Ravenna. *Gesta municipalia* e procedure di insinuazione', in *L'Héritage byzantine en Italie (VIIIe–XIIe siècle). I La Fabrique documentaire* (Rome 2011), pp. 9–32; G. Nicolaj, 'Breve viaggio fra i documenti altomedievali dell'Italia bizantina (cenni di sintesi)', in the same volume, pp. 169–87.

11. Jones, *LRE* II, pp. 737–9, 747.

12. Jones, *LRE* II, pp. 752–7. With the arrival of Odoacer and then the Gothic kings, Ravenna's council appears to have administered local government in the traditional style, but from 540 when Belisarius returned Ravenna to imperial rule, the city came under the closer control of officials appointed from the East, chiefly the praetorian prefect who resided there.

13. Ursus, originally buried in the Ursiana church of the Anastasis that he founded, but later moved (Agnellus is not sure), *LPR* c. 23, tr. p. 120. If the earlier date for his death is taken, the church would have been built between 370 and 396, a period when very little is recorded about Ravenna and there

is no evidence for such wealthy patrons and artistic brilliance. Deichmann, *Ravenna* III, pp. 169–70, argues for 396, Picard and Deliyannis for 426. Agnellus confuses two bishops named Peter, *LPR* c. 27, tr. p. 124, and this accounts for the discrepancy in various lists of bishops, e.g. as compiled by Deichmann, *Ravenna* III, pp. 173–4; D. M. Deliyannis, *Ravenna*, pp. 307–8, and Picard, *Le souvenir des évêques*, table 15, pp. 747–8.

14. *LPR* c. 23, tr. pp. 118–19. Agnellus identifies the north as the women's area, and the south as that for men, perhaps reflecting the places where they stood for the service.

15. *LPR* c. 23, tr. p. 119 (he reports that in the mid-ninth century nothing was left of this mechanism but an old stable, destroyed). *L'Acqua nei secoli altomedievali*, Settimana 55 (Spoleto 2008); *Cura Aquarum*, ed. G. Cuscito, *Antichità Altoatriatiche* 87 (2018).

16. Six suffragan bishops had been transferred to Ravenna by 451, when Vicohabentia, Forum Cornelii, Forum Livii, Faventia, Bononia and Mutina were no longer listed under Milan, Deichmann, *Ravenna* III, pp. 170–71.

17. Bischoff and Koehler, 'Eine illustrierte Ausgabe', p. 129 and the obverse of the fragment, col. 1.

CHAPTER 4

1. Olympiodoros is our main source for this period of Galla Placidia's life; on his point of view, see P. van Nuffelen, 'Olympiodorus of Thebes and Eastern Triumphalism', in *Theodosius II: Rethinking the Roman Empire in Late Antiquity*, ed. C. Kelly (Cambridge 2013), pp. 130–52. The barbarian escort is mentioned at fg. 38, tr. p. 203, probably a unit of Athaulf's private household cavalry (*bucellarii*).

2. Olympiodoros, fg. 33 (see also fgs. 7, 22, 24–6), tr. pp. 158–61, 184–5, 186–91, 196–7. By marrying an imperial princess Constantius now stood in line to succeed Honorius; M. Harlow, 'Galla Placidia: conduit of culture?' in *Women's Influence on Classical Civilisation*, ed. F. McHardy (London 2004), pp. 138–50, esp. 146, contrasting her fertility with Honorius' failure to produce children.

3. One year later Honorius issued a rescript concerning papal elections, which was designed to resolve such disputes. *LP* 44.1–4 tr. pp. 34–5. Galla Placidia's new mosaic decoration in the church of S. Croce in Gerusalemme, associated with Empress Helena, was recorded in an inscription now lost.

4. Olympiodoros and Philostorgius, fr. 33, tr. pp. 197–9. If this promotion was interpreted as making Constantius his successor, the eastern emperor Theodosius might have had grounds for objecting.

5. Olympiodoros, fr. 38, tr. p. 201.

6. J. Herrin, 'Late antique origins of the "Imperial Feminine": western and eastern empresses compared', *Byzantinoslavica* 74 (2016), pp. 5–24 at 13–14; J. Kent, *The Roman Imperial Coinage, vol. 10. The Divided Empire and the Fall of the Western Parts (395–491)* (London 1994), nos. 230–31, 263, 305, 426, 1804; D. Angelova, *Sacred Founders: Women, Men and Gods in the Discourse of Imperial Founding, Rome Through Early Byzantium* (Oakland 2014), pp. 193–5.

7. M. McEvoy, *Child Emperor Rule in the Roman West 367–455* (Oxford 2013).

8. Olympiodoros ends his history here, fg. 43; J. F. Matthews, *Laying Down the Law. A Study of the Theodosian Code* (New Haven 2000), pp. 3–4.

9. The classic study by P. Veyne, *Bread and Circuses: Historical Sociology and Political Pluralism* (London 1990) remains an unrivalled analysis of how Roman rulers developed this method of sustaining popular support. For the order of the factions, Cassiodorus, *Var.* III 51.5, tr. pp. 68–9; Alan Cameron, *Circus Factions* (Oxford 1976), p. 66.

10. In his funeral speech for Theodosius I in 395. On the power of empresses in late antiquity, see J. Herrin, 'The Imperial Feminine in Byzantium', *Past and Present* 169 (2000), pp. 3–35, repr. in *Unrivalled Influence: Women and Empire in Byzantium* (Princeton 2013), pp. 161–93; Herrin, 'Late antique origins of the "Imperial Feminine"'; L. James, *Empresses and Power in Early Byzantium* (London 2001); Anja Busch, *Die Frauen der theodosianischen Dynastie* (Stuttgart, 2015).

11. Kent, *The Roman Imperial Coinage 10.*

12. Tjäder, *Papyri* II, 59, pp. 252–3; a more detailed analysis in Tjäder, 'Ein Verhandlungsprotokoll aus dem Jahr 433 N Chr. (Pommersfelden, Papyrus Lat. 14R)', *Scriptorium* 12 (1958), pp. 3–43. Caecilius, *prodecurius*, is named as the official in charge, and Contius is the *notarius* of the church involved, cf. Ch. 3 n. 10 above. The *prodecurius* was one of the three *decurii sancti consistori*, officials each in charge of a group of ten *silentiarii*, Tjäder, *Papyri* I, pp. 277–8

13. *Annals of Ravenna*, p. 132.

14. *PLRE* IIA, p. 220, Bassus may have been responsible for a case brought against Pope Sixtus, *LP* 46.1–2, tr. p. 36. The document may be a forgery, and there is a contradiction between the alleged date of the case and his position as praetorian prefect.

15. C. Pietri, 'Les aristocraties de Ravenne (Ve–VIe s.)', *Studi Romagnoli* (1983), pp. 643–73, at 647–9; on Consentius, *PLRE* IIA, pp. 308–9.

16. No named official is recorded as *magister officiorum, quaestor sacri palatii, comes sacrarum largitionum, praepositus sacri cubiculi, magister scriniorum* or *agens in rebus* between 425 and 437, and no *quaestor, comes rei privatae* or *magister scriniorum* in the 18 years, 437 to 455. Valentinian appointed 2 or 3 *magistri officiorum* but no officials under them.

17. Marcellinus, anno 430/31, tr. p. 14, notes the death of Felix, which Agnellus attributes to Aetius, *LPR* c. 31, tr. p. 134; John of Antioch fg 201 (3), tr. Gordon p. 50; *PLRE* IIA, pp. 461–2 (Felix), IIA, 22–9 (Aetius).

18. *LPR* c. 49, tr. pp. 159–61.

19. Matthews, *Laying Down the Law*, pp. 24–5, with n. 52 citing T. Honoré, *Law in the Crisis of Empire, 377–455 AD: The Theodosian Dynasty and its Quaestors* (Oxford 1998), pp. 249–51; F. Millar, *A Greek Roman Empire: Power and Belief under Theodosius II (408–450)* (Berkeley 2006), pp. 56–7, is more sceptical and emphasizes the eastern pressure behind all the laws issued in the West between 425 and 429, including the *Law of Citations*.

20. Honoré sees the hand of Galla Placidia behind the law and attributes its authorship to Antiochus, *Law in the Crisis of Empire*, pp. 249–51, 255; S. Corcoran, 'Roman law in Ravenna', in *Ravenna, Its Role in Earlier Medieval Change and Exchange*, eds. J. Herrin and J. Nelson (London 2016), pp. 163–97, at 164–5, suggesting that Helion, *magister officiorum*, might have been the author.

21. Orosius, *Historia adversus paganos*, 7.43.

22. Matthews, *Laying Down the Law*, pp. 13–16.

23. Ibid., pp. 4–5, on the commemoration of the marriage displayed in the mosaic decoration described by Merobaudes, see F. M. Clover, *Flavius Merobaudes* (Philadelphia 1971), pp. 11, 16–27 for the poem.

24. Corcoran, 'Roman law in Ravenna', pp. 165–6.

25. T. Honoré on Galla Placidia's responsibility, picked up by J. Salisbury, *Rome's Christian Empress: Galla Placidia Rules at the Twilight of the Empire* (Baltimore 2015), pp. 148–9; Matthews, *Laying Down the Law*, pp. 6–7, 24–8, 76, 87.

26. On the Law of Citations, see Matthews, *Laying Down the Law*, pp. 24–6, 96–7, 100, for their place in the *CTh*, and pp. 101–18 on the first 5 books of *CTh*, in which the law is cited; S. Oost, *Galla Placidia Augusta: A Biographical Essay* (Chicago 1968), p. 219. On the importance of the *Breviary of Alaric*, Matthews, *Laying Down the Law*, pp. 87–9.

27. Matthews, *Laying Down the Law*, p. 247, n. 114.

CHAPTER 5

1. Deichmann, *Ravenna* II/1, pp. 90–93; Deliyannis, *Ravenna in Late Antiquity*, pp. 74–84; Jäggi, *Ravenna*, pp. 102–16; wonderful photographs in M. David, *Ravenna Eterna* (Milan 2013), pp. 75–101.

2. G. Pavan, 'I mosaici della chiesa di S. Croce a Ravenna: vecchie e nuovi ritrovamenti', *Felix Ravenna* ser. 4, 127–30, (1984/5), pp. 341–80; M. David, 'La Basilica di S. Croce. Nuovi contributi per Ravenna tardoantica', *Biblioteca di Felix Ravenna* 15 (Ravenna 2013). A fragment of plaster with

tesserae excavated from S. Croce, now in the National Museum, captures the skill of the mosaicist setting a starry sky similar to the dome of the Mausoleum.

3. *LPR* c. 41, tr. pp. 148–50.

4. G. Mackie, 'The Mausoleum of Galla Placidia: a possible occupant', *Byzantion* 65 (1995), pp. 396–404; *eadem*, 'New light on the so-called St Lawrence Panel at the Mausoleum of Galla Placidia, Ravenna', *Gesta* 29.1 (1990), pp. 54–60, identifying the figure as St Vincent, a Spanish saint beloved by Galla Placidia. On the many theories and Mackie's proposal that Placidia's first-born son Theodosius was brought back to be buried here, see D. M. Deliyannis, ' "Bury me in Ravenna". Appropriating Galla Placidia's body in the Middle Ages', *Studi Medievali* scr 3, XLII.1 (2001), pp. 289–99.

5. On the use of the Mausoleum for tourism, see B. M. Thomas, *Ravenna as a Capital: Art and Display as Discourse in Late Antiquity and Beyond*. PhD, University of Leicester (2018), online at https://lra.le.ac.uk/bitstream /2381/42512/1/2018ThomasBMPhD.pdf.

6. C. Fiori and E. Tozzola, *San Giovanni Evangelista a Ravenna* (Ravenna 2014), pp. 18–19, noting that it would be doubtful for Honoria to be represented in the apse after her scandalous approach to Attila (which is here dated to 434). Much later medieval sources describe the naval storm in great detail, the assistance of Placidia's confessor, St Barbaziano, and the miraculous acquisition of a relic of St John (his sandal), which facilitated the dedication of the church, see E. Schoolman, *Rediscovering Sainthood in Italy: Hagiography and the Late Antique Past in Ravenna*, new edn (New York 2016).

7. Fiori and Tozzola, *San Giovanni Evangelista*, with reconstructions of the way the inscriptions and portraits were displayed, figs. 13–16, pp. 34, 35, 37, 38. Also in Deliyannis, *Ravenna*, pp. 63–70 and Jäggi, *Ravenna*, pp. 91–101.

8. Fiori and Tozzola, *San Giovanni Evangelista*, coloured photos, pp. 67–78. Photos of the WW2 bombing, e.g. Jäggi, *Ravenna*.

9. Such as S. Maria Maggiore (432–40) in Rome, or the original church of Hagia Sophia, Holy Wisdom, in the eastern capital.

10. *LPR* c. 41, tr. p. 149.

11. *LPR* c. 27, tr. p. 124 and glossary under *scenofactor* pp. 337–8; *LPR*, Nauerth, *Bischofsbuch* I, pp. 148–9.

12. Theodoretos, letter 112 to Domnus, bishop of Antioch, *PG* 83, 1309–11, lists the most important bishops of the West as Milan, Aquileia and Ravenna; Deichmann, *Ravenna* II/3, pp. 170–71.

13. *St Peter Chrysologus*, CCL 24B Sermones II, ed. A. Olivar (1975), p. 799; *Selected Sermons*, tr. G. E. Ganss, *Fathers of the Church* 17 (Washington DC 1953), p. 130.

14. Many of these pre-Christian rites continued despite ecclesiastical canons against them, see, CCL 24B, sermo. 155, pp. 962–8, tr. Ganss, pp. 261–4; sermo. 129, tr. Ganss, p. 214; B. Filotas, *Pagan Survivals: Superstitions and Popular Cultures in Early Medieval Pastoral Literature* (Toronto 2005), pp. 157–8, 161–2, 168–71; and note the costume of Winter in the Seasons' mosaic floor in the *Domus dei Tappeti*, G. Montevecchi, *Archeologia Urbana a Ravenna. La 'Domus dei Tappeti di Pietra'* (Ravenna 2004), pp. 107–8.

15. E. Swift and A. Alwis, 'The role of late antique art in early Christian worship: a reconsideration of the iconography of the "starry sky" in the "Mausoleum" of Galla Placidia', *PBSR* 78 (2010), pp. 193–217 and 352–4; *LPR* c. 150, tr. p. 274, on Archbishop Felix advising clerics to use the sermons which he had edited.

16. Cassiodorus, *Var.* XI 1.9, tr. p. 147.

17. *LPR* c. 40, tr. p. 148; Deichmann, *Ravenna* II/3, pp. 223–4, on the theatre, circus and games celebrated at Ravenna. On the proximity of palace to Hippodrome, M. C. Carile, *The Vision of the Palace of the Byzantine Emperors as a Heavenly Jerusalem* (Spoleto 2012), p. 5 n. 18, p. 12 n. 63, p. 21; Cirelli, *Archeologia*, pp. 86–7, 90–92. Valentinian may indeed have inaugurated his new palace at the Laurel with celebratory games but most of Agnellus' information about Valentinian and his mother is very confused, although he claims to have found it in a history written by Bishop Maximian, now lost.

18. Sidonius Apollinaris, *Poems* I, tr. W.B. Anderson (Loeb 1936), pp. 296, 298, 302–12, cf. ch. 3.

19. P. Heather, *The Fall of the Roman Empire. A New History* (London 2005), cites the different accounts, pp. 335–6; A. Richlin, 'Julia's Jokes, Galla Placidia, and the Roman Use of Women as Political Icons', in *Arguments from Silence: Writing the History of Roman Women* (Ann Arbor 2014), pp. 81–109, esp. 102–9; M. McEvoy, *Child Emperor Rule in the Roman West 367–455* (Oxford 2013) for the suggestion that Honoria could have been 'held in reserve', just in case Valentinian III died young and without heirs.

20. Famously observed by Priscus during his embassy to the Huns in 449, *Fragmentary historians*, pp. 246–95.

21. Placidia persuaded her daughter to marry the elderly senator Herculanus and the marriage may have been one of the reasons for the court's move to Rome in 450. Although Attila never went to Ravenna, Agnellus preserves an entirely imaginary account of his visit to the city, another example of his inventiveness, which may be modelled on the entry of Theoderic in 493.

22. *Life* of Germanus of Auxerre, tr. F. R. Hoare, *The Western Fathers* (London 1954), chs. 35–6, pp. 313–20.

23. *Var.* XI 1.9

24. In a very confused account of the *Life* of St Peter Chrysologus, Agnellus alludes to this letter to the Council of Chalcedon that met in 451, when both he and Placidia were dead, *LPR* c. 48, tr. pp. 157–8. In fact, Peter had written to sup-

port the condemnation of Nestorios and in support of Flavian, see G. E. Ganss, *St Peter Chrysologus Selected Sermons* (New York 1953), Appendix pp. 285–7. After the flurry of correspondence which preserves the two instances of Placidia's literary capacity, there is no further instance of her letter-writing.

25. Roman influence is clear in Theoderic's palace church (scenes of the Gospel stories) and in Bishop Ecclesius' foundation, S. Maria Maggiore (522–32), Cirelli, *Archeologia*, p. 100. M. Clayton, *The Cult of the Virgin Mary in Anglo-Saxon England* (Cambridge 2002), pp. 26–37, on a feast in her honour that was celebrated on the Sunday before Christmas in Milan and Ravenna in the seventh century, possibly the Immaculate Conception (8 or 9 December).

26. *Acts of the Council of Chalcedon*, tr. R. Price and M. Gaddis, 3 vols. (Liverpool 2005), II, no. 22, pp. 14–24, III, 161–2.

27. *Acts of the Council of Chalcedon*, III, 160, 169.

28. D. MacCulloch, *A History of Christianity: The First Three Thousand Years* (London 2009), pp. 227–8 (distinguishing *mono physis*, only nature, from the *mia physis*, one nature).

29. Letter 56 of the letters of Pope Leo I, tr. C. L. Feltoe, in *A Select Library of Nicene and post Nicene Fathers of the Christian Church*, ed. P. Scaff, 2nd series, vol. 12 (Oxford/New York 1895), p. 58; and letter 58, tr. F. Millar, *A Greek Roman Empire: Power and Belief Under Theodosius II (408–450)* (Berkeley 2006), pp. 37–8; S. Oost, *Galla Placidia Augusta: A Biographical Essay* (Chicago 1968), p. 291 n. 137.

30. Theodosius II and Eudocia had a son, Arcadius, and another daughter, Flacilla, who both died young. Their surviving daughter Licinia Eudoxia had been married to Valentinian III. In 438 Empress Eudocia had gone to Jerusalem and settled there after a scandal. Theodosius did not remarry or adopt an heir.

31. *The Acts of the Council of Chalcedon*, II, pp. 14–24; Pulcheria's letters in vol. I, pp. 93–4, 107–8; Millar, *Greek Roman Empire*, Appendix on the material included in the council proceedings, clarifies the different versions of the letters (Latin and Greek translations), which are presented in a more complex fashion by E. Schwarz in the edition of the *Acta Conciliorum Oecumenicorum*.

32. Prosper Cont. c. 12, MGH *AA XI Chronica Minora* I, p. 489.

CHAPTER 6

1. M. Humphries, 'Valentinian III and the City of Rome, 425–55', in *The Two Romes: Rome and Constantinople in Late Antiquity*, eds. L. Grig and G. Kelly (Oxford 2012), pp. 161–82, citing letters of Leo I, nos. 55–58 (see Ch. 5, n. 29 above); D. Barritt, 'The Roman revolution: Leo I, Theodosius II and the contest for power in the fifth century', in *Trends and Turning Points: Constructing the Late Antique and Byzantine World*,

ed. M. Kinloch (Leiden 2019), pp. 115–32, completely ignores the period of Valentinian III's minority when the court in Ravenna was run by Galla Placidia, 425–38. During his sole rule of 17 years, Valentinian spent more than half in Ravenna and only the last 5 years continuously in Rome.

2. He withheld his approval of Marcian's accession until March 452, Prosper Cont. c. 21, MGH *A A XI Chronica Minora* I, p. 490 (the icons of Emperor Marcian were received at Rome).

3. Priscus, fg. Book I, 9.3, 2,100 lbs gold; and I, 9.4, 6,000 lbs gold and 1,000 lbs annual tribute, *Fragmentary Historians* II, pp. 236–7, 240–41.

4. Dagron, *Naissance d'une capitale: Constantinople et ses institutions de 330 à 451* (Paris 1974), pp. 48–76.

5. Priscus, fg. Book V. 30, *Fragmentary Historians* II, pp. 326–31.

6. Ibid., pp. 330–31 and n. 135 p. 393.

7. By Henri Grégoire, a revolutionary Catholic bishop, who opposed Robespierre and wrote treatises against slavery and racism, see https://en.wikipedia.org/wiki/Henri_Gr%C3%A9goire (consulted 21 Sept 2019).

8. Tjäder, *Papyri* I, 1 pp. 172–8 = Marini 73, *CLA* XX, 705. The record consists of three fragments.

9. G. Fasoli, 'Il patrimonio della Chiesa Ravennate', in *Storia di Ravenna* II, 1, pp. 389–400, citing the evidence from Pope Gregory the Great; L. Ruggini, *Economia e Società nell' 'Italia annonaria': rapporti fra agricoltura e commercio dal IV al VI secolo d.C.* (Milan 1961, repr. Bari 1995), pp. 103–5, cf. 262–4 on Theoderic's *annona* in grain raised from Sicily and sent to Gaul in 509–10, which was shipwrecked.

10. *LPR* c. 111, tr. p. 228, and Fasoli, 'Il patrimonio'.

11. Tjäder, *Papyri* I, 1 (as above); the ship is mentioned on p. 174.

12. *LPR* c. 28, tr. p. 125.

13. Deichmann, *Ravenna*, II/1, p. 17.

14. *LPR* c. 28, tr. p. 125.

15. A. Wharton, 'Ritual and reconstructed meaning: the Neonian Baptistery in Ravenna', *Art Bulletin* 69 (1987), pp. 358–75.

16. *LPR* c. 24, tr. p. 121.

17. *LPR* c. 25, tr. pp. 121–22.

18. *LPR* c. 30, tr. pp. 129–33. Presumably the image showed Christ with a strong arm, perhaps like the St Menas' icon where Christ has his protective arm around the saint's shoulder.

19. *LP* 46.4, tr. p. 37. Before 455 Valentinian III presented one to St Peter's in Rome, which showed Christ surrounded by the 12 apostles shown in 12 portals, all gold and decorated with very precious jewels, in thanks for prayers answered; it was associated with 400 lbs of silver that decorated the same area of the tomb of St Peter. Compare this with the 1,610 lbs of silver used on a silver colonnaded screen (*fastigium*) at the Constantinian

basilica which the same emperor provided after the barbarians (Vandals) had removed the original.

20. Bawit icon of St Menas in the Louvre, Paris, reproduced in colour in *Christian Egypt*, ed. M. Capuani (Cairo 2002), pl. 4, p. 35, and the wall paintings of the Red Monastery now brilliantly restored, *The Red Monastery Church: Beauty and Asceticism in Upper Egypt* , ed. E. Bolman (New Haven 2016).

21. Dennis Trout, 'Inscribing identity: the Latin epigraphic habit in Late Antiquity', in *A Companion to Late Antiquity*, ed. P. Rousseau (Chichester 2009), pp. 327–41, cf. *LPR* c. 29, tr. pp. 126–7.

22. LPR c. 29, tr. p. 127, Deichmann, *Ravenna*, II/2, pp. 314–15; M. Mazzotti, 'La cripta della chiesa ravennate di S. Francesco dopo le ultime esplorazioni', *CARB* (1974), pp. 217–30, esp. 227–8; J.-P. Caillet, *L'évergetisme monumental chrétienne en Italie et à ses marges* (Rome 1993), pp. 43–7, cf. the long sections on donors of so many feet of floor mosaic at Aquileia, Grado, Trieste and Parenzo.

23. An episcopal palace of the church of St George existed 'at the time of the Arians', *LPR* c. 70, tr. p. 186. This normally seems to refer to the 'barbarian' period of later kings, but there were certainly Arians in Ravenna throughout the fifth century.

24. *Scholies ariennes*, ed. R. Gryson, 3 vols. (Turnhout 1980); *idem, Le recueil arien de Vérone. MS LI de la Bibliothèque capitale* (Turnhout 1982); *idem, Les palimpsestes ariens de Bobbio* (Turnhout 1983); P. Heather and J. Matthews, *The Goths in the Fourth Century* (Liverpool 1991), pp. 156–73.

25. W. H. Bennett, *The Gothic Commentary on the Gospel of John* (New York 1960), pp. 67–70.

26. Jews are recorded in sixth- , seventh- and eighth-century Ravenna and a synagogue was converted into a church of St Paul, *LPR* c. 119, tr. p. 238, c. 133 tr. p. 257 (the conversion of a Jew), and c. 143 tr. p. 268 (the Jewish merchant who was asked by Charlemagne to put a value on the crown, one that disappeared under Bishop George). On the amphora with a Jewish inscription, see p. 123.

CHAPTER 7

1. Sidonius, Ep. I, v. 3–5 to Heronius, in Sidonius Apollinarius, *Poems and Letters*, tr. W. B. Anderson, 2 vols. (Loeb 1936), vol. I, pp. 354–7.

2. Sidonius, Ep. I, viii to Candidianus, vol. I, pp. 380–83.

3. Marcellinus, anno 466–7, tr. p. 24.

4. Sidonius, Ep. I, v. 5–6, to Heronius, vol. I, pp. 356–7; Martial on scarcity of drinking water, cf. lots of wine and tender wild asparagus, even better than the cultivated variety, *Epigrams* Book XIII, 21. CHECK epigram 66 on the great wines but not enough water.

5. Jan-Olaf Tjäder, ed., *Die nichtliterarischen lateinischen papyri Italiens aus der Zeit 445–700*, 3 vols. (Lund 1954–82), updating Marini's earlier edition, and now reprinted with facsimile reproductions, updated bibliography and corrections in *Chartae Latinae Antiquiores (CLA)*, organized geographically by archive. The family names occur in numerous documents from the late fifth century onwards, see the prosopographies constructed by Brown, *Gentlemen and Officers*, from 554–800, and S. Cosentino, *PiB* (only the first two volumes have appeared).

6. S. D. W. Lafferty, *Law and Society in the Age of Theoderic the Great. A study of the* Edictum Theoderici (Cambridge 2013), pp. 112–14.

7. See F. Santoni, 'I Papiri di Ravenna. *Gesta municipalia e* procedure di insinuazione', in *L'Héritage byzantine en Italie (VIIIe –XIIe siècle). I La Fabrique documentaire* (Rome 2011), pp. 9–32; G. Nicolaj, 'Breve viaggio fra i documenti altomedievalli dell'Italia bizantina (cenni di sintesi)', in the same volume, pp. 169–87.

8. Tjäder, *Papyri* I, 4–5 = Marini 74/74A, *CLA* XXIX, 878. This is a list of wills recopied in the mid-sixth century and identified by sections. B II 7–B III 4–8, pp. 208–10, dated before 474, concerns Pascasia, *honesta femina,* possibly the widow of Constantius.

9. Tjäder, *Papyri* I, 4–5, B III 8–IV 2–6, pp. 206–8, dated 480, cf. two more that survive from the late fifth century, A and B1, = Marini 74/74A, *CLA* XXIX, 878.

10. Such as Pascasia, see note 8 above.

11. Petition of Maria, Tjäder, *Papyri* I, 12, pp. 294–8 = Marini 84, *CLA* XXV 791, dated 491.

12. *LPR* c. 31, tr. p. 134.

13. P. Heather, *The Fall of the Roman Empire. A New History* (London 2005), pp. 418–19, 422–3, and see the introduction to the *Poems and Letters* of Sidonius, vol. I, pp. xlii–lii.

14. *LPR* c. 37, tr. pp. 139–44

15. Ibid., c. 33, tr. p. 135; J.-C. Picard, *Le souvenir des évêques* (Rome 1988), pp. 161 and pl. 33.

16. Sidonius, *Poem* XXIII, vol. I, pp. 296, 302–4.

CHAPTER 8

1. B. Ward Perkins, *The Fall of Rome and the End of Civilization* (Oxford 2005) most particularly and others not so emphatically, e.g. J. M. H. Smith, *Europe after Rome* (Oxford 2005). Cf. C. Wickham, *The Inheritance of Rome. A History of Europe from 400 to 1000* (London 2009), pp. 3–12.

2. Priscus, fg. 62 = John of Antioch, fg. 207, and Priscus, fg. 64 = John of Antioch, fg. 209, tr. pp. 370–73.

3. P. MacGeorge, *Late Roman Warlords* (Oxford 2002), pp. 167–268.
4. He decorated, or possibly founded, an Arian church in Rome, St Agata, between 459 and 471, which served as a model for Theoderic, MacGeorge, as above, pp. 180–81; R. W. Mathisen, 'Ricimer's church in Rome: How an Arian Barbarian Prospered in a Nicene World', in *The Power of Religions in Late Antiquity*, eds. A. Cain and N. Lenski (Farnham 2009), pp. 307–25. It served as a model for Theoderic – see similarity with the apostles in S. Apollinare Nuovo. R. Coates-Stephens, 'Dark Age Architecture in Rome', *PBSR* 65 (1997), pp. 177–232.
5. Marcellinus notes Glycerius was made emperor 'more by presumption than election' (tr. p. 26). He records that Julius Nepos was elevated at Rome, and then Romulus Augustulus at Ravenna.
6. Procopius, *Wars* III, vii, 16–17, tr. vol. II, p. 69.
7. Priscus, fg. 65 (John of Antioch, fg. 209.2), tr. pp. 372–4, claims that Gundobad (nephew of Ricimer) established Glycerius as emperor and Leo I (died 18 January 474) decided to send Nepos to remove him. His successor Zeno (474–91) had to deal with Glycerius and his successors. The convoluted history of these years would require a very lengthy analysis.
8. W. V. Harris, *Roman Power: A Thousand Years of Empire* (Cambridge 2016), pp. 220–26; *Le migrazioni nell'Alto Medioevo*, Settimana 66 (Spoleto 2019).
9. Marcellinus, anno 476, tr. pp. 26–27; *Anon. Vales* 8.38, 10.45, mentions the pension of 6,000 *solidi*.
10. *PLRE* IIB, pp. 791–3 and Addenda, xxxix: Odoacer's coinage suggests that he did recognize Julius Nepos as emperor (but did nothing to assist his return to Italy); D. Henning, *Periclitans res publica. Kaisertum und Eliten in der Krise des Weströmischen Reiches 454/5–493 n. Chr.* (Stuttgart 1999), pp. 178–84.
11. Malchus, fg. 13 records that Onulf (described as Odoacer's brother) was descended from the Theuringi (Thuringians) and on his mother's side from the Sciri, *Fragmentary Historians*, pp. 418–19.
12. *Anon. Vales* 10.46 tr. p. 537 claims that Odoacer offered to grant any wish he might have. As a result a certain Ambrose was pardoned and allowed to return from exile – precisely the sort of intervention a holy man was likely to make.
13. Malchus, fg. 14, *Fragmentary Historians*, p. 419. P. Heather, *The Fall of the Roman Empire. A New History* (London 2005), pp. 428–30.
14. If a tomb of 'Singledia' mentioned by Agnellus may be identified as Sunigilda's, then she was eventually buried at the church of S. Croce, which had been taken under Arian control, *LPR* c. 41, tr. pp. 148–9; *PLRE* IIB, pp. 1040–41. John of Antioch 214a, tr. S. Mariev, *Ioannis Antiocheni fragmenta quae supersunt omnia* (Berlin 2008), pp. 386–9; Gordon, pp. 182–3, claims that Theoderic starved her to death.

15. Jones, *LRE* I, p. 253; *LPR* ch. 39, tr. p. 146 and ch. 40 tr p. 148; Deichmann, *Ravenna*, II/ 3, p. 18.
16. Jones, *LRE* I, pp. 255, 425.
17. Jones, *LRE* I, p. 254.
18. J. Conant, *Staying Roman. Conquest and Identity in Africa and the Mediterranean, 439–700* (Cambridge 2015), p. 38, relates this development to Geiseric using Eudocia's claim on her father's imperial inheritance, which was abandoned once her marriage to Huneric had been recognized; Candidus, ll. 84–8, *Fragmentary Historians*, p. 469.
19. Tjäder, *Papyri* I, 10–11 = Marini 82–3, *CLA* XX 703, cf. *Regesta* Addendum no. 1, in *Storia di Ravenna* II.1, p. 545.
20. Candidus, ll. 84–8, *Fragmentary Historians*, p. 469; A. Chastagnol, *Le Sénat romain sous le règne d'Odoacre* (Bonn 1966), pp. 98–9; Thomas S. Burns, *A History of the Ostrogoths* (Bloomington 1984), pp. 74–7; J. Moorhead, *Theoderic in Italy* (Oxford 1993), pp. 54, 231–2; and the full entries for individual senators in *PLRE* IIA and B.
21. Ennodius, *Life of Epiphanius*, in *Early Christian Biographies,* Fathers of the Church series, tr. R. J. Deferrari (Washington DC 1964), vol. 15, pp. 329–45 on embassies to Ravenna.
22. *LP* 53 (Symmachus), tr. p. 46, cf. *LP* 50.1 and 4, tr. pp. 43–4. After this mention of Odoacer, a combined dating reference to 'the time of King Theoderic and the emperor Zeno' (or Anastasios) ruling in Constantinople, is later made more specific with the addition of the years of western consuls ('from the consulship of Paulinus to that of Senator'. The *Life* of Felix III was written in about 535, over 50 years later, see H. Geertman, 'La genesi del *Liber pontificalis romano*: un processo di organizzazione della memoria', in *Liber, gesta, histoire. Ecrire l'histoire des évêques et des papes de l'Antiquité au XXI siècle*, eds. F. Bougard and M. Sot (Turnhout 2009), pp. 37–108.
23. P. Amory, *People and Identity in Ostrogothic Italy 489–554* (Cambridge 2003), pp. 251–6, the largest number come from a single papyrus. Later Amory draws a distinction between the royal Vandal church in Africa, which persecuted Catholics, and the cultural church of the Goths, which spread its liturgy to all Arian believers largely in Latin, pp. 259–60. See S. Cohen, 'Religious Diversity' in *A Companion to Ostrogothic Italy,* pp. 503–32, esp. pp. 510–21, showing how the term 'Arian' became polemical, and G. Berndt and R. Steinacher, 'The *ecclesia legis Gothorum* and the Role of Arianism in Ostrogothic Italy', in G. Berndt and R. Steinacher, eds., *Arianism: Roman Heresy and Barbarian Creed* (Farnham 2014), 219–29.
24. *LPR* c. 37, tr. pp. 141–4. J. Martinez Pizarro demonstrates with consummate skill how this story draws on Pope Leo I's embassy to Attila, which was reworked in numerous later versions, see *Writing Ravenna. The* Liber pontificalis *of Andrea Agnellus* (Michigan 1995), pp. 106–19.

25. *LP* 50.2.4 (Felix III), tr. pp. 443–4; *LP* 51.4 (Gelasius) and the end of the Acacian schism under Hormisdas, 54.5–8, tr. pp. 49–50.
26. *LP* 51.1 (Gelasius I), tr. p. 44; 53.5 (Symmachus), tr. p. 46; 54.9 (Hormisdas), tr. p. 50 (all burning books of Manichaeans, plus hostility to all heretics, including Arians).
27. *LP* 51.6, tr. p. 45.

CHAPTER 9

1. W. Ensslin, *Theoderich der Grosse* 2nd edn (Munich 1959) has a useful chapter on this period; J. Shepard, 'Manners maketh Romans? Young barbarians at the emperor's court', in *Byzantine Style, Religion and Civilization in Honour of Sir Steven Runciman*, ed. E. Jeffreys (Cambridge 2006), pp. 135–58, esp. 135–41.
2. D. Braund, *Rome and the Friendly Kings* (London/New York 1984); J. Allen, *Hostages and Hostage-taking in the Roman Empire* (Cambridge 2006).
3. Instead of learning Roman ways, he and his eunuch friends provoked anger and the martyrs of Sebasteia assisted his escape from the Great Palace. See *Life of Peter the Iberian*, tr. C. Horn and R. R. Phenix Jr. (Leiden 2008), pp. 25–35; *PLRE* Petrus 13, Proclus 3; M. McCormick, 'Emperor and Court', *The Cambridge Ancient History*, vol. XIV (Cambridge 2001), ch. 6, pp. 154–5.
4. In this way Sebastian, son-in-law of the general Boniface, who supported Galla Placidia against Aetius, spent a decade at the court of Theodosius II between 433 and 443.
5. J. Herrin, 'Constantinople and the treatment of hostages, refugees and exiles in Late Antiquity', *Constantinople réelle et imaginaire. Autour de l'oeuvre de Gilbert Dagron, Travaux et Mémoires* 22/1 (2018), pp. 739–56.
6. A. Kosto, *Hostages in the Middle Ages* (Oxford 2012); *idem*, 'Transformation of hostageship in late antiquity', *Antiquité Tardive*, 21 (2013), pp. 265–82.
7. See Ensslin, *Theoderich der Grosse*, pp. 14–33; he might have been taught by Cledonius, an established *grammaticus* and professor of Latin, resident in Constantinople at about the same time, see *PLRE* IIA, p. 302, Cledonius 2; or Theoctistus, *grammaticus*, a second teacher, see *PLRE* IIB, p. 1066, Theoctistus 5.
8. Peter Heather has recently provided a most convincing account of how Constantinople may have appeared to Theoderic, *The Restoration of Rome. Barbarian Popes and Imperial Pretenders* (London 2013), pp. 14–17.
9. Malalas, *Chronicle*, records these events in bk 14.42–3, tr. pp. 205–6.
10. Mango, *Art*, pp. 34–5. It could have been based on an earlier example, but this one was erected inside the new chapel.

11. Marcellinus, anno 469, tr. p. 25; citing *Chronikon Paschale*, ed. and tr. Michael and Mary Whitby (Liverpool 1989), anno 468, tr. p. 90.

12. Marcellinus, anno 469, tr. p. 25.

13. Heather, *Restoration of Rome*, pp. 25–32 with map on p. 31.

14. Jordanes, *Getica* 57, gives a lyrical account of Theoderic's reception by Zeno, who treated his military ally to a triumph, seated him among the princes of his palace, adopted him as his son-at-arms and awarded him the rank of consul ordinary and *patricius* with an equestrian statue to the glory of this great man (pp. 289–91). Wolfram, *Goths*, pp. 277–8 on the run up to 487.

15. Jordanes, *Getica* 57, quoted by P. Sarris, *Empires of Faith* (Oxford 2011), pp. 100–101.

16. Wolfram, *Goths*, pp. 279–80, on the departure in autumn with the harvest to sustain them through the winter of 488–9.

17. S. Lazard, 'Goti e Latini a Ravenna', in *Storia di Ravenna* II/1, pp. 109–33; Wolfram, *Goths*, p. 279 suggests that about 100,000 Goths may have participated in the exodus and 10,000 probably settled in Ravenna.

18. Wolfram, *Goths*, p. 282 (noting that Odoacer had 'marched to Rome to have his son [Thela] proclaimed caesar', in order to secure the succession); Bury, *LRE* I, p. 424, suggests that this victory on the Adda persuaded the Senate to abandon Odoacer.

19. John of Antioch fg. 214a, tr. in C. D. Gordon, *The Age of Attila. Fifth-Century Byzantium and the Barbarians* (Ann Arbor 1972), pp. 182–3; S. Mariev, *Ioannis Antiocheni fragmenta quae supersunt omnia* (Berlin 2008), pp. 386–9.

20. *Anon. Vales* 60, tr. p. 545.

21. *Epistulae Theodericianae*, MGH *AA* XII, p. 390; J. Moorhead, *Theoderic in Italy* (Oxford 1993), pp. 89–90, 96.

22. *LPR* cc. 34–46, tr. pp. 136–56.

23. Moorhead, *Theoderic in Italy*, p. 25, accepts that Odoacer used Bishop John to negotiate the terms of the city's surrender, though other sources do not mention it. Possibly Agnellus wished to enhance the role of the Catholic bishop in welcoming an Arian ruler, *LPR* c. 39.

24. Moorhead, *Theoderic in Italy*, pp. 36–7, this was also unsuccessful. Only the third embassy, also led by Festus, obtained Anastasios' approval of Theoderic as king. On Festus, *PLRE* II, pp. 467–9.

25. Moorhead, *Theoderic in Italy*, pp. 33–4 discusses the thirds, 'tertiae', which are now interpreted as taxes not territory, confirmed by Heather, *Restoration of Rome*, pp. 64–7. In *The Fall of the Roman Empire* (London 2005), pp. 428–9, Heather supposes that Liberius was in charge as he had also arranged the settlement of Odoacer's followers after 476.

26. Lazard, 'Goti e Latini', pp. 128–9 and n. 165, citing Guillou, *Régionalisme*, p. 79. On the very long career of Liberius, *PLRE* II, pp. 677–81 and the study by J. J. O'Donnell, 'Liberius the patrician', *Traditio* 37 (1981), pp. 31–72.

27. *LPR* c. 70, tr. p. 185 on Unimundus/Uvimundus, bishop in the 24th year of Theoderic's reign; P. Amory, *People and Identity in Ostrogothic Italy 489–554* (Cambridge 2003), p. 429.

28. Deliyannis, *Ravenna,* pp. 17–18 on impost blocks and polygonal apse forms typical of Constantinople and the eastern Mediterranean.

29. *Anon. Vales* 11.53, 12.63, tr. pp. 543, 549.

30. S. D. W. Lafferty, *Law and Society in the Age of Theoderic the Great* (Cambridge 2013), p. 104, citing Cassiodorus, *Variae* III. 20.

31. Amory, *People and Identity*, pp. 251–6, stressing the formulaic use of Gothic by four members, which contrasts with the six who sign in much freer forms of Latin. A further five members make the sign of the cross, indicating that they are illiterate, though two plead 'weakness of the eyes', implying that they are blind. Lazard, 'Goti e Latini', p. 114, however, points out that at least one Goth, Hildevara, is known to have converted to the Catholic faith before 523.

32. Lazard, 'Goti e Latini', p. 121, citing a papyrus of 591 (Tjäder, *Papyri*, no. 37) as an example of intermarriage.

33. Amory, *People and Identity*, pp. 43–59, on the innovative combination of Gothic and Roman; Lafferty, *Law and Society*, also contrasts the ideals conveyed by Cassiodorus and the practical features of Theoderic's *Edict*.

34. Thomas S. Burns, *A History of the Ostrogoths* (Bloomington 1984), p. 219: 'although he built his regime upon Roman foundations, he made the bureaucracy function more efficiently and replaced outmoded concepts and institutions with Gothic innovations and personnel'.

CHAPTER 10

1. On Theoderic's kingdom in general see the many useful articles in *A Companion to Ostrogothic Italy*, eds. J. J. Arnold, M. S. Bjornlie and K. Stessa (Leiden 2016). Cassiodorus, *Var.* III 23.3 on the appointment of Colosseus, probably a Roman, to Sirmium, S. D. W. Lafferty, *Law and Society in the Age of Theoderic the Great* (Cambridge 2013), p. 103.

2. J. Moorhead, *Theoderic in Italy* (Oxford 1993), pp. 39–40, connects this with the Gothic *reiks*.

3. J. J. Arnold, *Theoderic and the Roman Imperial Restoration* (Cambridge 2014), pp. 84, 88–91, 111–13, 273. The municipal bronze coinage used in everyday exchange has the personified and turreted city of Ravenna on the obverse and the monogram of 'Felix Ravenna' (Fortunate Ravenna) on the reverse (see Plate 20).

4. Three such eunuchs are recorded: Seda, *ignuchus et cubicularis*, commemorated in a magnificent tomb; Wiliarit 2 and Triwila, *praepositus sacri cubiculi*, see *PLRE* IIB, pp. 987, 1126–7, 1167; and Helpidius 6, *PLRE* IIA, p. 537.

5. Wolfram, *Goths*, pp. 292–3; M. S. Bjornlie, 'Governmental administration' in *A Companion to Ostrogothic Italy*, eds. Arnold, Bjornlie and Stessa, pp. 47–72; Lafferty, *Law and Society*, p. 39, on the *saio* Unigilis who arranged provisions for the court when Theoderic visited Liguria, see Cassiodorus, *Var.* II 20.

6. Such as counts Cassine, Tzalicone, Assuin, Suna and Osuin, see S. Lazard, 'Goti e Latini a Ravenna', in *Storia di Ravenna* II.1, p. 119.

7. Thomas S. Burns, *A History of the Ostrogoths* (Bloomington 1984), pp. 83–4, 171–9, for many names of counts and *saiones* (e.g. Triwilla, Wilia, Tezutzaton); Pythius, *comes Gothorum;* Fridibad, *comes* of Savia; *comes* Marabad in Provence; *comes* Gildias in Sicily; Tancila (in Pavia?), p. 83. Oppas, ?*bucellarius*, who revolted against Theoderic, p. 176. Cf. Moorhead, *Theoderic in Italy*, pp. 77–8; Lazard, 'Goti e Latini', pp. 114–15, 119, 121. Pitzia was the military commander against the Gepids who took Thrasarich and his mother captive, see Burns, *Ostrogoths*, p. 175.

8. *PLRE* IIB, pp. 677–81 for his amazingly long career; and J. J. O'Donnell, 'Liberius the patrician', *Traditio* 37 (1981), pp. 31–72.

9. *PLRE* IIA, pp. 467 and 454.

10. Arnold's *Theoderic and the Roman Imperial Restoration* is particularly clear on this aspect.

11. M. S. Bjornlie, *Politics and Tradition between Rome, Ravenna and Constantinople* (Cambridge 2013); a selection of the letters are translated by S. Barnish, *Cassiodorus:* Variae (Liverpool 1992).

12. A. Chastagnol, *Le Sénat romain sous le règne d'Odoacre* (Bonn 1966), pp. 96–9; C. Pietri, 'Les aristocraties de Ravenne (Ve–VIe s.)', *Studi Romagnoli* (1983), pp. 643–73, esp. 656–7. For Gaudentius, see Marini, *Papyri* 139. *Magistri officiorum*: Andromachus in 489; Anicius Probus Faustus Niger 492–4; Rufius P. N. Cethegnus early sixth century, and praetorian prefects of Italy: Liberius to 500, Theodorus 500, Faustus Albinus 500–503. Lafferty, *Law and Society*, pp. 110–12 on the significance of provincial governors, judges who formed backbone of the administration and were sent out on circuit to provide legal resource for local people. The *Edict* has regulations to prevent them imposing for too long on local hospitality.

13. *PLRE* IIA, p. 482.

14. *PLRE* IIA, pp. 414–16.

15. Pietri, 'Les aristocraties de Ravenne', p. 659; *PLRE* IIA, pp. 350, 567–8.

16. Bjornlie, *Politics and Tradition*, pp. 128–30, argues that these low born professional *apparitores* could rise to higher posts in the bureaucracy in an *ordo* opposed to the Roman aristocrats. Moorhead also sees a shift from Roman senators to administrators from Gaul, pp. 151, 154–6.

17. P. Fabbri, 'Il controllo delle acque tra tecnica ed economia', in *Storia di Ravenna* II.1, pp. 9–25; Y. Murano, ' "Watered ... by the life-giving wave". Aqueducts and water management in Ostrogothic Italy', in *Owner-*

ship of Land and Natural Resources in the Roman World, eds. P. Erdkamp, K. Verhhoeven and A. Zuiderhoek (Oxford 2015), pp. 150–69; *Acqua, Settimana* 55 (Spoleto 2008); *Cura Aquarum*, ed. G. Cuscito, *Antichità Altoatriatiche* 87 (2018).

18. A. Urbano, 'Donation, dedication and *damnatio memoriae*. The Catholic reconciliation of Ravenna and the church of S. Apollinare Nuovo', *Journal of Early Christian Studies* 13 (2005), pp. 71–110. Later changes include a fine eleventh-century bell tower at the south-west corner, a medieval cloister also on the south side, and a Renaissance portico built onto the western entrance.

19. Deichmann, *Ravenna* II/I, p. 135 on masons' marks; Moorhead, *Theoderic in Italy*, pp. 158–9 on senator Festus charged with the transport of marbles from the Pinciana palace in Rome to Ravenna. He was also the supporter of Laurentius for pope and sheltered the unsuccessful candidate on his country estates, Moorhead, *Theoderic in Italy*, p. 207.

20. *LP* 53.7, tr. p. 47.

21. Procopius, *Wars* V i, 16–18, Deliyannus, *Ravenna*, pp. 46–7 on the channel that brought seawater into the city. Guillou, *Régionalisme*, pp. 59–61; P. Squatriti, 'Marshes and mentalities in early medieval Ravenna', *Viator* 23 (1992), pp. 1–16; *idem, Water and Society in Early Medieval Italy: AD 400–1000* (Cambridge 1998).

22. *LPR* c. 94, tr. p. 205, it was a mosaic image of Theoderic on horseback in the vault of the apse, probably of a reception hall.

23. Acclamations, ILS no. 827; *CIL* VI, no. 1794; *CIL* X, nos. 6850–52, praising Theoderic as 'most glorious'. P. Heather, *The Restoration of Rome. Barbarian Popes and Imperial Pretenders* (London 2013), pp. 60–61, 62 on the sense of *Romanitas*; Moorhead, *Theoderic in Italy*, pp. 47–8; *CIL* VI, no. 1794; *CIL* X, nos. 6850–52 on use of *augustus*.

24. Procopius, *Wars* V xxiv, 22, where Theoderic is described as an *archon*, and the gradual collapse of the image (*eikon*, of exceedingly small stones tinted with nearly every colour) is taken to predict the ending of Gothic rule in Italy.

25. Cassiodorus, *Var.* I 45 and 46, tr. pp. 20–23, 24.

26. Moorhead, *Theoderic in Italy*, pp. 169–70; *PLRE* IIB, p. 939 (Renatus); *PLRE* IIB, p. 1098 (Theodorus 63). The copyist is probably to be identified with Flavius Lucius Theodorus, an official in the *scrinium epistularium* (department of letters) and assistant to the *quaestor* in Constantinople, who corrected a copy of Boethius' translation of the *Categories* of Aristotle. He also copied the *Ars grammatica* of Priscian in Constantinople, finishing the work on 29 May 527.

27. J. Tjäder, 'Der Codex Argenteus in Uppsala und der Buchmeister Viliaric in Ravenna', in *Studia Gothica*, ed. U. E. Hagberg (Stockholm 1972), pp. 144–64, esp. 147–51. It arrived in Sweden after many adventures and has lost several of its original pages.

28. He may be the same as Viliaric, *antiquarius*, that is, someone interested in and capable of copying ancient texts.
29. *Var.* IX 24.
30. *Var.* IV 1, tr. p. 74, and cf. *Var.* II 2 above.
31. F. Staab, 'Ostrogothic geographers at the court of Theodoric the Great: a study of some sources of the Anonymous Ravenna Cosmographer', *Viator* 7 (1976), pp. 27–64, esp. 33–54, now much criticized by L. Dillemann, *La Cosmographie du Ravennate*, Latomus 235 (Brussels, 1997).
32. *Var.* IV 1, tr. p. 74; Arnold, *Theoderic and the Roman Imperial Restoration*, pp. 213–18 on the unfamiliar beasts, *voluptates exquisitas*.
33. *Var.* III 51, tr. p. 71.
34. *Var.* II 24 and 25, cf. III 8, IV, 10.
35. Tjäder, *Papyri*, no. 4–5, B 2, Marini, 74/74A, *CLA* XXIX, no. 878 (with the names Aelius, Aurelius, Melminius and Hernilius).
36. Bjornlie, *Politics and Tradition*, p. 113.
37. Tjäder, *Papyri* I, 29 = Marini 113 after 5 Feb 504, dated by reference to Rufius Petronius Nicomagus Cethegus, consul in 504; *PLRE* IIA, pp. 281–2.
38. Lafferty, *Law and Society*, pp. 111–12, and 114, *Edictum Theodericis*, cc. 52 and 53 (which also mentions the *duumvir* and *quiquennalis,* appointed every fifth year 'to perform local census'). See *Var.* VII 11 for the formula for the appointment of the *defensor*. Jones, *LRE* I, p. 145 traces their creation back to Valentinian I for the defence of the plebs against the powerful.
39. Text of the Will of Aurelian, Tjäder, *Papyri* I, 4–5, section B IV–V 7–11, pp. 210–12 = Marini, 74/74A, *CLA* XVII, no. 653; *Pros. Chrét. Italie* I, 232–3.
40. *Var.* III 19.
41. Senarius' epitaph in Ravenna, MGH *AA* XII, p. 499; and Liberius' in Rimini, *CIL* XI, no. 382.

CHAPTER 11

1. P. Heather, *The Restoration of Rome* (London 2013), pp. 70–79.
2. Cassiodorus, *Var.* IV 1, 1-2, tr. p. 74.
3. *Var.* II 41; III 1-4, tr. pp. 43–8.
4. N. Davies, *Vanished Kingdoms: The History of Half-forgotten Europe* (London 2011).
5. *Var.* IX 1; J. Conant, *Staying Roman. Conquest and Identity in Africa and the Mediterranean, 439–700* (Cambridge 2015), p. 40.
6. *Var.* II 40, tr. p. 42 (at the end of a long letter about the power of music to tame the savage hearts of the barbarians, 43, n. 31).
7. *Var.* I 45 and 46, tr. pp. 20–24.
8. *Var.* V 35, 39, tr. pp. 162–6, directed to the *comes* Liviritus and the *vir illustris* Ampelius (*NCMH* I, pp. 176–7).

9. *Var.* III 7, VIII 12.

10. J. Moorhead, *Theoderic in Italy* (Oxford 1993), pp. 189-90; Heather, *Restoration*, pp. 80-81. *Vita Caesarii episcopi Arelatensis,* ed. B. Krusch, *MGH SMR* III, ch. 36, pp. 470-71, ch. 38, pp. 471-2.

11. *CIL* X, no. 6850; ILS no. 827; *Var.* II 32, tr. pp. 35-7.

12. *Var.* II 20, tr. p. 30.

13. J. J. Arnold, *Theoderic and the Roman Imperial Restoration* (Cambridge 2014), pp. 285-7, citing *Var.* IV 5 1-2; *Var.* IV 26 1-2.

14. *Var.* II 40, tr. pp. 38-43.

15. *Var.* I 1; Moorhead, *Theoderic in Italy*, pp. 44, 186; cf. Heather, *Restoration*, pp. 3, 72; Arnold, *Theoderic and the Roman Imperial Restoration*, pp. 78-82 (claiming that the *princeps* when used by Theoderic meant in effect *imperator*). But the concept remained concealed. J. Prostko-Prostynski, *Utraque res publicae. Anastasius I's Gothic Policy (491-518)* (Poznan 1994).

16. *Anagnosticum* (502), in MGH *AA* XII, pp. 425-6. On 23 October 501 the assembled bishops, all 76, signed their agreement with the document, Peter of Ravenna again at the second place.

17. R. Lizzi Testa, 'Bishops, ecclesiastical institutions and the Ostrogothic regime', in *A Companion to Ostrogothic Italy,* eds. J. J. Arnold, M. S. Bjornlie and K. Stessa (Leiden 2016), pp. 451-79.

18. *LPR* c. 50, tr. pp. 161-2.

19. Agnellus on the inscription, *LPR* c. 57, tr. p. 171.

20. *Var.* II 27, tr. p. 35: 'Religionem imperare non possumus, quia nemo cogitur ut credat invitus.' On the rights of Jews in general, see the finely crafted lecture by L. Cracco Ruggini, 'Tolleranza et intolleranza nella società tardoantica', *Ricerche di Storia Sociale e Religiosa,* n.s. 23 (1983), pp. 27-44; *Gli Ebrei nell'alto Medioevo,* Settimana 26 (Spoleto 1980); S. D. W. Lafferty, *Law and Society in the Age of Theoderic the Great* (Cambridge 2013), pp. 32-3; S. Cohen, 'Religious Diversity' in *A Companion to Ostrogothic Italy,* pp. 503-32, stressing the king's need to uphold order and *civilitas,* rather than a principled tolerance, and showing how 'Arian' was used as a polemical term.

21. This was in accordance with Roman law.

22. D. Noy, *Jewish Inscriptions of Western Europe,* vol. I (Cambridge 1993), no. 10, pp. 17-18 (my thanks to Sebastian Brock for this reference). For the conversion of a synagogue, *LPR* c. 119, tr. p. 238.

23. Moorhead, *Theoderic in Italy*, pp. 97-9, 217.

24. Cracco Ruggini, 'Tolleranza e intolleranza', pp. 37-8, draws attention to the comparison.

25. *The Chronicle of Pseudo-Zachariah Rhetor,* bk 9, section a, ed. G. Greatrex, tr. R. R. Phenix and C. B Horn (Liverpool 2011), p. 365 and n. 278. While the dates of Dominic's disagreements with Theoderic are quite unclear, the author of *Ps-Zachariah* believed that 'the tyrant' had driven his opponent

out. Dominic may be the same person as a Domnicus who signed the acts of a council held in 536 against the Monophysite/Miaphysite leader Severus.

26. *Var.* V 1, tr. p. 83, gifts of armour, furs and fair-haired slave boys to secure peace.

CHAPTER 12

1. S. D. W. Lafferty, *Law and Society in the Age of Theoderic the Great* (Cambridge 2013), p. 181; C. Wickham, *Framing the Early Middle Ages* (Oxford 2005), p. 34.

2. W. Pohl, 'Early medieval Romanness – a multiple identity', in *Transformations of Romanness: Early Medieval Regions and Identities*, ed. W. Pohl (Berlin 2018), pp. 3–39.

3. Alan Cameron, *The Last Pagans of Rome* (Oxford, 2011), p. 791.

4. Ibid., pp. 787–93.

5. *LP* 55.2 tr. pp. 51–2 (the life of Pope John I) when he becomes 'the heretic king'. H. Geertman, 'La genesi del *Liber pontificalis romano*: un processo di organizzazione della memoria', in *Liber, gesta, histoire. Ecrire l'histoire des évêques et des papes de l'Antiquité au XXI siècle*, eds. F. Bougard and M. Sot (Turnhout 2009).

6. *LP* 53.2, tr. p. 45.

7. MGH *AA* XII, pp. 399–415, a synod of 66 bishop and 81 Roman priests and deacons.

8. J. Moorhead, *Theoderic in Italy* (Oxford 1993), p. 61.

9. *Anon. Vales* 65–7, tr. pp. 549–551.

10. M. S. Bjornlie, *Politics and Tradition between Rome, Ravenna and Constantinople* (Cambridge 2013), p. 129 on the senatorial duty to provide *Annona*; Moorhead, *Theoderic in Italy*, pp. 61–3.

11. Cassiodorus, *Var.* I 18, tr. p. 16.

12. Lafferty, *Law and Society*. Though it has been attributed to other rulers named Theoderic, this recent study makes a very strong case for its Ostrogothic origin and composition, which points to the long visit to Rome as a very likely moment for its publication.

13. *Prologue*, tr. Lafferty, *Law and Society*, p. 248; cf. *Var.* IV 42 to Argolicus, the urban prefect; VIII 3 written in Athalaric's name to the people of Rome; X 4 and 5 from Theodohad to the Senate, all stressing the idea of *ius commune*.

14. Lafferty, *Law and Society*, pp. 147–55.

15. Ibid., pp. 102–4, 110–12 on courts and justice.

16. *Var.* I 18.

17. Their names are not recorded, though from 503 a series of *quaestores* is identified.

18. M. T. G. Humphreys, *Law, Power, and Imperial Ideology in the Iconoclast Era* (Oxford 2015); *idem, The Laws of the Isaurian Era: The* Ecloga *and its Appendices* (Liverpool 2017).
19. Moorhead, *Theoderic in Italy*, p. 116.
20. MGH *A A* XII, pp. 438–55, 80 bishops and 36 local Roman clerics; the first two Gothic stewards are identified as *'sublimes viros, majores domus nostrae cum Conzortrer'*; *LP* 53.5 for the violence against women; *LP* 53. 3–4 on the visitor Peter of Altinum sent in by Theoderic.
21. Felix III specifically condemned the church of Constantinople for usurping the rights of other ecclesiastical provinces as well as its close co-operation with Peter Mongos, the Monophysite patriarch of Alexandria and the *Henotikon, LP* 50.2–4, tr. pp. 43–4. Despite diplomatic efforts, the Acacian schism was still in force when Felix died in 492 and his successors, Gelasius (492–6), Anastasius II (496–8) and Symmachus (498–514) had no success in ending it.
22. *LP* 54.2–3, 5–6.
23. Moorhead, *Theoderic in Italy*, pp. 155–6, associates the shift with the quarrels provoked by Laurentius' dissatisfaction with his bishopric. C. Radtki, 'The Senate at Rome in Ostrogothic Italy' in *A Companion to Ostrogothic Italy*, eds. J. J. Arnold, M. S. Bjornlie and K. Stessa (Leiden 2016), pp. 121–46, esp. 129, 133–37.
24. *LP* 55.1–2, tr. p. 51.
25. *Anon. Vales* 85, tr. pp. 563–5.
26. *LP* 55.6, tr. p. 52.
27. Bjornlie, *Politics and Tradition*, p. 149, n. 130.
28. Ibid., pp. 147 (n. 122) and 149 emphasizes Gothic hostility to Rusticiana on account of this destruction, which Teia's troops wanted to avenge 20 years later in 546. Her departure for Constantinople was part of the family's 'retrenchment' in the Mediterranean world ruled from the East rather than Rome.
29. H.-U. Wiemer, *Theoderich der Grosse: König der Goten, Herrscher der Römer: eine Biographie* (Munich 2018); later writers elaborated the torturous method of his murder.
30. J. J. O'Donnell, *The Ruin of the Roman Empire* (London/New York 2009), pp. 164–70; P. Heather, 'A tale of two cities: Rome and Ravenna under Gothic rule', in *Ravenna, Its Role in Earlier Medieval Change and Exchange*, eds. J. Herrin and J. L. Nelson (London 2016), pp. 15–37, esp. 32–7.

CHAPTER 13

1. Jäggi has a drawing of the problems in raising such a huge weight, *Ravenna*, pp. 214–15; cf. other photos of the bath and internal decoration, pp. 208–9.

2. M. J. Johnson, 'Toward a history of Theoderic's building program', *DOP* 42 (1988), pp. 73–96 esp. 94–6 on imperial models in Constantinople; photo and description, Jäggi, *Ravenna*, pp. 206–7. A saddle fitting found in a Gothic grave close to the mausoleum provided a clear parallel (though this was later stolen from the local museum and has disappeared).

3. J. J. Arnold, *Theoderic and the Roman Imperial Restoration* (Cambridge 2014), pp. 74–7.

4. *Anon. Vales* 60, tr. p. 545, adding 'or a Valentinian', see Arnold on which Valentinian, p. 73 n. 51.

5 Ennodius, II, 14, Ennode de Pavie, *Lettres*, ed. and tr. S. Gioanni (Paris 2006), written in the name of Pope Symmachus to the bishops of Africa exiled in Sardinia, pp. 67–8; cf. Ennodius, *Life* of Epiphanius, in *Early Christian Biographies,* Fathers of the Church series, tr. R. J. Deferrari (Washington DC 1964), vol. 15, pp. 329–45; Arnold, *Theoderic and the Roman Imperial Restoration,* pp. 181–90.

6. S. Rota, *Panegirico del clementissimo re Teodorico. Opusc. 1* (Rome 2002); *Life* of Epiphanius, tr. Deferrari, ch. 7, p. 143 quoted by Arnold, *Theoderic and the Roman Imperial Restoration,* p. 190.

7. Born in 516, Jordanes, *Getica* 304–5, more likely to be correct than Procopius who puts his birth two years later in 518.

8. Cassiodorus, *Var.* VIII 1.

9. *Var.* VIII 15. He also urged people to rejoice that the bishop's seat was occupied, rather than dwelling on the competition between rival candidates.

10. *Var.* VIII 31, 33, possibly exaggerating the agricultural riches of southern Italy, and the positive aspects of parents selling their children as slaves.

11. *De origine actibusque Getarum,* MGH *AA* V, and the translation by C. C. Mierow, *The Gothic History of Jordanes* (Princeton 1915).

12. The kingdom of Toulouse, brilliantly described by Sidonius Apollinarius, is memorably enshrined as a vanished kingdom by Norman Davies in his book of the same name. Cf. P. Heather, 'The barbarian in late antiquity: image, reality and transformation', in *Constructing Identities in Late Antiquity,* ed. R. Miles (London 1999), pp. 234–58; W. Pohl, *Integration und Herrschaft: enthnische Identität und soziale Organisation im Frühmittelalter* (Vienna 2002); *idem*, ed., *Transformation of Romanness: Early Medieval Regions and Identities* (Berlin 2018).

13. *Var.* XI 1, 1 Sept. 533 (his eulogy of the queen), tr. pp. 145–50; M. Vitiello, *Amalasuintha: The Transformation of Queenship in the Post-Roman World* (Philadelphia 2017); V. Fauvinet-Ranson, 'Portrait d'une régente: Un panégyrique d'Amalasonthe', *Cassiodorus* IV (1998), pp. 267–308; S. Joye and A. Knaepen, 'L'image d'Amalasonthe chez Procope de Césarée et Grégoire de Tours: portraits contrastés entre Orient et Occident', *Le Moyen Age* 106.2 (2005), pp. 229–57; C. la Rocca, '"Consors regni": A Problem of Gender?', in P. Stafford et al. eds., *Gender and Historiography in*

the Earlier Middle Ages in Honour of Pauline Stafford (London 2017), pp. 27–143.

14. Procopius, *Wars* V ii. 3, on Amalasuintha; K. Cooper, 'Amalasuentha', in *A Companion to Ostrogothic Italy*, eds. J. J. Arnold, M. S. Bjornlie and K. Stessa (Leiden 2016), pp. 296–315; Vitiello, *Amalasuintha*, pp. 172–213; D. Harrison, *The Age of Queens and Abbesses. Gender and Political Culture in Early Medieval Europe* (Lund 1998).

15. *Var.* IX 21.

16. Procopius, *Wars* V ii. 5; Edict and letters of Athalaric, *Var.* IX 18, tr. pp. 116–20, and IX 19 and 20 to the Senate and provincial governors to ensure enforcement of the Edict, tr. pp. 120–21.

17. *Var.* VIII 12 (526), tr. pp. 102–4 (Cassiodorus, writing in the name of Athalaric, here extends the notion of the Gothic kingdom).

18. *Var.* IX. 1.

19. S. Gelichi, 'Ravenna, ascesa e declino di una capitale', in *Sedes regiae (ann. 400–800)*, eds. G. Ripoll and J. M. Gurt (Barcelona 2000) pp. 109–34. Amalasuintha sent a Gothic agent, Calogenitus, to the East to purchase marble and other materials, *Var.* X 8–9.

20. Procopius, *Wars* V xiii 2 on the flight of Amalaberga (possibly after death of Amalasuintha). The family's safe exile in Constantinople resulted in the betrothal of her daughter (probably Rodelinda) to Audoin, king of the Lombards, an alliance arranged by Justinian to strengthen his relations with this relatively new force in the West.

21. *LPR* c. 60, tr. pp. 172–7. He quotes the letter of Pope Felix from the copy preserved in Ravenna.

22. Their names are given at the end of the pope's document and it's interesting to note that Ecclesius' successor, Ursicinus, is not among them. Agnellus also knew very little about this bishop. He records that Ursicinus built the church of St Apollinaris at Classis with the help of Julianus the *argentarius*, and contributed to the construction of the *Tricollis*, which took many years to complete, *LPR* c. 62, tr. p. 178. This *Life* is especially short and confused. Agnellus does not report that Ursicinus is one of the bishops depicted with three others in between the apse windows of S. Apollinare in Classe, suggesting that these figures may be an addition from the time of Maximianus, who distinguished between the two early bishops, now saints (Severus and Ursus), and his two predecessors, Ursicinus and Ecclesius, Jäggi, *Ravenna*, p. 276.

23. Novel 123, para 3 (on entry fees), see D. J. D. Miller and P. Sarris, *The Novels of Justinian, A Complete and Annotated English Translation* (Cambridge 2018), vol. 2, pp. 804–5. In churches with an income of 30 lbs of gold, the incoming bishop should pay 100 gold *solidi* for enthronement fees and 300 to the notaries of the man who appointed him. Cf. Jones, *LRE* II, pp. 906–7, 908 and 911 on Pope Felix IV, who shows that the leading bishops of the empire, like Ravenna, commanded salaries

comparable to highest civilian officials, and regularly had staffs of up to 80 clergy (Apamea in Syria). Theoderic's toleration of Catholics becomes even clearer from their intensive building and increase in ecclesiastical wealth.

24. Jones, *LRE* II, p. 907.

25. *LPR* c. 60, tr. p. 175, where the seven notaries are mentioned, *primicerius*, *secundicerius*, and so on (just as in Rome).

26. *LPR* c. 61, tr. pp. 175-7.

27. Deliyannis, *Ravenna*, p. 118, n. 88; Var. III 19.

28. *LPR* c. 62, tr. p. 178, it is called a *monasterium*.

29. By this date the church gradually took over responsibility for widows and orphans. T. S. Miller, *The Orphans of Byzantium: Child Welfare in the Christian Empire* (Washington DC 2003).

30. Amalasuintha's interventions in Rome are clear from letters written in Athalaric's name, see Ch. 12 n. 13 above. Later Theodahad accepted a bribe to impose Silverius as pope, *LP* 60.1, showing the opposite style of secular intervention in the church of Rome.

31. *Var.* XII 22, 24, 26, on cross-Adriatic contacts and Cassiodorus' letters to the Istrians, to the tribunes of the coast and to Paul, his strong man (*vir strenuous*) in the Venetia when crops failed (tr. pp. 175-9, 181-2); S. Cosentino, 'L'approvvigionamento annonario di Ravenna dal V all'VIII secolo: l'organizzazione e i riflessi socio-economici', in *Ravenna: da capitale imperiale a capitale esarcale* (Spoleto 2005), vol. 1, pp. 405-34.

32. Procopius, *Wars* V ii. 23-9. In 533 when Gelimer feared that imperial forces would conquer North Africa, he also loaded his treasure onto a ship to be sailed to Spain, but due to inclement conditions it had to remain in port and was captured by Belisarius, *Wars* IV iv. 34-41.

33. *Var.* X 3, tr. pp. 131-2; M. Vitiello, *Theodahad: A Platonic King at the Collapse of Ostrogothic Italy* (Toronto 2014).

34. *Var.* X 20, tr. pp. 137-8.

35. Procopius, *Wars* V ii. 1-iii. 9; *Wars* V iv. 4-31. Cf. *LP* 60.2, on Justinian's fury at the killing of Amalasuintha, 'who had entrusted herself to him'. P. Heather, *The Restoration of Rome. Barbarian Popes and Imperial Pretenders* (London 2013), pp. 149-53, a racy account of these years; Bury, *LRE* II, p. 206, on Peter the patrician and Athanasios, Justinian's ambassadors who were imprisoned at Ravenna for 4 years; Y. A. Marano, ' "Watered . . . with the Life-giving Wave". Aqueducts and water management in Ostrogothic Italy', in *Ownership of Land and Natural Resources in the Roman World*, eds. P. Erdkamp, K. Verhhoeven and A. Zuiderhoek (Oxford 2015), p. 158, on the fortified residence Theodahad built for himself on Lake Bolsena where Amalasuintha was probably murdered.

CHAPTER 14

1. Procopius, *Wars* I xxiv. 36–7, tr. pp. 231–3.
2. *Chronikon Paschale*, ed. and tr. Michael and Mary Whitby (Liverpool 1989), p. 127. W. Brandes, 'Der Nika-Aufstand, Senatorenfamilien un Justinians Bauprogramm', in *Liber, gesta, histoire. Ecrire l'histoire des évêques et des papes de l'Antiquité au XXI siècle*, eds. F. Bougard and M. Sot (Turnhout 2009), pp. 239–65. Brandes, following M. Meier, *Das andere Zeitalter Justinians: Kontingenzerfahrung und Kontingenzbewältigung im 6. Jahrhundert n. Chr.* (Göttingen 2003) emphasizes the destructive and tyrannical elements of the emperor's reign, claiming that what Procopius recorded in the *Secret History* is absolutely correct.
3. R. D. Scott, 'Chronicles versus classicizing history: Justinian's East and West', in his *Byzantine Chronicles and the Sixth Century* (Farnham 2012).
4. Procopius, *Wars* III xiv, 3–17, II, 126–31 (where Procopius claims responsibility for discovering this crucial information about the Vandal fleet); P. Heather, *The Restoration of Rome. Barbarian Popes and Imperial Pretenders* (London 2013), p. 142.
5. My special thanks to Salvatore Cosentino for reminding me of the figures. F. E. Schlosser, 'The exarchates of Africa and Italy: Justinian's arrangements for Africa after the reconquest', *JÖB* 53 (2003), pp. 27–45.
6. C. Wickham, *Framing the Early Middle Ages* (Oxford 2005), pp. 706, 709–13; J. Conant, *Staying Roman. Conquest and Identity in Africa and the Mediterranean, 439–700* (Cambridge 2012), pp. 91–5, 336–7.
7. A. Sarantis, 'The Geopolitical Role of Dalmatia in Justinian's Balkan and Gothic Wars', paper given at Split, 2018. I thank Alex for sharing this paper prior to publication.
8. P. Heather, *Rome Resurrected. War and Empire in the Age of Justinian* (Oxford 2018), esp. pp. 165–79.
9. Procopius, *Wars* V. 27.
10. Cassiodorus, *Var.* X 32 2–3, tr. p. 144, from Witigis to Justinian, cites Queen Amalasuintha of divine memory, and her daughter, arguing that the emperor's troops should have restored her to her kingdom, which he, Witigis, has now done: 'By a marvellous design, God made us acquainted with each other before reaching the summit of rule', so Justinian should be influenced by their love which has brought Matasuntha to her inheritance!
11. MGH *AA* XII 483, tr. in Vitiello, *Amalasuintha. The Transformation of Queenship in the Post-Roman World* (Philadelphia 2017), pp. 100–101.
12. *Var.* X 31 and 32, tr. pp. 142, 144, emphasizing the commonwealth, *res publica restaurata*.
13. *Var.* X 31, tr. p. 143, *Geticus populus Martium*.

14. Tjader, *Papyri* II, 30 = Marini 114, *CLA*, XX no. 706; P. Amory, *People and Identity in Ostrogothic Italy 489–554* (Cambridge 2003), pp. 421–2, identifies her as a Catholic Goth and the sum is specified in gold coins of full weight (*dominicos, probitos, obriziacos, pensantes*).

15. On Secundus and Andreas (deceased), *dromonarii and* Witterit, *scutarius* see Amory, *People and Identity*, pp. 359, 412, 440; on Julianus and his father John, *PLRE* IIIA, pp. 730–31. Deichmann, *Ravenna*, II/1, pp. 21–7 believes this is the famous *argentarius* who financed the Ravenna churches; S. Barnish, 'The wealth of Iulianus Argentarius: late antique banking and the Mediterranean economy', *Byzantion* 55 (1985), pp. 5–38; S. Cosentino, 'Le fortune di un banchiere tardoantico. Giuliano argentario e l'economia di Ravenna nel VI secolo', in *Santi, banchieri, re. Ravenna e Classe nel VI secolo. San Severo il tempio ritrovato* (catalogue), eds. A. Augenti and C. Bertelli (Milan 2006), pp. 43–8.

16. Serapio, Petrus, *collectarius*; Latinus, *possessorum parens corporis*, and Eusebius; the remaining witnesses, Opilio *vir strenuus strator inlustris*; Candidianus *vir laudabilis*; Armentarius *inlustris*, and Generosus *augustalis*, an official working for the praetorian prefect, are all of more elevated rank than the Goths.

17. Tjäder, *Papyri* II 31.3 = Marini 115, and Regesta, no. 4 (p. 492). The *sorte barbari* is a reference to the lands redistributed to the Goths at the end of the fifth century.

18. All those involved appear to be Italo-Romans, though there are problems in using names to establish ethnic origin, see Amory (1997) which sparked a great controversy, and S. Lazard, 'Goti e Latini a Ravenna', in *Storia di Ravenna*, II/1, pp. 109–33.

19. The status of an *argentarius* obviously could vary, one is *honestus*, another *clarissimus* – perhaps from changing money some became more like bankers and rose to grander positions. M. S. Bjornlie, 'Governmental administration', in *A Companion to Ostrogothic Italy*, eds. J. J. Arnold, M. S. Bjornlie and K. Stessa (Leiden 2016), pp. 47–73.

20. Procopius, *Wars* VI i. 11–19; VI ii. 24–33 medical treatment; VI iii. 6, 14, 21–30 Antonina in Naples and Vesuvius.

21. *Wars* VI x. 7–20; Alex Sarantis paper to Adriatic conference on the importance of the fleet; J. Pryor, 'The Mediterranean breaks up: 500–1000', in *The Mediterranean in History*, ed. D. Abulafia (London 2003), notes that Osimo guards the approach to Ravenna.

22. *Wars* VI xxix. 1–31; Heather, *Restoration of Rome*, p. 178, sees Witigis as responsible for the offer, which might have permitted him to hang on to some vestige of his regal power.

23. *Wars* VI xxix. 32–4.

24. *Wars* VI xxx. 7.

25. Procopius, *Buildings* I x. 5, 16–17, tr. in Mango, *Art*, p. 109.

26. His last victory occurred in 559 when he drove the Kutrigurs back across the Danube.

27. The novel was first published in 1938 and is part of a persistent curiosity about Belisarius, see, for example, an opera by Donizetti, and recent studies by Ian Hughes, R. Boss and J. Ludlow. Also the Wikipedia entry: https://en.wikipedia.org/wiki/Belisarius#Later_life_and_campaigns.

CHAPTER 15

1. Tjäder, *Papyri* II, 33 = Marini 117, *CLA* XXV no. 793, dated after 16 July 541. An *uncia/oncia* is one-twelfth of a *jugerum* (acre), the regular land measurement. Isacius the soap maker/merchant was probably of Jewish and possibly eastern origin. On the Arian clergy, see R. T. Mathisen, 'Barbarian "Arian" Clergy, Church Organisation and Church Practices', in G. Berndt and R. Steinacher, eds., *Arianism: Roman Heresy and Barbarian Creed* (Farnham 2014), 145–91.

2. *LPR* c. 66 on Bishop Victor.

3. *LPR* c. 66, tr. p. 182, so the baths were probably still functioning in the ninth century, see Cirelli, *Archeologia,* pp. 112–13. Finally, at Classis, Agnellus adds that the same bishop decorated the tall, four-sided baptistery built by Peter Chrysologus next to the Petriana church, where two little medallions recorded the words 'by our holy lord' and 'father Victor' in gold letters, *LPR* c. 67, cf. *LPR* c. 50, tr. p. 161, on Peter's wonderful monument, 'with doubled walls and high walls built with mathematical art'.

4. G. Cavallo's brilliant survey, 'La cultura scritta tra Tarda Antichità e Alto Medioevo', in *Storia di Ravenna,* II/2, pp. 79–125, esp. 110–14; J. Herrin, *The Formation of Christendom* (Princeton 1989), pp. 111–13 on the slow acceptance of the Dionysian system of calculation.

5. S. Ćurčić, 'Design and structural innovation in Byzantine architecture before Hagia Sophia', in *Hagia Sophia From the Age of Justinian to the Present*, eds., R. Mark and A. Çakmak (Cambridge 1992), pp. 16–40. Whether the basilica of St Polyeuktos was also domed, remains unclear.

6. V. Shalev-Hurvitz, *Holy Sites Encircled. The Early Byzantine Concentric Churches of Jerusalem* (Oxford 2015), pp. 78–102 on the church of the Ascension, and on the wider impact pp. 294–9; pl. 20 and fgs. 39–40.

7. Procopius, *Buildings* I i. 27–50; Mango, *Art*, pp. 72–96 (including later descriptions). The dome of St Peter's has a diameter of 41.4m (136 ft).

8. S. Cosentino, 'Le fortune di un banchiere tardoantico. Giuliano argentario e l'economia di Ravenna nel VI secolo', in *Santi, banchieri, re. Ravenna e Classe nel VI secolo. San Severo il tempio ritrovato* (catalogue), eds. A. Augenti and C. Bertelli (Milan 2006), pp. 43–8; and the funerary

inscription of Giorgius, *argentarius*, son of the Petrus, *vir clarissimus*, *argentarius*, who died in 581, ibid. p. 189.

9. M. J. Johnson, *San Vitale in Ravenna and Octagonal Churches in Late Antiquity* (2018); Deichmann, *Ravenna* II/1, pp. 21–7, esp. 24–6 on their rising social status, from *strenui* to *clarissimi*; *idem, Ravenna* II/2, pp. 3–7, 21–7, 48 on Ioulianos; *PLRE* IIIA, pp. 730–31.

10. *LPR* c. 61, tr. p. 177, the epitaph of Ecclesius. *Rerum Italicarum Scriptores*, ed. L. Muratori, 1.2 (Milan 1725), pp. 558–60, a *Passio* attributed to Ps-Ambrosius; cf. Jäggi, *Ravenna*, pp. 240–43. On Ambrose's visit to Bologna, N. B. McLynn, *Ambrose of Milan. Church and Court in a Christian Capital* (Berkeley/Los Angeles/London 1994), pp. 347–50.

11. E. Cirelli, 'Spolia e riuso di materiali tra tardo Antichità e l'alto Medioevo a Ravenna', *Hortus Artium Medievalium* 17 (2011), pp. 39–48, esp. 42–3 on these 'giulianei', bricks of a new size, 4.45cm, employed with a larger amount of mortar and a double drawing of the joins between them; *idem, Archeologia*, pp. 101–2.

12. D. Deliyannis, 'Ecclesius of Ravenna as donor in text and image', in *Envisioning the Bishop. Image and the Episcopacy in the Middle Ages*, eds. S. Danielson and E. A. Gatti (Turnhout 2014), pp. 41–62, with a discussion about the contemporary portrait of Pope Felix IV in Ss Cosmas and Damian in Rome, and giving that church priority as the first to portray the pope as donor, ibid., pp. 52–3; Deichmann, *Ravenna* III, pp. 315–19.

13. On the status of mosaicists, R. Browning, 'Education in the Roman Empire', *Cambridge Ancient History* vol. XIV, p. 880: the Edict on Maximum Prices of 314 stipulates a daily rate of 150 *denarii* for portrait painters, 75 for mural painters, 60 for mosaicists, and 50 for masons and carpenters, well below the rates for professional teachers like the grammarians (Latin and Greek) who received 200, or lawyers. On the training of mosaicists, see W. Wootton, 'A portrait of the artist as mosaicist under the Roman Empire', in *Beyond Boundaries: Connecting Visual Cultures in the Provinces of Ancient Rome*, eds. S. E. Alcock et al. (Los Angeles 2016), pp. 62–76, on family groups, father and son mosaicists.

14. Y. Marano, 'The circulation of marble in the Adriatic Sea at the time of Justinian', in *Ravenna, Its Role in Earlier Medieval Change and Exchange*, eds. J. Herrin and J. Nelson (London 2016), pp. 111–32. Such export trade is clear from a ship that was wrecked off the coast of Sicily (Marzamemi) with complete marble fittings for church.

15. Deichmann, *Ravenna* II/2, pp. 96–100 on the monograms of Victor and Ioulianos; *idem, Ravenna* II/3, pp. 116–18 on the marble and stucco decoration of the apse at San Vitale.

16. On the imperial regalia, see A. M. Stout, 'Jewelry as a symbol of status in the Roman Empire', in *The World of Roman Costume*, eds. J. L. Sebesta and L. Bonfante (Madison Wisc. 1994), pp. 77–100, esp. 83–98.

17. I. Andreescu-Treadgold and W. Treadgold, 'Procopius and the Imperial Panels of S. Vitale', *Art Bulletin* 79 (1997), pp. 708–23. Cf. Charles Barber, 'The Imperial Panels at S. Vitale: a reconsideration', *BMGS* 14 (1990), pp. 19–42; S. G. MacCormack, *Art and Ceremony in Late Antiquity* (Berkeley/Los Angeles/London 1981), pp. 259–66; Deichmann, *Ravenna* II/2, pp. 180–87; O. Simpson, *Sacred Fortress: Byzantine Art and Statecraft in Ravenna* (Chicago 1948, repr. Princeton 1987), pp. 36–9.

18. Antonina had accompanied her husband through both the Vandal and the Gothic wars and her husband Belisarius was depicted on mosaics in Constantinople that celebrated his victories. But as the extent of the mosaic replacement is not clear, it may be fanciful to identify the figures beside the imperial pair as the victorious general and his wife.

19. Agnellus reports this delegation of clerics and citizens travelling to Constantinople (the date is not accurately fixed, *c.* 544), *LPR* c. 70, tr. p. 185.

20. *LPR* c. 71, tr. p. 187, *primates urbis, magni, pusilli, et mediocres.*

21. If only the head of Maximian and the new inscription had to be added, the work could easily have been accomplished during the first three months of 547.

22. *LPR* c. 73, tr. pp. 188–9; Nauerth, *Bishofsbuch*, I, p. 312 suggests that the legend of supplies arriving overnight might derive from the speed of the work noted in an inscription.

23. A. R. Terry and H. Maguire, *Dynamic Splendor: The Wall Mosaics in the Cathedral of Eufrasius at Poreč* (University Park PA 2007) and personal observation.

24. L. James, *Mosaics in the Medieval World* (Cambridge 2017), p. 245 thinks this likely.

25. Ibid., pp. 243–5. In 553 Pope Pelagius I condemned a bishop named Eufrasius for committing numerous crimes and holding heretical views, but this may not be the same person who built the church. Cf. Picard, *Le souvenir des évêques*, pp. 652–4; *Pros. Chrét. Italie*, I, p. 672.

26. Mango, *Art*, pp. 34–5. This icon was painted for the dedication of the chapel of the Mother of God in the Blachernai church, called the *soros* (reliquary), that was built to house it. Another reference to an icon of them crowned by John the Baptist, which adorned the church they founded at Ephesus, is also known from verses, *The Greek Anthology* 1, bk I, 91, tr. p. 39.

27. Paul the silentiarios, Description of Hagia Sophia, 563, tr. in Mango, *Art*.

28. *Var.* X 20, 21, letters of Theodahad to the empress.

CHAPTER 16

1. Procopius, *Wars* VI, VII and VIII (although he was not an eyewitness to the events recorded, he provides the same degree of detail).

2. M. P. Canepa, *The Two Eyes of the Earth: Art and Ritual of Kingship Between Rome and Sasanian Iran* (Berkeley/Los Angeles/London 2009); Procopius, *Wars* II covers this second Persian campaign against the empire.

3. D. Stathakopoulos, *Famine and Pestilence in the Late Roman and Byzantine Empire* (Ashgate 2004); K. Harper, *The Fate of Rome. Climate, Disease and the End of an Empire* (Princeton 2017). But cf. L. Mordechai and M. Eisenberg, 'Rejecting catastrophe: the case of the Justinianic plague', *Past and Present* 244 (2019), pp. 3–50.

4. R. D. Scott, 'Chronicles versus classicizing history: Justinian's West and East', in his *Byzantine Chronicles and the Sixth Century* (Farnham 2012), pp. 1–25.

5. *Wars* VII; J. Conant, *Staying Roman. Conquest and Identity in Africa and the Mediterranean, 439–700* (Cambridge 2012), p. 238 lists four more who all served in Italy: Herodian 1, Innocentius 1, Ioannes 46, nephew of Vitalian, and Magnus 1, *PLRE* III, pp. 593–5, 621, 652–61, 804–5.

6. J. Pryor, 'The Mediterranean breaks up: 500–1000', in *The Mediterranean in History* ed. D. Abulafia (London 2003), p. 156.

7. *Wars* VII, ix. 13–14.

8. *Wars* VII iii. 4–6. It's very hard to untangle the various spheres of interest and complicated relations between imperially and locally appointed administrators in Ravenna. The city must have grown much larger, as it extended its capacity to lodge military forces: 12,000 men under 11 leaders (*archontes*) were involved in the campaign against Verona.

9. D. Stathakopoulos, 'Travelling with the plague', in *Travel in the Byzantine World*, ed. R. Macrides (Aldershot 2002), pp. 99–106; *LPR* c. 68, tr. pp. 183–4 (although when Agnellus says that all Victor's good work has now been undone through 'evil men and false Christians', with the apocalyptic description of the 'end and destruction of the world', he could be referring to his own mid-ninth-century time).

10. *PLRE* IIIB, pp. 912–28.

11. *Wars* VIII xxvi. 22–5. Although Procopius was no longer an eyewitness of these campaigns, his account of Narses' military strategy and skills as a commander is matched by reliable reports of Totila's opposing tactics.

12. *Wars* VIII, xxxi. 18–20; P. Sarris, *Empires of Faith* (Oxford 2011), pp. 118–20.

13. 'Pragmatic Sanction', a constitution of 554, tr. in D. J. D. Miller and P. Sarris, *The Novels of Justinian, A Complete and Annotated English Translation* (Cambridge 2018), vol. 2, Appendix 7, pp. 1117–30. Cf. *CJC* I 27. Many laws, edicts or constitutions were described as pragmatic. This was allegedly prompted by a petition of Pope Vigilius, but in 554 he was on his way back to Rome, utterly defeated by the Fifth Oecumenical Council, and died at Syracuse in 555.

14. Miller and Sarris, *Novels of Justinian*, vol. 1, pp. 20–23, on the sixth-century Latin translations of the Novels and their use for teaching in law schools; ibid., vol. 2, Appendix 7, cc. 11, 15, 17, 19, 22, 25, 27 for specific regulations.

15. Pragmatic Sanction, c. 12, Miller and Sarris, *Novels of Justinian*, vol. 2, pp. 1122–3. Justin II extended the new form of choosing provincial governors to the whole empire, Novel 149 in 569.

16. S. Cosentino, 'L'approvvigionamento annonario di Ravenna dal V all'VIII secolo: l'organizzazione e i riflessi socio-economici', in *Ravenna da capitale imperiale a capitale esarcale*, 2 vols. (Spoleto 2005), vol. 1, pp. 405–34 (numbers based on a comparison with Justinian's earlier arrangements for Africa).

17. Novel 86 (539), Miller and Sarris, *Novels of Justinian*, vol. 1, pp. 587–90; *CJC* I 4 on episcopal courts, esp. 4.21 and 31. Online at https://droitro main.univ-grenoble-alpes.fr/Corpus/CJ1.htm#4.

18. *LPR* c. 79, tr. p. 193 (the Goths held out against Narses in Verona longer than any other city). Manichaeans had also been identified in Rome under popes Gelasius, Symmachus and Hormisdas, between 492 and 523, who had ordered them to be sent into exile and had their heretical writings burned in public; *LPR* c. 90, tr. p. 203 under Bishop Agnellus.

19. Tjäder, *Papyri* I 4–5, B V 11–B VIII 7 (will of George), *CLA* XVII, no. 653; I, 13 (553) *CLA* XXIX, no. 880; and I, 8 (564) *CLA* XVII, no. 652. A similar case of protection for two young sons occurred in neighbouring Rieti in 557, when Gundihild, *inlustris femina* and widow of Gudahal, requested the council to appoint a tutor for her young sons. This was a legal obligation for city councils and in this case Flavianus, *vir honestus*, was appointed, *Papyri* I, 7 = Marini, 79, *CLA* XX, no. 71.

20. Tjäder, *Papyri* 8 (564) = Marini, 80, *CLA* XVII, no. 652; see a full list of the contents and their value in Thomas S. Burns, *A History of the Ostrogoths* (Bloomington 1984), pp. 132–4.

21. F. Borrei, 'Duces e magistri militum nell'Italia esarcale (VI-VIII secolo)', *Reti Medievali Rivista* 6/2 (2005), pp. 19–60.

22. Paul the deacon, *HL* II 3.

23. *PLRE* IIIB, p. 925, he had been recalled by Justin II and was replaced by Longinus. He had accumulated a great treasure which made some jealous.

24. *LP* 63.3–5, tr. p. 62; John of Ephesus, bk I. 39 records Narses' foundation of the monastery called Kathara in Bithynia before he was sent to Italy. After his many victories, his bones were brought back and deposited there in the presence of *reges* (King Justin and Queen Sophia) who took part in the funeral procession and in his canonization as the founder. John of Ephesus online@archive.org, pp. 75–6. He died in 574, *PLRE* IIIB, p. 926; see L. H. Fauber, *Narses, Hammer of the Goths: The Life and Times of Narses the Eunuch* (Gloucester/New York 1990).

CHAPTER 17

1. Justinian had condemned them in imperial edicts of 535, 541 and 542, which repeated earlier laws including *CJC*, I, 5, 12.4, see D. J. D. Miller and P. Sarris, *The Novels of Justinian, A Complete and Annotated English Translation* (Cambridge 2018), vol. 1, pp. 353–7 (Novel 37), vol. 2, pp. 711–13, 739–41 (Novels 109 and 115).

2. D. Angelov and J. Herrin, 'The Christian imperial tradition – Greek and Latin', in *Universal Empire*, eds. P. F. Bang and D. Kolodziejczyk (Cambridge 2012), pp. 149–74.

3. J. Herrin, 'The Pentarchy: theory and reality in the ninth century', *Cristianità d'Occidente e Cristianità d'Oriente (secoli VI–XI)*, Settimana 51 (Spoleto 2004), pp. 591–626, repr. in *Margins and Metropolis. Authority across the Byzantine Empire* (Princeton 2013), pp. 239–66. This was one reason why the Monothelete Council of 662 was considered illegitimate – neither Jerusalem nor Rome participated, indeed it is not clear that they had been invited.

4. *LP* 61, tr. pp. 58–61. The account of his life, composed in Rome, claims that Narses put pressure on Justinian to permit the pope to return.

5. E. Chrysos, *Die Bischöflisten des V. Ökumenischen Konzils (553)* (Bonn 1966), pp. 128–38 (Milan was the only other Italian see represented at the council); J. Herrin, *The Formation of Christendom* (Princeton 1989), pp. 121–3.

6. C. Sotinel, 'The Three Chapters and the transformations of Italy', in *The Crisis of the Oikoumene: The Three Chapters and the Failed Quest for Unity in the Sixth-century Mediterranean*, eds. C. Chazelle and C. Cubitt (Turnhout 2007), pp. 84–120, at 92.

7. *LPR* c. 81, tr. pp. 194–5 (Deliyannis, p. 212, suggests that this would have been one of the earliest uses of the Vulgate translation in Italy).

8. C. Jäggi, 'Ravenna in the sixth century: the archaeology of change', in *Ravenna, Its Role in Earlier Medieval Change and Exchange*, eds. J. Herrin and J. Nelson (London 2016), pp. 87–111, esp. 102–4, makes this point most convincingly. E. Schoolman *Rediscovering Sainthood in Italy: Hagiography and the Late Antique Past in Ravenna* (New York 2016), on the creation of this life of St Apollinaris, ed. L. Muratori, *Rerum Italicarum Scriptores* 1.2 (Milan 1725), pp. 538–46; the Passio in *AASS* Iul V, 345–50, and sermon 128 of St Peter Chrysologus on the annual celebration of the saint, CCL 24B Sermones II, ed. A. Olivar (1975), pp. 789–91.

9. *LPR* cc. 69–71, 78 for his quote from the *Histories*.

10. *LPR* cc. 75–6, tr. pp. 189–90.

11. *LPR* c. 76, tr. p. 190.

12. *LPR* c. 74, tr. p. 189 on *vistrum*.
13. *ACO* ser 1, 4 part 2, pp. 224–5; C. Kelly, *Ruling the Later Roman Empire* (Cambridge MA and London 2004), p. 171, gifts of two and even four ivory thrones, cf. Jones, *LRE* I, p. 346 (no mention of thrones, just lots of gold with the list of recipients).
14. These are documented in the famous account *On Buildings,* ed. and tr. H. B. Dewing with G. Downey (London 1961); see also *De Aedificiis: le texte de Procope et les réalités,* eds. C. Roueché, M. Carrié and N. Duval (Turnhout 2001).
15. *LPR* c. 77, tr. p. 191.
16. *LPR* cc. 63 and 77, tr. pp. 178–9, 191; Jäggi, *Ravenna*, pp. 276–7; *eadem*, 'Ravenna in the sixth century', pp. 87–109, esp. 100–106.
17. *LPR* c. 72, tr. pp. 187–8; Deliyannis, *Ravenna*, p. 188, n. 11 thinks these would have been monograms like that of Victor in S. Vitale.
18. *LPR* c. 77, tr. p. 192; tr. and ed. Nauerth, I, p. 314, n. 315. The rector of the church of Pola was closely connected to Maximian, who appears to have exercised rights to taxation in the region. Possibly the rector was responsible for bringing this revenue to Ravenna, and the house where he lived was actually there, rather than in Pola (see the contrast between *istius rector ecclesiae in ipsa civitate*).
19. See Deliyannis, *Ravenna*, pp. 212–13. Maximian might have written a list of all the bishops of Ravenna, which would have formed the basis for Agnellus' later record, in contrast to his chronicle which would have been a secular one.
20. *LPR* c. 80, tr. pp. 193–4.
21. *LPR* c. 77, tr as 'First Flag' by Deliyannis, p. 191, and might therefore be identified with the *numerus* called First Banner. The Latin *bandus* seems interchangeable with *numerus*, see Brown, *Gentlemen and Officers*, p. 97, who finds these terms used for meeting places and halls. This barracks of Maximian's time would have been one of them.
22. *LPR* c. 140, tr. p. 265.
23. *LPR* c. 83, tr. p. 197.
24. MGH *Epp* III no. 6, Pope Pelagius to the patrician Valerianus (445–6) about the *schismaticos* that Valerius and his brother John, *patricius*, have to discipline; P. M. Gassó and C. M. Batlle, eds., *Pelagii I Papae epistulae quae supersunt, 556–561* (Montserrat 1956), no. 59, cf. no. 52 to Valerius and no. 53 to John.
25. Pelagius II, MGH *Epp* III nos. 9, 10, and 11, Gassó and Batlle, nos. 37, 50 and 74 to Agnellus of Ravenna.

CHAPTER 18

1. *LPR* c. 84, tr. p. 198.
2. Justinian, Novel 37, tr. D. J. D. Miller and P. Sarris, *The Novels of Justinian, A Complete and Annotated English Translation* (Cambridge 2018), vol. 1, pp. 353–7; Procopius, *Wars* IV xiv. 11–12, on the large numbers of Arian soldiers of Herulian origin who were serving in the Roman army in Libya, and 13–16, emphasizing the anxiety when Easter approached and the Arians were not allowed to baptize their children; J. Conant, *Staying Roman. Conquest and Identity in Africa and the Mediterranean, 439–700* (Cambridge 2015), pp. 316–24.
3. *LPR* c. 85, tr. pp. 198–9; this is the only reference to an imperial instruction.
4. *LPR* c. 86, tr. p. 199.
5. See Ch. 11; A. Urbano, 'Donation, dedication and *damnatio memoriae*. The Catholic reconciliation of Ravenna and the church of S. Apollinare Nuovo', *Journal of Early Christian Studies* 13 (2005), pp. 71–110; Jäggi, *Ravenna*, pp. 177–92, esp. 184–5 showing which sections of the mosaics are original.
6. See the old photo which shows the feet, now removed, and pictures of the hands of courtiers, in Jäggi, *Ravenna*, p. 184.
7. Deichmann, *Ravenna* II/1, pp. 149–54 attributed all the saints and martyrs to the 560s, though the most unusual posture of the Virgin Mary, raising her right hand in blessing, while the Christ Child does not, is attributed to the original of *c.* 500. The cult of St Martin was well-developed in Ravenna – Archbishop Maximian had constructed a church dedicated to the saint. Stephen was also linked with Protasius and Gervasius, the sons of S. Vitale, in another chapel close to the church of S. Lorenzo in Caesarea, and other monuments. Originally the procession of men included St Stephen, the first martyr, who was represented gesturing towards the enthroned Christ.
8. A. R. Terry and H. Maguire, *Dynamic Splendor: The Wall Mosaics in the Cathedral of Eufrasius at Poreč* (University Park PA 2007).
9. *LPR* c. 88, tr. pp. 201–2, with additional interpretation of the colours of their cloaks.
10. Since both portraits have been heavily restored, it is hard to imagine the original depictions.
11. Tjäder, *Papyri* I, 13 = Marini 86, also *Regesta* no. 7, *CLA* XXIX, 880; the record was drawn up in the house of law by Severus, the *scribtor* and *forensis* of Ravenna, and witnessed by the donor and her husband who made the sign of the cross (for they could not write) and four other witnesses with typically Roman names.

12. P. Amory, *People and Identity in Ostrogothic Italy 489–554* (Cambridge 2003), pp. 409 (Ranilo) and 355 (Ademunt), with the suggestion that the bequest reflected a recent conversion to the Catholic faith.

13. S. Cosentino, 'Social instability and economic decline of the Ostrogothic community in the aftermath of the imperial victory: the papyri evidence', in *Ravenna, Its Role in Earlier Medieval Change and Exchange*, eds. J. Herrin and J. Nelson (London 2016), pp. 133–49.

14. Tjäder, *Papyri* I, 9 = Marini 141, *CLA* XX 710; Amory, *People and Identity*, p. 415.

15. *Papyri* II, 34 = Marini, 119, *CLA* XX 704; *eclesie legis Gothorum sanctae Anastasie*, or *aclisie gotice sancte Anastasie*.

16. *Papyri* I, 8 = Marini 80, *CLA* XVII 652; see Amory, *People and Identity*, pp. 251–5, 475; S. Lazard, 'Goti e Latini in Ravenna', in *Storia di Ravenna* II/1, pp. 109–43.

17. CJC I, 5 12 4, and Novel 37, in Miller and Sarris, *Novels of Justinian*, vol. I, pp. 353–7; Cosentino, 'Social instability . . . the papyri evidence', pp. 133–49.

18. Tjäder, *Papyri* I, 28 B = Marini 108, *CLA* IV 232 (Wililiwa); *LP* 65, tr. 63 (Unigildus); *LPR* c. 198, tr. pp. 283–4.

19. *Papyri* I, 14–15 = Marini 88/88A, *CLA* XXI 713; *Papyri* 20 = Marini 93, *CLA* XXI 717; *Papyri* 21 = Marini 94, *CLA* XXII 720.

20. *Papyri* I, 3 = Marini 137, *CLA* XX 709; cf. *Papyri* 34 = Marini 119 and *Regesta* no. 6 of 551, *CLA* XX 704. Only about a fifth of a much longer 3–5m roll survives.

21. *LPR* cc. 88–9, tr. pp. 202–3.

22. *LPR* c. 91, tr. p. 203.

23. *LPR* c. 84, tr. p. 198.

24. Tjäder, *Papyri* I, 2 (565–70) = Marini no. 87, *CLA* XX 711.

25. L. Pietri, 'Venance Fortunat et ses commanditaires: un poète italien dans la société gallo-franque', Settimana 39 (Spoleto 1992), pp. 729–58 disputes the theory that Venantius may have been sent to Metz as a spy for Emperor Justin II. He seems to have gone in search of patrons and ended up in Poitiers, close to St Radegund.

26. M. Herren, *The Humblest Sparrow. The Poetry of Venantius Fortunatus* (Ann Arbor 2009), p. 7.

27. Tjäder, *Papyri* I, 6 = Marini 75, *CLA* XXI 714.

28. *Papyri* I, 8 (564) = Marini 80, *CLA* XVII 652; Marini 120 (572); *CIL* XI 317 (before 574).

29. *Papyri* I, 14–15 A–B = Marini 88/88A, *CLA* XXIX 889 record Gunderit, *exceptor*, and Liberius, *tabellionus huius civitates ravennae*.

30. Herren, *The Humblest Sparrow*, p. 62.

CHAPTER 19

1. T. Hodgkin, *Italy and her Invaders*, 8 vols. (Oxford 1880–99), vol. 5, bk 6, pp. 80–164; G. Ausenda et al., eds., *The Langobards before the Frankish Conquest: An Ethnographic Perspective* (Woodbridge 2009).

2. N. Christie, 'Invasion or invitation? The Longobard occupation of northern Italy 568–569', *Romanobarbarica* 11 (1990), pp. 79–108.

3. L. H. Fauber, *Narses, Hammer of the Goths* (Gloucester/New York 1990); *PLRE* IIIB, p. 797, Longinus 5.

4. Roman hostility to the 'Greeks' and Narses as the man who represented them becomes a trope in anti-Constantinopolitan sentiment.

5. Paul the deacon, *HL* II 6–12, 14, 25–28.

6. In contrast, J. Moorhead, 'Ostrogothic Italy and the Lombard invasions', in *NCMH* I, p. 160, describes Ravenna as 'A branch office of a corporation controlled in Constantinople and staffed at the highest levels by non-natives' – typical of the presumed decline of the city.

7. *HL* III 8; *PLRE* III, p. 1159. Moorhead, 'Ostrogothic Italy', pp. 155–6; L. Paroli, 'La cultura materiale nella prima età longobarda', in *Visigoti e Longobardi*, eds. J. Arce and P. Delogu (Florence 2011), 257–304, including a necklace made entirely of Justinianic *solidi*.

8. *HL* II 25 on Lombard invasion of Liguria (569), 26–27 on siege and capture of Pavia.

9. *HL* II 28–30.

10. T. C. Lounghis, *Les ambassades byzantines en Occident . . . (407–1096)* (Athens 1980), pp. 89–93; *Le Relazioni Internazionali nell'Alto Medioevo*, Settimana 58 (Spoleto 2011).

11. *LP* 64, tr. p. 62. On the Lombard advance, *HL* II 25–27, pp. 79–81, and very brief mention in *LPR* c. 94, tr. p. 205; J. Jarnut, 'Gens, rex and regnum of the Lombards', in *Regna and Gentes: The Relationship between Late Antique and Early Medieval Peoples and Kingdoms in the Transformation of the Roman World*, eds. H. W. Goetz et al. (Leiden 2002), pp. 409–27.

12. *LPR* c. 51, p. 163, records its consecration by Peter Chrysologus, more than a century earlier, when Galla Placidia is supposed to have had a confessor named Barbatianus, see E. Schoolman, *Rediscovering Sainthood in Italy: Hagiography and the Late Antique Past in Ravenna* (New York 2016); M. Verhoeven, *The Early Christian Monuments of Ravenna. Transformations and Memory* (Turnhout 2011), pp. 80–84.

13. *HL* III 18 and 19, with the long verse epitaph on his grave in San Vitale, pp. 118–20. J. Conant, *Staying Roman. Conquest and Identity in Africa and the Mediterranean, 439–700* (Cambridge 2015), table 4.6, p. 227, adds him to potential commanders in Africa in 598.

14. *HL* III 19. Cf. Brown, *Gentlemen and Officers*, p. 41.

15. The Visigoths are identified as *'hostes barbaros'* in an inscription of 589/90 in Carthagena.
16. *LPR* c. 93, tr. p. 205.
17. *LPR* c. 93, tr. p. 205, *in regione ... Vico Salutaris*, see A. Augenti and E. Cirelli, 'San Severo and religious life in Ravenna during the ninth and tenth centuries', in *Ravenna, Its Role in Earlier Medieval Change and Exchange*, eds. J. Herrin and J. Nelson (London 2016), pp. 297–321. NB in the same year Agnellus notes that the Veneto was occupied by the Lombards and the Romans expelled, Pavia was captured, and there was an outbreak of pestilence that killed many cows.
18. *LPR* c. 98, tr. pp. 213–14.
19. These African exiles produced the most sophisticated theological opposition to Constantinople, see J. Herrin, *The Formation of Christendom* (Princeton 1989), pp. 122–3, 160–61; F. R. Whelan, *Being Christian in Vandal Africa: The Politics of Orthodoxy in the Post-Imperial West* (Oakland CA 2007).
20. *Epistulae Pelagii*, ed. Thiel, MGH *Epp.* III; *HL* III 20. On the background, see C. Sotinel, *Rhétorique de la faute et pastorale de la réconciliation dans la lettre apologétique contre Jean de Ravenna* (Rome 1994), pp. 68–147.
21. *HL* III 26 on Smaragdus.
22. *HL* III 26.
23. Sotinel, *Rhétorique de la faute,* esp. pp. 23–4.
24. Tjäder, *Papyri* I, 6 = Marini 75, *CLA* XXI 714.
25. Tjäder, *Papyri* I, 14–15 = Marini 88/88A, *CLA* XXIX 889; Amory, *People and Identity*, Gunderit 3, p. 382. Originally *exceptor* was a shorthand writer attached to the fiscal offices of the *res privata* and *comes rerum patrimonium* – by the sixth century probably a scribe with specific city responsibilities.
26. *ad Monita auri in porticum sacri palati*, Tjäder, *Papyri* II, 36 = Marini 121, *CLA* XXI 715, a sale made between 575 and 591. Similar designations occur in records from Rome, see *Papyri* I, 18–19 = Marini 92 *CLA* XXII 718.
27. A. Augenti, *La basilica e il monastero di San Severo a Classe* (Ravenna 2000); *idem*, 'Ravenna e Classe: archeologica di due città tra la tarda Antichità et l'alto Medieoevo', in *Le città italiane trà la tardo Antichità e l'alto Medioevo*, ed. A. Augenti (Florence 2006), pp. 185–217.
28. *LPR* c. 97, tr. p. 213.

CHAPTER 20

1. J. Conant, *Staying Roman. Conquest and Identity in Africa and the Mediterranean, 439–700* (Cambridge 2015), table 4.4, p. 218.

2. Brown, *Gentlemen and Officers*, pp. 46–8, emphasizing the long drawn out development of the exarchate; L. Brubaker and J. Haldon, *Byzantium in the Iconoclast Era c. 680–850. A History* (Cambridge 2011), pp. 723–8, confirm the same lengthy process of establishing *themata*. The extent to which in the West this promoted the military landholding system identified as 'feudalism' is unclear, but the conflicts that pitted imperial against local forces clearly contributed to the division of territory into smaller units under military command.

3. *CIL* VI no. 1200, see Ch. 25 for details.

4. *PLRE* IIIB pp. 1164–6 on the career of Smaragdus.

5. E. Martinori, *Via Flaminia, Studio storico topografico* (Rome 1929) with splendid ancient photographs.

6. *Il Corridoio bizantino e la via Amerina in Umbria nell'Alto Medioevo*, ed. E. Menestò (Spoleto 1999), esp. the long introductory chapter and the following one by Carile.

7. P. Arthur, *Naples from Roman Town to City State: An Archaeological Perspective* (London 2002).

8. Brown, *Gentlemen and Officers,* on *magistri militum*, who appear frequently in the correspondence of Pope Gregory I (590–604); F. Borrei, 'Duces e magistri militum nell'Italia esarcale (VI-VIII secolo)', *Reti Medievali Rivista 6/2* (2005), pp. 19–60.

9. On *bucellarii*, Jones, *LRE*, pp. 275, 290, 665–57.

10. Brown, *Gentlemen and Officers*, pp. 86, 88, 220.

11. Ibid., pp. 84–6, 89–90, 92–3; Guillou, *Régionalisme*, pp. 153–61. A document of *c.* 600 names one witness, Adquisitus *vir clarissimus*, who was commander (*optio*) of the Milan *numerus*, Tjäder, *Papyri* I, 20, *CLA* XXI 717.

12. Brown, *Gentlemen and Officers*, p. 93; *numerus* is the equivalent of Greek *arithmos,* used interchangeably with *bandus*. Reduced reliance on mercenaries meant a greater use of native-born troops, recruited and trained in the regions that gave them their names, e.g. the *numerus Tergetinus*, from Trieste.

13. Tjäder, *Papyri* I, 16 = Marini 90 *CLA* IV 240; Brown, *Gentlemen and Officers*, p. 89; *PLRE* III p. 700, Ioannes 228, *primicerius felicum numeri Theodosiacus* (sic), *spatharios* and *adiutor*.

14. As above, the banker is called *chrysokatalaktis* and the judicial clerk, *exceptor*.

15. Brown, *Gentlemen and Officers*, pp. 92–3 on the *signa* and *bandora* of Istria that played the same role.

16. *Strategikon* of Maurice, tr. G. Dennis (Vienna 1981), p. 83 on military feints.

17. Emphasized by Brown, *Gentlemen and Officers*, pp. 50–51.

18. Tjäder, *Papyri* I, 28 B 5, *CLA* IV 232; Wililiwa has a Germanic name and identifies herself as *guta*, Goth. Tjäder, *Papyri*, I, 21, *CLA* XXII 720, for the donation of Deusdedit and Melissa.

19. Tjäder, *Papyri* I, 22 = Marini 95 = *Regesta* no. 25, *CLA* XXIX 887; the soldier Paulacis made a gift of 36 gold *solidi*.

20. Bury, *LRE*, II p. 282.

21. Brown, *Gentlemen and Officers*, pp. 48–51.

22. Gregory of Tours, *Histories*, bk X 2.

23. Paul the deacon, *HL* III 13.

24. *HL* IV 32 on Smaragdus making peace with Agilulf for 12,000 *solidi*, while the cities of Tuscany were taken by Lombards, and then Agilulf made another peace treaty for three years.

25. Letters of King Childebert II and replies by an exarch (Romanus or Smaragdus), MGH *Epp* III, nos. 37, 40, 41 and 46, pp. 110–53.

26. *HL* IV 23.

CHAPTER 21

1. R. A. Marcus, *Gregory the Great and his World* (Cambridge 1997); *idem*, *The End of Ancient Christianity* (Cambridge 1990), pp. 223–8; P. Brown, *The Rise of Western Christendom* (Oxford 1996), pp. 133–47, rev. 10th anniversary edition with an important new preface (Chichester 2013), pp. 190–215; S. Boesch Gajano, *Gregorio Magno. Alle origini del Medio-evo* (Rome 2004); J. Herrin, *The Formation of Christendom* (Princeton 1989), pp. 145–82.

2. Maurice's letters to Gregory reveal the complaints of the schismatic bishops, T. C. Lounghis, *Les ambassades byzantines en Occident . . . (407–1096)* (Athens 1980), pp. 466–7 citing Gregory the Great, *Regesten* I 16, II 45 (online at Christian Classics Ethereal Library, *NPNF* vol. 212) and tr. J. R. C. Martyn, *The Letters of Gregory the Great*, 3 vols. (Toronto 2004).

3. *The Crisis of the Oikoumene. The Three Chapters and the Failed Quest for Unity in the Sixth-century Mediterranean*, eds. C. Chazelle and C. Cubitt (Turnhout 2007). Gregory, *Regesten* II 32 to Albio, *mm gloriosus* (592); *PLRE* III 40–41 identifies him with Aldio, also mentioned in *Regesten* II 27, cf IX 103.

4. Gregory, *Regesten* II 46 to John the Roman in Ravenna about Severus of Aquileia, with instructions to use funds to ransom free men taken prisoner by the Lombards at Fanum.

5. Gregory, *Regesten* V 23 to Castorius; V 25 to Severus, bishop of Ficulum, who was instructed to visit the bereaved church and ensure the correct promotion; V 48 concerning the election of Marinianus.

6. Gregory, *Regesten* VI 2.

7. *LPR* c. 100, tr. p. 215. *The Book of Pastoral Rule*, tr. G. Demacopoulos (Crestwood NY 2007); Boesch Gajano, *Gregorio Magno*, pp. 77–80.

8. Agnellus claims that when a bishopric has to be filled, some ecclesiastics employ spies to find out how much their rivals are willing to pay, and then offer twice the sum in order to secure the appointment of their own protégé (and the sums are not trivial, 500 and 1000 *solidi!*).

9. Gregory, *Regesten* VI 34; cf. IX 167; XIV 11. *Pros. Chrét. Italie* I p. 25 on Adeodatus, pp. 800–801 on Felix. In 599 Archbishop Marinianus had sent his deacon Florentinus to Rome to explain the situation.

10. Gregory, *Regesten* VI 1; VI 24; VI 29; XII 6 (January 602).

11. *LP* 66, tr. p. 63, cf. Paul the deacon, *HL* IV 8 records that Romanus went from Ravenna to Rome and on the way back he captured these cities.

12. *HL* IV 2, Paul makes much of the rivalry between Smaragdus and Gallicinus, *HL* IV 28.

13. *HL* IV 28, but then she died in childbirth.

14. *HL* IV 32.

15. Gregory's letters to the participants in the Salona scandal and to those in Ravenna, also alluding to Emperor Maurice's intervention, *Regesten* VI 25 and 26. On Callinicus, see *PLRE* IIIA, p. 264; he campaigned against some of the Slavs and received a letter of congratulation from Gregory, *Regesten*. IX, 154.

16. *HL* VI 14.

17. *LPR* prefatory verse, cc. 26 and 86, tr. pp. 96, 123, 199.

CHAPTER 22

1. *PLRE* IIIB, pp. 1164–6, for his career, cf. Ch. 24. Smaragdus may have been a eunuch since he held the position of *praepositus sacri palatii*. Cf. inscription below.

2. Gregory, *Regesten* XIII 32, 39 congratulations to Phokas; XIII 40 to Empress Leontia (July 603); tr. J. R. C. Martyn, *The Letters of Gregory the Great*, 3 vols. (Toronto 2004), vol. III, App. 8 on the reception of the imperial icons. S. Boesch Gajano, *Gregorio Magno. Alle origini del Medioevo* (Rome 2004), pp. 31, 119.

3. E. Thunø, 'The Pantheon in the Middle Ages', online at https://erenow.net/ancient/the-pantheon-from-antiquity-to-the-present/8.php. S. de Blaauw, 'Das Pantheon als christlicher Tempel' in *Bild und Formensprache der spätantiken Kunst. Hugo Brandenburg zum 65 Geburtstag* (Münster 1994), pp. 13–26; the church of Sts Cosmas and Damian under Pope Felix IV (526–30) involved the re-dedication of a secular building. *LP* 69, tr. p. 64; *LPR* c. 107, tr. p. 224.

4. *CIL* VI no. 1200, on the column see F. A. Bauer, *Stadt, Platz und Denkmal in der Spätantike*, (Mainz 1996), pp. 43–7.

5. Several exarchs of Ravenna are known only from their seals, see Zacos I, i 732, for the seal of Akataphronius, using a Greek inscription and a Latin title.

6. Brown, *Gentlemen and Officers*, p. 87, cites the *Life* of Gregory by John the deacon which records cuts in military pay. On the dangers provoked by such cuts or arrears in paying the army, Jones, *LRE* II, pp. 677-8.

7. *LP* 70, tr. p. 65, here noting the soldiers (*militibus*) of the exarch Eleutherios (possibly of the army of Ravenna); *LPR* c. 106, tr. p. 224, on his death at Lucioli. Agnellus comments that it was quite inappropriate for a eunuch to set himself up as emperor.

8. Paul the deacon, *HL* IV 38 with the story of his murder of two dukes of Friuli at Opitergium (Opitergo), cf. *PLRE* IIIB p. 1218.

9. Theophanes, *Chronographia*, AM 6103, tr. p. 429. They captured all the eastern mints leaving Constantinople and the western mints in Ravenna, Rome and Catania (Sicily) as the sole suppliers of coin.

10. J. Howard-Johnston, *Witnesses to a World Crisis: Historians and Histories of the Middle East in the Seventh Century* (Oxford 2010), pp. 436-45.

11. First noted on an edict of 629 and marking a distinct shift from Latin to Greek in Constantinople.

12. Pope Honorius had negotiated the re-use of bronze roof tiles from the temple of Rome, an act that required imperial permission, and his *Life* refers to Herakleios as the pious emperor, *LP* 72.2, tr. p. 66.

13. *LP* 73, tr. pp. 67-8.

14. *HL* IV 42, 45. According to Fredegarius, *Chronica*, MGH *SRM* II, pp. 155-6; *The Fourth Book of the Chronicle of Fredegar*, ed. and tr. J. Wallace-Hadrill (London 1960), IV 69, the imperial tribute paid annually to the Lombards was reduced from three to two *kentenaria*. On the shifting Lombard religious allegiances, see T. S. Brown, 'Lombard religious policy in the late sixth and seventh centuries: the Roman dimension', in *The Langobards Before the Frankish Conquest: An Ethnographic Perspective* (San Marino 2009), pp. 289-308, including an interesting discussion.

15. *L'année épigraphique* 1973, p. 245, dated by the 28th year of Herakleios, indiction 13; G. Caputo, *Torcello alle Origini di Venezia* (Venice 2009), pp. 46-7, with commentary by G. Cuscito.

16. *HL* V 29; and Nikephoros and Theophanes, Guillou, *Régionalisme*, pp. 102-3.

17. *LP* 75, tr. pp. 68-9.

18. *CIG* IV no. 9869.

19. Another at Perugia contains the bones of a local saint. In the early ninth century Charlemagne's daughters chose an early Roman sarcophagus with the rape of Proserpina depicted on it for his burial, and even 200 years later it was considered appropriate to bury a holy man like Christodoulos, founder of the eleventh-century monastery on Patmos, in a similar pre-Christian tomb.

20. G. Cavallo, 'La cultura scritta a Ravenna tra Tarda Antichità e Alto Medioevo', in *Storia di Ravenna* II/ 2, p. 121 and pl. 34.
21. Laurent, Médaillier no 98,
22. MGH Epp III, *Epistulae Langobardorum*, no. 2, p. 694, Pope Honorius' letter of 625 to Isaac *patricius et exarcus Italiae* in Latin, requesting his assistance in curbing those bishops who were supporting Ariopaltus, *tyrannus*, rather than Adulubaldus *rex*; no. 3, pp. 694-6, to the bishops of Venetia and Istria (628).
23. *CIG* IV no. 9870; A. Guillou, *Recueil des inscriptions grecs médiévales d'Italie* (Rome 1996), no. 108, *PiB* II 75, *c*. 625-43, i.e. under Isaac.
24. Tjäder, *Papyri* I, 22 = Marini 95 = *Regesta* no. 25, *CLA* XXIX 887, on Paulacis; Tjäder, *Papyri* I, 24 = Marini 110, *CLA* XXIX 865, on Gaudiosus *defensor* of the Roman church who signs his name in Greek and gives a garden, witnessed by a *vir honestus*, *scholaris* of the military *schole gentilium* at Classis.

CHAPTER 23

1. Tjäder, *Papyri* II, 35 = Marini 120 = *Regesta* no. 12, *CLA* III 181, a sale of land in 572 witnessed by Eugenius, a court official who identified himself as the son of doctor Leontios; I. Mazzini, 'Les traductions latines d'Oribase et d'Hippocrate', in *Les écoles médicales à Rome*, eds. P. Mundry and J. Pigeaud (Geneva 1991), pp. 286-93.
2. The formula for appointing a *comes archiatrorum* refers to disputes (*mutuae contentionis*) between doctors that had to be resolved, Cassiodorus, *Var.* VI 19, cf. IV 41 to John *archiatro*, MGH *AA* XIII, pp. 191-2.
3. L. G. Westerink et al., tr. *Agnellus of Ravenna. Lectures on Galen's* de sectis, Arethusa monographs VIII (Buffalo NY 1981), date the doctor between *c*. 550, when the Olympiodorean type of commentary would have been available in Ravenna, and *c*. 700. Cf. N. Palmieri, tr. *Agnellus de Ravenna: Lectures galéniques* (St Etienne 2005). The manuscript is discussed and illustrated by G. Cavallo, 'La cultura scritta a Ravenna tra Tarda Antichità e Alto Medioevo', *Storia di Ravenna* II/2, pp. 79-125, esp. 94-5, 97-8. Simplicius' manuscript (Bibl. Ambrosiana G 108 Inf) is a ninth-century copy of an earlier record; Claudia Bolgia, *Rome across Time and Space. Cultural Transmission and Exchange of Ideas c. 500-1400* (Cambridge 2011), esp. p. 54.
4. N. Palmieri, 'Les commentaires de Galen', in *Les Ecoles médicales*, eds. Mundry and Pigeaud, pp. 286-309, esp. 300, n. 48 and 306.
5. N. Palmieri, 'Prise en compte de l'environnement dans le premier galénisme alexandrin', in *Conserver la santé ou la rétablir? Le rôle de l'environnement dans la médecine antique et médiévale* (St Etienne 2012),

pp. 62–78; S. Musitelli et al., 'The Medical School at Ravenna', *American Journal of Nephrology* 14.4–6 (1994), pp. 317–19.

6. Palmieri, 'Les commentaires de Galen', p. 296; *Agnellus of Ravenna, Lectures* 11–33, mention the differences between medical schools, e.g. pp. 47, 61, 97. On the pulse as a key feature of diagnosis, see *Lectures galéniques: le 'De pulsibus ad tirones'*, ed. N. Palmieri (St Etienne 2005), I. 4: 'the pulse is the most true messenger of natural operations which take place invisibly within (the body)'.

7. M. Frampton, *Embodiments of Will: Anatomical and Physiological Theories of Voluntary Animal Motion from Greek Antiquity to the Latin Middle Ages, 400 BC–AD 1300* (Saarbrücken 2008), p. 222. To compare Ravenna to Alexandria is to give it an extremely high status, since recent archaeological discoveries of the schools and lecture halls in the Egyptian centre confirm its vibrant intellectual atmosphere. On the medical curriculum at Alexandria, see A. Z. Iskandar, 'An attempted reconstruction of the late Alexandrian medical curriculum', *Medical History* 20.3 (1976) pp. 235–58, from Ibn Ridwan, an Arabic source. The transmission of ancient medicine in the West is paralleled in the East, where Syriac scribes introduced ancient Greek medicine to the Islamic world through translations into Arabic.

8. Palmieri, 'Prise en compte de l'environnement', pp. 61–85, esp. 70–71.

9. *L'Ars Medica (Tegni) de Galien: Lectures antiques et médiévales*, ed. N. Palmieri (St Etienne 2008), II. 2, pp. 52–3, and introduction, pp. 35–6; Philip van der Eijk, 'The Art of Medicine. Nemesius of Emesa and early brain mapping', *Lancet* 372, August 2008, pp. 440–41, on the late fourth-century bishop from Syria who assigned sensation and imagination to the frontal, thought to the central and memory to the posterior cavities. Posidonios of Byzantium, a medical writer, had observed the same brain structure in his study of phrenitis.

10. *L'Ars Medica*, ed. Palmieri, II. 2. 1, pp. 53–9, and introduction, pp. 36–8.

11. Ibid., III. 3. 1–4, pp. 62–5, and introduction, pp. 47–9.

12. Palmieri, 'Les commentaires de Galen', p. 295, n. 30.

13. Y. Modéran, *Les Maures et l'Afrique romaine* (Rome 2003), pp. 63–119; P. Gautier-Dalché, 'Les "quatre sages" de Jules César et la "mesure du monde" selon Julius Honorius, II la tradition médiévale', *Journal des Savants* (1987), pp. 184–209.

14. Mazzini, 'Les traductions latines', pp. 300–301.

15. Ibid., pp. 290–93; Cavallo, 'La cultura scritta' on all the mss. including these medical ones, esp. pp. 94–5, 97–8. Of course, translators were also working in other centres, such as Naples, and their mss. are now found in Rome (the Vatican library), Lucca and Verona.

16. This is the second Latin version of Oribasios' *Euporista*, made in Ravenna, see Cavallo, 'La cultura scritta'.

17. *'quas Greci dicent . . . nos enim dicimus'*, see Palmieri, 'Les commentaires de Galen', p. 302. Mazzini, 'Les traductions latines', pp. 290–91, indicates particular forms of the comparative, passive participles and unusual genders which don't reappear in later Romance languages and suggest a school of proficient translators.
18. Palmieri, 'Les commentaires de Galen', pp. 303–4, untangling the numerous different commentaries and their translations into Latin.
19. Mazzini, 'Les traductions latines', p. 293.
20. Musitelli et al., 'The Medical School at Ravenna', p. 319.
21. G. Bafforio, 'Frammenti liturgici nell'Ambrosiana', in *Testi di medicina latini antichi: problemi filologici e storici*, eds. I. Mazzini and F. Fusco (Rome 1985), pp. 99–108, esp. 103.
22. V. van Büren, 'La place du ms. Ambr. L 99 sup dans la transmission des Etymologies d'Isidore de Séville', in *Testi di medicina latini antichi*, eds. Mazzini and Fusco, pp. 25–44, esp. 27–8. M. Bassetti, ' "Total Eclipse of the Text". Stories of palimpsests in Verona, Ravenna and Bobbio between Late Antiquity and Early Middle Ages', in *Identity of Text*, ed. F. Santi (Florence 2019), cites Galen's *De Alimentorum Facultatibus* as a Greek text that could only have come to Verona from Ravenna, cf. two Greek Gospel books, fragments of *Codices Guelferbytani A* and *B*, and of the Latin *Praefationes Hieronymi*, and commentaries on the Book of Job. The Pommersfelden collection of papyri also contains a fragment of the *Digest* of Justinian, originally issued in Greek and Latin, which may be associated with Ravenna, and a Greek formula, which could well have been found in Ravenna after 540.
23. Cavallo, 'La cultura scritta', pp. 90–101, has collected a large number and has attributed the Oribasios to Ravenna, not Visigothic Spain as Lowe thought.
24. Tjäder, *Papyri* II, 30 = Marini 114, *CLA* XX 706, cf. Maximus, another local pharmacist.
25. J. Riddle, catalogustranslationum.org online resource, vol. IV, pp. 1–144, esp. p. 6, discussion of Munich ms Clm 377 as one of three copies of the Old Latin translation, which some attribute to Ostrogothic Ravenna, others to Carthage.
26. Riddle, catalogustranslationum.org online resource, pp. 6–7, 20–21.
27. Cavallo, 'La cultura scritta', p. 99. Ravenna is also known as the place where an illustrated ms. of the Roman *agrimensores* originated; under Louis the Pious it was used at Aachen, ibid. p. 96. Cf. P. C. Berger, *The Insignia of the Notitia Dignitatum* (New York/London 1981), pp. 142–74, where the illustrations are attributed to Ravenna. Bassetti, 'Total Eclipse' on the debate over the Euclid translation, on Cassiodorus' *Complexiones*, which went from Ravenna to Verona, the Codex of Justinian, an ancient second-century legal text of Gaius, and Tribonian's *Institutiones*, as well as the more familiar *Institutiones* of Justinian in a late sixth- or early seventh-century copy.

28. N. Everett, *The Alphabet of Galen. Pharmacy from Antiquity to the Middle Ages* (Toronto 2012), p. 23; Alan Cameron, 'Vergil illustrated between pagans and Christians', *Journal of Roman Archaeology* 17 (2004), pp. 501–25, esp. 522–5, emphasized the role of Ravenna in the transmission of classical texts and asserted that it could well be the place where the illustrated Vergil ms. was produced, as well as the Greek interpolations in Priscian's massive grammar.

29. In his study of Lombard Italy, *Literacy in Lombard Italy ca. 568–774* (Cambridge 2003), Everett concludes that 'Ravenna stands out as a possible link in the chain of transmission' of medical knowledge in the medieval West. Cf. Cavallo, *La cultura scritta*, p. 357, on the lack of evidence for book production in the city.

30. *L'Ars Medica*, ed. Palmieri, pp. 7–8.

CHAPTER 24

1. *Chronikon Paschale*, ed. and tr. Michael and Mary Whitby (Liverpool 1989), pp. 182–3.

2. J. Howard-Johnston, *Witnesses to a World Crisis: Historians and Histories of the Middle East in the Seventh Century* (Oxford 2010), pp. 447–73; R. Hoyland, *Seeing Islam as Others Saw It: A Survey and Evaluation of Christian, Jewish and Zoroastrian Writings on Early Islam* (Princeton 1997), expanding the stimulating approach of P. Crone and M. Cook, *Hagarism and the Making of the Islamic World* (Cambridge 1977); P. Sarris, *Empires of Faith* (Oxford 2011), pp. 268–72.

3. Sarris, *Empires of Faith*, pp. 259–68 on the background. M. Cook, *Muhammad* (Oxford 1983); G. Fowden, *Before and after Muhammad* (Princeton 2014), pp. 1–5, 18–20, 188–94.

4. M. F. Hendy, *Studies in the Byzantine Monetary Economy c. 300–1450* (Cambridge 1985), pp. 618–19, calculated up to two-thirds of the tax revenue; J. Haldon, *The Empire That Would Not Die. The Paradox of Eastern Roman Survival 640–740* (Cambridge MA 2016), pp. 27–9; A. Laiou and C. Morrisson, *The Byzantine Economy* (Cambridge 2007).

5. Fredegar, *Chronicarum libri 4*, IV 81, MGH *SRM*, p. 162; Continuator I, anno 731, p. 175, tr. J. Wallace-Hadrill, *The Fourth Book of the Chronicle of Fredegar: with its continuations* (London 1960); Bede, *Ecclesiastical History of the English People*, eds. B. Colgrave and R. A. B. Mynors (Oxford 1969), p. 557, on Saracens ravaging Gaul; K. B. Wolf, *Conquerors and Chroniclers of Early Medieval Spain* (Liverpool 1990), pp. 32–3, 58–60; *Chronicle of 754* c. 8, 113–14.

6. The first mention of Saracens occurs in the *Life* of Pope Martin, when the exarch Olympios went off to Sicily to fight them, *LP* 76.7, tr. p. 72, with no

sense of the devastation of Christian communities in the East Mediterranean; Paul the deacon, *HL* VI 10–11, tr. p. 258.

7. An excellent summary of Pirenne's importance in P. Horden and N. Purcell, *The Corrupting Sea. A Study of Mediterranean History* (Oxford 2000), pp. 153–60; D. Abulafia, *The Great Sea. A Human History of the Mediterranean* (London 2011), pp. 237, 246–7, 252–4; L. Zavagno, *Cyprus Between Late Antiquity and the Early Middle Ages (ca. 600–800): An Island in Transition* (Abingdon 2017).

8. E. Cirelli, on an imported cooking dish from Cyprus.

9. *The Armenian History attributed to Sebeos*, tr. R. W. Thomson (Liverpool 1999), vol. I c. 50, pp. 144–6; vol. II *Historical Commentary*, J. Howard-Johnston and T. Greenwood, pp. 274–6.

10. J. Herrin, *The Formation of Christendom* (Princeton 1989), pp. 207–11 (though it was the addition of the phrase, 'who was crucified for us' to the Trisagion that led to so much debate, p. 208).

11. P. Booth, *Crisis of Empire. Doctrine and Dissent at the End of Late Antiquity* (Berkeley/Los Angeles/London 2014), pp. 260–61, and Herrin, *Formation of Christendom*, pp. 214–17, on western opposition to Monotheletism (and the embarrassment caused by Pope Honorius' cautious welcome of the one energy theory, *monoenergeia*, later condemned in the West and never mentioned in the Roman *Book of the Pontiffs*); *LP* 74, tr. p. 68 on John IV and his attention to Dalmatian captives and saints.

12. Booth, *Crisis of Empire*, pp. 262–4 on the Palestinian refugees; p. 275 on their emphasis on Rome as 'the sole patriarchate to denounce the monothelete innovation'; p. 277 on the growth of the idea of Rome's total secession from Constantinople. E. Patlagean, 'Les Moines grecs d'Italie et l'apologie des thèses pontificales (VIIIe–IXe siècles)', *Studi Medievali* 3e serie, 5/2 (1964), pp. 579–602; A. Ekonomou, *Byzantine Rome and the Greek Popes: Eastern Influences on Rome and the Papacy from Gregory the Great to Zacharias A D 590–752* (Lanham 2007).

13. Booth, *Crisis of Empire*, pp. 266–76 and 285–7 on the development of Monotheletism; on the link between the debate and Exarch Gregory's rebellion against Constans II, pp. 287–9; J. Tannous, 'In search of Monotheletism', *DOP* 68 (2014), pp. 29–67.

14. *LP* 75.3, tr. p. 69; *LP* 75.6, tr. p. 70, he was eventually restored to the patriarchate. Booth, *Crisis of Empire*, pp. 290–91.

15. See the list of exarchs, whose seals are recorded in both Greek and Latin.

16. *The Adriatic Between Venice and Byzantium c. 700–1453*, ed. M. Skoblar (Cambridge 2020); *Between Two Seas*, eds. R. Hodges and S. Gelichi (Turnhout 2012).

17. *LP* 76, tr. pp. 70–72; *LP* 76.1–2, tr. pp. 70–71.

18. *ACO*, ser. II vol. 1, *Acts of the Lateran Council, 649*, ed. R. Riedinger, originally composed in Greek with Maximos' assistance, and then trans-

lated into Latin, in which form they circulated throughout the West tr. R. Price et al. (Liverpool 2014), with detailed commentary.

19. *LP* 76.5, the soldier (*spatharius*) later affirmed under oath that he had not been able to see the pontiff 'distributing communion to the exarch or giving him the Peace', and thus avoided shedding blood in church.

20. *LP* 76.3–7, tr. pp. 71–2. Constans had spies in Rome who informed him of the situation (Eupraxios and Platon the patrician). The army of Ravenna is not recorded in the Sicilian campaign and probably returned to the city.

21. *LP* 76.8, tr. p. 72, the briefest account; Theophanes, *Chronographia*, AM 6150, tr. p. 485. Cf. P. Allen and B. Neil, *Maximus the Confessor and His Companions: Documents from Exile* (Oxford 2002).

22. *LP* 77, *Life* of Eugenius, 654–7, tr. p. 73.

23. Since it was later condemned, the records of this meeting have not survived, but Marek Jankowiak has reconstructed its probable form, see M. Jankowiak, 'The *Notitia* I and the impact of Arab invasions in Asia Minor', *Millennium* 10 (2013), pp. 435–61; *idem, Essai d'histoire politique du monothélisme*, PhD thesis, Paris-Warsaw (2009), pp. 351–9; *idem*, 'The first Arab siege of Constantinople', *Travaux et Mémoires* 17 (2013), pp. 237–320.

24. Booth, *Crisis of Empire*, pp. 292–3, 302, 323; Herrin, *Formation of Christendom*, p. 218, on Anastasius.

25. Haldon, *The Empire That Would Not Die*, pp. 4–5 with reference to the debates about this term.

CHAPTER 25

1. *LP* 78.1, tr. p. 73.

2. The main focus of the *Life* of Bishop Maurus is this long battle for freedom from Rome, *LPR* c. 110, tr. p. 227.

3. Maurus later declared his belief in the two operations and two wills in the two natures, human and divine, in the one person of Christ, *ACO*, ser. II, vol. 1, *Concilium Lateranense a. 649 celebratum*, ed. R. Riedinger (Berlin 1984), pp. 23, 27; F. Winkelmann, *Die monenergetisch-monotheletische Streit* (Berlin 2001), no. 109.

4. *LPR* c. 110, tr. p. 227.

5. This long civil war, called the first *fitna* (division), determined whether the succession to supreme authority should follow the Prophet's family, represented by his son-in-law Ali, or should be chosen by the entire community (leaving the way for an unrelated but successful military leader). It gave Constans II several years in which to plan the reorganization of his military forces, P. Sarris, *Empires of Faith* (Oxford 2011), pp. 286–8.

6. *LP* 78.2, tr. p. 73; ships attached to Sicily remained the only part of the Byzantine navy that had not been damaged in the disaster at Phoinike (Phoenix).

7. C. Zuckerman, 'Learning from the enemy and more: studies in "Dark Centuries" Byzantium', *Millennium* 2 (2006), pp. 79–135.

8. *LP* 78.2–3, tr. pp. 73–4. Mizizios was in Sicily with the eastern army, *LP* 79.2, tr. p. 74 reports his rebellion, unrelated to the murder of Constans, which is dated to July of the twelfth indication, 669.

9. *LP* 78.4, tr. p. 74; Zuckermann, 'Learning from the enemy'; Sarris, *Empires of Faith*, pp. 289–90; V. Prigent, 'La Sicile de Constant II: l'apport des sources sigillographique', in *La Sicile de Byzance à l'Islam*, eds. A. Nef and V. Prigent (Paris 2010), pp. 157–88.

10. V. Ortenberg West-Harling, 'The church of Ravenna, Constantinople and Rome in the seventh century', in *Ravenna, Its Role in Earlier Medieval Change and Exchange*, eds. J. Herrin and J. Nelson (London 2016), pp. 199–210, esp. 206–7; S. Cosentino, 'Constans II, Ravenna's autocephaly and the Panel of the Privileges in S. Apollinare in Classe: a reappraisal', in *Aureus. Volume for E. Chrysos* (Athens 2014), pp. 153–70.

11. Honorius had elevated Ravenna by transferring six sees from Milan, but this forgery made much larger claims.

12. *LPR* c. 110, tr. p. 227; Consentino argues that similar privileges had already been granted but this is the only surviving document, 'Constans II, Ravenna's autocephaly and the Panel of the Privileges', pp. 162–3.

13. *LPR* c. 113, tr. p. 231. This independence may also be related to the recording of the liturgy of the church of Ravenna on a magnificent roll, the Rotulus, whose creation is attributed to Archbishop Maurus, see *Santi, banchieri, re: Ravenna e Classe nel VI secolo: S. Severo il tempio ritrovato*, eds. A. Augenti et al. (Milan 2006), pp. 176, 179.

14. *LPR* c. 115, tr. p. 234.

15. Cosentino, 'Constans II, Ravenna's autocephaly and the Panel of the Privileges', pp. 163–5, from markings on the right shoulder of this figure that could be read as a Greek monogram of Theodore.

16. *LPR* c. 114, tr. p. 231, where Maurus also recorded the history of St Apollinaris on silver sheets in the centre of the church. Cosentino, 'Constans II, Ravenna's autocephaly and the Panel of the Privileges', pp. 165–6, neatly links the *translatio* with the construction of a ciborium, represented by Theodore's model.

17. The panels probably replaced earlier ones, but as with the mosaics of S. Apollinare Nuovo, there is no way of establishing what has now been obliterated.

18. On the importance of Melchizedek in imperial ideology, see G. Dagron, *Emperor and Priest. The Imperial Office in Byzantium* (Cambridge 2003), pp. 173–84.

19. C. Jäggi, 'Ravenna in the Sixth Century", in *Ravenna*, eds. Herrin and Nelson, esp. p. 108; cf. *eadem*, *Ravenna* (Regensburg 2013), pls. 170 and 190, pp. 254 and 277. The city's status is confirmed in a visit of Georgian

monks, who had been on a pilgrimage to Rome and then went to Ravenna, see G. Garitte, 'Histoires édifiantes géorgiennes', *Byzantion* 36 (1999), pp. 396–423.

20. *LPR* c. 112, tr. p. 230; c. 114, tr. p. 233. The account of his death includes the phrase 'they cut the top of the fetter of the right foot', which relates to the cutting of episcopal shoe straps to symbolize the loss of authority. After his trial in Constantinople Pope Martin's shoe straps were cut in this way to disqualify him from office, and Constantine, the anti-pope of 767–8, was subjected to the same ritual when all his episcopal costume was removed. *Life* of Stephen III, *LP* 96.3, tr. p. 94 and n. 32.

21. *PG* 90, 114; Brown, *Gentlemen and Officers*, pp. 65, 68, 165.

22. Mansi, X, cols. 849, 851

23. Tjäder, *Papyri* II, 44 = Marini 132 = *Regesta* no. 27, *CLA* XXII 721, dated 642–66, cf. Brown, *Gentlemen and Officers*, p. 136, dates it more closely to 648–61. The act was drawn up by Paul, *notarius* of the bishop, unnamed but probably Maurus; Apollenarius/Apolenaris, identified as *eminentissimae memoriae vir*, implies a definite distinction, if not praetorian prefect, ibid., 64. The annual rent for the lease is seven gold *solidi infiguratos*.

24. Laurent, *Médaillier*, nos. 100–101, and Schlumberger, *Seals*, 211. Since his wife and sons are included in the papyrus document, the family remained settled in Rimini.

25. M. Jankowiak, *Essai d'histoire politique du monothélisme*, PhD thesis, Paris-Warsaw (2009), pp. 605–6.

26. Jankowiak, *Etude,* pp. 364–73; *idem, Essai,* pp. 364–4; S. Cosentino, 'Byzantine Sardinia between West and East', *Millennium* 1 (2004) pp. 329–67.

27. Theophanes, *Chronographia,* AM 6164 and 6165 = AD 671–3, tr. pp. 493–4, recording the final years of a seven-year siege, was incorrectly placed in his narrative, see the major revision by Jankowiak, *Essai,* p. 392, and appendix 2, pp. 545–605; *idem,* 'The first Arab siege of Constantinople', *Travaux et Mémoires* 17 (2013), pp. 237–320. Cf. J. Haldon, *The Empire That Would Not Die. The Paradox of Eastern Roman Survival 640–740* (Cambridge MA 2016), pp. 42–3.

28. It is unclear whether factions in Byzantium supported the coup in Syracuse, angry at the emperor's long stay in the West while they faced renewed Arab threats, Theophanes, AM 6160, tr. pp. 490–91. *Chronicle of 754,* ed. K. B. Wolf, para. 29, tr. p. 122, on the emperor's two-year absence; M. Jankowiak, 'The *Notitia* I and the impact of Arab invasions in Asia Minor', *Millennium* 10 (2013), pp. 435–61. It seems very unlikely that Constantine IV immediately set sail for Sicily to avenge his father's murder, as Theophanes claims, AM 6160, tr. p. 491. Instead he ordered the exarch, probably Gregory, to impose control. *LP* 79.2 records an unambiguous reaction: the army of Italy, drawn from Istria, Campania, Africa and

Sardinia, united in Syracuse to kill Mizizios. Although no exarch is named, Gregory II probably commanded this force, loyal to the dynasty of Herakleios rather than the rebel Mizizios.

29. Theophanes AM 6164, tr. p. 493 on the fire ships and AM 6165, tr. p. 494 on Kallinikos, an architect from Syria, who manufactured the naval fire.

30. Theophanes AM 6160, tr. p. 491 on the return of the court from Syracuse to Constantinople.

31. *LPR* c. 120, tr. pp. 238–40.

32. *LPR* c. 125, tr. pp. 247–8.

33. *LPR* c. 121, tr. pp. 240–43.

34. *LPR* c. 122, tr. pp. 243–4.

35. *LPR* c. 123, tr. p. 245.

36. A. M. Orselli, *L'Immaginario religioso della città medievale* (Ravenna 1985), esp. 'Vita religioso nella città medievale italiana tra dimensione ecclesiastica e cristianesimo civico. Un'esemplificazione', pp. 355–412, esp. 353, 390. This brilliant analysis shows how at this moment the united clergy formed the Christian community of Ravenna, and illustrates their perception of the emperor's authority, whether the story is true or not.

37. *LPR* cc. 122–3, tr. pp. 243–5.

38. *LPR* c. 124, tr. pp. 245–6, also noted in the Roman *liber pontificalis* under Pope Agatho (678–81): 'Theodore archbishop of Ravenna after the passage of many years presented himself to the apostolic see', *LP* 81.1, tr. p. 76; Cf. *LP* 80.1, tr. p. 75, under Pope Donus (676–8), on the church of Ravenna 'which had separated itself from the Roman church to achieve independence, brought itself back into subjection to the ancient apostolic see'.

39. *LP* 80.2, tr. p. 75 under Pope Donus, confirmed under Pope Leo II, *LP* 82.4, tr. pp. 80–81.

40. *LPR* c. 124, tr. p. 246.

41. *LPR* c. 119, tr. p. 238. Plate 46 illustrates the exceptionally fine sarcophagus re-used by Archbishop Theodore of Ravenna, who died 691/2.

CHAPTER 26

1. Theophanes, *Chronographia*, AM 6169, and Nikephoros, *Short Chronicle* c. 34 record the terms: annual payments of 3,000 gold coins, 50 captives and 50 horses, cf. n. 3 about the much higher figures, cited in AM 6176, given in another treaty of 683/4, of 365,000 gold coins, 365 slaves and 365 horses (one for every day of the year). While both chroniclers have very inaccurate accounts, the victory off Syllaion was clearly a major triumph for the new imperial naval forces, M. Jankowiak, *Essai d'histoire politique du monothélisme*, PhD thesis, Paris-Warsaw (2009), pp. 392–3.

2. Ibid., pp. 392–402.

3. J. L. Van Dieten, *Geschichte der Patriarchen von Sergios I bis Johannes VI, 610–715* (Amsterdam 1972), pp. 120–30.

4. *LP* 81.10, tr. p. 78 cites this number, confirmed in the records of the Sixth Council.

5. *ACO* ser. II, vol. 2, part 2, *Concilium universale Constantinopolitanum tertium*, ed. R. Riedinger (Berlin 1992), actio 18, p. 754, cf. pp. 778–9. At 8th position, Theodore signs as presbyter and representative of Theodore, archbishop of Ravenna.

6. Because the order of signing established a hierarchy of ecclesiastical sees throughout the Christian world, to be accorded such a high position was a great honour.

7. An eyewitness account of how the council met in Constantinople fills many sections of the *Life* of Agatho, *LP* 81.4–15, tr. pp. 76–9, cf. the official record in *ACO* ser. II, vol. 2, in 3 parts (Berlin 1990–92).

8. *Notitia episcopatuum Ecclesiae Constantinopolitanae*, ed. J. Darrouzes (Paris 1981); M. Jankowiak, 'The *Notitia* I and the impact of Arab invasions in Asia Minor', *Millennium* 10 (2013), pp. 435–61.

9. The lists are printed in *ACO* ser. II, vol. 2, part 3, ed. Riedinger (Berlin 1992) and H. Ohme, *Concilium Constantinopolitanum a. 691/2 in trullo habitum (Concilium quinisextum)*, *ACO* ser. II, vol. 4 (Berlin 2013).

10. The list was published by Marini, *Papyri* no. 146, p. 211. R. Riedinger, 'Die Präsenz- und Subskriptionsliste des VI Ökumenischen Konzils (680/1) under der Papyrus Vind. G 3', in *Sitzungsberichte der Bayerischen Akademie der Wissenschaften, Philos.-Hist. Klasse, Abhandlung* 85 (1979), pp. 22–7, and *idem*, *ACO* ser. II, vol. 2, introduction pp. xx–xxi. A new edition by O. Kresten is promised.

11. *ACO* ser. II, vol. 2, part 2, pp. 754–97, for the subscriptions to the final actio; Jankowiak, *Essai*, pp. 457–60.

12. Jankowiak, *Essai*, pp. 474–81 has made sense of these interconnected events: Bulgarian campaign, military revolt and exile of the two junior emperors, drawing attention to the contradictions in Theophanes AM 6173, tr. p. 502, and the earlier incorrect entry at AM 6161, dated 668/9, tr. pp. 491–2. Cf. L. Brubaker and J. Haldon, *Byzantium in the Iconoclast Era c. 680–850. A History* (Cambridge 2011), pp. 27–8, dating the revolt to 681 but not associating it with opposition to the Sixth Council.

13. Two of these Monotheletes (Anastasios, a priest, and Leontios, a deacon), were readmitted to the church under Pope Leo II (682–3), though Makarios, Stephanos, Polychronios and another Anastasios refused to abandon Monotheletism and remained confined to different monasteries in Rome, see *LP* 82.2, tr. p. 80. Paul the deacon notes the appearance of a comet (usually a bad sign), and in 680 an eclipse of the moon and the sun at almost the same time, followed by a severe outbreak of pestilence that killed many (*HL* VI 4–5).

14. *Iussio* of 687 (Latin text) *ACO* ser. II, vol. 2, part 2, 886–7.
15. He is named as exarch during a disputed papal election in 686 (*LP* 85.1–2, tr. pp. 83–4 under Conon), see Ch. 25 above.
16. *LP* 85.1, tr. p. 83, *Life* of Conon; 86.3–4, tr. p. 86, *Life* of Sergius.
17. *LP* 87.1–2, tr. pp. 89–90; Brown, *Gentlemen and Officers*, pp. 212–13.
18. Tjäder, *Papyri* I, 23 = Marini 109 = *Regesta* no. 31, *CLA* IX 405 (fragmentary). Since most thriving cities had nunneries, its existence is not very surprising, but it provides the first definite proof and the name of the *abbatissa*, Johannia.
19. There are few references to them, but note the papyrus of 767, *Regesta* no. 42.
20. Tjäder, *Papyri* I, 24 = Marini 110, *CLA* XXIX 865 dated in the mid-seventh century. The *schole gentilium* refers to a garrison of non-local troops, identified by Tjäder as Germanic, ibid., p. 376. This is the last signature in Greek, see E. Schoolman, 'Local Networks and Witness Subscriptions in Early Medieval Ravenna', *Viator* 44/3 (2013), 21–41.

CHAPTER 27

1. *Itineraria romana*, eds. J. Schnetz and O. Cuntz, 2 vols. (Leipzig 1929–42, repr. 1990) vol. 2, bk I, 1; N. Lozovsky, *'The Earth is Our Book': Geographical Knowledge in the Latin West ca. 400–1000* (Ann Arbor 2000), pp. 145–6 stressing the importance the Cosmographer attached to written authority rather than the experience of travellers.
2. On city epithets, Ausonius, *Ordo urbium nobelium* (Turnhout 2010) Ebook; and José Luis Canazar Palacios, ' "From vetus Byzantion to urbs regia" (Amm. 22. 8. 8). Representation of Constantinople in late Roman emperors' laws", in *New Perspectives on Late Antiquity in the East Roman Empire,* eds. Ana de Francisco Heredero et al. (Newcastle 2014), pp. 280–310. My thanks to Michael-Jeffrey Featherstone for alerting me to this helpful text.
3. Joseph Schnetz dated it to *c.* 700; Lozovsky to the early eighth century: *The Earth is Our Book*, p. 59.
4. He mentions Emperor Trajan, the conqueror of Dacia.
5. *Liber Guidonis compositus de variis historiis*, ed. M. Campopiano (Florence 2008).
6. The 1860 edition by M. Pinder and G. Parthey is available online: https://archive.org/stream/ravennatisanonymoogeoguoft/ravennatisanonymoogeo guoft_djvu.doc. Cf. *Itineraria romana*, eds. Schnetz and Cuntz, vol. 2. Schnetz also translated the text into German, *Cosmographia: Eine Erdbeschreibung um das Jahr 700* (Uppsala 1951).

7. *Christo auxilante/adiuvante,* a common explanation in Christian texts. There is no trace of the battle, which had raged in Alexandria in the mid-sixth century, between the ancient Greek theory of the eternity of the world and this Christian view of creation.

8. Bk I, 9.

9. S. Mazzarino, 'Da Lollianus et Arbetio al mosaico storico di S. Apollinare in Classe', *Rivista di studi bizantini e neoellenici,* new series 2–3 (1965–6), pp. 99–117, esp. 102, repr. in *Antico, tardo antico ed èra costantiniana* (Bari 1980), pp. 325–33.

10. R. J. A Talbert, *Rome's World. The Peutinger Map Reconsidered* (Cambridge 2010), pp. 138–9.

11. Bk I, 10 (*tantummodo deo nostro est cognitum*). He then continues that the night journey of the sun permits him to set down the arctic regions along the edge of the Ocean shore that surrounds the universe, where he records them.

12. Bk I, 14.

13. Bk IV, 30.

14. Talbert, *Rome's World. The Peutinger Map Reconsidered,* with the entire map online at http://peutinger.atlantides.org/map-a/; B. Salway, 'The nature and genesis of the Peutinger Map', *Imago Mundi* 57, pt 2 (2005), pp. 119–35.

15. L. Dillemann, *La Cosmographie du Ravennate,* ed. J. Janvier, Collection Latomus 235 (Brussels 1997), on reliance on Castorius, pp. 48, 52–3. Dillemann suggests that this Castorius could be a *notarius* and *diaconus* cited by Gregory the Great, cf. Miller's identification with a late sixth-century bishop of Rimini.

16. It differs from the Peutinger table with some additional material especially in book V, and the complete western-most sections, thus preserving much information about Britain, Dillemann, *La Cosmographie,* pp. 20, 24.

17. P. Arnaud, 'L'origine, la date de rédaction et la diffusion de l'archétype de la Table de Peutinger', *Bulletin des Antiquitaires de France* (1988), pp. 302–21, esp. 316.

18. Lozovsky, *The Earth is Our Book,* pp. 30–31; similarly, maps attached to earlier geographic texts do not survive.

19. F. Staab, 'Ostrogothic geographers at the court of Theodoric the Great: a study of some sources of the Anonymous Ravenna Cosmographer', *Viator* 7 (1976), pp. 27–64, was determined to associate them with the court of Theoderic, a view dismissed by Dillemann, *La Cosmographie,* pp. 50, 57–8. Lozovsky points out that Jordanes, who provides so much information to the Cosmographer, also cited Ablavius, a famous describer of the Gothic race, among his sources, and gives greater credence to the Gothic geographers, Lozovsky, *The Earth is Our Book,* pp. 81–6.

20. C. Falluomini, 'Zum gotischen Fragment aus Bologna II', *Zeitschrift für deutsches Altertum und deutsche Literatur* 146 (2017), pp. 284–94, which records the Gothic word for lion; M. Bassetti, ' "Total Eclipse of the Text".

Stories of palimpsests in Verona, Ravenna and Bobbio between Late Antiquity and the Early Middle Ages', in *Identity of Text*, ed. F. Santi (forthcoming Florence, 2020). Ravenna also supplied the Greek text of Galen and certain legal texts to Verona.

21. Parthey and later studies of the Anonymous Cosmograher, Arnaud, 'L'origine, la date de rédaction et la diffusion de l'archétype de la Table de Peutinger', pp. 302–21.

22. G. A. Mansuelli, 'I geographici ravennati', *CARB* 19 (1973), pp. 331–46, esp. 334, 338–40, but refuted by Dillemann, *La Cosmographie*.

23. Einhard, *Vita Caroli Magni*, ed. O. Holder-Egger, MGH *SRG* (Hanover 1911), para. 33, Einhard and Notker the Stammerer, *Two Lives of Charlemagne* (Harmondsworth 1969), p. 89.

24. *LPR* c. 160, tr. p. 285.

25. B. Bachrach, *Charlemagne's Early Military Campaigns (768–777). A Diplomatic and Military Analysis* (Leiden 2013), pp. 306–7, 465, 474.

26. C. R. Whittaker, *Rome and its Frontiers: The Dynamic of Empire* (London 2004), p. 79; *Liber Guidonis*, ed. Campopiano, Introduction, pp. xciii–xciv.

27. This manuscript was acquired by Venetian ambassadors to the Council of Basel (1431–49), which is just 115km downstream from the monastery of Reichenau and may have been the source of this copy, see Salway, 'Nature and genesis', pp. 119–35, esp. 127.

28. This map shares with the Anonymous Cosmographer the city name *Forum Alieni*, in addition to 'Greek letters in many parts', features which may plausibly have been added in Ravenna. Although Prisciani found it difficult to read them, at some stage the itineraries of the Tabula Peutingeriana had been enhanced by Greek names of cities/regions that derived from the Ravenna Cosmographer.

29. Bachrach, *Charlemagne*, p. 307, citing E. Albu, 'Imperial geography and the medieval Peutinger Map', *Imago Mundi* 57 (2005), pp. 136–48. Cf. Salway, 'Nature and genesis', p. 127.

30. Brown, *Gentlemen and Officers*, p. 188, citing J. Tjäder, 'Et ad latus . . .', *Studi Romagnoli* 24 (1973), pp. 91–124, at 112, for the suggestion that Constantinople's practice, adopted in Ravenna, may have influenced that of the papal chancellery in Rome.

31. G. Sarti, *Un libro ravennate di spiritualità monastica dell'inizio del secolo VIII nell'Archivio Storico Diocesano di Ravenna-Cervia* (Ravenna 2017), with a very helpful introduction by R. Savigni. See Plate 44.

CHAPTER 28

1. The acts of the council are not preserved: only the bishops' address to the emperor (*prosphonetikos logos*), the text of the canons, and the signatures of

those present survive, see the translation by G. Nedungatt and M. Feather-stone, *The Council in Trullo Revisited* = *Kanonika* 6 (Rome 1995); and the new edition by H. Ohme, *ACO* ser. II, vol. 2, part 4 (Berlin 2013). On this occasion, the archbishops of Nea Ioustinianoupolis, Thessalonike, Caesarea, Sardinia and Ephesus were placed ahead of Ravenna, but its position was still higher than Herakleias of Thrace, Corinth and Gortyna, ibid., pp. 63-4.

2. Ohme, *ACO* ser. II, vol. 2, part 4, pp. 62-4. A. Fallier's review in *REB* 49 (1991), p. 287, criticized the way Ohme presented the documents, cf. N. Dura, 'The Ecumenicity of the Council in Trullo', in Nedungatt and Featherstone, *The Council in Trullo*, pp. 241-2. Originally, references to the expected signatures of the pope and other western bishops had been placed in the margin of the manuscript, and this is indicated in Mansi XI, 989B, in italics. Later copyists, however, moved these references into the main text, as if the spaces had been deliberately created.

3. The pope's representatives 'had been deceived into subscribing' the acts, *LP* 86.6, tr. p. 86.

4. J. Herrin, *The Formation of Christendom* (Princeton 1989), pp. 284-7; J. Haldon, *The Empire That Would Not Die. The Paradox of Eastern Roman Survival 640-740* (Cambridge MA 2016), pp. 128-30.

5. Married men could be ordained as priests in the East, for instance, whereas a nominal celibacy was required of priests in the West.

6. *LP* 86.6, tr. p. 86.

7. *LP* 86.15, tr. p. 89.

8. *LP* 86.6-7, tr. pp. 86-7.

9. *LP* 86.7-9, tr. p. 87; V. Ortenberg West-Harling, 'The church of Ravenna, Constantinople and Rome in the seventh century', in *Ravenna, Its Role in Earlier Medieval Change and Exchange*, eds. J. Herrin and J. Nelson (London 2016), pp. 199-210.

10. *LP* 86.9, tr. p. 87.

11. On the transfer of East Illyricum, L. Brubaker and J. Haldon, *Byzantium in the Iconoclast Era c. 680-850. A History* (Cambridge 2011), pp. 174-5, 257-8. Ohme thought Justinian II responsible and found evidence in the 692 acts.

12. Theophanes, *Chronographia*, AM 6187, tr. pp. 514-15; *LPR* c. 137, tr. p. 259 claims 'some citizens of Ravenna' assisted at this mutilation.

13. Noted by Paul the deacon, *HL* VI 12, tr. p. 259.

14. *HL* VI 32, tr. p. 275.

15. Theophanes AM 6190, tr. pp. 516-17; Nikephoros, *Short Chronicle* 41, pp. 98-100; J. Conant, *Staying Roman. Conquest and Identity in Africa and the Mediterranean, 439-700* (Cambridge 2015), pp. 358-9.

16. J.-M. Sansterre, *Les moines grecs et orientaux à Rome aux époques byzantine et carolingienne* (Brussels 1983), pp. 30-31, 39-40 on refugees from Africa.

17. V. Prigent, 'La Sicile de Constant II: l'apport des sources sigillographique', in *La Sicile de Byzance à l'Islam*, eds. A. Nef and V. Prigent (Paris 2010), pp. 157–88; *idem*, 'La circulation monétaire en Sicile (VI–VII siècle)' ", in D. Michaelides et al. eds., *The Insular System of the Early Byzantine Mediterranean* (Oxford 2013), pp. 139–60; *idem*, 'Monnaie et circulation monétaire en Sicile du début du VIIIe siècle à l'avènement de la domination musulmane', in *L'Héritage byzantin en Italie (VIIIe–XIIe siècle)*, eds. J.-M. Martin et al. (Rome 2012), vol. 2, pp. 455–82.

18. Theophanes AM 6197–6198, tr. pp. 522–3, with details of the punishment of both Leo/Leontios and Apsimar/Tiberios, the blinding of Patriarch Kallinikos, who was exiled to Rome, and the impaling and beheading of many civilian and military officials accused of supporting the previous regimes, cf. AM 6190, tr. p. 517.

19. Theophanes AM 6198, tr. p. 523; see also Nikephoros, *Short Chronicle* 42, tr. pp. 101–5; *LP* 88.4, tr. p. 91.

20. *LP* 88.5, tr. p. 91, records that gaining the pope's agreement to the canons of 692 was his most pressing concern.

21. *LP* 90.3, tr. p. 92.

22. *LRP* c. 137, tr. pp. 259–60. NB Agnellus is the only medieval writer to record the gold covers allegedly worn by the emperor over his nose *and* ears, though similar mutilations of nose and ears are well known.

23. *LP* 90.2, tr. p. 92, cf. *LPR* c. 137, tr. pp. 260–62. The role of the western fleet based in Sicily reinforced the increasing importance of the island and the promotion of its governor. *LP* 90.2, tr. p. 92 believes that Felix's disobedience towards Pope Constantine was responsible for the raid and blinding, cf. C. Head, *Justinian II of Byzantium* (Madison 1972), pp. 137–41. There is no trace of this vindictive attack, the burning of the city and subsequent punishment of the leaders in eastern sources, but a similar punishment was devised for Cherson and took the eastern fleet into the Black Sea, Theophanes AM 6203, tr. p. 527; *LPR* c. 137 tr. pp. 259–60.

24. *LPR* c. 137, tr. pp. 259–62. Cf. the outstanding analysis by J. M. Pizarro, *Writing Ravenna. The* Liber pontificalis *of Andrea Agnellus* (Michigan 1995), pp. 171–92, esp. 173 suggesting that Johannicis *may* have taken part in the mutilation of Justinian II in 695. There is no suggestion that an exarch was in post at the time.

25. *LPR* c. 140, tr. p. 265. Brown, *Gentlemen and Officers,* p. 98, n. 34 on the chronological difficulties of this period.

26. Brown insists that these twelve units already existed, with their own soldiers, and the innovation was to base each one in a particular quarter of the city, to which the local population was associated: *Gentlemen and Officers*, p. 97.

27. *LPR* c. 140, tr. p. 264 (*ex Bizantie ponto . . . bibimus venenum. Et tumidis corde Danais* (i.e. Greeks) *terga non demus*, ed. Nauerth, II, p. 502).

28. *LPR* c. 140, tr. p. 264.
29. Guillou, *Régionalisme*, pp. 216–18, on the rebellion.
30. *LPR* c. 139, tr. p. 263.
31. *LP* 90.4, tr. p. 92. The sequence of officials sent from Constantinople is rather unclear until October 710, when John Rizokopos arrived. If the emperor ordered a punitive raid before that moment, it could have coincided with a period when there was no exarch in post.
32. *LP* 90.4, tr. p. 92.
33. Theophanes AM 6203, tr. p. 529 reports that the *spatharios* Romanos was charged with the duty of taking the head 'to the countries of the West'.
34. *LPR* c. 142, tr. p. 267.

CHAPTER 29

1. *LPR* c. 134, tr. p. 257.
2. *LPR* c. 125, tr. p. 247.
3. *LPR* cc. 127–9, tr. pp. 248–52.
4. Illustrations of such fist fights confirm the public entertainment involved. This sort of communal violence is associated with urban traditions that go back to much earlier times and extend to the fist fighting recorded in the area that later became Venice, see J. Herrin, 'Urban riot or civic ritual?' in *Raum und Performanz. Rituale in Residenzen von der Antike bis 1815*, eds. D. Boschung, K.-J. Hölkeskamp and C. Sode (Stuttgart 2015), pp. 219–40. On Latronum *LPR* c. 129, tr. p. 252; Lepers, *LPR* c. 151, tr. p. 275.
5. *LPR* c. 134, tr. p. 257.
6. Ibid.
7. Paul the deacon, *HL* VI 3, also records that Radoald the rightful duke of Friuli sought refuge in Istria, sailed from there to Ravenna and went on to Pavia – proof that the port facility and the route to Pavia up the Po was still working.
8. *LP* 86.15, tr. p. 89; copied by Paul the deacon, *HL* VI 14, tr. p. 260. See C. Sotinel, 'The Three Chapters and the transformations of Italy', in *The Crisis of the Oikoumene: The Three Chapters and the Failed Quest for Unity in the Sixth-century Mediterranean*, eds. C. Chazelle and C. Cubitt (Turnhout 2007), pp. 84–120.
9. *HL* VI 43, tr. p. 285, cf. *LP* 88.3, tr. p. 91, where the document recording the gift to Pope John VII (705–7) is said to have been written in gold letters, and the act is attributed to King Aripert. It was confirmed by Liutprand, who was persuaded by Pope Gregory II to return Sutri in Latium and other hill towns 'to the blessed apostles Peter and Paul', *LP* 91.21, tr. II, p. 14.

10. *HL* VI 48, tr. pp. 288–9; R. Balzaretti, *Dark Age Liguria. Regional Identity and Local Power c. 400–1020* (London 2013), p. 97, on the route used to bring such precious relics to Pavia.

11. *HL* VI 44.

12. *LP* 91.13, tr. II, p. 9 (where many ships, *classes*, may be confused with the port city of Classis).

13. *The Council in Trullo revisited = Kanonika* 6, eds. G. Nedungatt and M. Featherstone (Rome 1995), pp. 162–4 (Greek text and tr. of canon 82).

14. *LP* 86.14, tr. p. 89.

15. L. James, *Mosaics in the Medieval World* (Cambridge 2017), p. 180; T. Mathews, *Clash of Gods* (Princeton 1993), pp. 115–41 on 'Chameleon Christ'; cf. B. Brenk, 'Mit was für Mitteln kann einem Physisch Anonymen Auctoritas vergleichen werden?' *East and West: Modes of Communication*, eds. E. Chrysos and I. Wood (Leiden 1999), pp. 143–72, esp. pp. 162–6.

16. C. Foss, 'Arab-Byzantine coins: money as cultural continuity', in *Byzantium and Islam. Age of Transition*, eds. H. Evans and B. Ratliff (New York 2012), pp. 136–7; *Byzantium and the Arabs* (Thessalonike 2011), Museum of Byzantine Culture, exhibition catalogue, with excellent illustrations; C. F. Robinson, *'Abd al-Malik* (Oxford 2005), pp. 71–9; P. Sarris, *Empires of Faith* (Oxford 2011), pp. 298–300 on the establishment of a specifically Muslim character within the Caliphate under Abd al-Malik.

17. Robinson, *'Abd al-Malik*, pp. 1–9; James, *Mosaics*, pp. 256–72; H. Maguire, *Nectar and Illusion. Nature in Byzantine Art and Literature* (Oxford 2012), pp. 35–41 on iconoclasm; J. Tannous, 'In search of Monotheletism', *DOP* 68 (2014), pp. 29–67.

18. *LPR* c. 133, tr. p. 257.

19. This issue is more fully discussed in Ch. 32.

20. *LPR* c. 131, tr. p. 253, he was John, priest and abbot of the monastery of St John *Ad Titum* (also called *Pinum* by the ignorant, *rustici nescientes*) in Classis (Nauerth, *Bishofbuch* 2, p. 476). The Anonymous Cosmographer notes similar changes of consonant which may suggest comparable linguistic developments – the settlement Pina = Tinna.

21. *LPR* c. 131, tr. pp. 253–6.

22. *LPR* c. 134, tr. p. 258.

23. G. Bovini, *Mosaici di Ravenna* (Milan 1957), p. 51, fragments of episcopal garments decorated with uncial inscriptions and dated to the late seventh or early eighth century.

CHAPTER 30

1. *Liber diurnus Romanorum pontificium*, ed. H. P. Foerster (Bern 1958), pp. 128–37, three formulae devised by the papal chancellery for the cor-

rect form of words to be used by subordinate bishops at their consecration, cf. A. T. Hack, *Codex Carolinus: Studien zur päpstlichen Epistolographie im 8. Jahrhundert*, 2 vols (Stuttgart 2006–7), I, 143–55.

2. *LP* 90.2, tr. p. 92.
3. According to Guillou, *Régionalisme*, pp. 212–14, the judicial officers appointed by the exarch in Ravenna forced him to do this.
4. *LP* 90.2, tr. p. 92; *LPR* cc. 137–8, tr. pp. 259–63, here Agnellus preserves a completely different account, not mentioning the issue of Bishop Felix and the bond, or the murder of the exarch, but claiming that some citizens of Ravenna had participated in the overthrow and mutilation of Justinian II in 695. While the *LP* interprets this attack on Ravenna as divine punishment for opposing the see of St Peter, it is not mentioned in Greek sources.
5. *LPR* c. 148, tr. p. 272, and J. M. Pizarro, *Writing Ravenna. The Liber pontificalis of Andrea Agnellus* (Michigan 1995), pp. 171–83, 187–8, on Agnellus' attempt to build up his relative by comparison with Boethius and as a counter to Felix. The name *Jericomium* (from Greek *hierokomion*) refers to a holy monastery that probably also served as a charitable home for old people, perhaps another indication of the influence Johannicis had brought from his first period in Constantinople.
6. *LPR* c. 36, tr. pp. 258–9 on *vicedominus* of monastery of St Bartholomew.
7. G. Cavallo's masterly analysis of the texts possibly written in Ravenna, 'La cultura scritta tra Antichità e Alto Medioevo', in *Storia di Ravenna* II/1, pp. 79–125, demonstrates the constant production and copying of manuscripts such as the liturgical Rotolus and the copy of the Desert Fathers (*ibid.* plates 21 and 22), as well as Felix's volumes, cf. M. Bassetti, 'Total Eclipse of Text', in *Identity of Text*, ed. F. Santi (forthcoming).
8. L. Brubaker and J. Haldon, *Byzantium in the Iconoclast Era c. 680–850. A History* (Cambridge 2011), pp. 575–87 on the new social elite. Older families of aristocratic and senatorial status appear to have avoided such nicknames and names derived from provincial origins, such as Koloneias, Paphlagonitis or Helladikos.
9. *LPR* c. 138, tr. p. 262, on the Empress Theodora's additions to the crown of Justinian II. In the same way imperial women wove ceremonial belts similarly adorned with jewels. In the late sixth century Sophia and Constantina made a precious crown for Emperor Maurice and were distressed when he hung it above the altar in the Hagia Sophia on a triple chain of gold and precious stones, Theophanes, *Chronographia*, AM 6093, tr. pp. 406–7.
10. *LPR* c. 138, tr. pp. 262–3 on Felix, and c. 141, tr. pp. 265–6 on Johannicis.
11. *LPR* c. 139, tr. p. 263.
12. *LPR* c. 148, tr. p. 272; Pizarro, *Writing Ravenna*, pp. 172–83 shows how Agnellus tries to match the sanctity of Archbishop Felix with similar skills displayed by Johannicis, though his are more intellectual than spiritual. He

also suggests, most convincingly, that the story of Boethius and his conflict with Theoderic provides a possible model for his hero.

13. The complex history of Cherson's role in this coup d'état draws attention to the importance of this Byzantine settlement, which had been used as place of exile for Pope Martin, Justinian II and Archbishop Felix.

14. *LP* 90.8 and 10, tr. pp. 93 and 94. J. Herrin, 'Philippikos "the Gentle"', in *Margins and Metropolis. Authority across the Byzantine Empire* (Princeton 2013), pp. 192–205.

15. *LPR* c. 143, tr. p. 268.

16. *LP* 90.9, tr. p. 94, 'fiunt indicula et fidei expositiones', probably written on papyrus which is then put into the tomb.

17. *LP* 90.11, tr. p. 94; J. Herrin, 'Philippikos and the Greens', in *Margins and Metropolis*, pp. 179–91.

18. The House of Felix existed until the twelfth century, see *LPR* c. 145, tr. p. 270 and n. 22.

19. *LPR* c. 163, tr. p. 269.

20. *LPR* c. 148, tr. p. 273. The reference to a chest of cypress wood might suggest that some of the relics were deposited in it.

21. Tjäder, *Papyri* I, 23 = Marini 109 = *Regesta* no. 31, *CLA* IX 405, but he didn't read the feminine ending of Johannia.

22. Marini 111, *CLA* XXIX 877 of 750–800. Apolenaris *domesticus numeri Invicti* signs as a witness, together with Vitalis *primicerius bandi secondi Tiberiaci*. This is probably the Second Tiberian rather than the Second Banner unit created by George. The *Persoarmeniaci* are known from Tjäder *Papyri*: II, 37 = Marini 122, *CLA* XXI 716 (Tzitas, prob of Armenian origin), but the *numerus Armeniorum* is documented from 639, cf. Tjäder, *Papyri* I, 23.

23. Donation of Eudocia *ancilla dei*, *Regesta* no. 42. A *domesticus numeri felicum letorum*, with two other *viri clarissimi*, a *domesticus* and another *scol(aris)* from the *scole gentilium* appear as witnesses of the time. Brown, *Gentlemen and Officers*, p. 84, no. 8 adds to the incomplete lists in Guillou, *Régionalisme*, p. 302.

24. *Codice Bavaro. Codex traditionum Ecclesiae Ravennatis (Breviarium Ecclesiae Ravennatensis)*, ed. E. Baldetti (Ancona 1983), no. 94, pp. 133–41.

25. *LPR* c. 153, tr. p. 277; cf. *LPR* c. 139, tr. p. 263.

26. Paul Dilley, 'Christian icon practice in apocryphal literature: consecration and conversion of synagogues into churches', *Journal of Roman Archaeology* 23 (2010), pp. 85–302 (very interesting on the significance of icons in such conversions and clear about the number of synagogues that were converted to Christian use).

27. *LPR* c. 136, tr. p. 258 on the 'day of judgment' text, and *LPR* c. 150, tr. p. 274 on the books of Peter Chrysologus.

28. *LPR* c. 150, tr. pp. 274–5.

CHAPTER 31

1. By 751 Islamic forces met those of imperial China in Transoxiana, see R. Hatch, '751CE. Watershed events in the Carolingian, Byzantine, Abbasid and Tang empires', in *Paradigm Shifts during the Global Middle Ages and the Renaissance*, ed. A. Classen (Turnhout 2019), pp. 1–15.

2. As Gibbon foresaw in his memorable counterfactual: that the Koran would now be taught in Oxford University, see *The History of the Decline and Fall of the Roman Empire*, ed. J. B. Bury, 7. vols. (London 1896–1900), vol. VI, p. 15.

3. Theophanes, *Chronographia*, AM 6208, tr. p. 540; Nikephoros, *Short Chronicle* 52, tr. p. 121, Leo had advanced to Chrysopolis opposite Constantinople. Anastasios II had already sent families that could not provide soldiers or had inadequate stores to survive a siege into the countryside, Theophanes AM 6202, tr. p. 534.

4. Theophanes AM 6209, tr. pp. 545–6. The victory was celebrated every year as a triumph, which kept alive the memory of Leo's defence.

5. Theophanes AM 6210, tr. pp. 549–50.

6. Against those historians who interpret Ravenna's opposition to Constantinople as an attempt to break away from the empire in 727, Francesco Borri convincingly shows how closely the Italian exarchate was related to the imperial capital, '*Duces e magistri militum* nell'Italia exarcale (VI–VII secolo)', *Reti Medievali Rivista* VI (2005), pp. 19–60, esp. 29.

7. Theophanes AM 6216, 6218, 6219, 6222, 6223, 6224, 6226, 6228, 6229, 6230–39 (brief notices of Arab attacks from 723–41), tr. pp. 554–76.

8. *LP* 91.14, tr. II, p. 10; *PmbZ* 4817

9. Theophanes AM 6211 and 6212, tr. pp. 551–2, 554.

10. J. Herrin, 'The historical context of Iconoclast reform', in *Margins and Metropolis. Authority across the Byzantine Empire* (Princeton 2013), pp. 206–19; for the new coin, ibid. n. 29; P. Grierson *Byzantine Coinage* (Washington DC 1999), pp. 13–14.

11. *LP* 91.15, tr. II, p. 10; cf. Theophanes AM 6217, tr. p. 558, Pope Gregory withheld the taxes of Italy and Rome. There is considerable debate about the issue.

12. Theophanes AM 6224, tr. p. 568. These additional measures follow the account of the naval expedition led by Manes and may also be an interpolation.

13. *LP* 91.16, tr. II, p. 10, connected to the exarch Paul and his instruction to kill the pontiff.

14. The count has been identified with Marinus, *komes tou Opsikiou*, known from his seal, which also mentions the exarch. V. Prigent, 'Une note sur

l'administration de l'Exarchat de Ravenna', *Nea Rome* 2 (2005), pp. 78–88, argues that a high-ranking official had been transferred to the West to assist the campaign, while C. Zuckerman, 'Marinos (*PmbZ* 4797), Count of the Opsikion and Exarch of Italy', in *Mélanges Jean-Claude Cheynet, Travaux et Mémoires* 21/1 (2017), pp. 803–6, supposes that Marinus held both titles at the same time and dates the seal in the seventh century. *LP* 91.16, tr. II, p. 11, implies that the anonymous count was under Paul's orders.

15. *LP* 91.16, tr. II, p. 11 n. 48, quoting T. F. X. Noble, *The Republic of St Peter. The Birth of the Papal State 680–825* (Philadelphia 1984), p. 29, but Exarch Paul had not led this effort and was in Ravenna when the emperor's mandates arrived later.

16. *LP* 91.15–18, tr. II, pp. 10–12, adds a theological dimension, claiming that the division was between those who supported 'the emperor's iniquity' and those 'who kept the faith'.

17. *LP* 91.18, tr. II, pp. 12–13; S. Cosentino, *Storia dell'Italia bizantina (VI–XI secolo)* (Bologna 2008), p. 242, reports a temporary occupation by Liutprand *c.* 728–32. O. Bertolini, 'Quale fu il vero oggiettivo assegnato da Leone III "Isaurico" all'armata di Manes, stratego dei Cibyrreoti?' *Byzantinische Forschungen* 2 (1967), pp. 15–49, dates the occupation to 732.

18. *LP* 91.21, tr. II, p. 14.

19. *LP* 91.22, tr. II, p. 15.

20. *LPR* cc. 151 and 89, tr. pp. 277 and 202.

21. *LPR* c. 155, tr. pp. 279–80. And he reports that much later the Lombard King Aistulf began the reconstruction of the Petriana, setting up the bases, which remained into the ninth century.

22. *LPR* c. 153, tr. p. 276. The regions of the Venetiae (plural, not the singular name for the city of Venice, which did not yet exist) were normally loyal to Constantinople rather than Rome. Possibly this quite unprecedented case of exile might reflect the more securely documented flight of Eutychios the exarch, who was forced by a Lombard attack to seek the help of the people of the Venetiae (see below). The story may have been constructed to account for John's absence.

23. Cosentino, *PiB*, for the name and office of Epiphanius (not in *PmbZ*) and Eutychios, also noted with his seals in *PmbZ* 1870 and 1871.

24. *LPR* cc. 151–2, tr. pp. 275–6. Cf. J. M. Pizarro, *Writing Ravenna. The Liber pontificalis of Andrea Agnellus* (Michigan 1995), pp. 40, 52. The whole story seems more fantasy than history, perhaps an invention of Agnellus to make sense of a story that Archbishop John had fled to the Venetiae at some point?

25. In 729 Eutychios was in Rome where he is recorded as assisting King Liutprand in his campaign against the dukes of Spoleto and Benevento, and putting down another revolt in Tuscany. He had abandoned any effort to

remove Pope Gregory II and sent the head of the Tuscan rebel to Constantinople as proof of his other success. *LP* 91.22–3 (which is placed before the news of Leo III's dismissal of Patriarch Germanos in January 730, *LP* 91.24, tr. II, pp. 15–16).

26. Marini-Mai, *Nova Collectio* V (Rome 1831), pp. 228–9; clearly analysed by Guillou, *Régionalisme*, pp. 272–7; cf. Cavallo, 'La cultura scritta . . .', pp. 117–18.

27. *LP* 91.17, 91.23–4, tr. II, pp. 13, 15–16, which notes the arrival of the emperor's mandates to remove icons, to take down and burn them, and his dismissal of Patriarch Germanos and replacement by Anastasios, before the death of Gregory II on 13 February 731. In the 740s, when the *Life* of Gregory III was compiled in Rome, the author(s) thought the persecution of icon venerators was raging, *LP* 92.2, tr. II, p. 19.

28. Pizarro, *Writing Ravenna*, pp. 170–71, 186–7, summarizes the event and provides interesting commentary.

29. *LPR* c. 153, tr. pp. 276–8. The commander is given the title '*monstratico*' (*monostrategos*) and is reported as returning again 'to depopulate Ravenna'. His forces are identified as '*Grecorum exercitum*' and '*Bizanteos*', so they were quite definitely Greek. But the repetition of the battle with such a total victory for the Ravennati is distinctly odd, perhaps an invention of Agnellus.

30. There seems to be no connection with another naval expedition led by the commander Manes, but on this see W. Brandes, 'Das Schweigen des *Liber Pontificalis*. Die "Enteignung" der päpstlichen Patrimonien Siziliens und Unteritaliens in der 50er Jahren des 8. Jahrhunderts', *Fontes Minores* 12 (2014), pp. 97–203, where both are considered imaginary.

CHAPTER 32

1. Theophanes, *Chronographia*, AM 6209, tr. pp. 542–4, provides a long novelistic account of his escapades.

2. Theophanes AM 6217, 6218, tr. pp. 558, 559; Nikephoros, *Short Chronicle* cc. 59–60, tr. pp. 128–31.

3. Theophanes AM 6218, tr. pp. 560–61; Nikephoros, *Short Chronicle* cc. 61, tr. pp. 130–31.

4. Exod. 20.4–5, repeated in Deut. 5.8–9, and restated in Isaiah 44.9–19, with much commentary on the fate of those who make idols, molten or graven images, and fall down before them. Cf. Ezekiel, 14.3, who specifies the same danger to 'men who set up idols in their heart', or 44.10–12 on the Levites 'who ministered before their idols and caused the house of Israel to fall into iniquity'.

5. Theophanes AM 6221, tr. pp. 563–4; Nikephoros, *Short Chronicle* cc. 62, tr. pp. 130–31. The imperial 'mandates' noted in the Roman *Liber pontificalis*

probably refer to these orders of 730, as there is no convincing evidence for an earlier order to remove icons.

6. J. Herrin, 'Women and the faith in icons in early Christianity', in *Unrivalled Influence. Women and Empire in Byzantium* (Princeton 2013), pp. 38–79; cf. L. Brubaker and J. Haldon, *Byzantium in the Iconoclast Era c. 680–850. A History* (Cambridge 2011), pp. 53–63.

7. T. F. Mathews, *The Dawn of Christian Art* (Los Angeles 2016), pp. 14–20; *idem*, *The Clash of Gods* 2nd edn (Princeton 1999), pp. 177–90.

8. And we have seen how such images functioned as imperial propaganda, for instance when Philippikos replaced portraits of church leaders with those of Monothelete patriarchs and bishops.

9. For example, when the imperial portraits of Phokas and his wife were welcomed into Rome (see Ch. 24); J. Herrin, 'The icon corner in medieval Byzantium', in *Unrivalled Influence*, pp. 281–301; Mathews, *The Dawn of Christian Art*, pp. 131–4, 221.

10. Herrin, 'The icon corner', p. 284; *eadem*, 'Women and the faith in icons', pp. 42–7. See also E. Doxiadis, *The Mysterious Fayum Portraits. Faces from Ancient Egypt* (London 1995), repr. with additions, *Facing Eternity. From the Fayum Portraits to the Early Christian Icons* (Heraklion 2019).

11. H. Maguire, *Nectar and Illusion. Nature in Byzantine Art and Literature* (Oxford 2012), pp. 11–47, esp. 23–8. When the Hebrews made the Golden Calf and danced around it, that was an act of sheer idolatry, anathematized by Moses when he came down from the Holy Mountain of Sinai as comparable to venerating the idols of ancient Egyptian or Greek gods.

12. Gregory the Great, *Regesten* IX 209, XI 10, and C. Chazelle, 'Pictures, books and the illiterate: Pope Gregory I's letters to Serenus of Marseilles', *Word and Image* 6 (1990), pp. 138–53. It was prompted by Bishop Serenus, whose spontaneous acts of iconoclasm horrified the pope.

13. Mango, *Art*, pp. 133–41, for a collection of texts referring to the painting and veneration of icons.

14. For the two bishops' letters, Brubaker and Haldon, *Byzantium*, pp. 94–105.

15. Ibid., pp. 98–101. Theophanes later claims that the impious Leo was too ignorant to understand the difference between relative veneration (*schetike proskynesis*) and the full worship of God (*latreia*), AM 6218, tr. p. 561.

16. *LP* 91.17, tr. II, p. 11, the event is dated after the tax revolt, at some point 'later'.

17. *LP* 91.23, tr. II, p. 15. This account of the destruction with great bonfires or whitewashing of churches, and the excessively violent punishment of Leo's opponents, is exaggerated in many ninth-century sources so hostile to the emperor.

18. *LP* 91.17, tr. II, p. 11; this provoked all the regions to elect their own dukes in order to achieve freedom for themselves and the pontiff. In western sources

such as the *Book of the Pontiffs* and Paul the deacon's *History of the Lombards*, the emperor is held specifically responsible for this development.

19. *LP* 91.17, tr. II, pp. 11–12 (the chronology is confused).

20. D. Deliyannis, 'Agnellus of Ravenna and iconoclasm: theology and politics in a ninth-century historical text', *Speculum* 71 (1996), pp. 449–76.

21. Theophanes AM 6210, tr. p. 550, on Umar's forced conversion of Christians. C. Sahner, 'The first iconoclasm in Islam: a new history of the Edict of Yazid II (AH 104/AD 723)', *Der Islam* 94 (2017), pp. 5–56; Brubaker and Haldon, *Byzantium*, pp. 114–16 persist in distinguishing Islamic from Christian iconoclasm and deny the existence of Yazid II's edict, p. 116 n. 147 citing P. Speck, *Ich bin's nicht. Kaiser Konstantin ist es gewesen. Die Legenden vom Einfluss des Teufels, des Juden und des Moslem auf den Ikonoklasmus* (Bonn 1990), pp. 35ff and 73ff. Cf. D. Reynolds, 'Rethinking Palestinian iconoclasm', *DOP* 71 (2017), pp. 1–64.

22. Brubaker and Haldon, *Byzantium*, pp. 98–100, 102–4, 105–17 on possible external influence.

23. S. Naef, 'Islam and images: a complex relation', in *L'aniconisme dans l'art religieux byzantin*, eds. M. Campagnolo et al. (Geneva 2014), pp. 49–58; F. B. Flood, 'Faith, religion, and the material culture of early Islam', in *Byzantium and Islam. Age of Transition*, eds. H. Evans and B. Ratliff (New York 2012), pp. 244–57. See also *Byzantium and the Arabs*, Museum of Byzantine Culture exhibition catalogue (Thessalonike 2011).

24. C. Zuckerman's memorable phrase, 'Learning from the enemy . . .', *Millennium* 2 (2006), pp. 79–135.

CHAPTER 33

1. *LP* 93.2, 4, 12, tr. II, pp. 35, 37, 41 and n. 46 where Davis claims that this shows Duke Stephen to be a subordinate of the pope, responsible to him rather than the exarch in Ravenna.

2. *LP* 91.22, tr. II. p. 14. Cf. *LP* 91.4 when Liutprand confirmed the restoration of the patrimony of the Cottian Alps to the pope (Paul the deacon *HL* VI 44); and *LP* 91.7 on the purchase of the castle of Cumae.

3. *HL* VI 58, tr. p. 304 on the foundation of St Anastasios.

4. M. Lauxtermann, 'A Lombard epigram in Greek', in *Inscribing Texts in Byzantium: Continuities and Transformations*, eds. M. Lauxtermann and I. Toth (forthcoming). On the icon, see H. Belting, *Likeness and Presence* Eng. trans. (Chicago 1994), pp. 142–3. The verse was copied many years later by a German pilgrim.

5. At this date the term consul was used by the highest military aristocracy in provincial society, so these four individuals represented a local leadership below the level of exarch.

6. *Codex Carolinus* 2, *MGH Epp* III, p. 477. He also sent a letter (dated 739) to Charles Martel, which expresses the pope's regret at the destruction of Ravenna by Hildebrand and Peredo.

7. Pope Gregory III's letter to Patriarch Antonius of Grado, MGH *Epp*. III, no. 1, p. 703.

8. *HL* VI 54, tr. pp. 297–8; the letter requesting help was known to John the deacon, who wrote the earliest history of Venice (in the late tenth/early eleventh century). In a fascinating forgery, the fourteenth-century chronicler Andrea Dandolo changed the addressee so that Doge Ursus (Orso) was the person to whom the pope had appealed – an obvious attempt to establish Ursus as the first holder of this title and leader of the nascent Venetian community. It passed into later historical memory and Ursus was retrospectively endowed with the Byzantine title *hypatos* (consul), and a commanding power between 726 to 737. He was also connected with a popular revolt against the imperial policy of iconoclasm and was allegedly assassinated on the orders of the exarch Eutychios, D. M. Nicol, *Byzantium and Venice: A Study in Diplomatic and Cultural Relations* (Cambridge 1988), pp. 10–11.

9. *HL* VI 55, tr. pp. 299–30; *LP* 92.15, tr. II, pp. 27–8.

10. *LP* 93.1 (n. 1, he is likely to have assisted at the synod of 732 as a deacon); J. Osborne, 'Papal Court Culture during the Pontificate of Zacharias (AD 741–52)', in *Court Culture in the Early Middle Ages: The Proceedings of the First Alcuin Conference*, ed. C. Cubitt (Turnhout 2003), pp. 223–34.

11. *LP* 93.2, tr. II, p. 35. Amelia, Orte and Bomarzo lie either side of the main road north from Rome to Orvieto; Blera is further to the west – presumably all four were castles that controlled the surrounding area.

12. *LP* 93.25 and 26, tr. II, pp. 48–9, and enormous bibliography on this development, summarized by Davis in II, pp. 31–4 cf. T. F. X. Noble, *The Republic of St Peter. The Birth of the Papal State 680–825* (Philadelphia 1984), pp. 246–9; F. Marazzi, 'La configurazione istituzionale del potere pontificio', in *L'héritage byzantin en Italie (VIIe au XIIe siècle) II. Les cadres juridiques et sociaux et les institutions publiques*, ed. J.-M. Martin et al. (Rome 2012), pp. 261–78. Zacharias extended the *domuscultae* by purchase and protected them by apostolic decrees that they should never be alienated from the church of Rome, very important steps highlighted by Marazzi, ibid., pp. 273–4.

13. *LP* 93.9, tr. II, p. 39. Some historians have seen in Sergius the future bishop of the city, who succeeded John in 744, but all these names are very commonly used by the Ravenna population.

14. *LP* 93.12, tr. II, p. 40.

15. Suggested by R. Davis, *LP*, II p. 41 n. 47), cf. *Il corridoio bizantino e la via Amerina in Umbria nell'Alto Medioevo*, ed. E. Menestò (Spoleto 1999).

16. *LP* 93.12–13, tr. II, p. 41.

17. *LPR* c. 155, tr. p. 279. But his account of the visit doesn't fit well with the Roman record of the same event, which fails to mention the church of S. Apollinare in Classe. Deliyannis has combined the two references, see *LPR* tr. p. 279, n. 3, and the gift of a purple altar cloth does suggest a very wealthy donor. But, as Agnellus confuses Zacharias with later popes such as Stephen II, his account is unreliable.

18. *LP* 93.14–17, tr. II, pp. 41–4 (quote at the end of 93.16, tr. II, p. 43).

19. *LP* 93.20, tr. II, pp. 45–6. Normally it should have been addressed to the patriarch.

20. *LP* 93.20, tr. II, p. 46. The donation is recorded in the lifetime of Zacharias, therefore before 752, but is connected with the fall of Ravenna to the Lombards in 751, an event not recorded in the *LP*.

21. *LP* 93.23, tr. II, p. 47.

22. *LP* 93.23, tr. II pp. 47–8. Noble, *Republic of St Peter*, pp. 55–7, emphasizes the pro-Roman and deeply Christian character of Ratchis, previously duke of Friuli. His wife and children were similarly dedicated to the Christian life.

23. Possibly Ratchis had developed a serious illness from which he died shortly after, see *SRL*, the Continuators of Paul the deacon's *Historia Langobardorum*, 1 the Casinensis, pp. 198–200, which records his death at the monastery of St Benedict, Montecassino, and his widow Tasia and daughter Rattruda, who endowed and directed a female monastery in Plumbariola.

24. *LP* 94.15, tr. II, p. 58 (indeed, this has been used by the author of the *Life of Pope Stephen* to justify his appeal to the Franks). In 751, as Aistulf was at the gates of Ravenna, Constantine V was capturing Theodosioupolis and Melitene in eastern Asia Minor. He went on to conquer the Armenians, and returned with numerous captives and much booty, Nikephoros, *Short Chronicle* 70, tr. p. 143; Theophanes, *Chronographia*, AM 6243, tr. p. 590.

25. J. Herrin, 'Constantinople, Rome and the Franks in the seventh and eighth centuries', repr. in *Margins and Metropolis. Authority across the Byzantine Empire* (Princeton 2013), pp. 220–38; M. McCormick, 'Textes, images et iconoclasme dans le cadre des relations entre Byzance et l'Occident carolingien', *Settimana di Spoleto* 41 (1994), pp. 95–158; M.-F. Auzépy, 'Constantin V, l'empereur Isaurien et les Carolingiens', in *Les assises du pouvoir: Temps médiévaux, territoires africains*, eds. O. Redon and B. Rosenberger (Paris 1994), pp. 49–65.

26. *LPR* c. 155, tr. pp. 279–80. For the diploma for Farfa monastery signed by Aistulf, *'in palatio'*, *Codice diplomatico longobardo* III/1, ed. C. Brühl (Rome 1970), no. 23, pp. 111–15; but the monastery did not become dependent on royal patronage, see M. Costambeys, *Power and Patronage in Early Medieval Italy: Local Society, Italian Politics and the Abbey of Farfa c. 700–900* (Cambridge 2007), p. 119.

27. Some historians have seen in his abandonment of Ravenna a treacherous arrangement with the Lombard ruler.

28. Theophanes records the development under Leo III, AM 6224, tr. p. 568, and reports that a major tax revenue of 25,200 gold *solidi* (or possibly 410,400, according to several mss.) was thus transferred from the church of Rome to the public treasury, for use by Constantinople. Nikephoros, *Short Chronicle* 76, doesn't mention the transfer but does note that in 761/2 when Constantine V celebrated a victory over the Bulgarians in the Hippodrome, he displayed 'two golden basins that had been made in the island of Sicily, each one weighing 800 lbs of gold', tr. p. 151. Could these have been found on one of the Sicilian papal estates and sent to Constantinople as part of the transfer? Since the papacy did not comment on this loss until the pontificate of Hadrian I (772–95), there is no precise record of the date of confiscation.

29. Most recently and convincingly argued by W. Brandes, 'Das Schweigen des *Liber Pontificalis*. Die "Enteignung" der päpstlichen Patrimonien Siziliens und Unteritaliens in der 50er Jahren des 8. Jahrhunderts', *Fontes Minores* 12 (2014), pp. 97–203.

CHAPTER 34

1. *LPR* c. 154, tr. p. 278.
2. '*more Graecorum*', *LPR* ed. Nauerth, II, p. 540; *CSEL* 332.26–8; tr. p. 279.
3. W. Woodfin, *The Embodied Icon: Liturgical Vestments and Sacramental Power in Byzantium* (Oxford 2012), p. 6, on Greek liturgical dress.
4. *ODB*, III, 1553 (*orarion*). This garment corresponds to the *ephod*, part of Aaron's priestly attire described in the Book of Leviticus.
5. G. Lobrichon, 'Le vêtement liturgique des évêques au IXe siècle', in *Costume et Société dans l'Antiquité et le haut Moyen Âge*, eds. F. Chausson and H. Ingelbert (Paris 2003), pp. 129–41, esp. 134–6, citing E. Palazzo, *L'évêque et son image: l'illustration du pontifical au Moyen Âge* (Turnhout 1999). In identifying it as a large decorated stole worn around the shoulders, Bede may have been misled by images of the prophets like Zachariah, who are shown wearing the *ephod* in the church at Parenzo. On Greek monastic traditions in Ravenna, J.-M. Sansterre, 'Monaci e monasteri greci a Ravenna', *Storia di Ravenna* II/2, pp. 323–39; E. Morini, 'Le strutture monastiche a Ravenna', *Storia di Ravenna* II/2, pp. 305–21.
6. *LPR* c. 154, tr. pp. 278–9; Guillou, *Régionalisme*, pp. 172–9, 221–3.
7. *LPR* c. 155, tr. p. 279. Such demonstrations of devotion to the church were not unusual, cf. a similar donation made by Pope Zacharias of an altar cloth of pure purple decorated with pearls given to the church of S. Apollinare, or

later gifts made by Charlemagne. The *Liber pontificalis* emphasizes Aistulf's mighty savagery, 94.5, tr. II, p. 54; pernicious savagery, 94.6, tr. II, p. 55; Aistulf the criminal, atrocious, boiling with mighty rage, 94.8 and 10, tr. II, pp. 56–7.

8. *LP* 94.15–17, tr. II, pp. 58–9: ed. Duchesne, I, p. 444, the Pope faced the 'pestiferum Langobardorum regem' and knew that no help would come from the imperial power, 'ab eo nihil hac de re obtinueret'.

9. *LP* 94.31, tr. II, p. 66 and n. 70, the term is first mentioned in CC 6, p. 489, written in 755; see. T. F. X. Noble, *The Republic of St Peter. The Birth of the Papal State 680–825* (Philadelphia 1984), pp. 95–7.

10. *LP* 94.11, tr. II, p. 57; cf. T. F. X. Noble, *Images, Iconoclasm and the Carolingians* (Philadelphia 2009), pp. 127–8.

11. *LP* 94.19–24, tr. II, pp. 60–63.

12. *LP* 94.23, tr. II, pp. 61–2.

13. J. L. Nelson, *King and Emperor. A New Life of Charlemagne* (London 2019), pp. 69–75.

14. RFA, a. 754; *LP* 94.27, tr. II, p. 64; J. Herrin, *The Formation of Christendom* (Princeton 1989), pp. 373–5; C. Goodson, 'To be the daughter of Saint Peter: S. Petronilla and forging the Franco-Papal alliance', *Three Empires, Three Cities: Identity, Material Culture and Legitimacy in Venice, Ravenna, and Rome , 750–1000*, ed. V. Ortenberg West-Harling (Turnhout 2015), pp. 159–82.

15. Theophanes, *Chronographia*, AM 6245, tr. pp. 591–2; Nikephoros, *Short Chronicle* c. 72, tr. pp. 143–5; *Die ikonoklastische Synode von Hiereia 754: Einleitung, Text, Übersetzung und Kommentar ihres Horos*, eds. T. Krannich, C. Schubert and C. Sode (Tübingen 2002).

16. Herrin, *Formation of Christendom*, pp. 377–81; Noble, *Images, Iconoclasm and the Carolingians*, pp. 63–8, though he notes that Hiereia was not followed up by serious destruction in the East, although some iconophile monks were attacked.

17. *LP* 94.32–7, tr. II, pp. 66–8.

18. *LP* 94.41–5.

19. Stephen II, *LP* 94.44–5, tr. II, p. 71. The king said that 'he could not steal what he had once given to St Peter'. George, who held the position of chief secretary, *protasekretis*, claimed that Aistulf had illegally occupied imperial territory.

20. Herrin, *Formation of Christendom*, pp. 303–4, 374–9.

21. *LP* 94.47, tr. II, p. 73. The names of the cities were later copied into another record preserved in Charles's archive.

22. *LP* 94.47, tr. II, p. 72.

23. *LRP* c. 157, tr. p. 280 where King Aistulf is also held responsible for betraying Sergius. Cf. O. Bertolini, 'Sergio arcivescovo di Ravenna (744–69) e i papi del suo tempo', *Studi Romagnoli* 1 (1950), pp. 43–88, esp. 60–64.

24. *LRP* c. 157, tr. pp. 280–81. The reference to secular favour might relate to the role of local aristocrats in choosing him to be their archbishop. The synod is not listed in W. Hartmann, *Die Synode der Karolingerzeit im Frankenreich und in Italien* (Paderborn 1989), so it was probably considered a merely local judicial case, not worthy of the name.

25. *praecepta actionum*, CC 49, p. 569 (Hadrian to Charles); cf. Noble, *Republic of St Peter* p. 106.

26. *LP* 95.1–2, tr. II, p. 80. His election was disputed by Theophylact, the archdeacon, and there was a delay of 35 days before Paul was consecrated.

27. Noble, *Republic of St Peter*, p. 106.

28. *LPR* c. 157, tr. p. 282; *LPR* ed. Nauerth, II, p 548; *CSEL* 335, pp. 126–7, *modica gratulatoria fuit et modica quies*.

29. Bertolini, O. 'Sergio arcivescovo di Ravenna (744– 69) e i papi del suo tempo', *Studi Romagnoli* 1 (1950), pp. 43–88, esp. pp. 72–3, 76–8.

30. On the papyrus of 767, see A. Vasina, 'La Romagna estense. Genesi e sviluppo dal Medioevo all'età moderna', *Studi Romagnoli* 21 (1970), pp. 47–68, esp. pp. 53–5; repr. *Regesta* no. 42, p. 413, where the term *hegoumenos* is interpreted as representing the name of an earlier abbot, Erguminus, cf. Deichmann, *Ravenna* II/1 p. 252. My thanks to Caroline Goodson for pointing out the use of the term *hegoumenos* in Naples. Dating by the regnal years of eastern emperors had been abandoned in Rome from Leo III's years of iconoclast activity in favour of dating from the Incarnation, though the *Life* of Paul refers in neutral manner to the reigns of Leo III and Constantine V, *LP* 95.2, tr. II, p. 80. Later, *LP* 95.3, tr. II, p. 83, records Pope Paul's many embassies and letters to the emperors, begging them to restore the veneration of icons. CC 36 mentions these (now lost) letters to Constantinople and Constantine V's reply.

31. *LPR* c. 159, tr. p. 284, cf. S. Gelichi, 'Lupicinius presbitur. Una breve nota sulle istituzioni ecclesiastiche comacchiesi delle origini', in *Ricerca come incontro. Archeologi, paleografi e storici per Paolo Delogu*, eds. G. Barone et al. (Rome 2013), pp. 41–60, on the church at Comacchio which came under Ravenna's control.

CHAPTER 35

1. CC 15–17, pp. 512–17; P. Delogu, 'Il regno Lombardo', in *Storia d'Italia*, vol 1. *Longobardi e Bizantini*, ed. G. Galasso (Turin 1980).

2. CC 21, 29–31, pp. 522–4, 533–7 indicating Desiderius' duplicitous dealings and begging Pippin to restore all that was promised to Pope Stephen II.

3. T. S. Brown, 'Byzantine Italy, *c*.680–*c*.876', in *NCMH* II, pp. 328–9.

4. *LP* 96.5–15, tr. II, pp. 90–95, with full details of the murders, blindings and imprisonment on starvation rations, which caused many deaths; R. McKitterick, 'The *Damnatio memoriae* of Pope Constantine II (767–68)',

in *Italy and Early Medieval Europe. Papers for Chris Wickham*, eds. R. Balzaretti et al. (Oxford 2018), pp. 231-48.

5. *LP* 96.13, tr. II, p. 94 (they all confessed their sin in not resisting the unholy ordination of Constantine).

6. *LP* 96.17, tr. II, p. 97.

7. *LP* 96.20, tr. II, p. 99. All this takes up chapters 2-22.

8. *LP* 96.16-24, tr. II, pp. 95-101. S. Scholz, *Politik-Selbstverständnis-Selbstdarstellung: die Päpste in karolingischer und ottonischer Zeit* (Stuttgart 2006), pp. 74-6, records 13 Franks, cf. T. F. X. Noble, *The Republic of St Peter. The Birth of the Papal State 680-825* (Philadelphia 1984), pp. 117-19, which says a total of 49 bishops, the Italians all from sees close to Rome, its suburbs, Roman Tuscany and Campania, and 12 from Francia.

9. M. McCormick, 'Textes, images et iconoclasme dans le cadre des relations entre Byzance et l'Occident carolingien', Settimana 41 (Spoleto 1994), pp. 95-158; the presence of the eunuch Synesios at Gentilly in 767 confirms that this meeting's purpose was to negotiate a marriage between Constantine V's son Leo and Pippin's daughter Gisela.

10. The fragmentary nature of the evidence is assembled by Pope Hadrian in later letters to the Franks, and more was unearthed in the papal archive by Anastasius Bibliothecarius in the ninth century, who added the text attributed to Ambrose of Milan. Its iconophile message hinges on the recognition of a saint from his portrait in a painting, see *MGH Concilia* II.1, 78, and W. Hartmann, ed., *Die Synoden der Karolingerzeit im Frankenreich und in Italien* (Paderborn 1989); F. Hartmann, *Hadrian I (772-795): frühmittelalterliches Adelspapsttum und die Lösung Roms vom byzantinischen Kaiser* (Stuttgart 2006).

11. J. L. Nelson, *King and Emperor. A New Life of Charlemagne* (London 2019), pp. 101-7.

12. The marriage was very short, Nelson, ibid., pp. 107-10, and probably involved sending Desiderius' daughter back to his court in Pavia, a public insult, so that Charles could marry Hildegard, a noble Alaman, and thus strengthen a link with her people.

13. *LP* 96.26, tr. II, p. 102.

14. CC 85, pp. 621-2, a papal letter to Charles, devoted to the correct way of electing the archbishop of Ravenna, which recapitulates the history of Michael 'the intruder'.

15. J. T. Hallenbeck, 'Paul Afiarta and the papacy: an analysis of politics in eighth-century Rome', *Archivum Historiae Pontificiae* 12 (1974), pp. 22-54, suggests Leo was acting as the pope's lieutenant in the papal 'state' created by Pippin's donation of 755/6, but Sergius was 'more rebellious than cooperative', p. 54, n. 69. Archbishop Leo was generally unwilling to co-operate with the pope; he later imprisoned a papal official sent to govern Gavello.

16. R. McKitterick, *Charlemagne. The Formation of a European Identity* (Cambridge 2008), pp. 43–6; Nelson, *King and Emperor*, pp. 119–27; A. Hack, *Codex Carolinus: päpstliche Epistolographie im 8. Jahrhundert*, 2 vols. (Stuttgart 2006–7).

17. CC 86, pp. 622–3, and 88, pp. 624–5, both dated 787–91. Hadrian asks Charles to expel the *Venetici negotiatores* from Ravenna and to campaign against Duke Garamannus, who has occupied church lands.

18. B. Bachrach, *Charlemagne's Early Military Campaigns (768–777). A Diplomatic and Military Analysis* (Leiden 2013), pp. 277, 290–92. These well-established ways over the Alpine barriers are also mentioned in the 806 division of Charles's territories, which stipulated what lands were to be ruled by his three eldest sons with Hildegard: Louis (Aquitaine), Charles the Younger (the major central part), Pippin (Italy). Coming from the West Louis would normally use the Susa route, Charles, the Great St Bernard/Aosta route, and Pippin could move north through the Norican alps towards Chur (Curia), see McKitterick, *Charlemagne*, pp. 96–7.

19. *LPR* c. 160, tr. p. 285. T. S. Brown, 'Louis the Pious and the papacy – a Ravenna perspective', in *Charlemagne's Heir*, eds. P. Godman and R. Collins (Oxford 1990), pp. 297–307, considers this 'clearly mythical' but a reflection of Ravenna's close contacts with the Franks.

20. RFA a. 773, 774, tr. pp. 49–50; P. Delogu, 'Lombard and Carolingian Italy', in *NCMH* II, pp. 302–3; *LP* 97.29, cf. 97.32, the *exercitus Francorum* defeated the *exercitus Langobardorum*.

21. *LP* 97.44, tr. II, p. 144.

22. *LP* 97.35–43, tr. II, pp. 138–42 (a splendid description of the king's visit to Rome) and a claim that the donation repeated Pippin's, when Pope Stephen II first went to Francia, 97.42, tr. II, pp. 141–2. Nelson, *King and Emperor*, pp. 135–41.

23. Nelson, *King and Emperor*, pp. 146–8 on the treatment of Desiderius and his wife Ansa.

24. Ibid., pp. 181–6. After Bernard's rebellion in 817, Louis gave the kingdom to his own son, Lothar, though he preferred to share the imperial title with his father. From 829 to 839, however, Lothar ruled in Italy and was succeeded by his son, Louis II, who in 844 received the crown of the Lombards from Pope Pascal and was anointed in Rome.

25. Nelson, *King and Emperor*, pp. 151–4.

26. J. L. Nelson, 'Charlemagne and Ravenna', in *Ravenna, Its Role in Earlier Medieval Change and Exchange*, eds. J. Herrin and J. Nelson (London 2016), pp. 239–52, pointing out how unusual this use of an embolum is in papal correspondence. In CC 55, EMBOLUM is printed in capital letters spread right across the page, 'Annex about the insolence of Archbishop Leo', pp. 579–80.

27. CC 60, p. 587.
28. CC 75, p. 606 (783). Cf. Charles's efforts to prevent the sale of slaves in Rome and the activity of Venetian merchants at Ravenna, which was in turn related to the sale of enslaved people, Noble, *Republic of St Peter*, p. 282.
29. CC 61, 64; cf. CC 94, pp. 632–6, esp. p. 635.
30. T. S. Brown, 'The church of Ravenna and the imperial administration in the seventh century', *English Historical Review* 94 (1979), pp. 1–28, at 27, makes this connection with Ravenna.
31. F. Hartmann, *Hadrian I*, pp. 182–93, esp. p. 195. Cf. J. Herrin, *The Formation of Christendom* (Princeton 1989), pp. 385–6, though the suggestion that the pontificate of Paul I was the most plausible context for the fabrication requires correction.
32. The genesis and later use of the document remained highly disputed, see J. Fried, *'Donation of Constantine' and 'Constitutum Constantini': The Misinterpretation of a Fiction and its Original Meaning* (Berlin 2007), pp. 103–9 arguing for a short, forged *Constitution* in the mid-eighth century, elaborated in the longer *Donation*, concocted at the abbey of Corbie in 830–34, and now sharply and convincingly criticized by C. Goodson and J. Nelson, 'The Roman contexts of the "Donation of Constantine". Review article', *Early Medieval Europe* 18.4 (2010), pp. 446–67.
33. CC 60, pp. 586–7.
34. Nelson, *King and Emperor*, pp. 182–6. See further in the Conclusion.
35. Possibly first expressed in Alcuin's view that Charles was the father of Europe, *pater Europas*, D. Bullough, 'Europae pater: Charlemagne and his achievement in the light of recent scholarship', *English Historical Review* 85 (1970), pp. 59–105.

CHAPTER 36

1. A tribune, Peter, mentioned in the 780s may have held such a position, *LPR* c. 163, tr. p. 289.
2. *LPR* c. 162, tr. p. 287, Leo *ipatus* (*hypatos*), the traditional Greek term for consul.
3. S. Cosentino, 'Potere e autorità nell'Esarcato in età post-bizantina', in *L'Héritage byzantin en Italie VIIIe–XIIe siècle*, II (Rome 2012), pp. 279–95; Edward Schoolman, 'Nobility, aristocracy and status in early medieval Ravenna', in *Ravenna, Its Role in Earlier Medieval Change and Exchange*, eds. J. Herrin and J. Nelson (London 2016), pp. 211–38.
4. He used this route in 776 when he put down the Lombard rebellion of Count Hrodgaud, RFA, a. 776, tr. p. 53.
5. J. L. Nelson, *King and Emperor. A New Life of Charlemagne* (London 2019), pp. 159–61. Charles took Lombard hostages back to Francia (including the

brother of Paul the deacon) and intended to make sure their wives kept all their rights.

6. CC 60, pp. 586–7, and 61, pp. 588–9, warning Charles of a possible Arab attack, the *nefandissimi* Beneventans and the *patricius* of Sicily, cf. ch. 35 note 27 above.

7. RFA, a. 781, tr. p. 59; Nelson, *King and Emperor,* pp. 181–6

8. In 814 Pippin's son, Bernard, was granted permission to remain king of Italy, see Ch. 35 n. 24.

9. Hartmann, *Papst Hadrian I,* and A. T. Hack, *Codex Carolinus: Studien zur päpstlichen Epistolographie im 8. Jahrhundert,* 2 vols. (Stuttgart 2007).

10. Theophanes, *Chronographia,* AM 6274, tr p. 628.

11. J. Shepard, 'Courts in East and West', in *The Medieval World,* eds. P. Linehan and J. L. Nelson (London 2001), pp. 14–36; Y. Hen, *Roman Barbarians. The Royal Court and Culture in the Early Medieval West* (Basingstoke 2007), 166–72; J. Herrin, 'Constantinople, Rome, and the Franks in the seventh and eighth centuries', repr. in *Margins and Metropolis. Authority across the Byzantine Empire* (Princeton 2013), pp. 220–38. There are drawings of such an organ in use in the Utrecht Psalter produced in Reims in about 830, but the mechanism of the bellows to create water pressure was not widely understood.

12. Theophanes AM 6274, tr. p. 628; Annales mosellani, a. 781, *MGH SS* XVI, p. 497.

13. J. Fried, *Charlemagne* (Cambridge MA/London 2016), pp. 139, 144–6 (an account that attributes to the fifteen-year-old Constantine VI a furious reaction to the failure of the alliance and the invasion of southern Italy in 787). In contrast, Theophanes, AM 6281, tr. pp. 637–8, records the breaking of the alliance and Constantine's marriage to Maria of Amnia in November 788, the same year as the Byzantine invasion of southern Italy, which ended disastrously. I thank Jinty Nelson for her advice on this, Nelson, *King and Emperor,* pp. 227–30.

14. P. Dutton, *Charlemagne's Mustache* (New York 2004), pp. 164–5.

15. Elsewhere I've explained why female rulers, who were a notable feature of Byzantium throughout its long history, were responsible for the restoration of icons in 787, and again in 843 by Irene's great-niece Theodora, see J. Herrin *Women in Purple* (London 2001); *eadem, Unrivalled Influence. Women and Empire in Byzantium* (Princeton 2013). On Irene's invitation to Pope Hadrian, see Nelson, *King and Emperor,* pp. 225–6.

16. As was usual, representatives of the pentarchy were informed, together with all the bishops under Irene's control. The idea that Charlemagne and the Franks should have been invited to the 786–7 council misunderstands the tradition of the pentarchy as the final arbiter of doctrine, and Rome's claim to represent all the Christians of the West. It may, however, have developed from the practice instituted by Pope Stephen III in 769,

when the Franks were specifically invited to the Roman council to discuss problems raised by the illegitimate Pope Constantine, *LP* 96.16–24, tr. II, pp. 95–101.

17. *LP* 97.88, tr. II, pp. 168–9. Rome was of course the leading western bishopric represented at the Council. Pope Hadrian sent delegates who knew Greek and could follow the debate over icons. Since the area of East Illyricum had already been transferred to the patriarch of Constantinople, bishops from that region attended as his subordinates. Nineteen from Sicily and Calabria participated and provided evidence for the justification of icon veneration.

18. J. Herrin, *The Formation of Christendom* (Princeton 1989), pp. 434–9; T. F. X. Noble, *Images, Iconoclasm and the Carolingians* (Philadelphia 2009), pp. 159–83, 183–206 for analysis of *opus caroli Regis*. Cf. Fried, *Charlemagne*, pp. 382, 390–91.

19. Fried, *Charlemagne*, p. 146; Nelson, *King and Emperor*, pp. 225–6.

20. Fried, *Charlemagne*, pp. 145–6, citing the *Gesta abbatum Fontinellensium* c. 12, *MGH SS* II (Hannover 1929), p. 29, which claims this embassy was provoked by Constantine's desire to marry Charles's daughter. R. McKitterick, *Charlemagne. The Formation of a European Identity* (Cambridge 2008), pp. 113–14 shows how difficult it was for Charles to gain real control of Lombard areas.

21. Final session of the Council of Nicaea, *ACO* ser. III, pts 1–3, ed. E. Lamberz (Berlin 2008–16).

22. J. Herrin, 'Mothers and daughters in the medieval Greek world', in *Unrivalled Influence*, pp. 80–114, esp. 87–8.

23. Adelchis was known as Theodotos in Byzantium, where he stayed as an honoured guest at the imperial court for fourteen years, see J. Herrin, 'Constantinople and the treatment of hostages, refugees and exiles during late antiquity', in *Constantinople réelle et imaginaire. Autour de l'oeuvre de Gilbert Dagron. Travaux et Mémoires* 22/1 (2018), pp. 257–74. The campaign to restore him is represented in Theophanes as part of Irene's new foreign policy against Charles. In contrast, later western sources present Constantine VI, a young teenager, invading Italy in a great fury.

24. Just as the area they were fighting to regain became known as Longobardia! *Regesta Imperii*, eds. J.-F. Boehmer and E. Mühlbacher (1908, repr. 1966), pp. 120–23; *MGH Epistolae* III, CC 82, pp. 615–20.

25. *The Life of St Philaretos the Merciful, written by his grandson Niketas*, c. 4, ed. L. Rydén (Uppsala 2002), pp. 82–93; R.-J. Lilie, *Byzanz unter Eirene und Konstantin VI, 780–802* (Frankfurt 1996), pp. 199–205.

26. *LPR* c. 164, tr. p. 290.

27. Ibid. Agnellus loves to repeat these entertaining stories, which may not have any historical foundation but fill out his account of otherwise unknown figures.

28. *LPR* c. 165, tr. pp. 290–91, probably all invented, but Charles must have visited Ravenna to have solicited building materials, see his letter to Hadrian, A. T. Hack, *Codex Carolinus: päpstliche Epistolographie im 8. Jahrhundert*, 2 vols. (Stuttgart 2006–7), II, pp. 840–41, 970; Nelson, *King and Emperor*, pp. 231–2.

29. Agnellus himself had taken advantage of these *spolia* for his own building activity. At Aachen columns that do not come from Rome or Ravenna have been identified, so the *spolia* from Italy may have provided decoration for the palace itself, see J. Ley, '*Aquis palatium*: Spätantiker Palast oder frühmittelalterliche Pfalz? Architekturhistorische überlegungen zur Ikonographie der Aachener Pfalz', in *The Emperor's House*, eds. M. Featherstone et al. (Berlin 2015), pp. 237–46; D. Kinney, 'Roman architectural spolia', *Proceedings of the American Philosophical Society* 145/2 (2001), pp. 138–61, esp. pp. 147–9 on Aachen.

30. CC no. 94, dated 790–91, pp. 632–6. C. Gantner, 'The label "Greeks" in the papal diplomatic repertoire in the eighth century', in *Strategies of Identification: Ethnicity and Religion in Early Medieval Europe*, eds. W. Pohl and G. Heydemann (Turnhout 2013), pp. 303–49.

31. RFA, a. 793, tr. p. 71 records the embassy.

32. J. Story et al., 'Charlemagne's black marble: the origin of the epitaph of Pope Hadrian I', *PBSR* 73 (2005), pp. 157–90.

33. RFA, a. 796, tr. p. 74; Nelson, *King and Emperor*, pp. 362–4.

CHAPTER 37

1. Charles's power is set in a wider perspective by J. Preiser-Kapeller, *Jenseits von Rom und Karl dem Grossen. Aspekte der globalen Verflechtung in der langen Spätantike, 300–800 n. Chr.* (Vienna 2018); W. Scheidel, *Escape from Rome. The Failure of Empire and the Road to Prosperity* (Princeton/Oxford 2019), esp. pp. 132–8, 154–6, 508–10, a global history designed to belittle any post-Roman effort to preserve imperial structures, whether by Charlemagne or the East Roman empire.

2. M. Thompson, 'The monogram of Charlemagne in Greek', *American Numismatic Society, Museum Notes* 12 (1966), pp. 125–7 and fig. b; P. Grierson, *Coins of Medieval Europe* (London 1991), pp. 34–5. Instead of a mint mark, these silver pennies have Charles's full titles up to the year 800: CAROLUSREXFR/LANGOACPATROM – Charles, king of the Franks and the Lombards, and patrician of the Romans. See now A. Rovelli, *Coinage and Coin Use in Medieval Italy* (Farnham 2012). My thanks to Cécile Morrisson for her help with these issues.

3. J. Fried, *Charlemagne* (Cambridge MA/London 2016), pp. 442–3, 444–5; M. MacCormick, *Charlemagne's Survey of the Holy Land* (Washington DC 2011).

4. Although blinding was not widespread in Francia, when Count Hardrad rebelled against Charles in 785–6, he and the other leaders were punished by blinding, J. L. Nelson, *King and Emperor. A New Life of Charlemagne* (London 2019), pp. 214–20, and blinding remained a regular punishment for rebels: Louis the Pious had his uncle blinded in 818, see J. Herrin, 'Blinding in Byzantium', *Polyplevros nous. Miscellanea für Peter Schreiner zu seinem 60. Geburtstag*, eds. C. Scholz and G. Makris (Leipzig 2000), pp. 56–68.

5. RFA, a. 798, tr. pp. 76–7.

6. Einhard, *Vita Caroli (Life of Charlemagne)*, para 16, tr. p. 70; Paul Dutton, *Charlemagne's Mustache* (London 2004), pp. 59–61.

7. *Parastaseis syntomoi chronikai*, cc. 17, 37; see *Constantinople in the Early Eighth Century*, eds. A. Cameron and J. Herrin (Leiden 1984), pp. 80–81, 98–101; Otto III used an elephant silk as a shroud for Charlemagne, Dutton, *Charlemagne's Mustache*, pp. 61–2.

8. RFA, a. 802, tr. p. 82.

9. Possibly Daniel the envoy sent by Michael the *strategos* of Sicily could have carried this message, RFA, a. 799, tr. p. 78, cf. Theophanes AM 6293 and 6294, tr. pp. 653–4, where Charles's offer to marry Irene and thus unite East and West is stressed. The issue is much debated, see Nelson, *King and Emperor*, pp. 359–62 (a desperate attempt by Irene), and J. Herrin *Women in Purple* (London 2001); pp. 117–18, 122–5 (a more considered political strategy).

10. Fried, *Charlemagne*, p. 407; R. McKitterick, *Charlemagne. The Formation of a European Identity* (Cambridge 2008), pp. 116–17.

11. *LP* 98.11–19, tr. II, pp. 184–9, describing the pontiff's escape; RFA, a. 800, tr. p. 80 on Charlemagne's arrival outside Rome, specifying 'seven days', enough time for Pope Leo to prepare his welcome.

12. RFA, a. 800 and 801, tr. pp. 80–81; J. L. Nelson, 'Why are there so many different accounts of Charles' imperial coronation?', in *Courts, Elites and Gendered Power in the Early Middle Ages* (Aldershot 2007), no. XII.

13. LP 98.24–5, tr. II, pp. 191–2, no silk cloths are mentioned.

14. At Spoleto he avoided a serious earthquake on 30 April, RFA, a. 801, tr. p. 81.

15. RFA, a. 801, 802, tr. pp. 81–2.

16. P. Classen, '*Romanum gubernans imperium*: zur Vorgeschichte des Kaisertitulatur des Karls des Grossen', *Deutsches Archiv für Erforschung des Mittelalters* 9 (1951), pp. 103–21, repr. in *Ausgewählte Aufsätze von Peter Classen*, eds. J. Fleckenstein et al. (Sigmaringen 1983). And wouldn't this have been a neat way for a female regent like Galla Placidia to claim supreme authority?

17. The phrase 'had long been current in parts of Italy', Nelson, *King and Emperor*, p. 383.

18. Einhard, *Vita Caroli*, para 28, tr. p. 81.

19. Classen, '*Romanum gubernans imperium*'. Although very few records documenting this title have survived, in the eighth and ninth centuries there were many in the archives at Ravenna where Charles might have seen them.

20. McKitterick, *Charlemagne*, pp. 169, 339 sees Ravenna as an inspiration for Charles, but not Theoderic. On the other hand, his advisers also compared him to Justinian.

21. *LPR* c. 94, tr. p. 207; confirmed by Walafrid Strabo's 829 description of it in precisely the same relationship to the palace as in Ravenna, Deliyannis, *Ravenna in Late Antiquity*, p. 298.

22. *LP* 98.27, tr. II, p. 193 (the mosaic is only known from drawings, see J. Herrin, *The Formation of Christendom* (Princeton 1989), p. 461).

23. This is reported in a letter of Leo III to Charles sent in 808, *MGH Epp Karolini Aevi* III, no. 2 pp. 87–8. It is another occasion when the pope uses the EMBOLUM to denounce the activity of Charles's officials.

24. *MGH Epp Karolini Aevi* III, nos. 9 and 10, pp. 100–102, 102–4, written between 808 and 814 repeat a similar charge. Charles's *missi* made a *magis damnum* by removing all the produce and leaving nothing for the pope's *missus*, a bishop John, ibid. p. 101; and their *malas machinationes*, which he compared to the horror of separating a child from its mother! He warns of the judgment of St Peter who holds the keys to the kingdom of Heaven, and orders Charles to uphold the *oblatio* made by King Pippin which Charles had confirmed. See T. S. Brown, 'Louis the Pious and the papacy. A Ravenna perspective', in *Charles' Heir*, eds. P. Godman and R. Collins (Oxford 1990), pp. 297–307, esp. 302.

25. RFA, a. 804, tr. p. 84, not mentioned in the *Life* of Leo III. Nelson, *King and Emperor*, 415–18.

26. *LP* 98.106, tr. II, pp. 227–8 (these gifts are very insignificant in comparison with others made to churches of Rome).

27. *MGH Epp Karolini Aevi* III, nos. 2, 9 and 10.

28. *LPR* c. 70, tr. p. 186; M. C. Miller, *The Bishop's Palace: Architecture and Authority in Medieval Italy* (Ithaca NY 2000), pp. 57–8.

29. Deliyannis, *Ravenna in Late Antiquity*, pp. 294–5; Jäggi, *Ravenna*, 268–71. Identical columns are preserved in the portico of the church of S. Spirito in Ravenna, suggesting that previously all of them may have adorned a building such as the two episcopal palaces that dated back to the time of the Arians.

30. *LPR* c. 169, tr. p. 297.

31. '*uacula argentea totam expletem mensem factam in diodum platani*'. The table had been made during the reign of Archbishop Valerius.

32. *LPR* c. 167, tr. p. 296.

33. Ibid. (presumably this was the price of an abbacy). If the 200 gold *solidi* and more were used in making this *chrismatarion*, it would compare with the two small ones made by Maximian, *LPR* c. 80, tr. pp. 193–4, one of which weighed 14 lbs.

34. M. C. Carile, 'Production, promotion and reception: the visual culture of Ravenna between late antiquity and the Middle Ages', in *Ravenna, Its Role in Earlier Medieval Change and Exchange*, eds. J. Herrin and J. Nelson (London 2016), pp. 53-85, esp. 75, on the damage, which must be related to Martin's repair of the roof.

35. *LPR* c. 168, tr. pp. 296-7, cf. *LP* 98.106, tr. II, p. 228, for the description of the church's roofing with 'square colonnades'.

36. *LPR* c. 168, tr. p. 296; Cirelli, *Archeologia*, pp. 104-5, fig. 86.

37. The 'irregularities' may well have concerned rights to land or areas of northern Italy, which the pope believed should lie within his own jurisdiction, but which the archbishop of Ravenna was ruling as his own. Leo's letters indicate the removal of actual workmen as well as produce, *MGH Epp Karolini Aevi* III, nos. 9 and 10.

38. *LPR* c. 169, tr. p. 297; Brown, 'Louis the Pious and the papacy', pp. 297-307, esp. 302-3.

39. *LPR* c. 170, tr. p. 298 (in the fifth century a sandal attributed to St John the Evangelist was the chief relic of Galla Placidia's church, so these new relics appear to have been 'discovered' later, a true 'invention' in the sense of a miracle).

40. Ibid.

41. Einhard, *Vita Caroli*, para 33, tr. p. 89. In his will Charlemagne stipulated that the first square silver table was to go to Rome, the second, circular, to Ravenna, and the third 'which is far superior to the others . . . which shows the entire universe in three concentric circles' to be added to the part for his heirs, plus the big, heavy golden table.

42. D. Deliyannis, 'Charlemagne's silver tables: the ideology of an imperial capital', *Early Medieval Europe* 12 (2003), pp. 159-77.

43. McKitterick, *Charlemagne*, pp. 372, 374-5.

44. Einhard, *Vita Caroli*, para 33, tr. pp. 88-9. His will also made complex arrangements for the use of the final third that had been retained for his own basic expenses while alive, and for his heirs, the poor, palace servants and additions to the twenty-one metropolitan sees after his death.

45. R. J. Belletzkie, 'Pope Nicholas I and John of Ravenna. The struggle for ecclesiastical rights', *Church History* 49/2 (1980), pp. 262-72.

46. *LPR* c. 113, tr. p. 231.

47. *LPR* c. 1, tr. p. 103; ed. Nauerth, I, p. 98; Cirelli, *Archeologia*, pp. 159-60.

48. P. Delogu, 'Lombard and Carolingian Italy', in *NCMH* II, p. 310: 'Cities were concerned with their own independence and saw the bishop above all as a local power capable of understanding their own needs and of representing them before the king.'

49. M. McCormick, 'Byzantium and the West, 700-900', in *NCMH* II, pp. 349-80, on the decline of 'Greek' merchants, and increasing connections

between the West and the Islamic world, visible in the dominance of the *mancus* 'along the edges of Byzantine Italy', pp. 358–9.

CONCLUSION

1. R. Hatch, '751CE. Watershed events in the Carolingian, Byzantine, Abbasid and Tang Empires', in *Paradigm Shifts during the Global Middle Ages and the Renaissance*, ed. A. Classen (Turnhout 2019), pp. 1–15.

2. *LPR* c. 42, tr. p. 150. Agnellus also quotes a section of the Chronicle where Maximian describes his travels to Alexandria when Timothy was patriarch and there was an earthquake that destroyed Nazarba in Cilicia, c. 78, tr. p. 192 (dated about 525). On forgetting, see M. Verhoeven, *The Early Christian Monuments of Ravenna: Transformations and Memory* (Turnhout 2011).

3. M. S. Bjornlie, *Politics and Tradition between Rome, Ravenna and Constantinople* (Cambridge 2013).

4. Cassiodorus, *Institutions of Divine and Secular Learning* and *On the Soul*, tr. J. W. Halporn (Liverpool 2004), and esp. the Introduction by M. Vessey, pp. 1–101.

5. *LPR* c. 94, tr. p. 206; ed. Nauerth, II, pp. 356–7, suggests that this figure may have been Constantinople, not Ravenna.

6. W. V. Harris, *Roman Power. A Thousand Years of Empire* (Cambridge 2016), pp. 219–21, stressing the distinct features of each period of decline; P. Sarris, *Empires of Faith. The Fall of Rome to the Rise of Islam, 500–700* (Oxford 2011), pp. 41–68 on the West, 275–306 on the East.

7. J. Herrin, 'From bread and circuses to soup and salvation', in *Margins and Metropolis. Authority across the Byzantine Empire* (Princeton 2013), pp. 267–98.

8. Bryan Ward-Perkins for the catastrophists: *The Fall of Rome and the End of Civilization* (Oxford 2005), v. Walter Pohl et al. on more gradual assimilation, see *The Transformation of Frontiers from Late Antiquity to the Carolingians*, ed. W. Pohl (Leiden/Boston 2001); *Regna and Gentes. The Relationship Between Late Antique and Early Medieval Peoples and Kingdoms in the Transformation of the Roman World*, ed. H.-W. Goertz (Leiden/Boston 2003); *Transformations of Romanness: Early Medieval Regions and Identities*, ed. W. Pohl (Berlin/Boston 2018). M. Kolakowski, *Imperial Tragedy. From Constantine's Empire to the Destruction of Roman Italy* (London 2019), on Justinian as the final blow against the West. In his tenth anniversary edition of *The Rise of Western Christendom: Triumph and Diversity, AD 200–1000* (Wiley-Blackwell ebook 2013), Peter Brown elegantly demonstrates the weakness of the catastrophists.

9. Italian cities suffered less than others further north, C. Wickham, *The Inheritance of Rome: a history of Europe from 400–1000* (London 2009), pp. 95–108; *idem, Framing the Middle Ages. Europe and the Mediterranean 400–800* (Oxford 2009), pp. 644–55; E. Cirelli, 'Ravenna: rise of a late antique capital', in *Debating Urbanism. Within and Beyond the Walls. AD 300–700*, eds. D. Sani and G. Speed (Leicester 2010), pp. 239–64.

10. A. H. M. Jones, *The Decline of the Ancient World* (London 1966); R. Krautheimer, *Rome: Profile of a City 312–1308* (Princeton 1980), pp. 62–4; B. Ward-Perkins, *From Classical Antiquity to the Middle Ages: Urban Public Building in Northern and Central Italy, AD 300–850* (Oxford 1984).

11. C. Goodson, 'Roman archaeology in medieval Rome', in *Rome: Continuing Encounters between Past and Present*, eds. D. Caldwell and L. Caldwell (Farnham 2011), pp. 17–34, on the appreciation and adaptation of old buildings; R. Coates-Stephens, 'Epigraphy as *spolia* – the re-use of inscriptions in early medieval buildings', *PBSR* 70 (2002), pp. 275–96.

12. 'Father of Europe', R. McKitterick, *Charlemagne. The Formation of a European Identity* (Cambridge 2008), pp. 1–5, 140–41; N. Davies, *Europe. A History* (Oxford 1996), esp. pp. 302, 305–6, 307.

Acknowledgements

My first and heartfelt acknowledgement is to the A. G. Leventis Foundation and to Howard and Roberta Ahmanson, who have supported my research on Ravenna for many years. I deeply appreciate their patience and confidence. I'm especially grateful to Roberta for her enthusiastic interest and regular attention to its progress, and for putting me in touch with Kieran Dodds, whose brilliant photographs add so much to the volume.

In Ravenna, Gian Luca Bandini provided continuous practical advice and organized the crew of intrepid yachtsmen who sailed me across the Adriatic – Ing. Stefano Luciani, Dr Mauro Marabini and himself, captained by Dr. Enzo Bruni. He also introduced me to Giovanna Montevecchi, who gave me invaluable assistance in negotiating with the authorities that control the major monuments of the city. Antonio and Consuelo Bandini lent us their house; Antonio Carile and Alba Maria Orselli took me to visit the manuscripts and Dante's bones in the Biblioteca Classense; and I was greatly helped by Andrea Augenti, Maria Cristina Carile, Salvatore Cosentino and Enrico Cirelli (whose book *Ravenna: Archeologia di una città* has been a constant companion and most instructive guide). In Poreč I was fortunate to discuss the mosaics of the Eufrasiana with Ivan Matejčić, and Jeremy Hardie and Kirsteen Stewart took me on an exciting visit to Aachen.

Over the period of writing, many have helped me with a great variety of advice, copies of articles, references, corrections and that critical element of moral support for which I am most grateful: Anne Alwis, Charalambos and Demetra Bakirtzis, Henrietta Batchelor, David Blackman, Petros Bouras-Valliantos, Sebastian Brock, Bruno Callegher, Averil Cameron, Nicky Coldstream, Franca Ela Consolino, Deborah Deliyannis, Kieran Dodds, Nicholas and Matti Egon, Vera von Falkenhausen, Michael Jeffrey Featherstone, Sauro Gelichi, Cathrine Gomani, Elizabeth Jeffreys, Maria Lidova, Jamie Mackay, Neil McLynn, Paul Magdalino, Yuri Marano, Marina Marks, Tom Mathews, Cécile Morrisson, Jinty Nelson, Vivian Prigent, Claudia Rapp, Charlotte Roueché,

Teo Ruiz, Bennet Salway, Alex Sarantis, Ned Schoolman, Roger Scott, Roger Scruton, Julia Smith, Dennis Stathakopoulos, Gonda van Steen, Eva Synek, Rick Trainor, Miranda Tufnell, Maria Vrij, Bryan Ward-Perkins, Marina Warner, Chris Wickham, Constantin Zuckerman and my colleagues and the all-important staff at King's College London.

I tested arguments explored in the book at the University of New Mexico, Albuquerque; the International Byzantine Congress held in Sofia, Bulgaria; the Center for Medieval and Renaissance Studies, UCLA; the Byzantine Studies Conference at the Italian Academy, Columbia University, New York; the Institut fur Byzantinistik und Neogräzistik, Vienna; the 'After Rome' seminar at the University of Oxford; the Byzantine seminar of Ioanna Rapti at the Sorbonne, Paris; the conference 'Byzantium in the Adriatic' at Split; the 'Byzantine Worlds' seminar at the University of Cambridge, and at the Leventis Municipal Museum Nicosia, in Cyprus, and I thank the organizers and audiences for their comments.

The staff of the Bodleian Library, Oxford, the Warburg Institute and Institute of Classical Studies, London, and the Vienna Institut were exceptionally helpful. I also benefitted from very kind librarians of Corpus Christi College, Brasenose College and Hertford College, who assisted me in finding books unavailable in other Oxford libraries at short notice.

It is a particular pleasure to acknowledge the immense support, critical improvements and vital input of my editor, Stuart Proffitt, at Penguin/ Random House; his colleagues Alice Skinner, Charlotte Ridings and Richard Duguid, who brought the book into publishable form; and Cecilia Mackay, who not only found many of the illustrations for the book but also persisted in obtaining the most effective layouts. At Princeton University Press, I am indebted to Brigitta van Rheinberg for her lengthy support and to Eric Crahan and Thalia Leaf for looking after the American edition. Anonymous readers' reports commissioned by Princeton, as well as the two solicited by Penguin/Random House from Tom Brown and Caroline Goodson, were invaluable and contributed many improvements.

Families often suffer from authors' neglectful absence, and mine was forced to share a long obsession while *Ravenna* came into focus. To Tamara and Portia Barnett-Herrin, Jay Basu, Seb Smith and my beloved, Anthony Barnett, who accompanied me on adventures to drive along the via Flaminia, to find the River Isonzo crossing and to sail across the Adriatic from Poreč to Ravenna, I can never thank you enough and could not have completed the book without your insistent support.

Index

Agnellus, Archbishop of Ravenna
　　xxxi, 190, 191, 193, 195, 197,
　　197–8, 205, 209
Agnellus (consul) 336
Agnellus (doctor, *yatrosophista*)
　　xxxi, 239–44, 307
Agnellus (historian)
　　as abbot of S. Maria *ad Blachernas*
　　　229, 267, 381–2
　　as abbot of St Bartholomew's 306
　　on Amalasuintha 145
　　on Archbishop Agnellus 198
　　on Archbishop Damianus 297–9,
　　　302–3
　　on Archbishop Felix 306–9, 311
　　on Archbishop Gratiosus 370
　　on Archbishop John V 323, 324–5
　　on Archbishop Martin 382
　　on Archbishop Maximian 387
　　on Archbishop Sergius 341–2, 349
　　on Archbishop Theodore 265, 266
　　on Baduarius 207
　　on Bishop John and Theoderic 96
　　Book of the Pontiffs of Ravenna
　　　xxxii, 26, 41, 143, 241, 388–9
　　and building materials 108
　　on Carolingians 384
　　on Charlemagne's gifts to
　　　Ravenna 383
　　on churches in Ravenna 229
　　on death of Pope Pelagius 180
　　distinguished from namesakes xxxi
　　on districts of Ravenna 299
　　on equestrian statue of
　　　Theoderic 379
　　on Exarch Theodore II 266–7
　　on independence of Ravenna from
　　　Rome 259
　　on inhabitants of Ravenna 169
　　on inscriptions 390
　　on Johannicis 264
　　on Justinian II 293

　　on Justinian's letter on Arian
　　　churches 192
　　Life of Archbishop Felix 306
　　on Marinianus 225
　　on Mausoleum of Galla Placidia
　　　47, 49
　　on Maximian 185–7, 188–9,
　　　387, 389
　　on mosaics of Theoderic 391
　　on pestilence 176
　　on Petriana icon 68
　　on Pope Zacharias 338
　　on power of emperor 304
　　on Ravenna's defence systems 294–5
　　on S. Apollinare Nuovo 106, 193,
　　　390–91
　　on St Agnes church 75
　　on St Probus church 213
　　on statue of Theoderic in Pavia 109
　　on tomb of Bishop John 76
　　on Ursiana church 29–31, 160–61
　　use of term 'Melisenses' 312
Agnese, St 192
Aistulf, King of the Lombards
　　339–40, 342–7, 353, 469*n*21,
　　474*n*24
Akakios, Patriarch of Constantinople
　　106, *see also* Acacian schism
　　Henotikon (with Peter Mongos) 84,
　　　132–3
Akroinon, *map 1*
　　battle of 339
Alamud 195
Alans 18, 93, 326
Alaric I, King of the Visigoths xxxvi,
　　9, 12, 19, 20–21, 36
Alaric II, King of the Visigoths 44,
　　95, 116, 117
Albania 263
Albanionus 211
Albenga *map 2*, 235
Albinus 104, 134, 135